THIRD EDITION

Strategic Management

Frank T. Rothaermel

Georgia Institute of Technology

Mc
Graw
Hill
Education

STRATEGIC MANAGEMENT, THIRD EDITION

Published by McGraw-Hill Education, 2 Penn Plaza, New York, NY 10121. Copyright © 2017 by McGraw-Hill
Education. All rights reserved. Printed in the United States of America. Previous editions © 2015 and 2013.
No part of this publication may be reproduced or distributed in any form or by any means, or stored in a
database or retrieval system, without the prior written consent of McGraw-Hill Education, including, but not
limited to, in any network or other electronic storage or transmission, or broadcast for distance learning.

Some ancillaries, including electronic and print components, may not be available to customers outside
the United States.

This book is printed on acid-free paper.

1 2 3 4 5 6 7 8 9 DOW 21 20 19 18 17 16

ISBN 978-1-259-25549-6
MHID 1-259-25549-2

DEDICATION

To my eternal family for their love, support, and sacrifice: Kelleyn, Harris, Winston, Roman, Adelaide, and Avery

—FRANK T. ROTHAERMEL

CONTENTS IN BRIEF

MINICASES AND FULL-LENGTH CASES

MINICASES /

FULL-LENGTH CASES /

All available through McGraw-Hill Create, www.McGrawHillCreate.com/Rothaermel

* NEW TO THE THIRD EDITION ➡ REVISED AND UPDATED FOR THE THIRD EDITION + THIRD-PARTY CASE

CHAPTERCASES & STRATEGY HIGHLIGHTS

CONTENTS

ABOUT THE AUTHOR

Frank T. Rothaermel
Georgia Institute of Technology

© Kelleyn Rothaermel

FRANK T. ROTHAERMEL (PH.D.) is a professor of strategy, holds the Russell and Nancy McDonough Chair in the Scheller College of Business at the Georgia Institute of Technology (GT), and is an Alfred P. Sloan Industry Studies Fellow. He received a National Science Foundation (NSF) CAREER award, which "is a Foundation-wide activity that offers the National Science Foundation's most prestigious awards in support of . . . those teacher-scholars who most effectively integrate research and education" (NSF CAREER Award description).

Frank's research interests lie in the areas of strategy, innovation, and entrepreneurship. Frank has published over 30 articles in leading academic journals such as the *Strategic Management Journal, Organization Science, Academy of Management Journal, Academy of Management Review,* and elsewhere. He has received several recognitions for his research, including the Sloan Industry Studies Best Paper Award, the Academy of Management Newman Award, the Strategic Management Society Conference Best Paper Prize, the DRUID Conference Best Paper Award, and the Israel Strategy Conference Best Paper Prize.

Thomson Reuters identified Frank as one of the "world's most influential scientific minds" for having published in the top 1% of citation-based journal articles. He was listed among the top-100 scholars for his more than decade-long impact in both economics and business. *Businessweek* named Frank one of Georgia Tech's Prominent Faculty in their national survey of business schools. The Kauffman Foundation views Frank as one of the world's 75 thought leaders in entrepreneurship and innovation.

To inform his research Frank has conducted extensive field work and executive training with leading corporations such as Amgen, Daimler, Eli Lilly, Equifax, GE Energy, GE Healthcare, Hyundai Heavy Industries (South Korea), Kimberly-Clark, Microsoft, McKesson, NCR, Turner (TBS), UPS, among others. Frank regularly translates his research findings for wider audiences in articles in *Forbes, MIT Sloan Management Review, Wall Street Journal,* and elsewhere.

Frank has a wide range of executive education experience, including teaching in programs at Georgia Institute of Technology, Georgetown University, ICN Business School (France), Politecnico di Milano (Italy), St. Gallen University (Switzerland), and the University of Washington. He received numerous teaching awards for excellence in the classroom including the GT institute-wide Georgia Power Professor of Excellence award. When launched (in 2012), Frank's *Strategic Management* textbook received the McGraw-Hill 1st Edition of the Year Award in Business & Economics.

Frank holds a PhD degree in strategic management from the University of Washington; a MBA from the Marriott School of Management at Brigham Young University; and a M.Sc. (Diplom-Volkswirt) in economics from the University of Duisburg-Essen, Germany. Frank completed training in the case teaching method at the Harvard Business School. He was a visiting professor at the University of St. Gallen, Switzerland, and an Erasmus Scholar at Sheffield Hallam University, UK.

VISIT THE AUTHOR AT: http://ftrStrategy.com/

Strategic Management is a research- and application-based strategy text that covers issues facing managers in a globalized and turbulent 21st century.

When the first edition published, the market response was overwhelmingly enthusiastic, and I was grateful for the strong vote of confidence. When the second edition published, the enthusiasm was even greater; I remain ever grateful for the sustained support. In this third edition, I build upon the unique strengths of the text and continue to add improvements based upon hundreds of insightful reviews and important feedback from professors, students, and professionals.

The strategy textbook market has long been separated into two overarching categories: traditional, application-based and research-based. Traditional, application-based strategy books represent the first-generation texts whose first editions were published in the 1980s. The research-based strategy books represent the second-generation texts whose first editions were published in the 1990s. This text represents a new category of strategy textbook—a third-generation text that *combines* the student accessible, application-oriented framework of the first-generation texts with the research-based framework of the second-generation texts. It integrates core concepts, frameworks, and analysis techniques in strategy with functional course offerings; it also aims to help students become managers capable of making well-reasoned strategic decisions.

To facilitate an enjoyable and refreshing reading experience that enhances learning, I synthesize and integrate theory, empirical research, and practical applications with current real-world examples. This approach and emphasis on real-world examples offers students a learning experience that uniquely combines rigor and relevance. As Dr. John Media of the University of Washington's School of Medicine and life-long researcher on how the mind organizes information, explains:

> How does one communicate meaning in such a fashion that learning is improved? A simple trick involves the liberal use of relevant real-world examples, thus peppering main learning points with meaningful experiences. . . . Numerous studies show this works. . . . The greater the number of examples . . . the more likely the students were to remember the information. It's best to use real-world situations familiar to the learner. . . . Examples work because they take advantage of the brain's natural predilection for pattern matching. Information is more readily processed if it can be immediately associated with information already present in the brain. We compare the two inputs, looking for similarities and differences as we encode the new information. Providing examples is the cognitive equivalent of adding more handles to the door. [The more handles one creates at the moment of learning, the more likely the information can be accessed at a later date.] Providing examples makes the information more elaborative, more complex, better encoded, and therefore better learned.*

Strategic Management brings theory to life via examples that cover products and services from companies with which students are familiar, such as Facebook, Google, Starbucks, Apple, and Uber. Use of such examples aids in making strategy relevant to students' lives and helps them internalize strategy concepts and frameworks.

The hallmark features of this text continue to be:

- Use of a holistic *Analysis, Formulation, and Implementation (AFI)* Strategy Framework.
- Synthesis and integration of empirical research and practical applications combined with relevant strategy material to focus on *what is important* for the student and *why it is important.*

*Source: Medina, J. (2014). *Brain Rules: 12 Principles for Surviving and Thriving at Work, Home, and School* (pp. 139–140). Pear Press. Kindle Edition.

- Comprehensive but concise presentation of core concepts, frameworks, and techniques.
- Combination of traditional and contemporary strategy concepts.
- Up-to-date examples and discussion of current topics within a global context.
- Stand-alone chapter on competitive advantage, including a focus on *triple bottom line* and sustainability.
- Direct applications of strategy to careers and lives (including the popular *my*Strategy modules at the end of each chapter).
- Inclusion of *Strategy Term Project* (end-of-chapter) and interactive *Running Case* on HP (in Connect).
- Industry-leading digital delivery options and adaptive learning systems (Create, SmartBook, LearnSmart, and Connect)
- High-quality **Cases**, well integrated with textbook chapters and standardized, high-quality teaching notes; there are two types of cases:
  - **ChapterCases** begin and end each chapter, framing the chapter topic and content.
  - 28 **MiniCases** (Part 4 of the book), all based on original research, provide dynamic opportunities for students to apply strategy concepts by assigning them as add-ons to chapters, either as individual assignments or as group work, or by using them for class discussion.

I have taken pride in authoring all of the ChapterCases, Strategy Highlights, and Mini-Cases. This additional touch allows quality control and ensures that chapter content and cases use one voice and are closely interconnected. Both types of case materials come with sets of questions to stimulate class discussion or provide guidance for written assignments. The instructor resources offer sample answers that apply chapter content to the cases.

In addition to these in-text cases, 21 full-length cases, authored or co-authored by me specifically to accompany this textbook, are available through McGraw-Hill's custom-publishing *Create*™ program (www.McGrawHillCreate.com/Rothaermel). Full-length cases **New** to the third edition are: Delta, General Electric, and Google. Popular cases about Apple, Amazon.com, IBM, Facebook, McDonald's, Tesla Motors, and Better World Books among several others are significantly updated and revised. Robust and standardized case teaching notes are also available and accessible through Create; financial data for these cases may be accessed from the Instructor Resource site on Connect.

What's New in the Third Edition?

I have revised and updated the third edition in the following ways, many of which were inspired by conversations and feedback from the many users and reviewers of the first and second editions.

OVERVIEW OF IMPORTANT CHANGES IN 3E:

- New section on blue ocean strategy (Chapter 6), with application examples and strategy canvas.
- More global coverage included throughout, with a stronger Asian focus both on the continent as well as its global competitors.
- Stronger focus on sustainable business.
- Increased the total number of MiniCases to 28 (15 brand new, 13 revised).
- New, completely revised, or updated ChapterCases and Strategy Highlights.

- Stronger integration and expanded discussion of ChapterCases throughout.
- Increased emphasis on practice and applications of strategy concepts and frameworks.
- Updated or new firm, product, and service examples to afford more in-depth discussion.
- Enhanced graphic design and rendering of exhibits throughout entire text.

In detail:

CHAPTER 1

- New ChapterCase about Twitter's rise and current challenges.
- New Strategy Highlight 1.1 discussing Threadless and its use of crowdsourcing to help produce better products and maintain competitive advantage.
- Updated Strategy Highlight 1.2 about BP's Gulf Coast oil spill and systemic safety issues over the last decade.

CHAPTER 2

- New ChapterCase about Yahoo's CEO Marissa Mayer and the attempted turnaround under her leadership.
- Created new and stand-alone sections on each vision, mission, and values.
- Updated Strategy Highlight 2.1 on Merck's core values and the development of drugs to treat river blindness and the challenges with the Vioxx recall.
- Added a new table comparing and contrasting top-down strategic planning, scenario planning, and strategy as planned emergence (brief descriptions, pros and cons, where best used); see Exhibit 2.9.
- Added new sections to expand discussion of autonomous actions, serendipity, and resource allocation process as part of strategy as planned emergence.
- Added new ethical/social issues question focusing on Merck's responsibility to meet the needs of both its customers and its shareholders.

CHAPTER 3

- Updated ChapterCase about Tesla Motors and the U.S. automotive industry.
- Separate discussion of political and legal factors in the PESTEL framework.
- Sharpened the discussion of PESTEL framework overall.
- New Strategy Highlight 3.1: "BlackBerry's Bust."
- Updated the discussion of competition in the U.S. domestic airline industry throughout the chapter, and in Strategy Highlight 3.2: "The Five Forces in the Airline Industry."

CHAPTER 4

- New ChapterCase about Dr. Dre, and multi-billion-dollar Apple acquisition of Beats Electronics.
- Fresh examples of core competencies and their applications.
- Interlocution of the concept of *Core Rigidities.*
- Expanded discussion on dynamic capabilities, including new Strategy Highlight 4.2: "Dynamic Capabilities at IBM."

- Included new Exhibit 4.6 showing IBM's successful transition throughout several technological discontinuities over the last 125 years.
- Sharpened discussion of SWOT, including moving (an updated version of) the SWOT application to McDonald's in the Instructor Manual.

CHAPTER 5

- New ChapterCase, focusing on Apple vs. Microsoft and their quest for competitive advantage over time.
- Extended discussion of Apple and Microsoft (turnaround under new CEO Satya Nadella) throughout the chapter.
- Sharpened discussion of competitive advantage and firm performance.
- Expanded discussion of business models to include new popular applications and examples, with a more in-depth discussion.
- New Strategy Highlight 5.2 on Airbnb and its novel business model.

CHAPTER 6

- New ChapterCase about JetBlue and how its straddling of different strategy positions led to being "Stuck in the Middle" and a competitive disadvantage.
- New section on Blue Ocean Strategy.
- Application of the Blue Ocean Strategy canvas to the U.S. domestic airline industry.
- Discussion of the *Eliminate-Reduce-Raise-Create* framework from Blue Ocean Strategy and application to IKEA.
- New Strategy Highlight 6.1: "Dr. Shetty: The Henry Ford of Heart Surgery," focusing on cost reductions in healthcare.
- New Strategy Highlight 6.2: "How JCPenney Sailed into the Red Ocean."
- Dropped the section "The Dynamics of Competitive Positioning"
- New *my*Strategy module, comparing and contrasting low-cost and differentiated workplaces.

CHAPTER 7

- New ChapterCase on Netflix and the disruption in the TV industry.
- Coverage of innovation process expanded with a stronger focus on how to manage innovation.
- More in-depth coverage of product and process innovation over the entire industry life cycle, including revision of Exhibit 7.6 "Product and Process Innovation throughout an Industry Life Cycle."
- Revision of Exhibit 7.9 "Features and Strategic Implications of the Industry Life Cycle."
- New Strategy Highlight 7.1: "How Dollar Shave Club Is Disrupting Gillette."
- Dropped the section "The Internet as Disruptive Force: The Long Tail."
- Revised the *my*Strategy module and end-of-chapter section around debate on whether college adds to potential success of entrepreneurs.

CHAPTER 8

- New ChapterCase on how Amazon.com diversified over time to become the "Everything Store," including a detailed exhibit showing Amazon.com's key strategic initiatives and stock market valuation from the idea of in 1994 to 2015 (Exhibit 8.1).

- New section titled, "Why Firms Need to Grow."
- New Strategy Highlight 8.1 "Is Coke Becoming a Monster?"
- More in-depth discussion of Exhibit 8.4 "Alternatives on the Make-or-Buy Continuum" in the text.
- New subsection on "When Does Vertical Integration Make Sense?"
- Revised section of "Types of Corporate Diversification" to sharpen discussion and provide graphic support as Rumelt's framework categorizing different types of diversification is developed (Exhibit 8.8).
- Expanded discussion to clarify more fully the sources of value creation and costs of vertical integration and diversification (Exhibit 8.11).

CHAPTER 9

- Revised and updated ChapterCases focusing on Disney's attempt to build billion-dollar franchises, with strategic alliances, and mergers and acquisitions as critical to corporate strategy execution.
- Changed macro structure of chapter by moving the Build-Borrow-Buy Framework upfront to guide and frame the discussion corporate strategy execution using.
- Discussion of strategic alliances before mergers and acquisitions.
- Included a new section entitled "How Firms Achieve Growth."
- New Strategy Highlight 9.1 "IBM and Apple: From Big Brother to Big Alliance Partner."
- Revised to *my*Strategy module to sharpen the discussion of network strategy in terms of career management.

CHAPTER 10

- New ChapterCase on IKEA, with a focus on the question whether the Swedish furniture retailer's success is sustainable while competing globally.
- Reorganization of section "What Is Globalization" into two subsections, focusing on the stage and state of globalization respectively.
- New Strategy Highlight 10.1 "The Gulf Airlines Are Landing in the United States."

CHAPTER 11

- Revised and updated ChapterCase "Zappos: From Happiness to Holacracy."
- Included discussion on Holacracy as new organization structure.
- Expanded discussion with detailed visual support of section "Organizational Inertia: The Failure of Established Firms."
- New Strategy Highlight 11.1 "The Premature Death of a Google-like Search Engine at Microsoft."
- Dropped section on using SWOT analysis for strategy implementation.

CHAPTER 12

- New ChapterCase on Uber and its ethical lapses.
- Strong integration of Uber ChapterCase throughout the body of the chapter.
- Updated Strategy Highlight 12.1 "GE's Board of Directors," including discussion chairperson—CEO duality in the body of the chapter.
- Updated Strategy Highlight 12.2 "Did Goldman Sachs and the Fabulous Fab Commit Securities Fraud?"

MINICASES

- Added 15 brand-new MiniCases.
- Updated 13 MiniCases from second edition.
- Stronger focus on non-U.S. firms, especially on global competitors from Asia.
- Stronger focus on competing in China and India, facing strong domestic competitors.

FULL-LENGTH CASES

- Added three brand-new, full-length Cases: Delta Air Lines, General Electric after GE Capital, and Google.
- Revised and updated: Amazon.com, Apple, Best Buy, Better World Books, Facebook, IBM, McDonald's, Merck, Tesla Motors, and Better World Books, among others.
- Also included is an updated version of the popular case "The Movie Exhibition Industry" by Steve Gove and Brett Matherne.
- **All cases**—including the new and revised cases plus all cases from the first and second editions that were authored by Frank T. Rothaermel—**are available through McGraw-Hill Create**: http://www.mcgrawhillcreate.com/Rothaermel.
- Cases include financial data in e-format for analysis.

Instructor Resources

Connect, McGraw-Hill's online assignment and assessment system, offers a wealth of content for both students and instructors. Students will find the following:

- **Running case**, an activity that begins with a review of a specific company and its applied strategy using appropriate tools (e.g., PESTEL, Porter's Five Forces, VRIO, SWOT, and others). The analysis progresses from a broad perspective to the appropriate company-level perspective—i.e., from global to industry to strategic group to company. Students will develop a strategy analysis for the company and consider several scenarios for improving the company's competitive advantage. The scenarios will include a financial analysis and justification and ultimately provide a specific recommendation.
- **Interactive applications** (such as click-drag activities, video cases, and—new in this edition—case analyses for each of the MiniCases) that require students to *apply* key concepts; instant feedback and progress tracking are also available.
- **Resources for analysis** (such as financial ratios, templates for strategic financial analysis, and financial review activities) that provide students with the tools they need to compare performance between firms and to refresh or extend their working knowledge of major financial measures in a strategic framework.
- **LearnSmart and SmartBook**, which has been significantly improved for this edition to provide students with more opportunity to probe concepts at a higher level of thinking.

Under the **Instructor's Resources tab**, instructors will find tested and effective tools that enable automatic grading and student-progress tracking and reporting, and a trove of content to support teaching:

- The **Combined Instructor Manual (IM)** includes thorough coverage of each chapter, support for newer and experienced faculty, as well as guidance for integrating Connect—all in a single resource. Included in this newly combined IM is the appropriate level of theory, recent application or company examples, teaching tips, PowerPoint references, critical discussion topics, and answers to end-of-chapter exercises.

- The **PowerPoint (PPT)** slides provide comprehensive lecture notes, video links, and company examples not found in the textbook. There will be instructor media-enhanced slides as well as notes with outside application examples.

- The **Test Bank** includes 100–150 questions per chapter, in a range of formats and with a greater-than-usual number of comprehension, critical-thinking, and application (or scenario-based) questions. It's tagged by learning objectives, Bloom's Taxonomy levels, and AACSB compliance requirements.

- The **Video Guide** is new for this edition and includes video links that relate to concepts from chapters. The video links include sources such as Big Think, Stanford University's Entrepreneurship Corner, *The McKinsey Quarterly,* ABC, BBC, CBS, CNN, ITN/Reuters, MSNBC, NBC, PBS, and YouTube.

CREATE, McGraw-Hill's custom-publishing program, is where you access the full-length cases that accompany *Strategic Management* (**http://www.mcgrawhillcreate.com/Rothaermel**). Through CREATE, you will be able to select from 20 author-written cases that go specifically with this textbook as well as cases from Harvard, Ivey Darden, NACRA, and much more! You can: *Assemble your own course,* selecting the chapters, cases, and readings that will work best for you. Or *choose from several ready-to-go, author-recommended complete course solutions,* which include chapters, cases, and readings, pre-loaded in CREATE. Among the **pre-loaded** solutions, you'll find options for undergrad, MBA, accelerated, and other strategy courses.

ACKNOWLEDGMENTS

Any list of acknowledgments will almost always be incomplete, but I would like to thank some special people without whom this text would not have been possible. First and foremost, my wife Kelleyn, and our children: Harris, Winston, Roman, Adelaide, and Avery. Over the last few years, I have worked longer hours than when I was a graduate student to conduct the research and writing necessary for this text and accompanying case studies and other materials. I sincerely appreciate the sacrifice this has meant for my family.

The Georgia Institute of Technology provided a conducive, intellectual environment and superb institutional support to make this project possible. I thank Russell and Nancy McDonough for generously funding the endowed chair that I am honored to hold. I'm grateful for Dean Maryam Alavi and Senior Associate Dean Peter Thompson for providing the exceptional leadership that allows faculty to fully focus on research, teaching, and service. I have been at Georgia Tech for over a decade, and could not have had better colleagues—all of whom are not only great scholars but also fine individuals whom I'm fortunate to have as friends: Marco Ceccagnoli, Annamaria Conti, Stuart Graham, Matt Higgins, David Ku, John McIntyre, Alex Oettl, Henry Sauermann, Eunhee Sohn, Jerry Thursby, and Marie Thursby. We have a terrific group of current and former PhD students, many of whom had a positive influence on this project, including Shanti Agung (Drexel University), Drew Hess (Washington and Lee University), Kostas Grigoriou (Florida International University), Jaiswal Mayank, Nicola McCarthy, German Retana (INCAE Business School, Costa Rica), Briana Sell, (Mercer University) Jose Urbina, Carrie Yang (University of Chicago), and Wei Zhang (Singapore Management University).

I was also fortunate to work with McGraw-Hill, and the best editorial and marketing team in the industry: Michael Ablassmeir (Director), Susan Gouijnstook (Managing Director), Lai T. Moy (Senior Product Developer), Casey Keske (Senior Marketing Manager), Mary E. Powers and Keri Johnson (Content Project Managers), and Matt Diamond (Designer). Bill Teague, Freelance Content Development Editor, worked tirelessly and carefully on the third edition manuscript. Thank you to senior management at McGraw-Hill Education, especially Kurt Strand (Senior Vice President, Products & Markets), who assembled this fine team.

I'm more than grateful to work with a number of great colleagues on various resources that accompany this text:

- Marne Arthaud-Day (Kansas State University) on some *Cases* and *Case Teaching Notes*
- Heidi Bertels (College of Staten Island, CUNY) on *SmartBook* and *LearnSmart*
- John Burr (Purdue University) on the *Video Guide*
- Melissa Francisco (University of Central Florida) on the *PowerPoint Slide Decks*
- Anne Fuller (California State University, Sacramento), on *Connect Interactives, Connect Instructor Manual,* and *End-of-Chapter Material*
- David R. King (Iowa State University) on *MiniCase Teaching Notes* as well as on select *Full-length Cases* and *Full-length Case Teaching Notes*
- Stuart Napshin (Kennesaw State University) on *Connect Interactives*
- Louise Nemanich (Arizona State University) on the *Instructor Manual*
- Chris Papenhausen (University of Massachusetts, Dartmouth) on *Strategic Financial Analysis*
- Robert Porter (University of Central Florida) on the *Running Case* in *Connect*

I'd also like to thank the students at Georgia Tech, in the undergraduate and full-time day MBA, and the evening and executive MBA programs, as well as the executive MBA students from the ICN Business School in Nancy, France, on whom the materials were beta-tested. Their feedback helped fine-tune the content and delivery.

Last, but certainly not least, I wish to thank the reviewers and focus group attendees who shared their expertise with us, from the very beginning when we developed the prospectus to the final text and cases that you hold in your hands. The reviewers have given us the greatest gift of all—the gift of time! These very special people are listed starting on page xxiii.

Frank T. Rothaermel
Georgia Institute of Technology

Web: http://ftrStrategy.com/
Strategy Blog: http://www.facebook.com/ftrStrategy
Twitter: @ftrStrategy

THANK YOU . . .

This book has gone through McGraw-Hill Education's thorough development process. Over the course of several years, the project has benefited from numerous developmental focus groups and symposiums, from hundreds of reviews from reviewers across the country, and from beta-testing of the first-edition manuscript as well as market reviews of the second edition on a variety of campuses. The author and McGraw-Hill wish to thank the following people who shared their insights, constructive criticisms, and valuable suggestions throughout the development of this project. Your contributions have improved this product.

REVIEWERS AND SYMPOSIUM ATTENDEES

Joshua R. Aaron
East Carolina University

Moses Acquaah
University of North Carolina at Greensboro

Garry Adams
Auburn University

Todd Alessandri
Northeastern University

M. David Albritton
Northern Arizona University

Benjamin N. Alexander
Tulane University

Brent B. Allred
The College of William & Mary

Semiramis Amirpour
University of Texas at El Paso

Cory J. Angert
University of Houston-Downtown

Melissa Appleyard
Portland State University

Jorge A. Arevalo
William Paterson University

Asli Arikan
Kent State University

Marne Arthaud-Day
Kansas State University

Bindu Arya
University of Missouri-St. Louis

Seung Bach
California State University, Sacramento

David Baker
Kent State University

LaKami T. Baker
Auburn University

Jeffery Bailey
University of Idaho

Dennis R. Balch
University of North Alabama

Edward R. Balotsky
Saint Joseph's University

Kevin Banning
Auburn University at Montgomery

Jeff Barden
Oregon State University

Patricia Beckenholdt
University of Maryland University College

Geoff Bell
University of Minnesota, Duluth

Heidi Bertels
City University of New York, College of Staten Island

Tim Blumentritt
Kennesaw State University

William C. Bogner
Georgia State University

Nathan A. Bragaw
Louisiana State University

Dorothy Brawley
Kennesaw State University

Michael G. Brizek
South Carolina State University

James W. Bronson
University of Wisconsin-Whitewater

Jill A. Brown
Bentley University

Barry Bunn
Valencia College

Richard A. L. Caldarola
Troy University

Janice F. Cerveny
Florida Atlantic University

Clint Chadwick
University of Alabama in Huntsville

Kenneth H. Chadwick
Nicholls State University

Betty S. Coffey
Appalachian State University

Anne N. Cohen
University of Minnesota

Jay P. Chandran
Northwood University

Yi-Yu Chen
New Jersey City University

Steve Childers
Radford University

Valerie L. Christian
Sacred Heart University

Brent Clark
University of South Dakota

Timothy S. Clark
Northern Arizona University

Anne N. Cohen
University of Minnesota

Brian Connelly
Auburn University

W. J. Conwell
University of Texas at El Paso

Cynthia S. Cycyota
United States Air Force Academy

Parthiban David
American University

Irem Demirkan
Northeastern University

Geoffrey Desa
San Francisco State University

Edward Desmarais
Salem State University

Samuel DeMarie
Iowa State University

Michael E. Dobbs
Eastern Illinois University

Mark Dobeck
Cleveland State University

Darla Domke-Damonte
Coastal Carolina University

Stephen A. Drew
Florida Gulf Coast University

Derrick E. D'Souza
University of North Texas

Mohinder Dugal
Western Connecticut State University

Arthur J. Duhaime III
Nichols College

David Duhon
University of Southern Mississippi

Danielle Dunne
Fordham University

Loretta S. Duus
Midlands Technical College

Jason Scott Earl
Brigham Young University Hawaii

Andrew G. Earle
University of New Hampshire

Helen Eckmann
Brandman University

Linda F. Edelman
Bentley University

Alan Ellstrand
University of Arkansas-Fayetteville

David Epstein
University of Houston Downtown

Michael M. Fathi
Georgia Southwestern State University

Kevin Fertig
University of Illinois at Urbana, Champaign

James Fiet
University of Louisville

Robert S. Fleming
Rowan University

Daniel Forbes
University of Minnesota

Isaac Fox
University of Minnesota

Susan Fox-Wolfgramm
Hawaii Pacific University

William Foxx
Troy University

Charla S. Fraley
Columbus State Community College

W.A. Franke
College of Business, Northern Arizona University

Steven A. Frankforter
Winthrop University

Anne W. Fuller
California State University, Sacramento

Venessa Funches
Auburn University, Montgomery

Jeffrey Furman
Boston University

John E. Gentner
University of Dayton

Devi R. Gnyawali
Virginia Tech

Sanjay Goel
University of Minnesota, Duluth

Steve Gove
University of Vermont

Patrick Greek
Macomb Community College

Shirley A. Green
Indian River State College

Regina A. Greenwood
Nova Southeastern University

Robert D. Gulbro
Athens State University

Michael Gunderson
University of Florida

Craig Gustin
American InterContinental University

Stephen F. Hallam
University of Akron

Marcia McLure Hardy
Northwestern State Univesity-Louisiana

Ahma Hassan
Morehead State University

Scott D. Hayward
Appalachian State University

Jon Timothy Heames
West Virginia University

Richard A. Heiens
University of South Carolina, Aiken

Duane Helleloid
University of North Dakota

Kurt A. Heppard
United States Air Force Academy

Theodore T. Herbert
Rollins College

Ken Hess
Metropolitan State University

Scott Hicks
Liberty University

Glenn Hoetker
Arizona State University

Phyllis Holland
Valdosta State University

R. Michael Holmes, Jr.
Florida State University

Stephen V. Horner
Arkansas State University

George Hruby
Cleveland State University

Tammy Huffman
Utah Valley University

Tobias M. Huning
Columbus State University

Tammy G. Hunt
University of North Carolina Wilmington

Ana Elisa Iglesias
University of Wisconsin-La Crosse

Syeda Noorein Inamdar
Singapore Management University

John G. Irwin
Troy University

Carol K. Jacobson
Purdue University

Sean Jasso
University of California, Riverside

Scott Johnson
Oklahoma State University

Mahesh P. Joshi
George Mason University

Jon Kalinowski
Minnesota State University, Mankato

Necmi Karagozoglu
California State University, Sacramento

Joy Karriker
East Carolina University

J. Kay Keels
Coastal Carolina University

Franz Kellermanns
University of North Carolina, Charlotte

Theodore A. Khoury
Portland State University

Brent Kinghorn
Missouri State University

Jerry Kopf
Radford University

Frank Kozak
Bowling Green State University

Mario Krenn
Louisiana State University

Bruce C. Kusch
Brigham Young University, Idaho

Melody LaPreze
Missouri State University

Mariana J. Lebrón
Towson University

K. Blaine Lawlor
University of West Florida

Marty Lawlor
Rochester Institute of Technology

John Lawrence
University of Idaho

Hun Lee
George Mason University

Mina Lee
Xavier University

Charles J. F. Leflar
University of Arkansas-Fayetteville

Jon Lehman
Vanderbilt University

David Leibsohn
California State University, Fullerton

Aristotle T. Lekacos
Stony Brook University

Jun Lin
State University of New York (SUNY), New Paltz

Joseph Mahoney
University of Illinois at Urbana-Champaign

David Major
Indiana University

Paul Mallette
Colorado State University

Tatiana S. Manolova
Bentley University

Daniel B. Marin
Louisiana State University

Louis Martinette
University of Mary Washington

Anthony U. Martinez
San Francisco State University

Sarah Marsh
Northern Illinois University

Patricia Matuszek
Troy University-Montgomery

David McCalman
University of Central Arkansas

Jeffrey E. McGee
The University of Texas at Arlington

Jean McGuire
Louisiana State University

Rick McPherson
University of Washington

Michael Merenda
University of New Hampshire

John M. Mezias
University of Miami

Grant Miles
University of North Texas

Douglas R. Miller
University of North Carolina

Michael Miller
University of Illinois at Chicago

Elouise Mintz
Saint Louis University

Raza Mir
William Paterson University

Kelly Mollica
University of Memphis

Mike Montalbano
Bentley University

Gwen Moore
University of Missouri-St. Louis

James P. Morgan
Webster University, Fort Leonard Wood

Richard T. Mpoyi
Middle Tennessee State University

John Mullane
Middle Tennessee State University

Chandran Mylvaganam
Northwood University-Michigan

Louise Nemanich
Arizona State University

Charles Newman
University of Maryland University College

Don O. Neubaum
Oregon State University

Kuei-Hsien Niu
California State University, Sacramento

Jill Novak
Indian River State College

Frank Novakowski
Davenport University

Jeffrey R. Nystrom
University of Colorado Denver

Kenny (Kyeungrae) Oh
University of Missouri-St. Louis

Don A. Okhomina
Fayetteville State University

Kevin J. O'Mara
Elon University

Eren Ozgen
Troy University-Dothan

James M. Pappas
Oklahoma State University

Chris Papenhausen
University of Massachusetts, Dartmouth

Audrey Parajon
Wilmington University

Ronaldo Parente
Florida International University

Srikanth Paruchuri
Pennsylvania State University

Christine Cope Pence
University of California, Riverside

Luis A. Perez-Batres
Central Michigan University

Clifford R. Perry
Florida International University

Keith Perry
San Jose State University

Antoaneta Petkova
San Francisco State University

JoDee Phillips
Kaplan University

Michael Pitts
Virginia Commonwealth University

Erin Pleggenkuhle-Miles
University of Nebraska-Omaha

Robert Porter
University of Central Florida

Richard A. Quinn
University of Central Florida

Vasudevan Ramanujam
Case Western Reserve University

Krishnan Ramaya
College of Business, Pacific University

Annette L. Ranft
University at Tennessee

Christopher R. Reutzel
Sam Houston State University

Gary B. Roberts
Kennesaw State University

Simon Rodan
San Jose State University

Elton Scifres
Stephen F. Austin State University

Yassir M. Samra
Manhattan College

Michael D. Santoro
Lehigh University

Tim Schoenecker
Southern Illinois University-Edwardsville

Gary Scudder
Vanderbilt University

Wendell Seaborne
Franklin University

Deborah Searcy
Florida Atlantic University

Jim Sena
California Polytechnic State University, San Luis Obispo

Anju Seth
Virginia Tech

Deepak Sethi
Old Dominion University

Jennifer Sexton
West Virginia University

Mark Sharfman
University of Oklahoma

Thomas Shirley
San Jose State University

Eugene Simko
Monmouth University

Faye A. Sisk
Mercer University, Atlanta

Lise Anne D. Slatten
University of Louisiana, Lafayette

Garry D. Smith
Mississippi State University

Ned Smith
University of Michigan

James D. Spina
University of Maryland

Peter A. Stanwick
Auburn University

Mark Starik
San Francisco State University

Warren Stone
University of Arkansas at Little Rock

Mohan Subramaniam
Boston College

Ram Subramanian
Montclair State University

Jing'an Tang
Sacred Heart University

Linda F. Tegarden
Virginia Tech

Paul W. Thurston, Jr.
Siena College

Thuhang Tran
Middle Tennessee State University

Kim K. J. Tullis
University of Central Oklahoma

Rashada Houston Turner
Florida A&M University

Beverly B. Tyler
North Carolina State University

Jorge Walter
The George Washington University

Isaiah O. Ugboro
North Carolina A&T State University

Bruce Walters
Louisiana Tech University

Jia Wang
California State University, Fresno

Andrew Ward
Lehigh University

Vincent Weaver
Greenville Technical College

Joel West
Claremont Graduate University

McGraw-Hill Connect®
Learn Without Limits

Connect is a teaching and learning platform that is proven to deliver better results for students and instructors.

Connect empowers students by continually adapting to deliver precisely what they need, when they need it, and how they need it, so your class time is more engaging and effective.

Course outcomes improve with Connect.

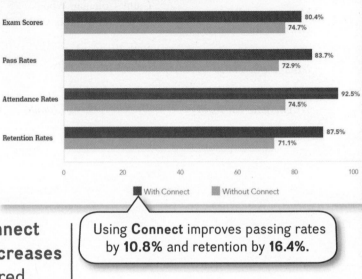

	With Connect	Without Connect
Exam Scores	80.4%	74.7%
Pass Rates	83.7%	72.9%
Attendance Rates	92.5%	74.5%
Retention Rates	87.5%	71.1%

88% of instructors who use **Connect** require it; instructor satisfaction **increases** by 38% when **Connect** is required.

Using **Connect** improves passing rates by **10.8%** and retention by **16.4%**.

Analytics

Connect Insight®

Connect Insight is Connect's new one-of-a-kind visual analytics dashboard—now available for both instructors and students—that provides at-a-glance information regarding student performance, which is immediately actionable. By presenting assignment, assessment, and topical performance results together with a time metric that is easily visible for aggregate or individual results, Connect Insight gives the user the ability to take a just-in-time approach to teaching and learning, which was never before available. Connect Insight presents data that empowers students and helps instructors improve class performance in a way that is efficient and effective.

Connect helps students achieve better grades

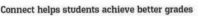

	A	B	C	D	F
With Connect	36%	29.5%	22%	4.3%	8.2%
Without Connect	22.2%	22.3%	25.6%	9.8%	20%

Based on McGraw-Hill Education Connect Effectiveness Study 2013

Students can view their results for any **Connect** course.

Mobile

Connect's new, intuitive mobile interface gives students and instructors flexible and convenient, anytime–anywhere access to all components of the Connect platform.

Adaptive

THE FIRST AND ONLY **ADAPTIVE READING EXPERIENCE** DESIGNED TO TRANSFORM THE WAY STUDENTS READ

More students earn **A's** and **B's** when they use McGraw-Hill Education **Adaptive** products.

SmartBook®

Proven to help students improve grades and study more efficiently, SmartBook contains the same content within the print book, but actively tailors that content to the needs of the individual. SmartBook's adaptive technology provides precise, personalized instruction on what the student should do next, guiding the student to master and remember key concepts, targeting gaps in knowledge and offering customized feedback, and driving the student toward comprehension and retention of the subject matter. Available on smartphones and tablets, SmartBook puts learning at the student's fingertips—anywhere, anytime.

Over **4 billion questions** have been answered, making McGraw-Hill Education products more intelligent, reliable, and precise.

STUDENTS WANT

SMARTBOOK®

95% of students reported **SmartBook** to be a more effective way of reading material

100% of students want to use the Practice Quiz feature available within **SmartBook** to help them study

100% of students reported having reliable access to off-campus wifi

90% of students say they would purchase **SmartBook** over print alone

95% reported that **SmartBook** would impact their study skills in a positive way

*Findings based on a 2015 focus group survey at Pellissippi State Community College administered by McGraw-Hill Education

Analysis

The AFI Strategy Framework

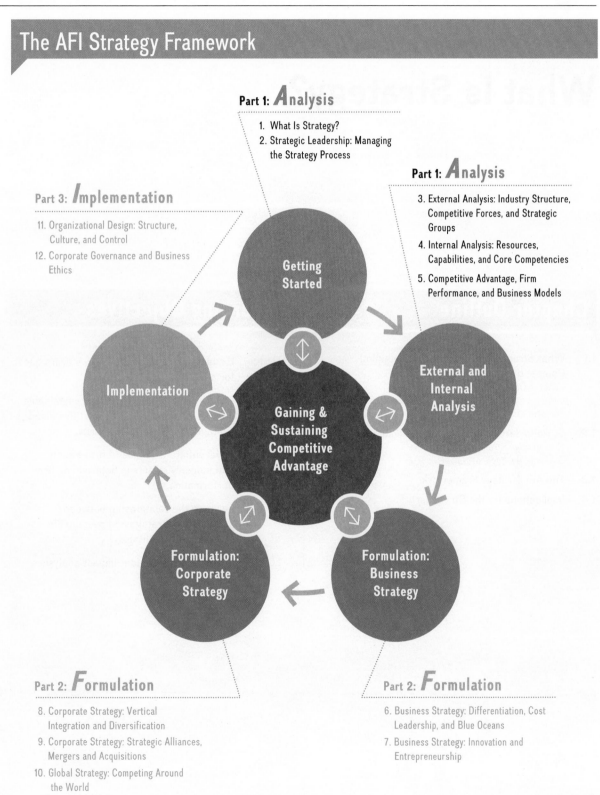

Part 1: *A*nalysis

1. What Is Strategy?
2. Strategic Leadership: Managing the Strategy Process

Part 1: *A*nalysis

3. External Analysis: Industry Structure, Competitive Forces, and Strategic Groups
4. Internal Analysis: Resources, Capabilities, and Core Competencies
5. Competitive Advantage, Firm Performance, and Business Models

Part 3: *I*mplementation

11. Organizational Design: Structure, Culture, and Control
12. Corporate Governance and Business Ethics

Getting Started

External and Internal Analysis

Implementation

Gaining & Sustaining Competitive Advantage

Formulation: Corporate Strategy

Formulation: Business Strategy

Part 2: *F*ormulation

8. Corporate Strategy: Vertical Integration and Diversification
9. Corporate Strategy: Strategic Alliances, Mergers and Acquisitions
10. Global Strategy: Competing Around the World

Part 2: *F*ormulation

6. Business Strategy: Differentiation, Cost Leadership, and Blue Oceans
7. Business Strategy: Innovation and Entrepreneurship

What Is Strategy?

Chapter Outline

Learning Objectives

LO 1-1 Explain the role of strategy in a firm's quest
for competitive advantage.

LO 1-2 Define competitive advantage, sustainable
competitive advantage, competitive disadvantage, and competitive parity.

LO 1-3 Differentiate the roles of firm effects
and industry effects in determining firm
performance.

LO 1-4 Evaluate the relationship between
stakeholder strategy and sustainable
competitive advantage.

LO 1-5 Conduct a stakeholder impact analysis.

Does Twitter Have a Strategy?

TWITTER IS NOT FLYING HIGH. In the summer of 2015, Twitter's stock price was 50 percent lower than what it was shortly after the social networking service went public November 7, 2013. Twitter's disappointing performance led to the departure of its CEO, Dick Costolo, who served from 2010 to 2015. Co-founder Jack Dorsey was brought back as Twitter's CEO. With several high-profile departures and continuing unabated demotions, the young company faced turmoil among its executive ranks.

Jack Dorsey, co-founder and CEO of Twitter.
© Thomas Samson/Getty Images

Launched in 2006, Twitter is often called the "SMS of the Internet" because it allows users to send short messages or "tweets" restricted to 140 characters with pictures and videos often attached.[1] Twitter's leader described the social media service as an "indispensable companion to life in the moment" and "the world's largest information network."[2] Users can follow other people on the social network. For example, Katy Perry, the American singer, song-

CEO of Square; Dick Costolo, CEO of Twitter, 2010–2015.
© AP Photo/Lionel Cironneau

writer, and actress, has more than 70 million followers. Justin Bieber (with 65 million) and President Barack Obama (with 60 million) round out the top three in terms of followers. When a user follows another, she can see that person's status updates in her Twitter feed.

Twitter has some 300 million worldwide active users, that is, people who log in at least once a month. Core users stay connected pretty much permanently, providing multiple status updates throughout the day. Although most tweets cover trivia, Twitter's claim to significance rises from its role in political revolutions such as the Arab Spring or live coverage of breaking news, including the raid on Osama bin Laden's compound in Pakistan. Twitter also appears constantly in the mass media. TV channels show tweets of athletes, politicians, or other celebrities, often live during their shows. Some 20 percent of smartphone users in the United States, and close to 10 percent internationally, use Twitter regularly.

Twitter's business model is to grow its user base and then charge advertisers for promoting goods and services to that base of users. Individual users pay nothing. Their tweets give Twitter free user-generated content to drive more traffic. Companies pay for "promoted tweets" that are directly inserted into a user's news stream. Advertisers value how Twitter can deliver their ads in real time. In one famous episode, when a blackout halted the 2013 Super Bowl for over half an hour, Nabisco promoted Oreo cookies by tweeting, "Power out? No problem. You can still dunk in the dark." Advertisers can also target their ads based on the user's interests or location, the time of day, and so on.

Twitter faces several challenges that make its future prospects highly uncertain. Amid turnover and reshuffling in the management and engineering ranks, Twitter struggles to grow its user base. Compare Twitter's

300 million monthly users to Facebook's 1.5 billion. Twitter needs a larger user base to attract more online advertisers and better monetize its social media service. When serving as CEO, Costolo made the tweet-worthy declaration that Twitter's "ambition is to have the largest audience in the world."[3] Yet, the trend runs in the opposite direction as Twitter's user growth has slowed considerably while Facebook is getting even larger, with a steep rise in users on mobile devices. If Twitter fails to grow in user size to increase the value of the communication platform for online advertisers, it might become either a takeover target for much larger digital advertising companies such as Google or be overtaken by a new social media news app.[4]

You will learn more about Twitter by reading the chapter; related questions appear on page 23.

▲ **WHY IS TWITTER STRUGGLING?** In contrast, why are Facebook and Google so successful? For that matter, why is any company successful? What enables some firms to gain and then sustain their competitive advantage over time? Why do once-great firms fail? How can managers influence firm performance? These are the big questions that define strategic management. Answering these questions requires integrating the knowledge you've obtained in your studies of various business disciplines to understand what leads to superior performance, and how you can help your organization achieve it.

strategic management
An integrative management field that combines analysis, formulation, and implementation in the quest for competitive advantage.

Strategic management is the integrative management field that combines *analysis, formulation,* and *implementation* in the quest for competitive advantage. Mastery of strategic management enables you to view a firm in its entirety. It also enables you to think like a general manager to help position your firm for superior performance. The *AFI strategy framework* (shown on page 3) embodies this view of strategic management. It will guide our exploration of strategic management through the course of your study.

In this chapter, we lay the groundwork for the study of strategic management. We'll introduce foundational ideas about strategy and competitive advantage and then consider the role of business in society. Next, we take a closer look at the components of the AFI framework and provide an overview of the entire strategic management process. We conclude this introductory chapter, as we do with all others in this text, with a section titled "Implications for the Strategist." Here we provide practical applications and considerations of the material developed in the chapter. Let's begin the exciting journey to understand strategic management and competitive advantage.

LO 1-1

Explain the role of strategy in a firm's quest for competitive advantage.

1.1 What Strategy Is: Gaining and Sustaining Competitive Advantage

strategy
The set of goal-directed actions a firm takes to gain and sustain superior performance relative to competitors.

Strategy is a set of goal-directed actions a firm takes to gain and sustain superior performance *relative* to competitors.[5] To achieve superior performance, companies compete for resources: New ventures compete for financial and human capital. Existing companies compete for profitable growth. Charities compete for donations, and universities compete for the best students and professors. Sports teams compete for championships, while celebrities compete for media attention. As highlighted in the ChapterCase, Twitter is competing for more users against other social media such as SnapChat, Facebook and its messaging service WhatsApp, and others. In any competitive situation, therefore, a *good strategy* enables a firm to achieve superior performance. This leads to the question: What is a good strategy?

A *good strategy* consists of three elements:[6]

1. A *diagnosis* of the competitive challenge. This element is accomplished through *analysis* of the firm's external and internal environments (Part 1 of the AFI framework).

2. A *guiding policy* to address the competitive challenge. This element is accomplished through strategy *formulation,* resulting in the firm's corporate, business, and functional strategies (Part 2 of the AFI framework).

3. A *set of coherent actions* to implement the firm's guiding policy. This element is accomplished through strategy *implementation* (Part 3 of the AFI framework).

Let's revisit ChapterCase 1 to see whether Twitter is pursuing a good strategy. A quick rereading indicates that Twitter appears to be underperforming, and thus its strategy does not seem to be a good one. Let's take a closer look at the three elements of a good strategy to see how Twitter's CEO could turn a bad strategy into a winning one.[7]

THE COMPETITIVE CHALLENGE. A good strategy needs to start with a clear and critical diagnosis of the competitive challenge. ChapterCase 1 indicates that the biggest competitive challenge for Twitter is to grow its user base to become more valuable for online advertisers. With some 300 million active users compared to Facebook's roughly 1.5 billion monthly users, Twitter is viewed by advertisers as a niche application. Companies direct the bulk of their digital ad dollars to Facebook and Google rather than Twitter. Moreover, Twitter suffers in comparison to Facebook for reasons other than sheer scale. Facebook allows advertisers to target their online ads much more precisely based on a host of demographic data that the social network collects and infers about each user, including birth year, university affiliation, network of friends, interests, and so on.

A GUIDING POLICY. Next, after the diagnosis of the competitive challenge, the strategist needs to formulate an effective guiding policy in response. The formulated strategy needs to be consistent, often backed up with strategic commitments such as sizable investments or changes to an organization's incentive and reward system—big changes that cannot be easily reversed. Without consistency in a firm's guiding policy, a firm's employees become confused and cannot make effective day-to-day decisions that support the overall strategy. Without consistency in strategy, moreover, other stakeholders, including investors, also become frustrated.

Here is where Twitter's problems begin. While its leaders are well aware of the competitive challenge it faces and have diagnosed this challenge correctly, they still lack a clear, guiding policy for facing this challenge. They could respond to it by taking steps to accelerate user sign-ups and usage. For example, such steps could include making the sign-up process and use of the services easier, explaining the sometimes idiosyncratic conventions on Twitter to a broader audience, and rooting out offensive content. However, rather than formulating a guiding policy to grow active core users, Twitter has emphasized defining its user base more broadly. When serving as CEO, Costolo specifically declared that the company should be seen as "three geometrically [con]centric circles" reflecting three types of users. The first inner circle represents direct users of the social media service; the second, visitors to the Twitter site who do not log in; and the third, people who view Twitter content on affiliate sites such as cable news networks, live sportscasts, and other websites. Twitter decided that it should henceforth pursue all three types of users.

The goal of providing a new definition of Twitter users is clear: To expand the perception of its reach so as to compare more favorably to Facebook. Changing the definition of users, however, is not sufficient to address the competitive challenge of growing the base of core users. Moreover, users in the second and third circle are harder to track, and more importantly, they are also much less valuable to advertisers than core users.

COHERENT ACTIONS. Finally, a clear guiding policy needs to be implemented with a set of coherent actions. Changing the goalpost of which users to go after not only confused management, but it also limited functional guidance for employees in day-to-day operations. Consequences of an unclear mission followed: Frustration among managers and engineers increased, leading to turnover of key personnel. Internal turmoil was further stoked by a number of management demotions as well as promotions of close personal friends of the respective CEO. From its inception, Twitter's culture has been hampered by infighting and public intrigues among co-founders and other early leaders.

In summary, a good strategy is more than a mere goal or a company slogan. Declaring that Twitter's "ambition is to have the largest audience in the world"[8] is not a good strategy; it is no strategy at all. Rather it is a mere statement of desire. In creating a good strategy, three steps are crucial. First, a good strategy defines the competitive challenges facing an organization through a critical and honest assessment of the status quo. Second, a good strategy provides an overarching approach on how to deal with the competitive challenges identified. The approach needs to be communicated in policies that provide clear guidance for all employees involved. Last, a good strategy requires effective implementation through a coherent set of actions.

LO 1-2

Define competitive advantage, sustainable competitive advantage, competitive disadvantage, and competitive parity.

WHAT IS COMPETITIVE ADVANTAGE?

Competitive advantage is always *relative,* not absolute. To assess competitive advantage, we compare firm performance to a *benchmark*—that is, either the performance of other firms in the same industry or an industry average. A firm that achieves superior performance relative to other competitors in the same industry or the industry average has a **competitive advantage**.[9] Google has a competitive advantage over Facebook, Twitter, and Yahoo in digital advertising. In smartphones, Apple has achieved a competitive advantage over Samsung, Microsoft, and BlackBerry. A firm that is able to outperform its competitors or the industry average over a prolonged period of time has a **sustainable competitive advantage**.

If a firm underperforms its rivals or the industry average, it has a **competitive disadvantage**. For example, a 15 percent return on invested capital may sound like superior firm performance. In the consulting industry, though, where the average return on invested capital is often above 20 percent, such a return puts a firm at a competitive disadvantage. In contrast, if a firm's return on invested capital is 2 percent in a declining industry, like newspaper publishing, where the industry average has been negative (-5 percent) for the past few years, then the firm has a competitive advantage. Should two or more firms perform at the same level, they have **competitive parity**. In Chapter 5, we'll discuss in greater depth how to evaluate and assess competitive advantage and firm performance.

To gain a competitive advantage, a firm needs to provide either goods or services consumers value more highly than those of its competitors, or goods or services similar to the competitors' at a lower price.[10] The rewards of superior value creation and capture are profitability and market share. Sam Walton was driven by offering lower prices than his competitors. Steve Jobs wanted to "put a ding in the universe"—making a difference by delivering products and services people love. Mark Zuckerberg built Facebook to make the world more open and connected. Google co-founders Larry Page and Sergey Brin are motivated to make the world's information universally accessible. For Walton, Jobs, Zuckerberg, Page, Brin, and numerous other entrepreneurs

---

competitive advantage
Superior performance relative to other competitors in the same industry or the industry average.

sustainable competitive advantage
Outperforming competitors or the industry average over a prolonged period of time.

competitive disadvantage
Underperformance relative to other competitors in the same industry or the industry average.

competitive parity
Performance of two or more firms at the same level.

and businesspeople, creating shareholder value and making money is the *consequence* of filling a need and providing a product, service, or experience consumers wanted, at a price they could afford.

The important point here is that strategy is about creating superior value, while containing the cost to create it. Managers achieve this combination of value and cost through *strategic positioning.* That is, they stake out a unique position within an industry that allows the firm to provide value to customers, while controlling costs. The greater the difference between value creation and cost, the greater the firm's *economic contribution* and the more likely it will gain competitive advantage.

Strategic positioning requires *trade-offs,* however. As a low-cost retailer, Walmart has a clear strategic profile and serves a specific market segment. Upscale retailer Nordstrom has also built a clear strategic profile by providing superior customer service to a higher end, luxury market segment. Although these companies are in the same industry, their customer segments overlap very little, and they are not direct competitors. Walmart and Nordstrom have each chosen a distinct but different strategic position. The managers make conscious trade-offs that enable each company to strive for competitive advantage in the retail industry, using different competitive strategies: leadership versus differentiation. In regard to the customer service dimension, Walmart provides acceptable service by low-skill employees in a big-box retail outlet offering "everyday low prices," while Nordstrom provides a superior customer experience by professional salespeople in a luxury setting. A clear strategic profile—in terms of product differentiation, cost, and customer service—allows each retailer to meet specific customer needs. Competition focuses on creating value for customers (through lower prices or better service and selection, in this example) rather than destroying rivals. Even though Walmart and Nordstrom compete in the same industry, both can win if they achieve a clear strategic position through a well-executed competitive strategy.

Since clear strategic positioning requires trade-offs, strategy is as much about deciding what *not* to do, as it is about deciding what to do.[11] Because resources are limited, managers must carefully consider their strategic choices in the quest for competitive advantage. Trying to be everything to everybody will likely result in inferior performance.

Given Twitter's new emphasis on its target audience as comprising three discrete segments, many employees at Twitter lament confusion in deciding how to serve all three. As Twitter attempts to be more attractive to different types of users simultaneously, it encounters trade-offs that are hard if not impossible to reconcile. Consider the functionality of an application such as search or mobile use, for example: Core users have very different needs from the needs of casual visitors or passive viewers of Twitter content. In an attempt to match Facebook's scale, Twitter is attempting to be everything to everybody, without considering the strategic trade-offs. This resulted not only in low employee morale, but also in inferior performance. In contrast, Facebook is fully committed to providing a superior user experience for its 1.5 billion active core users on mobile devices.[12]

The key to successful strategy is to combine a set of activities to stake out a *unique position* within an industry. Competitive advantage has to come from performing different activities or performing the same activities differently than rivals are doing. Ideally, these activities reinforce one another rather than create trade-offs. For instance, Walmart's strategic activities strengthen its position as cost leader: Big retail stores in rural locations, extremely high purchasing power, sophisticated IT systems, regional distribution centers, low corporate overhead, and low base wages and salaries combined with employee profit sharing reinforce each other, to maintain the company's cost leadership. Strategy Highlight 1.1 takes a closer look at how the online startup Threadless used different activities than rivals to gain a competitive advantage in the apparel industry.

Strategy Highlight 1.1

Threadless: Leveraging Crowdsourcing to Design Cool T-Shirts

Jacob DeHart, left, and Jake Nickell, center, (co-founders) and Jeffrey Kalmikoff (early CEO) created Threadless, an online company that sells millions of dollars' worth of T-shirts annually.
© Jason Wambsgans/MCT/Newscom

Threadless, an online design community and apparel store (www .threadless.com), was founded in 2000 by two students with $1,000 as start-up capital. Jake Nickell was then at the Illinois Institute of Art and Jacob DeHart at Purdue University. After Jake had won an online T-shirt design contest, the two entrepreneurs came up with a business model to leverage user-generated content. The idea is to let consumers "work for you" and turn consumers into *prosumers*, a hybrid between producers and consumers.

Members of the Threadless community, which is some 2.5 million strong, do most of the work, which they consider fun: They submit T-shirt designs online, and community members vote on which designs they like best. The designs receiving the most votes are put in production,

printed, and sold online. Each Monday, Threadless releases 10 new designs and reprints more T-shirts throughout the week as inventory is cleared out. The cost of Threadless T-shirts is a bit higher than that of competitors, about $25.

Threadless leverages *crowdsourcing,* a process in which a group of people voluntarily perform tasks that were traditionally completed by a firm's employees. Rather than doing the work in-house, Threadless outsources its T-shirt design to its website community. The concept of leveraging a firm's own customers via Internet-enabled technology to help produce better products is explicitly included in the Threadless business model. In particular, Threadless is leveraging the *wisdom of the crowds,* where the resulting decisions by many participants in the online forum are often better than decisions that could have been made by a single individual. To more effectively leverage this idea, the crowds need to be large and diverse.

At Threadless, the customers play a critical role across the entire value chain, from idea generation to design, marketing, sales forecasting, and distribution. The Threadless business model translates real-time market research and design contests into quick sales. Threadless produces only T-shirts that were approved by its community. Moreover, it has a good understanding of market demand because it knows the number of people who participated in each design contest. In addition, when scoring each T-shirt design in a contest, Threadless users have the option to check "*I'd buy it.*" These features give the Threadless community a voice in T-shirt design and also coax community members into making a prepurchasing commitment. Threadless does not make any significant investments until the design and market size are determined, minimizing its downside.

Not surprisingly, Threadless has sold every T-shirt that it has printed. Moreover, it has a cult-like following and is outperforming established companies American Eagle, Old Navy, and Urban Outfitters with their more formulaic T-shirt designs.[13]

In addition, operational effectiveness, marketing skills, and other functional expertise all strengthen a unique strategic position. Those capabilities, though, do not substitute for competitive strategy. Competing to be similar but just a bit better than your competitor is likely to be a recipe for cut-throat competition and low profit potential. Let's take this idea to its extreme in a quick thought experiment: If all firms in the same industry pursued a low-cost position through application of competitive benchmarking, all firms would have identical cost structures. None could gain a competitive advantage. Everyone would be running faster, but nothing would change in terms of relative strategic positions.

There would be little if any value creation for customers because companies would have no resources to invest in product and process improvements. Moreover, the least-efficient firms would be driven out, further reducing customer choice.

To gain a deeper understanding of what strategy is, it may be helpful to think about what strategy is *not*.[14] Be on the lookout for the following major hallmarks of what strategy is NOT:

1. *Grandiose statements are not strategy.* You may have heard firms say things like, "Our strategy is to win" or "We will be No. 1." Twitter declared its "ambition is to have the largest audience in the world." Such statements of desire, on their own, are not strategy. They provide little managerial guidance and often lead to goal conflict and confusion. Moreover, such wishful thinking frequently fails to address economic fundamentals. As we will discuss in the next chapter, an effective vision and mission *can* lay the foundation upon which to craft a good strategy. This foundation must be backed up, however, by strategic actions that allow the firm to address a competitive challenge with clear consideration of economic fundamentals, in particular, value creation and costs.

2. *A failure to face a competitive challenge is not strategy.* If the firm does not define a clear competitive challenge, managers have no way of assessing whether they are making progress in addressing it. Managers at the now-defunct video rental chain Blockbuster, for example, failed to address the competitive challenges posed by new players Netflix, Redbox, Amazon Prime, and Hulu.

3. *Operational effectiveness, competitive benchmarking, or other tactical tools are not strategy.* People casually refer to a host of different policies and initiatives as some sort of strategy: pricing strategy, Internet strategy, alliance strategy, operations strategy, IT strategy, brand strategy, marketing strategy, HR strategy, China strategy, and so on. All these elements may be a *necessary* part of a firm's functional and global initiatives to support its competitive strategy, but these elements are *not sufficient* to achieve competitive advantage. In this text, though, we will reserve the term *strategy* for describing the firm's overall efforts to *gain and sustain competitive advantage*.

INDUSTRY VS. FIRM EFFECTS IN DETERMINING FIRM PERFORMANCE

Firm performance is determined primarily by two factors: industry and firm effects. **Industry effects** describe the underlying economic structure of the industry. They attribute firm performance to the industry in which the firm competes. The structure of an industry is determined by elements common to all industries, elements such as entry and exit barriers, number and size of companies, and types of products and services offered. In a series of empirical studies, academic researchers have found that about 20 percent of a firm's profitability depends on the industry it's in.[15] In Chapter 3, when studying external analysis, we'll gain a deeper understanding of an industry's underlying structure and how it affects firm performance.

Firm effects attribute firm performance to the actions managers take. In Chapter 4, we'll look inside the firm to understand why firms within the same industry differ, and how differences among firms can lead to competitive advantage.

For now, the key point is that managers' actions tend to be more important in determining firm performance than the forces exerted on the firm by its external environment.[16] Empirical research studies indicate that a firm's strategy can explain up to 55 percent of its performance.[17] Exhibit 1.1 shows these findings.

LO 1-3

Differentiate the roles of firm effects and industry effects in determining firm performance.

industry effects Firm performance attributed to the structure of the industry in which the firm competes.

firm effects Firm performance attributed to the actions managers take.

Other Effects
(Business Cycle Effects,
Unexplained Variance)

~25%

Up to 55% **Firm Effects**

~20%

Industry Effects

Although a firm's industry environment is not quite as important as the firm's strategy within its industry, they jointly determine roughly 75 percent of overall firm performance. The remaining 25 percent relates partly to business cycles and other effects.

Competition—the ongoing struggle among firms to gain and sustain competitive advantage—does not take place in isolation. Managers therefore must understand the relationship between strategic management and the role of business in society, which we will turn to next.

1.2 Stakeholders and Competitive Advantage

Companies with a good strategy generate value for society. When firms compete in their own self-interest while obeying the law and acting ethically, they ultimately create value. Value creation occurs because companies with a good strategy are able to provide products or services to consumers at a price point that they can afford while making a profit at the same time. Both parties benefit from this trade as each captures a part of the value created. In so doing, they make society better.[18] Value creation in turn lays the foundation for the benefits that successful economies can provide: education, public safety, and health care, among others. Superior performance allows a firm to reinvest some of its profits and to grow, which in turn provides more opportunities for employment and fulfilling careers. Although Google started as a research project in graduate school by Larry Page and Sergey Brin, it is worth roughly $350 billion and employs some 55,000 people worldwide, not to mention the billions of people across the world who rely on it for information gathering.[19]

Strategic failure, in contrast, can be expensive. Once a leading technology company, Hewlett-Packard was known for innovation, resulting in superior products. The "HP way of management" included lifetime employment, generous benefits, work/life balance, and freedom to explore ideas, among other perks.[20] However, HP has not been able to address the competitive challenges of mobile computing or business IT services effectively. As a result, HP's stakeholders suffered. Shareholder value was destroyed. The company also had to lay off tens of thousands of employees in recent years. Its customers no longer received the innovative products and services that made HP famous.

The contrasting examples of Google and HP illustrate the relationship between individual firms and society at large. Recently, this relationship received more critical scrutiny due to some major shocks to free-market capitalism.

In the first decade of the 21st century, several **black swan events** eroded the public's trust in business as an institution and capitalism as an economic system.[21] In the past, most people assumed that all swans are white, so when they first encountered swans that were black, they were surprised. Today, the metaphor of a black swan describes the *high impact of a highly improbable event.*[22] Examples of black swan events include the fall of the Berlin Wall and the subsequent collapse of the Soviet Union, the 9/11 terrorist attacks, the Fukushima nuclear disaster in Japan, and the Arab Spring. Such events were considered to be highly improbable and thus unexpected, but when they did occur, each had a very profound impact.

The implicit trust relationship between the corporate world and society at large has deteriorated because of the arrival of several black swans. One of the first black swan events of the 21st century occurred when the accounting scandals at Enron, Arthur Andersen, WorldCom, Tyco, Adelphia, and Parmalat (of Italy) came to light. Those events led to bankruptcies, large-scale job loss, and the destruction of billions of dollars in shareholder value. As a result, the public's trust in business and free market capitalism began to erode.

Another black swan event occurred in the fall of 2008 with the global financial crisis, which shook the entire free market system to its core.[23] A real estate bubble had developed in the United States, fueled by cheap credit and the availability of subprime mortgages. When that bubble burst, many entities faced financial stress or bankruptcy—those who had unsustainable mortgages, investors holding securities based on those mortgages, and the financial institutions that had sold the securities. Some went under, and others were sold at fire-sale prices. Home foreclosures skyrocketed as a large number of borrowers defaulted on their mortgages. House prices in the United States plummeted by roughly 30 percent. The Dow Jones Industrial Average (DJIA) lost about half its market value, plunging the United States into a deep recession.

The impact was worldwide. The freezing of capital markets during the global financial crisis triggered a debt crisis in Europe. Some European governments (notably Greece) defaulted on government debt; other countries were able to repay their debts only through the assistance of other, more solvent European countries. This severe financial crisis not only put Europe's common currency, the euro, at risk, but also led to a prolonged and deep recession in Europe.

In the United States, the Occupy Wall Street protest movement was born out of dissatisfaction with the capitalist system. Issues of income disparity, corporate ethics, corporate influence on governments, and ecological sustainability were key drivers. The Occupy movement, organized through social media platforms such as Twitter and Facebook, eventually expanded around the world.

Although these black swan events in the business world differed in their specifics, two common features are pertinent to our study of strategic management.[24] First, these events demonstrate that managerial actions can affect the economic well-being of large numbers of people around the globe. Most of the events resulted from executive actions (or inactions) within a single organization, or compounded across a specific industry or government.

The second pertinent feature relates to **stakeholders**—organizations, groups, and individuals that can affect or be affected by a firm's actions.[25] This leads us to *stakeholder strategy,* which we discuss next.

© Krys Bailey/Alamy

black swan events
Incidents that describe highly improbable but high-impact events.

stakeholders
Organizations, groups, and individuals that can affect or are affected by a firm's actions.

STAKEHOLDER STRATEGY

Stakeholders have a vested claim or interest in the performance and continued survival of the firm. Stakeholders can be grouped by whether they are internal or external to a firm. As shown in Exhibit 1.2, *internal stakeholders* include stockholders, employees (including executives, managers, and workers), and board members. *External stakeholders* include customers, suppliers, alliance partners, creditors, unions, communities, governments at various levels, and the media.

All stakeholders make specific contributions to a firm, which in turn provides different types of benefits to different stakeholders. Employees contribute their time and talents to the firm, receiving wages and salaries in exchange. Shareholders contribute capital in the hope that the stock will rise and the firm will pay dividends. Communities provide real estate, infrastructure, and public safety. In return, they expect that companies will pay taxes, provide employment, and not pollute the environment. The firm, therefore, is embedded in a multifaceted *exchange relationship* with a number of diverse internal and external stakeholders.

If any stakeholder withholds participation in the firm's exchange relationships, it can negatively affect firm performance. The aerospace company Boeing, for example, has a long history of acrimonious labor relations, leading to walk-outs and strikes. This in turn has not only delayed production of airplanes but also raised costs. Borrowers who purchased subprime mortgages are stakeholders (in this case, customers) of financial institutions. When they defaulted in large numbers, they threatened the survival of these financial institutions and, ultimately, of the entire financial system.

Stakeholder strategy is an integrative approach to managing a diverse set of stakeholders effectively in order to gain and sustain competitive advantage.[26] The unit of analysis is the web of exchange relationships a firm has with its stakeholders (see Exhibit 1.2). Stakeholder strategy allows firms to analyze and manage how various external and internal stakeholders interact to jointly create and trade value.[27] A core tenet of stakeholder strategy is that a single-minded focus on shareholders alone exposes a firm to undue risks. Simply putting shareholder interest above all else can undermine economic performance and even threaten the very survival of the enterprise. The strategist, therefore, must understand the complex web of exchange relationships among different stakeholders. With that understanding, the firm can proactively shape the various relationships to maximize the

stakeholder strategy
An integrative approach to managing a diverse set of stakeholders effectively in order to gain and sustain competitive advantage.

EXHIBIT 1.2 /

Internal and External Stakeholders in an Exchange Relationship with the Firm

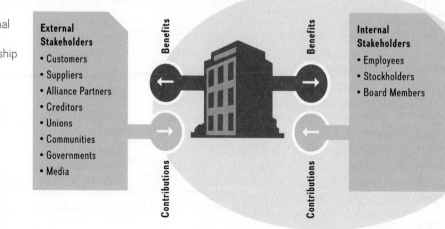

joint value created and manage the distribution of this larger pie in a fair and transparent manner. Effective stakeholder management exemplifies how managers can act to improve firm performance, thereby enhancing the firm's competitive advantage and the likelihood of its continued survival.[28]

Target Corporation has gathered numerous awards that reflect its strong relationship with its stakeholders. It has been named on lists such as best places to work, most admired companies, most ethical companies, best in class for corporate governance, and grassroots innovation. Since its founding, Target has contributed 5 percent of its profits to education, the arts, and social services in the communities in which it operates and reached the milestone of contributing $4 million per week in 2012. To demonstrate its commitment to minorities and women, Target launched a program to bring minority- and women-owned businesses into its supply chain. Volunteerism and corporate giving strengthen the relationship Target has with its employees, consumers, local communities, and suppliers. These actions, along with many others, can help Target gain competitive advantage as a retailer as long as the benefits Target accrues from its stakeholder strategy exceed the costs of such programs.[29]

Strategy scholars have provided several arguments as to why effective stakeholder management can benefit firm performance:[30]

- Satisfied stakeholders are more cooperative and thus more likely to reveal information that can further increase the firm's value creation or lower its costs.
- Increased trust lowers the costs for firms' business transactions.
- Effective management of the complex web of stakeholders can lead to greater organizational adaptability and flexibility.
- The likelihood of negative outcomes can be reduced, creating more predictable and stable returns.
- Firms can build strong reputations that are rewarded in the marketplace by business partners, employees, and customers. Most managers do care about public perception of the firm, and frequently celebrate and publicize high-profile rankings such as the "World's Most Admired Companies" published annually by *Fortune*.[31] In 2014, the top five companies in this ranking were Apple, Amazon, Google, Berkshire Hathaway (the conglomerate led by Warren Buffett), and Starbucks. Because of its continued innovation in products, services, and delivery, Apple has been ranked as the world's most admired company for the past several years by *Fortune*.

STAKEHOLDER IMPACT ANALYSIS

Conduct a stakeholder impact analysis.

The key challenge of stakeholder strategy is to effectively balance the needs of various stakeholders. The firm needs to ensure that its primary stakeholders—the firm's shareholders and other investors—achieve their objectives. At the same time, the firm needs to recognize and address the concerns of other stakeholders—employees, suppliers, and customers—in an ethical and fair manner, so that they too are satisfied. This all sounds good in theory, but how can managers go about this in practice?

Stakeholder impact analysis provides a decision tool with which managers can recognize, prioritize, and address the needs of different stakeholders. This tool helps the firm achieve a competitive advantage while acting as a good corporate citizen. Stakeholder impact analysis takes managers through a five-step process of recognizing stakeholders' claims. In each step, managers must pay particular attention to three important stakeholder attributes: *power, legitimacy,* and *urgency.*[32]

- A stakeholder has *power* over a company when it can get the company to do something that it would not otherwise do.

stakeholder impact analysis
A decision tool with which managers can recognize, prioritize, and address the needs of different stakeholders, enabling the firm to achieve competitive advantage while acting as a good corporate citizen.

■ A stakeholder has a *legitimate claim* when it is perceived to be legally valid or otherwise appropriate.

■ A stakeholder has an *urgent claim* when it requires a company's immediate attention and response.

Exhibit 1.3 depicts the five steps in stakeholder impact analysis and the key questions to be asked. Let's look at each step in detail.

STEP 1: IDENTIFY STAKEHOLDERS. In step 1, the firm asks, "Who are our stakeholders?" In this step, the firm focuses on stakeholders that currently have, or potentially can have, a material effect on a company. This prioritization identifies the most powerful internal and external stakeholders as well as their needs. For public-stock companies, key stakeholders are the shareholders and other suppliers of capital. If shareholders are not satisfied with returns to investment, they will sell the company's stock, leading to depreciation in the firm's market value. If this process continues, it can make the company a takeover target, or launch a vicious cycle of continued decline.

A second group of stakeholders includes customers, suppliers, and unions. Local communities and the media are also powerful stakeholders that can materially affect the smooth operation of the firm. Any of these groups, if their needs are not met, can materially affect the company's operations.

For example, Boeing opened a new airplane factory in South Carolina in 2011 to move production away from its traditional plant near Seattle, Washington. In contrast to Washington state, in South Carolina the work force is nonunionized, which should lead to fewer work interruptions due to strikes, higher productivity, and improvements along other performance dimensions (like on-time delivery of new airplanes). In 2014, Boeing announced that its new 787 Dreamliner jet would be exclusively built in its nonunionized South Carolina factory.[33]

STEP 2: IDENTIFY STAKEHOLDERS' INTERESTS. In step 2, the firm asks, "What are our stakeholders' interests and claims?" Managers need to specify and assess the interests and claims of the pertinent stakeholders using the power, legitimacy, and urgency criteria

EXHIBIT 1.3 / Stakeholder Impact Analysis

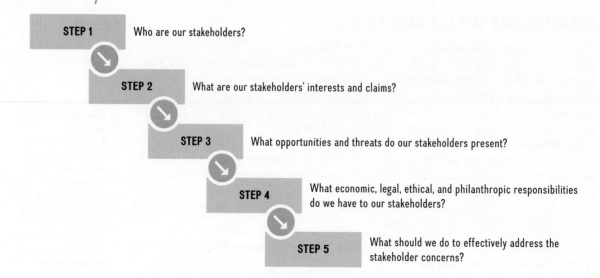

STEP 1 Who are our stakeholders?

STEP 2 What are our stakeholders' interests and claims?

STEP 3 What opportunities and threats do our stakeholders present?

STEP 4 What economic, legal, ethical, and philanthropic responsibilities do we have to our stakeholders?

STEP 5 What should we do to effectively address the stakeholder concerns?

introduced earlier. As the legal owners, shareholders have the most legitimate claim on a company's profits. However, the wall separating the claims of ownership (by shareholders) and of management (by employees) has been eroding. Many companies incentivize top executives by paying part of their overall compensation with stock options. They also turn employees into shareholders through *employee stock ownership plans (ESOPs)*. These plans allow employees to purchase stock at a discounted rate or use company stock as an investment vehicle for retirement savings. For example, Coca-Cola, Google, Microsoft, Southwest Airlines, Starbucks, Walmart, and Whole Foods all offer ESOPs. Clearly, the claims and interests of stakeholders who are employed by the company, and who depend on the company for salary and other benefits, will be somewhat different from those of stakeholders who merely own stock. The latter are investors who are primarily interested in the increased value of their stock holdings through appreciation and dividend payments. Executives, managers, and workers tend to be more interested in career opportunities, job security, employer-provided health care, paid vacation time, and other perks.

Even within stakeholder groups there can be significant variation in the power a stakeholder may exert on the firm. For example, public companies pay much more attention to large investors than to the millions of smaller, individual investors. *Shareholder activists,* such as Carl Icahn, Daniel Loeb, or T. Boone Pickens, tend to buy equity stakes in a corporation that they believe is underperforming to put public pressure on a company to change its strategy. Examples include the takeover battle at Dell Computer (which founder Michael Dell subsequently took private), the pressure on PepsiCo to spin off its Frito-Lay brand, or on eBay to sell PayPal, which it did. Even top-performing companies are not immune to pressure by shareholder activists.[34] As a result of a sustained competitive advantage over the last decade, Apple had not only become the most valuable company on the planet but also amassed some $200 billion in cash in the process. Apple CEO Tim Cook faced significant pressure from Carl Icahn, who held roughly $4 billion worth of Apple stock, to buy back more of its shares and thus to further raise Apple's share price.

Although both individual and activist investors may claim the same legitimacy as stockholders, shareholder activists have much more power over a firm. They can buy and sell a large number of shares at once, or exercise block-voting rights in the *corporate-governance process* (which we'll discuss in detail in Chapter 12). Shareholder activists frequently also demand seats on the company's boards to more directly influence its corporate governance, and with it exert more pressure to change a company's strategy. These abilities make activist investors potent stakeholders.

STEP 3: IDENTIFY OPPORTUNITIES AND THREATS. In step 3, the firm asks, "What opportunities and threats do our stakeholders present?" Since stakeholders have a claim on the company, opportunities and threats are two sides of the same coin. Consumer boycotts, for example, can be a credible threat to a company's behavior. Some consumers boycotted Nestlé products when the firm promoted infant formula over breast milk in developing countries. PETA[35] called for a boycott of McDonald's due to alleged animal-rights abuses.

In the best-case scenario, managers transform such threats into opportunities. Sony Corp., for example, was able to do just that.[36] During one holiday season, the Dutch government blocked Sony's entire holiday season shipment of PlayStation game systems, valued at roughly $500 million, into the European Union because of a small but legally unacceptable amount of toxic cadmium discovered in one of the system's cables. This incident led to an 18-month investigation in which Sony inspected over 6,000 supplier factories around the world to track down the source of the problem. The findings allowed Sony to redesign and develop a cutting-edge supplier management system that now adheres to a stringent extended value chain responsibility.

STEP 4: IDENTIFY SOCIAL RESPONSIBILITIES. In step 4, the firm asks, "What economic, legal, ethical, and philanthropic responsibilities do we have to our stakeholders?" To identify these responsibilities more effectively, scholars have advanced the notion of **corporate social responsibility (CSR).** This framework helps firms recognize and address the economic, legal, ethical, and philanthropic expectations that society has of the business enterprise at a given point in time.[37] According to the CSR perspective, managers need to realize that society grants shareholders the right and privilege to create a publicly traded stock company. Therefore, the firm owes something to society.[38] Moreover, CSR provides managers with a conceptual model that more completely describes a society's expectations and can guide strategic decision making more effectively. In particular, CSR has four components: economic, legal, ethical, and philanthropic responsibilities.[39]

> **corporate social responsibility (CSR)** A framework that helps firms recognize and address the economic, legal, social, and philanthropic expectations that society has of the business enterprise at a given point in time.

Economic Responsibilities. The business enterprise is first and foremost an economic institution. Investors expect an adequate return for their risk capital. Creditors expect the firm to repay its debts. Consumers expect safe products and services at appropriate prices and quality. Suppliers expect to be paid in full and on time. Governments expect the firm to pay taxes and to manage natural resources such as air and water under a decent stewardship. To accomplish all this, firms must obey the law and act ethically in their quest to gain and sustain competitive advantage.

Legal Responsibilities. Laws and regulations are a society's codified ethics, embodying notions of right and wrong. They also establish the rules of the game. For example, business as an institution can function because property rights exist and contracts can be enforced in courts of law. Managers must ensure that their firms obey all the laws and regulations, including but not limited to labor, consumer protection, and environmental laws.

One far-reaching piece of U.S. legislation in terms of business impact, for example, is the Patient Protection and Affordable Care Act (PPACA), more commonly known as Affordable Care Act (ACA) or Obamacare. Key provisions of this federal law include, among others, that firms with 50 or more full-time employees must offer affordable health insurance to their employees and dependents, or pay a fine for each worker. This will make it harder for entrepreneurs to grow their ventures above this threshold. One reaction of many small businesses has been to reduce the number of full-time workers to 49 employees and add part-time employees only, which do not fall under this provision. Another reaction of employers is to offer lower wages to compensate for higher health care costs. Moreover, health insurance providers are no longer allowed to deny coverage based on preexisting medical conditions. Some observers are concerned that this may drive up health care premiums further as the overall risk pool of insurers will be less healthy. In an attempt to balance the risk pool, however, the ACA also includes the so-called individual mandate, which requires every individual, including young and healthy people, to carry health insurance or pay a fine. People who cannot afford health insurance will receive government subsidies.[40]

Ethical Responsibilities. Legal responsibilities, however, often define only the minimum acceptable standards of firm behavior. Frequently, managers are called upon to go beyond what is required by law. The letter of the law cannot address or anticipate all possible business situations and newly emerging concerns such as Internet privacy or advances in DNA testing, genetic engineering, and stem-cell research.

A firm's ethical responsibilities, therefore, go beyond its legal responsibilities. They embody the full scope of expectations, norms, and values of its stakeholders. Managers are called upon to do what society deems just and fair. Starbucks, for example, developed an ethical sourcing policy to help source coffee of the highest quality, while adhering to fair trade and responsible growing practices. On the other hand, Starbucks has been criticized for not paying an adequate amount of taxes in the United Kingdom. Albeit entirely legal, Starbucks did pay very little in corporate income taxes since opening its first store in the UK in 1998 (around $13.5 million total). In an attempt to silence the critics, to stop protests, and to please its British customers, Starbucks volunteered an additional tax payment of $16 million for the 2013–14 tax year, despite having no legal obligation to do so.[41]

Philanthropic Responsibilities. Philanthropic responsibilities are often subsumed under the idea of *corporate citizenship,* reflecting the notion of voluntarily giving back to society. Over the years, Microsoft's corporate philanthropy program has donated more than $3 billion in cash and software to people who can't afford computer technology.[42]

The pyramid in Exhibit 1.4 summarizes the four components of corporate social responsibility.[43] Economic responsibilities are the foundational building block, followed by legal, ethical, and philanthropic responsibilities. Note that society and shareholders *require* economic and legal responsibilities. Ethical and philanthropic responsibilities result from a society's expectations toward business. The pyramid symbolizes the need for firms to carefully balance their social responsibilities. Doing so ensures not only effective strategy implementation, but also long-term viability.

STEP 5: ADDRESS STAKEHOLDER CONCERNS. Finally, in step 5, the firm asks, "What should we do to effectively address any stakeholder concerns?" In the last step in stakeholder impact analysis, managers need to decide the appropriate course of action for the firm, given all of the preceding factors. Thinking about the attributes of power, legitimacy, and urgency helps to prioritize the legitimate claims and to address them accordingly. Strategy Highlight 1.2 describes how the U.S. government legitimized claims by thousands of businesses and individuals in the aftermath of the BP oil spill in the Gulf of Mexico, causing the claims to become of great urgency to BP.

Philanthropic Responsibilities — Corporate citizenship

Ethical Responsibilities — Do what is right, just, and fair

Legal Responsibilities — Laws and regulations are society's codified ethics / Define minimum acceptable standard

Economic Responsibilities — Gain and sustain competitive advantage

EXHIBIT 1.4

The Pyramid of Corporate Social Responsibility

Source: Adapted from A. B. Carroll (1991), "The pyramid of corporate social responsibility: Toward the moral management of organizational stakeholders," *Business Horizons,* July–August: 42.

Strategy Highlight 1.2

BP "Grossly Negligent" in Gulf of Mexico Disaster

On April 20, 2010, an explosion occurred on BP's Deepwater Horizon oil drilling rig off the Louisiana coastline, killing 11 workers. The subsequent oil spill continued unabated for over three months. It released an estimated 5 million barrels of crude oil into the Gulf of Mexico, causing the largest environmental disaster in U.S. history. Two BP employees even faced manslaughter charges. The cleanup alone cost BP $14 billion. Because of the company's haphazard handling of the crisis, Tony Hayward, BP's CEO at the time, was fired.

Technical problems aside, many experts argued that BP's problems were systemic, because management had repeatedly failed to put an adequate safety culture in place. In 2005, for example, BP experienced a catastrophic accident at a Texas oil refinery, which killed 15 workers. A year later, a leaking BP pipeline caused the largest oil spill ever on Alaska's North Slope. BP's strategic focus on cost reductions, initiated a few years earlier, may have significantly compromised safety across the board. In a fall 2014 ruling, a federal judge declared that BP's measures to cut costs despite safety risks "evince an extreme deviation from the standard of care and a conscious disregard of known risks."[44]

In the aftermath of the gulf oil spill, BP faced thousands of claims by many small business owners in the tourism and seafood industries. These business owners were not powerful individually, and pursuing valid legal claims meant facing protracted and expensive court proceedings. As a collective organized in a potential class-action lawsuit, however, they were powerful. Moreover, their claims were backed by the U.S. government, which has the power to withdraw BP's business license or cancel current permits and withhold future ones. Collectively, the small business owners along the Gulf Coast became powerful

Source: U.S. Coast Guard

BP stakeholders, with a legitimate claim that needed to be addressed. In response, BP agreed to pay over $25 billion to settle their claims and cover other litigation costs.

Even so, this was not the end of the story for BP. Additional fines and other environmental costs added another $8.5 billion. BP's total tab for the Gulf of Mexico disaster was some $43 billion.[45] To make matters worse, BP was found to have committed "gross negligence" (reckless and extreme behavior) by a federal court in the fall of 2014. This could result in an additional pollution fine of around $18 billion, bringing the total to a staggering $60 billion. BP CEO Bob Dudley sold about $40 billion in assets so far, turning BP into a smaller company that aims to become more profitable in coming years.

Moreover, claiming that BP displayed a "lack of business integrity" in handling the gulf oil spill, the Environmental Protection Agency (EPA) banned BP from any new contracts with the U.S. government. If the EPA decision stands, the ban would put BP at a major competitive disadvantage. It would be unable to acquire new leases for oil field exploration in the United States, or to continue as a major supplier of refined fuel to the armed forces.[46]

1.3 The AFI Strategy Framework

How do firms craft and execute a strategy that enhances their chances of achieving superior performance? A successful strategy details a set of actions that managers take to gain and sustain competitive advantage. Effectively managing the strategy process is the result of three broad tasks:

1. Analyze (A)
2. Formulate (F)
3. Implement (I)

The tasks of analyze, formulate, and implement are the pillars of research and knowledge about strategic management. Although we will study each of these tasks one at a time, they are highly interdependent and frequently happen simultaneously. Effective managers do not formulate strategy without thinking about how to implement it, for instance. Likewise, while implementing strategy, managers are analyzing the need to adjust to changing circumstances.

We've captured these interdependent relationships in the **AFI strategy framework** shown in Exhibit 1.5. This framework (1) explains and predicts differences in firm performance, and (2) helps managers formulate and implement a strategy that can result in superior performance. In each of the three broad management tasks, managers focus on specific *questions,* listed below. We address these questions in specific chapters, as indicated.

> **AFI strategy framework**
> A model that links three interdependent strategic management tasks—analyze, formulate, and implement—that, together, help managers plan and implement a strategy that can improve performance and result in competitive advantage.

Strategy Analysis *(A)* Topics and Questions

- Strategic leadership and the strategy process: *What roles do strategic leaders play? What are the firm's vision, mission, and values? What is the firm's process for creating strategy and how does strategy come about?* (Chapter 2)
- External analysis: *What effects do forces in the external environment have on the firm's potential to gain and sustain a competitive advantage? How should the firm deal with them?* (Chapter 3)

EXHIBIT 1.5

The AFI Strategy Framework

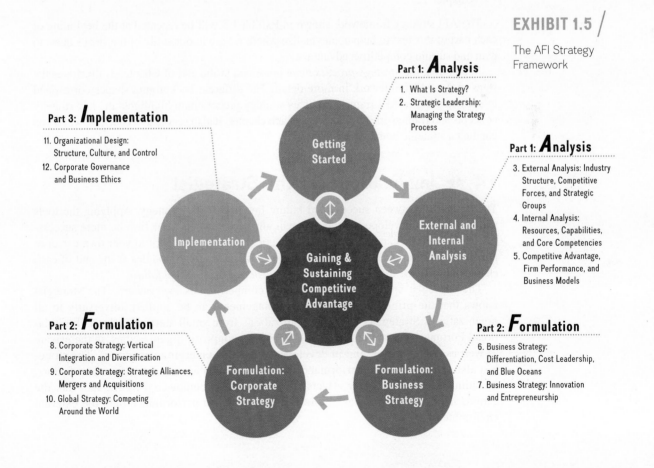

Part 1: Analysis

1. What Is Strategy?
2. Strategic Leadership: Managing the Strategy Process

Part 1: Analysis

3. External Analysis: Industry Structure, Competitive Forces, and Strategic Groups
4. Internal Analysis: Resources, Capabilities, and Core Competencies
5. Competitive Advantage, Firm Performance, and Business Models

Part 2: Formulation

6. Business Strategy: Differentiation, Cost Leadership, and Blue Oceans
7. Business Strategy: Innovation and Entrepreneurship

Part 3: Implementation

11. Organizational Design: Structure, Culture, and Control
12. Corporate Governance and Business Ethics

Part 2: Formulation

8. Corporate Strategy: Vertical Integration and Diversification
9. Corporate Strategy: Strategic Alliances, Mergers and Acquisitions
10. Global Strategy: Competing Around the World

Getting Started

External and Internal Analysis

Gaining & Sustaining Competitive Advantage

Implementation

Formulation: Corporate Strategy

Formulation: Business Strategy

- Internal analysis: *What effects do internal resources, capabilities, and core competencies have on the firm's potential to gain and sustain a competitive advantage? How should the firm leverage them for competitive advantage?* (Chapter 4)
- Competitive advantage, firm performance, and business models: *How does the firm make money? How can one assess and measure competitive advantage? What is the relationship between competitive advantage and firm performance?* (Chapter 5)

Strategy Formulation *(F)* Topics and Questions

- Business strategy: *How should the firm compete: cost leadership, differentiation, or value innovation* (Chapters 6 and 7)
- Corporate strategy: *Where should the firm compete: industry, markets, and geography?* (Chapters 8 and 9)
- Global strategy: *How and where should the firm compete: local, regional, national, or international?* (Chapter 10)

Strategy Implementation *(I)* Topics and Questions

- Organizational design: *How should the firm organize to turn the formulated strategy into action?* (Chapter 11)
- Corporate governance and business ethics: *What type of corporate governance is most effective? How does the firm anchor strategic decisions in business ethics?* (Chapter 12)

The AFI strategy framework shown in Exhibit 1.5 will be repeated at the beginning of each part of this text to help contextualize where we are in our study of the firm's quest to gain and sustain competitive advantage.

In addition, the *strategy process map,* presented at the end of Chapter 1, illustrates the steps in the AFI framework in more detail. The different background shades correspond to each step in the AFI framework. This strategy process map highlights the key strategy concepts and frameworks we'll cover in each chapter. It also serves as a checklist when you conduct a strategic management analysis.

1.4 ◀▶ Implications for the Strategist

The difference between success and failure lies in a firm's strategy. Applying the tools and frameworks developed in this text will allow you to help your firm be more successful. Moreover, you can also apply the strategic management toolkit to your own career to pursue your professional and other goals (see the *my*Strategy modules at the end of each chapter). Basically, *strategy is the art and science of success and failure.*

The strategist appreciates the fact that competition is *everywhere.* The strategist knows that the principles of strategic management can be applied universally to all organizations. Strategists work in organizations from small startups to large, multinational Fortune 100 companies, from for-profit to nonprofit organizations, in the private as well as public sector, and in developed as well as emerging economies. The strategist also knows that firm performance is determined by a set of interdependent factors, including firm and industry effects. The strategist is empowered by the fact that the actions he or she creates have more influence on firm performance than the external environment.

CHAPTERCASE 1 / Consider This...

The excitement was high when Twitter went public in the fall of 2013. Twitter's share price soared from $26 at its initial public offering (IPO) to over $73 within a few short weeks. But a year and a half later, after ups and downs, Twitter was trading well under the IPO price. To add insult to injury, Twitter's debt was rated "junk," reflecting the higher risk of default in relation to investment-grade bonds. At the same time, Twitter's market capitalization was about $25 billion (share price × outstanding shares) with annual revenues of $1.4 billion, while losing roughly $1 billion a year.

By the summer of 2015, Dick Costolo was coming under increasing pressure because of Twitter's lack of user and revenue growth. As a consequence, he was forced to resign July 1. A former improv comedian, Costolo's leadership style involved not only frequent but also often unexpected and rapid shifts in strategy. This may have worked well in Twitter's early days when he turned the rough-and-tumble startup into a highly sought-after candidate by Wall Street for an initial public offering (IPO). Costolo struggled to define a clear and consistent strategy for a business that continued to lose money despite a tremendous cultural impact. This led to frustration and confusion among Twitter employees and other stakeholders. What Twitter needs, they argued, is a leader who takes a more proactive and strategic stance, as Mark Zuckerberg did when he declared that services on mobile devices is the future of Facebook and backed up this commitment with a high level of investments. In July 2015, Twitter co-founder Jack Dorsey returned as CEO; Dick Costolo tweeted "Welcome back, @jack!!" The question remains whether Jack Dorsey, who serverd as Twitter's CEO from 2008 to 2010, can turn the company around. He is quite busy, because he is also the CEO of Square, a mobile payment services company.[47]

Questions

1. Why is Twitter struggling? What role do industry and firm effects play here?

2. What grade would you give Dick Costolo, Twitter's CEO from 2010 to 2015? Support your decision with specifics. Also, list some of his leadership strengths and weaknesses. What recommendations would you have for the new Twitter CEO to be a more effective strategic leader?

3. Why is a *good strategy* so important, especially at high-tech startups like Twitter? Why is crafting a *good strategy* at Twitter so difficult? What are some of the pitfalls that a CEO of a company such as Twitter needs to watch out for when crafting and implementing a strategy?

4. Apply the three-step process for developing a *good strategy* outlined above (diagnose the competitive challenge, derive a guiding policy, and implement a set of coherent actions) to Twitter's situation today. Which recommendations would you have for Twitter to outperform its competitors in the future?

To be more effective, the strategist follows a three-step process:

1. Analyze the external and internal environments.
2. Formulate an appropriate business and corporate strategy.
3. Implement the formulated strategy through structure, culture, and controls.

Keep in mind that the strategist is making decisions under conditions of uncertainty and complexity. As the strategist is following the AFI steps, he or she maintains an awareness of key stakeholders and how they can affect or be affected by the decisions that are made. The strategist then monitors and evaluates the progress toward key strategic objectives and makes adjustments by fine-tuning the strategy as necessary. We discuss how this is done in the next chapter where we focus on *strategic leaders* and *the strategic management process.*

TAKE-AWAY CONCEPTS

This chapter defined strategy and competitive advantage and discussed the role of business in society. It also set the stage for further study of strategic management, as summarized by the following learning objectives and related take-away concepts.

LO 1-1 / Explain the role of strategy in a firm's quest for competitive advantage.

- Strategy is the set of goal-directed actions a firm takes to gain and sustain superior performance relative to competitors.
- A good strategy enables a firm to achieve superior performance. It consists of three elements:
  1. A diagnosis of the competitive challenge.
  2. A guiding policy to address the competitive challenge.
  3. A set of coherent actions to implement the firm's guiding policy.
- A successful strategy requires three integrative management tasks—analysis, formulation, and implementation.

LO 1-2 / Define competitive advantage, sustainable competitive advantage, competitive disadvantage, and competitive parity.

- Competitive advantage is always judged relative to other competitors or the industry average.
- To obtain a competitive advantage, a firm must either create more value for customers while keeping its cost comparable to competitors, or it must provide the value equivalent to competitors but at a lower cost.
- A firm able to outperform competitors for prolonged periods of time has a sustained competitive advantage.
- A firm that continuously underperforms its rivals or the industry average has a competitive disadvantage.
- Two or more firms that perform at the same level have competitive parity.
- An effective strategy requires that strategic trade-offs be recognized and addressed—for example, between value creation and the costs to create the value.

LO 1-3 / Differentiate the roles of firm effects and industry effects in determining firm performance.

- A firm's performance is more closely related to its managers' actions (firm effects) than to the external circumstances surrounding it (industry effects).
- Firm and industry effects, however, are interdependent. Both are relevant in determining firm performance.

LO 1-4 / Evaluate the relationship between stakeholder strategy and sustainable competitive advantage.

- Stakeholders are individuals or groups that have a claim or interest in the performance and continued survival of the firm. They make specific contributions for which they expect rewards in return.
- *Internal stakeholders* include stockholders, employees (for instance, executives, managers, and workers), and board members.
- *External stakeholders* include customers, suppliers, alliance partners, creditors, unions, communities, governments at various levels, and the media.
- Several recent black swan events eroded the public's trust in business as an institution and in free market capitalism as an economic system.
- The effective management of stakeholders—the organization, groups, or individuals that can materially affect or are affected by the action of a firm—is necessary to ensure the continued survival of the firm and to sustain any competitive advantage.

LO 1-5 / Conduct a stakeholder impact analysis.

- Stakeholder impact analysis considers the needs of different stakeholders, which enables the firm to perform optimally and to live up to the expectations of good citizenship.
- In a stakeholder impact analysis, managers pay particular attention to three important stakeholder attributes: power, legitimacy, and urgency.

■ Stakeholder impact analysis is a five-step process that answers the following questions for the firm:

1. Who are our stakeholders?
2. What are our stakeholders' interests and claims?
3. What opportunities and threats do our stakeholders present?

4. What economic, legal, ethical, and philanthropic responsibilities do we have to our stakeholders?
5. What should we do to effectively address the stakeholder concerns?

KEY TERMS

AFI strategy framework *(p. 21)*

Black swan events *(p. 13)*

Competitive advantage *(p. 8)*

Competitive disadvantage *(p. 8)*

Competitive parity *(p. 8)*

Corporate social responsibility (CSR) *(p. 18)*

Firm effects *(p. 11)*

Industry effects *(p. 11)*

Stakeholders *(p. 13)*

Stakeholder impact analysis *(p. 15)*

Stakeholder strategy *(p. 14)*

Strategic management *(p. 6)*

Strategy *(p. 6)*

Sustainable competitive advantage *(p. 8)*

DISCUSSION QUESTIONS

1. Consider the brief description of Target's stakeholder relationships and combine that information with your experience shopping in a Target store. How might Target's stakeholders, in particular its employees, customers, local communities, and suppliers, influence the manager's decisions about building competitive advantage in the analysis stage of the AFI framework? How might Target gather information from its stakeholders to inspire a better customer experience in the formulation stage in order to differentiate? Or in order to lower costs? Brainstorm by jotting down as many ideas as you can think of about how key stakeholders may affect or be affected by the implementation stage.

2. BP's experience in the Gulf of Mexico has made it the poster company for how *not* to manage stakeholder relationships effectively (see Strategy Highlight 1.2). What advice would you give to BP's managers to help them continue to rebuild stakeholder relationships in the gulf region and beyond? How can BP repair its damaged reputation? Brainstorm ways that top management might leverage the experience gained by reactions in the gulf and use that knowledge to motivate local managers and employees in other locales to build stakeholder relationships proactively so that BP avoids this type of negative publicity.

3. As noted in the chapter, research found that firm effects are more important than industry effects. What does this mean? Can you think of situations where this might not be true? Explain.

4. Choose an industry with a clear leader, and then examine the differences between the leader and one or two of the other competitors in the industry. How do the strategies differ? What has the leader done differently? Or what different things has the leader done?

ETHICAL/SOCIAL ISSUES

1. Choose one of the companies discussed in the chapter (including BP, Target, Threadless, Twitter, or Facebook). By looking at the company's annual report on its website or conducting an Internet search for news about the company, identify instances where the company

has acted ethically or showed its interest in a key stakeholder—or where it has failed to do so.

2. Corporate leaders are responsible for setting the firm's strategies to gain and sustain a competitive advantage. Should managers be concerned only about the company's financial performance? What responsibility do company managers have for other consequences of their strategies? For example, should Walmart try to mitigate the negative impact its arrival in

communities can have on small locally owned stores? Should Apple be concerned about the working conditions at Foxconn (the company that manufactures the iPhone and the iPad in China)? Why or why not? Explain.

3. Other than Whole Foods, think of company examples where "doing things right" and acting in the interests of broader stakeholders (rather than just stockholders alone) have produced a stronger competitive advantage. Why was this the case?

SMALL GROUP EXERCISES

//// Small Group Exercise

Form small groups of three to four students. Search the Internet on the following topic and debate your findings.

The chapter includes a discussion of black swan events that were improbable and unexpected yet had an extreme impact on the well-being of individuals, firms, and nations. Nassim Nicholas Taleb, author of *The Black Swan,* has argued that policy makers and decision makers need to focus on building more robust organizations or systems rather than on improving predictions of events. This notion is reflected in the response to the predicted increase in powerful storms and storm surges. Hurricanes Katrina (which

devastated New Orleans and parts of the Gulf Coast) and Sandy (which wreaked havoc on the New Jersey coast) have stimulated discussions about how to not only build a more resilient infrastructure and buildings, but also develop more flexible and effective responses.

Each group should search the Internet about options and plans to (1) build more sustainable communities that will help threatened areas cope with superstorms, storm surges, or drought conditions, and (2) organize responses to black swan events (including natural disasters or terrorist attacks) more effectively. Brainstorm additional recommendations that you might make to policy makers.

STRATEGY TERM PROJECT

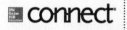 *The* HP Running Case, *a related activity for each strategy term project module, is available in Connect.*

//// Project Overview

The goal of the strategy term project is to give you practical experience with the elements of strategic management. This can be done individually or in a study group. Each end-of-chapter assignment requires data collection and analysis relating the material discussed in the chapter to the firm you select here for study throughout the course. At the end of each chapter, we make additional stages of a strategic analysis available. The goal of this term-long project is to give you a tangible application of many of the concepts discussed in the text. By the end of the project, you will not only have practice in using key strategic management components and processes

to increase your understanding of the material, but you will also be able to conduct a complete strategic management analysis of any company.

The "HP Running Case," a related activity for each strategy term project module, is available in Connect.

//// Module 1: Initial Firm Selection and Review

In this first module, you will identify a firm to study for this project. We suggest you select one company and use it for each module in this term project. Choose a firm that you find interesting or one that is part of an industry you would like to know more about. Throughout the modules, you will be required to obtain and analyze a significant amount of data about the firm. Therefore, a key criterion is also to choose a firm that has data available for you to gather.

The primary approach to this project is to select a publicly held firm. Many large firms (for example, Apple, Google, and GE) have been widely reported on in the business and popular press, and a wealth of information is available on them. Other medium-sized public firms, such as Tesla Motors, Netflix, and Black-Berry, can be used as example firms for this project. One cautionary note: For firms that are less than three years public or in industries that are not well-defined, it will take extra effort to properly identify such items as competitors and suppliers. But if it is a firm you are truly motivated to study, the effort can be quite rewarding.

Relevant data on all public firms can be freely obtained using web services such as Edgar (www.sec .gov/edgar.shtml). (For guidance on how to pull data from the Securities and Exchange Commission (SEC) website, ask your instructor to download instructions from the Instructor's Resources tab in Connect at www .mhhe.com/ftrStrategy3e.) Annual reports for firms also are a treasure trove of information. These reports and other quarterly update materials are often available from the firm's own website (look for "about us" or "investor relations" tabs, often located at the bottom of the company's website). Additionally, most university and public libraries have access to large databases of articles from many trade publications. (Factiva and ABI/Proquest are two examples.) Company profiles of a variety of publicly listed firms are available at reliable websites such as Hoovers.com and finance.yahoo. com. Also, many industries have quite active trade associations that will have websites and publications that can also be useful in this process. Your local librarian can likely provide you with additional resources that may be licensed for library use or that are otherwise not available online. Examples of these are Value Line Ratings & Reports and Datamonitor.

A second approach to this project is to select a smaller firm in your area. These firms may have coverage in the local press. However, if the firm is not public, you will need to ensure you have access to a wide variety of data from the firm. If this is a firm for which you have worked or where you know people, please check ahead of time to be sure the firm is willing to share its information with you. This approach can work well, especially if the firm is interested in a detailed analysis of its strategic position. But to be successful with this project, be sure you will have access to a broad range of data and information (perhaps including interviews of key managers at the firm).

If you are in doubt on how to select a firm, check with your instructor before proceeding. In some instances, your instructor will assign firms to the study groups.

For this module, complete or answer the following:

1. Provide a brief history of the company.

2. List the top management of the firm and note what experience and leadership skills the executives bring to the firm. If it is a larger conglomerate, list both the corporate and business managers.

3. What is the principal business model of the firm? (How does the firm make most of its profits?)

*my*STRATEGY

How to Position Yourself for Career Advantage

As presented in the chapter, firm-level decisions have a significant impact on the success or failure of organizations. Industry-level effects, however, can also play an important role (see Exhibit 1.1). Many considerations go into deciding what career choices you make during your working life. Exhibit MS 1.1 provides a sample of revenue growth rates in various industries for a recent five-year period. It shows the data for the top-25 and bottom-25 industries, including the total industry average (out of roughly 100 industries tracked). Using that table, answer the following questions.

1. If you are about to embark on a new career or consider switching careers, what effect should the likelihood of industry growth play in your decision?

2. Why could growth rates be an important consideration? Why not?

3. The data in the table show the most recent five years available. How do you expect this list to look five years from now? Which three to five industries do you expect to top the list, and which three to five industries will be at the bottom of the list? Why?

EXHIBIT MS1.1 / Top-25 and Bottom-25 Industries (by Revenue Growth Rates), 2010–2014[48]

Top Segments			Bottom Segments		
Rank	**Industry**	**Growth**	**Rank**	**Industry**	**Growth**
1	Auto & Truck	30.26%	71	Advertising	5.44%
2	Electrical Equipment	29.39%	72	Engineering/Construction	5.04%
3	Green & Renewable Energy	28.92%	73	Insurance (Life)	4.98%
4	Real Estate (Development)	28.52%	74	Insurance (General)	4.83%
5	Oil/Gas (Production and Exploration)	26.59%	75	Recreation	4.79%
6	Reinsurance	26.15%	76	Oil/Gas (Integrated)	4.72%
7	Precious Metals	23.22%	77	Beverage (Soft)	4.72%
8	Oil/Gas Distribution	22.80%	78	Computers/Peripherals	4.34%
9	Real Estate (General/Diversified)	20.70%	79	Rubber & Tires	4.31%
10	Real Estate Investment Trust (R.E.I.T.)	19.18%	80	Retail (Grocery and Food)	4.11%
11	Oilfield Svcs/Equip.	18.31%	81	Business & Consumer Services	4.10%
12	Real Estate (Operations & Services)	17.24%	82	Aerospace/Defense	4.07%
13	Farming/Agriculture	17.02%	83	Metals & Mining	3.76%
14	Drugs (Biotechnology)	16.84%	84	Retail (General)	3.67%
15	Environmental & Waste Services	16.37%	85	Telecom (Wireless)	3.51%
16	Drugs (Pharmaceutical)	16.29%	86	Education	3.27%
17	Entertainment	16.26%	87	Cable TV	3.16%
18	Software (System & Application)	15.90%	88	Electronics (Consumer & Office)	2.20%
19	Investments & Asset Management	15.73%	89	Unclassified	2.00%
20	Heathcare Information and Technology	14.92%	90	Software (Entertainment)	1.95%
21	Transportation	14.50%	91	Office Equipment & Services	1.72%
22	Chemical (Basic)	14.17%	92	Coal & Related Energy	1.20%
23	Banks (Regional)	13.45%	93	Utility (General)	0.45%
24	Retail (Distributors)	13.32%	94	Publishing & Newspapers	0.12%
25	Homebuilding	13.29%	95	Shipbuilding & Marine	−0.18%

Note: During this five-year period, the average revenue growth across U.S. industrial segments was 11.5 percent.

ENDNOTES

1. SMS stands for short message service, by which cell phone users text one another.

2. Koh, Y., and K. Grind, "Twitter CEO Dick Costolo struggles to define vision," *The Wall Street Journal,* November 6, 2014; Koh, Y., "Twitter CEO Dick Costolo stepping down," *The Wall Street Journal,* June 11, 2015; and "Twitter's future: How high can it fly?" *The Economist,* November 8, 2014.

3. "Twitter's future," *The Economist.*

4. This ChapterCase is based on: Koh, Y., and T.W. Martin, "Twitter's debt is rated as junk," *The Wall Street Journal,* November 14, 2014; "Twitter's future," *The Economist;* Koh and Grind, "Twitter CEO Dick Costolo struggles to

define vision"; Bilton, N. (2013), *Hatching Twitter: A True Story of Money, Power, Friendship, and Betrayal* (London, UK: Sceptre); Guynn, J., "Twitter CEO Dick Costolo is determined to get the last laugh," *Los Angeles Times,* January 30, 2011; and http://www.wolframalpha.com/input/?i=Twitter.

5. This section draws on: McGrath, R.G. (2013), *The End of Competitive Advantage: How to Keep Your Strategy Moving as Fast as Your Business* (Boston, MA: Harvard Business Review Press); Rumelt, R. (2011), *Good Strategy, Bad Strategy: The Difference and Why It Matters* (New York: Crown Business); Porter, M.E. (2008), "The five competitive forces that shape strategy," *Harvard Business Review,* January: 78–93; Porter, M.E.

(1996), "What is strategy?" *Harvard Business Review,* November–December: 61–78; and Porter, M.E. (1980), *Competitive Strategy: Techniques for Analyzing Competitors* (New York: The Free Press).

6. Rumelt, *Good Strategy, Bad Strategy.*

7. This section draws on: "Twitter's future," *The Economist;* Koh and Grind, "Twitter CEO Dick Costolo"; and Bilton, *Hatching Twitter.*

8. "Twitter's future," *The Economist.*

9. This section draws on Porter, "The five competitive forces," "What is strategy?" and *Competitive Strategy.*

10. Ibid.

11. Rumelt, *Good Strategy, Bad Strategy;* and Porter, "What is strategy?"

12. Albergotti, R., "Facebook vows aggressive spending," *The Wall Street Journal,* October 28, 2014.

13. Nickell, J. (2010), *Threadless: Ten Years of T-shirts from the World's Most Inspiring Online Design Community* (New York: Abrams); Howe, J. (2008), *Crowdsourcing: Why the Power of the Crowd Is Driving the Future of Business* (New York: Crown Business); and Surowiecki, J. (2004), *The Wisdom of Crowds* (New York: Anchor Books).

14. Rumelt, *Good Strategy, Bad Strategy;* Porter, "What is strategy?" and Porter, *Competitive Strategy.*

15. This interesting debate unfolds in the following articles, among others: Misangyi, V.F., H. Elms, T. Greckhamer, and J.A. Lepine (2006), "A new perspective on a fundamental debate: A multilevel approach to industry, corporate, and business unit effects," *Strategic Management Journal* 27: 571–590; Hawawini, G., V. Subramanian, and P. Verdin (2003), "Is performance driven by industry- or firm-specific factors? A new look at the evidence," *Strategic Management Journal* 24: 1–16; McGahan, A.M., and M.E. Porter (1997), "How much does industry matter, really?" *Strategic Management Journal* 18: 15–30; Rumelt, R.P. (1991), "How much does industry matter?" *Strategic Management Journal* 12: 167–185; and Hansen, G.S., and B. Wernerfelt (1989), "Determinants of firm performance: The relative importance of economic and organizational factors," *Strategic Management Journal* 10: 399–411.

16. Ibid.

17. Ibid.

18. Smith, A. (1776), *An Inquiry into the Nature and Causes of the Wealth of Nations,* 5th ed. (published 1904) (London: Methuen and Co.).

19. Levy, S. (2011), *In The Plex: How Google Thinks, Works, and Shapes Our Lives* (New York: Simon & Schuster); and www.wolframalpha.com/input/?i=google.

20. "The HP Way," see www.hpalumni.org/hp_way.htm; and Packard, D. (1995), *HP Way: How Bill Hewlett and I Built Our Company* (New York: Collins).

21. This discussion draws on: Carroll, A.B., and A.K. Buchholtz (2012), *Business & Society. Ethics, Sustainability, and Stakeholder Management* (Mason, OH: South-Western Cengage); Porter, M.E., and M.R. Kramer (2011), "Creating shared value: How to reinvent capitalism—and unleash innovation and growth," *Harvard Business Review,* January–February; Parmar, B.L., R.E. Freeman, J.S. Harrison, A.C. Wicks, L. Purnell, and S. De Colle (2010), "Stakeholder theory: The state of the art," *Academy of Management Annals* 4: 403–445; and Porter, M.E., and M.R. Kramer (2006), "Strategy and society: The link between competitive advantage and corporate social responsibility," *Harvard Business Review,* December: 80–92.

22. Talib, N.N. (2007), *The Black Swan: The Impact of the Highly Improbable* (New York: Random House).

23. See the discussion by Lowenstein, R. (2010), *The End of Wall Street* (New York: Penguin Press); Paulson, H.M. (2010), *On the Brink: Inside the Race to Stop the Collapse of the Global Financial System* (New York: Business Plus); and Wessel, D. (2010), *In FED We Trust: Ben Bernanke's War on the Great Panic* (New York: Crown Business).

24. Parmar et al., "Stakeholder theory."

25. Phillips, R. (2003), *Stakeholder Theory and Organizational Ethics* (San Francisco: Berrett-Koehler); Freeman, E.R., and J. McVea (2001), "A stakeholder approach to strategic management," in Hitt, M.A., E.R. Freeman, and J.S. Harrison (eds.), *The Blackwell Handbook of Strategic Management* (Oxford, UK: Blackwell), 189–207; Freeman, E.R. (1984), *Strategic Management: A Stakeholder Approach* (Boston, MA: Pitman).

26. To acknowledge the increasing importance of *stakeholder strategy,* the Strategic Management Society (SMS)—the leading association for academics, business executives, and consultants interested in strategic management—has recently created a *stakeholder strategy* division; see http://strategicmanagement.net/. Also see Anderson, R.C. (2009), *Confessions of a Radical Industrialist: Profits, People, Purpose—Doing Business by Respecting the Earth* (New York: St. Martin's Press); Sisodia, R.S., D.B. Wolfe, and J.N. Sheth (2007), *Firms of Endearment: How World-Class Companies Profit from Passion and Purpose* (Upper Saddle River, NJ: Prentice-Hall Pearson); and Svendsen, A. (1998), *The Stakeholder Strategy: Profiting from Collaborative Business Relationships* (San Francisco: Berrett-Koehler).

27. Parmar et al., "Stakeholder theory," 406.

28. Ibid.

29. Kapner, S., L. Stevens, and S. Germano, "Wal-Mart and Target take fight to Amazon for holiday sales," *The Wall Street Journal,* November 28, 2014.

30. Parmar et al., "Stakeholder theory," 406

31. *Fortune 2014 The World's Most Admired Companies,* http://fortune.com/worlds-most-admired-companies/.

32. Eesley, C., and M.J. Lenox (2006), "Firm responses to secondary stakeholder action," *Strategic Management Journal* 27: 765–781; and Mitchell, R.K., B.R. Agle, and D.J. Wood (1997), "Toward a theory of stakeholder identification and salience," *Academy of Management Review* 22: 853–886.

33. Ostrower, J., "Boeing to build stretched 787-10 in South Carolina," *The Wall Street Journal,* July 30, 2014.

34. Benoit, D., "Icahn ends Apple push with hefty profit," *The Wall Street Journal,* February 10, 2014.

35. People for the Ethical Treatment of Animals (PETA) is an animal-rights organization.

36. This example is drawn from: Esty, D.C., and A.S. Winston (2006), *Green to Gold: How Smart Companies Use Environmental Strategy to Innovate, Create Value, and Build Competitive Advantage* (Hoboken, NJ: Wiley).

37. This discussion draws on: Carroll, A.B., and A.K. Buchholtz (2012), *Business & Society:*

Ethics, Sustainability, and Stakeholder Management (Mason, OH: South-Western Cengage); Carroll, A.B. (1991), "The pyramid of corporate social responsibility: Toward the moral management of organizational stakeholders," *Business Horizons,* July–August: 39–48; and Carroll, A.B. (1979), "A three-dimensional, conceptual model of corporate social performance," *Academy of Management Review* 4: 497–505.

38. For an insightful but critical treatment of this topic, see the 2003 Canadian documentary film *The Corporation.*

39. For recent empirical findings concerning the relationship between corporate social responsibility and firm performance, see Barnett, M.L., and R.M. Salomon (2012), "Does it pay to be really good? Addressing the shape of the relationship between social and financial performance," *Strategic Management Journal,* 33: 1304–1320; Wang, T., and Bansal, P. (2012), "Social responsibility in new ventures: profiting from a long-term orientation," *Strategic Management Journal,* 33: 1135–1153; and Jayachandran, S., K. Kalaignanam, and M. Eilert (2013), "Product and environmental social performance: Varying effect on firm performance," *Strategic Management Journal,* 34: 1255–1264.

40. "Will Obamacare destroy jobs?" *The Economist,* August 21, 2013; and Patton, M., "Obamacare: Seven major provisions and how they affect you," *Forbes,* November 27, 2013.

41. "Wake up and smell the coffee: Starbucks's tax troubles are a sign of things to come for multinationals," *The Economist,* December 15, 2012.

42. Gates, B., "How to help those left behind," *Time,* August 11, 2008.

43. Carroll, "The pyramid of corporate social responsibility," 39–48.

44. Gilbert, D., and J. Scheck, "BP is found grossly negligent in Deepwater Horizon disaster," *The Wall Street Journal,* September 4, 2014.

45. The total listed here ran to $47.5 billion, but BP was able to recover some $5 billion in the process. Gilbert and Scheck, "BP is found grossly negligent."

46. Gilbert and Scheck; Gara, T., "U.S. government slams BP's 'lack of business integrity,'" *The Wall Street Journal,* November 28, 2012; "BP and the Deepwater Horizon disaster," *The Economist,* November 15, 2012; Fowler, T., "BP slapped with record fine," *The Wall Street Journal,* November 15, 2012; and Fowler, T., "BP, plaintiffs reach settlement in Gulf oil spill," *The Wall Street Journal,* March 4, 2012.

47. Rusli, E.M., "Profitable learning curve for Facebook CEO Mark Zuckerberg," *The Wall Street Journal,* July 5, 2014; Albergotti, "Facebook vows aggressive spending"; Koh and Grind, "Twitter CEO Dick Costolo"; Koh, "Twitter CEO Dick Costolo stepping down"; "Twitter's future," *The Economist;* and Koh and Martin, "Twitter's debt is rated as junk."

48. Compiled from Value Line data by A. Damodaran, NYU, used as of January 2015, at http://people.stern.nyu.edu/adamodar/New_Home_Page/datafile/histgr.html.

The Strategic Management Process Map

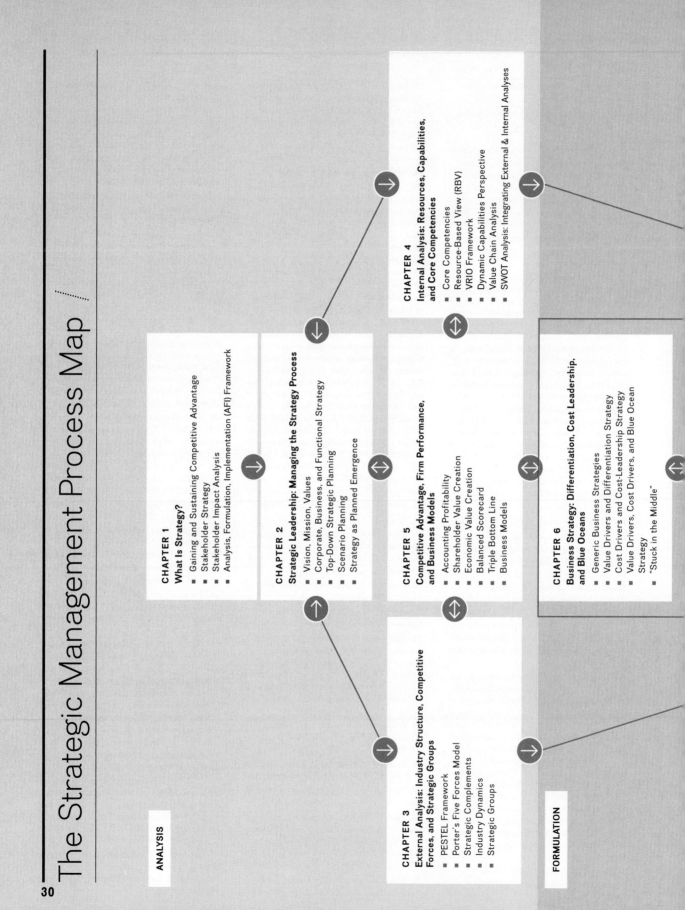

ANALYSIS

CHAPTER 1
What Is Strategy?
- Gaining and Sustaining Competitive Advantage
- Stakeholder Strategy
- Stakeholder Impact Analysis
- Analysis, Formulation, Implementation (AFI) Framework

CHAPTER 2
Strategic Leadership: Managing the Strategy Process
- Vision, Mission, Values
- Corporate, Business, and Functional Strategy
- Top-Down Strategic Planning
- Scenario Planning
- Strategy as Planned Emergence

CHAPTER 3
External Analysis: Industry Structure, Competitive Forces, and Strategic Groups
- PESTEL Framework
- Porter's Five Forces Model
- Strategic Complements
- Industry Dynamics
- Strategic Groups

CHAPTER 4
Internal Analysis: Resources, Capabilities, and Core Competencies
- Core Competencies
- Resource-Based View (RBV)
- VRIO Framework
- Dynamic Capabilities Perspective
- Value Chain Analysis
- SWOT Analysis: Integrating External & Internal Analyses

CHAPTER 5
Competitive Advantage, Firm Performance, and Business Models
- Accounting Profitability
- Shareholder Value Creation
- Economic Value Creation
- Balanced Scorecard
- Triple Bottom Line
- Business Models

CHAPTER 6
Business Strategy: Differentiation, Cost Leadership, and Blue Oceans
- Generic Business Strategies
- Value Drivers and Differentiation Strategy
- Cost Drivers and Cost-Leadership Strategy
- Value Drivers, Cost Drivers, and Blue Ocean Strategy
  - "Stuck in the Middle"

FORMULATION

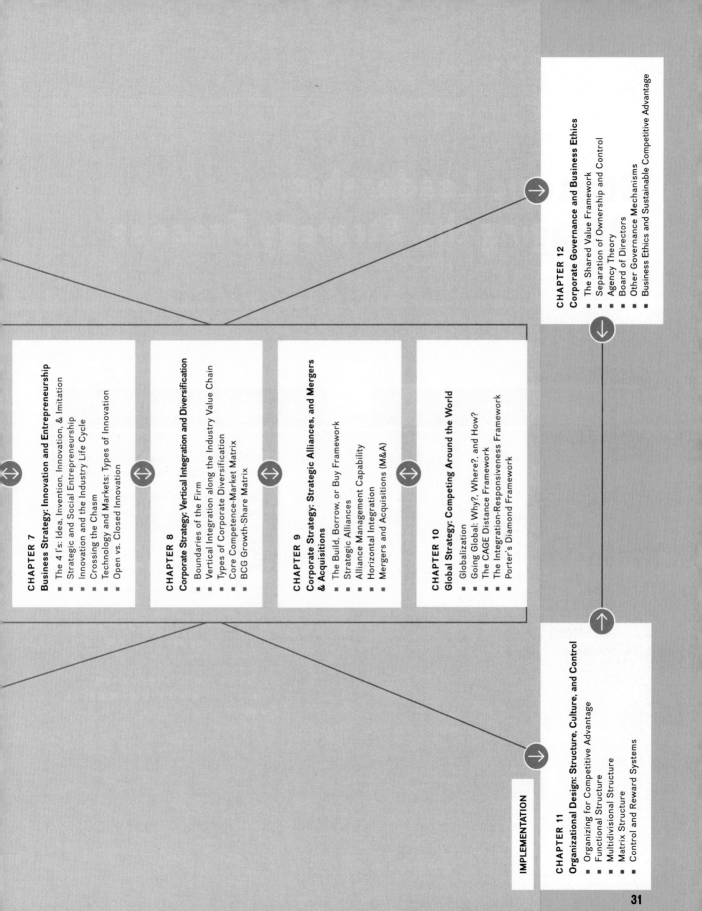

CHAPTER 7

Business Strategy: Innovation and Entrepreneurship

- The 4 I's: Idea, Invention, Innovation, & Imitation
- Strategic and Social Entrepreneurship
- Innovation and the Industry Life Cycle
- Crossing the Chasm
- Technology and Markets: Types of Innovation
- Open vs. Closed Innovation

CHAPTER 8

Corporate Strategy: Vertical Integration and Diversification

- Boundaries of the Firm
- Vertical Integration along the Industry Value Chain
- Types of Corporate Diversification
- Core Competence-Market Matrix
- BCG Growth-Share Matrix

CHAPTER 9

Corporate Strategy: Strategic Alliances, and Mergers & Acquisitions

- The Build, Borrow, or Buy Framework
- Strategic Alliances
- Alliance Management Capability
- Horizontal Integration
- Mergers and Acquisitions (M&A)

CHAPTER 10

Global Strategy: Competing Around the World

- Globalization
- Going Global: Why?, Where?, and How?
- The CAGE Distance Framework
- The Integration-Responsiveness Framework
- Porter's Diamond Framework

PART 3

IMPLEMENTATION

CHAPTER 11

Organizational Design: Structure, Culture, and Control

- Organizing for Competitive Advantage
- Functional Structure
- Multidivisional Structure
- Matrix Structure
- Control and Reward Systems

CHAPTER 12

Corporate Governance and Business Ethics

- The Shared Value Framework
- Separation of Ownership and Control
- Agency Theory
- Board of Directors
- Other Governance Mechanisms
- Business Ethics and Sustainable Competitive Advantage

31

Chapter 2

Strategic Leadership: Managing the Strategy Process

Learning Objectives

LO 2-1 Describe the roles of vision, mission, and values in the strategic management process.

LO 2-2 Evaluate the strategic implications of product-oriented and customer-oriented vision statements.

LO 2-3 Explain why anchoring a firm in ethical core values is essential for long-term success.

LO 2-4 Outline how managers become strategic leaders.

LO 2-5 Describe the roles of corporate, business, and functional managers in strategy formulation and implementation.

LO 2-6 Evaluate top-down strategic planning, scenario planning, and strategy as planned emergence.

Marissa Mayer: Turnaround at Yahoo?

APPOINTED CEO IN 2012, Marissa Mayer has just one job at Yahoo: Turn it around.

Yahoo was once the go-to Internet leader, a web portal with e-mail and finance, sports, social media, and video-sharing services. Advertisers loved it. During the peak of the Internet boom, Yahoo's share price reached an all-time high of close to $120. In 2000 when the bubble burst, Yahoo's stock sank to $5. Despite rebounding as high as $40 in the mid-2000s, the stock had long hovered around $15 by the time Mayer got the job. From its peak to Mayer's hiring, Yahoo's stock valuation (share price × number of outstanding shares) lost more than 80 percent, falling from $125 billion to a mere $20 billion.

Marissa Mayer, CEO Yahoo.
© AP Photo/Julie Jacobson

You can measure Yahoo's challenges by CEO turnover. When Mayer took the job, she became the fifth CEO in three years. So who is Marissa Mayer to break the Yahoo CEO jinx? How is she turning Yahoo around?

PRE-YAHOO

Mayer grew up in Wausau, Wisconsin, but took her higher education and built her career in California's Silicon Valley. She entered Stanford University in 1993, majoring in symbolic systems, a discipline that combines cognitive sciences, artificial intelligence, and human–computer interaction. Still at Stanford, Mayer earned a master's degree in computer science. On graduation in 1999, she declined over a dozen job offers, ranging from prestigious consulting firms to top-tier universities. Instead she went to a garage that housed a small startup with a handful of employees, just a few months old. It was called Google.

Google's 20th hire and its first female engineer, Mayer became a star. With a superior skill set and strong work ethic, she rose quickly to the rank of vice president. She helped develop many of Google's best known features: Gmail, images, news, and maps. In particular, she designed the functionality and uncluttered look and feel of Google's iconic search site. Mayer is known for her attention to detail, her commitment of time, and her desire to provide the very best user experience possible, putting products before profits. She maintains that if you build the best products possible, profits will come.

In 2012 Yahoo's site had long been stale. The former search leader was third in traffic behind Google and Bing. No doubt Mayer's pedigree at Google appealed to the Yahoo board. She was deeply involved in everything that Google had done right. And she was ready.

AT YAHOO

Mayer's first acts at Yahoo revolved around culture and cash. To change Yahoo's culture, she retooled the company's vision and mission statements. (We'll visit them later in the chapter.) She also took on Yahoo's organizational culture. Yahoo had become overly bureaucratic and lost the zeal characteristic of high-tech startups. Many Yahoo employees worked from home. For those who worked in the office, weekends began Thursday afternoons, leaving empty parking garages at Yahoo's campus in Sunnyvale, California.

In response, Mayer withdrew the option to work remotely. All of Yahoo's 12,000 employees would have to come to the office. She also installed a weekly town-hall style meeting called FYI to review Yahoo's progress and take questions. All Yahoo employees were expected to attend, either in person or via satellite link if they did not work in the Sunnyvale offices—every Friday afternoon.

To raise cash, Mayer sold part of Yahoo's ownership stake in Alibaba, the Chinese e-commerce company, for over $6 billion. Mayer spent about $2 billion acquiring more than three dozen tech ventures, including $1.1 billion for microblogging and social networking site Tumblr and $640 million for video ad company BrightRoll. The acquisitions filled gaps in product line and brought in new engineering talent.

Is it working? A number of signs are positive. By 2015, Yahoo's various websites had more than 800 million monthly visitors, with 400 million of those on mobile devices, up from a mere 160 million in 2014. Yahoo's market cap has more than doubled to over $45 billion, and its share price has more than tripled since Mayer's appointment as CEO.[1]

You will learn more about Yahoo by reading this chapter; related questions appear on page 55.

HOW DO STRATEGIC LEADERS like Marissa Mayer develop and implement a vision for their company to achieve strategic goals? How do they guide and motivate employees? In Chapter 2, we move from thinking about why strategy is important to considering how firms and other organizations define their vision, mission, and values, and how strategic leaders manage the strategy process across different levels in the organization. We also explore some of the frameworks they use to develop strategy. And finally, we summarize some of the most important practical insights in our "Implications for the Strategist."

2.1 Vision, Mission, and Values

LO 2-1

Describe the roles of vision, mission, and values in the strategic management process.

An effective **strategic management process** lays the foundation for sustainable competitive advantage. Strategic leaders design a process to formulate and implement strategy. **Strategic leadership** pertains to executives' use of power and influence to direct the activities of others when pursuing an organization's goals.[2] The first step in this process is to define a firm's vision, mission, and values.

To define these basic principles, strategic leaders can ask these questions:

- **Vision.** What do we want to accomplish ultimately?
- **Mission.** How do we accomplish our goals?
- **Values.** What commitments do we make, and what guardrails do we put in place, to act both legally and ethically as we pursue our vision and mission?

strategic management process
Method put in place by strategic leaders to formulate and implement a strategy, which can lay the foundation for a sustainable competitive advantage.

strategic leadership
Executives' use of power and influence to direct the activities of others when pursuing an organization's goals.

Because the vision succinctly identifies the primary goal of the organization, it is the first item to define. Strategic leaders need to begin with the end in mind.[3] In fact, early on strategic success is created *twice*. Leaders create the vision in the abstract by formulating strategies that enhance the chances of gaining and sustaining competitive advantage, before any actions of strategy implementation are taken in a second round of strategy creation. This process is similar to building a house. The future owner must communicate her vision to the architect, who draws up a blueprint of the home for her review. The process is iterated a couple of times until all the homeowner's ideas have been translated into the blueprint. Only then does the building of the house begin. The same holds for strategic success; it is first created through strategy formulation based on careful analysis before any actions are taken. Because the vision succinctly identifies the primary objective of the organization, it is the first item to define. Let's look at this process in more detail.

VISION

A **vision** captures an organization's aspiration and spells out what it ultimately wants to accomplish. An effective vision pervades the organization with a sense of winning and motivates employees at all levels to aim for the same target, while leaving room for individual and team contributions. Marissa Mayer developed a new vision for Yahoo—*to make the world's daily habits more inspiring and entertaining*—to help reinvigorate Yahoo's employees and get its customers excited again. Mayer's vision attempts to inspire Yahoo's employees to resume leadership in online advertising.

Employees in visionary companies tend to feel part of something bigger than themselves. An inspiring vision helps employees find meaning in their work. Beyond monetary rewards, it allows employees to experience a greater sense of purpose. People have an intrinsic motivation to make the world a better place through their work activities.[4] This greater individual purpose can in turn lead to higher organizational performance.[5] Basing actions on its vision, a firm will build the necessary resources and capabilities through continuous organizational learning, including learning from failure, to translate into reality what begins as a stretch goal or *strategic intent.*[6]

To provide meaning for employees in pursuit of the organization's ultimate goals, vision statements should be forward-looking and inspiring. Consider, for example, the vision of the nonprofit organization Teach for America (TFA): *One day, all children in this nation will have the opportunity to attain an excellent education.*[7] That vision effectively and clearly communicates what TFA ultimately wants to accomplish, while providing an inspiring target.

It's not surprising that vision statements can be inspiring and motivating in the nonprofit sector. Many people would find meaning in wanting to help children attain an excellent education (TFA) or wanting *to be always there,* touching the lives of people in need, the vision of the American Red Cross. But what about for-profit firms?

Many companies in the for-profit sector measure success primarily by financial performance. However, this is not always the case. Visionary companies, such as 3M, General Electric, Procter & Gamble (P&G), and Walmart, provide more aspirational ideas that are not exclusively financial. The upscale retailer Nordstrom's vision, for example, is *to provide outstanding service every day, one customer at a time.* Visionary companies often outperform their competitors over the long run. Tracking the stock market performance of companies over several decades, strategy scholars found that visionary companies outperformed their peers by a wide margin.[8] A truly meaningful and inspiring vision makes employees feel they are part of something bigger. This is highly motivating and, in turn, can improve financial performance.

Moreover, more companies big and small are responding to the desire of society and individual employees to find meaning in work, beyond financial success.[9] While sometimes the effort results in overreach, the trend appears to be positive. For example, Travelzoo CEO Chris Loughlin is convinced that, "If we all traveled, there would be significantly more peace on Earth." Less specific but also lofty is the take of a motorcycle marketing director at a recent investor conference: "There is a higher purpose to the Harley-Davidson brand that is more than motorcycles." One possible explanation for this shift has to do with the increasing demands of work. "In part, professionals are demanding more meaning from their careers

© AP Photo/J.Pat Carter

vision
A statement about what an organization ultimately wants to accomplish; it captures the company's aspiration.

because work simply takes up more of life than before, thanks to longer hours, competitive pressures and technological tethers of the modern job."[10]

MISSION

mission
Description of what an organization actually does—the products and services it plans to provide, and the markets in which it will compete.

Building on the vision, organizations establish a **mission**, which describes what an organization actually does—that is, the products and services it plans to provide, and the markets in which it will compete. People sometimes use the terms *vision* and *mission* interchangeably, but in the strategy process they differ.

■ A vision defines what an organization wants to accomplish ultimately, and thus the goal can be described by the verb *to*. For instance, TFA's vision is *to attain an excellent education for all children.*

■ A mission describes what an organization does; it defines the means *by* which vision is accomplished. Accordingly, TFA says it will achieve its vision *by enlisting our nation's most promising future leaders in the effort.*

strategic commitments
Actions to achieve the mission that are costly, long-term oriented, and difficult to reverse.

To be effective, firms need to back up their visions and missions with **strategic commitments**, in which the enterprise puts its money where its mouth is. Such commitments are costly, long-term oriented, and difficult to reverse.[11] For instance, the vision of EADS, the parent company of Airbus, is *to be the world's leading aerospace company.* Airbus translates this ultimate goal into its mission *by manufacturing the world's best aircraft, with passengers at heart and airlines in mind.* In service of its mission, Airbus spent 10 years and $15 billion to develop the A380 super jumbo, which can accommodate over 850 passengers and fly almost 10,000 miles, a sufficient range to fly non-stop from New York to Singapore. The company's vision is backed by a powerful strategic commitment. However noble the mission statement, for competitive advantage companies still need strategic actions informed by economic fundamentals of value creation.

Consider the strategic commitments made by Mayer to help turn Yahoo around. Its sale of Alibaba holdings and purchases of various startups show the kind of bold commitment required of strategic leaders. To retain existing talent and restore morale, she also had to sell her workers on the new vision and mission. She did so by sharing this mantra with them via tweets and other means: *People then products then traffic then revenue.* Employees understood they were the start of the transformation.

VALUES

core values statement
Statement of principles to guide an organization as it works to achieve its vision and fulfill its mission, for both internal conduct and external interactions; it often includes explicit ethical considerations.

While many companies have powerful vision and mission statements, they are not enough. An organization's values should also be clearly articulated in the strategy process. A **core values statement** matters because it provides touchstones for the employees to understand the company culture. It offers bedrock principles that employees at all levels can use to deal with complexity and to resolve conflict. Such statements can help provide the organization's employees with a moral compass.

Consider that much of unethical behavior, while repugnant, may not be illegal. Often we read the defensive comment from a company under investigation or fighting a civil suit that "we have broken no laws." However, any firm that fails to establish extra-legal, ethical standards will be more prone to behaviors that can threaten its very existence. A company whose culture is silent on moral lapses breeds further moral lapses. Over time such a culture could result in a preponderance of behaviors that cause the company to ruin its reputation, at the least, or slide into outright legal violations with resultant penalties and punishment, at the worst.

EXHIBIT 2.1 / Teach for America: Vision, Mission, and Values

VISION	One day, all children in this nation will have the opportunity to attain an excellent education.
MISSION	Teach for America is growing the movement of leaders who work to ensure that kids growing up in poverty get an excellent education.
VALUES	**Transformational Change:** We seek to expand educational opportunity in ways that are life-changing for children and transforming for our country. Given our deep belief in children and communities, the magnitude of educational inequity and its consequences, and our optimism about the solvability of the problem, we act with high standards, urgency, and a long-term view.
	Leadership: We strive to develop and become the leaders necessary to realize educational excellence and equity. We establish bold visions and invest others in working towards them. We work in purposeful, strategic, and resourceful ways, define broadly what is within our control to solve, and learn and improve constantly. We operate with a sense of possibility, persevere in the face of challenges, ensure alignment between our actions and beliefs, and assume personal responsibility for results.
	Team: We value and care about each other, operate with a generosity of spirit, and have fun in the process of working together. To maximize our collective impact, we inspire, challenge, and support each other to be our best and sustain our effort.
	Diversity: We act on our belief that the movement to ensure educational equity will succeed only if it is diverse in every respect. In particular, we value the perspective and credibility that individuals who share the racial and economic backgrounds of the students with whom we work can bring to our organization, classrooms, and the long-term effort for change.
	Respect & Humility: We value the strengths, experiences, and perspectives of others, and we recognize our own limitations. We are committed to partnering effectively with families, schools, and communities to ensure that our work advances the broader good for all children.

Source: www.teachforamerica.org.

To see how all three components—vision, mission, and values—work together, see Exhibit 2.1, which provides a snapshot of aspirations at Teach for America.

Do vision statements help firms gain and sustain competitive advantage? It depends. The effectiveness of vision statements differs based on type. *Customer-oriented* vision statements allow companies to adapt to changing environments. *Product-oriented* vision statements often constrain this ability. This is because customer-oriented vision statements focus employees to think about how best to solve a problem for a consumer.[12] Clayton Christensen shares how a customer focus let him help a fast-food chain increase sales of milk shakes.[13] The company approached Christensen after it had made several changes to its milk-shake offering based on extensive customer feedback but sales failed to improve. Rather than asking customers what kind of milk shake they wanted, he thought of the problem in a different way. He observed customer behavior and then asked customers, "What job were you trying to do that caused you to hire that milk shake?"[14] He wanted to know what problem the customers were trying to solve. Surprisingly he found that roughly half of the milk shakes were purchased in the mornings, because customers wanted an easy breakfast to eat in the car and a diversion on long commutes. Based on the insights gained from this problem-solving perspective, the company expanded its milk-shake offerings to include healthier options with fruit chunks and provided a prepaid dispensing machine to speed up the drive-through, and thus improve customers' morning commute. A customer focus made finding a solution much easier.

You could say that the restaurant company had a product orientation that prevented its executives from seeing unmet customer needs. Product-oriented vision statements focus employees on improving existing products and services without consideration of

LO 2-2

Evaluate the strategic implications of product-oriented and customer-oriented vision statements.

underlying customer problems to be solved. Our environments are ever-changing and sometimes seem chaotic. The increased strategic flexibility afforded by customer-oriented vision statements can provide companies with a competitive advantage.[15] Let's look at both types of vision statements in more detail.

PRODUCT-ORIENTED VISION STATEMENTS. A product-oriented vision defines a business in terms of a good or service provided. Product-oriented visions tend to force managers to take a more myopic view of the competitive landscape. Consider the strategic decisions of U.S. railroad companies. Railroads are in the business of moving goods and people from point A to point B by rail. When they started in the 1850s, their short-distance competition was the horse or horse-drawn carriage. There was little long-distance competition (e.g., ship canals or good roads) to cover the United States from coast to coast. Because of their monopoly, especially in long-distance travel, these companies were initially extremely profitable. Not surprisingly, the early U.S. railroad companies saw their vision as being in the railroad business, clearly a product-based definition.

However, the railroad companies' monopoly did not last. Technological innovations changed the transportation industry dramatically. After the introduction of the automobile in the early 1900s and the commercial jet in the 1950s, consumers had a wider range of choices to meet their long-distance transportation needs. Rail companies were slow to respond; they failed to redefine their business in terms of services provided to the consumer. Had they envisioned themselves as serving the full range of transportation and logistics needs of people and businesses across America (a customer-oriented vision), they might have become successful forerunners of modern logistics companies such as FedEx or UPS.

Recently, the railroad companies seem to be learning some lessons: CSX Railroad is now redefining itself as a green-transportation alternative. It claims it can move one ton of freight 423 miles on one gallon of fuel. However, its vision remains product-oriented: *to be the safest, most progressive North American railroad.*

CUSTOMER-ORIENTED VISION STATEMENTS. *A customer-oriented vision* defines a business in terms of providing solutions to customer needs. For example, "We provide solutions to professional communication needs." Companies with customer-oriented visions can more easily adapt to changing environments. Exhibit 2.2 provides additional examples of companies with customer-oriented vision statements. In contrast, companies that define themselves based on product-oriented statements (e.g., "We are in the typewriter business") tend to be less flexible and thus more likely to fail. The lack of an inspiring needs-based vision can cause the long-range problem of failing to adapt to a changing environment.

EXHIBIT 2.2 /

Companies with Customer-Oriented Vision Statements

Amazon: To be earth's most customer centric company; to build a place where people can come to find and discover anything they might want to buy online.

Alibaba: To make it easy to do business anywhere.

GE: To turn imaginative ideas into leading products and services that help solve some of the world's toughest problems.

Google: To organize the world's information and make it universally accessible and useful.

IBM: To be the best service organization in the world.

Microsoft: To enable people and businesses throughout the world to realize their full potential.

Nike: To bring inspiration and innovation to every athlete in the world.

Walmart: To give ordinary folk the chance to buy the same thing as rich people.

Yahoo: To make the world's daily habits more inspiring and entertaining.

Customer-oriented visions identify a critical need but leave open the means of how to meet that need. Customer needs may change, and the *means* of meeting those needs can change. The future is unknowable, and innovation may provide new ways to meet needs that we cannot fathom today.[16] For example, consider the need to transmit information over long distances. Communication needs have persisted throughout the millennia, but the technology to solve this problem has changed drastically over time.[17] During the reign of Julius Caesar, moving information over long distances required papyrus, ink, a chariot, a horse, and a driver. During Abraham Lincoln's time, railroads handled this task, while an airplane was used when Franklin Delano Roosevelt was president. Today, we use connected mobile devices to move information over long distances at the speed of light. The problem to be solved—moving information over long distance—has remained the same over the millennia, but the technology employed to do this job has changed quite drastically. Christensen recommends that strategic leaders think hard about how the means of getting a job done have changed over time and ask themselves, "Is there an even better way to get this job done?"

It is critical that an organization's vision should be flexible to allow for change and adaptation. Consider how Ford Motor Company has addressed the problem of personal mobility over the past 100 years. Before Ford entered the market in the early 1900s, people traveled long distances by horse-drawn buggy, horseback, boat, or train. But Henry Ford had a different idea. In fact, he famously said, "If I had listened to my customers, I would have built a better horse and buggy."[18] Instead, Henry Ford's original vision was *to make the automobile accessible to every American.* He succeeded, and the automobile dramatically changed how mobility was achieved.

Fast-forward to today: Ford Motor Company's vision is *to provide personal mobility for people around the world.* Note that it does not even mention the automobile. By focusing on the consumer need for personal mobility, Ford is leaving the door open for exactly how it will fulfill that need. Today, it's mostly with traditional cars and trucks propelled by gas-powered internal combustion engines, with some hybrid electric vehicles in its lineup. In the near future, Ford is likely to provide vehicles powered by alternative energy sources such as electric power or hydrogen. In the far-reaching future, perhaps Ford will get into the business of individual flying devices. Throughout all of this, its vision would still be relevant and compel its managers to engage in future markets. In contrast, a product-oriented vision would have greatly constrained Ford's degree of strategic flexibility.

MOVING FROM PRODUCT-ORIENTED TO CUSTOMER-ORIENTED VISION STATEMENTS. In some cases, product-oriented vision statements do not interfere with the firm's success in achieving superior performance and competitive advantage. Consider Intel Corporation, one of the world's leading silicon innovators. Intel's early vision was *to be the preeminent building-block supplier of the PC industry.* Intel designed the first commercial microprocessor chip in 1971 and set the standard for microprocessors in 1978. During the personal computer (PC) revolution in the 1980s, microprocessors became Intel's main line of business. Intel's customers were original equipment manufacturers that produced consumer end-products, such as computer manufacturers HP, IBM, Dell, and Compaq.

In the Internet age, though, the standalone PC as the end-product has become less important. Customers want to stream video and share selfies and other pictures online. These activities consume a tremendous amount of computing power. To reflect this shift, Intel in 1999 changed its vision to focus on being *the preeminent building-block supplier to the Internet economy.* Although its product-oriented vision statements did not impede performance or competitive advantage, in 2008 Intel fully made the shift to a customer-oriented vision: *to delight our customers, employees, and shareholders by relentlessly delivering the platform and technology advancements that become essential to the way we work and live.*

Part of this shift was reflected by the hugely successful "Intel Inside" advertising campaign in the 1990s that made Intel a household name worldwide.

Intel accomplished superior firm performance over decades through continuous adaptations to changing market realities. Its formal vision statement lagged behind the firm's strategic transformations. Intel regularly changed its vision statement *after* it had accomplished each successful transformation.[19] In such a case, vision statements and firm performance are clearly not related to one another.

Taken together, empirical research shows that sometimes vision statements and firm performance are *associated* with one another. A positive relationship between vision statements and firm performance is more likely to exist under certain circumstances:

- The visions are customer-oriented.
- Internal stakeholders are invested in defining the vision.
- Organizational structures such as compensation systems align with the firm's vision statement.[20]

The upshot is that an effective vision statement can lay the foundation upon which to craft a strategy that creates competitive advantage.

Organizational core values are the ethical standards and norms that govern the behavior of individuals within a firm or organization. Strong ethical values have two important functions. First, they form a solid foundation on which a firm can build its vision and mission, and thus lay the groundwork for long-term success. Second, values serve as the guardrails put in place to keep the company on track when pursuing its vision and mission in its quest for competitive advantage.

The values espoused by a company provide answers to the question, *how do we accomplish our goals?* They help individuals make choices that are both ethical and effective in advancing the company's goals. Strategy Highlight 2.1, featuring the pharmaceutical company Merck, provides an example of how values can drive strategic decision making, and what can happen if a company deviates from its core values.

One last point about organizational values: Without commitment and involvement from top managers, any statement of values remains merely a public relations exercise. Employees tend to follow values practiced by strategic leaders. They observe the day-to-day decisions of top managers and quickly decide whether managers are merely paying lip service to the company's stated values. Organizational core values must be lived with integrity, especially by the top management team. Unethical behavior by top managers is like a virus that spreads quickly throughout an entire organization. It is imperative that strategic leaders set an example of ethical behavior by living the core values. Since strategic leaders have such a strong influence in setting an organization's vision, mission, and values, we next discuss strategic leadership.

2.2 Strategic Leadership

Strategic leadership describes the executives' successful use of power and influence to direct the activities of others when pursuing an organization's goals. Executives whose vision and actions enable their organizations to achieve competitive advantage demonstrate strategic leadership.[21] Marissa Mayer demonstrated strategic leadership in defining a new vision and mission for Yahoo. To put Yahoo's new vision and mission into action, she worked to rejuvenate Yahoo's bureaucratic culture and engaged in more open and frequent communication, with weekly FYI town-hall meetings where she and other executives provide updates and field questions.[22] All employees are expected to attend and encouraged to participate in the Q&A. Questions are submitted online during the week, and the employees vote which questions executives should respond to.

Strategy Highlight 2.1

Merck: Reconfirming Its Core Values

Merck's vision is *to preserve and improve human life.* The words of founder George W. Merck still form the basis of the company's values today: *We try to never forget that medicine is for the people. It is not for profits. The profits follow, and if we have remembered that, they have never failed to appear.*[23]

ENDING RIVER BLINDNESS   In 1987, Ray Vagelos, a former Merck scientist turned CEO, announced that the company would donate its recently discovered drug Mectizan, without charge, to treat river blindness. For centuries, river blindness—a parasitic disease that leads to loss of eyesight—plagued remote communities in Africa and other parts of the world. Merck's executives formed a novel private-public partnership, the Mectizan Donation Program (MDP), to distribute the drug in remote areas, where health services are often not available.

After 25 years, more than 1 billion treatments, and some 120,000 communities served, the disease had effectively been eradicated. Merck's current CEO, Kenneth Frazier, announced himself "humbled" by the result of the company's value-driven actions.[24]

WITHDRAWING VIOXX   In the case of another drug, though, Merck's values were brought into question. Vioxx was a painkiller developed to produce fewer gastrointestinal side-effects than aspirin or ibuprofen. Once the Food and Drug Administration (FDA) approved the new drug in 1999, Merck engaged in typical big pharma promotional practices:

- Heavy direct-to-consumer advertising via TV and other media.
- Luxury doctor inducements, including consulting contracts and free retreats at exotic resorts.

Merck's new drug was a blockbuster, generating revenues of $2.5 billion a year by 2002 and growing fast.

Allegations began to appear, however, that Vioxx caused heart attacks and strokes. Critics alleged that Merck had suppressed evidence about Vioxx's dangerous side-effects from

Merck CEO Kenneth Frazier
© The Star-Ledger/Saed Hindash/The Image Works

early clinical trials. In 2004, Merck voluntarily recalled the drug. Merck's CEO at the time, Raymond Gilmartin, framed the situation in terms of knowledge learned *after* the initial release. He said he received a phone call from the head of research. "He told me that our long-term safety study of Vioxx was showing an increased risk of cardiovascular events compared to placebo, and the trial was being discontinued . . . After analyzing the data further and consulting with outside experts, the Merck scientists recommended that we voluntarily withdraw the drug."[25]

Regardless of what Merck knew when, the voluntary withdrawal reconfirmed in a costly way its core value that patients come before profits. Merck's reputation damaged, its stock fell almost 30 percent to $33, eradicating $27 billion in market value almost overnight—an amount much greater than the estimated net present value of the profits that Merck would have obtained from continued sales of Vioxx. Merck has been hit by lawsuits ever since; legal liabilities have cost the company up to $30 billion thus far.

Some corporate social responsibility experts argue that Merck should have never put Vioxx on the market in the first place, or that it should have at least provided up-front, clear assessments of the risks associated with Vioxx.[26]

Mayer took some heat when she announced that Yahoo employees could no longer work from home, but needed to come into the office instead. Her rationale is that working in the same shared space encourages collaboration, teamwork, and the creative spark to foster innovation. She moved out of her corner office and instead works in a cubicle among other Yahoo rank-and-file employees. To ease the transition into now being required to work on the Yahoo campus in Sunnyvale, California, Mayer ordered a renovation and upgrade to Yahoo's cafeteria. Now, gourmet meals—breakfast, lunch, and dinner—are available free for all Yahoos.

There are other less-than-popular changes. Where before Yahoos enjoyed a casual work culture, now they faced a stacked ranking system of employee performance. Managers had to grade their direct reports along a bell curve, with a fixed percentage as "underperforming." Team leaders were now to rank their employees in defined groups: 10 percent in "greatly exceeds," 25 percent in "exceeds," 50 percent in "achieves," 10 percent in "occasionally misses," and 5 percent in "misses." Unintended consequences ensued. High performers refused to work with one another in the same team. Managers cynically traded team members to fill their quotas. Political infighting increased.[27]

While the effect of strategic leaders varies, they still matter to firm performance.[28] Think of great business founders and their impact on the companies they built—Jack Ma at Alibaba, Steve Jobs at Apple, Jeff Bezos at Amazon, and so on. There are also strategic leaders who have shaped and revitalized existing businesses: Tim Cook at Apple, Chung Mong-Koo at Hyundai, Satya Nadella at Microsoft, etc.[29] Or continue with the example of Marissa Mayer. In 2014, *Forbes* listed her as number eight in its annual ranking of the most powerful women in business, just behind other great business leaders such as Mary Barra (GM), Sheryl Sandberg (Facebook), and Virginia Rometty (IBM), among others. One of the world's top business leaders, Mayer, born 1975, is one of the youngest.

At the other end of the spectrum, some CEOs have massively destroyed shareholder value: Charles Prince at Citigroup, Richard Wagoner at GM, Robert Nardelli at The Home Depot and later Chrysler, Martin Winterkorn at VW, and Ron Johnson at JCPenney, among many others.

Why do some leaders create great companies or manage them to greatness, while others lead them into decline and sometimes even demise? To answer that question, let's first consider what strategic leaders actually do.

WHAT DO STRATEGIC LEADERS DO?

What do strategic leaders do that makes some strategic leaders more effective than others? In a recent study of more than 350 CEOs, strategy scholars found that they spend, on average, 67 percent of their time in meetings, 13 percent working alone, 7 percent on e-mail, 6 percent on phone calls, 5 percent on business meals, and 2 percent on public events such as ribbon-cutting for a new factory (see Exhibit 2.3).[30] Other studies have also found that

EXHIBIT 2.3 /

How CEOs Spend Their Days

Source: Data from O. Bandiera, A. Prat, and R. Sadun (2012), "Management capital at the top: Evidence from the time use of CEOs," London School of Economics and Harvard Business School Working Paper.

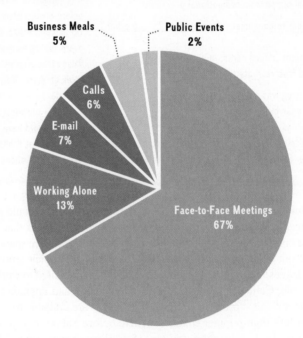

Business Meals 5%

Public Events 2%

Calls 6%

E-mail 7%

Working Alone 13%

Face-to-Face Meetings 67%

most managers prefer oral communication: CEOs spend most of their time "interacting—talking, cajoling, soothing, selling, listening, and nodding—with a wide array of parties inside and outside the organization."[31] Surprisingly given the advances in information technology, CEOs today spend most of their time in face-to-face meetings. They consider face-to-face meetings most effective in getting their message across and obtaining the information they need. Not only do meetings present data through presentations and verbal communications, but they also enable CEOs to pick up on rich nonverbal cues such as facial expressions, body language, and mood, that are not apparent to them if they use e-mail or Skype, for example.[32]

HOW DO YOU BECOME A STRATEGIC LEADER?

Is becoming an ethical and effective strategic leader innate? Can it be learned? According to the **upper-echelons theory**, organizational outcomes including strategic choices and performance levels reflect the values of the top management team.[33] These are the individuals at the upper echelons, or levels, of an organization. The theory states that executives interpret situations through the lens of their unique perspectives, shaped by personal circumstances, values, and experiences. Their leadership actions reflect characteristics of age, education, and career experiences, filtered through personal interpretations of the situations they face. The upper-echelons theory favors the idea that strong leadership is the result of both innate abilities *and* learning.

> **upper-echelons theory**
> A conceptual framework that views organizational outcomes—strategic choices and performance levels—as reflections of the values of the members of the top management team.

In the bestseller *Good to Great,* Jim Collins explored over 1,000 *good* companies to find 11 *great* ones. He identified *great companies* as those that transitioned from average performance to sustained competitive advantage. He measured that transition as "cumulative stock returns of almost seven times the general market in the 15 years following their transition points."[34] A lot has happened since the book was published over a decade ago. Today only a few of the original 11 stayed all that great, specifically Kimberly-Clark and Walgreens. Some fell back to mediocrity; a few no longer exist in their earlier form or at all. Anyone remember Circuit City or Fannie Mae? Let's agree that competitive advantage is hard to achieve and even harder to sustain. But the book remains valuable for its thought-provoking observations. Studying these large corporations, Collins found consistent patterns of leadership among the top companies, as pictured in the **Level-5 leadership pyramid** in Exhibit 2.4.[35] The pyramid is a conceptual framework that shows leadership progression through five distinct, sequential levels. Collins found that all the companies he identified as *great* were led by Level-5 executives. So if you are interested in becoming an ethical and strategic leader, the leadership pyramid suggests the areas of growth required.

> **Level-5 leadership pyramid**
> A conceptual framework of leadership progression with five distinct, sequential levels.

According to the Level-5 leadership pyramid, effective strategic leaders go through a natural progression of five levels. Each level builds upon the previous one; the manager can move on to the next level of leadership only when the current level has been mastered. On the left (in Exhibit 2.4) are the capabilities associated with each level. But not all companies are Fortune 500 behemoths. On the right we suggest that the model is valuable as well to the individual looking to develop the capacity for greater success.

FORMULATING STRATEGY ACROSS LEVELS: CORPORATE, BUSINESS, AND FUNCTIONAL MANAGERS

Describe the roles of corporate, business, and functional managers in strategy formulation and implementation.

According to the upper-echelons theory, the top management team primarily determines a firm's ability to gain and sustain a competitive advantage through the strategies they pursue. Given the importance of such strategies, we need to gain a deeper understanding of how they are formed.

EXHIBIT 2.4 / Strategic Leaders: The Level-5 Pyramid

Adapted to compare corporations and entrepreneurs

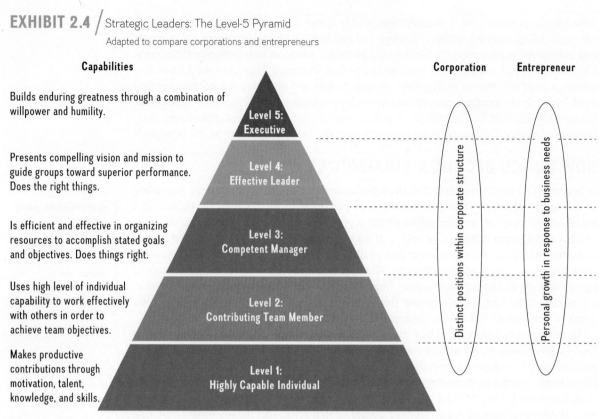

Source: Adapted from J. Collins (2001), *Good to Great: Why Some Companies Make the Leap . . . And Others Don't* (New York: HarperCollins), 20.

strategy formulation
The part of the strategic management process that concerns the choice of strategy in terms of where and how to compete.

strategy implementation
The part of the strategic management process that concerns the organization, coordination, and integration of how work gets done, or strategy execution.

Strategy formulation concerns the choice of strategy in terms of *where and how to compete.* In contrast, **strategy implementation** concerns the organization, coordination, and integration of *how work gets done.* In short, it concerns the *execution of strategy.* It is helpful to break down strategy formulation and implementation into three distinct areas—corporate, business, and functional.

■ *Corporate strategy* concerns questions relating to where to compete in terms of industry, markets, and geography.

■ *Business strategy* concerns the question of how to compete. Three generic business strategies are available: cost leadership, differentiation, or value innovation.

■ *Functional strategy* concerns the question of how to implement a chosen business strategy.

Exhibit 2.5 shows the three areas of strategy formulation.

Although we generally speak of the firm in an abstract form, individual employees make strategic decisions—whether at the corporate, business, or functional level. *Corporate executives* at headquarters formulate corporate strategy. Think of corporate executives including Mukesh Ambani (Reliance Industries), Ursula Burns (Xerox), Sheryl Sandberg (Facebook), or Marillyn Hewson (Lockheed Martin). Corporate executives need to decide in which industries, markets, and geographies their companies should compete. They need to formulate a strategy that can create synergies across business units that may be quite different, and determine the boundaries of the firm by deciding whether to enter certain industries and markets and whether to sell certain divisions. They are responsible for setting

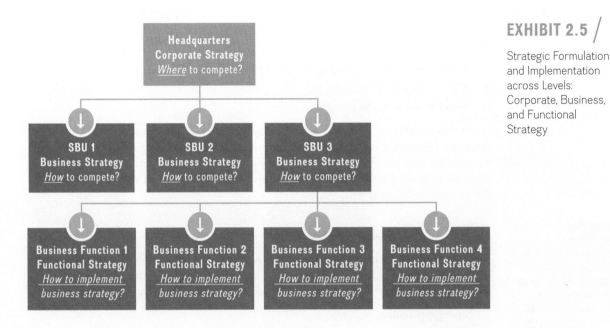

EXHIBIT 2.5 /

Strategic Formulation
and Implementation
across Levels:
Corporate, Business,
and Functional
Strategy

overarching strategic objectives and allocating scarce resources among different business divisions, monitoring performance, and making adjustments to the overall portfolio of businesses as needed. The objective of corporate-level strategy is to increase overall corporate value so that it is higher than the sum of the individual business units.

Business strategy occurs within **strategic business units**, or **SBUs**, the standalone divisions of a larger conglomerate, each with its own profit-and-loss responsibility. General managers in SBUs must answer business strategy questions relating to how to compete in order to achieve superior performance. Within the guidelines received from corporate headquarters, they formulate an appropriate generic business strategy, including cost leadership, differentiation, or value innovation, in their quest for competitive advantage.

Rosalind Brewer, CEO of Sam's Club, pursues a somewhat different business strategy from the strategy of parent company Walmart. By offering higher-quality products and brand names with bulk offerings and by prescreening customers via required Sam's Club memberships to establish creditworthiness, Brewer is able to achieve annual revenues of roughly $60 billion. This would place Sam's Club in the top 50 in the Fortune 500 list. Although as CEO of Sam's Club, Brewer is responsible for the performance of this strategic business unit, she reports to Walmart's CEO, C. Douglas McMillon, who as corporate executive oversees Walmart's entire operations, with close to $500 billion in annual revenues and over 11,000 stores globally.

Within each strategic business unit are various business *functions:* accounting, finance, human resources, product development, operations, manufacturing, marketing, and customer service. Each *functional manager* is responsible for decisions and actions within a single functional area. These decisions aid in the implementation of the business-level strategy, made at the level above.

Returning to our ChapterCase, CEO Marissa Mayer determines Yahoo's corporate strategy and is responsible for the performance of the entire organization. The far-flung Yahoo has its own wide range of Internet services and products, and it owns parts of several

strategic business unit (SBU)
A standalone division of a larger conglomerate, with its own profit-and-loss responsibility.

Rosalind Brewer,
Sam's Club CEO
© AP Photo/April L. Brown

foreign-based Internet companies, including Yahoo Japan and Alibaba of China. Mayer decides

- What types of products and services to offer.
- Which industries to compete in.
- Where in the world to compete.

To successfully turn around Yahoo, Mayer identified four future growth areas for investing significant resources and attention: mobile advertising, video, social media advertising, and native advertising. *Native advertising* is online advertising that attempts to present itself as naturally occurring editorial content rather than a search-driven paid placement.

LO 2-6

Evaluate top-down strategic planning, scenario planning, and strategy as planned emergence.

2.3 The Strategic Management Process

We have gained some insight into the corporate, business, and functional levels of strategy. Next, we turn to the process or method by which strategic leaders formulate and implement strategy. When strategizing for competitive advantage, managers rely on three approaches:

1. Strategic planning.
2. Scenario planning.
3. Strategy as planned emergence.

This order also reflects how these approaches were developed: strategic planning, then scenario planning, and then strategy as planned emergence. The first two are relatively formal, top-down planning approaches. The third approach begins with a strategic plan but offers a less formal and less stylized approach. Each approach has its strengths and weaknesses, depending on the circumstances under which it is employed.

TOP-DOWN STRATEGIC PLANNING

The prosperous decades after World War II resulted in tremendous growth of corporations. As company executives needed a way to manage ever more complex firms more effectively, they began to use strategic planning.[36] **Top-down strategic planning**, derived from military strategy, is a rational process through which executives attempt to program future success.[37] In this approach, all strategic intelligence and decision-making responsibilities are concentrated in the office of the CEO. The CEO, much like a military general, leads the company strategically through competitive battles.

top-down strategic planning
A rational, data-driven strategy process through which top management attempts to program future success.

Exhibit 2.6 shows the three steps of analysis, formulation, and implementation in a traditional top-down strategic planning process. Strategic planners provide detailed analyses of internal and external data and apply it to all quantifiable areas: prices, costs, margins, market demand, head count, and production runs. Five-year plans, revisited regularly, predict future sales based on anticipated growth. Top executives tie the allocation of the annual corporate budget to the strategic plan and monitor ongoing performance accordingly. Based on a careful analysis of these data, top managers reconfirm or adjust the company's vision, mission, and values before formulating corporate, business, and functional strategies. Appropriate organizational structures and controls as well as governance mechanisms aid in effective implementation.

Top-down strategic planning more often rests on the assumption that we can predict the future from the past. The approach works reasonably well when the environment does not change much. One major shortcoming of the top-down strategic planning approach is that the formulation of strategy is separate from implementation, and thinking about strategy is separate from doing it. Information flows one way only: from the top down. Another shortcoming of the strategic planning approach is that we simply cannot know the future. There is no data. Unforeseen events can make even the most scientifically developed and formalized plans obsolete. Moreover, strategic leaders' visions of the future can be downright wrong; a few notable exceptions prove the rule, however.

At times, strategic leaders impose their visions onto a company's strategy, structure, and culture from the top down to create and enact a desired future state. Under its co-founder and longtime CEO, Steve Jobs, Apple was one of the few successful tech companies using a top-down strategic planning process.[38] Jobs felt that he knew best what the next big thing should be. Under his top-down, autocratic leadership, Apple did not engage in market research, because Jobs firmly believed that "people don't know what they want until you show it to them."[39] This traditional top-down strategy process served Apple well as it became the world's most valuable company. Since Jobs' death, however, Apple's strategy process has become more flexible under CEO Tim Cook, and the company is now trying to incorporate the possibilities of different future scenarios and bottom-up strategic initiatives.[40]

EXHIBIT 2.6 / Top-Down Strategic Planning in the AFI Framework

*A*nalysis
- Vision, Mission, and Values
- External Analysis
- Internal Analysis

*F*ormulation
- Corporate Strategy
- Business Strategy
- Functional Strategy

*I*mplementation
- Structure, Culture, & Control
- Corporate Governance & Business Ethics

SCENARIO PLANNING

Given that the only constant is change, should managers even try to strategically plan for the future? The answer is yes—but they also need to expect that unpredictable events will happen. We can compare strategic planning in a fast-changing environment to a fire department operation.[41] There is no way to know where and when the next emergency will arise, nor can we know its magnitude beforehand. Nonetheless, fire chiefs put contingency plans in place to address a wide range of emergencies along different dimensions.

In the same way, **scenario planning** asks those "what if" questions. Similar to top-down strategic planning, scenario planning also starts with a top-down approach to the strategy process. In addition, in scenario planning, top management envisions different scenarios, to anticipate plausible futures in order to derive strategic responses. For example, new laws might restrict carbon emissions or expand employee health care. Demographic shifts may alter the ethnic diversity of a nation; changing tastes or economic conditions will affect consumer behavior. Technological advance may provide completely new products, processes, and services. How would any of these changes affect a firm, and how should it respond? Scenario planning takes place at both the corporate and business levels of strategy.

Typical scenario planning addresses both optimistic and pessimistic futures. For instance, strategy executives at UPS recently identified a number of issues as critical to shaping its future competitive scenarios: (1) big data analytics; (2) being the target of a terrorist attack, or having a security breach or IT system disruption; (3) large swings in energy prices, including gasoline, diesel and jet fuel, and interruptions in supplies of these commodities; (4) fluctuations in exchange rates or interest rates; and (5) climate change.[42] Managers then formulate strategic plans they could activate and implement should the envisioned optimistic or pessimistic scenarios begin to appear.

scenario planning
Strategy-planning activity in which top management envisions different what-if scenarios to anticipate plausible futures in order to derive strategic responses.

EXHIBIT 2.7 /

Scenario Planning
within the AFI
Strategy Framework

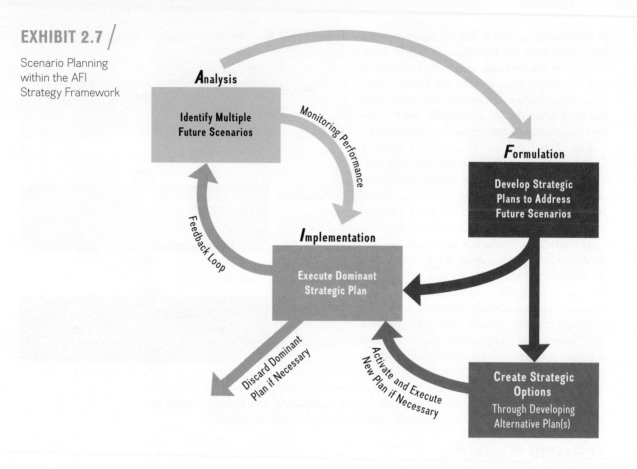

To model the scenario-planning approach, place the elements in the AFI strategy frame-work in a continuous feedback loop, where Analysis leads to Formulation to Implementa-tion and back to Analysis. Exhibit 2.7 elaborates on this simple feedback loop to show the dynamic and iterative method of scenario planning.

The goal is to create a number of detailed and executable strategic plans. This allows the strategic management process to be more flexible and more effective than the more static strategic-planning approach with one master plan. In the *analysis stage,* managers brainstorm to identify possible future scenarios. Input from several different hierarchies within the organization and from different functional areas such as R&D, manufacturing, and marketing and sales is critical. UPS executives considered, for example, how they would compete if the price of a barrel of oil was $35, or $100, or even $200. Managers may also attach probabilities (highly likely versus unlikely, or 85 percent likely versus 2 percent likely) to different future states.

Although managers often tend to overlook pessimistic future scenarios, it is imperative to consider negative scenarios carefully. An exporter such as Boeing, Harley-Davidson, or John Deere would want to analyze the impact of shifts in exchange rates on profit margins. They go through an exercise to derive different strategic plans based on large exchange rate fluctuations of the U.S. dollar against major foreign currencies such as the euro, Japanese yen, or Chinese yuan. What if the euro depreciated to below $1 per euro, or the Chinese yuan depreciated rather than appreciated? How would Disney compete if the dollar were to appreciate so much as to make visits by foreign tourists to its California and Florida theme parks prohibitively expensive? Managers might also consider how black swan events (discussed in Chapter 1) might affect their strategic planning. The BP oil spill was such a black swan for many businesses on the Gulf Coast, including the tourism, fishing, and energy industries.

In the *formulation stage* in scenario planning, management teams develop different strategic plans to address possible future scenarios. This kind of what-if exercise forces managers to develop detailed contingency plans before events occur. Each plan relies on an entire set of analytical tools, which we will introduce in upcoming chapters. They capture the firm's internal and external environments and answer several key questions:

- What resources and capabilities do we need to compete successfully in each future scenario?
- What strategic initiatives should we put in place to respond to each respective scenario?
- How can we shape our expected future environment?

By formulating responses to the varying scenarios, managers build a portfolio of future options. They then continue to integrate additional information over time, which in turn influences future decisions. Finally, managers transform the most viable options into full-fledged, detailed strategic plans that can be activated and executed as needed. The scenarios and planned responses promote strategic flexibility for the organization. This is because if a new scenario should emerge, the company won't lose any time coming up with a new strategic plan. It can activate a new plan quickly based on careful scenario analysis done earlier.

In the *implementation stage,* managers execute the **dominant strategic plan**, the option that top managers decide most closely matches the current reality. If the situation changes, managers can quickly retrieve and implement any of the alternate plans developed in the formulation stage. The firm's subsequent performance in the marketplace gives managers real-time feedback about the effectiveness of the dominant strategic plan. If performance feedback is positive, managers continue to pursue the dominant strategic plan, fine-tuning it in the process. If performance feedback is negative, or if reality changes, managers consider whether to modify further the dominant strategic plan in order to enhance firm performance or to activate an alternative strategic plan.

> **dominant strategic plan**
> The strategic option that top managers decide most closely matches the current reality and which is then executed.

The circular nature of the scenario-planning model in Exhibit 2.7 highlights the continuous interaction among analysis, formulation, and implementation. Through this interactive process, managers can adjust and modify their actions as new realities emerge. The interdependence among analysis, formulation, and implementation also enhances organizational learning and flexibility.

STRATEGY AS PLANNED EMERGENCE: TOP-DOWN *AND* BOTTOM-UP

Critics of top-down and scenario planning argue that *strategic planning* is not the same as *strategic thinking.*[43] In fact, they argue the strategic-planning processes are often too regimented and confining. As such, they lack the flexibility needed for quick and effective response. Managers engaged in a more formalized approach to the strategy process may also fall prey to an **illusion of control**, which describes a tendency by managers to overestimate their ability to control events.[44] Hard numbers in a strategic plan can convey a false sense of security. According to critics of strategic planning, to be successful, a strategy should be based on an inspiring vision and not on hard data alone. They advise that managers should focus on all types of information sources, including soft sources that can generate new insights, such as personal experience, deep domain expertise, or the insights of front-line employees. The important work, according to this viewpoint, is to synthesize all available input from different internal and external sources into an overall strategic vision. This vision in turn should then guide the firm's strategy, as discussed earlier in this chapter.

> **illusion of control**
> A tendency by people to overestimate their ability to control events.

In today's complex and uncertain world, the future cannot be predicted from the past with any degree of certainty. Black swan events can profoundly disrupt businesses and society. Moreover, the other approaches to planning just discussed do not account sufficiently for the role employees at all levels of the hierarchy may play. This is because lower-level employees not only implement the given strategy, but they also frequently come up with initiatives on their own that may alter a firm's strategy. In many instances, front-line employees have unique insights based on constant customer feedback that may elude the more removed top executives. Moreover, hugely successful strategic initiatives are occasionally the result of serendipity, or unexpected but pleasant surprises.

In 1990, for example, online retailing was nonexistent. Today, almost all Internet users have purchased goods and services online. As a total of all sales, online retailing is approaching 10 percent in 2015, with an annual growth rate of almost 20 percent.[45] Given the success of Amazon as the world's leading online retailer and eBay as the largest online marketplace in the United States, brick-and-mortar companies such as Best Buy, The Home Depot, JCPenney, Kmart, Sears, and Walmart have all been forced to respond and adjust their strategy. Others such as Circuit City and RadioShack went out of business. In the business-to-business online space, Alibaba is emerging as the leading Internet-based wholesaler connecting manufacturing businesses in China to buyers in the West. In a similar fashion, Uber and Lyft, the app-based taxi hailing services, are disrupting the existing taxi and limousine businesses in many metropolitan areas across the world. Having been protected by decades of regulations, existing taxi and limo services scramble to deal with the unforeseen competition. Many try to block Uber and Lyft using the court or legislative system, alleging the app-based services violate safety and other regulations.

The critics of more formalized approaches to strategic planning, most notably Henry Mintzberg, propose a third approach to the strategic management process. In contrast to the two top-down approaches discussed above, this one is a less formal and less stylized approach to the development of strategy. To reflect the reality that strategy can be planned *or* emerge from the bottom up, Exhibit 2.8 shows a more integrative approach to managing the strategy process. Please note that even in strategy as planned emergence, the overall strategy process still unfolds along the AFI framework of analysis, formulation, and implementation.

EXHIBIT 2.8 /

Realized Strategy Is a Combination of Top-Down Intended Strategy and Bottom-Up Emergent Strategy

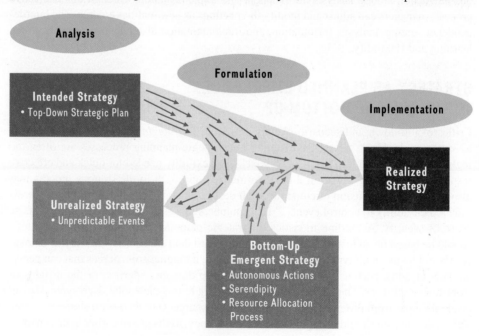

According to this more holistic model, the strategy process also begins with a top-down strategic plan based on analysis of external and internal environments. This analysis completes the first stage of the AFI framework (see Exhibit 2.8). Top-level executives then design an **intended strategy**—the outcome of a rational and structured, top-down strategic plan. Exhibit 2.8 illustrates how parts of a firm's *intended strategy* are likely to fall by the wayside because of unpredictable events and turn into *unrealized strategy*.

A firm's **realized strategy** is generally formulated through a combination of its top-down strategic intentions and bottom-up emergent strategy. An **emergent strategy** describes any unplanned strategic initiative bubbling up from the bottom of the organization. If successful, emergent strategies have the potential to influence and shape a firm's overall strategy.

The strategic initiative is a key feature in the strategy as a planned emergence model. A **strategic initiative** is any activity a firm pursues to explore and develop new products and processes, new markets, or new ventures. Strategic initiatives can come from anywhere. They could be the result of a response to external trends or come from internal sources. As such, strategic initiatives can be the result of top-down planning by executives, or they can also emerge through a *bottom-up process*. The arrows in Exhibit 2.8 represent different strategic initiatives. In particular, strategic initiatives can bubble up from deep within a firm through:

- Autonomous actions.
- Serendipity.
- Resource-allocation process (RAP).[46]

AUTONOMOUS ACTIONS. **Autonomous actions** are strategic initiatives undertaken by lower-level employees on their own volition and often in response to unexpected situations. Strategy Highlight 2.2 illustrates that successful emergent strategies are sometimes the result of *autonomous actions* by lower-level employees.

intended strategy
The outcome of a rational and structured top-down strategic plan.

realized strategy
Combination of intended and emergent strategy.

emergent strategy
Any unplanned strategic initiative bubbling up from the bottom of the organization.

strategic initiative
Any activity a firm pursues to explore and develop new products and processes, new markets, or new ventures.

autonomous actions
Strategic initiatives undertaken by lower-level employees on their own volition and often in response to unexpected situations.

Strategy Highlight 2.2

Starbucks' CEO: "It's Not What We Do"

Diana, a Starbucks store manager in Southern California, received several requests a day for an iced beverage offered by a local competitor. After receiving more than 30 requests one day, she tried the beverage herself. Thinking it might be a good idea for Starbucks to offer a similar iced beverage, she requested that headquarters consider adding it to the product lineup. Diana had an internal champion in Howard Behar, then one of Starbucks' top executives. Behar presented this strategic initiative to the Starbucks executive committee. The committee voted down the idea in a 7:1 vote. Starbucks' CEO Howard Schultz commented, "We do coffee, we don't do iced drinks."

Diana, however, was undeterred. She experimented until she created the iced drink, and then she began to offer it in her store. When Behar visited Diana's store, he was shocked to see this new drink on the menu—all Starbucks stores were supposed to offer only company-approved drinks. But Diana told him the new drink was selling well.

© Bloomberg/Getty Images

Behar flew Diana's team to Starbucks headquarters in Seattle to serve the iced-coffee drink to the executive committee. They liked its taste, but still said no. Then Behar pulled out the sales numbers that Diana had carefully kept. The drink was selling like crazy: 40 drinks a day the first week, 50 drinks a day the next week, and then 70 drinks a day in the third week after introduction. They had never seen such growth numbers. These results persuaded the executive team to give reluctant approval to introduce the drink in all Starbucks stores.

You've probably guessed by now that we're talking about Starbucks' Frappuccino. Frappuccino is now a billion-dollar business for Starbucks. At one point, this iced drink brought in more than 20 percent of Starbucks' total revenues, which were $17 billion in 2014.[47]

Functional managers such as Diana, the Starbucks store manager featured in Strategy Highlight 2.2, are much closer to the final products, services, and customers than the more removed corporate- or business-level managers. As a result, functional managers may start strategic initiatives based on autonomous actions that can influence the direction of the company. To be successful, however, top-level executives need to support emergent strategies that they believe fit with the firm's vision and mission. Diana's autonomous actions might not have succeeded or might have got her in trouble if she did not garner the support of a senior Starbucks executive. This executive championed her initiative and helped persuade other top executives.

Although emergent strategies can arise in the most unusual circumstances, it is important to emphasize the role that top management teams play in this type of strategy process. In the strategy-as-planned-emergence approach, executives need to decide which of the bottom-up initiatives to pursue and which to shut down. This critical decision is made on the basis of whether the strategic initiative fits with the company's vision and mission, and whether it provides an opportunity worth exploiting. At General Electric, CEO Jeffrey Immelt decided to move ahead with a strategic initiative to buy the wind energy company Enron Wind from the bankruptcy proceedings of Enron, because he saw the acquisition as supporting the company's vision and mission.[48] But the initiative only survived to get Immelt's attention because of the tireless persistence of a mid-level engineer who saw its value during a transition of leadership from Jack Welch to Immelt. GE provided appropriate resources and structures to grow this emergent strategy into a major strategic initiative that's now worth billions of dollars.

| serendipity
| Any random events,
| pleasant surprises,
| and accidental
| happenstances that can
| have a profound impact
| on a firm's strategic
| initiatives.

SERENDIPITY. **Serendipity** describes random events, pleasant surprises, and accidental happenstances that can have a profound impact on a firm's strategic initiatives.

There are dozens of examples where serendipity had a crucial influence on the course of business and entire industries. The discovery of 3M's Post-it Notes or Pfizer's Viagra, first intended as a drug to treat hypertension, are well known.[49] Less well known is the discovery of potato chips.[50] The story goes that in the summer of 1853, George Crum was working as a cook at the Moon Lake Lodge resort in Saratoga Springs, New York. A grumpy patron ordered Moon's resort signature fried potatoes. These potatoes were served in thick slices and eaten with a fork as was in the French tradition. When the patron received the fries, he immediately returned them to the kitchen, asking for them to be cut thinner. Crum prepared a second plate in order to please the patron, but this attempt was returned as well. The third plate was prepared by an annoyed Crum who, trying to mock the patron, sliced the potatoes sidewise as thin as he could and fried them. Instead of being offended, the patron was ecstatic with the new fries and suddenly other patrons wanted to try them as well. Crum later opened his own restaurant and offered the famous "Saratoga Chips," which he set up in a box and some clients simply took home. Today, PepsiCo's line of Frito-Lay's chips are a multibillion-dollar business.

| resource-allocation
| process (RAP)
| The way a firm allocates
| its resources based
| on a predetermined
| policies, which can be
| critical in shaping its
| realized strategy.

RESOURCE-ALLOCATION PROCESS. A firm's **resource-allocation process (RAP)** determines the way it allocates its resources and can be critical in shaping its realized strategy.[51] Emergent strategies can result from a firm's resource-allocation process (RAP).[52] Intel Corp. illustrates this concept.[53] Intel was founded in 1968 to produce DRAM (dynamic random-access memory) chips. From the start, producing these chips was the firm's top-down strategic plan, and initially it worked well. In the 1980s, Japanese competitors brought better-quality chips to the market at lower cost, threatening Intel's position and obsoleting its top-down strategic plan. However, Intel was able to pursue a strategic transformation because of the way it set up its resource-allocation process. In a sense, Intel was using functional-level managers to drive business and corporate strategy in a bottom-up fashion. In particular, during this time Intel had only a few fabrication plants (called "fabs") to produce silicon-based products. It would have taken several years and billions of dollars to build additional capacity by bringing new fabs online.

With constrained capacity, Intel had implemented the production-decision rule *to maximize margin-per-wafer-start.* Each time functional managers initiated a new production run, they were to consider the profit margins for DRAM chips and for semiconductors, the "brains" of personal computers. The operations managers then could produce *whichever product* delivered the higher margin. By following this simple rule, front-line managers shifted Intel's production capacity away from the lower-margin DRAM business to the higher-margin semiconductor business. The firm's focus on semiconductors emerged from the bottom up, based on resource allocation. Indeed, by the time top management finally approved the de facto strategic switch, the company's market share in DRAM had dwindled to less than 3 percent.[54]

Taken together, a firm's realized strategy is frequently a combination of top-down strategic intent and bottom-up emergent strategies, as Exhibit 2.8 shows. This type of strategy process is called **planned emergence**. In that process, organizational structure and systems allow bottom-up strategic initiatives to emerge and be evaluated and coordinated by top management.[55] These bottom-up strategic initiatives can be the result of autonomous actions, serendipity, or the resource allocation process.

planned emergence
Strategy process in which organizational structure and systems allow bottom-up strategic initiatives to emerge and be evaluated and coordinated by top management.

2.4 ◄► Implications for the Strategist

Two ingredients are needed to create a powerful foundation upon which to formulate and implement a strategy in order to gain and sustain a competitive advantage: First, the firm needs an inspiring vision and mission backed up by ethical values. Customer-oriented or problem-defining vision statements are often correlated with firm success over long periods of time. This is because they allow firms strategic flexibility to change in order to meet changing customer needs and exploit external opportunities. Second, the strategic leader must put an effective strategic management process in place.

Each of the three strategy processes introduced in this chapter has its strengths and weaknesses. The effectiveness of the chosen strategy process is *contingent* upon the rate of change in the internal and external environments of the firm. In a slow-moving and stable environment, top-down strategic planning might be the most effective approach. Besides the rate of change, a second dimension is firm size. Larger firms tend to use either a top-down strategic-planning process or scenario planning. For a nuclear power provider such as Areva in France that provides over 75 percent of the country's energy and has the long-term backing of the state, for instance, using a top-down strategy approach might work well. Given that nuclear accidents are rare, but when they occur they have a tremendous impact such as in Chernobyl, Russia, and Fukushima, Japan, Areva might use scenario planning to prepare for black swan events. In fast-moving environments, in contrast, Internet-based companies such as Alibaba, Facebook, Google, Dropbox, Pinterest, Twitter, or Uber tend to use the strategy-as-planned-emergence process.

Another important implication of our discussion is that all employees should be involved in setting an inspiring vision and mission to create more meaningful work. Belief in a company's vision and mission motivates its employees. Moreover, every employee plays a strategic role. Lower-level employees focus mainly on strategy implementation when a firm is using top-down or scenario planning. As the examples have shown, however, *any employee,* even at the entry level, can have great ideas that might become *strategic initiatives* with the potential to transform companies. Exhibit 2.9 compares and contrasts the three different approaches to the strategic management process: top-down strategic planning, scenario planning, and strategy as planned emergence.

Here we conclude our discussion of the strategic management process, which marks the end of the "getting started" portion of the AFI framework. The next three chapters cover the analysis part of the framework, where we begin by studying external and internal analyses before taking a closer look at competitive advantage, firm performance, and business models.

EXHIBIT 2.9 / Comparing and Contrasting Top-Down Strategic Planning, Scenario Planning, and Strategy as Planned Emergence

Strategy Process	Description	Pros	Cons	Where Best Used
Top-Down Strategic Planning	A rational strategy process through which top management attempts to program future success; typically concentrates strategic intelligence and decision-making responsibilities in the office of the CEO.	• Provides a clear strategy process and lines of communication. • Affords coordination and control of various business activities. • Readily accepted and understood as process is well established and widely used. • Works relatively well in stable environments.	• Fairly rigid and inhibits flexibility. • Top-down, one-way communication limits feedback. • Assumes that the future can usually be predicted based on past data. • Separates elements of AFI framework so that top management (analysis & formulation) are removed from line employees (implementation).	• Highly regulated and stable industries such as utilities, e.g., Georgia Power in Southeast United States or Areva, state-owned nuclear operator in France. • Government • Military
Scenario Planning	Strategy-planning activity in which top management envisions different what-if scenarios to anticipate plausible futures in order to plan optimal strategic responses.	• Provides a clear strategy process and lines of communication. • Affords coordination and control of various business activities. • Readily accepted and understood as process is well established and widely used. • Provides some strategic flexibility.	• Top-down, one-way communication limits feedback. • Separates elements of AFI framework so that top management (analysis & formulation) are removed from line employees (implementation). • As the future is unknown, responses to all possible events cannot be planned. • Leaders tend to avoid planning for pessimistic scenarios.	• Fairly stable industries, often characterized by some degree of regulation such as airlines, logistics, or medical devices, e.g., American Airlines, Delta Air Lines and United Airlines; FedEx and UPS; Medtronic. • Larger firms in industries with a small number of other large competitors (oligopoly).

Strategy Process	Description	Pros	Cons	Where Best Used
Strategy as Planned Emergence	Blended strategy process in which organizational structure and systems allow both top-down vision and bottom-up strategic initiatives to emerge for evaluation and coordination by top management.	• Combines all elements of the AFI framework in a holistic and flexible fashion. • Provides provisional direction through intended strategy. • Accounts for unrealized strategy (not all strategic initiatives can be implemented). • Accounts for emergent strategy (good ideas for strategic initiatives can bubble up from lower levels of hierarchy through autonomous actions, serendipity, and RAP). • The firm's realized strategy is a combination of intended and emergent strategy. • Highest degree of strategic flexibility and buy-in by employees.	• Unclear strategy process and lines of communication can lead to employee confusion and lack of focus. • Many ideas that bubble up from the bottom may not be worth pursuing. • Firms may lack a clear process of how to evaluate emergent strategy, increasing the chances of missing mega opportunities or pursuing dead ends; may also contribute to employee frustration and lower morale.	• New ventures and smaller firms. • High-velocity industries such as technology ventures. • Internet companies (e.g., Alibaba, Amazon, Baidu, Facebook, eBay, Google, Salesforce.com, Twitter, Uber, and Yahoo. • Biotech companies (e.g., Amgen, Biogen, Gilead Sciences, Genentech, and Genzyme).

CHAPTER**CASE 2** / Consider This...

LET'S TAKE ONE more look at Yahoo. Once a leader in online advertising in the Web 1.0 portal world, Yahoo had fallen to third place, behind Google and Facebook, well before its current CEO took charge. As CEO, Marissa Mayer wants Yahoo to "own" (be the market leader in) the mobile Internet in creating the best user experience, just as Yahoo once owned the user experience in the early days of the Internet for desktop users.

But much has changed. In the early days, the Internet was hard to use. Yahoo provided a web portal that solved this problem for millions of users worldwide. It was their first stop once they logged in. With successful Yahoo products like Yahoo Mail, Yahoo Finance, and Yahoo Sports, many users spent their entire time online at Yahoo. In the first decade of the Internet, this made Yahoo extremely attractive for online advertisers.

By 2012, however, the Internet had undergone a dramatic shift from the Web 1.0 on personal computers to a Web 2.0 on mobile devices. The mobile experience, and with it mobile advertising, had become the new frontier.

The difficulty that Mayer encountered as the new Yahoo CEO was that Google, Facebook, and Twitter all had moved faster and more successfully into the mobile space and thus mobile advertising.

To generate much-needed cash for the turnaround and to keep investors happy, Mayer sold part of Yahoo's ownership in Alibaba Group, when the Chinese Internet company went public in the fall of 2014. In 2015, Mayer announced that Yahoo would spin out the remaining 15 percent ownership of Alibaba, valued at close to $40 billion out of the roughly $45 billion market value for Yahoo.[56] With this strategic move, Mayer may be trying to buy herself even more time to turn Yahoo around. Unfortunately, Yahoo continues to decline in its core advertising business. Some of the money will be returned to shareholders, some will be used to buy more companies to strengthen Yahoo's technical capabilities and engineering skills, especially in the four key areas of focus: mobile, video, social media, and native advertising.

Perhaps the thorniest problem that Mayer faces is that investors still don't see much value in Yahoo's core business. Given Yahoo's $45 billion market capitalization, some analysts argue that Yahoo's holdings in Alibaba and in Yahoo Japan account for *all* of the value in Yahoo, if not more.

They say if you subtract the value of Yahoo's remaining equity holdings from its market cap, the true valuation of Yahoo's core business is zero or less than zero. And financial results on Yahoo's core business continues to decline.

Questions

1. In an attempt to turn around Yahoo, Mayer defined a new vision and mission for the Internet company. How useful are the new vision and mission in Yahoo's turnaround attempt?

2. What are some of the major changes Mayer has undertaken to turn Yahoo around? How do you evaluate them?

3. What "grade" would you give Mayer for her job performance as strategic leader? What are her strengths and her weaknesses? Where would you place her on the Level-5 pyramid of strategic leaders (see Exhibit 2.4), and why? Support your answers.

4. Some investors remain skeptics about Yahoo's future, essentially valuing the company close to zero dollars were it to sell its stake in Alibaba. Do you share their pessimism, or do you think that Mayer will be able turn Yahoo around? Why or why not?

TAKE-AWAY CONCEPTS

This chapter explained the role of vision, mission, and values in the strategic management process. It provided an overview of strategic leadership and explained different processes to create strategy, as summarized by the following learning objectives and related take-away concepts.

LO 2-1 / Describe the roles of vision, mission, and values in the strategic management process.

- A vision captures an organization's aspirations. An effective vision inspires and motivates members of the organization.

- A mission statement describes what an organization actually does—what its business is—and why and how it does it.

- Core values define the ethical standards and norms that should govern the behavior of individuals within the firm.

LO 2-2 / Evaluate the strategic implications of product-oriented and customer-oriented vision statements.

- Product-oriented vision statements define a business in terms of a good or service provided.

- Customer-oriented vision statements define business in terms of providing solutions to customer needs.

- Customer-oriented vision statements provide managers with more strategic flexibility than product-oriented missions.

- To be effective, visions and missions need to be backed up by hard-to-reverse strategic commitments and tied to economic fundamentals.

LO 2-3 / Explain why anchoring a firm in ethical core values is essential for long-term success.

- Ethical core values form a solid foundation on which a firm can build its vision and mission, and thus lay the groundwork for long-term success.

■ Ethical core values are the guardrails that help keep the company on track when pursuing its mission and its quest for competitive advantage.

LO 2-4 / Outline how managers become strategic leaders.

■ To become an effective strategic leader, a manager needs to develop skills to move sequentially through five different leadership levels: highly capable individual, contributing team member, competent manager, effective leader, and executive.

■ The Level-5 strategic leadership pyramid applies to both distinct corporate positions and personal growth.

LO 2-5 / Describe the roles of corporate, business, and functional managers in strategy formulation and implementation.

■ Corporate executives must provide answers to the question of *where to compete,* whether in industries, markets, or geographies, and *how to create synergies* among different business units.

■ General managers in strategic business units must answer the strategic question of *how to compete*

in order to achieve superior performance. They must manage and align the firm's different functional areas for competitive advantage.

■ Functional managers are responsible for *implementing business strategy* within a single functional area.

LO 2-6 / Evaluate top-down strategic planning, scenario planning, and strategy as planned emergence.

■ Top-down strategic planning is a sequential, linear process that works reasonably well when the environment does not change much.

■ In scenario planning, managers envision what-if scenarios and prepare contingency plans that can be called upon when necessary.

■ Strategic initiatives can be the result of top-down planning or can emerge through a bottom-up process from deep within the organization. They have the potential to shape a firm's strategy.

■ A firm's realized strategy is generally a combination of its top-down intended strategy and bottom-up emergent strategy, resulting in planned emergence.

KEY TERMS

Autonomous actions *(p. 51)*

Core values statement *(p. 36)*

Dominant strategic plan *(p. 49)*

Emergent strategy *(p. 51)*

Illusion of control *(p. 49)*

Intended strategy *(p. 51)*

Level-5 leadership pyramid *(p. 43)*

Mission *(p. 36)*

Organizational core values *(p. 40)*

Planned emergence *(p. 53)*

Realized strategy *(p. 51)*

Resource-allocation process (RAP) *(p. 52)*

Scenario planning *(p. 47)*

Serendipity *(p. 52)*

Strategic business unit (SBU) *(p. 45)*

Strategic commitments *(p. 36)*

Strategy formulation *(p. 44)*

Strategy implementation *(p. 44)*

Strategic initiative *(p. 51)*

Strategic leadership *(p. 34)*

Strategic management process *(p. 34)*

Top-down strategic planning *(p. 46)*

Upper-echelons theory *(p. 43)*

Vision *(p.35)*

DISCUSSION QUESTIONS

1. What characteristics does an effective mission statement have?

2. In what situations is top-down planning likely to be superior to bottom-up emergent strategy development?

3. This chapter introduces three different levels appropriate for strategic considerations (see Exhibit 2.5). In what situations would some of these levels be more important than others? For example, what issues might be considered

by the corporate level? What do you see as the primary responsibilities of corporate-level executives? When might the business-level managers bear more responsibility for considering how to respond to an issue? In what situations might the functional-level managers have a primary responsibility for considering an issue? How should the organization ensure the proper attention to each level of strategy as needed?

4. Identify an industry that is undergoing intense competition or is being featured in the business press. Discuss how scenario planning might be used by companies to prepare for future events. Can some industries benefit more than others from this type of process? Explain why.

ETHICAL/SOCIAL ISSUES

1. In the discussion about Merck (Strategy Highlight 2.1), it is clear the firm has followed a socially responsible path by donating more than 1 billion drug treatments to remedy river blindness in remote African communities. Yet Merck must also meet shareholder responsibilities (as discussed in Chapter 1) and make profits on drugs in use in more affluent societies. How should a responsible firm make these trade-offs? What steps can strategic leaders take to guide organizations on these challenging issues?

2. The list below shows a sample of various vision/ mission statements. Match the company with their statements. Also, identify whether the statements are principally customer-oriented or product-oriented.

	Vision/Mission Statement	Type of Statement	Matched Company	#	Company
a	To be the world's best quick service restaurant			1	AutoNation
b	To be the most respected global financial services company.			2	Avon
c	To become the beauty company most women turn to worldwide.			3	Barnes & Noble
d	To provide a global trading platform where practically anyone can trade practically anything.			4	CarMax
e	To operate the best specialty retail business in America, regardless of the product we sell.			5	Citibank
f	To provide our customers great quality cars at great prices with exceptional customer service.			6	Darden Restaurants
g	To nourish and delight everyone we serve.			7	eBay
h	To be America's best run, most profitable automotive retailer.			8	Estee Lauder
i	Bringing the best to everyone we touch			9	Facebook
j	[To be] the world's largest & best platform for online communities to share & connect.			10	Kelly Services
k	To give everyone the power to create and share ideas and information instantly, without barriers.			11	KFC
l	To be the best worldwide provider of higher-value staffing services and the center for quality employment opportunities.			12	Manpower
m	To sell food in a fast, friendly environment that appeals to pride-conscious, health-minded consumers			13	McDonald's
n	To serve our customers, employees, shareholders and society by providing a broad range of staffing services and products.			14	Reddit
o	To give the people the power to share and make the world more open and connected.			15	Twitter

SMALL GROUP EXERCISES

//// Small Group Exercise 1

A popular topic in education and public policy is the need to support the STEM disciplines (science, technology, engineering, mathematics) as the key to U.S. competitiveness. These disciplines generate innovative ideas and build new companies—and perhaps new industries. As you have learned in this chapter, innovative ideas can help sustain competitive advantage. Many American businesses, however, are concerned about whether there will be an adequate supply of STEM workers in the future because the growth in job opportunities for STEM occupations is expected to be nearly three times as fast as for non-STEM occupations. A key advocate for federal support for funding STEM education is the STEM Education Coalition, which expresses its mission as "to ensure that STEM education is recognized as a national policy priority."

The skills and expertise of the STEM occupations will be critical in dealing with the National Intelligence Council's Global Trends 2030 initiatives, which will confront the global community over the next 15 years. In particular, the key trends include a need for new communication and manufacturing technologies, cybersecurity, health care advances and preparations to manage pandemic threats, innovative and sustainable designs for infrastructure improvements, and improvements in the production and management of food, water, and energy that will meet the needs of a growing population. Business organizations may find opportunities to build sustainable competitive advantages by responding to these trends, but they will need adequate STEM expertise in order to create innovative and appropriate responses to these challenges. With innovation and cooperation, these trends can be confronted peacefully in order to benefit geopolitical stability.

1. Discuss within your group methods that the STEM Education Coalition might use to gain partners, particularly business organizations, that will help make sure STEM education is a national policy priority. Given the budget crisis, how can the coalition persuade congressional representatives to support funding?

2. How does funding for STEM education affect job opportunities for business majors?

3. Although group members may not be STEM majors, brainstorm ideas about how you might advise businesses to modify their operations or to expand/transform their operations in order to find opportunities in the Global Trends initiatives over the next 15 years. Choose a business of interest to the group. Then consider scenarios in which the business may thrive as one of the five trends develop. For example, the majority of businesses might want to ask, "What if threats to cybersecurity increase?" Or, "What if water resources become more scarce? How would this affect production or demand for the goods produced?" Your group may also consider businesses or industries that may decline as a result of the trends.

4. What additional developmental opportunities might prepare business majors for playing key roles in facing the Global Trends 2030? What skills will you need in order to manage effectively the STEM employees who are central to innovation?

//// Small Group Exercise 2

In many situations, promising ideas emerge from the lower levels of an organization, only to be discarded before they can be implemented. It was only extraordinary tenacity and disregard for the policy of selling only corporate-approved drinks that permitted the Frappuccino to "bloom" within Starbucks (see Strategy Highlight 2.2).

Some scholars have suggested that companies set aside up to 2 percent of their budgets for *any* manager with budget control to be able to invest in new ideas within the company.[57] Thus, someone with a $100,000 annual budget to manage would be able to invest $2,000 in cash or staff time toward such a project. Multiple managers could go in together for somewhat larger funds or time amounts. Through such a process, the organization could generate a network of "angel investors." Small funds or staff time could be invested in a variety of projects. Approval mechanisms would be easier for these small "seed-stock" ideas, to give them a chance to develop before going for bigger funding at the top levels of the organization.

What problems would need to be addressed to introduce this angel-network idea into a firm? Use a firm someone in your group has worked for or knows well to discuss possible issues of widely distributing small funding level approvals across the firm.

STRATEGY TERM PROJECT

connect *The HP Running Case, a related activity for each strategy term project module, is available in Connect.*

//// Module 2: Mission, Goals, and the Strategic Management Process

1. Search for a vision, mission statement, and statement of values for your chosen firm. Note that not all organizations publish these statements specifically, so you may need to make inferences from the available information. Relevant information is often available at the firm's website (though it may take some searching) or is contained in its annual reports. You may also interview a manager of the firm or contact investor relations. You may also be able to compare the official statement with the business press coverage of the firm.

2. Identify the major goals of the company. What are its short-term versus long-term goals? What resources must the firm acquire to achieve its long-term goals?

3. Trace any changes in strategy that you can identify over time. Try to determine whether the strategic changes of your selected firm are a result of intended strategies, emergent strategies, or some combination of both.

my STRATEGY

How Much Are Your Values Worth to You?

How much are you willing to pay for the job you want? This may sound like a strange question, since your employer will pay you to work, but think again. Consider how much you value a specific type of work, or how much you would want to work for a specific organization because of its values.

A recent study shows scientists who want to continue engaging in research will accept some $14,000 less in annual salary to work at an organization that permits them to publish their findings in academic journals, implying that some scientists will "pay to be scientists." This finding appears to hold in the general business world, too. In a recent survey, 97 percent of Stanford MBA students indicated they would forgo some 14 percent of their expected salary, or about $11,480 a year, to work for a company that matches their own values with concern for stakeholders and sustainability. According to Monster.com, an online career service, about 92 percent of all undergraduates want to work for a "green" company. These diverse examples demonstrate that people put a real dollar amount on pursuing careers in sync with their values.

On the other hand, certain high-powered jobs such as management consulting or investment banking pay very well, but their high salaries come with strings attached. Professionals in these jobs work very long hours, including weekends, and often take little or no vacation time. These workers "pay for pay" in that they are often unable to form stable relationships, have little or no leisure time, and sometimes even sacrifice their health. People "pay for"—make certain sacrifices for—what they value, because strategic decisions require important trade-offs.[58]

1. Identify your personal values. How do you expect these values to affect your work life or your career choice?

2. How much less salary would (did) you accept to find employment with a company that is aligned with your values?

3. How much are you willing to "pay for pay" if your dream job is in management consulting or investment banking?

ENDNOTES

1. This ChapterCase is based on: "Google's Marissa Mayer," *Vogue,* March 28, 2012; "A makeover made in Google's image," *The Wall Street Journal,* August 9, 2012; "Mayer culpa," *The Economist,* March 2, 2013; "Is Alibaba or SoftBank about to buy Yahoo?" *Forbes,* July 23, 2014; Jackson, E., "How do you solve a problem like Marissa?" *Forbes,* July 29, 2014; "Alibaba IPO to give Yahoo windfall," *The Wall Street Journal,* September 19, 2014; "Yahoo CEO set to refresh turn-around plan," *The Wall Street Journal,* October 19, 2014; "Yahoo sales, profit gains may allay Mayer critics," *The Wall Street Journal,* October 22, 2014; "Yahoo to spin off remaining Alibaba stake," *The Wall Street Journal,* January 28, 2015; "Yahoo 2013 Annual Report," www.sec.gov; Levy, S. (2011), *In The Plex: How Google Thinks, Works, and Shapes Our Lives* (New York: Simon & Schuster); Edwards, D. (2012), *I'm Feeling Lucky: The Confessions of Google Employee Number 59* (New York: Houghton Mifflin Harcourt); Thiel, P. (2014), *Zero to One. Notes on Startups or How to Build the Future* (New York: Crown Business); and Carlson, N. (2015), *Marissa Mayer and the Fight to Save Yahoo!* (New York: Hachette Book Group).

2. Finkelstein, S., D.C. Hambrick, and A.A. Cannella (2008), *Strategic Leadership: Theory and Research on Executives, Top Management Teams, and Boards* (Oxford, UK: Oxford University Press); and Yulk, G. (1998), *Leadership in Organizations,* 4th ed. (Englewood Cliffs, NJ: Prentice Hall).

3. Covey, S.R. (1989), *The 7 Habits of Highly Effective People: Powerful Lessons in Personal Change* (New York: Simon & Schuster).

4. Frankl, V.E. (1984), *Man's Search for Meaning* (New York: Simon & Schuster).

5. Pink, D.H. (2011), *The Surprising Truth about What Motivates Us* (New York: Riverhead Books).

6. Hamel, G., and C.K. Prahalad (1989), "Strategic intent," *Harvard Business Review* (May–June): 64–65; Hamel, G., and C.K. Prahalad (1994), *Competing for the Future* (Boston, MA: Harvard Business School Press); and Collins, J.C., and J.I. Porras (1994), *Built to Last: Successful Habits of Visionary Companies* (New York: Harper Collins).

7. www.teachforamerica.org.

8. Collins and Porras (1994), *Built to Last;* Collins, J.C. (2001), *Good to Great: Why Some Companies Make the Leap . . . And Others Don't* (New York: HarperBusiness).

9. Feintzeig, R., "I don't have a job, I have a higher calling," *The Wall Street Journal,*

February 24, 2015, http://www.wsj.com/articles/corporate-mission-statements-talk-of-higher-purpose-1424824784.

10. Ibid.

11. Dixit, A., and B. Nalebuff (1991), *Thinking Strategically: The Competitive Edge in Business, Politics, and Everyday Life* (New York: Norton); and Brandenburger, A.M., and B.J. Nalebuff (1996), *Co-opetition* (New York: Currency Doubleday).

12. For academic work on using a problem-solving perspective as the basis for understanding the firm, see Nickerson, J., and T. Zenger (2004), "A knowledge-based theory of the firm—the problem-solving perspective," *Organization Science,* 15: 617–632.

13. This example is drawn from Clayton Christensen's work as described in Kane, Y.I. (2014), *Haunted Empire: Apple After Steve Jobs* (New York: HarperCollins), 191.

14. Ibid.

15. Germain, R., and M.B. Cooper (1990), "How a customer mission statement affects company performance," *Industrial Marketing Management* 19(2): 47–54; Bart, C.K. (1997), "Industrial firms and the power of mission," *Industrial Marketing Management* 26(4): 371–83; and Bart, C.K. (2001), "Measuring the mission effect in human intellectual capital," *Journal of Intellectual Capital* 2(3): 320–330.

16. Christensen, C. (1997), *The Innovator's Dilemma* (New York: HarperCollins).

17. Kane, *Haunted Empire,* 191.

18. "The three habits . . . of highly irritating management gurus," *The Economist,* October 22, 2009.

19. Burgelman, R.A., and A.S. Grove (1996), "Strategic dissonance," *California Management Review* 38: 8–28; and Grove, A.S. (1996), *Only the Paranoid Survive: How to Exploit the Crisis Points that Challenge Every Company* (New York: Currency Doubleday).

20. Bart, C.K., and M.C. Baetz (1998), "The relationship between mission statements and firm performance: An exploratory study," *Journal of Management Studies* 35: 823–853.

21. Finkelstein, Hambrick, and Cannella, *Strategic Leadership,* 4.

22. See note 1.

23. As quoted in: Collins, J. (2009), *How the Mighty Fall. And Why Some Companies Never Give In* (New York: Harper Collins), 53.

24. http://www.merck.com/about/featured-stories/mectizan1.html.

25. Gilmartin, R.V., "The Vioxx recall tested our leadership," *Harvard Business Review Blog Network,* October 6, 2011.

26. The Merck river blindness case and the quote by CEO Kenneth Frazier draws from: http://www.merck.com/about/featured-stories/mectizan1.html. The Vioxx example draws from "Jury finds Merck liable in Vioxx death and awards $253 million," *The New York Times,* August 19, 2005; Heal, G. (2008), *When Principles Pay: Corporate Social Responsibility and the Bottom Line* (New York: Columbia Business School); Collins, *How the Mighty Fall;* and Wang, T., and P. Bansal (2012), "Social responsibility in new ventures: profiting from a long-term orientation," *Strategic Management Journal,* 33: 1135–1153.

27. Carlson, *Marissa Mayer and the Fight to Save Yahoo!*

28. Hambrick, D.C., and E. Abrahamson (1995), "Assessing managerial discretion across industries: A multimethod approach," *Academy of Management Journal* 38: 1427–1441.

29. "The 100 best performing CEOs in the World," *Harvard Business Review,* January–February 2013.

30. Bandiera, O., A. Prat, and R. Sadun (2012), "Managerial capital at the top: Evidence from the time use of CEOs," *London School of Economics and Harvard Business School Working Paper;* and "In defense of the CEO," *The Wall Street Journal,* January 15, 2013. The patterns of how CEOs spend their time have held in a number of different studies across the world.

31. Finkelstein, Hambrick, and Cannella, *Strategic Leadership,* 17.

32. Ibid.

33. Hambrick, D.C. (2007), "Upper echelons theory: An update," *Academy of Management Review* 32: 334–343; and Hambrick, D.C., and P.A. Mason (1984), "Upper echelons: The organization as a reflection of its top managers," *Academy of Management Review* 9: 193–206.

34. Collins, *Good to Great,* 3.

35. Ibid.

36. For a superb treatise of the history of strategy, see Freedman, L. (2013), *Strategy: A History* (New York: Oxford University Press).

37. This discussion is based on Mintzberg, H. (1993), *The Rise and Fall of Strategic Planning: Reconceiving Roles for Planning, Plans, and Planners* (New York: Simon & Schuster); and Mintzberg, H. (1994), "The fall and rise of strategic planning," *Harvard Business Review,* January–February: 107–114.

38. Isaacson, W. (2011), *Steve Jobs* (New York: Simon & Schuster). See also: Isaacson, W. (2012), "The real leadership lessons of Steve Jobs," *Harvard Business Review,* April.

39. Jobs, S., "There is sanity returning," *BusinessWeek,* May 25, 1998.

40. "CEO Tim Cook pushes employee-friendly benefits long shunned by Steve Jobs," *The Wall Street Journal,* November 12, 2012.

41. Grove, *Only the Paranoid Survive.*

42. UPS 2014 Investor Conference Presentations, Thursday, November 13; and UPS 2013 Annual Report.

43. Mintzberg, *The Rise and Fall of Strategic Planning,* and "The fall and rise of strategic planning."

44. Thompson, S.C. (1999), "Illusions of Control: How We Overestimate Our Personal Influence," *Current Directions in Psychological Science* 8: 187–190.

45. Data from the U.S. Census Bureau, "US e-commerce sales as percent of retail sales," http://ycharts.com/indicators/ ecommerce_sales_as_percent_retail_sales.

46. Arthur, B.W. (1989), "Competing technologies, increasing returns, and lock-in by historical events," *Economic Journal* 99: 116–131; and Brown, S.L., and K.M. Eisenhardt (1998), *Competing on the Edge: Strategy as Structured Chaos* (Boston, MA: Harvard Business School Press); Bower, J.L. (1970), *Managing the Resource Allocation Process* (Boston, MA: Harvard Business School Press); Bower, J.L., and C.G. Gilbert (2005), *From Resource Allocation to Strategy* (Oxford, UK: Oxford University Press); Burgelman, R.A. (1983), "A model of the interaction of strategic behavior, corporate context, and the concept of strategy," *Academy of Management Review* 8: 61–71; and Burgelman, R.A. (1983), "A process model of internal corporate venturing in a major diversified firm," *Administrative Science Quarterly* 28: 223–244.

47. Based on Howard Behar (retired president, Starbucks North America and Starbucks International) (2009), Impact Speaker Series Presentation, College of Management, Georgia Institute of Technology,October 14. See also Behar, H. (2007), *It's Not About the Coffee: Leadership Principles from a Life at Starbucks* (New York: Portfolio).

48. John Rice, GE vice chairman, president, and CEO, GE Technology Infrastructure (2009), presentation at Georgia Institute of Technology, May 11.

49. See MiniCase "Strategy and Serendipity: A Billion-Dollar Bonanza," http://mcgrawhill-create.com/rothaermel.

50. This example is drawn from: "Crispy 'Saratoga chips' potato chips invented in Saratoga," at www.saratoga.com/news/saratoga-chips.cfm; and "George Crum," at http://lemelson.mit.edu/resources/george-crum.

51. Bower and Gilbert, *From Resource Allocation to Strategy.*

52. Bower, *Managing the Resource Allocation Process;* Bower and Gilbert, *From Resource Allocation to Strategy;* Burgelman, "A model of the interaction of strategic behavior"; and Burgelman, "A process model."

53. Burgelman, R.A. (1994), "Fading memories: A process theory of strategic business exit in dynamic environments," *Administrative Science Quarterly* 39: 24–56.

54. Burgelman and Grove, "Strategic dissonance."

55. Grant, R.M. (2003), "Strategic planning in a turbulent environment: Evidence from the oil majors," *Strategic Management Journal* 24: 491–517; Brown, S.L., and K.M. Eisenhardt (1997), "The art of continuous change: Linking complexity theory and time-based evolution in relentlessly shifting organizations," *Administrative Science Quarterly* 42: 1–34; Farjourn, M. (2002), "Towards an organic perspective on strategy," *Strategic Management Journal* 23: 561–594; Mahoney, J. (2005), *Economic Foundation of Strategy* (Thousand Oaks, CA: Sage); and Burgelman, R.A., and A.S. Grove (2007), "Let chaos reign, then reign in chaos—repeatedly: Managing strategic dynamics for corporate longevity," *Strategic Management Journal* 28(10): 965–979.

56. "Yahoo to spin off remaining Alibaba stake."

57. Hamel, G. (2007), *The Future of Management* (Boston, MA: Harvard Business School Publishing).

58. Based on Stern, S. (2004), "Do scientists pay to be scientists?" *Management Science* 50(6): 835–853; and Esty, D.C., and A.S. Winston (2009), *Green to Gold: How Smart Companies Use Environmental Strategy to Innovate, Create Value, and Build Competitive Advantage,* revised and updated (Hoboken, NJ: John Wiley).

Chapter 3

External Analysis: Industry Structure, Competitive Forces, and Strategic Groups

Learning Objectives

LO 3-1 Generate a PESTEL analysis to evaluate the impact of external factors on the firm.

LO 3-2 Apply Porter's five competitive forces to explain the profit potential of different industries.

LO 3-3 Explain how competitive industry structure shapes rivalry among competitors.

LO 3-4 Describe the strategic role of complements in creating positive-sum co-opetition.

LO 3-5 Appraise the role of industry dynamics and industry convergence in shaping the firm's external environment.

LO 3-6 Generate a strategic group model to reveal performance differences between clusters of firms in the same industry.

Tesla Motors and the U.S. Automotive Industry

THE BIG THREE—GM, Ford, and Chrysler—ruled the U.S. car market for most of the 20th century. Protected by high entry barriers, highly profitable GM had over half of the U.S. market to itself. Ford and Chrysler both did well too. Then, in the 1960s and 1970s, foreign carmakers entered the U.S. market, at first mainly by importing vehicles from overseas plants. Foreign makes included the German brands Volkswagen (also owner of the Porsche and Audi brands), Daimler, and BMW, and the Japanese brands Toyota, Honda, and Nissan. By the 1980s, these foreign entrants had intensified competition and threatened the Big Three's market share, such that the U.S. Congress passed significant import restrictions. Not to be stopped, the new players responded by building U.S. plants to comply with the new rules. More recently, Korean carmakers Hyundai and Kia have begun making and selling cars in the United States.

© Johannes Eisele/AFP/Getty Images

Although globalization paved the way for significant new entry into the U.S. auto market, the worldwide car manufacturing industry has seen few new entrants. In fact, no new major car manufacturers have emerged in the past couple of decades simply because few industrial products, save for jet airplanes and nuclear power plants, are as complex to build as traditional cars powered by internal combustion engines. Large-scale production is necessary for car manufacturers to be cost-competitive. Taken together, these factors create significant entry barriers into the car manufacturing industry. Would you say, then, that a Silicon Valley technology startup, attempting to break into this industry, might be running a fool's errand?

Enter serial entrepreneur Elon Musk, who creates and runs new ventures to address not only economic but also social and environmental challenges. Musk looms large in the public imagination and has even been likened to the fictional Tony Stark, aka the Iron Man, Marvel Comics' eccentric inventor. Indeed, Musk made a cameo appearance in *Iron Man 2*. During the Internet boom, Musk made his fortune by developing an early version of Google maps and by co-founding the online payment system PayPal. The sale of both companies amounted to close to $2 billion, and Musk's share allowed him to focus on his lifelong passions in science, engineering, and space.

His most recent companies include SpaceX, the first private company to deliver a cargo payload to the International Space Station; SolarCity, basically the Walmart of solar panel installations; and, of course, Tesla Motors. Currently, Tesla receives most of Musk's attention.

Faced with the formidable entry barrier of large-scale production, Tesla sidesteps the hurdle by producing all-electric cars. Compared to complex gasoline engines, electric power trains use relatively simple motors and gearboxes with few parts. The Tesla Roadster, a $110,000 sports coupe with faster acceleration than a Porsche 911 GT, served as a prototype to demonstrate that electric vehicles can be more than mere golf carts.

After selling some 2,500 Roadsters, Tesla discontinued its production to focus on its next car: the Model S, a four-door family sedan, with a base price of $71,000 before tax credits. The line appeals to a larger market and thus allows for larger production runs to drive down unit costs. The Model S received an outstanding market reception. It was awarded not only the 2013 *Motor Trend* Car of the Year, but also received the highest score of any car ever tested by *Consumer Reports* (99/100). Tesla manufactures the Model S in the Fremont, California, factory that it purchased from Toyota. By 2015, it had sold some 60,000 of the Model S worldwide. Tesla is also working on a newly designed seven-seat electric vehicle—the Model X—in an attempt to combine the best features of an SUV with the benefits of a minivan; the first deliveries are scheduled for 2016. The third model in Tesla's lineup is a smaller vehicle that will cost around $35,000 and has a range of 200 miles per battery charge. The Model 3 is slated to go on sale in 2017.[1]

You will learn more about Tesla Motors by reading this chapter; related questions appear on page 95.

▲ **THE TESLA MOTORS** ChapterCase illustrates that competitive forces in an industry have a direct bearing on a firm's profit potential. Globalization led to extensive entry by foreign car manufacturers in the U.S. auto market, increasing the number of competitors and competitive rivalry. The Japanese automakers, for example, were successful in the U.S. market early on because their cars were generally of better quality, their production systems were more efficient, and they were more responsive to changes in customer preferences. Today, Korean carmakers are attempting to duplicate this feat. At the same time, U.S. automakers Ford and GM are experiencing a resurgence. Moreover, technological innovations have allowed startups such as Tesla Motors to enter the electric car segment (or strategic group), effectively circumventing high entry barriers into the broader automotive market. With more firms vying for a share of the U.S. auto market, competitive intensity is likely to increase.

In this chapter, we present a set of frameworks to analyze the firm's *external environment*—that is, the industry in which the firm operates, and the competitive forces that surround the firm from the outside. We move from a more macro perspective to a more micro understanding of how the external environment affects a firm's quest for competitive advantage.

We begin with the PESTEL framework, which allows us to scan, monitor, and evaluate changes and trends in the firm's macroenvironment. Next, we study Porter's five forces model of competition, which helps us to determine an industry's profit potential. Depending on the firm's strategic position, these forces can affect its performance for good or ill. We then move from a static analysis of a firm's industry environment to a dynamic understanding of how industries and competition change over time. Next we introduce the strategic group model for understanding performance differences among clusters of firms in the same industry. Finally, we offer practical "Implications for the Strategist."

3.1 The PESTEL Framework

LO 3-1

Generate a PESTEL analysis to evaluate the impact of external factors on the firm.

A firm's external environment consists of all the factors that can affect its potential to gain and sustain a competitive advantage. By analyzing the factors in the external environment, managers can mitigate threats and leverage opportunities. One common approach to understanding how external factors impinge upon a firm is to consider the source or proximity of these factors. For example, external factors in the firm's *general environment* are ones that managers have little direct influence over, such as macroeconomic factors (e.g., interest or currency exchange rates). In contrast, external factors in the firm's *task environment* are ones that managers do have some influence over, such as the composition of their strategic groups (a set of close rivals) or the structure of the industry. We will now look at each of these environmental layers in detail, moving from a firm's general environment to its task environment. Following along in Exhibit 3.1, we will be working from the outer ring to the inner ring.

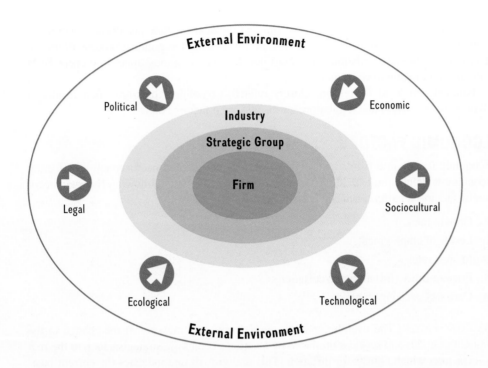

EXHIBIT 3.1

The Firm within Its External Environment, Industry, and Strategic Group, Subject to PESTEL Factors

The **PESTEL model** groups the factors in the firm's general environment into six segments:

- **Political**
- **Economic**
- **Sociocultural**
- **Technological**
- **Ecological**
- **Legal**

> **PESTEL model**
> A framework that categorizes and analyzes an important set of external factors (political, economic, sociocultural, technological, ecological, and legal) that might impinge upon a firm. These factors can create both opportunities and threats for the firm.

Together these form the acronym PESTEL. The PESTEL model provides a relatively straightforward way to *scan, monitor,* and *evaluate* the important external factors and trends that might impinge upon a firm. With more open markets and international trade in recent decades, the PESTEL factors have become more global. Such factors create both opportunities and threats.

POLITICAL FACTORS

Political factors result from the processes and actions of government bodies that can influence the decisions and behavior of firms.[2]

While political factors are located in the firm's general environment, where firms traditionally wield little influence, companies nevertheless increasingly work to shape and influence this realm. They do so by applying *nonmarket strategies*—that is, through lobbying, public relations, contributions, litigation, and so on, in ways that are favorable to the firm.[3] For example, traditional car dealers have been challenging Tesla's build-to-order sales model that allows customers to purchase a Tesla vehicle online and have it delivered to their home, anywhere in the United States.[4] Traditional car dealers, which often benefit from geographic monopolies, are not so much concerned about Tesla Motors as they are that their own brand names, such as GM or Ford, will also adopt an online, direct-to-consumer sales model, thus cutting out the dealers. Auto dealers and their associations are powerful lobbying forces that are influencing the political process to invoke decade-old laws and regulations or to craft new legislation in most states to prevent Tesla from selling directly to consumers.

Political and legal factors are closely related, as political pressure often results in changes in legislation and regulation; we discuss legal factors below.

ECONOMIC FACTORS

Economic factors in a firm's external environment are largely macroeconomic, affecting economy-wide phenomena. Managers need to consider how the following five macroeconomic factors can affect firm strategy:

- Growth rates.
- Levels of employment.
- Interest rates.
- Price stability (inflation and deflation).
- Currency exchange rates.

GROWTH RATES. The overall economic *growth rate* is a measure of the change in the amount of goods and services produced by a nation's economy. Strategists look to the *real growth rate,* which adjusts for inflation. This real growth rate indicates the current business cycle of the economy—that is, whether business activity is expanding or contracting. In periods of economic expansion, consumer and business demands are rising, and competition among firms frequently decreases. During economic booms, businesses expand operations to satisfy demand and are more likely to be profitable. The reverse is generally true for recessionary periods, although certain companies that focus on low-cost solutions may benefit from economic contractions because demand for their products or services rises in such times. For customers, expenditures on luxury products are often the first to be cut during recessionary periods. For instance, you might switch from a $4 venti latte at Starbucks to a $1 alternative from McDonald's.

Occasionally, boom periods can overheat and lead to speculative asset bubbles. In the early 2000s, the United States experienced an asset bubble in real estate.[5] Easy credit, made possible by the availability of subprime mortgages and other financial innovations, fueled an unprecedented demand in housing. Real estate, rather than stocks, became the investment vehicle of choice for many Americans, propelled by the common belief that house prices could only go up. When the housing bubble burst, the deep economic recession of 2008–2009 began, impacting in some way nearly all businesses in the United States and worldwide.

LEVELS OF EMPLOYMENT. Growth rates directly affect the *level of employment.* In boom times, unemployment tends to be low, and skilled human capital becomes a scarce and more expensive resource. In economic downturns, unemployment rises. As more people search for employment, skilled human capital is more abundant and wages usually fall.

INTEREST RATES. Another key macroeconomic variable for managers to track is real *interest rates*—the amount that creditors are paid for use of their money and the amount that debtors pay for that use, adjusted for inflation. The economic boom during the early years in the 21st century, for example, was fueled by cheap credit. Low real interest rates have a direct bearing on consumer demand. When credit is cheap because interest rates are low, consumers buy homes, automobiles, computers, and vacations on credit; in turn, all of this demand fuels economic growth. During periods of low real interest rates, firms can easily borrow money to finance growth. Borrowing at lower real rates reduces the cost of capital and enhances a firm's competitiveness. These effects reverse, however, when real interest rates are rising. Consumer demand slows, credit is harder to come by, and firms find it more difficult to borrow money to support operations, possibly deferring investments.

PRICE STABILITY. *Price stability*—the lack of change in price levels of goods and services—is rare. Therefore, companies will often have to deal with changing price levels, which is a direct function of the amount of money in any economy. When there is too much money in an economy, we tend to see rising prices—*inflation.* Indeed, a popular economic definition of inflation is *too much money chasing too few goods and services.*[6] Inflation tends to go with lower economic growth. Countries such as Argentina, Brazil, Mexico, and Poland experienced periods of extremely high inflation rates in recent decades.

Deflation describes a decrease in the overall price level. A sudden and pronounced drop in demand generally causes deflation, which in turn forces sellers to lower prices to motivate buyers. Because many people automatically think of lower prices from the buyer's point of view, a decreasing price level seems at first glance to be attractive. However, deflation is actually a serious threat to economic growth because it distorts expectations about the future.[7] For example, once price levels start falling, companies will not invest in new production capacity or innovation because they expect a further decline in prices. In recent decades, the Japanese economy has been plagued with persistent deflation.

CURRENCY EXCHANGE RATES. The *currency exchange rate* determines how many dollars one must pay for a unit of foreign currency. It is a critical variable for any company that buys or sells products and services across national borders. For example, if the U.S. dollar appreciates against the euro, and so increases in real value, firms need more euros to buy one dollar. This in turn makes U.S. exports such as Boeing aircraft, Intel chips, or John Deere tractors more expensive for European buyers and reduces demand for U.S. exports overall. This process reverses when the dollar depreciates (decreases in real value) against the euro. In this scenario it would take more dollars to buy one euro, and European imports such as LVMH luxury accessories or BMW automobiles become more expensive for U.S. buyers.

In a similar fashion, if the Chinese yuan appreciates in value, Chinese goods imported into the United States are relatively more expensive. At the same time, Chinese purchasing power increases, which in turn allows their businesses to purchase more U.S. capital goods such as sophisticated machinery and other cutting-edge technologies.

In summary, economic factors affecting businesses are ever-present and rarely static. Managers need to fully appreciate the power of these factors, in both domestic and global markets, to assess their effects on firm performance.

SOCIOCULTURAL FACTORS

Sociocultural factors capture a society's cultures, norms, and values. Because sociocultural factors not only are constantly in flux but also differ across groups, managers need to closely monitor such trends and consider the implications for firm strategy. In recent years, for example, a growing number of U.S. consumers have become more health-conscious about what they eat. This trend led to a boom for businesses such as Chipotle, Subway, and Whole Foods. At the same time, traditional fast-food companies McDonald's and Burger King, along with grocery chains such as Albertsons and Kroger, have all had to scramble to provide healthier choices in their product offerings.

Demographic trends are also important sociocultural factors. These trends capture population characteristics related to age, gender, family size, ethnicity, sexual orientation, religion, and socioeconomic class. Like other sociocultural factors, demographic trends present opportunities but can also pose threats. The most recent U.S. census revealed that 51 million Americans (16.4 percent of the total population) are Hispanic. It is now the second-largest ethnic group in the United States and growing fast. On average, Hispanics are also younger and their incomes are climbing quickly. This trend is not lost on companies trying to benefit from this opportunity. For example, MundoFox and ESPN Deportes (specializing in soccer) have joined Univision and NBC's Telemundo in the Spanish-language television market. In the United States, Univision is now the fifth most popular network overall, just behind the four major English-language networks (ABC, NBC, CBS, and Fox). Likewise, advertisers are pouring dollars into the Spanish-language networks to promote their products and services.[8]

TECHNOLOGICAL FACTORS

Technological factors capture the application of knowledge to create new processes and products. Major innovations in process technology include lean manufacturing, Six Sigma quality, and biotechnology. The nanotechnology revolution, which is just beginning, promises significant upheaval for a vast array of industries ranging from tiny medical devices to new-age materials for earthquake-resistant buildings.[9] Recent product innovations include the smartphone, computer tablets, and high-performing electric cars such as the Tesla Model S. Recent service innovations include social media and online search engines that respond to voice commands. If one thing seems certain, technological progress is relentless and seems to be picking up speed.[10] Not surprisingly, changes in the technological environment bring both opportunities and threats for companies. Given the importance of a firm's innovation strategy to competitive advantage, we discuss the effect of technological factors in greater detail in Chapter 7.

Strategy Highlight 3.1 details how BlackBerry fell victim by not paying sufficient attention to the PESTEL factors.

ECOLOGICAL FACTORS

Ecological factors involve broad environmental issues such as the natural environment, global warming, and sustainable economic growth. Organizations and the natural environment coexist in an interdependent relationship. Managing these relationships in a responsible and sustainable way directly influences the continued existence of human societies and the organizations we create. Managers can no longer separate the natural and the business worlds; they are inextricably linked.[11]

Negative examples come readily to mind, as many business organizations have contributed to the pollution of air, water, and land, as well as depletion of the world's natural resources. BP's infamous oil spill in the Gulf of Mexico destroyed fauna and flora along the U.S. shoreline from Texas to Florida. This disaster led to a decrease in fish and wildlife populations, triggered a decline in the fishery and tourism industries, and threatened the livelihood of thousands of people. It also cost BP some $50 billion and one-half of its market value (see Strategy Highlight 1.2).

Strategy Highlight 3.1

BlackBerry's Bust

A pioneer in smartphones, BlackBerry was the undisputed industry leader in the early 2000s. IT managers preferred BlackBerry. Its devices allowed users to receive e-mail and other data in real time globally, with enhanced security features. For executives, a BlackBerry was not just a tool to increase productivity—and to free them from their laptops—but also an important status symbol. As a consequence, by 2008 BlackBerry's market cap had peaked at $75 billion. Yet by 2015, this valuation had fallen more than 90 percent, to less than $7 billion. What happened?

Being Canadian, BlackBerry's longtime co-CEO, Jim Balsillie, not surprisingly sees ice hockey as his favorite sport. He likes to quote Wayne Gretzky, "The Great One," whom many consider the best ice hockey player ever: "Skate to where the puck is going to be, not to where it is." Alas, BlackBerry did not follow that advice. BlackBerry fell victim to two important PESTEL factors in its external environment: sociocultural and technological.

Let's start with technology. The introduction of the iPhone by Apple in 2007 changed the game in the mobile device industry. Equipped with a camera, the iPhone's slick design offered a user interface with a touchscreen including a virtual keyboard. The iPhone connected seamlessly other cellular networks and Wi-Fi. Combined with thousands of

Wayne Gretzky: Skate to where the puck is going to be, not to where it is.
© AP Photo/Jim Rogash

apps via the Apple iTunes store, the iPhone provided a powerful user experience, or as the late Steve Jobs said, "the Internet in your pocket."

However, BlackBerry engineers and executives initially dismissed the iPhone as a mere toy with poor security features. Everyday users thought differently. They had less concern for encrypted software security than they had desire for having fun with a device that allowed them to text, surf the web, take pictures, play games, and do e-mail. Although BlackBerry devices were great in productivity applications, such as receiving and responding to e-mail via typing on its iconic physical keyboard, they provided a poor mobile web browsing experience.

The second external development that helped erode BlackBerry's dominance was sociocultural. Initially, mobile devices were issued top-down by corporate IT departments. The only available device for execs was a company-issued BlackBerry. This made life easy for IT departments, ensuring network security. Consumers, however, began to bring their personal iPhones to work and used them for corporate communication and productivity applications. This bottom-up groundswell of the BYOT ("bring your own technology") movement forced corporate IT departments to open up their services beyond the BlackBerry.

Caught in the oncoming gale winds of two PESTEL factors—technological and sociocultural—BlackBerry was pushed backward in the smartphone market. Unlike Gretzky, it failed to skate where the puck was going to be and therefore continued to focus on its existing customer base of corporate IT departments and government. Later, feeble modifications in product lineup appeared to be a "too little, too late." Apple continued to drive innovation in the smartphone industry by bringing out more advanced iPhone models and enhancing the usefulness of its apps for the various business and productivity applications.[12]

Let's think about the rapid progress in mobile computing. BlackBerry, once an undisputed leader in the smartphone industry, did not recognize early enough or act upon changes in the external environment. Consumer preferences changed quickly as the iPhone and later the iPad became available. Professionals brought their own Apple or other devices to work instead of using company-issued BlackBerrys. Although the Canadian technology company made a valiant effort to make up lost ground with its new BlackBerry 10 operating system and several new models, it was too little, too late.

The relationship between organizations and the natural environment need not be adversarial, however. Ecological factors can also provide business opportunities. As we saw in the ChapterCase, Tesla Motors is addressing environmental concerns regarding the carbon emissions of gasoline-powered cars by building zero-emission battery-powered vehicles. The question of how to generate the power needed to charge the batteries in a sustainable way, however, still needs to be addressed.

LEGAL FACTORS

Legal factors include the official outcomes of political processes as manifested in laws, mandates, regulations, and court decisions—all of which can have a direct bearing on a firm's profit potential. In fact, regulatory changes tend to affect entire industries at once. Many industries in the United States have been deregulated over the last few decades, including airlines, telecom, energy, and trucking, among others.

As noted earlier, legal factors often coexist with or result from political will. Governments especially can directly affect firm performance by exerting both political pressure and legal sanctions, including court rulings and industry regulations. Consider how several European countries and the European Union (EU) apply political and legal pressure on U.S. tech companies. European targets include Apple, Amazon, Facebook, Google, and Microsoft—the five largest U.S. tech companies—but also startups such as Uber, the taxi-hailing mobile app. Europe's policy makers seek to retain control over important industries ranging from transportation to the Internet to ensure that profits earned in Europe by Silicon Valley firms are taxed locally. The EU parliament even proposed legislation to break up "digital monopolies" such as Google. This proposal would require Google to offer search services independently as a standalone company from its other online services, including Google Drive, a cloud-based file storage and synchronization service. But the EU wariness extends beyond tax revenue: The Eurozone has much stronger legal requirements and cultural expectations concerning data privacy. Taken together, political/legal environments can have a direct bearing on a firm's performance.

Amazon is preparing to use drones for package delivery.
© Amazon/Zuma Press/ Newscom

LO 3-2

Apply Porter's five competitive forces to explain the profit potential of different industries.

Governments can often wield positive legal and political mechanisms to achieve desired changes in consumer behavior. For example, to encourage consumers to buy zero-emission vehicles, the U.S. government offers a $7,500 federal tax credit with the purchase of a new electric vehicle such as the Chevy Bolt, Nissan Leaf, or Tesla Model S.

You see the influence of multiple PESTEL factors affecting the implementation of drones for commercial purposes. Amazon and Alibaba were initially bullish on drones for doorstep delivery of products, but governmental, legal, and technological factors are proving a serious challenge and are delaying the introduction of drones for commercial applications.[13]

industry
A group of incumbent companies that face more or less the same set of suppliers and buyers.

industry analysis
A method to (1) identify an industry's profit potential and (2) derive implications for a firm's strategic position within an industry.

3.2 Industry Structure and Firm Strategy: The Five Forces Model

We now move one step closer to the firm (in the center of Exhibit 3.1) and come to the industry in which it competes. An **industry** is a group of incumbent companies facing more or less the same set of suppliers and buyers. Firms competing in the same industry tend to offer similar products or services to meet specific customer needs. Although the PESTEL framework allows us to scan, monitor, and evaluate the external environment to identify opportunities and threats, **industry analysis** provides a more rigorous basis not only to identify an industry's profit potential—the level of profitability that can be expected for the *average* firm—but also to derive implications for one firm's strategic position within an industry. A firm's **strategic position** relates to its ability to create value for customers (*V*) while containing the cost to do so (*C*). Competitive advantage flows to the firm that is able to create as large a gap as possible between the value the firm's product or service generates and the cost required to produce it (*V* − *C*).

Michael Porter developed the highly influential **five forces model** to help managers understand the profit potential of different industries and how they can position their respective firms to gain and sustain competitive advantage.[14] By combining theory from industrial organization economics with hundreds of detailed case studies, Porter derived two key insights that form the basis of his seminal five forces model:

1. Rather than defining competition narrowly as the firm's closest competitors to explain and predict a firm's performance, competition must be viewed more broadly, to also encompass the other forces in an industry: buyers, suppliers, potential new entry of other firms, and the threat of substitutes.

2. The profit potential of an industry is neither random nor entirely determined by industry-specific factors. Rather, it is a function of the five forces that shape competition: *threat of entry, power of suppliers, power of buyers, threat of substitutes,* and *rivalry among existing firms.*

> **strategic position**
> A firm's strategic profile based on the difference between value creation and cost (*V* − *C*).
>
> **five forces model**
> A framework that identifies five forces that determine the profit potential of an industry and shape a firm's competitive strategy.

COMPETITION IN THE FIVE FORCES MODEL

Because the five forces model has especially powerful implications for strategy and competitive advantage, we will explore it in some detail. We start with the concept of competition. The first major insight this model provides is that competition involves more than just creating economic value; firms must also capture a significant share of it or they will see the economic value they create lost to suppliers, customers, or competitors. Firms create economic value by expanding as much as possible the gap between the value (*V*) the firm's product or service generates and the cost (*C*) to produce it. *Economic value* thus equals *V* minus *C*. To succeed, creating value is not enough. Firms must also be able to capture a significant share of the value created to gain and sustain a competitive advantage.

In Porter's five forces model, competition is more broadly defined beyond the firm's closest competitors (e.g., Nike vs. Under Armour, The Home Depot vs. Lowe's, Merck vs. Pfizer, and so on) to include other industry forces: buyers, suppliers, potential new entry of other firms, and the threat of substitutes. Competition describes the struggle among these forces to capture as much of the economic value created in an industry as possible. A firm's managers, therefore, must be concerned not only with the intensity of rivalry among direct competitors, but also with the strength of the other competitive forces that are attempting to extract part or all of the economic value the firm creates. When faced with competition in this broader sense, strategy explains how a firm is able to achieve superior performance.

The second major insight from the five forces model is that it enables managers to not only understand their industry environment but also shape their firm's strategy. As a rule of thumb, *the stronger the five forces, the lower the industry's profit potential*—making the industry less attractive for competitors. The reverse is also true: *the weaker the five forces, the greater the industry's profit potential*—making the industry more attractive. Therefore, from the perspective of a manager of an existing firm competing for advantage in an established industry, the company should be positioned in a way that relaxes the constraints of strong forces and leverages weak forces. The goal of crafting a strategic position is of course to improve the firm's ability to achieve a competitive advantage.

Strategy Highlight 3.2 provides an overview of the five competitive forces that shape strategy, with an application to the U.S. domestic airline industry. We will take up the topic of competitive positioning in Chapter 6 when studying business-level strategy.

Strategy Highlight 3.2

The Five Forces in the Airline Industry

Although many of the mega-airlines such as American, Delta, and United have lost billions of dollars over the past few decades and continue to struggle to generate consistent profitability, other players in this industry have been quite profitable because they were able to extract some of the economic value created. The airlines, however, benefited from a windfall because the prices for jet fuel fell from a high of $3.25 per gallon (in 2011) to $1.50 (in 2015), giving some reprieve to cash-strapped airlines.

Regardless, the *nature of rivalry* among airlines is incredibly intense, as consumers primarily make decisions based on price. In inflation-adjusted dollars, ticket prices have been falling since industry deregulation in 1978. Thanks to Internet travel sites such as Orbitz, Travelocity, and Kayak, price comparisons are effortless. Consumers benefit from cut-throat price competition between carriers and capture significant value. Low switching costs and nearly perfect information combine to strengthen buyer power. Moreover, large corporate customers can contract with airlines to serve all of their employees' travel needs; such *powerful buyers* further reduce profit margins for air carriers.

Entry barriers are relatively low, resulting in a number of new airlines popping up. To enter the industry (on a small scale, serving a few select cities), a prospective new entrant needs only a couple of airplanes, which can be rented; a few pilots and crew members; some routes connecting city pairs; and gate access in airports. Indeed, despite notoriously low industry profitability, Virgin America entered the U.S. market in 2007. Virgin America is the brainchild of Sir Richard Branson, founder and chairman of the Virgin Group, a UK conglomerate of hundreds of companies using the Virgin brand, including the international airline Virgin Atlantic. Its business strategy is to offer low-cost service between major metropolitan cities on the American East and West Coasts.

In the airline industry, the *supplier power* is also strong. The providers of airframes (e.g., Boeing or Airbus), makers of aircraft engines (e.g., GE or Rolls-Royce), aircraft maintenance companies (e.g., Goodrich), caterers (e.g., Marriott), labor unions, and airports controlling gate access all bargain away the profitability of airlines.

To make matters worse, *substitutes* are also readily available: If prices are seen as too high, customers can drive their cars or use the train or bus. As an example, the route between Atlanta and Orlando (roughly 400 miles) used to be one of the busiest and most profitable ones for Delta. Given the increasing security delays at airports, more and more people now prefer to drive. Taken together, the competitive forces are quite unfavorable for generating a profit potential in the airline industry: low entry barriers, high supplier power, high buyer power combined with low customer switching costs, and the availability of low-cost substitutes. This type of hostile environment leads to intense rivalry among existing airlines and low overall industry profit potential.

The surprising conclusion is that while the mega-airlines themselves (i.e., American, Delta, and United) frequently struggle to make a profit, the other players in the industry—such as the suppliers of aircraft engines, aircraft maintenance companies, IT companies providing reservation and logistics services, caterers, airports, and so on—are quite profitable, all extracting significant value from the air transportation industry. Customers also are better off, as ticket prices have decreased and travel choices increased.[15]

Taking a closer look at the U.S. domestic airline industry in Strategy Highlight 3.2 shows how the five forces framework is a powerful and versatile tool to analyze industries. The five forces model allows managers to analyze all players using a wider industry lens, which in turn enables a deeper understanding of an industry's profit potential. Moreover, a five forces analysis provides the basis for how a firm should position itself to gain and sustain a competitive advantage. We are now ready to take a deep dive and look closer at each of the five competitive forces.

As Exhibit 3.2 shows, Porter's model identifies five key competitive forces that managers need to consider when analyzing the industry environment and formulating competitive strategy:

1. Threat of entry.
2. Power of suppliers.

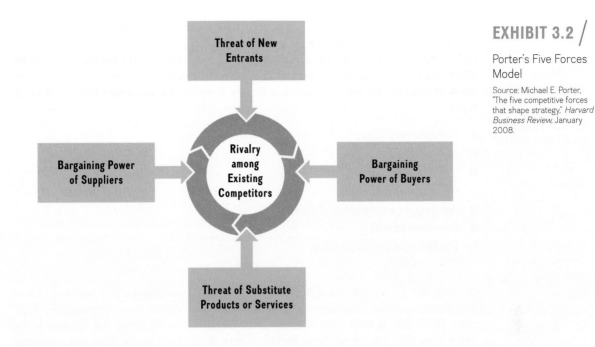

EXHIBIT 3.2 /

Porter's Five Forces
Model

Source: Michael E. Porter,
"The five competitive forces
that shape strategy," *Harvard
Business Review,* January
2008.

3. Power of buyers.
4. Threat of substitutes.
5. Rivalry among existing competitors.

THE THREAT OF ENTRY

The **threat of entry** describes the risk that potential competitors will enter the industry. Potential new entry depresses industry profit potential in two major ways:

1. With the threat of additional capacity coming into an industry, incumbent firms may lower prices to make entry appear less attractive to the potential new competitors, which would in turn reduce the overall industry's profit potential, especially in industries with slow or no overall growth in demand. Consider the market for new microwaves. Demand consists of the replacement rate for older models and the creation of new households. Since this market grows slowly, if at all, any additional entry would likely lead to excess capacity and lower prices overall.

2. The threat of entry by additional competitors may force incumbent firms to spend more to satisfy their existing customers. This spending reduces an industry's profit potential, especially if firms can't raise prices. Consider how Starbucks has chosen to constantly upgrade and refresh its stores and service offerings. Starbucks has over 11,000 U.S. stores and 22,000 globally. By raising the value of its offering in the eyes of the consumers, it slows others from entering the industry or from rapidly expanding. This allows Starbucks to hold at bay smaller regional competitors, such as Peet's Coffee & Tea, with fewer than 200 stores mostly on the West Coast, and prevents smaller national chains, such as Caribou Coffee, with 415 stores nationally, from increasing the level of competition. Starbucks is willing to accept a lower profit margin to maintain its market share.

> **threat of entry**
> The risk that potential competitors will enter an industry.

entry barriers
Obstacles that determine how easily a firm can enter an industry and often significantly predict industry profit potential.

Of course, the more profitable an industry, the more attractive it is for new competitors to enter. There are, however, a number of important barriers to entry that raise the costs for potential competitors and reduce the threat of entry. **Entry barriers**, which are advantageous for incumbent firms, are obstacles that determine how easily a firm can enter an industry. Incumbent firms can benefit from several important sources of entry barriers:

- Economies of scale.
- Network effects.
- Customer switching costs.
- Capital requirements.
- Advantages independent of size.
- Government policy.
- Credible threat of retaliation.

ECONOMIES OF SCALE. *Economies of scale* are cost advantages that accrue to firms with larger output because they can spread fixed costs over more units, employ technology more efficiently, benefit from a more specialized division of labor, and demand better terms from their suppliers. These factors in turn drive down the cost per unit, allowing large incumbent firms to enjoy a cost advantage over new entrants who cannot muster such scale.

We saw the important relationship between scale and production cost in the Tesla ChapterCase. Usually entrants into the broad automobile industry need large-scale production to be efficient. Tesla Motors leveraged new technology to circumvent this entry barrier. Yet, reaching sufficient manufacturing scale to be cost-competitive is critical for Tesla as it is moving more into the mass market.

To benefit from economies of scale, Tesla is introducing new models, helping it move away from small-scale and costly production of niche vehicles to larger production runs of cars with a stronger mass-market appeal. Tesla's first vehicle, the Roadster (costing over $110K) was more or less a prototype to prove the viability of an all-electric car that outperforms high-performance traditional sports cars. For consumers, it created a new mind-set of what electric cars can do. Tesla ended production of the Roadster to focus more fully on its next model: the family sedan, Model S (over $70K). Tesla's manufacturing scale increased more than 20-fold, from some 2,500 Roadsters to 60,000 Model S's. The all-electric car company is hoping for an even broader customer appeal with its Model X, a crossover between an SUV and a family van. Finally, Tesla is betting that its next model, the smaller and lower-priced Model 3 ($35K) will allow the new company to break into the mass market and manufacture many more cars. Tesla CEO Musk set an audacious goal of selling 500,000 cars a year by 2020, which is needed for the company to be profitable.[16] Tesla's new product introductions over time are motivated by an attempt to capture benefits that accrue to economies of scale.

network effects
The value of a product or service for an individual user increases with the number of total users.

NETWORK EFFECTS. **Network effects** describe the positive effect that one user of a product or service has on the value of that product or service for other users. When network effects are present, the value of the product or service increases with the number of users. The threat of potential entry is reduced when network effects are present.

For example, Facebook, with some 1.5 billion active users worldwide, enjoys tremendous network effects, making it difficult for more recent entrants such as Google Plus to compete effectively. We will discuss network effects in more detail in Chapter 7.

CUSTOMER SWITCHING COSTS. *Switching costs* are incurred by moving from one supplier to another. Changing vendors may require the buyer to alter product specifications, retrain employees, and/or modify existing processes. Switching costs are onetime sunk costs, which can be quite significant and a formidable barrier to entry.

For example, a firm that has used enterprise resource planning (ERP) software from SAP for many years will incur significant switching costs when implementing a new ERP system from Oracle.

CAPITAL REQUIREMENTS. *Capital requirements* describe the "price of the entry ticket" into a new industry. How much capital is required to compete in this industry, and which companies are willing and able to make such investments? Frequently related to economies of scale, capital requirements may encompass investments to set up plants with dedicated machinery, run a production process, and cover start-up losses.

Tesla Motors made a sizable capital investment of roughly $150 million when it purchased the Fremont, California, manufacturing plant from Toyota and upgraded it with a highly automated production process using robots to produce cars of the highest quality at large scale.[17] This strategic commitment, however, is dwarfed by the $5 billion that Tesla is investing to build its battery "gigafactory" in Nevada.[18] The new factory allows Tesla to not only secure supplies of lithium-ion batteries, the most critical and expensive component of an all-electric car, but also build as many as 500,000 vehicles a year.[19] In such cases, the likelihood of entry is determined by not only the level of capital investment required to enter the industry, but also the expected return on investment. The potential new entrant must carefully weigh the required capital investments, the cost of capital, and the expected return. Taken together, the threat of entry is high when capital requirements are low in comparison to the expected returns. If an industry is attractive enough, efficient capital markets are likely to provide the necessary funding to enter an industry. Capital, unlike proprietary technology and industry-specific know-how, is a fungible resource that can be relatively easily acquired in the face of attractive returns.

ADVANTAGES INDEPENDENT OF SIZE. Incumbent firms often possess cost and quality advantages that are independent of size. These advantages can be based on brand loyalty, proprietary technology, preferential access to raw materials and distribution channels, favorable geographic locations, and cumulative learning and experience effects.

Tesla Motors has loyal customers, which strengthens its competitive position and reduces the threat of entry into the all-electric car segment, at least by other start-up companies.[20] Unlike GM or Ford, which spend billions each year on advertising, Tesla doesn't have a large marketing budget. Rather, it relies on word of mouth. It luckily has its own "cool factor" of being different, similar to Apple in its early days. Tesla can back this perception with beautifully designed cars of top-notch quality made domestically in California. Indeed, when *Consumer Reports* tested the Model S, the usually understated magazine concluded: "The Tesla Model S is the best car we ever tested."[21] In addition, many Tesla owners feel an emotional connection to the company because they deeply believe in the company's vision "to accelerate the advent of sustainable transport by bringing compelling mass market electric cars to market as soon as possible."[22]

Patents and trade secrets, such as the original Coke formula, are examples of proprietary technology and know-how that can also reduce the threat of entry. The value of trade secrets to a firm is reflected in the efforts to improve cybersecurity so that trade secrets cannot be stolen by hacking into corporate computers.

Preferential access to raw materials and key components can bestow absolute cost advantages. As mentioned, lithium-ion batteries are not only the most expensive and critical parts of an all-electric vehicle, but they are also in short supply. Tesla's new battery "gigafactory" will afford it independence from the few worldwide suppliers, such as Panasonic of Japan, and also likely bestow an absolute cost advantage.[23] This should further reduce the threat of new entry in the all-electric vehicle segment, assuming no radical technological changes are to be expected in battery-cell technology in the next few years.

Favorable locations, such as Silicon Valley for Tesla Motors, often present advantages that other locales cannot match easily, including access to human and venture capital, and world-class research and engineering institutions.

Finally, incumbent firms often benefit from cumulative learning and experience effects accrued over long periods of time. Tesla Motors now has more than 10 years of experience in designing and building high-performance all-electric vehicles of superior quality and design. Attempting to obtain such deep knowledge within a shorter time frame is often costly, if not impossible, which in turn constitutes a formidable barrier to entry.

GOVERNMENT POLICY. Frequently government policies restrict or prevent new entrants. Until recently, India did not allow foreign retailers such as Walmart or IKEA to own stores and compete with domestic companies in order to protect the country's millions of small vendors and wholesalers. China frequently requires foreign companies to enter joint ventures with domestic ones and to share technology.

In contrast, deregulation in industries such as airlines, telecommunications, and trucking have generated significant new entries. Therefore, the threat of entry is high when restrictive government policies do not exist or when industries become deregulated.

CREDIBLE THREAT OF RETALIATION. Potential new entrants must also anticipate how incumbent firms will react. A credible threat of retaliation by incumbent firms often deters entry. Should entry still occur, however, incumbents are able to retaliate quickly, through initiating a price war, for example. The industry profit potential can in this case easily fall below the cost of capital. Incumbents with deeper pockets than new entrants are able to withstand price competition for a longer time and wait for the new entrants to exit the industry—then raise prices again. Other weapons of retaliation include increased product and service innovation, advertising, sales promotions, and litigation.

Potential new entrants should expect a strong and vigorous response beyond price competition by incumbent firms in several scenarios. If the current competitors have deep pockets, unused excess capacity, reputational clout with industry suppliers and buyers, a history of vigorous retaliation during earlier entry attempts, or heavy investments in resources specific to the core industry and ill-suited for adaptive use, then they are likely to press these advantages. Moreover, if industry growth is slow or stagnant, incumbents are more likely to retaliate against new entrants to protect their market share, often initiating a price war with the goal of driving out these new entrants.

In contrast, the threat of entry is high when new entrants expect that incumbents will not or cannot retaliate. For example, in the southeastern United States, TV cable company

Comcast has entered the market for residential and commercial telephone services and Internet connectivity (as an ISP, Internet service provider), emerging as a direct competitor for AT&T. Comcast also acquired NBC Universal, combining delivery and content. AT&T responded to Comcast's threat by introducing U-verse, a product combining high-speed Internet access with cable TV and telephone service, all provided over its fast fiber-optic network.

THE POWER OF SUPPLIERS

The bargaining power of suppliers captures pressures that industry suppliers can exert on an industry's profit potential. This force reduces a firm's ability to obtain superior performance for two reasons: Powerful suppliers can raise the cost of production by demanding higher prices for their inputs or by reducing the quality of the input factor or service level delivered. Powerful suppliers are a threat to firms because they reduce the industry's profit potential by capturing part of the economic value created.

To compete effectively, companies generally need a wide variety of inputs into the production process, including raw materials and components, labor (via individuals or labor unions, when the industry faces collective bargaining), and services. The relative bargaining power of suppliers is high when

- The suppliers' industry is more concentrated than the industry it sells to.
- Suppliers do not depend heavily on the industry for a large portion of their revenues.
- Incumbent firms face significant switching costs when changing suppliers.
- Suppliers offer products that are differentiated.
- There are no readily available substitutes for the products or services that the suppliers offer.
- Suppliers can credibly threaten to forward-integrate into the industry.

In Strategy Highlight 3.2, we noted that the airline industry faces strong supplier power. Let's take a closer look at one important supplier group to this industry: Boeing and Airbus, the makers of large commercial jets. The reason airframe manufacturers are powerful suppliers to airlines is because their industry is much more concentrated (only two firms) than the industry it sells to. Compared to two airframe suppliers, there are hundreds of commercial airlines around the world. Given the trend of large airlines merging to create even larger mega-airlines, however, increasing buyer power may eventually balance this out a bit. Nonetheless, the airlines face nontrivial switching costs when changing suppliers because pilots and crew would need to be retrained to fly a new type of aircraft, maintenance capabilities would need to be expanded, and some routes may even need to be reconfigured due to differences in aircraft range and passenger capacity. Moreover, while some of the aircraft can be used as substitutes, Boeing and Airbus offer differentiated products. This fact becomes clearer when considering the most recent models from each company. Boeing introduced the 787 Dreamliner to capture long-distance point-to-point travel (close to an 8,000-mile range, sufficient to fly non-stop from Los Angeles to Sydney), while Airbus introduced the A-380 Superjumbo to focus on high-volume transportation (close to 900 passengers) between major airport hubs (e.g., Tokyo's Haneda Airport and Singapore's International Airport). When considering long-distance travel, there are no readily available substitutes for commercial airliners, a fact that strengthens supplier power.

All in all, the vast strengths of these factors lead us to conclude that the supplier power of commercial aircraft manufacturers is quite significant. This puts Boeing and Airbus in a strong position to extract profits from the airline industry, thus reducing the profit potential of the airlines themselves.

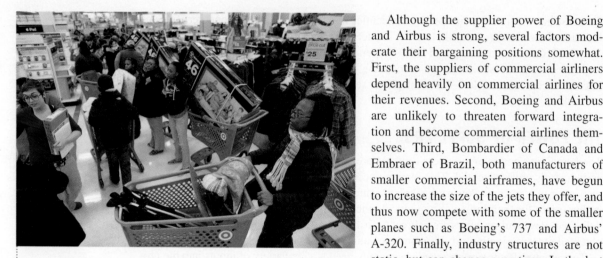

Retailers claim they schedule Black Friday sales events because the buyers demand it. We can see this phenomenon as one example of the power of buyers demanding discounted goods, thus reducing the ability of retailers to retain the economic value they have created.
© John Gress/Corbis

Although the supplier power of Boeing and Airbus is strong, several factors moderate their bargaining positions somewhat. First, the suppliers of commercial airliners depend heavily on commercial airlines for their revenues. Second, Boeing and Airbus are unlikely to threaten forward integration and become commercial airlines themselves. Third, Bombardier of Canada and Embraer of Brazil, both manufacturers of smaller commercial airframes, have begun to increase the size of the jets they offer, and thus now compete with some of the smaller planes such as Boeing's 737 and Airbus' A-320. Finally, industry structures are not static, but can change over time. In the last few years, several of the remaining large domestic U.S. airlines have merged (Delta and Northwest, United and Continental, and American and U.S. Airways), which changed the industry structure in their favor. There are now fewer but even larger airlines remaining. This fact increases their buyer power, which we turn to next.

THE POWER OF BUYERS

In many ways, the bargaining power of buyers is the flip side of the bargaining power of suppliers. Buyers are the customers of an industry. The power of buyers concerns the pressure an industry's customers can put on the producer's margins in the industry by demanding a lower price or higher product quality. When buyers successfully obtain price discounts, it reduces a firm's top line (revenue). When buyers demand higher quality and more service, it generally raises production costs. Strong buyers can therefore reduce industry profit potential and a firm's profitability. Powerful buyers are a threat to the producing firms because they reduce the industry's profit potential by capturing part of the economic value created.

As with suppliers, an industry may face many different types of buyers. The buyers of an industry's product or service may be individual consumers—like you or me when we decide which provider we want to use for our wireless devices. In many areas, you can choose between several providers such as AT&T, Sprint, T-Mobile, or Verizon. Although we might be able to find a good deal when carefully comparing their individual service plans, as individual consumers we generally do not have significant buyer power. On the other hand, large institutions such as businesses or universities have significant buyer power when deciding which provider to use for their wireless services, because they are able to sign up or move several thousand employees at once.

The power of buyers is high when

- There are a few buyers and each buyer purchases large quantities relative to the size of a single seller.
- The industry's products are standardized or undifferentiated commodities.
- Buyers face low or no switching costs.
- Buyers can credibly threaten to backwardly integrate into the industry.

In addition, companies need to be aware of situations when buyers are especially price sensitive. This is the case when:

- The buyer's purchase represents a significant fraction of its cost structure or procurement budget.
- Buyers earn low profits or are strapped for cash.
- The quality (cost) of the buyers' products and services is not affected much by the quality (cost) of their inputs.

The retail giant Walmart provides perhaps the most potent example of tremendous buyer power. Walmart is not only the largest retailer worldwide (with over 11,000 stores and 2.2 million employees), but it is also one of the largest companies in the world (with $485 billion in revenues in 2014). Walmart is one of the few large big-box global retail chains and frequently purchases large quantities from its suppliers. Walmart leverages its buyer power by exerting tremendous pressure on its suppliers to lower prices and to increase quality or risk losing access to shelf space at the largest retailer in the world. Walmart's buyer power is so strong that many suppliers co-locate offices directly next to Walmart's headquarters in Bentonville, Arkansas, because such proximity enables Walmart's managers to test the supplier's latest products and negotiate prices.

© niloo138/123RF

The bargaining power of buyers also increases when their switching costs are low. Having multiple suppliers of a product category located close to its headquarters allows Walmart to demand further price cuts and quality improvements because it can easily switch from one supplier to the next. This threat is even more pronounced if the products are non-differentiated commodities from the consumers' perspective. For example, Walmart can easily switch from Rubbermaid plastic containers to Sterlite containers by offering more shelf space to the producer that offers the greatest price cut or quality improvement.

Buyers are also powerful when they can credibly threaten backward integration. Backward integration occurs when a buyer moves upstream in the industry value chain, into the seller's business. Walmart has exercised the threat to backward-integrate by producing a number of products as private-label brands such as Equate health and beauty items, Ol'Roy dog food, and Parent's Choice baby products. Taken together, powerful buyers have the ability to extract a significant amount of the value created in the industry, leaving little or nothing for producers.

In regard to any of the five forces that shape competition, it is important to note that their relative strengths are context-dependent. For example, the Mexican multinational CEMEX, one of the world's leading cement producers, faces very different buyer power in the United States than domestically. In the United States, cement buyers consist of a few large and powerful construction companies that account for a significant percentage of CEMEX's output. The result? Razor-thin margins. In contrast, the vast majority of CEMEX's customers in its Mexican home market are numerous, small, individual customers facing a few large suppliers, with CEMEX being the biggest. CEMEX earns high profit margins in its home market. With the same undifferentiated product, CEMEX competes in two different industry scenarios in terms of buyer strength.

THE THREAT OF SUBSTITUTES

Substitutes meet the same basic customer needs as the industry's product but in a different way. The threat of substitutes is the idea that products or services available from *outside the given industry* will come close to meeting the needs of current customers.[24] For example, many software products are substitutes to professional services, at least at the lower end. Tax preparation software such as Intuit's TurboTax is a substitute for professional services offered by H&R Block and others. LegalZoom, an online legal documentation service, is a threat to professional law firms. Other examples of substitutes are energy drinks versus coffee, videoconferencing versus business travel, e-mail versus express mail, gasoline versus biofuel, and wireless telephone services versus Voice over Internet Protocol (VoIP), offered by Skype or Vonage.

A high threat of substitutes reduces industry profit potential by limiting the price the industry's competitors can charge for their products and services. The threat of substitutes is high when:

- The substitute offers an attractive price-performance trade-off.
- The buyer's cost of switching to the substitute is low.

The movie rental company Redbox, which uses 44,000 kiosks in the United States to make movie rentals available for just $1.50, is a substitute for buying movie DVDs. For buyers, video rental via Redbox offers an attractive price-performance trade-off with low switching costs in comparison to DVD ownership. Moreover, for customers that view only a few movies a month, Redbox is also a substitute for Netflix's on-demand Internet movie streaming service, which costs $7.99 a month. Rather than a substitute, however, Redbox is a direct competitor to Netflix's DVD rental business, where plans also cost $7.99 a month (for one DVD out at a time).

In addition to a lower price, substitutes may also become more attractive by offering a higher value proposition.[25] In Spain, some 6 million people travel annually between Madrid and Barcelona, roughly 400 miles apart. The trip by car or train takes most of the day, and 90 percent of travelers would choose to fly, creating a highly profitable business for local airlines. This all changed when the Alta Velocidad Española (AVE), an ultra-modern high-speed train, was completed in 2008. Taking into account total time involved, high-speed trains are faster than short-haul flights. Passengers travel in greater comfort than airline passengers and commute from one city center to the next, with only a short walk or cab ride to their final destinations.

The AVE example highlights the two fundamental insights provided by Porter's five forces framework. First, competition must be defined more broadly to go beyond direct industry competitors. In this case, rather than defining competition narrowly as the firm's closest competitors, airline executives in Spain must look beyond other airlines and consider substitute offerings such as high-speed trains. Second, any of the five forces on its own, if sufficiently strong, can extract industry profitability. In the AVE example, the threat of substitutes is limiting the airline industry's profit potential. With the arrival of the AVE, the airlines' monopoly on fast transportation between Madrid and Barcelona vanished, and with it the airlines' high profits. The strong threat of substitutes in this case increased the rivalry among existing competitors in the Spanish air transportation industry.

LO 3-3

Explain how competitive industry structure shapes rivalry among competitors.

RIVALRY AMONG EXISTING COMPETITORS

Rivalry among existing competitors describes the intensity with which companies within the same industry jockey for market share and profitability. It can range from genteel to cut-throat. The other four forces—threat of entry, the power of buyers and suppliers, and the threat of substitutes—all exert pressure upon this rivalry, as indicated by the arrows pointing toward the center in Exhibit 3.2. The stronger the forces, the stronger the expected competitive intensity, which in turn limits the industry's profit potential.

Competitors can lower prices to attract customers from rivals. When intense rivalry among existing competitors brings about price discounting, industry profitability erodes. Alternatively, competitors can use non-price competition to create more value in terms of product features and design, quality, promotional spending, and after-sales service and support. When non-price competition is the primary basis of competition, costs increase, which can also have a negative impact on industry profitability. However, when these moves create unique products with features tailored closely to meet customer needs and willingness to pay, then average industry profitability tends to increase because producers are able to raise prices and thus increase revenues and profit margins.

The intensity of rivalry among existing competitors is determined largely by the following factors

- Competitive industry structure.
- Industry growth.
- Strategic commitments.
- Exit barriers.

COMPETITIVE INDUSTRY STRUCTURE. The **competitive industry structure** refers to elements and features common to all industries. The structure of an industry is largely captured by

- The number and size of its competitors.
- The firms' degree of pricing power.
- The type of product or service (commodity or differentiated product).
- The height of entry barriers.[26]

> **competitive industry structure**
> Elements and features common to all industries, including the number and size of competitors, the firms' degree of pricing power, the type of product or service offered, and the height of entry barriers.

Exhibit 3.3 shows different industry types along a continuum from fragmented to consolidated structures. At one extreme, a *fragmented industry* consists of many small firms and tends to generate low profitability. At the other end of the continuum, a *consolidated industry* is dominated by a few firms, or even just one firm, and has the potential to be highly profitable. The four main competitive industry structures are

(1) perfect competition,

(2) monopolistic competition,

(3) oligopoly, and

(4) monopoly.

Perfect Competition. A *perfectly competitive* industry is fragmented and has many small firms, a commodity product, ease of entry, and little or no ability for each individual firm to raise its prices. The firms competing in this type of industry are approximately similar in size and resources. Consumers make purchasing decisions solely on price, because the commodity product offerings are more or less identical. The resulting performance of the industry shows low profitability. Under these conditions, firms in perfect competition have difficulty achieving even a temporary competitive advantage and can achieve only competitive parity. Although perfect competition is a rare industry structure in its pure form, markets for commodities such as natural gas, copper, and iron tend to approach this structure.

Modern high-tech industries are also not immune to the perils of perfect competition. Many Internet entrepreneurs learned the hard way that it is difficult to beat the forces of perfect competition. Fueled by eager venture capitalists, about 100 online pet supply stores such as *pets.com, petopia.com,* and *pet-store.com* had sprung up by 1999, at the height of the Internet bubble.[27] Cut-throat competition ensued, with online retailers selling products

EXHIBIT 3.3 / Industry Competitive Structures along the Continuum from Fragmented to Consolidated

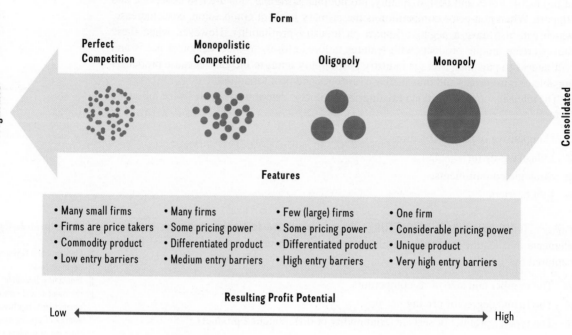

below cost. When there are many small firms offering a commodity product in an industry that is easy to enter, no one is able to increase prices and generate profits. To make matters worse, at the same time, category-killers such as PetSmart and PetCo were expanding rapidly, opening some 2,000 brick-and-mortar stores in the United States and Canada. The ensuing price competition led to an industry shakeout, leaving online retailers in the dust. Looking at the competitive industry structures depicted in Exhibit 3.3, we might have predicted that online pet supply stores were unlikely to be profitable.

Monopolistic Competition. A *monopolistically competitive* industry has many firms, a differentiated product, some obstacles to entry, and the ability to raise prices for a relatively unique product while retaining customers. The key to understanding this industry structure is that the firms now offer products or services with unique features.

The computer hardware industry provides one example of monopolistic competition. Many firms compete in this industry, and even the largest of them (Apple, ASUS, Dell, HP, or Lenovo) have less than 20 percent market share. Moreover, while products between competitors tend to be similar, they are by no means identical. As a consequence, firms selling a product with unique features tend to have some ability to raise prices. When a firm is able to differentiate its product or service offerings, it carves out a niche in the market in which it has some degree of monopoly power over pricing, thus the name "monopolistic competition." Firms frequently communicate the degree of product differentiation through advertising.

Oligopoly. An *oligopolistic* industry is consolidated with a few large firms, differentiated products, high barriers to entry, and some degree of pricing power. The degree of pricing power depends, just as in monopolistic competition, on the degree of product differentiation.

A key feature of an oligopoly is that the competing firms are *interdependent*. With only a few competitors in the mix, the actions of one firm influence the behaviors of the others. Each competitor in an oligopoly, therefore, must consider the strategic actions of the other competitors. This type of industry structure is often analyzed using *game theory,* which attempts to predict strategic behaviors by assuming that the moves and reactions of competitors can be anticipated.[28] Due to their strategic interdependence, companies in oligopolies have an incentive to coordinate their strategic actions to maximize joint performance. Although explicit coordination such as price fixing is illegal in the United States, tacit coordination such as "an unspoken understanding" is not.

The express-delivery industry is an example of an oligopoly. The main competitors in this space are FedEx and UPS. Any strategic decision made by FedEx (e.g., to expand delivery services to ground delivery of larger-size packages) directly affects UPS; likewise, any decision made by UPS (e.g., to guarantee next-day delivery before 8:00 a.m.) directly affects FedEx. Other examples of oligopolies include the soft drink industry (Coca-Cola vs. Pepsi), airframe manufacturing business (Boeing vs. Airbus), home-improvement retailing (The Home Depot vs. Lowe's), toys and games (Hasbro vs. Mattel), and detergents (P&G vs. Unilever).[29]

Companies in an oligopoly tend to have some pricing power if they are able to differentiate their product or service offerings from those of their competitors. *Non-price competition,* therefore, is the preferred mode of competition. This means competing by offering unique product features or services rather than competing based on price alone. When one firm in an oligopoly cuts prices to gain market share from its competitor, the competitor typically will respond in kind and also cut prices. This process initiates a price war, which can be especially detrimental to firm performance if the products are close rivals.

In the early years of the soft drink industry, for example, whenever Pepsi lowered prices, Coca-Cola followed suit. These actions only resulted in reduced profitability for both companies. In recent decades, both Coca-Cola and Pepsi have repeatedly demonstrated that they have learned this lesson. They shifted the basis of competition from price-cutting to new product introductions and lifestyle advertising. Any price adjustments are merely short-term promotions. By leveraging innovation and advertising, Coca-Cola and Pepsi have moved to non-price competition, which in turn allows them to charge higher prices and to improve industry and company profitability.[30]

Monopoly. An industry is a *monopoly* when there is only one, often large firm supplying the market. The firm may offer a unique product, and the challenges to moving into the industry tend to be high. The monopolist has considerable pricing power. As a consequence, firm and thus industry profit tends to be high. The one firm is the industry.

In some instances, the government will grant one firm the right to be the sole supplier of a product or service. This is often done to incentivize a company to engage in a venture that would not be profitable if there was more than one supplier. For instance, public utilities incur huge fixed costs to build plants and to supply a certain geographic area. Public utilities supplying water, gas, and electricity to businesses and homes are frequently monopolists. As examples, Georgia Power is the only supplier of electricity for some 2.5 million customers in the southeastern United States. Philadelphia Gas Works is the only supplier of natural gas in the city of Philadelphia, Pennsylvania, serving some 500,000 customers. These are so-called *natural monopolies.* Without them, the governments involved believe the market would not supply these products or services. In the past few decades, however, more and more of these natural monopolies have been deregulated in the United States, including airlines, telecommunications, railroads, trucking, and ocean transportation. This deregulation has allowed competition to emerge, which frequently leads to lower prices, better service, and more innovation.

While natural monopolies appear to be disappearing from the competitive landscape, so-called *near monopolies* are of much greater interest to strategists. These are firms that have accrued significant market power, for example, by owning valuable patents or proprietary technology. In the process, they are changing the industry structure in their favor, generally from monopolistic competition or oligopolies to near monopolies. These near monopolies are firms that have accomplished product differentiation to such a degree that they are in a class by themselves, just like a monopolist. The European Union, for example, views Google with its 90 percent market share in online search as a "digital monopoly."[31] This is an enviable position in terms of the ability to extract profits by leveraging its data to provide targeted online advertising and other customized services, so long as Google can steer clear of monopolistic behavior, which may attract antitrust regulators and lead to legal repercussions.

INDUSTRY GROWTH. Industry growth directly affects the intensity of rivalry among competitors. In periods of high growth, consumer demand rises, and price competition among firms frequently decreases. Because the pie is expanding, rivals are focused on capturing part of that larger pie rather than taking market share and profitability away from one another. The demand for knee replacements, for example, is a fast-growing segment in the medical products industry. In the United States, robust demand is driven by the need for knee replacements for an aging population as well as for an increasingly obese population.

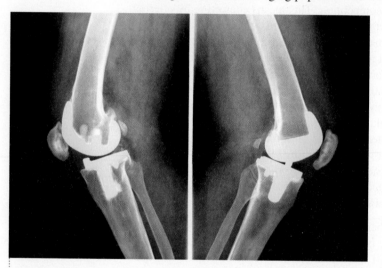

Competition in the knee replacement industry is primarily based on innovative design, improved implant materials, and differentiated products.
© BSIP/UIG/Getty Images

The leading competitors are Zimmer Biomet, DePuy, and Stryker, with significant share held by Smith & Nephew. Competition is primarily based on innovative design, improved implant materials, and differentiated products such as gender solutions and a range of high-flex knees. With improvements to materials and procedures, younger patients are also increasingly choosing early surgical intervention. Competitors are able to avoid price competition and, instead, focus on differentiation that allows premium pricing.

In contrast, rivalry among competitors becomes fierce during slow or even negative industry growth. Price discounts, frequent new product releases with minor modifications, intense promotional campaigns, and fast retaliation by rivals are all tactics indicative of an industry with slow or negative growth. Competition is fierce because rivals can gain only at the expense of others; therefore, companies are focused on taking business away from one another. Demand for traditional fast food providers such as McDonald's, Burger King, and Wendy's has been declining in recent years. Consumers have become more health-conscious and demand has shifted to alternative restaurants such as Subway, Chick-fil-A, and Chipotle. Attempts by McDonald's, Burger King, and Wendy's to steal customers from one another include frequent discounting tactics such as dollar menus. Such competitive tactics are indicative of cut-throat competition and a low profit potential in the traditional hamburger fast food industry.

Competitive rivalry based solely on cutting prices is especially destructive to profitability because it transfers most, if not all, of the value created in the industry to the customers—leaving little, if anything, for the firms in the industry. While this may appear attractive to customers, firms that are not profitable are not able to make the investments necessary to upgrade their product offerings or services to provide higher value, and they eventually leave the industry. Destructive price competition can lead to limited choices, lower product quality, and higher prices for consumers in the long run if only a few large firms survive.

STRATEGIC COMMITMENTS. If firms make strategic commitments to compete in an industry, rivalry among competitors is likely to be more intense. We defined *strategic commitments* (in Chapter 2) as firm actions that are costly, long-term oriented, and difficult to reverse. Strategic commitments to a specific industry can stem from large, fixed cost requirements, but also from non-economic considerations.[32]

For example, significant strategic commitments are required to compete in the airline industry when using a hub-and-spoke system to provide not only domestic but also international coverage. U.S. airlines Delta, United, and American have large fixed costs to maintain their network of routes that affords global coverage, frequently in conjunction with foreign partner airlines. These fixed costs in terms of aircraft, gate leases, hangars, maintenance facilities, baggage facilities, and ground transportation all accrue before the airlines sell any tickets. High fixed costs create tremendous pressure to fill empty seats. An airline seat on a specific flight is perishable, just like hotel rooms not filled. Empty airline seats are often filled through price-cutting. Given similar high fixed costs, other airlines respond in kind. Eventually, a vicious cycle of price-cutting ensues, driving average industry profitability to zero, or even negative numbers (where the companies are losing money). To make matters worse, given their strategic commitments, airlines are unlikely to exit an industry. Excess capacity remains, further depressing industry profitability.

In other cases, strategic commitments to a specific industry may be the result of more political than economic considerations. Airbus, for example, was created by a number of European governments through direct subsidies to provide a countervailing power to Boeing. The European Union in turn claims that Boeing is subsidized by the U.S. government indirectly via defense contracts. Given these political considerations and large-scale strategic commitments, neither Airbus nor Boeing is likely to exit the aircraft manufacturing industry even if industry profit potential falls to zero.

EXIT BARRIERS. The rivalry among existing competitors is also a function of an industry's **exit barriers,** the obstacles that determine how easily a firm can leave that industry. Exit barriers comprise both economic and social factors. They include fixed costs that must be paid regardless of whether the company is operating in the industry or not. A company exiting an industry may still have contractual obligations to suppliers, such as employee health care, retirement benefits, and severance pay. Social factors include elements such as emotional attachments to certain geographic locations. In Michigan, entire communities still depend on GM, Ford, and Chrysler. If any of those carmakers were to exit the industry, communities would suffer. Other social and economic factors include ripple effects through the supply chain. When one major player in an industry shuts down, its suppliers are adversely impacted as well.

exit barriers
Obstacles that determine how easily a firm can leave an industry.

An industry with low exit barriers is more attractive because it allows underperforming firms to exit more easily. Such exits reduce competitive pressure on the remaining firms because excess capacity is removed. In contrast, an industry with high exit barriers reduces its profit potential because excess capacity still remains. All of the large airlines featured in Strategy Highlight 3.2 (American, Delta, and United) have filed for bankruptcy at one point. Due to a unique feature of U.S. Chapter 11 bankruptcy law, however, companies may continue to operate and reorganize while being temporarily shielded from their creditors and other obligations until renegotiated. This implies that excess capacity is not removed from the industry, and by putting pressure on prices further reduces industry profit potential.

To summarize our discussion of the five forces model, Exhibit 3.4 provides a checklist that you can apply to any industry when assessing the underlying competitive forces that

EXHIBIT 3.4 /

The Five Forces
Competitive Analysis
Checklist

The threat of entry is high when:

√ The minimum efficient scale to compete in an industry is low.

√ Network effects are not present.

√ Customer switching costs are low.

√ Capital requirements are low.

√ Incumbents do not possess:

- Brand loyalty.
- Proprietary technology.
- Preferential access to raw materials.
- Preferential access to distribution channels.
- Favorable geographic locations.
- Cumulative learning and experience effects.

√ Restrictive government regulations do not exist.

√ New entrants expect that incumbents will not or cannot retaliate.

The power of suppliers is high when:

√ Suppliers' industry is more concentrated than the industry it sells to.

√ Suppliers do not depend heavily on the industry for their revenues.

√ Incumbent firms face significant switching costs when changing suppliers.

√ Suppliers offer products that are differentiated.

√ There are no readily available substitutes for the products or services that the suppliers offer.

√ Suppliers can credibly threaten to forward-integrate into the industry.

The power of buyers is high when:

√ There are a few buyers and each buyer purchases large quantities relative to the size of a single seller.

√ The industry's products are standardized or undifferentiated commodities.

√ Buyers face low or no switching costs.

√ Buyers can credibly threaten to backwardly integrate into the industry.

The threat of substitutes is high when:

√ The substitute offers an attractive price–performance trade-off.

√ The buyers' cost of switching to the substitute is low.

The rivalry among existing competitors is high when:

√ There are many competitors in the industry.

√ The competitors are roughly of equal size.

√ Industry growth is slow, zero, or even negative.

√ Exit barriers are high.

√ Incumbent firms are highly committed to the business.

√ Incumbent firms cannot read or understand each other's strategies well.

√ Products and services are direct substitutes.

√ Fixed costs are high and marginal costs are low.

√ Excess capacity exists in the industry.

√ The product or service is perishable.

Source: Adapted from Porter, M.E. (2008), "The five competitive forces that shape strategy," *Harvard Business Review*, January.

shape strategy. The key take-away from the five forces model is that the stronger the forces, the lower the industry's ability to earn above-average profits, and correspondingly, the lower the firm's ability to gain and sustain a competitive advantage. Conversely, the weaker the forces, the greater the industry's ability to earn above-average profits, and correspondingly, the greater the firm's ability to gain and sustain competitive advantage. Therefore, managers need to craft a strategic position for their company that leverages weak forces into opportunities and mitigates strong forces because they are potential threats to the firm's ability to gain and sustain a competitive advantage.

A SIXTH FORCE: THE STRATEGIC ROLE OF COMPLEMENTS

As valuable as the five forces model is for explaining the profit potential and attractiveness of industries, the value of Porter's five forces model can be further enhanced if one also considers the availability of complements.[33]

A **complement** is a product, service, or competency that adds value to the original product offering when the two are used in tandem.[34] Complements increase demand for the primary product, thereby enhancing the profit potential for the industry and the firm. A company is a **complementor** to your company if customers value your product or service offering more when they are able to combine it with the other company's product or service.[35] Firms may choose to provide the complements themselves or work with another company to accomplish this.

For example, in the smartphone industry, Google complements Samsung. The Korean high-tech company's smartphones are more valuable when they come with Google's Android system installed. At the same time, Google and Samsung are increasingly becoming competitors. With Google's acquisition of Motorola Mobility, the online search company is planning to launch its own line of smartphones and Chromebooks. This development illustrates the process of **co-opetition**, which is cooperation by competitors to achieve a strategic objective. Samsung and Google cooperate as complementors to compete against Apple's strong position in the mobile device industry, while at the same time Samsung and Google are increasingly becoming competitive with one another.

3.3 Changes over Time: Industry Dynamics

Although the five-forces-plus-complements model is useful in understanding an industry's profit potential, it provides only a point-in-time snapshot of a moving target. With this model (as with other static models), one cannot determine the changing speed of an industry or the rate of innovation. This drawback implies that managers must repeat their analysis over time in order to create a more accurate picture of their industry. It is therefore important that managers consider industry dynamics.

Industry structures are not stable over time. Rather, they are dynamic. Since a consolidated industry tends to be more profitable than a fragmented one (see Exhibit 3.3), firms have a tendency to change the industry structure in their favor, making it more consolidated through horizontal mergers and acquisitions. Having fewer competitors generally equates to higher industry profitability. Industry incumbents, therefore, have an incentive to reduce the number of competitors in the industry. With fewer but larger competitors, incumbent firms can mitigate the threat of strong competitive forces such as supplier or buyer power more effectively.

The U.S. domestic airline industry (featured in Strategy Highlight 3.2) has witnessed several large, horizontal mergers between competitors, including Delta and Northwest,

---

LO 3-4

Describe the strategic role of complements in creating positive-sum co-opetition.

complement
A product, service, or competency that adds value to the original product offering when the two are used in tandem.

complementor
A company that provides a good or service that leads customers to value your firm's offering more when the two are combined.

co-opetition
Cooperation by competitors to achieve a strategic objective.

LO 3-5

Appraise the role of industry dynamics and industry convergence in shaping the firm's external environment.

United and Continental, Southwest and AirTran, as well as American and U.S. Airways. These moves allow the remaining carriers to enjoy a more benign industry structure. It also allows them to retire some of the excess capacity in the industry as the merged airlines consolidate their networks of routes. The merger activity in the airline industry provides one example of how firms can proactively reshape industry structure in their favor. A more consolidated airline industry is likely to lead to higher ticket prices and fewer choices for customers, but also more profitable airlines.

In contrast, consolidated industry structures may also break up and become more fragmented. This generally happens when there are external shocks to an industry such as deregulation, new legislation, technological innovation, or globalization. For example, the emergence of the Internet moved the stock brokerage business from an oligopoly controlled by full-service firms such as Merrill Lynch and Morgan Stanley to monopolistic competition with many generic online brokers such as Ameritrade, E*TRADE, and Scottrade.

industry convergence
A process whereby formerly unrelated industries begin to satisfy the same customer need.

Another dynamic to be considered is **industry convergence**, a process whereby formerly unrelated industries begin to satisfy the same customer need. Industry convergence is often brought on by technological advances. For years, many players in the media industries have been converging due to technological progress in IT, telecommunications, and digital media. Media convergence unites computing, communications, and content, thereby causing significant upheaval across previously distinct industries. Content providers in industries such as newspapers, magazines, TV, movies, radio, and music are all scrambling to adapt. Many standalone print newspapers are closing up shop, while others are trying to figure out how to offer online news content for which consumers are willing to pay.[36] Internet companies such as Google, Facebook, Instagram, LinkedIn, Snapchat, Pinterest, and Twitter are changing the industry structure by constantly morphing their capabilities and forcing old-line media companies such as News Corp., Time Warner, and Disney to adapt. Amazon's Kindle, Apple's iPad, Google's Chromebook, and Samsung's Galaxy Tab provide a new form of content delivery that has the potential to make print media obsolete.

LO 3-6

Generate a strategic group model to reveal performance differences between clusters of firms in the same industry.

3.4 Performance Differences within the Same Industry: Strategic Groups

In further analyzing the firm's external environment to explain performance differences, we now move to firms *within the same industry*. As noted earlier in the chapter, a firm occupies a place within a **strategic group**, a set of companies that pursue a similar strategy within a specific industry in their quest for competitive advantage (see Exhibit 3.1).[37] Strategic groups differ from one another along important dimensions such as expenditures on research and development, technology, product differentiation, product and service offerings, pricing, market segments, distribution channels, and customer service.

strategic group
The set of companies that pursue a similar strategy within a specific industry.

strategic group model
A framework that explains differences in firm performance within the same industry.

To explain differences in firm performance within the same industry, the **strategic group model** clusters different firms into groups based on a few key strategic dimensions.[38] Even within the same industry, firm performances differ depending on strategic group membership. Some strategic groups tend to be more profitable than others. This difference implies that firm performance is determined not only by the industry to which the firm belongs, but also by its strategic group membership.

The distinct differences across strategic groups reflect the business strategies that firms pursue. Firms in the same strategic group tend to follow a similar strategy. Companies in the same strategic group, therefore, are direct competitors. The rivalry among firms *within* the same strategic group is generally more intense than the rivalry *among* strategic groups: *intra-group rivalry exceeds inter-group rivalry.* The number of different business strategies pursued within an industry determines the number of strategic groups in that industry. In most industries, strategic groups can be identified along a fairly small number of dimensions. In many instances, two strategic groups are in an industry based on two different business strategies: one that pursues a low-cost strategy and a second that pursues a differentiation strategy (see Exhibit 3.5). We'll discuss each of these generic business strategies in detail in Chapter 6.

THE STRATEGIC GROUP MODEL

To understand competitive behavior and performance within an industry, we can map the industry competitors into strategic groups. We do this as shown:

- Identify the most important strategic dimensions such as expenditures on research and development, technology, product differentiation, product and service offerings, pricing, market segments, distribution channels, and customer service.

- Choose two key dimensions for the horizontal and vertical axes, which expose important differences among the competitors. The dimensions chosen for the axes should *not* be highly correlated.

- Graph the firms in the strategic group, indicating each firm's market share by the size of the bubble with which it is represented.[39]

The U.S. domestic airline industry (featured in Strategy Highlight 3.2) provides an illustrative example. Exhibit 3.5 maps companies active in this industry. The two strategic dimensions on the axes are prices and routes. As a result of this mapping, two strategic groups become apparent, as indicated by the dashed circles: Group A, low-cost, point-to-point airlines (Virgin Atlantic, Alaska Airlines, JetBlue, and Southwest Airlines) and Group B, differentiated airlines using a hub-and-spoke system (American, Delta, and United). The low-cost, point-to-point airlines are clustered in the lower-left corner because they tend to offer lower ticket prices but generally serve fewer routes due to their point-to-point operating system.

The differentiated airlines in Group B, offering full services using a hub-and-spoke route system, comprise the so-called legacy carriers. They are clustered in the upper-right corner because their frequently higher ticket prices reflect frequently higher cost structures. They usually offer many more routes than the point-to-point low-cost carriers, made possible by use of the hub-and-spoke system, and thus offer many different destinations. For example, Delta's main hub is in Atlanta, Georgia.[40] If you were to fly from Seattle, Washington, to Miami, Florida, you would stop to change planes in Delta's Atlanta hub on your way.

The strategic group mapping in Exhibit 3.5 provides some additional insights:

- **Competitive rivalry is strongest between firms that are within the same strategic group.** The closer firms are on the strategic group map, the more directly and intensely they are in competition with one another. After a wave of mergers, the remaining mega-airlines—American, Delta, and United—are competing head-to-head, not only in the U.S. domestic market but also globally. They tend to monitor one another's strategic actions closely. While Delta faces secondary competition from low-cost carriers such as Southwest Airlines (SWA) on some domestic routes, its primary competitive rivals remain the other legacy carriers. This is because they compete more on providing seamless global services within their respective airline alliances (SkyTeam for Delta, Oneworld for American, and Star Alliance for United) than on low-cost airfares for

EXHIBIT 3.5 /

Strategic Groups and
the Mobility Barrier
in the U.S. Domestic
Airline Industry

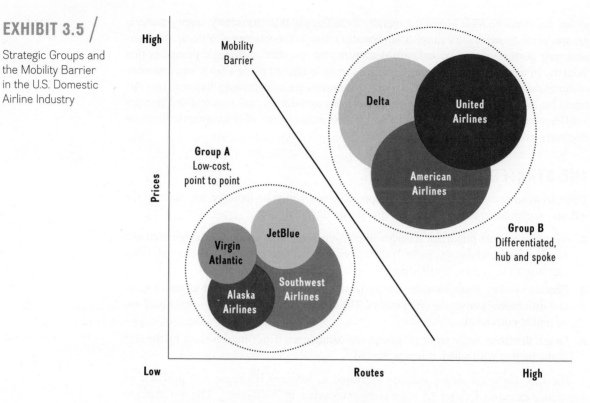

particular city pairs in the United States. Nonetheless, when Delta is faced with direct competition from SWA on a particular domestic route (say from Atlanta to Chicago), both tend to offer similar low-cost fares.

■ **The external environment affects strategic groups differently.** During times of economic downturn, for example, the low-cost airlines tend to take market share away from the legacy carriers. Moreover, given their generally higher cost structure, the legacy carriers are often unable to stay profitable during recessions, at least on domestic routes. This implies that external factors such as recessions or high oil prices favor the companies in the low-cost strategic group. On the other hand, given a number of governmental restrictions on international air travel, the few airlines that are able to compete globally usually make a tidy profit in this specific industry segment.

■ **The five competitive forces affect strategic groups differently.** *Barriers to entry,* for example, are higher in the hub-and-spoke (differentiated) airline group than in the point-to-point (low-cost) airline group. Following deregulation, many airlines entered the industry, but all of these new players used the point-to-point system. Since hub-and-spoke airlines can offer worldwide service and are protected from foreign competition by regulation to some extent, they often face weaker *buyer power,* especially from business travelers. While the hub-and-spoke airlines compete head-on with the point-to-point airlines when they are flying the same or similar routes, the *threat of substitutes* is stronger for the point-to-point airlines. This is because they tend to be regionally focused and compete with the viable substitutes of car, train, or bus travel. The threat of *supplier power* tends to be stronger for the airlines in the point-to-point, low-cost strategic group because they are much smaller and thus have weaker negotiation power when acquiring new aircraft, for example. To get around this, these airlines frequently purchase used aircraft from legacy carriers. This brief application of the five forces model leads us to conclude that rivalry among existing competitors in the low-cost, point-to-point strategic group is likely to be more intense than within the differentiated, hub-and-spoke strategic group.

■ **Some strategic groups are more profitable than others.** Historically, airlines clustered in the lower-left corner tend to be more profitable when considering the U.S. domestic market only. Why? Because they create similar, or even higher, value for their customers in terms of on-time departure and arrival, safety, and fewer bags lost, while keeping ticket costs below those of the legacy carriers. The point-to-point airlines have generally lower costs than the legacy carriers because they are faster in turning their airplanes around, keep them flying longer, use fewer and older airplane models, focus on high-yield city pairs, and tie pay to company performance, among many other activities that all support their low-cost business model. The point-to-point airlines, therefore, are able to offer their services at a lower cost and a higher perceived value, thus creating the basis for a competitive advantage.

MOBILITY BARRIERS

Although some strategic groups tend to be more profitable and therefore more attractive than others, **mobility barriers** restrict movement between groups. These are industry-specific factors that separate one strategic group from another.[41]

The two groups identified in Exhibit 3.5 are separated by the fact that offering international routes necessitates the hub-and-spoke model. Frequently, the international routes tend to be the remaining profitable routes left for the legacy carriers; albeit the up-and-coming Persian Gulf region carriers, in particular Emirates, Etihad Airways, and Qatar Airways, are beginning to threaten this profit sanctuary.[42]

This economic reality implies that if carriers in the lower-left cluster, such as SWA or JetBlue, would like to compete globally, they would likely need to change their point-to-point operating model to a hub-and-spoke model. Or, they could select a few profitable international routes and service them with long-range aircrafts such as Boeing 787s or Airbus A-380s. Adding international service to the low-cost model, however, would require significant capital investments and a likely departure from a well-functioning business model. Additional regulatory hurdles reinforce these mobility barriers, such as the difficulty of securing landing slots at international airports around the world.

Despite using its point-to-point operating system, SWA experienced these and many other challenges when it began offering international flights to selected resort destinations such as Aruba, Cabo San Lucas, Cancun, the Bahamas, and Jamaica: changes to its reservation system, securing passports for crew members, cultural-awareness training, learning instructions in foreign languages, and performing drills in swimming pools on how to evacuate passengers onto life rafts.[43]

mobility barriers
Industry-specific factors that separate one strategic group from another.

3.5 ◄► Implications for the Strategist

At the start of the strategic management process, it is critical for managers to conduct a thorough analysis of the firm's external environment to identify threats and opportunities. The initial step is to apply a PESTEL analysis to scan, monitor, and evaluate changes and trends in the firm's macroenvironment. This versatile framework allows managers to track important trends and developments based on the *source* of the external factors: political, economic, sociocultural, technological, ecological, and legal. When applying a PESTEL analysis, the guiding consideration for managers should be the question of how the external factors identified affect the firm's industry environment.

Exhibit 3.1 delineates external factors based on the *proximity* of these external factors by gradually moving from the general to the task environment. The next layer for managers to understand is the industry. Applying Porter's five forces model allows managers to understand the profit potential of an industry and to obtain clues on how to carve out a strategic position that makes gaining and sustaining a competitive advantage more likely. Follow these steps to apply the five forces model:[44]

1. **Define the relevant industry.** In the five forces model, industry boundaries are drawn by identifying a group of incumbent companies that face more or less the same suppliers and buyers. This group of competitors is likely to be an industry if it also has the same entry barriers and a similar threat from substitutes. In this model, therefore, an industry is defined by commonality and overlap in the five competitive forces that shape competition.

2. **Identify the key players in each of the five forces and attempt to group them into different categories.** This step aids in assessing the relative strength of each force. For example, while makers of jet engines (GE, Rolls-Royce, Pratt & Whitney) and local catering services are all suppliers to airlines, their strengths vary widely. Segmenting different players within each force allows you to assess each force at a fine-grained level.

3. **Identify the underlying drivers of each force.** Which forces are strong, and which are weak? And why? Keeping with the airline example, why is the supplier power of jet engine manufacturers strong? Because they are supplying a mission-critical, highly differentiated product for airlines. Moreover, there are only a few suppliers of jet engines worldwide and no viable substitutes.

4. **Assess the overall industry structure.** What is the industry's profit potential? Here you need to identify forces that directly influence industry profit potential, because not all forces are likely to have an equal effect. Focus on the most important forces that drive industry profitability.

The final step in industry analysis is to draw a strategic group map. This exercise allows you to unearth and explain *performance differences within the same industry.* When analyzing a firm's external environment, it is critical to apply the three frameworks introduced in this chapter (PESTEL, Porter's five forces, and strategic group mapping). Taken together, the external environment can determine up to roughly one-half of the performance differences across firms (see Exhibit 1.1).

Although the different models discussed in this chapter are an important step in the strategic management process, they are not without shortcomings. First, all of the models presented are *static.* They provide a snapshot of what is actually a moving target and do not allow for consideration of industry dynamics. However, changes in the external environment can appear suddenly, for example, through black swan events. Industries can be revolutionized by innovation. Strategic groups can be made obsolete through deregulation or technological progress. To overcome this important shortcoming, managers must conduct external analyses at different points in time to gain a sense of the underlying *dynamics.* The frequency with which these tools need to be applied is a function of the rate of change in the industry. The mobile app industry is changing extremely fast, while the railroad industry experiences a less volatile environment.

Second, the models presented in this chapter do not allow managers to fully understand *why* there are performance differences among firms in the *same* industry or strategic group. To better understand differences in firm performance, we must look *inside the firm* to study its resources, capabilities, and core competencies. We do this in the next chapter by moving from external to internal analysis.

CHAPTER**CASE 3** / Consider This...

ALTHOUGH TESLA MOTORS has successfully entered the U.S. automotive market using innovative new technology, its continued success will depend on other firm and industry factors. While industry forces have been favorable for a long time in the U.S. automotive industry, recent dynamics have lowered the profit potential of competing in this industry and thus reduced its attractiveness. Now that Tesla Motors has demonstrated how new technology can be used to circumvent entry barriers, other new ventures may soon follow. There are also nontraditional competitors entering the electric vehicle market. Google, for example, has been working on a self-driving car, unveiling a prototype in 2015. Apple is also investing in an electric car under the code name "Titan." None of these has the performance of a Tesla, but both are firms with established brands and credibility and significant financial resources. In addition, the old-line car companies are also adopting the new technology by introducing hybrid or all-electric cars, further increasing rivalry in the industry. The Nissan Leaf, with a sticker price of about $30,000 before tax incentives, is the world's best-selling all-electric vehicle worldwide, with more than 200,000 vehicles sold.

One of the biggest PESTEL factors impacting the all-electric car market, however, is that the price for crude oil declined steeply from over $110 per barrel in the summer of 2014 to about $40 by spring 2015. With it, prices for a gallon of regular gas in the United States fell from over $4 in the summer of 2008 to less than $2 by 2015. With low gas prices, Americans prefer to buy large SUVs and trucks, which benefits GM, Ford, and Chrysler. In addition, several states are reducing or phasing out tax credits for alternative-fuel vehicles.

Another external industry force that Tesla Motors currently addresses is the bargaining power of suppliers. Lithium-ion battery packs are not only in short supply but also the single most-expensive component for Tesla's electric engines. These critical inputs are supplied by only a few technology firms, including Panasonic in Japan. Given that these sources are few, the bargaining power of suppliers in the electric car segment is quite high, further limiting the industry's profit potential. To mitigate the strong bargaining power of key suppliers, however, Tesla has committed to building a 980-acre facility near Reno, Nevada, to produce its own lithium-ion batteries to supply its automobile assembly plant in Fremont, California. The new battery plant is slated to begin production in 2017 and requires a $5 billion investment to place the plant near sources of lithium and power it with renewable energy. Questions remain whether lithium-ion batteries will be able to provide the needed performance for battery life and recharging time, or whether a new technology will emerge, making this a large gamble.

Tesla Motors completed its IPO on June 29, 2010, the first IPO by an American automaker since Ford in 1956. On the first day of trading, Tesla's shares closed at $23.89 and generated $226.1 million for the company. By fall 2014, Tesla's stock had risen to over $285 per share before starting to slide below $200 in spring 2015. Nonetheless, Tesla's market capitalization is almost one-half that of GM, although Tesla revenues were a little over $3 billion in 2014, while GM's were $155 billion.[45]

Questions

1. Which PESTEL factors are the most salient for the electric vehicle segment of the car industry? Do you see a future for electric vehicles in the United States? Why or why not?

2. Looking at Porter's five forces of competition, how would you assess the profit potential of the U.S. car industry?

3. Using the five forces model, what implications can we derive for how Tesla Motors should compete in the U.S. car industry? What would be your top three recommendations for Elon Musk? Support your arguments.

4. Draw a strategic group map for the U.S. automotive industry. What are your conclusions?

5. Why do you think that Tesla's market capitalization (Share price × Number of outstanding shares) is roughly 50 percent that of GM, while GM's revenues are more than 50 times larger than that of Tesla Motors?

TAKE-AWAY CONCEPTS

This chapter demonstrated various approaches to analyzing the firm's *external environment,* as summarized by the following learning objectives and related take-away concepts.

LO 3-1 / Generate a PESTEL analysis to evaluate the impact of external forces on the firm.

- A firm's macroenvironment consists of a wide range of political, economic, sociocultural, technological, ecological, and legal (PESTEL) factors that can affect industry and firm performance. These external factors have both domestic and global aspects.
- Political factors describe the influence government bodies can have on firms.
- Economic factors to be considered are growth rates, interest rates, levels of employment, price stability (inflation and deflation), and currency exchange rates.
- Sociocultural factors capture a society's cultures, norms, and values.
- Technological factors capture the application of knowledge to create new processes and products.
- Ecological factors concern a firm's regard for environmental issues such as the natural environment, global warming, and sustainable economic growth.
- Legal factors capture the official outcomes of the political processes that manifest themselves in laws, mandates, regulations, and court decisions.

LO 3-2 / Apply Porter's five competitive forces to explain the profit potential of different industries.

- Competition must be viewed more broadly to encompass not only direct rivals but also a set of other forces in an industry: buyers, suppliers, the potential new entry of other firms, and the threat of substitutes.
- The profit potential of an industry is a function of the five forces that shape competition: (1) threat of entry, (2) power of suppliers, (3) power of buyers, (4) threat of substitutes, and (5) rivalry among existing competitors.
- The stronger a competitive force, the greater the threat it represents. The weaker the competitive force, the greater the opportunity it presents.
- A firm can shape an industry's structure in its favor through its strategy.

LO 3-3 / Explain how competitive industry structure shapes rivalry among competitors.

- The competitive structure of an industry is largely captured by the number and size of competitors in an industry, whether the firms possess some degree of pricing power, the type of product or service the industry offers (commodity or differentiated product), and the height of entry barriers.
- A perfectly competitive industry is characterized by many small firms, a commodity product, low entry barriers, and no pricing power for individual firms.
- A monopolistic industry is characterized by many firms, a differentiated product, medium entry barriers, and some pricing power.
- An oligopolistic industry is characterized by few (large) firms, a differentiated product, high entry barriers, and some degree of pricing power.
- A monopoly exists when there is only one (large) firm supplying the market. In such instances, the firm may offer a unique product, the barriers to entry may be high, and the monopolist usually has considerable pricing power.

LO 3-4 / Describe the strategic role of complements in creating positive-sum co-opetition.

- Co-opetition (co-operation among competitors) can create a positive-sum game, resulting in a larger pie for everyone involved.
- Complements increase demand for the primary product, enhancing the profit potential for the industry and the firm.
- Attractive industries for co-opetition are characterized by high entry barriers, low exit barriers, low buyer and supplier power, a low threat of substitutes, and the availability of complements.

LO 3-5 / Appraise the role of industry dynamics and industry convergence in shaping the firm's external environment.

- Industries are dynamic—they change over time.
- Different conditions prevail in different industries, directly affecting the firms competing in these industries and their profitability.
- In industry convergence, formerly unrelated industries begin to satisfy the same customer

need. Such convergence is often brought on by technological advances.

LO 3-6 / Generate a strategic group model to reveal performance differences between clusters of firms in the same industry.

- A strategic group is a set of firms within a specific industry that pursue a similar strategy in their quest for competitive advantage.
- Generally, there are two strategic groups in an industry based on two different business strategies: one that pursues a low-cost strategy and a second that pursues a differentiation strategy.

- Rivalry among firms of the same strategic group is more intense than the rivalry between strategic groups: intra-group rivalry exceeds inter-group rivalry.
- Strategic groups are affected differently by the external environment and the five competitive forces.
- Some strategic groups are more profitable than others.
- Movement between strategic groups is restricted by mobility barriers—industry-specific factors that separate one strategic group from another.

KEY TERMS

Competitive industry
   structure *(p. 83)*
Complement *(p. 89)*
Complementor *(p. 89)*
Co-opetition *(p. 89)*
Entry barriers *(p. 76)*

Exit barriers *(p. 87)*
Five forces model *(p. 73)*
Industry *(p. 72)*
Industry analysis *(p. 73)*
Industry convergence *(p. 90)*
Mobility barriers *(p. 93)*

Network effects *(p. 76)*
PESTEL model *(p. 67)*
Strategic group *(p. 90)*
Strategic group model *(p. 90)*
Strategic position *(p. 73)*
Threat of entry *(p. 75)*

DISCUSSION QUESTIONS

1. Why is it important for any organization (firms, nonprofits, etc.) to study and understand its external environment?

2. How do the five competitive forces in Porter's model affect the average profitability of the industry? For example, in what way might weak forces increase industry profits, and in what way do strong forces reduce industry profits? Identify an

industry in which many of the competitors seem to be having financial performance problems. Which of the five forces seems to be strongest?

3. What is a strategic group? How can studying such groups be useful in industry analysis?

4. How do mobility barriers affect the structure of an industry? How do they help us explain firm differences in performance?

ETHICAL/SOCIAL ISSUES

1. UBS, a venerable Swiss banking institution with global business activities, experienced the significant implications that political factors can have on the bottom line. The U.S. government alleged that by advertising its "tax savings" advantages to U.S. clients, UBS aided wealthy

Americans in siphoning off billions of dollars to a safe haven that the IRS cannot touch. The government requested from UBS the names of 52,000 U.S. citizens who it suspected were tax evaders. Initially, UBS declined to release names, citing Swiss banking laws and regulations that guarantee the privacy of customers. However, UBS was in a lose–lose situation: If it resisted the IRS, it risked losing its U.S. banking license. If it disclosed names of its customers, it would break the traditional Swiss banking secrecy and potentially violate Swiss law, which makes it a felony to improperly disclose client information. In 2009, after multiple rounds of intense negotiations, UBS finally relented to significant pressure by the U.S. government and released the names of 4,450 U.S. citizens who are suspected to have evaded taxes.

The U.S. government's case against UBS was helped immensely by a former employee at UBS who cooperated with prosecutors on details of how such transactions occur. The "whistle-blower," a U.S. citizen, has been lauded for his help in the investigation. Yet, in January 2010 he also began serving a 40-month prison sentence for his own guilty plea for helping his clients at UBS evade taxes.[46] Some in the industry believe such a surprisingly long prison term, despite his cooperation with investigators, will dramatically reduce motivation for other potential whistle-blowers to come forward.

a. What is the proper role for a multinational firm in cases where government regulations across countries are in conflict? For example, UBS executives claimed that releasing *any* names of U.S. customers would violate Swiss banking laws. A compromise was later reached that only the names of customers suspected of illegal activity were released.

b. What is the responsibility of individual employees to their employers and to their governments when there seems to be a conflict?

2. The chapter notes the U.S. federal government has provided incentives for consumers to purchase electric vehicles (EVs). Some state governments are also providing additional purchase incentives. However, other countries are also encouraging the purchase of EVs. Norway counts over 30 percent of its newly registered vehicles in the first quarter of 2015 as electric vehicles (compared to less than 1 percent for U.S. registrations). Norway waives a substantial automobile import tax on EVs sold inside the country.[47]

a. What is the appropriate role for governments to encourage or discourage certain purchasing behaviors? You may note many national governments have for decades collected additional taxes on tobacco and alcohol products as a measure to try to moderate consumption of these items.

b. As a strategist in a major firm, how would you seek to position your company in light of such current and potential future governmental policies?

SMALL GROUP EXERCISES

//// Small Group Exercise 1

Your group is a team of KraftHeinz Company (www.kraftheinzcompany.com) marketing interns. The company has asked you to propose new guidelines for helping it promote food to children in a socially responsible way. As the third-largest consumer packaged food and beverage company in North America, KraftHeinz's 2014 sales exceeded $29 billion. The company projects steady growth but would like your help in boosting growth. One of Kraft's largest brands is Oscar Mayer Lunchables, described as making lunch fun and targeted to busy parents who want a quick lunch to send with their children to school or keep on hand as an after-school snack. One of the options is Lunchables with Juice, Nachos Cheese Dip, and Salsa. However, there is a growing controversy about the social responsibility of directly marketing to children when the food is unhealthy—high in fat, sugar, and salt, but low in nutrition. There is a societal concern with the growing rate of obesity in children and the increased incidence of diabetes that results from childhood obesity. In response, most food and beverage companies have agreed to follow voluntary guidelines created by the Better Business Bureau, termed the Children's Food and Beverage Advertising Initiative (CFBAI). The guidelines ask for participating companies to pledge to advertise only healthy choices during children's programs, defined as those with an audience of 35 percent or more children under 12.

Kraft would like to have a reputation as a socially responsible company. Accordingly, Kraft would like to create internal guidelines that will help it market Lunchables (as well as other packaged food items) responsibly and gain the approval of medical professionals, parents, and watchdog groups.[48]

1. Visit the Kraft food website (www.lunchables .com) and review the Lunchables products, as well as other packaged food products that Kraft offers. Discuss among your group members the extent to which the product options are healthy choices.

2. What changes would you recommend to the CFBAI pledge in order to ensure that the primary audience watching advertisements for Kraft packaged foods will not be children? Describe alternative guidelines that Kraft might adopt.

3. Identify other actions that Kraft might take in order to demonstrate that it is a food company that genuinely cares about children's health and a company that would like to help reverse the trend of increasing childhood obesity.

4. If your group believes that the company is not responsible for personal choices that consumers make to eat unhealthy food, then describe how the company should respond to activist groups and public health officials that are urging companies to stop producing and marketing unhealthy foods.

//// Small Group Exercise 2

One industry with an impact on both undergraduate and MBA students is textbook publishing. On the one hand, traditional printed textbooks are being challenged by self-publishing firms offering very low prices for specific instructor materials, and on the other hand, a need to offer digital resources that substitute printed materials. Large textbook publishers are increasingly investing in adaptive learning systems such as WileyPLUS, Cengage MindTap, and McGraw-Hill Connect. Complicating factors for the publishers is the changing business model of renting textbooks (printed and electronic). U.S. university book rental was projected to top 25 percent of student purchasing volume in 2015.[49]

Use the five forces model (with complements) to think through the various impacts such technology shifts may have on the textbook industry. Include in your response answers to the following questions.

1. How should managers of a textbook publishing company respond to such changes?

2. Will the shifts in technology and business models be likely to raise or lower the textbook industry profits? Explain.

STRATEGY TERM PROJECT

Connect *The* HP Running Case, *a related activity for each strategy term project module, is available in Connect.*

//// Module 3: External Analysis

The "HP Running Case," a related activity for each strategy term project module, is available in Connect.

1. Study the external environment of the firm you have previously selected for this project. Are any changes taking place in the macroenvironment that might have a positive or negative impact on the industry in which your company is based? Apply the PESTEL framework to identify which factors may be the most important in

your industry. What will be the effect on your industry?

2. Apply the five forces model to your industry. What does this model tell you about the nature of competition in the industry?

3. Identify any strategic groups that might exist in the industry. How does the intensity of competition differ across the strategic groups you have identified?

4. How dynamic is the industry in which your company is based? Is there evidence that industry structure is reshaping competition, or has done so in the recent past?

*my*STRATEGY

Is My Job the Next One Being Outsourced?

The outsourcing of IT programming jobs to India is now commonly understood after years of this trend. However, more recently some accounting functions have also begun to flow into India's large technically trained and English-speaking work force. For example, the number of U.S. tax returns completed in India rose dramatically from 2003 to 2011 (25,000 in 2003 to 1.6 million in 2011). Some estimate that over 20 million U.S. tax returns will be prepared in India within the next few years. Outsourcing accounting functions may affect the job and career prospects for accounting-oriented business school graduates. Tax accountants in Bangalore, India, are much cheaper than those in Boston or Baltimore. Moreover, tax accountants in India often work longer hours and can therefore process many more tax returns than U.S.-based CPAs and tax accountants during the crunch period of the U.S. tax filing system.[50] Other services once thought to be immune to offshoring are also experiencing vulnerability. One example is the rise in medical tourism for major medical treatments to handle everything from joint replacements, weight loss, dental problems, and infertility. It is estimated that over 6 million patients traveled from one country to another seeking medical treatment in 2014.

1. Which aspects of accounting do you think are more likely to resist the outsourcing trends just discussed? Think about what aspects of accounting are the high-value activities versus the routine standardized ones. (If it's been a while since you took your accounting courses, reach out for information to someone in your strategy class who is an accounting major.)

2. What industries do you think may offer the best U.S. (or domestic) job opportunities in the future? Which industries do you think may offer the greatest job opportunities in the global market in the future? Use the PESTEL framework and the five forces model to think through a logical set of reasons that some fields will have higher job growth trends than others.

3. Do these types of macroenvironmental and industry trends affect your thinking about selecting a career field after college? Why or why not? Explain.

ENDNOTES

1. For an in-depth discussion of Tesla Motors and the U.S. car industry, see Rothaermel, F.T., and D. King (2015), Case MHE-FTR-032-1259420477, "Tesla Motors, Inc.," http://create.mheducation.com/.

2. For a detailed treatise on how institutions shape the economic climate and with it firm performance, see: North, D.C. (1990), *Institutions, Institutional Change, and Economic Performance* (New York: Random House).

3. De Figueireo, R.J.P., and G. Edwards (2007), "Does private money buy public policy? Campaign contributions and regulatory outcomes in telecommunications," *Journal of Economics & Management Strategy* 16: 547–576; and Hillman, A.J., G. D. Keim, and D. Schuler (2004), "Corporate political activity: A review and research agenda," *Journal of Management* 30: 837–857.

4. Ramsey, M. "Tesla closer to being able to have New Jersey dealerships," *The Wall Street Journal,* March 17, 2015.

5. Lowenstein, R. (2010), *The End of Wall Street* (New York: Penguin Press).

6. "Professor Emeritus Milton Friedman dies at 94," University of Chicago press release, November 16, 2006.

7. Lucas, R. (1972), "Expectations and the neutrality of money," *Journal of Economic Theory* 4: 103–124.

8. "Media companies are piling into the Hispanic market. But will it pay off?" *The Economist,* December 15, 2012.

9. Woolley, J.L., and R. M. Rottner (2008), "Innovation policy and nanotech entrepreneurship," *Entrepreneurship Theory and Practice* 32: 791–811; and Rothaermel, F.T., and

M. Thursby (2007), "The nanotech vs. the biotech revolution: Sources of incumbent productivity in research," *Research Policy* 36: 832–849.

10. Afuah, A. (2009), *Strategic Innovation: New Game Strategies for Competitive Advantage* (New York: Routledge); Hill, C.W.L., and F.T. Rothaermel (2003), "The performance of incumbent firms in the face of radical technological innovation," *Academy of Management Review* 28: 257–274; and Bettis, R., and M.A. Hitt (1995), "The new competitive landscape," *Strategic Management Journal* 16 (Special Issue): 7–19.

11. Academy of Management, ONE Division, 2013 domain statement; Anderson, R.C. (2009), *Confessions of a Radical Industrialist: Profits, People, Purpose—Doing Business by Respecting the Earth* (New York: St. Martin's Press); and Esty, D.C., and A.S. Winston (2009), *Green* *to Gold: How Smart Companies Use Environmental Strategy to Innovate, Create Value, and Build Competitive Advantage,* revised and updated (Hoboken, NJ: John Wiley).

12. For an in-depth discussion of BlackBerry and the smartphone industry, see Burr, J.F., F.T. Rothaermel, and J. Urbina (2015), Case MHE-FTR-020 (0077645065), "Make or Break at RIM: Launching BlackBerry 10, "http://create.mheducation.com; Dvorak, P., "BlackBerry maker's issue: Gadgets for work or play?" *The Wall Street Journal,* September 30, 2011; Dyer, J., H. Gregersen, C.M. Christensen (2011), *The Innovator's DNA: Mastering the Five Skills of Disruptive Innovators* (Boston, MA: Harvard Business Review Press); Ycharts.com.

13. Nicas, J., and G. Bensinger, "Delivery drones hit bumps on path to doorstep," *The Wall Street Journal,* March 20, 2015.

14. The discussion in this section is based on: Magretta, J. (2012), *Understanding Michael Porter: The Essential Guide to Competition and Strategy* (Boston, MA: Harvard Business Review Press); Porter, M.E. (2008), "The five competitive forces that shape strategy," *Harvard Business Review,* January; Porter, M.E. (1980), *Competitive Strategy: Techniques for Analyzing Industries and Competitors* (New York: Free Press); and Porter, M.E. (1979), "How competitive forces shape strategy," *Harvard Business Review,* March–April: 137–145.

15. Strategy Highlight 3.2 is drawn from: Porter, M.E. (2008), "The five competitive forces that shape strategy," *An Interview with Michael E. Porter: The Five Competitive Forces that Shape Strategy,* Harvard BusinessPublishing video; "Everyone else in the travel business makes money off airlines," *The Economist,* August 25, 2012; "How airline ticket prices fell 50% in 30 years (and nobody noticed)," *The Atlantic,* February 28, 2013; U.S. gallon of jet fuel prices http://www.indexmundi.com/commodities/ ?commodity=jet-fuel &months=60; author's interviews with Delta executives.

16. Stoll, D., and M. Ramsey, "Tesla first-quarter car deliveries rise above 10,000," *The Wall Street Journal,* April 3, 2015.

17. Hull, D., "Tesla idles Fremont production line for Model X upgrade," *San Jose Mercury News,* July 22, 2014; and Vance, A., "Why everybody loves Tesla," *Bloomberg Businessweek,* July 18, 2013.

18. Ramsey, M., "Tesla to choose Nevada for battery factory," *The Wall Street Journal,* September 3, 2014.

19. Ramsey, M., "Tesla plans $5 billion battery factory," *The Wall Street Journal,* February 26, 2014.

20. Walsh, T., "The cult of Tesla Motors Inc: Why this automaker has the most loyal customers," *The Motley Fool,* September 2, 2014.

21. *Consumer Reports:* Tesla Model S road test, http://www.consumerreports.org/cro/tesla/model-s/road-test.htm.

22. Musk, E., "The mission of Tesla," *Tesla Motors Blog,* November 18, 2013, http://www.teslamotors.com/blog.

23. Wang, U., "Tesla considers building the world's biggest lithium-ion battery factory," *Forbes,* November 5, 2013.

24. Whether a product is a substitute (complement) can be estimated by the cross-elasticity of demand. The cross-elasticity estimates the percentage change in the quantity demanded of good X resulting from a 1 percent change in the price of good Y. If the cross-elasticity of demand is greater (less) than zero, the products are substitutes (complements). For a detailed discussion, see: Allen, W.B., K. Weigelt, N. Doherty, and E. Mansfield (2009), *Managerial Economics Theory, Application, and Cases,* 7th ed. (New York: Norton).

25. This example, as with some others in the section on the five forces, is drawn from Magretta, J. (2012), *Understanding Michael Porter: The Essential Guide to Competition and Strategy* (Boston, MA: Harvard Business Review Press).

26. Because the threat of entry is one of the five forces explicitly recognized in Porter's model, we discuss barriers to entry when introducing the threat of entry above. The competitive industry structure framework is frequently referred to as the Structure-Conduct-Performance (SCP) model. For a detailed discussion, see: Allen, et al., *Managerial Economics;* Carlton, D.W., and J.M. Perloff (2000), *Modern Industrial Organization,* 3rd ed. (Reading, MA: Addison-Wesley); Scherer, F.M., and D. Ross (1990), *Industrial Market Structure and Economic Performance,* 3rd ed. (Boston, MA: Houghton Mifflin); and Bain, J.S. (1968), *Industrial Organization* (New York: John Wiley).

27. Besanko, D., E. Dranove, M. Hanley, and S. Schaefer (2010), *The Economics of Strategy,* 5th ed. (Hoboken, NJ: John Wiley).

28. Dixit, A., S. Skeath, and D.H. Reiley (2009), *Games of Strategy,* 3rd ed. (New York: Norton).

29. When there are only two main competitors, it's called a *duopoly* and is a special case of oligopoly.

30. Yoffie, D.B., and R.Kim, "Coca-Cola in 2011: In Search of a New Model," Harvard Business School Case 711-504, June 2011 (revised August 2012). See also earlier Yoffie and Y. Wang (2002), "Cola Wars Continue:

Coke and Pepsi in the Twenty-First Century," Harvard Business School Case 702-442, January 2002 (revised January 2004, et seq).

31. "Trustbusting in the Internet Age: Should digital monopolies be broken up?," *The Economist,* November 29, 2014; and "Internet monopolies: Everybody wants to rule the world," *The Economist,* November 29, 2014.

32. See Chang, S-J., and B. Wu (2013), "Institutional barriers and industry dynamics," *Strategic Management Journal* 35: 1103–1123. Discussion of this new and insightful research offers an opportunity to link the PESTEL analysis to the five forces analysis. The study focuses on the competitive interaction between incumbents and new entrants as a driver of industry evolution. It investigates the impact of institutional characteristics (political, legal, and sociocultural norms in PESTEL analysis) unique to China on productivity and exit hazards of incumbents versus new entrants. China's environment created a divergence between productivity and survival that shaped industry evolution. It also offers an illustration of the role that liability of newness plays in new entrant survival.

33. Brandenburger, A.M., and B. Nalebuff (1996), *Co-opetition* (New York: Currency Doubleday); and Grove, A.S. (1999), *Only the Paranoid Survive* (New York: Time Warner).

34. Milgrom, P., and J. Roberts (1995), "Complementarities and fit strategy, structure, and organizational change in manufacturing," *Journal of Accounting and Economics* 19(2-3): 179–208; and Brandenburger and Nalebuff, *Co-opetition.*

35. In this recent treatise, Porter also highlights positive-sum competition. See: Porter, M.E. (2008), "The five competitive forces that shape strategy," *Harvard Business Review,* January.

36. "Reading between the lines," *The Economist,* March 26, 2009; and "New York Times is near web charges," *The Wall Street Journal,* January 19, 2010.

37. Porter, M.E. (1980), *Competitive Strategy: Techniques for Analyzing Industries and Competitors* (New York: Free Press); Hatten, K.J., and D.E. Schendel (1977), "Heterogeneity within an industry: Firm conduct in the U.S. brewing industry," *Journal of Industrial Economics* 26: 97–113; and Hunt, M.S. (1972), *Competition in the Major Home Appliance Industry, 1960–1970,* unpublished doctoral dissertation, Harvard University.

38. This discussion is based on: McNamara, G., D.L. Deephouse, and R. Luce (2003), "Competitive positioning within and across a strategic group structure: The performance of core, secondary, and solitary firms," *Strategic Management Journal* 24: 161–181;

Nair, A., and S. Kotha (2001), "Does group membership matter? Evidence from the Japanese steel industry," *Strategic Management Journal* 22: 221–235; Cool, K., and D. Schendel (1988), "Performance differences among strategic group members," *Strategic Management Journal* 9: 207–223; Hunt, *Competition in the Major Home Appliance Industry;* Hatten and Schendel, "Heterogeneity within an industry: Firm conduct in the U.S. brewing industry"; and Porter, *Competitive Strategy.*

39. In Exhibit 3.5, United Airlines is the biggest bubble because it merged with Continental in 2010, creating the largest airline in the United States. Delta is the second-biggest airline in the United States after merging with Northwest Airlines in 2008.

40. American's hub is at Dallas–Fort Worth; Continental's is at Newark, New Jersey; United's is at Chicago, Illinois; and U.S. Airways' is at Charlotte, North Carolina.

41. Caves, R.E., and M.E. Porter (1977), "From entry barriers to mobility barriers," *Quarterly Journal of Economics* 91: 241–262.

42. Carey, S., "U.S. airlines battling gulf carriers cite others' experience," *The Wall Street Journal,* March 16, 2015.

43. Carey, S., "Steep learning curve for Southwest Airlines as it flies overseas," *The Wall Street Journal,* October 14, 2014.

44. Porter, "The five competitive forces that shape strategy"; and Magretta, *Understanding Michael Porter: The Essential Guide to Competition and Strategy,* pp. 56–57.

45. For an in-depth discussion of Tesla Motors and the U.S. car industry, see see Rothaermel, F.T., and D. King (2015), Case MHE-FTR-XXX-XXX, "Tesla Motors, Inc.," http://create.mheducation.com/.

46. "Crying foul, ex-UBS banker starts prison term," *The Wall Street Journal,* January 9, 2010.

47. "Norway leads global electric vehicle market, IHS says," Business Wire news, July 7, 2015.

48. Corporate website; Orciari, M., "Industry self-regulation permits junk food ads in programming popular with children," *Yale News,* March 12, 2013, accessed online; Moss, M., "How the fast food industry creates and keeps selling the crave," *The New York Times Magazine,* February 24, 2013.

49. Benson-Armer, R., J. Sarakatsannis and K. Wee; "The future of textbooks," *McKinsey on Society,* August 2014.

50. The myStrategy module is based on: Friedman, T. (2005), *The World Is Flat: A Brief History of the Twenty-first Century* (New York: Farrar, Strauss & Giroux); and *ValueNotes,* http://www.sourcingnotes.com/content/view/197/54/.

Chapter 4

Internal Analysis: Resources, Capabilities, and Core Competencies

Chapter Outline

Learning Objectives

LO 4-1 Differentiate among a firm's core competencies, resources, capabilities, and activities.

LO 4-2 Compare and contrast tangible and intangible resources.

LO 4-3 Evaluate the two critical assumptions behind the resource-based view.

LO 4-4 Apply the VRIO framework to assess the competitive implications of a firm's resources.

LO 4-5 Evaluate different conditions that allow a firm to sustain a competitive advantage.

LO 4-6 Outline how dynamic capabilities can enable a firm to sustain a competitive advantage.

LO 4-7 Apply a value chain analysis to understand which of the firm's activities in the process of transforming inputs into outputs generate differentiation and which drive costs.

LO 4-8 Conduct a SWOT analysis to generate insights from external and internal analysis and derive strategic implications.

Dr. Dre's Core Competency: Coolness Factor

IN 2014, DR. DRE—whose real name is Andre Young—became the first hip-hop billionaire after Apple acquired Beats Electronics for $3 billion. Dr. Dre has a long track record as a successful music producer, rapper, and entrepreneur. Known for his strong work ethic, he expects nothing less than perfection from the people he works with—similar to some of the personality attributes ascribed to the late Steve Jobs, co-founder and long-time CEO of Apple.

Although Dr. Dre created and subsequently sold several successful music record labels, as an entrepreneur he is best known as co-founder of Beats Electronics with Jimmy Iovine, also an entrepreneur and record and film producer. Both are considered to be some of the best-connected businesspeople in the music industry, with personal networks spanning hundreds of both famous and up-and-coming artists. Founded in 2008, Beats Electronics is known globally for its premium consumer headphones, Beats by Dr. Dre, which he claims allows the listeners to "hear all the music." Since early 2014, the company also offers the streaming music subscription service Beats Music. Beats' vision is to "bring the energy, emotion, and excitement of playback in the recording studio to the listening experience and introduce an entirely new generation to the possibilities of premium sound entertainment."[1] Many acoustics experts maintain, however, that playback of digitally compressed MP3 audio files is inferior in comparison to high fidelity. Moreover, the sound quality of Beats headphones is considered poor in comparison to other premium-brand headphones such as those by Bose, JBL, Sennheiser, and others.

Dr. Dre, right, and Jimmy Iovine, center, cofounders of Beats Electronics, with Luke Wood, president, on left.
© Kevin Mazur/Getty Images

Why then would Apple pay $3 billion to acquire Beats Electronics? This was by far the largest acquisition in Apple's history. Two main reasons: First, Apple is hoping that some of Beats' coolness will spill over to its brand, which has become somewhat stale. Apple's iPhones, for example, have become a standardized commodity given the successful imitation by Samsung, Xiaomi, and others. Second, although Apple is the world's largest music vendor with 800 million accounts on iTunes Store, the industry is being disrupted. Content delivery, especially in music but also video (think Netflix), is moving rapidly from ownership via downloads to streaming on demand. As a consequence, music downloads have been declining in the past few years.

BEATS COOLNESS FACTOR

Beats by Dr. Dre achieved an unprecedented coolness factor with celebrity endorsements not only from music icons but also athletes, actors, and other stars. Prior to Beats, no musician endorsed audio headphones in the same way as a basketball player such as Michael Jordan endorsed his line of Nike shoes, Air Jordan. Dr. Dre was the first legendary music producer to endorse premium headphones. In addition, he created custom Beats for stars such as Justin Bieber, Lady Gaga, and Nicki Minaj. Other music celebrities including Skrillex, Lil Wayne, and will.i.am endorsed Beats by wearing them in their music videos and at live events and mentioning them on social media. But Beats did not stop at musicians. Famous athletes—basketball superstars LeBron James and Kobe Bryant, tennis player Serena Williams, and soccer stars Cristiano Ronaldo and Neymar Jr.—are all wearing Beats by Dr. Dre in public and endorse the brand in advertisements.

Content delivery is rapidly moving from ownership through downloads to renting via online streaming. This disruption in the business model is most visible in movies as the success of Netflix demonstrates, but is also gaining steam in music. Apple is a laggard in music streaming when compared to leaders such as Pandora with 250 million users and Spotify with 60 million users. Apple's attempt at online music streaming service, iTunes Radio created in 2013, has been falling flat. After disrupting the music download space with iTunes in 2003, Apple is now being disrupted by others that lead in music streaming. It is hoping that by acquiring Beats Music it can become a leader in the music streaming space.[2]

You will learn more about Beats Electronics by reading this chapter; related questions appear on page 132.

ONE OF THE KEY messages of this chapter is that a firm's ability to gain and sustain competitive advantage is partly driven by *core competencies*—unique strengths that are embedded deep within a firm. Core competencies allow a firm to differentiate its products and services from those of its rivals, creating higher value for the customer or offering products and services of comparable value at lower cost. So what are core competencies of Beats by Dr. Dre? Beats succeeds not because it provides the best possible acoustic experience, but because it functions as a fashion statement that communicates coolness.[3] The iconic headphones are worn by celebrities from music, movies, and sports. Even fashion designer Marc Jacobs had models wear Beats headphones during runway shows. The extent to which Beats succeeds at product placements with celebrities across the world is unprecedented. The genius behind Beats is creating a perception that if you want to be as cool as one of your heroes, you need to shell out hundreds of dollars to wear plastic headphones in public.

Beats' unique strengths in establishing a brand that communicates coolness is built upon Dr. Dre's intuition and feel for music and cultural trends; Dr. Dre is one of music's savviest marketing minds. Although the sound quality of Beats headphones is good enough, they mainly sell as a fashion accessory for their coolness factor and brand image. Dr. Dre relies on gut instinct in making decisions, while shunning market research. This approach is quite similar to Apple's late co-founder Steve Jobs who made no secret of his disdain for market research because he believed that consumers don't really know what they want until someone else shows it to them.

Beats' core competency in marketing allows the company to differentiate its products from rival offerings because it is able to create higher perceived value for its customers. In turn, Beats' core competency affords the firm a competitive advantage. It is hugely successful: Beats holds some 65 percent market share in the premium headphone market, priced at $100 and up. Beats' competitive advantage was rewarded with a $3 billion acquisition by Apple.

In this chapter, we study analytical tools to explain why differences in firm performance exist even within the *same* industry. For example, why does Beats Electronics outperform Audio-Technica, Bose, JBL, Skullcandy, Sennheiser, and Sony in the high-end, premium headphone market? Since these companies compete in the same industry and face similar external opportunities and threats, the source for some of the observable performance difference must be found *inside the firm*. When discussing industry, firm, and other effects in explaining superior performance, we noted that up to 55 percent of the overall performance differences is explained by firm-specific effects (see Exhibit 1.1). Looking inside the firm to analyze its resources, capabilities, and core competencies allows us to understand the firm's strengths and weaknesses. Linking these insights from a firm's internal analysis to the ones derived in Chapter 3 on external analysis allows managers to determine their

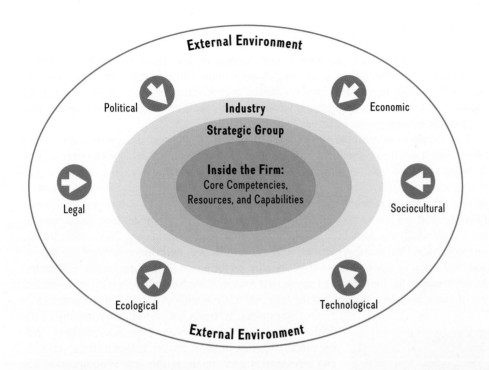

EXHIBIT 4.1 /

Inside the Firm:
Competitive
Advantage based on
Core Competencies,
Resources, and
Capabilities

strategic options. Ideally, firms want to leverage their internal strengths to exploit external opportunities, and to mitigate internal weaknesses and external threats.

Exhibit 4.1 depicts how and why we move from the firm's external environment to its internal environment. To formulate and implement a strategy that enhances the firm's chances of gaining and sustaining competitive advantage, the firm must have certain types of resources and capabilities that combine to form core competencies. The best firms conscientiously identify their core competencies, resources, and capabilities to survive and succeed. Firms then determine how to manage and develop internal strengths to respond to the challenges and opportunities in their external environment. In particular, firms conduct the evaluation and development of internal strengths in the context of external PESTEL forces and competition within its industry and strategic group.

The firm's response is dynamic. Rather than creating a onetime and thus a static fit, the firm's internal strengths need to change with its external environment in a *dynamic* fashion. At each point the goal should be to develop resources, capabilities, and competencies that create a *strategic fit* with the firm's environment. The forward motion of those environmental forces must also be considered. The chapter will provide a deeper understanding of the *sources* of competitive advantage that reside within a firm.

To gain a better understanding of why and how firm differences explain competitive advantage, we begin this chapter by taking a closer look at *core competencies.* Next, we introduce the *resource-based view* of the firm to provide an analytical model that allows us to assess resources, capabilities, and competencies and their potential for creating a sustainable competitive advantage. We discuss the *dynamic capabilities perspective,* a model that emphasizes a firm's ability to modify and leverage its resource base to gain and sustain a competitive advantage in a constantly changing environment. We then turn our attention to the *value chain analysis* to gain a deeper understanding of the internal activities a firm engages in when transforming inputs into outputs. We conclude with "Implications for the Strategist," with a particular focus on how to use the *SWOT analysis* to obtain strategic insights from combining external and internal analysis.

Differentiate among
a firm's resources,
capabilities, core
competencies, and
activities.

4.1 Core Competencies

Let's begin by taking a closer look at **core competencies**. These are unique strengths, embedded deep within a firm. Core competencies allow a firm to differentiate its products and services from those of its rivals, creating higher value for the customer or offering products and services of comparable value at lower cost. The important point here is that competitive advantage can be driven by core competencies.[4]

Take Honda as an example of a company with a clearly defined core competency. Its life began with a small two-cycle motorbike engine. Through continuous learning over several decades, and often from lessons learned from failure, Honda built the core competency to design and manufacture small but powerful and highly reliable engines for which it now is famous. This core competency results from superior engineering know-how and skills carefully nurtured and honed over several decades. Honda's business model is to find a place to put its engines. Today, Honda engines can be found everywhere: in cars, SUVs, vans, trucks, motorcycles, ATVs, boats, generators, snowblowers, lawn mowers and other yard equipment, and even small airplanes. Due to their superior performance, Honda engines have been the most popular in the Indy Racing League (IRL) since 2006. Not coincidentally, this was also the first year in its long history that the Indy 500 was run without a single engine problem.

One way to look at Honda is to view it as a company with a distinct competency in engines and a business model of finding places to put its engines. That is, underneath the products and services that make up the *visible* side of competition lies a diverse set of *invisible* competencies that make this happen. These invisible core competencies reside deep within the firm. Companies, therefore, compete as much in the product and service markets as they do in developing and leveraging core competencies. Although invisible by themselves, core competencies find their expression in superior products and services. Exhibit 4.2 identifies the core competencies of a number of companies, with application examples.

Since core competencies are critical to gaining and sustaining competitive advantage, it is important to understand how they are created. Companies develop core competencies through the interplay of resources and capabilities. Exhibit 4.3 shows this relationship. **Resources** are any assets such as cash, buildings, machinery, or intellectual property that a firm can draw on when crafting and executing a strategy. Resources can

Honda promotes its expertise with engines by sponsoring racecar driver Danica Patrick.
© AP Photo/Julio Cortez

be either tangible or intangible. **Capabilities** are the organizational and managerial skills necessary to orchestrate a diverse set of resources and to deploy them strategically. Capabilities are by nature intangible. They find their expression in a company's structure, routines, and culture.

As shown in Exhibit 4.3, such competencies are demonstrated in the company's activities, which can lead to competitive advantage, resulting in superior firm performance. **Activities** are distinct and fine-grained business processes such as order taking,

---

core competencies
Unique strengths, embedded deep within a firm, that are critical to gaining and sustaining competitive advantage.

resources
Any assets that a firm can draw on when formulating and implementing a strategy.

capabilities
Organizational and managerial skills necessary to orchestrate a diverse set of resources and deploy them strategically.

activities
Distinct and fine-grained business processes that enable firms to add incremental value by transforming inputs into goods and services.

EXHIBIT 4.2 / Company Examples of Core Competencies and Applications

Company	Core Competencies	Application Examples
Amazon.com	• Superior IT capabilities. • Superior customer service.	• Online retailing: Largest selection of items online. • Cloud computing: Largest provider through Amazon Web Services (AWS).
Apple	• Superior industrial design in integration of hardware and software. • Superior marketing and retailing experience. • Establishing an ecosystem of products and services that reinforce one another in a virtuous fashion.	• Creation of innovative and category-defining mobile devices and software services that take the user's experience to a new level (e.g., iMac, iPod, iTunes, iPhone, iPad, Apple Pay, and Apple Watch.)
Beats Electronics	• Superior marketing: creating a perception of coolness. • Establishing an ecosystem, combining hardware (headphones) with software (streaming service).	• Beats by Dr. Dre and Beats Music.
Coca-Cola	• Superior marketing and distribution.	• Leveraging one of the world's most recognized brands (based on its original "secret formula") into a diverse lineup of soft drinks. • Global availability of products.
ExxonMobil	• Superior at discovering and exploring fossil-fuel–based energy sources globally.	• Focus on oil and gas (fossil fuels only, not renewables).
Facebook	• Superior IT capabilities to provide reliable social network services globally on a large scale. • Superior algorithms to offer targeted online ads.	• Connecting 1.5 billion social media users worldwide. • News feed, timeline, and graph search.
General Electric	• Superior expertise in industrial engineering, designing and implementing efficient management processes, and developing and training leaders.	• Providing products and services to solve tough engineering problems in energy, health care, and aerospace, among other sectors.
Google	• Superior in creating proprietary algorithms based on large amounts of data collected online.	• Software products and services for the Internet and mobile computing, including some mobile devices (Chromebook). • Online search, Android mobile operating system, Chrome OS, Chrome web browser, Google Play, AdWords, AdSense, Google docs, Gmail, etc.
Honda	• Superior engineering of small but powerful and highly reliable internal combustion engines.	• Motorcycles, cars, ATVs, sporting boats, snowmobiles, lawn mowers, small aircraft, etc.
IKEA	• Superior in designing modern functional home furnishings at low cost. • Superior retail experience.	• Fully furnished room setups, practical tools for all rooms, do-it-yourself.
McKinsey	• Superior in developing practice-relevant knowledge, insights, and frameworks in strategy.	• Management consulting; in particular, strategy consulting provided to company and government leaders.
Netflix	• Superior in creating proprietary algorithms-based individual customer preferences.	• DVD-by-mail rentals, streaming media (including proprietary) content, connection to game consoles.
Tesla Motors	• Superior engineering expertise in designing high-performance battery-powered motors and power trains.	• Tesla Model S, Tesla Model X, and Tesla Model 3.
Uber	• Superior mobile-app–based transportation and logistics expertise focused on cities, but on global scale.	• Uber, UberX, UberBlack, UberLUX, UberSUV, etc.

EXHIBIT 4.3 /

Linking Core Competencies, Resources, Capabilities, and Activities to Competitive Advantage and Superior Firm Performance

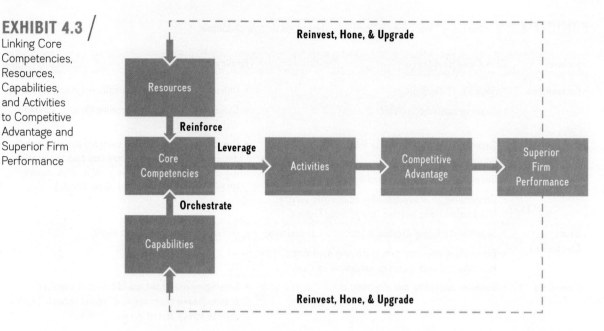

the physical delivery of products, or invoicing customers. Each distinct activity enables firms to add incremental value by transforming inputs into goods and services. In the interplay of resources and capabilities, resources reinforce core competencies, while capabilities allow managers to orchestrate their core competencies. Strategic choices find their expression in a set of specific firm activities, which leverage core competencies for competitive advantage. The arrows leading back from performance to resources and capabilities indicate that superior performance in the marketplace generates profits that can be reinvested into the firm (retained earnings) to further hone and upgrade a firm's resources and capabilities in its pursuit of achieving and maintaining a strategic fit within a dynamic environment.

We should make two more observations about Exhibit 4.3 before moving on. First, core competencies that are not continuously nourished will eventually lose their ability to yield a competitive advantage. And second, in analyzing a company's success in the market, it can be too easy to focus on the more *visible* elements or facets of core competencies such as superior products or services. While these are the outward manifestation of core competencies, what is even more important is to understand the *invisible* part of core competencies. As to the first point, we consider the consumer electronics industry. For some years, Best Buy outperformed Circuit City based on its strengths in customer-centricity (segmenting customers based on demographic, attitudinal, and value tiers, and configuring stores to serve the needs of the customer segments in that region), employee development, and exclusive branding. Although Best Buy outperformed Circuit City (which filed for bankruptcy in 2009), more recently Best Buy did not hone and upgrade its core competencies sufficiently to compete effectively against Amazon.com, the world's largest online retailer. Amazon does not have the overhead expenses associated with maintaining buildings or human sales forces; therefore, it can undercut in-store retailers on price. When a firm does not invest in continual upgrading or improving core competencies, its competitors are more likely to develop equivalent or superior skills, as did Amazon. This insight will allow us to explain differences between firms in the same industry, as well as competitive dynamics, over time. It also will help us identify the strategy with which firms gain and sustain a competitive advantage and weather an adverse external environment.

As to the second point, we will soon introduce tools to help bring more opaque aspects of a firm's core competencies into the daylight to be seen with clarity. We start by looking at both tangible and intangible resources.

4.2 The Resource-Based View

LO 4-2

Compare and contrast tangible and intangible resources.

To gain a deeper understanding of how the interplay between resources and capabilities creates core competencies that drive firm activities leading to competitive advantage, we turn to the **resource-based view** of the firm. This model systematically aids in identifying core competencies.[5] As the name suggests, this model sees resources as key to superior firm performance. As Exhibit 4.4 illustrates, resources fall broadly into two categories: tangible and intangible. **Tangible resources** have physical attributes and are visible. Examples of tangible resources are labor, capital, land, buildings, plant, equipment, and supplies. **Intangible resources** have no physical attributes and thus are invisible. Examples of intangible resources are a firm's culture, its knowledge, brand equity, reputation, and intellectual property.

Consider Google. Its tangible resources, valued at $16 billion, include its headquarters (The Googleplex)[6] in Mountain View, California, and numerous server farms (clusters of computer servers) across the globe.[7] The Google brand, an intangible resource, is valued at roughly $160 billion (number one worldwide)—10 times higher than the value of its tangible assets.[8]

Google's headquarters provides examples of both tangible and intangible resources. The Googleplex is a piece of land with a futuristic building, and thus a tangible resource. The *location* of the company in the heart of Silicon Valley is an *intangible resource* that provides access to a valuable network of contacts and gives the company several benefits. It allows Google to tap into a large and computer-savvy work force and access graduates and knowledge spillovers from a large number of universities, including San Francisco State University, San Jose State University, Santa Clara University, Stanford, and the University of California, Berkeley, among others, which

EXHIBIT 4.4 / Tangible and Intangible Resources

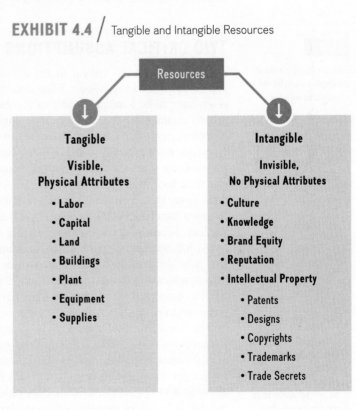

resource-based view
A model that sees certain types of resources as key to superior firm performance.

tangible resources
Resources that have physical attributes and thus are visible.

intangible resources
Resources that do not have physical attributes and thus are invisible.

adds to Google's technical and managerial capabilities.[9] Another benefit stems from Silicon Valley's designation as having the largest concentration of venture capital in the United States. This proximity benefits Google because venture capitalists tend to prefer local investments to ensure closer monitoring.[10] Google received initial funding from the well-known venture capital firms Kleiner Perkins Caufield & Byers and Sequoia Capital, both located in Silicon Valley.

Competitive advantage is more likely to spring from intangible rather than tangible resources. Tangible assets, such as buildings or computer servers, can be bought on the open market by any comers who have the necessary cash. However, a brand name must be built, often over long periods of time. Google (founded in 1998) and Amazon .com (founded in 1994) accomplished their enormous brand valuation fairly quickly due to a ubiquitous Internet presence, while the other companies in the global top-10 most valuable brands—Apple, IBM, Microsoft, McDonald's, Coca-Cola, Visa, AT&T, and Marlboro—took much longer to build value and have it recognized in the marketplace.[11]

Note that the resource-based view of the firm uses the term *resource* much more broadly than previously defined. In the resource-based view of the firm, a resource includes any assets as well as any capabilities and competencies that a firm can draw upon when formulating and implementing strategy. In addition, the usefulness of the resource-based view to explain and predict competitive advantage rests upon two critical assumptions about the nature of resources, to which we turn next.

LO 4-3

Evaluate the two critical assumptions behind the resource-based view.

resource heterogeneity
Assumption in the resource-based view that a firm is a bundle of resources and capabilities that differ across firms.

resource immobility
Assumption in the resource-based view that a firm has resources that tend to be "sticky" and that do not move easily from firm to firm.

TWO CRITICAL ASSUMPTIONS

Two assumptions are critical in the resource-based model: (1) *resource heterogeneity* and (2) *resource immobility*.[12] What does this mean? In the resource-based view, a firm is assumed to be a unique bundle of resources, capabilities, and competencies. The first critical assumption—**resource heterogeneity**—comes from the insight that bundles of resources, capabilities, and competencies differ across firms. This insight ensures that analysts look more critically at the resource bundles of firms competing in the *same* industry (or even the same strategic group), because each bundle is unique to some extent. For example, Southwest Airlines (SWA) and Alaska Airlines both compete in the same strategic group (low-cost, point-to-point airlines, see Exhibit 3.5). But they draw on different resource bundles. SWA's employee productivity tends to be higher than that of Alaska Airlines, because the two companies differ along human and organizational resources. At SWA, job descriptions are informal and employees pitch in to "get the job done." Pilots may help load luggage to ensure an on-time departure; flight attendants clean airplanes to help turn them around at the gate within 15 minutes from arrival to departure. This allows SWA to keep its planes flying for longer and lowers its cost structure, savings that SWA passes on to passengers in lower ticket prices.

The second critical assumption—**resource immobility**—describes the insight that resources tend to be "sticky" and don't move easily from firm to firm. Because of that stickiness, the resource differences that exist between firms are difficult to replicate and, therefore, can last for a long time. For example, SWA has enjoyed a sustained competitive advantage, allowing it to outperform its competitors over several decades. That resource difference is not due to a lack of imitation attempts, though. Continental and Delta both attempted to copy SWA, with Continental Lite and Song airline offerings, respectively. Neither airline, however, was able to successfully imitate the resource bundles and firm capabilities that make SWA unique. Combined, these insights tell us that resource bundles differ across firms, and such differences can persist for long periods. These two assumptions about resources are critical to explaining superior firm performance in the resource-based model.

Note, by the way, that the critical assumptions of the resource-based model are fundamentally different from the way in which a firm is viewed in the perfectly competitive industry structure introduced in Chapter 3. In perfect competition, all firms have access to the *same* resources and capabilities, ensuring that any advantage that one firm has will be short-lived. That is, when resources are freely available and mobile, competitors can move quickly to acquire resources that are utilized by the current market leader. Although some commodity markets approach this situation, most other markets include firms whose resource endowments differ. The resource-based view, therefore, delivers useful insights to managers about how to formulate a strategy that will enhance the chances of gaining a competitive advantage.

THE VRIO FRAMEWORK

LO 4-4

Apply the VRIO framework to assess the competitive implications of a firm's resources.

Our tool for evaluating a firm's resource endowments is a framework that answers the question of what resource attributes underpin competitive advantage. This framework is implied in the resource-based model, identifying certain *types of resources* as key to superior firm performance.[13] For a resource to be the basis of a competitive advantage, it must be

Valuable

Rare

Icostly to **I**mitate.

And finally, the firm itself must be

Organized to capture the value of the resource.

Following the lead of Jay Barney, one of the pioneers of the resource-based view of the firm, we call this model the **VRIO framework**.[14] According to this model, a firm can gain and sustain a competitive advantage only when it has resources that satisfy all of the VRIO criteria. Keep in mind that resources in the VRIO framework are broadly defined to include any assets *as well as* any capabilities and competencies that a firm can draw upon when formulating and implementing strategy. So to some degree, this presentation of the VRIO model summarizes all of our discussion in the chapter so far.

VRIO framework
A theoretical framework that explains and predicts firm-level competitive advantage.

Exhibit 4.5 captures the VRIO framework. You can use this decision tree to decide if the resource, capability, or competency under consideration fulfills the VRIO requirements. As you study the following discussion of each of the VRIO attributes, you will see that the attributes accumulate. Only if a firm's managers are able to answer "yes" four times to

EXHIBIT 4.5 / Applying the Resource-Based View: A Decision Tree Revealing Competitive Implications

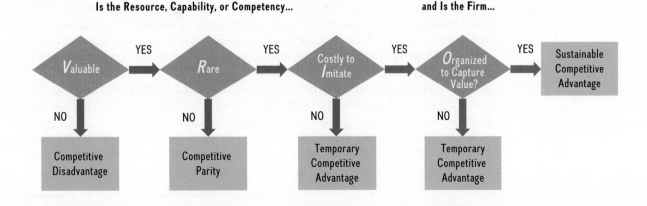

the attributes listed in the decision tree is the resource in question a core competency that underpins a firm's sustainable competitive advantage.

valuable resource
One of the four key criteria in the VRIO framework. A resource is valuable if it helps a firm exploit an external opportunity or offset an external threat.

VALUABLE. A **valuable resource** is one that enables the firm to exploit an external opportunity or offset an external threat. This has a positive effect on a firm's competitive advantage. In particular, a valuable resource enables a firm to increase its economic value creation $(V - C)$. Revenues rise if a firm is able to increase the perceived value of its product or service in the eyes of consumers by offering superior design and adding attractive features (assuming costs are not increasing). Production costs, for example, fall if the firm is able to put an efficient manufacturing process and tight supply chain management in place (assuming perceived value is not decreasing). Beats Electronics' ability to design and market premium headphones that bestow a certain air of coolness upon wearers is a valuable resource. The profit margins for Beats designer headphones are astronomical: The production cost for its headphones is estimated to be no more than $15, while they retail for $150 to $450, with some special editions over $1,000. Thus, Beats' competency in designing and marketing premium headphones is a valuable resource in the VRIO framework.

rare resource
One of the four key criteria in the VRIO framework. A resource is rare if the number of firms that possess it is less than the number of firms it would require to reach a state of perfect competition.

RARE. A resource is **rare** if only one or a few firms possess it. If the resource is common, it will result in perfect competition where no firm is able to maintain a competitive advantage (see discussion in Chapter 3). A resource that is valuable but not rare can lead to competitive parity at best. A firm is on the path to competitive *advantage* only if it possesses a valuable resource that is also rare. Beats Electronics' ability and reach in product placement and celebrity endorsements that build its coolness factor are certainly rare. No other brand in the world, not even Apple or Nike, has such a large number of celebrities from music, movies, and sports using its product in public. Thus, this resource is not only valuable but also rare.

costly-to-imitate resource
One of the four key criteria in the VRIO framework. A resource is costly to imitate if firms that do not possess the resource are unable to develop or buy the resource at a comparable cost.

COSTLY TO IMITATE. A resource is **costly to imitate** if firms that do not possess the resource are unable to develop or buy the resource at a reasonable price. If the resource in question is valuable, rare, and costly to imitate, then it is an internal strength and a core competency. If the firm's competitors fail to duplicate the strategy based on the valuable, rare, and costly-to-imitate resource, then the firm can achieve a temporary competitive advantage.

Beats' core competency in establishing a brand that communicates coolness is built upon the intuition and feel for music and cultural trends of Dr. Dre, one of music's savviest marketing minds. Although the sound quality of Beats headphones is good enough, they mainly sell as a fashion accessory for their coolness factor and brand image. Because its creator Dr. Dre relies on gut instinct in making decisions rather than market research, this resource is costly to imitate. Even if a firm wanted to copy Beats' core competency—how would it go about it? The music and trend-making talent as well as the social capital of Dr. Dre and Jimmy Iovine, two of the best-connected people in the music industry, might be impossible to replicate. Even Apple with its deep talent pool decided not to build its own line of premium headphones but rather opted to acquire Beats Electronics' line for $3 billion, and to put employment contracts in place that make Dr. Dre and Jimmy Iovine senior executives at Apple Inc. The combination of the three resource attributes $(V + R + I)$ has allowed Beats Electronics to enjoy a competitive advantage (see Exhibit 4.5).

A firm that enjoys a competitive advantage, however, attracts significant attention from its competitors. They will attempt to negate a firm's resource advantage by directly imitating the resource in question *(direct imitation)* or through working around it to provide a comparable product or service *(substitution).*

Direct Imitation. We usually see direct imitation, as a way to copy or imitate a valuable and rare resource, when firms have difficulty protecting their advantage. (We discuss barriers to imitation shortly.) Direct imitation is swift if the firm is successful and intellectual property (IP) protection such as patents or trademarks, for example, can be easily circumvented.

Crocs, the maker of the iconic plastic clog, fell victim to direct imitation. Launched in 2002 as a spa shoe at the Fort Lauderdale, Florida, boat show, Crocs experienced explosive growth, selling millions of pairs each year and reaching over $650 million in revenue in 2008. Crocs are worn by people in every age group and walk of life, including celebrities Sergey Brin, Matt Damon, Heidi Klum, Adam Sandler, and even Kate Middleton, the Duchess of Cambridge. To protect its unique shoe design, the firm owns several patents. Given Crocs' explosive growth, however, numerous cheap imitators have sprung up to copy the colorful and comfortable plastic clog. Despite the patents and celebrity endorsements, other firms were able to copy the shoe, taking a big bite into Crocs' profits. Indeed, Crocs' share price plunged from a high of almost $75 to less than $1 in less than 13 months.[15]

This example illustrates that competitive advantage cannot be sustained if the underlying capability can easily be replicated and can thus be *directly imitated.* Competitors simply created molds to imitate the shape, look, and feel of the original Crocs shoe. Any competitive advantage in a fashion-driven industry, moreover, is notoriously short-lived if the company fails to continuously innovate or build such brand recognition that imitators won't gain a foothold in the market. Crocs was more or less a "one-trick pony." Beats Electronics, on the other hand, created an ecosystem of hardware (Beats by Dr. Dre) and software (Beats Music) that positively reinforce one another. Beats by Dr. Dre are the installed base that drives demand for Beats Music. As Beats Music's music streaming and celebrity-curated playlists become more popular, demand for Beats headphones further increases. With increasing demand, Beats Music services also become more valuable as its proprietary algorithms have more data to work with. Continuous innovation by churning out new headphone designs combined with the unique coolness factor of Dr. Dre make direct imitation attempts more or less futile.

Substitution. The second avenue of imitation for a firm's valuable and rare resource is through *substitution.* This is often accomplished through *strategic equivalence.* Take the example of Jeff Bezos launching and developing Amazon.com.[16] Before Amazon's inception, the retail book industry was dominated by a few large chains and many independent mom-and-pop bookstores. As the Internet was emerging in the 1990s, Bezos was looking for options in online retail. He zeroed in on books because of their non-differentiated commodity nature and easiness to ship. In purchasing a printed book online, customers knew exactly what they would be shipped, because the products were identical, whether sold online or in a brick-and-mortar store. The only difference was the mode of transacting and delivery. Taking out the uncertainty of online retailing to some extent made potential customers more likely to try this new way of shopping.

Bezos realized, however, that he could not compete with the big-box book retailers directly and needed a different business model. The emergence of the Internet allowed him

Tiffany & Co. has developed a core competency—elegant jewelry design and craftsmanship delivered through a superior customer experience—that is valuable, rare, and costly for competitors to imitate. The company vigorously protects its trademarks, including its Tiffany Blue Box, but it never trademarked the so-called "tiffany setting" for diamond rings, used now by many jewelers. The term has been co-opted for advertising by other retailers (including Costco), which now maintain it is a generic term commonly used in the jewelry industry.
© Lucas Oleniuk/Getty Images

to come up with a new distribution system that negated the need for retail stores and thus high real-estate costs. Bezos' new business model of ecommerce not only substituted for the traditional fragmented supply chain in book retailing, but also allowed Amazon to offer lower prices due to its lower operating costs. Amazon uses a strategic equivalent substitute to satisfy a customer need previously met by brick-and-mortar retail stores.

Combining Imitation and Substitution. In some instances, firms are able to combine direct imitation and substitution when attempting to mitigate the competitive advantage of a rival. With its Galaxy line of smartphones, Samsung has been able to imitate successfully the look and feel of Apple's iPhones. Samsung's Galaxy smartphones use Google's Android operating system and apps from Google Play as an alternative to Apple's iOS and iTunes Store. Samsung achieved this through a combination of *direct imitation* (look and feel) and *substitution* (using Google's mobile operating system and app store).[17]

More recently, both Apple and Samsung are feeling the pressure from low-end disruptor Xiaomi, a Chinese smartphone company.[18] As a result of its explosive growth, Xiaomi is now the world's third-largest maker of smartphones. Xiaomi has been spectacularly successful in its Chinese home market where it is selling more smartphones than Apple or even Samsung.[19] Xiaomi also uses Google's Android system on its low-priced models that mimic the look and feel of both the Apple iPhone as well as the Samsung Galaxy line of phones.

ORGANIZED TO CAPTURE VALUE. The final criterion of whether a rare, valuable, and costly-to-imitate resource can form the basis of a sustainable competitive advantage depends on the firm's internal structure. To fully exploit the competitive potential of its resources, capabilities, and competencies, a firm must be **organized to capture value**— that is, it must have in place an effective organizational structure and coordinating systems. (We will study organizational design in detail in Chapter 11.) Before Apple or Microsoft had any significant share of the personal computer market, Xerox's Palo Alto Research Center (PARC) invented and developed an early word-processing application, the graphical user interface (GUI), the Ethernet, the mouse as a pointing device, and even the first personal computer. These technology breakthroughs laid the foundation of the desktop-computing industry.[20] Xerox's invention competency built through a unique combination of resources and capabilities was clearly valuable, rare, and costly to imitate with the potential to create a competitive advantage.

Due to a lack of appropriate organization, however, Xerox failed to appreciate and exploit the many breakthroughs made by PARC in computing software and hardware. Why? Because the innovations did not fit within the Xerox business focus at the time. Under pressure in its core business from Japanese low-cost competitors, Xerox's top management was busy pursuing innovations in the photocopier business. Xerox was not organized to appreciate the competitive potential of the valuable, rare, and inimitable resources generated at PARC, if not in the photocopier field. Such organizational problems were exacerbated by geography: Xerox headquarters is on the East Coast in Norwalk, Connecticut, across the country from PARC on the West Coast in Palo Alto, California.[21] Nor did it help that development engineers at Xerox headquarters had a disdain for the scientists engaging in basic research at PARC. In the meantime, both Apple and Microsoft developed operating systems, graphical user interfaces, and application software.

If a firm is not effectively organized to exploit the competitive potential of a valuable, rare, and costly-to-imitate (VRI) resource, the best-case scenario is a temporary competitive

organized to capture value
One of the four key criteria in the VRIO framework. The characteristic of having in place an effective organizational structure, processes, and systems to fully exploit the competitive potential of the firm's resources, capabilities, and competencies.

advantage (see Exhibit 4.5). In the case of Xerox, where management was not supportive of the resource, even a temporary competitive advantage would not be realized even though the resource meets the VRI requirements.

In summary, for a firm to gain and sustain a competitive advantage, its resources and capabilities need to interact in such a way as to create unique core competencies (see Exhibit 4.3). Ultimately, though, only a few competencies may turn out to be those *specific* core competencies that fulfill the VRIO requirements.[23] A company cannot do everything equally well and must carve out a unique strategic position for itself, making necessary trade-offs.[24] Strategy Highlight 4.1 demonstrates application of the VRIO framework.

Strategy Highlight 4.1

Applying VRIO: The Rise and Fall of Groupon

After graduating with a degree in music from Northwestern University, Andrew Mason spent a couple of years as a web designer. In 2008, the then 27-year-old founded Groupon, a daily-deal website that connects local retailers and other merchants to consumers by offering goods and services at a discount. Groupon creates marketplaces by bringing the brick-and-mortar world of local commerce onto the Internet. The company basically offers a "group-coupon." If more than a predetermined number of Groupon users sign up for the offer, the deal is extended to all Groupon users. For example, a local spa may offer a massage for $40 instead of the regular $80. If more than say 10 people sign up, the deal becomes reality. The users prepay $40 for the coupon, which Groupon splits 50-50 with the local merchant. Inspired by how Amazon.com has become the global leader in ecommerce, Mason's strategic vision for Groupon was *to be the global leader in local commerce.*

Measured by its explosive growth, Groupon became one of the most successful recent Internet startups, with over 260 million subscribers and serving over 500,000 merchants in the United States and some 50 countries. Indeed, Groupon's success attracted a $6 billion buyout offer by Google in early 2011, which Mason declined. In November 2011, Groupon held a successful initial public offering (IPO), valued at more than $16 billion with a share price of over $26. But a year later, Groupon's share price had fallen 90 percent to just $2.63, resulting in a market cap of less than $1.8 billion In early 2013, Mason posted a letter for Groupon employees on the web, arguing that it would leak anyway, stating, "After four and a half intense and wonderful years as CEO of Groupon, I've decided that I'd like to spend more time with my family. Just kidding—I was fired today."

Although Groupon is still in business, it is just one competitor among many, and not a market leader. What went wrong? The implosion of Groupon's market value can be explained using the VRIO framework. Its competency to drum up more business for local retailers by offering lower prices for its users was certainly *valuable.* Before Groupon, local merchants used online and classified ads, direct mail, yellow pages, and other venues to reach customers. Rather than using one-way communication, Groupon facilitates the meeting of supply and demand in local markets. When Groupon launched, such local market-making competency was also *rare.* Groupon, with its first-mover advantage, seemed able to use technology in a way so valuable and rare it prompted Google's buyout offer. But was it costly to imitate? Not so much.

The multibillion-dollar Google offer spurred potential competitors to reproduce Groupon's business model. They discovered that Groupon was more of a sales company than a tech venture, despite perceptions to the contrary. To target and fine-tune its local deals, Groupon relies heavily on human labor to do the selling. Barriers to entry in this type of business are nonexistent because Groupon's competency is built more on a tangible resource (labor) than on an intangible one (proprietary technology). Given that Groupon's valuable and rare competency was *not hard to imitate,* hundreds of new ventures (so-called Groupon clones) rushed in to take advantage of this opportunity. Existing online giants such as Google, Amazon (via LivingSocial), and Facebook also moved in. The spurned Google almost immediately created its own daily-deal version with Google Offers.

Also, note that the ability to imitate a rare and valuable resource is directly linked to barriers of entry, which is one of the key elements in Porter's five forces model *(threat of new entrants).* This relationship allows linking internal analysis using the resource-based view to external analysis

(continued)

with the five forces model, which also would have predicted low industry profit potential given low or no barriers to entry.

To make matters worse, these Groupon clones are often able to better serve the needs of local markets and specific population groups. Some daily-deal sites focus only on a specific geographic area. As an example, Conejo Deals meets the needs of customers and retailers in Southern California's Conejo Valley, a cluster of suburban communities. These hyper-local sites tend to have much deeper relationships and expertise with merchants in their specific areas. Since they are mostly matching local customers with local businesses, moreover, they tend to foster more repeat business than the one-off bargain hunters that use Groupon (based in Chicago). In addition, some daily-deal sites often target specific groups. They have greater expertise in matching their users with local retailers (e.g., Daily Pride serving LGBT communities; Black Biz Hookup serving

African-American business owners and operators; Jdeal, a Jewish group-buying site in New York City; and so on).

"Finding your specific group" or "going hyper local" allows these startups to increase the perceived value added for their users over and above what Groupon can offer. Although Groupon aspires to be the *global leader,* there is really no advantage to global scale in serving local markets. This is because daily-deal sites are best suited to market *experience goods,* such as haircuts at a local barber shop or a meal in a specific Thai restaurant. The quality of these goods and services cannot be judged unless they are consumed. Creation of experience goods and their consumption happens in the *same geographic space.*

Once imitated, Groupon's competency to facilitate local commerce using an Internet platform was neither valuable nor rare. As an application of the VRIO model would have predicted, Groupon's competitive advantage as a first mover would only be temporary at best (see Exhibit 4.5).[22]

LO 4-5

Evaluate different conditions that allow a firm to sustain a competitive advantage.

ISOLATING MECHANISMS: HOW TO SUSTAIN A COMPETITIVE ADVANTAGE

Although VRIO resources can lay the foundation of a sustainable competitive advantage, no competitive advantage can be sustained indefinitely. Several conditions, however, can offer some protection to a successful firm by making it more difficult for competitors to imitate the resources, capabilities, or competencies that underlie its competitive advantage:[25]

- Better expectations of future resource value.
- Path dependence.
- Causal ambiguity.
- Social complexity.
- Intellectual property (IP) protection.

isolating mechanisms
Barriers to imitation that prevent rivals from competing away the advantage a firm may enjoy.

These *barriers to imitation* are important examples of **isolating mechanisms** because they prevent rivals from competing away the advantage a firm may enjoy.[26] This link ties isolating mechanisms directly to one of the criteria in the resource-based view to assess the basis of competitive advantage: costly to imitate. If one, or any combination, of these isolating mechanisms is present, a firm may strengthen its basis for competitive advantage, increasing its chance to be sustainable over a longer period of time.

BETTER EXPECTATIONS OF FUTURE RESOURCE VALUE. Sometimes firms can acquire resources at a low cost, which lays the foundation for a competitive advantage later when expectations about the future of the resource turn out to be more accurate.

A real estate developer illustrates the role that the future value of a resource can play. She must decide when and where to buy land for future development. Her firm may gain a competitive advantage if she buys a parcel of land for a low cost in an undeveloped rural area 40 miles north of San Antonio, Texas—in anticipation that it will increase in value with shifting demographics. Let's assume, several years later, that an interstate highway is built near her firm's land. With the highway, suburban growth explodes as many new neighborhoods and shopping malls are built. Her firm is now able to develop this particular piece of property to build high-end office or apartment buildings. The value creation far exceeds the cost, and her firm gains a competitive advantage. The resource has suddenly become valuable, rare, and costly to imitate, gaining the developer's firm a competitive advantage. Other developers could have bought the land, but once the highway was announced, the cost of the developer's land and that of adjacent land would have risen drastically, reflecting the new reality and thus negating any potential for competitive advantage. The developer had better expectations than her competitors of the future value of the resource, in this case the land she purchased. If this developer can repeat such "better expectations" over time, she will have a sustainable competitive advantage. If she cannot, she was simply lucky. Although luck can play a role in gaining an initial competitive advantage, it is not a basis for a sustainable competitive advantage.

PATH DEPENDENCE. **Path dependence** describes a process in which the options one faces in a current situation are limited by decisions made in the past.[27] Often, early events—sometimes even random ones—have a significant effect on final outcomes. The U.S. carpet industry provides an example of path dependence.[28] Roughly 85 percent of all carpets sold in the United States and almost one-half of all carpets sold worldwide come from carpet mills located within 65 miles of one city: Dalton, Georgia. While the U.S. manufacturing sector has suffered in recent decades, the carpet industry has flourished. Companies not clustered near Dalton face a disadvantage because they cannot readily access the required know-how, skilled labor, suppliers, low-cost infrastructure, and so on needed to be competitive.

> **path dependence**
> A situation in which the options one faces in the current situation are limited by decisions made in the past.

But why Dalton? Two somewhat random events combined. First, the boom after World War II drew many manufacturers South to escape restrictions placed upon them in the North, such as higher taxation or the demands of unionized labor. Second, technological progress allowed industrial-scale production of tufted textiles to be used *as substitutes for the more expensive wool*. This innovation emerged in and near Dalton. Thus historical accident explains why today almost all U.S. carpet mills are located in a relatively small region, including world leaders Shaw Industries and Mohawk Industries.

Path dependence also rests on the notion that time cannot be compressed at will. While management can compress resources such as labor and R&D into a shorter period, the push will not be as effective as when a firm spreads out its effort and investments over a longer period. Trying to achieve the same outcome in less time, even with higher investments, tends to lead to inferior results, due to *time compression diseconomies*.[29]

Consider GM's problems in providing a competitive alternative to the highly successful Toyota Prius, a hybrid electric vehicle. Its problems highlight path dependence and time compression issues. The California Air Resource Board (CARB) in 1990 passed a mandate for introducing zero-emissions cars, which stipulated that 10 percent of new vehicles sold by carmakers in the state must have zero emissions by 2003. This mandate not only accelerated research in alternative energy sources for cars, but also led to the development of the first fully electric production car, GM's EV1. GM launched the car in California and Arizona in 1996. Competitive models followed, with the Toyota RAV EV and the Honda EV. In this case, regulations in the legal environment fostered innovation in the automobile industry (see discussion of PESTEL forces in Chapter 3).

Companies not only feel the nudge of forces in their environment but can also push back. The California mandate on zero emissions, for example, did not stand.[30] Several stakeholders, including the car and oil companies, fought it through lawsuits and other actions. CARB ultimately gave in to the pressure and abandoned its zero-emissions mandate. When the mandate was revoked, GM recalled and destroyed its EV1 electric vehicles and terminated its electric-vehicle program. This decision turned out to be a strategic error that would haunt GM a decade or so later. Although GM was the leader among car companies in electric vehicles in the mid-1990s, it did not have a competitive model to counter the Toyota Prius when its sales took off in the early 2000s. The Chevy Volt (a plug-in hybrid), GM's first major competition to the Prius, was delayed by over a decade because GM had to start its electric-vehicle program basically from scratch. Not having an adequate product lineup during the early 2000s, GM's U.S. market share dropped below 20 percent in 2009 (from over 50 percent a few decades earlier), the year it filed for bankruptcy. GM subsequently reorganized under Chapter 11 of the U.S. bankruptcy code, and relisted on the New York Stock Exchange in 2010.

While GM sold about 40,000 Chevy Volts worldwide, Toyota sold over 3.5 million Prius cars. Moreover, Nissan introduced its all-electric Leaf in 2010; GM did not have an all-electric vehicle in its lineup. In the meantime, Nissan sold over 200,000 Leafs worldwide, while GM is hoping to introduce its first all-electric vehicle, the Chevy Bolt, in the 2017 model year. Once the train of new capability development has left the station, it is hard to jump back on because of path dependence. Moreover, firms cannot compress time at will; indeed, learning and improvements must take place over time, and existing competencies must constantly be nourished and upgraded.

Strategic decisions generate long-term consequences due to path dependence and time-compression diseconomies; they are not easily reversible. A competitor cannot imitate or create core competencies quickly, nor can one buy a reputation for quality or innovation on the open market. These types of valuable, rare, and costly-to-imitate resources, capabilities, and competencies must be built and organized effectively over time, often through a painstaking process that frequently includes learning from failure.

causal ambiguity
A situation in which the cause and effect of a phenomenon are not readily apparent.

CAUSAL AMBIGUITY. **Causal ambiguity** describes a situation in which the cause and effect of a phenomenon are not readily apparent. To formulate and implement a strategy that enhances a firm's chances of gaining and sustaining a competitive advantage, managers need to have a hypothesis or theory of how to compete. This implies that managers need to have some kind of understanding about what causes superior or inferior performance. Understanding the underlying reasons of observed phenomena is far from trivial, however. Everyone can see that Apple has had several hugely successful innovative products such as the iMac, iPod, iPhone, and iPad, combined with its hugely popular iTunes services. These successes stem from Apple's set of *V, R, I,* and *O* core competencies that supports its ability to continue to offer a variety of innovative products and to create an ecosystem of products and services.

A deep understanding, however, of exactly *why* Apple has been so successful is very difficult. Even Apple's managers may not be able to clearly pinpoint the sources of their success. Is it the visionary role that the late Steve Jobs played? Is it the rare skills of Apple's uniquely talented design team around Jonathan Ive? Is it the timing of the company's product introductions? Is it Apple CEO Tim Cook who adds superior organizational skills and puts all the pieces together when running the day-to-day operations? Or is it a combination of these factors? If the link between cause and effect is ambiguous for Apple's managers, it is that much more difficult for others seeking to copy a valuable resource, capability, or competency.

SOCIAL COMPLEXITY. **Social complexity** describes situations in which different social and business systems interact. There is frequently no causal ambiguity as to how the *individual* systems such as supply chain management or new product development work in isolation. They are often managed through standardized business processes such as Six Sigma or ISO 9000. Social complexity, however, emerges when two or more such systems are *combined*. Copying the emerging complex social systems is difficult for competitors because neither direct imitation nor substitution is a valid approach. The interactions between different systems create too many possible permutations for a system to be understood with any accuracy. The resulting social complexity makes copying these systems difficult, if not impossible, resulting in a valuable, rare, and costly-to-imitate resource that the firm is organized to exploit.

Look at it this way. A group of three people has three relationships, connecting every person directly with one another. Adding a fourth person to this group *doubles* the number of direct relationships to six. Introducing a fifth person increases the number of relationships to 10.[31] This gives you some idea of how complexity might increase when we combine different systems with many different parts.

In reality, firms may manage thousands of employees from all walks of life. Their interactions within the firm's processes, procedures, and norms make up its culture. Although an observer may conclude that Zappos' culture, with its focus on autonomous teams in a flat hierarchy to provide superior customer service, might be the basis for its competitive advantage, engaging in reverse social engineering to crack Zappos' code of success might be much more difficult. Moreover, an organizational culture that works for online retailer Zappos, led by CEO and chief happiness officer Tony Hsieh, might seed havoc for an aerospace and defense company such as Lockheed Martin, led by CEO Marillyn Hewson. This implies that one must understand competitive advantage within its organizational and industry context. Looking at individual elements of success without taking social complexity into account is a recipe for inferior performance, or worse.

> **social complexity**
> A situation in which different social and business systems interact with one another.

INTELLECTUAL PROPERTY PROTECTION. **Intellectual property (IP) protection** is a critical intangible resource that can also help sustain a competitive advance. Consider the five major forms of IP protection: patents, designs, copyrights, trademarks, and trade secrets.[32]

The intent of IP protection is to prevent others from copying legally protected products or services. In many knowledge-intensive industries that are characterized by high research and development (R&D) costs, for example smartphones and pharmaceuticals, IP protection provides not only an incentive to make these risky and often large-scale investments in the first place, but also affords a strong isolating mechanism that is critical to a firm's ability to capture the returns to investment. Although the initial investments to create the first version of a new product or service is quite high in many knowledge-intensive industries, the *marginal cost* (i.e., the cost to produce the next unit) after initial invention is quite low. For example, Microsoft spends billions of dollars to develop a new version of its Windows operating system; once completed, the cost of the next "copy" is close to zero because it is just software code distributed online in digital form. In a similar fashion, the costs of developing a new prescription drug, a process often taking more than a decade, are estimated to be over $2.5 billion.[33] Rewards to IP-protected products or services, however, can be high. During a little over 14 years on the market, Pfizer's Lipitor, the world's best-selling drug, accumulated over $125 billion in sales.[34]

IP protection can make direct imitation attempts difficult, if not outright illegal. A U.S. court, for example, has found that Samsung infringed in some of its older models

> **intellectual property (IP) protection**
> A critical intangible resource that can provide a strong isolating mechanism, and thus help to sustain a competitive advantage.

on Apple's patents and awarded some $600 million in damages.[35] In a similar fashion, Dr. Dre attracted significant attention and support from other artists in the music industry when he sued Napster, an early online music file-sharing service, and helped shut it down in 2001 because of copyright infringements.

IP protection does not last forever, however. Once the protection has expired the invention can be used by others. Patents, for example, usually expire 20 years after a patent is filed with the U.S. Patent and Trademark Office. In the next few years, patents protecting roughly $100 billion in sales of proprietary drugs in the pharmaceutical industry are set to expire. Once this happens, producers of generics (drugs that contain the same active ingredients as the original patent-protected formulation) such as Teva Pharmaceutical Industries of Israel enter the market, and prices fall drastically. Pfizer's patent on Lipitor expired in 2011. Just one year later, of the 55 million Lipitor prescriptions, 45 million (or more than 80 percent) were generics.[36] Drug prices fall by 20 to 80 percent once generic formulations become available.[37]

Taken together, each of the five isolating mechanisms discussed here (or combinations thereof) allow a firm to extend its competitive advantage. Although no competitive advantage lasts forever, a firm may be able to protect its competitive advantage (even for long periods of time) when it has consistently better expectations about the future value of resources, when it has accumulated a resource advantage that can be imitated only over long periods of time, when the source of its competitive advantage is causally ambiguous or socially complex, or when the firm possesses strong intellectual property protection.

LO 4-6

Outline how dynamic capabilities can enable a firm to sustain a competitive advantage.

4.3 The Dynamic Capabilities Perspective

A firm's external environment is rarely stable (as discussed in Chapter 3). Rather, in many industries, change is fast and ferocious. Firms that fail to adapt their core competencies to a changing external environment not only lose a competitive advantage but also may go out of business.

We've seen the merciless pace of change in consumer electronics retailing in the United States. Once a market leader, Circuit City's core competencies in efficient logistics and superior customer service lost value because the firm neglected to upgrade and hone them over time. As a consequence, Circuit City was outflanked by Best Buy and online retailer Amazon, and went bankrupt. Earlier in the chapter we saw how Best Buy encountered the same difficulties competing against Amazon just a few years later. Core competencies might form the basis for a competitive advantage at one point, but as the environment changes, the very same core competencies might later turn into *core rigidities*, retarding the firm's ability to change.[38] A core competency can turn into a **core rigidity** if a firm relies too long on the competency without honing, refining, and upgrading as the environment changes.[39] Over time, the original core competency is no longer a good fit with the external environment, and it turns from an asset into a liability.

core rigidity
A former core competency that turned into a liability because the firm failed to hone, refine, and upgrade the competency as the environment changed.

This is the reason reinvesting, honing, and upgrading resources and capabilities are so crucial to sustaining any competitive advantage (see Exhibit 4.3). This ability lies at the heart of the dynamic capabilities perspective. At the beginning of this chapter, we defined *capabilities* as the organizational and managerial skills necessary to orchestrate a diverse set of resources and to deploy them strategically. Capabilities are by nature intangible. They find their expression in a company's structure, routines, and culture.

dynamic capabilities
A firm's ability to create, deploy, modify, reconfigure, upgrade, or leverage its resources in its quest for competitive advantage.

The dynamic capabilities perspective adds, as the name suggests, a *dynamic* or time element. In particular, **dynamic capabilities** describe a firm's ability to create, deploy, modify, reconfigure, upgrade, or leverage its resources over time in its quest for competitive advantage.[40] Dynamic capabilities are essential to move beyond a short-lived advantage and create a sustained competitive advantage. For a firm to sustain its advantage, any fit between its internal strengths and the external environment must be dynamic. That is, the firm must be able to change its internal resource base as the external environment changes. The goal should be to develop resources, capabilities, and competencies that create a *strategic fit* with the firm's environment. Rather than creating a static fit, the firm's internal strengths should change with its external environment in a *dynamic* fashion.

Not only do dynamic capabilities allow firms to adapt to changing market conditions, but they also enable firms to *create market changes* that can strengthen their strategic position. These market changes implemented by proactive firms introduce altered circumstances, to which more reactive rivals might be forced to respond. Apple's dynamic capabilities allowed it to redefine the markets for mobile devices and computing, in particular in music, smartphones, and media content. For the portable music market through its iPod and iTunes store, Apple generated environmental change to which Sony and others had to respond. With its iPhone, Apple redefined the market for smartphones, again creating environmental change to which competitors such as Samsung, BlackBerry, Google (with its Motorola Mobility unit), or Microsoft (with its Nokia unit) must respond. Apple's introduction of the iPad redefined the media and tablet computing market, forcing competitors such as Amazon and Microsoft to respond. With the introduction of the Apple Watch it is attempting to shape the market for computer wearables in its favor. Dynamic capabilities are especially relevant for surviving and competing in markets that shift quickly and constantly, such as the high-tech space in which firms such as Apple, Google, Microsoft, and Amazon compete. Strategy Highlight 4.2 shows how IBM developed dynamic capabilities to transform itself from a hardware company focused on mainframe computers to a global services company addressing major disruptions in the business world.

Strategy Highlight 4.2

Dynamic Capabilities at IBM

Virginia Rometty, CEO of IBM
© Jewel Samad/AFP/Getty Images

At its core, IBM is a solutions company. It solves data-based problems for its business clients, but the technology and problems both change over time. As an example, IBM helped kickstart the PC revolution in 1981 by setting an open standard in the computer industry with the introduction of the IBM PC running on an Intel 8088 chip and a Microsoft operating system (MS-DOS). Ironically, in the years following, IBM nearly vanished after experiencing the full force of that revolution, because its executives believed that the future of computing lay in mainframes and minicomputers that would be produced by fully integrated companies. However, with an open standard in personal computing, the entire industry value chain disintegrated, and many new firms entered its different stages. This led to a strategic misfit for IBM, which resulted in a competitive disadvantage.

Rather than breaking up IBM into independent businesses, newly installed CEO Lou Gerstner refocused the company on satisfying market needs, which demanded sophisticated IT services. Keeping IBM together as one entity allowed

(continued)

Gerstner to integrate hardware, software, and services to provide sophisticated solutions to customers' IT challenges. IBM was quick to capitalize on the emergence of the Internet to add further value to its business solutions. The company also moved quickly to sell its PC business when substitution from tablet computers was just beginning to impact demand. More recently, IBM also sold its server business, further shedding its legacy in hardware.

Exhibit 4.6 shows IBM's dynamic capability to successfully transform itself multiple times over its more than 100-year history—a history with periods of major disruptions in the data information industry, from mechanical calculators to the Internet. In contrast to IBM, note how at the bottom of Exhibit 4.6, strong competitors in one period drop from significance when a new wave of technology emerges.

Led by CEO Virginia Rometty, the IBM of today is an agile and nimble IT services company.[41] Rometty was promoted to CEO in 2012 from her position as senior vice president of sales, marketing, and strategy. Rather than just facing one technological transformation, IBM and its clients are currently facing three disruptions at once:

1. *Cloud computing:* By providing convenient, on-demand network access to shared computing resources such as networks, servers, storage, applications, and services, IBM attempts to put itself at the front of a trend now readily apparent in services that include Google Drive, Dropbox, or Microsoft 365. Increasingly, businesses are renting computer services rather than owning hardware and software and running their own networks. One of the largest cloud computing providers for businesses is Amazon Web Services (AWS), which beat out IBM in winning a high-profile CIA contract. This was seen as a major embarrassment given IBM's long history of federal contracts.

2. *Systems of engagement:* IBM now helps businesses with their systems of engagement, a term the company uses broadly to cover the transition from enterprise systems to decentralized systems or mobility. IBM identifies the traditional enterprise system as a "system of record" that passively provides information to the enterprise's knowledge workers. It contrasts that with systems of engagement that provide mobile computing platforms, often including social media apps such as Facebook or Twitter, that promote rapid and active collaboration. To drive adoption of mobile computing for business, IBM partnered with Apple to provide business productivity apps on Apple devices.

3. *Big data and analytics:* IBM now offers smarter analytics solutions that focus on how to acquire, process, store, manage, analyze, and visualize data arriving at high volume, velocity, and variety. Prime applications are in finance, medicine, law, and many other professional fields relying on deep domain expertise within fast-moving environments. IBM partnered with Twitter to provide IBM's business clients big data and analytics solutions in real time based on the vast amount of data produced on Twitter.

Critics of this strategic approach point out that IBM was slow to take advantage of these mega-opportunities, and they continue to watch IBM's stock performance with skepticism. The critics grew louder when Rometty received a pay increase and a $3.6 million bonus for her 2014 performance, during which revenue dropped about 6 percent and net income 27 percent. Overall, IBM's market cap plummeted by more than 60 percent: from a high of $240 billion in the spring of 2013 to some $150 billion early in 2015. And revenues for IBM have fallen for three straight years, from a high of $107 billion when Rometty became CEO to $93 billion by early 2015. During the same period, IBM's stock price fell by almost 10 percent, while the S&P 500 index rose by 67 percent.

Rometty, however, stays committed to IBM's new strategic focus and argues that she is transforming IBM for the long run. She views the most recent waves of technology disruptions as creating major business opportunities and has made sure that IBM invests heavily to take advantage of them. IBM has trained all of its consultants—over 100,000—in these three areas to help its business clients with their own transformation. If history is any guide, IBM is likely to master this three-pronged tech transformation also.[42]

EXHIBIT 4.6 / IBM Navigates Wave after Wave of Technological Change

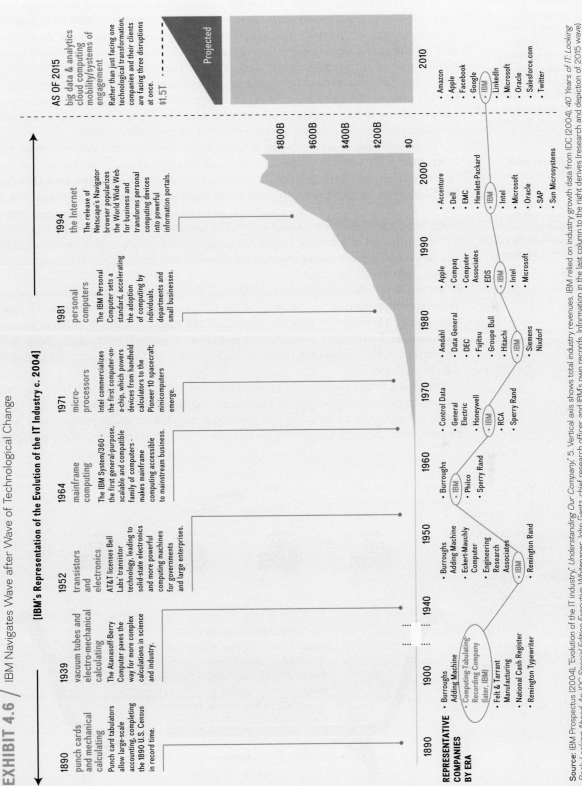

[IBM's Representation of the Evolution of the IT Industry c. 2004]

1890
punch cards and mechanical calculating
Punch card tabulators allow large-scale accounting, completing the 1890 U.S. Census in record time.

1939
vacuum tubes and electro-mechanical calculating
The Atanasoff-Berry Computer paves the way for more complex calculations in science and industry.

1952
transistors and electronics
AT&T licenses Bell Labs' transistor technology, leading to solid-state electronics and more powerful computing machines for governments and large enterprises.

1964
mainframe computing
The IBM System/360 - the first general-purpose, scalable and compatible family of computers - makes mainframe computing accessible to mainstream business.

1971
microprocessors
Intel commercializes the first computer-on-a-chip, which powers devices from handheld calculators to the Pioneer 10 spacecraft; minicomputers emerge.

1981
personal computers
The IBM Personal Computer sets a standard, accelerating the adoption of computing by individuals, departments and small businesses.

1994
the Internet
The release of Netscape's Navigator browser popularizes the World Wide Web for business and transforms personal computing devices into powerful information portals.

AS OF 2015
big data & analytics
cloud computing
mobility/systems of engagement
Rather than just facing one technological transformation, companies and their clients are facing three disruptions at once.

Projected

$1.5T

$800B
$600B
$400B
$200B
$0

1890 1900 1940 1950 1960 1970 1980 1990 2000 2010

REPRESENTATIVE COMPANIES BY ERA

- Burroughs Adding Machine
- Computing-Tabulating Recording Company (later, IBM)
- Felt & Tarrant Manufacturing
- National Cash Register
- Remington Typewriter

- Burroughs Adding Machine
- Eckert-Mauchly Computer
- Engineering Research Associates
- IBM
- Remington Rand

- Burroughs
- IBM
- Philco
- Sperry Rand

- Control Data
- General Electric
- Honeywell
- IBM
- RCA
- Sperry Rand

- Amdahl
- Data General
- DEC
- Fujitsu
- Groupe Bull
- Hitachi
- IBM
- Siemens Nixdorf

- Apple
- Compaq
- Computer Associates
- EDS
- IBM
- Intel
- Microsoft

- Accenture
- Dell
- EMC
- Hewlett-Packard
- IBM
- Intel
- Microsoft
- Oracle
- SAP
- Sun Microsystems

- Amazon
- Apple
- Facebook
- Google
- IBM
- LinkedIn
- Microsoft
- Oracle
- Salesforce.com
- Twitter

Source: IBM Prospectus (2004), "Evolution of the IT industry," *Understanding Our Company*; "Evolution of the IT industry," *Understanding Our Company*; 5. Vertical axis shows total industry revenues. IBM relied on industry growth data from IDC (2004), *40 Years of IT: Looking Back, Looking Ahead. An IDC Special Edition Executive Whitepaper*; John Gantz, chief research officer; and IBM's own records. Information in the last column to the right derives (research and depiction of 2015 wave) from author's analysis and estimate of industry growth from various industry sources. Red lines added to emphasize IBM's ongoing competitive standing.

dynamic capabilities perspective
A model that emphasizes a firm's ability to modify and leverage its resource base in a way that enables it to gain and sustain competitive advantage in a constantly changing environment.

resource stocks
The firm's current level of intangible resources.

resource flows
The firm's level of investments to maintain or build a resource.

In the **dynamic capabilities perspective,** competitive advantage is the outflow of a firm's capacity to modify and leverage its resource base in a way that enables it to gain and sustain competitive advantage in a constantly changing environment. Given the accelerated pace of technological change, in combination with deregulation, globalization, and demographic shifts, dynamic markets today are the rule rather than the exception. As a response, a firm may create, deploy, modify, reconfigure, or upgrade resources so as to provide value to customers and/or lower costs in a dynamic environment. The essence of this perspective is that competitive advantage is not derived from static resource or market advantages, but from a *dynamic reconfiguration* of a firm's resource base.

One way to think about developing dynamic capabilities and other intangible resources is to distinguish between resource stocks and resource flows.[43] In this perspective, **resource stocks** are the firm's current level of intangible resources. **Resource flows** are the firm's level of investments to maintain or build a resource. A helpful metaphor to explain the differences between resource stocks and resource flows is a bathtub that is being filled with water (see Exhibit 4.7).[44] The amount of water in the bathtub indicates a company's level of a specific *intangible resource stock*—such as its dynamic capabilities, new product development, engineering expertise, innovation capability, reputation for quality, and so on.[45]

Intangible resource stocks are built through investments over time. These resource flows are represented in the drawing by the different faucets, from which water flows into the tub. These faucets indicate investments the firm can make in different intangible resources. Investments in building an innovation capability, for example, differ from investments made in marketing expertise. Each investment flow would be represented by a different faucet.

How fast a firm is able to build an intangible resource—how fast the tub fills—depends on how much water comes out of the faucets and how long the faucets are left open. Intangible resources are built through continuous investments and experience over time. Organizational learning also fosters the increase of intangible resources. Many intangible

EXHIBIT 4.7

The Bathtub Metaphor: The Role of Inflows and Outflows in Building Stocks of Intangible Resources

Source: Figure based on metaphor used in I. Dierickx and K. Cool (1989), "Asset stock accumulation and sustainability of competitive advantage," *Management Science* 35: 1504–1513.

Inflows
Investments in Resources

Intangible Resource Stocks
(Dynamic Capabilities, New Product Development, Engineering Expertise, Innovation Capability, Reputation for Quality, Supplier Relationships, Employee Loyalty, Corporate Culture, Customer Goodwill, Know-How, Patents, Trademarks . . .)

Outflows
Leakage, Forgetting

resources, such as IBM's expertise in cognitive computing, take a long time to build. IBM's quest for cognitive computing began in 1997 after its Deep Blue computer (based on artificial intelligence) beat reigning chess champion Garry Kasparov. It has invested close to $25 billion to build a deep capability in cognitive computing with the goal to take advantage of business opportunities in big data and analytics. Its efforts were publicized when its Watson, a supercomputer capable of answering questions posed in natural language, went up against 74-time *Jeopardy!* quiz show champion Ken Jennings and won. Watson has demonstrated its skill in many professional areas where deep domain expertise is needed when making decisions in more or less real time: a wealth manager making investments, a doctor working with a cancer patient, an attorney working on a complex case, or even a chef in a five-star restaurant creating a new recipe. Moreover, cognitive computer systems get better over time as they learn from experience.

How fast the bathtub fills, however, also depends on how much water leaks out of the tub. The outflows represent a reduction in the firm's intangible resource stocks. Resource leakage might occur through employee turnover, especially if key employees leave. Significant resource leakage can erode a firm's competitive advantage. A reduction in resource stocks can occur if a firm does not engage in a specific activity for some time and forgets how to do this activity well.

According to the dynamic capabilities perspective, the managers' task is to decide which investments to make over time (i.e., which faucets to open and how far) in order to best position the firm for competitive advantage in a changing environment. Moreover, managers also need to monitor the existing intangible resource stocks and their attrition rates due to leakage and forgetting. This perspective provides a dynamic understanding of capability development to allow a firm's continuous adaptation to and superior performance in a changing external environment.

4.4 The Value Chain Analysis

The **value chain** describes the internal activities a firm engages in when transforming inputs into outputs.[46] Each activity the firm performs along the horizontal chain adds incremental value—raw materials and other inputs are transformed into components that are assembled into finished products or services for the end consumer. Each activity the firm performs along the value chain also adds incremental costs. A careful analysis of the value chain allows managers to obtain a more detailed and fine-grained understanding of how the firm's *economic value creation* $(V - C)$ breaks down into a distinct set of activities that help determine perceived value (V) and the costs (C) to create it. The value chain concept can be applied to basically any firm, from those in manufacturing industries to those in high-tech ones or service firms.

A firm's core competencies are deployed through its activities (see Exhibit 4.3). A firm's activities, therefore, are one of the key internal drivers of performance differences across firms. *Activities* are distinct actions that enable firms to add incremental value at each step by transforming inputs into goods and services. Managing a supply chain, running the company's IT system and websites, and providing customer support are all examples of distinct activities. Activities are narrower than functional areas such as marketing, because each functional area is made up of a set of distinct activities.

To build its uniquely cool brand image, Beats Electronics engages in a number of distinct activities. Its iconic Beats headphones are designed by Dr. Dre. To create special editions such as lightweight Beats for sports, Dr. Dre taps into his personal network and

LO 4-7

Apply a value chain analysis to understand which of the firm's activities in the process of transforming inputs into outputs generate differentiation and which drive costs.

value chain
The internal activities a firm engages in when transforming inputs into outputs; each activity adds incremental value.

works with basketball stars such as Kobe Bryant. Once designed, Beats manufactures its high-end headphones (before the Apple acquisition, that was done in conjunction with Monster Cable Products, a California-based company). Other distinct activities concern the marketing and sales of its products. Beats is not only marketing savvy in product placement and branding with a large number of celebrities across different fields, but it also focuses on other distinct activities such as packaging and product presentation to create a premium unboxing experience and superb displays in retail outlets, and now especially in Apple stores. In addition, Dr. Dre also works with celebrity musicians to have them curate playlists for the Beats Music streaming service. In sum, a number of distinct activities along the value chain are performed to create Beats by Dr. Dre, from initial design to a unique sales experience and after-sales service.

As shown in the generic value chain in Exhibit 4.8, the transformation process from inputs to outputs is composed of a set of distinct activities. When a firm's distinct activities generate value greater than the costs to create them, the firm obtains a profit margin (see Exhibit 4.8), assuming the market price the firm is able to command exceeds the costs of value creation. A generic value chain needs to be modified to capture the activities of a specific business. Retail chain American Eagle Outfitters, for example, needs to identify suitable store locations, either build or rent stores, purchase goods and supplies, manage distribution and store inventories, operate stores both in the brick-and-mortar world and online, hire and motivate a sales force, create payment and IT systems or partner with vendors, engage in promotions, and ensure after-sales services including returns. A maker of semiconductor chips such as Intel, on the other hand, needs to engage in R&D, design and engineer semiconductor chips and their production processes, purchase silicon and other ingredients, set up and staff chip fabrication plants, control quality and throughput, engage in marketing and sales, and provide after-sales customer support.

As shown in Exhibit 4.8, the value chain is divided into primary and support activities. The **primary activities** add value directly as the firm transforms inputs into outputs—from

primary activities
Firm activities that add value directly by transforming inputs into outputs as the firm moves a product or service horizontally along the internal value chain.

EXHIBIT 4.8 /

A Generic Value Chain: Primary and Support Activities

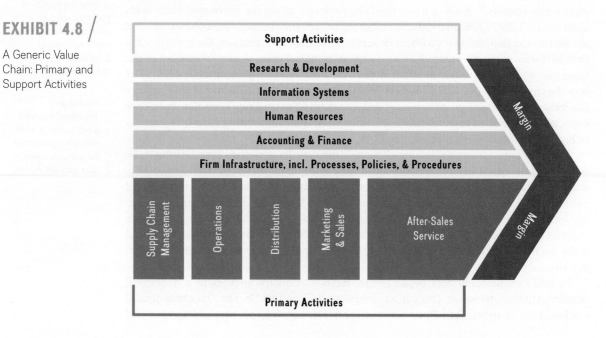

raw materials through production phases to sales and marketing and finally customer service, specifically

■ Supply chain management.
■ Operations.
■ Distribution.
■ Marketing and sales.
■ After-sales service.

Other activities, called **support activities**, add value indirectly. These activities include

■ Research and development (R&D).
■ Information systems.
■ Human resources.
■ Accounting and finance.
■ Firm infrastructure including processes, policies, and procedures.

support activities
Firm activities that add value indirectly, but are necessary to sustain primary activities.

To help a firm achieve a competitive advantage, each distinct activity performed needs to either add incremental value to the product or service offering or lower its relative cost. Discrete and specific firm activities are the basic units with which to understand competitive advantage because they are the drivers of the firm's relative costs and level of differentiation the firm can provide to its customers. Although the resource-based view of the firm helps identify the integrated set of resources and capabilities that are the building blocks of core competencies, the value chain perspective enables managers to see how competitive advantage flows from the firm's distinct set of activities. This is because a firm's core competency is generally found in a network linking different but distinct activities, each contributing to the firm's strategic position as either low-cost leader or differentiator.

Let's consider The Vanguard Group, one of the world's largest investment companies, with $3 trillion of assets under management.[47] It serves individual investors, financial professionals, and institutional investors such as state retirement funds. Vanguard's mission is *to help clients reach their financial goals by being their highest-value provider of investment products and services.*[48] It therefore emphasizes low-cost investing and quality service for its clients. Vanguard's average expense ratio (fees as a percentage of total net assets paid by investors) is generally the lowest in the industry.[49] Vanguard's core competency of low-cost investing while providing quality service for its clients is accomplished through a unique set of interconnected primary and support activities including strict cost control, direct distribution, low expenses with savings passed on to clients, a broad array of mutual funds, an efficient investment management approach, and straightforward client communication and education.

4.5 Implications for the Strategist

We've now reached a significant point: We can combine external analysis from Chapter 3 with the internal analysis just introduced. Together the two allow you to begin formulating a strategy that matches your firm's internal resources and capabilities to the demands of the external industry environment. Ideally, managers want to leverage their firm's internal strengths to exploit external opportunities, while mitigating internal weaknesses and external threats. Both types of analysis in tandem allow managers to formulate a strategy that is tailored to their company, creating a unique fit between the company's internal resources and the external environment. A *strategic fit* increases the likelihood that a firm is able to gain a competitive advantage. If a firm achieves a *dynamic* strategic fit, it is likely to be able to *sustain* its advantage over time.

USING SWOT ANALYSIS TO GENERATE INSIGHTS FROM EXTERNAL AND INTERNAL ANALYSIS

LO 4-8

Conduct a SWOT analysis to generate insights from external and internal analysis and derive strategic implications.

SWOT analysis
A framework that allows managers to synthesize insights obtained from an internal analysis of the company's strengths and weaknesses (S and W) with those from an analysis of external opportunities and threats (O and T) to derive strategic implications.

We synthesize insights from an internal analysis of the company's *strengths* and *weaknesses* with those from an analysis of external *opportunities* and *threats* using the **SWOT analysis**. Internal strengths (S) and weaknesses (W) concern resources, capabilities, and competencies. Whether they are strengths or weaknesses can be determined by applying the VRIO framework. A resource is a weakness if it is not valuable. In this case, the resource does not allow the firm to exploit an external opportunity or offset an external threat. A resource, however, is a strength and a core competency if it is valuable, rare, costly to imitate, and the firm is organized to capture at least part of the economic value created.

External opportunities (O) and threats (T) are in the firm's general environment and can be captured by PESTEL and Porter's five forces analyses (discussed in the previous chapter). An attractive industry as determined by Porter's five forces, for example, presents an external opportunity for firms not yet active in this industry. On the other hand, stricter regulation for financial institutions, for example, might represent an external threat to banks.

A SWOT analysis allows the strategist to evaluate a firm's current situation and future prospects by simultaneously considering internal and external factors. The SWOT analysis encourages managers to scan the internal and external environments, looking for any relevant factors that might affect the firm's current or future competitive advantage. The focus is on internal and external factors that can affect—in a positive or negative way—the firm's ability to gain and sustain a competitive advantage. To facilitate a SWOT analysis, managers use a set of strategic questions that link the firm's internal environment to its external environment, as shown in Exhibit 4.9, to derive strategic implications. In this SWOT matrix, the horizontal axis is divided into factors that are *external to the firm* (the focus of Chapter 3) and the vertical axis into factors that are *internal to the firm* (the focus of this chapter).

In a first step, managers gather information for a SWOT analysis in order to link internal factors *(Strengths* and *Weaknesses)* to external factors *(Opportunities* and *Threats)*. Next, managers use the SWOT matrix shown in Exhibit 4.9 to develop *strategic alternatives* for the firm using a four-step process:

1. Focus on the *Strengths–Opportunities* quadrant (top left) to derive "offensive" alternatives by using an internal strength in order to exploit an external opportunity.
2. Focus on the *Weaknesses–Threats* quadrant (bottom right) to derive "defensive" alternatives by eliminating or minimizing an internal weakness in order to mitigate an external threat.

	External to Firm	
Strategic Questions	**Opportunities**	**Threats**
Strengths	*How can the firm use internal strengths to take advantage of external opportunities?*	*How can the firm use internal strengths to reduce the likelihood and impact of external threats?*
Weaknesses	*How can the firm overcome internal weaknesses that prevent the firm from taking advantage of external opportunities?*	*How can the firm overcome internal weaknesses that will make external threats a reality?*

(leftmost label: **Internal to Firm**)

EXHIBIT 4.9

Strategic Questions within the SWOT Matrix

3. Focus on the *Strengths–Threats* quadrant (top right) to use an internal strength to minimize the effect of an external threat.

4. Focus on the *Weaknesses–Opportunities* quadrant (bottom left) to shore up an internal weakness to improve its ability to take advantage of an external opportunity.

In a final step, the strategist needs to carefully evaluate the pros and cons of each strategic alternative to select one or more alternatives to implement. Managers need to carefully explain their decision rationale, including why other strategic alternatives were rejected.

Although the SWOT analysis is a widely used management framework, however, a word of caution is in order. A problem with this framework is that a strength can also be a weakness and an opportunity can also simultaneously be a threat. Earlier in this chapter, we discussed the location of Google's headquarters in Silicon Valley and near several universities as a key resource for the firm. Most people would consider this a strength for the firm. However, California has a high cost of living and is routinely ranked among the worst of the U.S. states in terms of "ease of doing business." In addition, this area of California is along major earthquake fault lines and is more prone to natural disasters than many other parts of the country. So is the location a strength or a weakness? The answer is "it depends." In a similar fashion, is global warming an opportunity or threat for car manufacturers? If governments enact higher gasoline taxes and make driving more expensive, it can be a threat. If, however, carmakers respond to government regulations by increased innovation through developing more fuel-efficient cars as well as low- or zero-emission engines such as hybrid or electric vehicles, it may create more demand for new cars and lead to higher sales.

To make the SWOT analysis an effective management tool, the strategist must first conduct a thorough external and internal analysis, as laid out in Chapters 3 and 4. This sequential process enables the strategist to ground the analysis in rigorous theoretical frameworks before using SWOT to synthesize the results from the external and internal analyses in order to derive a set of strategic options.

You have now acquired the toolkit with which to conduct a complete strategic analysis of a firm's internal and external environments. In the next chapter, we consider various ways to assess and measure competitive advantage. That chapter will complete Part 1, on strategy analysis, in the AFI framework (see Exhibit 1.5).

CHAPTERCASE 4 / Consider This...

ALTHOUGH MANY OBSERVERS are convinced that Apple purchased Beats Electronics for the coolness of its brand and to gain a stronger position in the music industry, others are suggesting that what Apple is really buying are the talents that Beats co-founder Jimmy Iovine and Dr. Dre bring to the table. Since the death of Steve Jobs, Apple's visionary leader, the company has been lacking the kind of inspired personality it needs to remain a cultural icon. The critics argue that what Apple really needs is someone with a creative vision combined with a wide-reaching industry network and the ability to close a deal, especially in music where the personalities of its celebrities are known to be idiosyncratic. In music jargon, Apple is in need of a "front man." With the acquisition of Beats, it got two of the greatest creative talents in the music industry, with a long successful track record and deep and far-reaching networks.

Indeed, Iovine is of the opinion that Beats had always belonged with Apple. Iovine and Dr. Dre set out to model Beats Electronics after Apple's unique ability to marry culture and technology. Intriguingly, both Iovine and Dr. Dre are taking on senior positions at Apple. This indicates how much Apple's culture has changed under CEO Cook, because Iovine and Dr. Dre were not the first cool superstars from flashy industries he brought to Apple. In 2013, Apple hired former Burberry CEO Angela Ahrendts to head its retail operations. Bringing in superstars from the flashy industries of music or fashion to Apple, let alone into senior executive roles, would have been unthinkable under Jobs. Under his top-down leadership, only Apple products introduced to the public by himself in well-rehearsed theatrical launches were allowed to shine.

Questions

1. The ChapterCase argues that Beats Electronics' core competency lies in its marketing savvy and in Dr. Dre's coolness factor. Do you agree with this assessment? Why or why not?

2. If you believe that Apple bought Beats Electronics to bring Jimmy Iovine and Dr. Dre into Apple, what are the potential downsides of this multibillion-dollar "acqui-hire" (an acquisition to hire key personnel)?

3. If Beats Electronics' core competencies are indeed intangibles, such as coolness and marketing savvy, do you think these competencies will remain as valuable under Apple's ownership? Why or why not?

4. The ChapterCase provides at least three theories why Apple purchased Beats Electronics. Which of those do you believe are most accurate, and why?

TAKE-AWAY CONCEPTS

This chapter demonstrated various approaches to analyzing the firm's *internal environment,* as summarized by the following learning objectives and related take-away concepts.

LO 4-1 / Differentiate among a firm's core competencies, resources, capabilities, and activities.

- *Core competencies* are unique, deeply embedded, firm-specific strengths that allow companies to differentiate their products and services and thus create more value for customers than their rivals, or offer products and services of acceptable value at lower cost.

- *Resources* are any assets that a company can draw on when crafting and executing strategy.

- *Capabilities* are the organizational and managerial skills necessary to orchestrate a diverse set of resources to deploy them strategically.

- *Activities* are distinct and fine-grained business processes that enable firms to add incremental value by transforming inputs into goods and services.

LO 4-2 / Compare and contrast tangible and intangible resources.

■ *Tangible resources* have physical attributes and are visible.

■ *Intangible resources* have no physical attributes and are invisible.

■ Competitive advantage is more likely to be based on intangible resources.

LO 4-3 / Evaluate the two critical assumptions behind the resource-based view.

■ The first critical assumption—*resource heterogeneity*—is that bundles of resources, capabilities, and competencies differ across firms. The resource bundles of firms competing in the same industry (or even the same strategic group) are unique to some extent and thus differ from one another.

■ The second critical assumption—*resource immobility*—is that resources tend to be "sticky" and don't move easily from firm to firm. Because of that stickiness, the resource differences that exist between firms are difficult to replicate and, therefore, can last for a long time.

LO 4-4 / Apply the VRIO framework to assess the competitive implications of a firm's resources.

■ For a firm's resource to be the basis of a competitive advantage, it must have VRIO attributes: *valuable (V), rare (R),* and *costly to imitate (I).* The firm must also be able to *organize (O) in order to capture the value of the resource.*

■ A resource is valuable (V) if it allows the firm to take advantage of an external opportunity and/or neutralize an external threat. A valuable resource enables a firm to increase its economic value creation $(V - C)$.

■ A resource is rare (R) if the number of firms that possess it is less than the number of firms it would require to reach a state of perfect competition.

■ A resource is costly to imitate (I) if firms that do not possess the resource are unable to develop or buy the resource at a comparable cost.

■ The firm is organized (O) to capture the value of the resource if it has an effective organizational structure, processes, and systems in place to fully exploit the competitive potential.

LO 4-5 / Evaluate different conditions that allow a firm to sustain a competitive advantage.

■ Several conditions make it costly for competitors to imitate the resources, capabilities, or competencies that underlie a firm's competitive advantage: (1) *better expectations of future resource value,* (2) *path dependence,* (3) *causal ambiguity,* (4) *social complexity,* and (5) *intellectual property (IP) protection.*

■ These *barriers to imitation* are isolating mechanisms because they prevent rivals from competing away the advantage a firm may enjoy.

LO 4-6 / Outline how dynamic capabilities can enable a firm to sustain a competitive advantage.

■ To sustain a competitive advantage, any fit between a firm's internal strengths and the external environment must be dynamic.

■ *Dynamic capabilities* allow a firm to create, deploy, modify, reconfigure, or upgrade its resource base to gain and sustain competitive advantage in a constantly changing environment.

LO 4-7 / Apply a value chain analysis to understand which of the firm's activities in the process of transforming inputs into outputs generate differentiation and which drive costs.

■ The value chain describes the internal activities a firm engages in when transforming inputs into outputs.

■ Each activity the firm performs along the horizontal chain adds incremental value and incremental costs.

■ A careful analysis of the value chain allows managers to obtain a more detailed and fine-grained understanding of how the firm's economic value creation breaks down into a distinct set of activities that helps determine perceived value and the costs to create it.

■ When a firm's set of distinct activities is able to generate value greater than the costs to create it, the firm obtains a profit margin (assuming the market price the firm is able to command exceeds the costs of value creation).

LO 4-8 / Conduct a SWOT analysis to generate insights from external and internal analysis and derive strategic implications.

■ Formulating a strategy that increases the chances of gaining and sustaining a competitive advantage is based on synthesizing insights obtained from an internal analysis of the company's strengths (S) and weaknesses (W) with those from an analysis of external opportunities (O) and threats (T).

■ The strategic implications of a SWOT analysis should help the firm to leverage its internal strengths to exploit external opportunities, while mitigating internal weaknesses and external threats.

KEY TERMS

Activities *(p. 108)*

Capabilities *(p. 108)*

Causal ambiguity *(p. 120)*

Core competencies *(p. 108)*

Core rigidity *(p. 122)*

Costly-to-imitate resource *(p. 114)*

Dynamic capabilities *(p. 122)*

Dynamic capabilities perspective *(p. 126)*

Intangible resources *(p. 111)*

Intellectual property (IP) protection *(p. 121)*

Isolating mechanisms *(p. 118)*

Organized to capture value *(p. 116)*

Path dependence *(p. 119)*

Primary activities *(p. 128)*

Rare resource *(p. 114)*

Resource-based view *(p. 111)*

Resource flows *(p. 126)*

Resource heterogeneity *(p. 112)*

Resource immobility *(p. 112)*

Resource stocks *(p. 126)*

Resources *(p. 108)*

Social complexity *(p. 121)*

Support activities *(p. 129)*

SWOT analysis *(p. 130)*

Tangible resources *(p. 111)*

Valuable resource *(p. 114)*

Value chain *(p. 127)*

VRIO framework *(p. 113)*

DISCUSSION QUESTIONS

1. Why is it important to study the internal resources, capabilities, and activities of firms? What insights can be gained?

2. **a.** Conduct a value chain analysis for McDonald's. What are its primary activities? What are its support activities? Identify the activities that add the most value for the customer. Why? Which activities help McDonald's to contain cost? Why?

   b. In the past few years, McDonald's has made a lot of changes to its menu, adding more healthy choices and more higher-priced items, such as those offered in McCafé (e.g., premium roast coffee, frappé, and fruit smoothies), and has also enhanced its in-restaurant services (e.g., free, unlimited Wi-Fi; upgraded interiors). Did McDonald's new priorities—in terms of a broader, healthier menu and an improved in-restaurant experience—require changes to its traditional value chain activities? If so, how? Try to be as specific as possible in comparing the McDonald's from the recent past (focusing on low-cost burgers) to the McDonald's of today.

3. The resource-based view of the firm identifies four criteria that managers can use to evaluate whether particular resources and capabilities are core competencies and can, therefore, provide a basis for sustainable competitive advantage. Are these measures independent or interdependent? Explain. If (some of) the measures are interdependent, what implications does that fact have for managers wanting to create and sustain a competitive advantage?

ETHICAL/SOCIAL ISSUES

1. As discussed in this chapter, resources that are valuable, rare, and costly to imitate can help create a competitive advantage. In many cases, firms try to "reverse-engineer" a particular feature from a competitor's product for their own uses. It is common, for example, for smartphone manufacturers to buy the newest phones of their competitors and take them apart to see what new components/features the new models have implemented.

   As the competition between Google (www.google.com) and Baidu (www.ir.baidu.com) over Internet searches in China makes clear, however, this sort of corporate behavior does not stop with hardware products. With hundreds of millions of users and growing fast, China is considered to be one of the most lucrative online markets worldwide. Baidu, a Chinese web services company, has allegedly adapted many of the search tools that Google uses. Baidu, however, modifies its searches inside China (its major market) to accommodate government guidelines. In protest over these same guidelines, in 2010 Google left the Chinese market and is running its Chinese search operations from Hong Kong. Google no longer censors its online searches as requested by the Chinese government. Baidu has some78 percent market share in online search in China, and Google less than 15 percent.[50]

   It is legal to take apart publicly available products and services and try to replicate them and even develop work-arounds for relevant patents. But is it ethical? If a key capability protected by patents or trademarks in your firm is being reverse-engineered by the competition, what are your options for a response? Also, how do you evaluate Google's decision to move its servers to Hong Kong? For Google's values, see www.google.com/about/company/philosophy/.

2. The chapter mentions that one type of resource flow is the loss of key personnel who move to another firm. Assume that the human resources department of your firm has started running ads and billboards for open positions near the office of your top competitor. Your firm is also running Google ads on a keyword search for this same competitor. Is there anything unethical about this activity? Would your view change if this key competitor had just announced a major layoff?

SMALL GROUP EXERCISES

//// Small Group Exercise 1

Brand valuations were mentioned in the chapter as a potential key intangible resource for firms. Some product brands are so well established the entire category of products (including those made by competitors) may be called by the brand name rather than the product type. In your small group, develop two or three examples of this happening in the marketplace. In any of the cases noted, does such brand valuation give the leading brand a competitive advantage? Or does it produce confusion in the market for all products or services in that category? Provide advice to the leading brand as to how the firm can strengthen the brand name.

//// Small Group Exercise 2

Strategy Highlight 4.1 explains the rise and fall of Groupon. The company's strategic vision was *to be a global leader in local commerce*, based on a core competency that could be described as "local market-making." Numerous competitors took advantage of low barriers to entry and the easy imitation of Groupon's combined competency of some technology skills with sales skills, so that Groupon found that its competitive advantage was only temporary. Groupon continues to compete but needs your advice on how to build dynamic capabilities that might help it pursue the vision of becoming a global leader in local commerce. How might Groupon reinvest or upgrade its technology and sales skills so it builds a global customer base? For example, are there new products or services that would meet the needs of global clients in each of the local markets where the client does business? Brainstorm ways that Groupon might add value for its customers. How might Groupon build relationships with clients that are more socially complex, making Groupon's competencies more difficult to imitate?

STRATEGY TERM PROJECT

Mc Graw Hill Education **connect**

The HP Running Case *a related activity for each strategy term project module, is available in Connect.*

//// Module 4: Internal Analysis

1. Study the internal resources, capabilities, core competencies, and value chain of of the firm you have selected for this project. A good place to start with an internal firm analysis is to catalog the assets a firm has. List the firm's tangible assets. Then make a separate list of its intangible assets.

2. Now extend beyond the asset base and use the VRIO framework to identify the competitive position held by your firm. Which, if any, of these resources are helpful in sustaining the firm's competitive advantage?

3. Identify the core competencies that are at the heart of the firm's competitive advantage. (Remember, a firm will have only one, or at most a few, core competencies, by definition.)

4. Perform a SWOT analysis for your firm. Remember that strengths and weaknesses (S, W) are internal to the firm, and opportunities and threats (O, T) are external. Prioritize the strategic actions that you would recommend to your firm. Refer to the *Implications for the Strategist* section on how to conduct a SWOT analysis and provide recommendations building from strategic alternatives.

*my*STRATEGY

Looking Inside Yourself: What Is My Competitive Advantage?

We encourage you to apply what you have learned about competitive advantage to your career. Spend a few minutes looking at yourself to discover *your own* competitive advantage. If you have previous work experience, these questions should be from a work environment perspective. If you do not have any work experience yet, use these questions to evaluate a new workplace or as strategies for presenting yourself to a potential employer.

1. Write down your own strengths and weaknesses. What sort of organization will permit you to really leverage your strengths and keep you highly engaged in your work (person–organization fit)? Do some of your weaknesses need to be mitigated through additional training or mentoring from a more seasoned professional?

2. Personal capabilities also need to be evaluated over time. Are your strengths and weaknesses different today from what they were five years ago? What are you doing to make sure your capabilities are dynamic? Are you upgrading skills, modifying behaviors, or otherwise seeking to change your future strengths and weaknesses?

3. Are some of your strengths valuable, rare, and costly to imitate? How can you organize your work to help capture the value of your key strengths (or mitigate your weaknesses)? Are your strengths specific to one or a few employers, or are they more generally valuable in the marketplace? In general, should you be making investments in your human capital in terms of company-specific or market-general skills? Why should that distinction matter?

4. As an employee, how could you persuade your boss that you could be a vital source of sustainable competitive advantage? What evidence could you provide to make such an argument? If you are currently or previously employed, consider how your professional activities can help reinforce the key value-added activities in your department or organization.

ENDNOTES

1. www.beatsbydre.com/aboutus

2. www.beatsbydre.com; Eels, J., "Dr. Dre and Jimmy Iovine's school for innovation," *The Wall Street Journal,* November 5, 2014; Brownlee, M. (2014), "The truth about Beats by Dre!," August 30, YouTube video, www.youtube.com/watch?v=ZsxQxS0AdBY; "The sound of music," *The Economist,* August 24, 2014; Karp, H., "Apple's new Beat: What Steve Jobs and Dr. Dre have in common," *The Wall Street Journal,* June 6, 2014; Cohen, M., "Apple buys Beats to regain music mojo," *The Wall Street Journal,* May 29, 2014; "Can you feel the Beats?" *The Economist,* May 28, 2014; Karp, H., "Apple-Beats Electronics: The disrupter is disrupted," *The Wall Street Journal,* May 9, 2014; Karp, H., and D. Wakabayashi, "Dr. Dre, Jimmy Iovine would both join Apple in Beats deal," *The Wall Street Journal,* May 9, 2014; "Beats nicked," *The Economist,* May 13, 2014; and "The legacy of Napster," *The Economist,* September 13, 2013.

3. The discussion of Beats Electronics throughout the chapter is based on the sources above.

4. Prahalad, C.K., and G. Hamel (1990), "The core competence of the corporation," *Harvard Business Review,* May–June.

5. This discussion is based on: Amit, R., and P.J.H. Schoemaker (1993), "Strategic assets and organizational rent," *Strategic Management Journal* 14: 33–46; Peteraf, M. (1993), "The cornerstones of competitive advantage," *Strategic Management Journal* 14: 179–191; Barney, J. (1991), "Firm resources and sustained competitive advantage," *Journal of Management* 17: 99–120; and Wernerfelt, B. (1984), "A resource-based view of the firm," *Strategic Management Journal* 5: 171–180.

6. In 2015, Google sought permission to build a 3.4 million-square-foot campus across four pieces of land near the edge of San Francisco Bay. The futuristic site, to be completed in 2020, will be covered by canopy structures that can be rearranged in a flexible manner. See "Silicon Valley headquarters: Googledome, or temple of doom?" *The Economist,* March 7, 2015.

7. Tangible resources are listed under "Property and Equipment" in the Consolidated Balance Sheet, see Google Annual Report, 2013, https://investor.google.com/proxy.html.

8. "Top 100 most valuable global brands 2014," report by Millward Brown, WPP, www.millwardbrown.com/mb-global/brand-strategy/brand-equity/brandz/top-global-brands.

9. For a discussion on the benefits of being located in a technology cluster, see Rothaermel,

F.T., and D. Ku (2008), "Intercluster innovation differentials: The role of research universities," *IEEE Transactions on Engineering Management* 55: 9–22; and Saxenian, A. L. (1994), *Regional Advantage: Culture and Competition in Silicon Valley and Route 128* (Cambridge, MA: Harvard University Press).

10. Stuart, T., and O. Sorenson (2003), "The geography of opportunity: Spatial heterogeneity in founding rates and the performance of biotechnology firms," *Research Policy* 32: 229–253.

11. "Top 100 most valuable global brands 2014."

12. This discussion is based on Amit and Schoemaker, "Strategic assets and organizational rent"; Barney, "Firm resources and sustained competitive advantage"; Peteraf, "The cornerstones of competitive advantage"; and Wernerfelt, "A resource-based view of the firm."

13. This discussion is based on Barney, J., and W. Hesterly (2009), *Strategic Management and Competitive Advantage,* 3rd ed. (Upper Saddle River, NJ: Pearson Prentice Hall); Amit and Schoemaker, "Strategic assets and organizational rent"; Barney, "Firm resources and sustained competitive advantage"; Peteraf, "The cornerstones of competitive advantage"; and Wernerfelt, "A resource-based view of the firm."

14. Barney, J., and W. Hesterly (2014), *Strategic Management and Competitive Advantage,* 5th ed. (Upper Saddle River, NJ: Pearson Prentice Hall); and Barney, "Firm resources and sustained competitive advantage."

15. Crocs' share price hit an all-time high of $74.75 on October 31, 2007. By November 20, 2008, the share price had fallen to $0.94.

16. For a detailed history of the creation and growth of Amazon.com, see Stone, B. (2013), *The Everything Store: Jeff Bezos and the Age of Amazon* (New York: Little, Brown and Company).

17. "U.S. judge reduces Apple's patent award in Samsung case," *The Wall Street Journal,* March 1, 2013; and "Apple wins big in patent case," *The Wall Street Journal,* August 24, 2012.

18. Vazquez Sampere, J.P. (2014), "Xiaomi, not Apple, is changing the smartphone industry," *Harvard Business Review,* October 14.

19. Culpan, T., "Xiaomi smartphone sales surge to top Samsung as China's No. 1," *Bloomberg Businessweek,* February 17, 2015.

20. Chesbrough, H. (2006), *Open Innovation: The New Imperative for Creating and Profiting from Technology* (Boston, MA: Harvard Business School Press).

21. In 1968, Xerox moved its headquarters from Rochester, New York, to Norwalk, Connecticut.

22. Groupon Annual Report, 2012; Groupon investor deck, March 2013; "Don't weep for Groupon ex-CEO Andrew Mason," *The Wall Street Journal,* March 1, 2013; "Groupon CEO fired as daily-deals biz bottoms out," *WIRED,* February 28, 2013; "Struggling Groupon ousts its quirky CEO," *The Wall Street Journal,* February 28, 2013; "Why Groupon is over and Facebook and Twitter should follow," *Forbes,* August 20, 2012; "Groupon: Deep discount," *The Economist,* August 14, 2012; "The economics of Groupon," *The Economist,* October 22, 2011; "In Groupon's $6 billion wake, a fleet of startups," *The New York Times,* March 9, 2011; and Godin, S. (2008), *Tribes: We Need You to Lead Us* (New York: Portfolio).

23. Prahalad and Hamel, "The core competence of the corporation."

24. Porter, M.E. (1996), "What is strategy?" *Harvard Business Review,* November–December: 61–78.

25. This discussion is based on: ; Mahoney, J.T., and J.R. Pandian (1992), "The resource-based view within the conversation of strategic management," *Strategic Management Journal* 13: 363–380; Barney, "Firm resources and sustained competitive advantage"; Dierickx, I., and K. Cool (1989), "Asset stock accumulation and sustainability of competitive advantage," *Management Science* 35: 1504–1513; and Barney, J. (1986), "Strategic factor markets: Expectations, luck, and business strategy," *Management Science* 32: 1231–1241.

26. Lippman, S.A., and R. P. Rumelt (1982), "Uncertain imitability: An analysis of interfirm differences in efficiency under competition," *The Bell Journal of Economics* 13: 418–438.

27. Arthur, W.B. (1989), "Competing technologies, increasing returns, and lock-in by historical events," *Economics Journal* 99: 116–131; and Dierickx and Cool, "Asset stock accumulation and sustainability of competitive advantage."

28. Krugman, P. (1993), *Geography and Trade* (Cambridge, MA: MIT Press); and Patton, R.L. (2010), "A history of the U.S. carpet industry," *Economic History Association Encyclopedia,* http://eh.net/encyclopedia/article/patton.carpet.

29. Dierickx and Cool, "Asset stock accumulation and sustainability of competitive advantage."

30. For a detailed discussion of how several stakeholders influenced the CARB to withdraw zero-emissions standard, see Sony Pictures' documentary "Who Killed the Electric Car?," www.whokilledtheelectriccar.com/

31. More formally, the number of relationships (r) in a group is a function of its group members (n), with $r = n(n − 1)/2$. The assumption is that two people, A and B, have only one relationship (A ← → B), rather than two relationships (A → B and A ← 1 B). In the latter case, the number of relationships (r) in a group with n members doubles, where $r = n(n − 1)$.

32. This discussion is based on: Hallenborg, L., M. Ceccagnoli, and M. Clendenin (2008), "Intellectual property protection in the global economy," *Advances in the Study of Entrepreneurship, Innovation, and Economic Growth* 18: 11–34; and Graham, S.J.H. (2008), "Beyond patents: The role of copyrights, trademarks, and trade secrets in technology commercialization," *Advances in the Study of Entrepreneurship, Innovation, and Economic Growth* 18: 149–171.

33. "Cost to develop and win marketing approval for a new drug is $2.6 billion," *Tufts Center for the Study of Drug Development*, November 2014.

34. "Lipitor becomes world's top-selling drug," *Associated Press*, December 28, 2011.

35. Sherr, I., "U.S. judge reduces Apple's patent award in Samsung case," *The Wall Street Journal*, March 1, 2013; and Vascellaro, J.E., "Apple wins big in patent case," *The Wall Street Journal*, August 25, 2012.

36. Loftus, P., "Lipitor: Pfizer aims to sell over-the-counter version," *The Wall Street Journal*, March 2, 2014.

37. "Drug Prices to Plummet in Wave of Expiring Patents," Drugs.com, www.drugs. com/news/prices-plummet-wave-expiring-patents-32684.html

38. Leonard-Barton, D. (1992), "Core capabilities and core rigidities: A paradox in managing new product development," *Strategic Management Journal* 13: 111–125.

39. Leonard-Barton, D. (1995), *Wellsprings of Knowledge: Building and Sustaining the Sources of Innovation* (Boston, MA: Harvard Business School Press).

40. This discussion is based on Peteraf, M., G. Di Stefano, and G. Verona (2013), "The elephant in the room of dynamic capabilities: Bringing two diverging conversations together," *Strategic Management Journal* 34: 1389–1410; Rothaermel, F.T., and A.M. Hess (2007), "Building dynamic capabilities: Innovation driven by individual-, firm-, and network-level effects," *Organization Science* 18: 898–921; Eisenhardt, K.M., and Martin, J. (2000), "Dynamic capabilities: What are they?" *Strategic Management Journal* 21: 1105–1121; and Teece, D.J., G. Pisano, and A. Shuen (1997), "Dynamic capabilities and strategic management," *Strategic Management Journal* 18: 509–533.

41. This Strategy Highlight is based on: "Systems of Engagement and the Enterprise," IBM website; Hiltzik, M., "IBM redefines failure as 'success,' gives underachieving CEO huge raise," *Los Angeles Times*, February 2, 2015; Goldman, D., "IBM CEO Sam Palmisano to step down," *CNN Money*, October 25, 2011; Harreld, J.B., C.A. O'Reilly, and M. Tushman (2007), "Dynamic capabilities at IBM: Driving strategy into action," *California Management Review* 49: 21–43; Gerstner, L.V. (2002), *Who Says Elephants Can't Dance?* (New York: HarperBusiness); Grove, A.S. (1996), *Only the Paranoid Survive: How to Exploit the Crisis Points that Challenge Every Company and Every Career* (New York: Currency Doubleday); and various resources at ibm.com (diverse years).

42. Langley, M., "Behind Ginni Rometty's plan to reboot IBM," *The Wall Street Journal*, April 20, 2015.

43. Dierickx and Cool, "Asset stock accumulation and sustainability of competitive advantage."

44. Ibid.

45. Eisenhardt and Martin, "Dynamic capabilities: What are they?"

46. This discussion is based on: Porter, M.E. (1985), *Competitive Advantage: Creating and Sustaining Superior Performance* (New York: Free Press); Porter, "What is strategy?"; Siggelkow, N. (2001), "Change in the presence of fit: The rise, the fall, and the renaissance of Liz Claiborne," *Academy of Management Journal* 44: 838–857; and Magretta, J. (2012), *Understanding Michael Porter. The Essential Guide to Competition and Strategy.*

47. This discussion draws on: Porter, "What is strategy?"; and Siggelkow, N. (2002), "Evolution toward fit," *Administrative Science Quarterly* 47: 125–159.

48. https://careers.vanguard.com/vgcareers/why_vgi/story/mission.shtml.

49. "Funds: How much you're really paying," *Money*, November 2005; and https://personal. vanguard.com/us/content/Home/WhyVanguard/AboutVanguardWhoWeAreContent.jsp.

50. "Special report: China and the Internet," *The Economist*, April 6, 2013; and "How Baidu won China," *Bloomberg Businessweek*, November 11, 2010.; "China Search Engine Market Update for Q4 2013," *China Internet Watch*, March, 11, 2014.

Competitive Advantage, Firm Performance, and Business Models

Learning Objectives

LO 5-1 Conduct a firm profitability analysis using accounting data to assess and evaluate competitive advantage.

LO 5-2 Apply shareholder value creation to assess and evaluate competitive advantage.

LO 5-3 Explain economic value creation and different sources of competitive advantage.

LO 5-4 Apply a balanced scorecard to assess and evaluate competitive advantage.

LO 5-5 Apply a triple bottom line to assess and evaluate competitive advantage.

LO 5-6 Outline how business models put strategy into action.

The Quest for Competitive Advantage: Apple vs. Microsoft*

Apple and Microsoft have been fierce rivals since their arrival in the mid-1970s. Although Apple has been dominating more recently, in the early decades of the PC revolution, Microsoft was the undisputed leader. With its Windows operating system, Microsoft set the standard in the world of personal computers. Some 90 percent of all PCs run Windows. Once users are locked into a Microsoft operating system, which generally comes preloaded with the computer they purchased, they then want to buy applications that run seamlessly with the operating system. The obvious choice for users is Microsoft's Office Suite (containing Word, Excel, PowerPoint, OneNote, Outlook, Publisher, and Access), but they need to shell out several hundred dollars for the latest version. Microsoft's business model was to create a large installed base of users for its PC operating system and then make money from selling application software such as its ubiquitous Office Suite.

Steve Jobs and Bill Gates at All Things Digital 5 in 2007.
© Reprinted by permission of WSJ, Copyright July 8, 2007 Dow Jones & Company, Inc. All rights reserved worldwide.

Microsoft then went on to replicate with its corporate customers this hugely successful business model of setting the standard in operating systems combined with bundling discounted application suites. Once servers became ubiquitous in corporations, Microsoft offered IT departments e-mail systems, databases, and other business applications that were tightly integrated with Windows. As a consequence, some 80 percent of Microsoft's revenues were either tied directly or indirectly to its Windows franchise. Microsoft's strategy of focusing on setting the industry standard allowed it to create a favorable (monopoly) market position and thus to extract high profits for many years. For example, its bundling strategy with Microsoft Office, combining different application services that run seamlessly in one discounted product offering, allowed Microsoft to overtake IBM, once the most valuable tech company. By 2000, Microsoft was the most valuable company globally with some $510 billion in market capitalization.

In contrast, at roughly the same time, Apple was struggling to survive with less than 5 percent market share in the PC market. Near bankruptcy in 1997, Apple's revitalization took off in the fall of 2001 when it introduced the iPod, a portable digital music player. Eighteen months later, the Cupertino, California, company soared even higher when it opened the online store iTunes, quickly followed by its first retail stores. Apple's stores earn the highest sales per square foot of any retail outlets, including luxury stores such as jeweler Tiffany & Co. or LVMH, purveyor of fine handbags and other luxury goods.

Apple didn't stop there. In 2007, the company revolutionized the smartphone market with the introduction of the iPhone. Just three years later, Apple created the tablet computer industry by introducing the iPad, thus beginning to reshape the publishing and media industries. Further, for each of its iPod, iPhone, and iPad lines of businesses, Apple followed up with incremental product innovations extending each product category. By the fall of 2012, Apple had become the most valuable company in the world with some $620 billion market capitalization.

Two years later, in the fall of 2014, Apple introduced the hugely popular iPhone 6 and the iPhone 6 Plus, offering larger screens with higher resolution. In the spring of 2015, the high-tech company introduced Apple Watch, a watch that is fully integrated with the iOS Apple operating system, thus running basically all the apps available for the iPhone. Apple Watch also incorporates new fitness track-ing and other health-oriented capabilities. At the same time, Apple's market capitalization had further risen to almost $740 billion.

The comparison of Microsoft and Apple over time shows that competitive advantage is clearly transitory. Given the rough-and-tumble competition combined with relentless technological progress and innovation, it is hard to gain a competitive advantage in the first place, and it is even harder to sustain it.

You will learn more about Microsoft and Apple by reading the chapter; related questions appear on page 167.[1]

* A strategic financial analysis exercise related to this ChapterCase is available in Connect.

GAINING AND SUSTAINING competitive advantage is the defining goal of strategic management. Competitive advantage leads to superior firm performance. To explain differences in firm performance and to derive strategic implications—including new strategic initiatives—we must understand how to measure and assess competitive advantage. We devote this chapter to studying how to measure and assess firm performance. In particular, we introduce three frameworks to capture the multifaceted nature of competitive advantage. The three traditional frameworks to measure and assess firm performance are

- Accounting profitability.
- Shareholder value creation.
- Economic value creation.

We then will introduce two integrative frameworks, combining quantitative data with qualitative assessments:

- The balanced scorecard.
- The triple bottom line.

Next, we take a closer look at *business models* to understand more deeply how firms put their strategy into action in order to make money. We conclude the chapter with practical "Implications for the Strategist."

5.1 Competitive Advantage and Firm Performance

It is easy to compare two firms and identify the better performer as having competitive advantage. But simple comparisons have their limitations. How can we understand how and why a firm has competitive advantage? How can we measure it? How can we under-stand that advantage within the bigger picture of an entire industry and the ever-changing external environment? And what strategic implications for managerial actions do we derive from our assessments? These apparently simple questions do not have simple answers. Strategic management researchers have debated them intensely for at least 30 years.[2]

To address these key questions, we will develop a *multidimensional perspective* for assessing competitive advantage. Let's begin by focusing on the three standard performance dimensions:[3]

1. What is the firm's *accounting profitability*?
2. How much *shareholder value* does the firm create?
3. How much *economic value* does the firm generate?

These three performance dimensions tend to be correlated, particularly over time. Accounting profitability and economic value creation tend to be reflected in the firm's stock price, which in turn determines in part the stock's market valuation.

ACCOUNTING PROFITABILITY

Conduct a firm profitability analysis using accounting data to assess and evaluate competitive advantage.

As we discussed in Chapter 1, *strategy* is a set of goal-directed actions a firm takes to gain and sustain competitive advantage. Using accounting data to assess competitive advantage and firm performance is standard managerial practice. When assessing competitive advantage by measuring accounting profitability, we use financial data and ratios derived from publicly available accounting data such as income statements and balance sheets.[4] Since *competitive advantage* is defined as superior performance *relative* to other competitors in the same industry or the industry average, a firm's managers must be able to accomplish two critical tasks:

1. Accurately assess the performance of their firm.
2. Compare and benchmark their firm's performance to other competitors in the same industry or against the industry average.

Standardized financial metrics, derived from such publicly available accounting data as income statements and balance sheets, fulfill both these conditions. Public companies are required by law to release these data, in compliance with generally accepted accounting principles (GAAP) set by the Financial Accounting Standards Board (FASB), and as audited by certified public accountants. Publicly traded firms are required to file a Form 10-K (or 10-K report) annually with the U.S. Securities and Exchange Commission (SEC), a federal regulatory agency. The 10-K reports are the primary source of companies' accounting data available to the public. In the wake of the Sarbanes–Oxley Act of 2002, accounting data released to the public had to comply with even more stringent requirements. This in turn enhances the data's usefulness for comparative analysis.

Accounting data enable us to conduct direct performance comparisons between different companies. Some of the profitability ratios most commonly used in strategic management are *return on invested capital (ROIC), return on equity (ROE), return on assets (ROA),* and *return on revenue (ROR).* In the "How to Conduct a Case Analysis" module (at the end of Part 4, following the MiniCases), you will find a complete presentation of accounting measures and financial ratios, how they are calculated, and a brief description of their strategic characteristics.

One of the most commonly used metrics in assessing firm financial performance is *return on invested capital (ROIC),* where ROIC = (Net profits / Invested capital).[5] ROIC is a popular metric because it is a good proxy for *firm profitability.* In particular, the ratio measures how effectively a company uses its *total invested capital,* which consists of two components: (1) *shareholders' equity* through the selling of shares to the public, and (2) *interest-bearing debt* through borrowing from financial institutions and bondholders.

As a rule of thumb, if a firm's ROIC is greater than its cost of capital, it generates value; if it is less than the cost of capital, the firm destroys value. The *cost of capital* represents a firm's cost of financing operations from both equity through issuing stock and debt through issuing bonds. To be more precise and to be able to derive strategic implications, however, managers must compare their ROIC to other competitors.

APPLE VS. MICROSOFT To demonstrate the usefulness of accounting data in assessing competitive advantage and to derive strategic implications, let's revisit the comparison between Apple and Microsoft that we began in ChapterCase 5, and investigate the sources of performance differences in more detail. Exhibit 5.1 shows the ROIC for Apple and Microsoft (as of fiscal year 2014).[6] It further breaks down ROIC into its constituent

EXHIBIT 5.1

Comparing Apple and
Microsoft: Drivers of
Firm Performance
(2014)

Source: Analysis of publicly
available data.

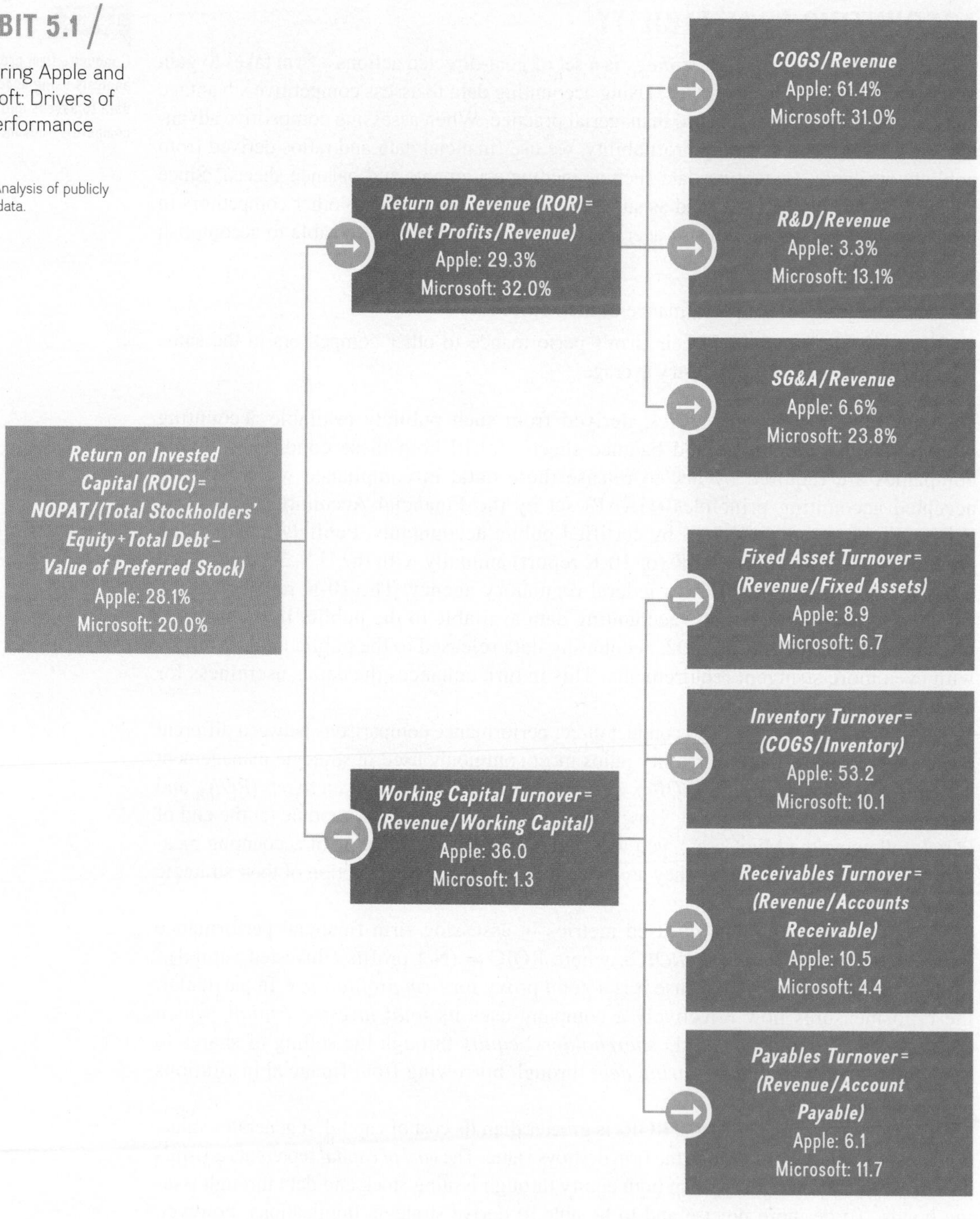

Return on Invested Capital (ROIC) =
NOPAT/(Total Stockholders' Equity + Total Debt − Value of Preferred Stock)
Apple: 28.1%
Microsoft: 20.0%

Return on Revenue (ROR) =
(Net Profits/Revenue)
Apple: 29.3%
Microsoft: 32.0%

COGS/Revenue
Apple: 61.4%
Microsoft: 31.0%

R&D/Revenue
Apple: 3.3%
Microsoft: 13.1%

SG&A/Revenue
Apple: 6.6%
Microsoft: 23.8%

Working Capital Turnover =
(Revenue/Working Capital)
Apple: 36.0
Microsoft: 1.3

Fixed Asset Turnover =
(Revenue/Fixed Assets)
Apple: 8.9
Microsoft: 6.7

Inventory Turnover =
(COGS/Inventory)
Apple: 53.2
Microsoft: 10.1

Receivables Turnover =
(Revenue/Accounts Receivable)
Apple: 10.5
Microsoft: 4.4

Payables Turnover =
(Revenue/Account Payable)
Apple: 6.1
Microsoft: 11.7

components. This provides important clues for managers on which areas to focus when attempting to improve firm performance relative to their competitors.

Apple's ROIC was 28.1 percent, which was more than 8 percentage points higher than Microsoft's (20.0 percent). This means that for every $1.00 invested in Apple, the company returned almost $1.28, while for every $1.00 invested in the company, Microsoft returned

$1.20. Since Apple was 40 percent more efficient than Microsoft at generating a return on invested capital, Apple had a clear competitive advantage over Microsoft. Although this is an important piece of information, managers need to know the underlying factors driving differences in firm profitability. Why is the ROIC for these two companies so different?

Much like detectives, managers look for clues to solve that mystery: They break down ROIC into its constituents (as shown in Exhibit 5.1)—*return on revenue* and *working capital turnover*—to discover the underlying drivers of the marked difference in firm profitability.

We start with the first component of ROIC. *Return on revenue (ROR)* indicates how much of the firm's sales is converted into profits. Apple's ROR was 29.3 percent, while Microsoft's ROR was 32 percent. For every $100 in revenues, Apple earns $29.30 in profit, while Microsoft earns $32 in profit. On this metric, Microsoft had a slight edge over Apple. Keep in mind, however, that Apple's 2014 revenues were $183 billion, while Microsoft's were $83 billion. Thus, Apple is 2.2 times larger than Microsoft in terms of annual sales. As we investigate the differences in ROIC further, we will also discover that Microsoft has a higher cost structure than Apple, and that Apple is able to charge a much higher margin for its products and services than Microsoft.

To explore further drivers of this difference, we break down return on revenue into three additional financial ratios:

- Cost of goods sold (COGS) / Revenue.
- Research & development (R&D) expense / Revenue.
- Selling, general, & administrative (SG&A) expense / Revenue.

The first of these three ratios, *COGS / Revenue,* indicates how efficiently a company can produce a good. On this metric, Microsoft turns out to be much more efficient than Apple, with a difference of over 30 percentage points (see Exhibit 5.1). This is because Microsoft's vast majority of revenues (87 percent) came from software and online services, with little cost attached to such digitally delivered products and services. In contrast, Apple's revenues were mostly from mobile devices, combining both hardware and software. In particular, the iPhone made up two-thirds (or over $120 billion) of Apple's total revenues (in 2014).

Even though Apple is more than two times as large as Microsoft in terms of revenues, it spends much less on research and development or on marketing and sales. Both of these help drive down Apple's cost structure. In particular, the next ratio, *R&D / Revenue,* indicates how much of each dollar that the firm earns in sales is invested to conduct research and development. A higher percentage is generally an indicator of a stronger focus on innovation to improve current products and services, and to come up with new ones.

Interestingly, Apple's R&D is much less intense than Microsoft's. Apple spent 3.3 percent on R&D for every dollar of revenue, while Microsoft spent almost four times as much (13.1 percent R&D). Even considering the fact that Microsoft's revenues were $83 billion versus Apple's $183 billion, Microsoft ($11 billion) spent more on R&D in absolute dollars than Apple ($6 billion). For every $100 earned in revenues Microsoft spent $13.10 on R&D, while Apple only spent $3.30. For more than a decade now, Microsoft generally spends the most on R&D in absolute terms among all technology firms.

In contrast, Apple has spent much less on research and development than other firms in the high-tech industry, in both absolute and relative terms. Apple's co-founder and long-time CEO, the late Steve Jobs, defined Apple's R&D philosophy as follows: "Innovation has nothing to do with how many R&D dollars you have. When Apple came up with the Mac, IBM was spending at least 100 times more on R&D. It's not about money. It's about the people you have, how you're led, and how much you get it."[7]

The third ratio in breaking down return on revenue, *SG&A / Revenue,* indicates how much of each dollar that the firm earns in sales is invested in sales, general, and administrative (SG&A) expenses. Generally, this ratio is an indicator of the firm's focus on marketing and sales to promote its products and services. Again, Microsoft ($20 billion) not only outspent Apple ($18.3 billion) in absolute terms in marketing and sales expenses, but its SG&A intensity was more than 3.5 times as high as Apple's. For every $100 earned in revenues Microsoft spent $23.80 on sales and marketing, while Apple spent $6.60.

The second component of ROIC is *working capital turnover* (see Exhibit 5.1), which is a measure of how effectively capital is being used to generate revenue. This is where Apple outperforms Microsoft by a wide margin (36.0 vs. 1.3). For every dollar that Apple puts to work, it realizes a whopping $36.00 of sales; this rate is more than 28 times higher than the conversion rate for Microsoft, which only realizes $1.30 in sales for each dollar invested.

This huge difference provides an important clue for Microsoft's managers to dig deeper to find the underlying drivers in working capital turnover. This enables managers to uncover which levers to pull in order to improve firm financial performance. In a next step, therefore, managers break down working capital turnover into other ratios, including *fixed asset turnover, inventory turnover, receivables turnover,* and *payables turnover.* Each of these metrics is a measure of how effective a particular item on the balance sheet is contributing to revenue.

Fixed asset turnover (Revenue / Fixed assets) measures how well a company leverages its fixed assets, particularly property, plant, and equipment (PPE). Microsoft's fixed assets contribute $6.70 of revenue for every dollar spent on PPE, while each dollar of Apple's fixed assets generates $8.90. This ratio indicates how much of a firm's capital is tied up in its fixed assets. Higher fixed assets often go along with lower firm valuations (more on this in the section "Shareholder Value Creation" later in this chapter).

The performance difference between Apple and Microsoft in regard to *inventory turnover (COGS / Inventory)* is even more striking. Cost of goods sold (COGS) captures the firm's production cost of merchandise it *has sold.* Inventory is the cost of the firm's merchandise *to be* sold. This ratio indicates how much of a firm's capital is tied up in its inventory. Apple turned over its inventory more than 53 times during 2014, which implies that the company had very little capital tied up in its inventory. Apple benefited from strong demand for its products, as well as an effective management of its global supply chain. The vast majority of Apple's manufacturing is done in China by low-cost producer Foxconn, which employs over 1.2 million people.

In stark contrast, Microsoft turned over its inventory only about 10 times during the year. The firm's cost of hardware products to be sold was very high, because Microsoft acquired Nokia's mobile phone business for over $7 billion to more effectively compete against Apple. With the Nokia purchase, however, came a huge pile of unsold Lumia phones, added to Microsoft's inventory of unsold Surface tablet computers, tying up billions of dollars. In addition, Microsoft has likely higher production costs than Apple. Rather than outsourcing manufacturing to Foxconn or other original equipment manufacturers (OEMs), Microsoft owns and operates its manufacturing facilities. They are also located in countries with a generally higher cost structure (e.g., Brazil and Mexico, among others) than China. In comparison to Microsoft, Apple turned over its inventory more than five times faster! This big difference can be explained by disappointing demand for Lumia phones and Surface tablet computers and the lack of any exciting new product launches. Consumers continued to migrate to Apple iPhones, especially its popular iPhone 6, which launched in 2014.

The final set of financial ratios displayed in Exhibit 5.1 concerns the effectiveness of a company's receivables and payables. These are part of a company's cash flow management; they indicate the company's efficiency in extending credit, as well as collecting debts.

Higher ratios of *receivables turnover (Revenue / Accounts receivable)* imply more efficient management in collecting accounts receivable and shorter durations of interest-free loans to customers (i.e., time until payments are due). In contrast, *payables turnover (Revenue / Accounts payable)* indicates how fast the firm is paying its creditors and how much it benefits from interest-free loans extended by its suppliers. A lower ratio indicates more efficient management in paying creditors and generating interest-free loans from suppliers.

In the two dimensions of cash flow management, Apple displays a clear advantage over Microsoft. *Apple is paid much faster than Microsoft.* This might be explained by the fact that Apple's customers are mainly individual consumers who tend to pay with cash or credit cards at the time of purchase, while Microsoft's most important customers are other businesses, in particular, OEMs that make PCs and corporate IT departments and governments (who request to be invoiced, and thus pay later). On the other hand, *Apple takes quite a bit longer to pay its creditors.* Due to its stronger negotiating power, Apple might also be able to extend its payment periods, while Microsoft may be required to pay its creditors more quickly.

Satya Nadella, CEO Microsoft
© Brian Smale/
Microsoft/Getty Images

A deeper understanding of the fundamental drivers for differences in firm profitability allows managers to develop strategic approaches. For example, Satya Nadella, Microsoft's CEO since 2014, could rework Microsoft's cost structure, in particular, its very high R&D and SG&A spending. Perhaps, R&D dollars could be spent more effectively? Apple generates a much higher return to its R&D spending. Microsoft's sales and marketing expenses also seem to be quite high, but may be needed to rebuild Microsoft's brand image with a new focus on mobile and cloud computing. One of the biggest drains on operating profits for Microsoft is the multibillion-dollar Nokia handset acquisition, resulting in low *working capital turnover* and *inventory turnover* ratios.

LIMITATIONS OF ACCOUNTING DATA Although accounting data tend to be readily available and we can easily transform them into financial ratios to assess and evaluate competitive performance, they also exhibit some important limitations:

- *All accounting data are historical and thus backward-looking.* Accounting profitability ratios show us only the outcomes from past decisions, and the past is no guarantee of future performance. There is also a significant time delay before accounting data become publicly available. Some strategists liken making decisions using accounting data to driving a car by looking in the rearview mirror.[8] While financial strength certainly helps, past performance is no guarantee that a company is prepared for market disruption. Rather, as we saw in Chapter 4, IBM survived over the last century only by complete transformation of its capabilities multiple times in response to radical technological innovations.

- *Accounting data do not consider off–balance sheet items.* Off–balance sheet items, such as pension obligations (quite large in some U.S. companies) or operating leases in the retail industry, can be significant factors. For example, one retailer may own all its stores, which would properly be included in the firm's assets; a second retailer may lease all its stores, which would *not be* listed as assets. All else being equal, the second retailer's return on assets (ROA) would be higher. Strategists address this shortcoming by adjusting accounting data to obtain an *equivalent* economic capital base, so that they can compare companies with different capital structures.

- *Accounting data focus mainly on tangible assets, which are no longer the most important.*[9] This limitation of accounting data is nicely captured in the adage: *Not everything that can be counted counts. Not everything that counts can be counted.*[10] Although accounting data capture some intangible assets, such as the value of intellectual property (patents, trademarks, and so on) and customer goodwill, many key intangible assets are not captured. Today, the most competitively important assets tend to be intangibles such as innovation, quality, and customer experience, which are not included in a firm's balance sheets. For example, Tesla's core competency in designing high-performance all-electric vehicles is not a balance sheet item, but nonetheless a critical foundation in its quest for competitive advantage.

INTANGIBLES AND THE VALUE OF FIRMS Intangible assets that are not captured in accounting data have become much more important in firms' stock market valuations over the last few decades. Exhibit 5.2 shows the firm's book value (accounting data capturing the firm's actual costs of assets minus depreciation) as part of a firm's total stock market valuation (number of outstanding shares times share price). The firm's book value captures the historical cost of a firm's assets, whereas market valuation is based on future expectations for a firm's growth potential and performance. For the firms in the S&P 500 (the 500 largest publicly traded companies by market capitalization in the U.S. stock market, as determined by Standard & Poor's, a rating agency), the importance of a firm's book value has declined dramatically over time. This decline mirrors a commensurate increase in the importance of intangibles that contribute to growth potential and yet are not captured in a firm's accounting data.

In 1980, about 80 percent of a firm's stock market valuation was based on its book value with 20 percent based on the market's expectations concerning the firm's future performance. This almost reversed by 2000 (at the height of the Internet bubble), when firm valuations were based only 15 percent on assets captured by accounting data. The important take-away is that intangibles not captured in firms' accounting data have become much more important to a firm's competitive advantage. By 2015, about 75 percent of a firm's market valuation was determined by its intangibles. This explains why Google ($365 billion) is valued over six times more than GM ($59 billion), or why Facebook ($234 billion) is valued more than twice as much as Boeing ($110 billion).

So what have we learned about accounting profitability? Key financial ratios based on accounting data give us an important tool with which to assess competitive advantage. In particular, they help us measure *relative* profitability, which is useful when comparing firms of different sizes over time. While not perfect, these ratios are an important starting point when analyzing the competitive performance of firms (and thus are a critical tool for case analysis). Again, see the "How to Conduct a Case Analysis" module (at the end of Part 4). We next turn to *shareholder value creation* as a second traditional way to measure and assess competitive advantage, attempting to overcome the shortcomings of a backward-looking internal focus on mostly tangible assets inherent in accounting profitability.

EXHIBIT 5.2 / The Declining Importance of Book Value in a Firm's Stock Market Valuation, 1980–2015

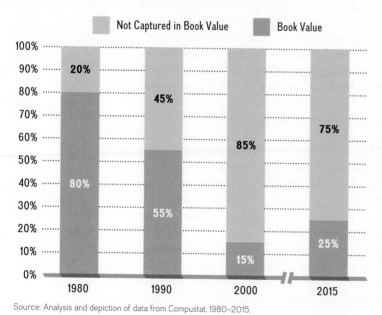

Source: Analysis and depiction of data from Compustat, 1980–2015.

SHAREHOLDER VALUE CREATION

Shareholders—individuals or organizations that own one or more shares of stock in a public company—are the legal owners of public companies. From the shareholders' perspective, the measure of competitive advantage that matters most is the return on their **risk capital**,[11] which is the money they provide in return for an equity share, money that they cannot recover if the firm goes bankrupt. In September 2008, the shareholders of Lehman Brothers, a global financial services firm, lost their entire investment of about $40 billion when the firm declared bankruptcy.

Investors are primarily interested in a company's **total return to shareholders**, which is the return on risk capital, including stock price appreciation plus dividends received over a specific period. Unlike accounting data, total return to shareholders is an *external* and *forward-looking* performance metric. It essentially indicates how the stock market views all available public information about a firm's past, current state, and expected future performance, with most of the weight on future growth expectations. The idea that all available information about a firm's past, current state, and expected future performance is embedded in the market price of the firm's stock is called the *efficient-market hypothesis.*[12] In this perspective, a firm's share price provides an objective performance indicator. When assessing and evaluating competitive advantage, a comparison of rival firms' share price development or market capitalization provides a helpful yardstick when used over the *long term.* **Market capitalization** (or market cap) captures the total dollar market value of a company's total outstanding shares at any given point in time (*Market cap = Number of outstanding shares × Share price*). If a company has 50 million shares outstanding, and each share is traded at $200, the market capitalization is $10 billion (50,000,000 × $200 = $10,000,000,000, or $10 billion).[13]

All public companies in the United States are required to report total return to shareholders annually in the statements they file with the Securities and Exchange Commission (SEC). In addition, companies must also provide benchmarks, usually one comparison to the industry average and another to a broader market index that is relevant for more diversified firms.[14] Since competitive advantage is defined in relative terms, these benchmarks allow us to assess whether a firm has a competitive advantage. In its annual reports, Microsoft, for example, compares its performance to two stock indices: the NASDAQ computer index and the S&P 500. The computer index includes over 400 high-tech companies traded on the NASDAQ, including Apple, Adobe, Google, Intel, and Oracle. It provides a comparison of Microsoft to the computer industry—broadly defined. The S&P 500 offers a comparison to the wider stock market beyond the computer industry. In its 2014 annual report, Microsoft shows that it *underperformed* in comparison to both, the NASDAQ computer index and the S&P 500 since 2009, with the gap widening over time.[15] This is one reason Satya Nadella was appointed Microsoft's CEO in early 2014, following Steve Ballmer, who had served as CEO since 2000.

Effective strategies to grow the business can increase a firm's profitability and thus its stock price.[16] Indeed, investors and Wall Street analysts expect continuous growth. A firm's stock price generally increases only if the firm's rate of growth exceeds investors' expectations. This is because investors discount into the present value of the firm's stock price whatever growth rate they foresee in the future. If a low-growth business like Comcast (in cable TV) is expected to grow 2 percent each year but realizes 4 percent growth, its stock price will appreciate. In contrast, if a fast-growing business like Apple in mobile computing is expected to grow by 10 percent annually but delivers "only" 8 percent growth, its stock price will fall.

Investors also adjust their expectations over time. Since the business in the slow-growth industry surprised them by delivering higher than expected growth, they adjust their expectations upward. The next year, they expect this firm to again deliver 4 percent growth. On the other hand, if the industry average is 10 percent a year in the high-tech business, the firm that delivered 8 percent growth will again be expected to deliver at least the industry average growth rate; otherwise, its stock will be further discounted.

In ChapterCase 5, we noted that Apple was the most valuable company on the planet. In early 2015, Apple's market cap was a whopping $727 billion, twice as high as the second most valuable company worldwide, Exxon Mobil with $360 billion in market cap. Considering stock market valuations (*Share price × Number of outstanding shares*) over the long term provides a useful metric to assess competitive advantage. Exhibit 5.3 shows the stock market valuations for Apple and Microsoft from 1990 until early 2015. Microsoft was once the most valuable company worldwide (in December 1999 with close to $600 billion in market cap), but since then its market valuation has dropped more than 40 percent. The valuation declined because investors now have lower expectations concerning Microsoft's ability to deliver profitable growth in the future. In particular, Microsoft struggles with the transition from desktop to mobile computing. CEO Satya Nadella vows to move Microsoft away from its Windows-only business model to compete more effectively in a "mobile-first, cloud-first world."[17] It appears that investors view this strategic shift in a positive way because they believe it will put Microsoft on a future growth trajectory. Since a low in Microsoft's market cap of about $220 billion in early 2013, it has grown by more than 50 percent to over $340 billion by spring 2015. Nonetheless, Microsoft remains well below Apple, as Exhibit 5.3 clearly shows using market cap as its metric. This shows again that it is difficult to gain a competitive advantage, and even harder to sustain it over a prolonged period of time. *Competitive advantage is transitory!*

LIMITATIONS OF SHAREHOLDER VALUE CREATION Although measuring firm performance through total return to shareholders and firm market capitalization has many advantages, just as with accounting profitability, it has its shortcomings:

■ *Stock prices can be highly volatile, making it difficult to assess firm performance, particularly in the short term.* This volatility implies that *total return to shareholders* is a better measure of firm performance and competitive advantage over the long term, because of the "noise" introduced by market volatility, external factors, and investor sentiment.

EXHIBIT 5.3

Stock Market Valuations of Apple and Microsoft, 1990–2015

Source: Depiction of publicly available data using YCHARTS; www.ycharts.com.

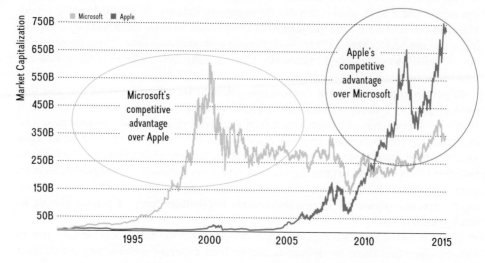

■ *Overall macroeconomic factors such as economic growth or contraction, the unem- ployment rate, and interest and exchange rates all have a direct bearing on stock prices.* It can be difficult to ascertain the extent to which a stock price is influenced more by external macroeconomic factors (as discussed in Chapter 3) than by the firm's strategy (see also Exhibit 1.1 highlighting firm, industry, and other effects in overall firm performance).

■ *Stock prices frequently reflect the psychological mood of investors, which can at times be irrational.* Stock prices can overshoot expectations based on economic fundamen- tals amid periods like the Internet boom, during which former Federal Reserve Chair- man Alan Greenspan famously described investors' buoyant sentiments as "irrational exuberance."[18] Similarly, stock prices can undershoot expectations during busts like the 2008–2009 global financial crisis, during which investors' sentiment was described as "irrational gloom."[19]

ECONOMIC VALUE CREATION

The relationship between *economic value creation* and competitive advantage is funda- mental in strategic management. It provides the foundation upon which to formulate a firm's competitive strategy for cost leadership or differentiation (discussed in detail in the next chapter). For now, it is important to note that a firm has a competitive advantage when it creates more *economic value* than rival firms. What does that mean?

Economic value created is the difference between a buyer's willingness to pay for a product or service and the firm's total cost to produce it. Let's assume you consider buying a laptop computer and you have a budget of $1,200. You have narrowed your search to two models, one offered by Firm A, the other by Firm B. Your subjective assessment of the ben- efits derived from owning Firm A's laptop is $1,000—this is the absolute maximum you'd be willing to pay for it, or the **reservation price**. For example, this could be a more or less generic, run-of-the-mill Dell laptop. In contrast, you value Firm B's laptop model at $1,200 because it has somewhat higher performance, is more user-friendly, and definitely has a higher "coolness-factor." Think of Apple's MacBook Pro with Retina display. Given that you value Firm B's laptop by $200 more than Firm A's model, you will purchase a laptop from Firm B (and, in this case, end up paying as much as your reservation price allows).

Let's move now from your individual considerations to the overall market for laptop com- puters in order to derive implications for firm-level competitive advantage. To simplify this illustration, only Firm A and Firm B are competing in the market for laptops. Assuming that both Firm A and Firm B have the same total unit cost of producing the particular laptop models under consideration ($400) and the market at large has preferences similar to yours, then Firm B will have a competitive advantage. This is because Firm B creates more eco- nomic value than Firm A (by $200), but has the same total cost, depicted in Exhibit 5.4. The amount of *total perceived consumer benefits* equals the *maximum willingness to pay,* or the *reservation price.* This amount is then split into economic value creation and the firm's total unit cost. Firm A and Firm B have identical total unit cost, $400 per laptop. However, Firm B's laptop (e.g., Apple's MacBook Pro) is perceived to provide more utility than Firm A's laptop (e.g., Dell's generic laptop), which implies that Firm B creates more economic value ($1,200 − $400 = $800) than Firm A ($1,000 − $400 = $600). Taken together, Firm B has a competitive advantage over Firm A because Firm B creates more economic value. This is because Firm B's offering has greater total perceived consumer benefits than Firm A's, while the firms have the same total cost. In short, Firm B's advantage is based on superior *differen- tiation* leading to higher perceived value. Further, the competitive advantage can be quanti- fied: It is $200 (or, $1,200 − $1,000) per laptop sold for Firm B over Firm A (see Exhibit 5.4).

LO 5-3

Explain economic value creation and different sources of competitive advantage.

economic value created Difference between value (*V*) and cost (*C*), or (*V − C*).

reservation price The maximum price a consumer is willing to pay for a product or service based on the total perceived consumer benefits.

EXHIBIT 5.4 / Firm B's Competitive Advantage: Same Cost as Firm A but Firm B Creates More Economic Value

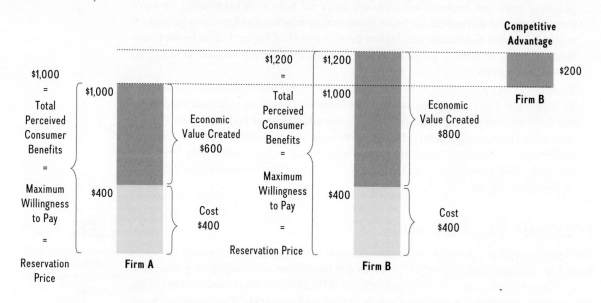

Exhibit 5.4 shows that Firm B's competitive advantage is based on greater economic value creation because of superior product differentiation. In addition, a firm can achieve competitive advantage through a second avenue. In particular, competitive advantage can also result from a relative *cost advantage* over rivals, assuming both firms can create the same total perceived consumer benefits.

As shown in Exhibit 5.5, two different laptop makers each offer a model that has the same perceived consumer benefits ($1,200). Firm C, however, creates economic value greater ($900, or $1,200 − $300) than that of Firm B ($600, or $1,200 − $600). This is because Firm C's total unit cost ($300) is lower than Firm D's ($600). Firm C has a relative cost advantage over Firm D, while both products provide identical total perceived consumer benefits ($1,200). In this example, Firm C could be Lenovo with lower cost structure than Firm D, which could be HP, but both firms offer the same value. As Exhibit 5.5 shows,

EXHIBIT 5.5 / Firm C's Competitive Advantage: Same Total Perceived Consumer Benefits as Firm D but Firm C Creates More Economic Value

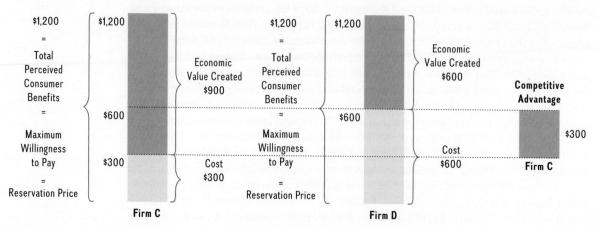

Firm C has a competitive advantage over Firm D because it has lower costs. Firm C's competitive advantage over Firm D is in the amount of $300 for each laptop sold. Here, the source of the competitive advantage is a relative cost advantage over its rival.

So far we have looked at situations in which products are priced at the maximum a consumer might be willing to pay. But markets generally don't work like that. More often, the economic value created is shared among the producer and the consumer. That is, most of the time consumers are able to purchase the product at a price point below the maximum they are willing to spend. Both the seller and the buyer benefit.

For ease in calculating competitive advantage, three components are needed. These will help us to further explain *total perceived consumer benefits* and *economic value created* in more detail:

1. Value (*V*)
2. Price (*P*)
3. Cost (*C*)

Value denotes the dollar amount (*V*) a consumer attaches to a good or service. Value captures a consumer's willingness to pay and is determined by the perceived benefits a good or service provides to the buyer. The cost (*C*) to produce the good or service matters little to the consumer, but it matters a great deal to the producer (supplier) of the good or service since it has a direct bearing on the profit margin.

Let's return to our laptop example from Exhibit 5.4, in which two firms sold their laptops at different prices ($1,000 for Firm A and $1,200 for Firm B), even though the costs were the same ($400). In each case, the price matched the consumer's maximum willingness to pay for the particular offering. Subtracting the costs, we found that Firm A created an economic value of $600 while Firm B created an economic value of $800, thus achieving a competitive advantage. In most market transactions, however, some of the economic value created benefits the consumer as well.

Again, let's revisit the example depicted in Exhibit 5.4. The consumer's preference was to buy the laptop from Firm B, which she would have done because it matched her reservation price. Let's assume Firm B's laptop is actually on sale for $1,000 (everything else remains constant). Assume the consumer again chose to purchase the laptop of Firm B rather than the one offered by Firm A (which she considered inferior). In this case, some of the economic value created by Firm B goes to the consumer. On a formula basis, total perceived value of Firm B's laptop ($1,200) splits into *economic value created* (*V* − *C* = $800) plus *total unit cost* (*C* = $400), or: $V = (V - C) + C$.

The difference between the price charged (*P*) and the cost to produce (*C*) is the **profit**, or **producer surplus**. In the laptop example in Exhibit 5.6, if the price charged is $1,000, the profit is $P - C = \$1,000 - \$400 = \$600$. The firm captures this amount as profit per unit sold. As the consumer, you capture the difference between what you would have been willing to pay (*V*) and what you paid (*P*), called **consumer surplus**. In our example, the consumer surplus is $V - P = \$1,200 - \$1,000$, or $200. *Economic value creation* therefore equals *consumer surplus* plus *firm profit*, or $(V - C) = (V - P) + (P - C)$. In the laptop example:

Economic Value Created ($1,200 − $400) = Consumer Surplus ($1,200 − $1,000) + Producer surplus ($1,000 − $400) = $200 + $600 = $800.

The relationship between consumer and producer surplus is the reason trade happens: Both transacting parties capture *some* of the overall value created. Note, though, that the distribution of the value created between parties need not be equal to make trade worthwhile. In the example above (illustrated in Exhibit 5.6), the consumer surplus was $200, while profit per unit sold was $600.

In some cases, where firms offer highly innovative products or services, the relationship can be even more skewed. The entry-level model of the Apple Watch retailed for $349

value
The dollar amount (*V*) a consumer attaches to a good or service; the consumer's maximum willingness to pay; also called *reservation price*.

profit
Difference between price charged (*P*) and the cost to produce (*C*), or (*P* − *C*); also called *producer surplus*.

producer surplus
Another term for profit, the difference between price charged (*P*) and the cost to produce (*C*), or (*P* − *C*); also called *profit*.

consumer surplus
Difference between the value a consumer attaches to a good or service (*V*) and what he or she paid for it (*P*), or (*V* − *P*).

EXHIBIT 5.6 / The Role of Consumer Surplus and Producer Surplus (Profit)

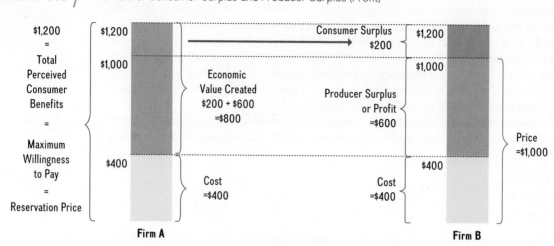

(in 2015), and the high-tech firm is predicted to sell millions of it. An analysis by an independent engineering team, however, revealed that the firm's total cost in terms of materials and labor for the Apple Watch is no more than $84.[20] Thus, Apple's profit for each watch sold is an estimated $265, with a profit margin of 315 percent.

The economic value creation framework shows that strategy is about

1. Creating economic value.
2. Capturing as much of it as possible.

In contrast to Apple, consider Amazon as a counter-example: It is creating a large amount of value for its customers, but it is not capturing much, if any, of it. Amazon has had several years of negative net income as it attempts to build a stronger position in a variety of businesses. Its cloud computing service offering, Amazon Web Services (AWS), for example, is creating huge value for the businesses that run its computing needs on AWS, businesses including Airbnb, Condé Nast, Comcast, Foursquare, HTC, NASA, Nokia, and Pfizer, but Amazon's "profit" margin is a negative 1 to 2 percent.[21] In this case, Amazon's customers are capturing the value that Amazon is creating.

Exhibit 5.7 illustrates how the components of economic value creation fit together conceptually. On the left side of the graph, *V* represents the total perceived consumer benefits, as captured in the consumer's maximum willingness to pay. In the lower part of the center bar, *C* is the cost to produce the product or service (the unit cost). It follows that the difference between the consumers' maximum willingness to pay and the firm's cost $(V - C)$ is the economic value created. The price of the product or service (P) is indicated in the dashed line. The economic value created $(V - C)$, as shown in Exhibit 5.7, is split between producer and consumer: $(V - P)$ is the value the consumer captures (*consumer surplus*), and $(P - C)$ is the value the producer captures (*producer surplus, or profit*).

Competitive advantage goes to the firm that achieves the largest economic value created, which is the difference between *V*, the consumer's willingness to pay, and *C*, the cost to produce the good or service. The reason is that a large difference between *V* and *C* gives the firm two distinct pricing options: (1) It can charge higher prices to reflect the higher value and thus increase its profitability, or (2) it can charge the same price as competitors and thus gain market share. Given this, the strategic objective is to maximize $(V - C)$, or the economic value created.

Applying the notion of *economic value creation* also has direct implications for firm financial performance. Revenues are a function of the value created for consumers and the

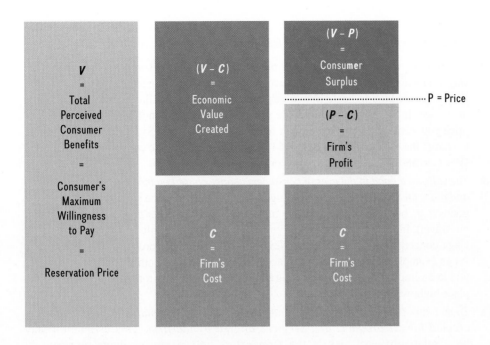

EXHIBIT 5.7

Competitive Advantage and Economic Value Created: The Role of Value, Cost, and Price

price of the good or service, which together drive the volume of goods sold. In this perspective, profit (*Π*) is defined as total revenues (*TR*) minus total costs (*TC*):

$$\Pi = TR - TC, \text{ where } TR = P \times Q, \text{ or price times quantity sold}$$

Total costs include both fixed and variable costs. *Fixed costs* are independent of consumer demand—for example, the cost of capital to build computer manufacturing plants or an online retail presence to take direct orders. *Variable costs* change with the level of consumer demand—for instance, components such as different types of display screens, microprocessors, hard drives, and keyboards.

Rather than merely relying on historical costs, as done when taking the perspective of *accounting profitability* (introduced earlier), in the *economic value creation* perspective, *all costs,* including *opportunity costs,* must be considered. **Opportunity costs** capture the value of the best forgone alternative use of the resources employed.

An entrepreneur, for example, faces two types of opportunity costs: (1) forgone wages she could be earning if she was employed elsewhere and (2) the cost of capital she invested in her business, which could instead be invested in, say, the stock market or U.S. Treasury bonds. At the end of the year, the entrepreneur considers her business over the last 12 months. She made an *accounting profit* of $70,000, calculated as total revenues minus expenses, which include all historical costs but not opportunity costs. But she also realizes she has forgone $60,000 in salary she could have earned as an employee at another firm. In addition, she knows she could have earned $15,000 in interest if she had bought U.S. Treasury bills with a 2 percent return instead of investing $750,000 in her business. The opportunity cost of being an entrepreneur was $75,000 ($60,000 + $15,000). Therefore, when considering all costs, including opportunity costs, she actually experienced an economic loss of $5,000 ($75,000 − $70,000). When considering her future options, she should stay in business only if she values her independence as an entrepreneur more than $5,000 per year, or thinks business will be better next year.

opportunity costs
The value of the best forgone alternative use of the resources employed.

LIMITATIONS OF ECONOMIC VALUE CREATION As with any tool to assess competitive advantage, the economic value creation framework also has some limitations:

■ *Determining the value of a good in the eyes of consumers is not a simple task.* One way to tackle this problem is to look at consumers' purchasing habits for their revealed preferences, which indicate how much each consumer is willing to pay for a product or service. In the earlier example, the value (V) you placed on the laptop—the highest price you were willing to pay, or your reservation price—was \$1,200. If the firm is able to charge the reservation price ($P = \$1,200$), it captures all the economic value created ($V - C = \$800$) as producer surplus or profit ($P - C = \$800$).

■ *The value of a good in the eyes of consumers changes based on income, preferences, time, and other factors.* If your income is high, you are likely to place a higher value on some goods (e.g., business-class air travel) and a lower value on other goods (e.g., Greyhound bus travel). In regard to preferences, you may place a higher value on a ticket for a Lady Gaga concert than on one for the New York Philharmonic orchestra (or vice versa). As an example of time value, you place a higher value on an airline ticket that will get you to an important business meeting tomorrow than on one for a planned trip to take place eight weeks from now.

■ *To measure firm-level competitive advantage, we must estimate the economic value created for all products and services offered by the firm.* This estimation may be a relatively easy task if the firm offers only a few products or services. However, it becomes much more complicated for diversified firms such as General Electric or the Tata Group that may offer hundreds or even thousands of different products and services across many industries and geographies. Although the performance of individual strategic business units (SBUs) can be assessed along the dimensions described here, it becomes more difficult to make this assessment at the corporate level (more on this in our discussion of diversification strategy in Chapter 8).

The economic value creation perspective gives us one useful way to assess competitive advantage. This approach is conceptually quite powerful, and it lies at the center of many strategic management frameworks such as the generic business strategies (which we discuss in the next chapter). However, it falls somewhat short when managers are called upon to operationalize competitive advantage. When the need for "hard numbers" arises, managers and analysts frequently rely on firm financials such as *accounting profitability* or *shareholder value creation* to measure firm performance.

We've now completed our consideration of the three standard dimensions for measuring competitive advantage—accounting profitability, shareholder value, and economic value. Although each provides unique insights for assessing competitive advantage, one drawback is that they are more or less one-dimensional metrics. Focusing on just one performance metric when assessing competitive advantage, however, can lead to significant problems, because each metric has its shortcomings, as listed earlier. We now turn to two more conceptual and qualitative frameworks—the balanced scorecard and the triple bottom line—that attempt to provide a more holistic perspective on firm performance.

THE BALANCED SCORECARD

LO 5-4

Apply a balanced scorecard to assess and evaluate competitive advantage.

Just as airplane pilots rely on a number of instruments to provide constant information about key variables—such as altitude, airspeed, fuel, position of other aircraft in the vicinity, and destination—to ensure a safe flight, so should managers rely on multiple yardsticks to more accurately assess company performance in an integrative way. The **balanced scorecard** is a framework to help managers achieve their strategic objectives more effectively.[22] This approach harnesses multiple internal and external performance metrics in order to balance both financial and strategic goals.

Exhibit 5.8 depicts the balanced-scorecard framework. Managers using the balanced scorecard develop appropriate metrics to assess strategic objectives by answering four key questions.[23] Brainstorming answers to these questions ideally results in a set of measures that give managers a quick but also comprehensive view of the firm's current state. The four key questions are:

1. *How do customers view us?* The customer's perspective concerning the company's products and services links directly to its revenues and profits. Consumers decide their reservation price for a product or service based on how they view it. If the customer views the company's offering favorably, she is willing to pay more for it, enhancing its competitive advantage (assuming production costs are well below the asking price). Managers track customer perception to identify areas to improve, with a focus on speed, quality, service, and cost. In the air-express industry, for example, managers learned from their customers that many don't really need next-day delivery for most of their documents and packages; rather what they really cared about was the ability to track the shipments. This discovery led to the development of steeply discounted second-day delivery by UPS and FedEx, combined with sophisticated real-time tracking tools online.

2. *How do we create value?* Answering this question challenges managers to develop strategic objectives that ensure future competitiveness, innovation, and organizational learning. The answer focuses on the business processes and structures that allow a firm to create economic value. One useful metric is the percentage of revenues obtained from new product introductions. For example, 3M requires that 30 percent of revenues must come from products introduced within the last four years.[24] A second metric, aimed at assessing a firm's external learning and collaboration capability, is to stipulate that a certain percentage of new products must originate from outside the firm's boundaries.[25] Through its Connect + Develop program, the consumer products company Procter & Gamble has raised the percentage of new products that originated (at least partly) from outside P&G, from 15 to 35 percent.[26]

3. *What core competencies do we need?* This question focuses managers internally, to identify the core competencies needed to achieve their objectives and the accompanying business processes that support, hone, and leverage those competencies. As mentioned in the last chapter, Honda's core competency is to design and manufacture small but powerful and highly reliable engines. Its business model is to find places to put its engines. Beginning with motorcycles in 1948, Honda nurtured this core competency over many decades and is leveraging it to reach stretch goals in the design, development, and manufacture of small airplanes.

> **balanced scorecard**
> Strategy implementation tool that harnesses multiple internal and external performance metrics in order to balance financial and strategic goals.

EXHIBIT 5.8 / Balanced-Scorecard Approach to Creating and Sustaining Competitive Advantage

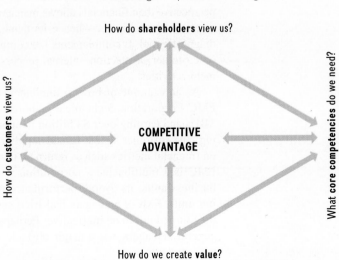

Today, consumers still value reliable, gas-powered engines made by Honda. If consumers start to value electric motors more because of zero emissions, lower maintenance costs, and higher performance metrics, among other possible reasons, the value of Honda's engine competency will decrease. If this happens, then Tesla's core competency in designing and building high-powered battery packs and electric drivetrains will become more valuable. In turn, Tesla might then be able to leverage this core competency into a strong strategic position in the emerging all-electric car and mobility industry.

4. *How do shareholders view us?* The final perspective in the balanced scorecard is the shareholders' view of financial performance (as discussed in the prior section). Some of the measures in this area rely on accounting data such as cash flow, operating income, ROIC, ROE, and, of course, total returns to shareholders. Understanding the shareholders' view of value creation leads managers to a more future-oriented evaluation.

By relying on both an internal and an external view of the firm, the balanced scorecard combines the strengths provided by the individual approaches to assessing competitive advantage discussed earlier: accounting profitability, shareholder value creation, and economic value creation.

ADVANTAGES OF THE BALANCED SCORECARD The balanced-scorecard approach is popular in managerial practice because it has several advantages. In particular, the balanced scorecard allows managers to:

- Communicate and link the strategic vision to responsible parties within the organization.
- Translate the vision into measurable operational goals.
- Design and plan business processes.
- Implement feedback and organizational learning to modify and adapt strategic goals when indicated.

The balanced scorecard can accommodate both short- and long-term performance metrics. It provides a concise report that tracks chosen metrics and measures and compares them to target values. This approach allows managers to assess past performance, identify areas for improvement, and position the company for future growth. Including a broader perspective than financials allows managers and executives a more balanced view of organizational performance—hence its name. In a sense, the balanced scorecard is a broad diagnostic tool. It complements the common financial metrics with operational measures on customer satisfaction, internal processes, and the company's innovation and improvement activities.

As an example of how to implement the balanced-scorecard approach, let's look at FMC Corporation, a chemical manufacturer employing some 5,000 people in different SBUs and earning over $3 billion in annual revenues.[27] To achieve its vision of becoming "the customer's most valued supplier," FMC's managers initially had focused solely on financial metrics such as return on invested capital (ROIC) as performance measures. FMC is a multibusiness corporation with several standalone profit-and-loss strategic business units; its overall performance was the result of both over- and underperforming units. FMC's managers had tried several approaches to enhance performance, but they turned out to be ineffective. Perhaps even more significant, short-term thinking by general managers was a major obstacle in the attempt to implement an effective business strategy.

Searching for improved performance, FMC's CEO decided to adopt a balanced-scorecard approach. It enabled the managers to view FMC's challenges and shortcomings from a holistic, company perspective, which was especially helpful to the general managers of different business units. In particular, the balanced scorecard allowed general managers to focus on market position, customer service, and new product introductions that could generate long-term value. Using the framework depicted in Exhibit 5.7, general managers had to answer tough follow-up questions such as: How do we become the customer's most valued supplier, and how can my division create this value for the customer? How do we become more externally focused? What are my division's core competencies and contributions to the company goals? What are my division's weaknesses?

Implementing a balanced scorecard allowed FMC's managers to align their different perspectives to create a more focused corporation overall. General managers now review progress along the chosen metrics every month, and corporate executives do so on a quarterly basis. Implementing a balanced-scorecard approach is not a onetime effort, but requires continuous tracking of metrics and updating of strategic objectives, if needed. It is a continuous process, feeding performance back into the strategy process to assess its effectiveness (see Chapter 2).

DISADVANTAGES OF THE BALANCED SCORECARD Though widely implemented by many businesses, the balanced scorecard is not without its critics.[28] It is important to note that the balanced scorecard is a tool for strategy *implementation,* not for strategy *formulation.* It is up to a firm's managers to formulate a strategy that will enhance the chances of gaining and sustaining a competitive advantage. In addition, the balanced-scorecard approach provides only limited guidance about which metrics to choose. Different situations call for different metrics. All of the three approaches to measuring competitive advantage— accounting profitability, shareholder value creation, and economic value creation— in addition to other quantitative and qualitative measures can be helpful when using a balanced-scorecard approach.

When implementing a balanced scorecard, managers need to be aware that a failure to achieve competitive advantage is not so much a reflection of a poor framework but of a strategic failure. The balanced scorecard is only as good as the skills of the managers who use it: They first must devise a strategy that enhances the odds of achieving competitive advantage. Second, they must accurately translate the strategy into objectives that they can measure and manage within the balanced-scorecard approach.[29]

Once the metrics have been selected, the balanced scorecard tracks chosen metrics and measures and compares them to target values. It does not, however, provide much insight into how metrics that deviate from the set goals can be put back on track.[30]

THE TRIPLE BOTTOM LINE

LO 5-5

Apply a triple bottom line to assess and evaluate competitive advantage.

Today, managers are frequently asked to maintain and improve not only the firm's economic performance but also its social and ecological performance. CEO Indra Nooyi responded by declaring PepsiCo's vision to be *Performance with Purpose* defined by goals in the social dimension (*human sustainability* to combat obesity by making its products healthier, and the *whole person at work* to achieve work/life balance) and ecological dimension (*environmental sustainability* in regard to clean water, energy, recycling, and so on), in addition to firm financial performance.

Being proactive along noneconomic dimensions can make good business sense. In anticipation of coming industry requirements for "extended producer responsibility," which requires the seller of a product to take it back for recycling at the end of its life, the German carmaker BMW was proactive. It not only lined up the leading car-recycling companies but also started to redesign its cars using a modular approach. The modular parts allow for quick car disassembly and reuse of components in the after-sales market (so-called refurbished or rebuilt auto parts).[31] Three dimensions—*economic, social, and ecological*—make up the **triple bottom line**, which is fundamental to a sustainable strategy. These three dimensions are also called the three Ps: profits, people, and planet:

triple bottom line
Combination of economic, social, and ecological concerns—*or profits, people, and planet*—that can lead to a sustainable strategy.

- **Profits.** The *economic dimension* captures the necessity of businesses to be profitable to survive.
- **People.** The *social dimension* emphasizes the people aspect, such as PepsiCo's initiative of the *whole person at work*.
- **Planet.** The *ecological dimension* emphasizes the relationship between business and the natural environment.

sustainable strategy
A strategy along the economic, social, and ecological dimensions that can be pursued over time without detrimental effects on people or the planet.

As the intersection of the three ovals (*profits, people,* and *planet*) in Exhibit 5.9 suggests, achieving positive results in all three areas can lead to a **sustainable strategy**. Rather than emphasizing sustaining a competitive advantage over time, *sustainable strategy* means a strategy that can be pursued over time without detrimental effects on people or the planet. Using renewable energy sources such as wind or solar power, for example, is sustainable over time. It can also be good for profits, or simply put "green is green," as Jeffrey Immelt, GE's CEO, is fond of saying. GE's renewable energy business brought in more than $6 billion in revenues in 2014 and made up roughly one quarter of GE's total business in its power and water division.[32]

business model
A firm's plan that details how it intends to make money.

Like the balanced scorecard, the triple bottom line takes a more integrative and holistic view in assessing a company's performance.[33] Using a triple-bottom-line approach, managers audit their company's fulfillment of its social and ecological obligations to stakeholders such as employees, customers, suppliers, and communities as conscientiously as they track its financial performance.[34] In this sense, the triple-bottom-line framework is related to *stakeholder theory,* an approach to understanding a firm as embedded in a network of internal and external constituencies that each make contributions and expect consideration in return (see the discussion in Chapter 1). For an example of how Interface, a global leader in the carpet industry, uses a triple-bottom-line approach to gain and sustain a competitive advantage, read Strategy Highlight 5.1.

LO 5-6

Outline how business models put strategy into action.

5.2 Business Models: Putting Strategy into Action

EXHIBIT 5.9 / Sustainable Strategy: A Focus on the Triple Bottom Line

The simultaneous pursuit of performance along social, economic, and ecological dimensions provides a basis for a triple-bottom-line strategy.

People

Sustainable **STRATEGY**

Planet

Profits

Strategy is a set of goal-directed actions a firm takes to gain and sustain superior performance relative to competitors or the industry average. The translation of strategy into action takes place in the firm's **business model**, which details the firm's competitive tactics and initiatives. Simply put, the firm's business model explains *how the firm intends to make money.* The business model stipulates how the firm conducts its business with its buyers, suppliers, and partners.[37]

How companies do business can sometimes be as important to gaining and sustaining competitive advantage as what they do. This also implies that *business model innovation* might be as important as product or process innovation.

Strategy Highlight 5.1

Interface: The World's First Sustainable Company

The Atlanta-based Interface Inc. is the world's largest manufacturer of modular carpet with annual sales of roughly $1 billion. What makes the company unique is its strategic intent to become the world's first *fully sustainable* company. In 1994, founder Ray Anderson set a goal for the company to be "off oil" entirely by 2020. That included not using any petroleum-based raw materials or oil-related energy to fuel the manufacturing plants.

According to Collins and Porras in *Built to Last,* their classic study of high-performing companies over long periods of time, this is a "BHAG—a big hairy audacious goal." BHAGs are bold missions declared by visionary companies and are a "powerful mechanism to stimulate progress."[35] Weaning Interface off oil by 2020 is indeed a BHAG. Many see the carpet industry as an extension of the petrochemical industry, given its heavy reliance on fossil fuels and chemicals in the manufacturing, shipping, and installation of its products.

Today, Interface is not only the global leader in modular carpet but also in sustainability. The company estimates that between 1996 and 2008, it saved over $400 million due to its energy efficiency and use of recycled materials. Its business model is changing the carpet industry. Speaking of sustainability as a business model, Mr. Anderson concluded:

> Sustainability has given my company a competitive edge in more ways than one. It has proven to be the most powerful marketplace differentiator I have known in my long career. Our costs are down, our profits are up, and our products are the best they have ever been. Sustainable design has provided an unexpected wellspring of innovation, people are galvanized around a shared higher purpose, better people are applying, the best people are staying and working with a purpose, the goodwill in the marketplace generated by our focus on sustainability far exceeds that which any amount of advertising or marketing expenditure could have generated—this company believes it has found a better way to a bigger and more legitimate profit—a better business model.[36]

Consider Netflix, the video-streaming service that allows people to watch movies and TV shows on almost any Internet-enabled device, such as a tablet, PC, TV, or smartphone. Netflix's business model is to grow its global user base as large as possible and then to monetize it via monthly subscription fees. The cost of establishing a large library of streaming content is more or less fixed, but the per unit cost falls drastically as more users join. Netflix has been hugely successful in attracting new users; as of spring 2015 it had more than 61 million subscribers worldwide. Yet, while providing a large selection of high quality online streaming is a necessity of the Netflix business model, this element can and has been easily duplicated by Amazon, Hulu, and premium services on YouTube.

To lock in its large installed base of users, however, Netflix has begun producing and distributing original content such as the hugely popular shows *House of Cards* and *Orange Is the New Black.* Netflix also releases all episodes of a new season of a series at once, allowing subscribers to watch what they want, when they want. This has given rise to the practice of "binge watching," where subscribers will dedicate a weekend to watching all episodes, rather than making a regular weekly time commitment to watch a particular show. This demonstrates that for a business model to be successful, it might need to consist of several reinforcing activities. Netflix remains a moving target for its competition, which allows it to monetize its large user base with monthly subscription fees. This has allowed Netflix to grow to over $5 billion in annual revenues and $35 billion in market cap, while producing a positive net income. The expectations are high that Netflix can further drive this business model to continue its success across the world.

To come up with an effective business model, a firm's managers first transform their strategy of how to compete into a blueprint of actions and initiatives that support the overarching goals. In a second step, managers implement this blueprint through structures, processes, culture, and procedures. If the company fails to translate a strategy into a profitable business model, the firm will run into trouble.

Take Zipcar, a member-based car-sharing company.[38] Zipcar came up with a new business model: It allowed its members to rent a vehicle online that was already in their vicinity for a few hours or a day. Users were charged for the duration of the use of the car, and gas and insurance are included in the rental fees. Zipcar appealed to urban dwellers and Millennials who prefer not to own a vehicle but need a car on occasion. The Zipcar member just paid for the service of access to a car as needed. The downside of Zipcar's business model is that it required a large amount of up-front investment to build the rental car fleet. Although Zipcar excelled in customer experience and technology, it was unable to obtain the capital necessary to scale its operation to be profitable. Given low barriers to imitation, numerous competitors have sprung up. The first competitors to Zipcar included traditional car rental companies and others that created Zipcar clones such as Hertz on Demand, Enterprise's WeCar, U-Haul's U Car Share, Avis On Location, and Daimler's Car2Go. Regional competitors also entered the industry, including City CarShare in the San Francisco Bay Area, I-GO in Chicago, and Mint in New York and Boston. Perhaps the most powerful competitors to Zipcar, however, were those that required no capital investment by the provider—ride-sharing services Uber, Lyft, and Sidecar. As a consequence, Zipcar's stock price fell rapidly. Zipcar was eventually acquired by rental car company Avis, which planned to combine its vast rental fleet with Zipcar's mobile technology and customer experience.

Often business model innovation combines new ideas with information technology. The sharing economy, for example, leverages information technology and Internet connectivity to offer peer-to-peer rental services such as ride sharing (Uber or Lyft), car rental (RelayRides), house cleaning (Handy), or someone running errands for you (TaskRabbit). Strategy Highlight 5.2 shows how Airbnb's business model revolutionized the hospitality and travel business.

Strategy Highlight 5.2

Airbnb: Tapping the Value of Unused Space

In 2007, the then unemployed Brian Chesky and Joe Gebbia became roommates in San Francisco. They could not afford their rent payments and had extra space and some inflatable mattresses in their loft. They decided to try renting out space on the mattresses and serving guests breakfast. After they got a few paying guests, they brought on web architect Nathan Blecharczyk to create a smooth web interface. They named the website "Air Bed and Breakfast," later shortened to Airbnb. The launch of their startup was timed to take advantage of the anticipated shortage of hotel rooms in Denver, Colorado, the site of the Democratic Party national convention in the summer of 2008.

After struggling initially, the Airbnb founders quickly realized that attractive photographs were the key to spaces being rented. The founders created a system whereby a professional photographer would take high-quality photographs of the location at no cost to the owner. Airbnb also streamlined the payment process between hosts and guests, profiting from a fee on the transaction. As a first mover in the peer-to-peer rental industry, Airbnb grew quickly. It also garnered fame and rave reviews for its unique accommodation offerings, including an airplane fuselage in Costa Rica, a chateau in France, a tree house in California, a cave in Spain, a windmill in Greece, and even a private island in Fiji.

Airbnb has allowed spaces that previously would have been unused to generate revenue, while also dramatically increasing the potential amount of accommodation space in the 191 countries (including Afghanistan, Cuba, and Iraq) where it has listings. As a result of a unique business model innovation, by spring 2015 Airbnb was valued at $20 billion.[39]

POPULAR BUSINESS MODELS

Given their critical importance to achieving competitive advantage, business models are constantly evolving. Below we will discuss the some of the more popular business models:[40]

- Razor-razorblades
- Subscription
- Pay as you go
- Freemium
- Wholesale
- Agency
- Bundling

Understanding the more popular business models today will increase the tools in your strategy toolkit.

- **Razor-razorblades**. The initial product is often sold at a loss or given away for free in order to drive demand for complementary goods. The company makes its money on the replacement part needed. As you might guess, it was invented by Gillette, which gave away its razors and sold the replacement cartridges for relatively high prices. The razor-razorblade model is found in many business applications today. For example, HP charges little for its laser printers but imposes high prices for its replacement toner cartridges.

- **Subscription**. The subscription model has been traditionally used for (print) magazines and newspapers. Users pay for access to a product or service whether they use the product or service during the payment term or not. Industries that use this model presently are cable television, cellular service providers, satellite radio, Internet service providers, and health clubs. Above we discussed Netflix, which uses a subscription model.

- **Pay as you go**. In the *pay-as-you-go business model,* users pay for only the services they consume. The pay-as-you-go model is most widely used by utilities providing power and water and cell phone service plans, but it is gaining momentum in other areas such as rental cars (e.g., Zipcar) and cloud computing. News providers such as *The New York Times* and *The Wall Street Journal* have created "pay walls" as a pay-as-you-go option.

- **Freemium**. The *freemium (free + premium) business model* provides the basic features of a product or service *free* of charge, but charges the user for *premium* services such as advanced features or add-ons.[41] For example, companies may provide a minimally supported version of their software as a trial (e.g., business application or video game) to give users the chance to try the product. Users later have the option of purchasing a supported version of software, which includes a full set of product features and product support.

- **Wholesale**. The traditional model in retail is called a wholesale model. Let's look at the book publishing industry as an example. Under the wholesale model, book publishers would sell books to retailers at a fixed price (usually 50 percent below the recommended retail price). Retailers, however, were free to set their own price on any book and profit from the difference between their selling price and the cost to buy the book from the publisher (or wholesaler).

- **Agency.** In this model the producer relies on an agent or retailer to sell the product, at a predetermined percentage commission. Sometimes the producer will also control the retail price. The agency model was long used in the entertainment industry, where agents place artists or artistic properties and then take their commission. More recently we see this approach at work in a number of online sales venues, as in Apple's pricing of book products or its app sales. (See further discussion following.)

■ **Bundling.** The bundling business model sells products or services for which demand is negatively correlated *at a discount*. Demand for two products is negatively correlated if a user values one product more than another. In the Microsoft Office Suite, a user might value Word more than Excel and vice versa. Instead of selling both products for $120 each, Microsoft bundles them in a suite and sells them combined at a discount, say $180. This bundling strategy allowed Microsoft to become the number-one provider of all major application software packages such as word processing, spreadsheets, slide show presentation, and so on. Before its bundling strategy, Microsoft faced strong competition in each segment. Indeed, Word Perfect was outselling Word, Lotus 1-2-3 was outselling Excel, and Harvard Graphics was outselling PowerPoint. The problem for Microsoft's competitors was that they did not control the operating system (Windows), which made their programs less seamless on this operating system. In addition, the competitor products to Microsoft were offered by three independent companies, so they lacked the option to bundle them at a discount.

DYNAMIC NATURE OF BUSINESS MODELS

Business models evolve dynamically, and we can see many combinations and permutations. Sometimes business models are tweaked to respond to disruptions in the market, efforts that can conflict with fair trade practices and may even prompt government intervention.

COMBINATION. Telecommunications companies such as AT&T or Verizon, to take one industry, combine the *razor-razorblade* model with the *subscription* model. They provide a basic cell phone at no charge, or significantly subsidize a high-end smartphone, when you sign up for a two-year wireless service plan. Telecom providers recoup the subsidy provided for the smartphone by requiring customers to sign up for lengthy service plans. This is why it is so critical for telecom providers to keep their *churn rate*—the proportion of subscribers that leave, especially before the end of the contractual term—as low as possible.

EVOLUTION. The freemium business model can be seen as an evolutionary variation on the razor-razorblade model. The base product is provided free, and the producer finds other ways to monetize the usage. The freemium model is used extensively by open-source software companies (e.g., Red Hat), mobile app companies, and other Internet businesses. Many of the free versions of applications include advertisements to make up for the cost of supporting nonpaying users. In addition, the paying premium users subsidize the free users. The freemium model is often used to build a consumer base when the marginal cost of adding another user is low or even zero (such as in software sales). Many online video games, including massive multiplayer online games and app-based mobile games, follow a variation of this model, allowing basic access to the game for free, but charging for power-ups, customizations, special objects, and similar things that enhance the game experience for users.

DISRUPTION. When introducing the agency model, we mentioned Apple and book publishing, and you may already know how severely Amazon disrupted the traditional wholesale model for publishers. Amazon took advantage of the pricing flexibility inherent in the wholesale model and offered many books (especially e-books) below the cost that other retailers had to pay to publishers. In particular, Amazon would offer newly released bestsellers, such as Dan Brown's novels, for $9.99 to promote its Kindle e-reader. Publishers and other retailers strongly objected because Amazon's retail price was lower than the wholesale price paid by retailers competing with Amazon. Moreover, the $9.99 e-book offer by Amazon made it untenable for other retailers to continue to charge $28.95 for newly released hardcover books (for which they had to pay $14 to $15 to the publishers). With its aggressive pricing, Amazon not only devalued the printed book, but also lost money on every book it sold. It did this to increase the number of users of its Kindle e-readers and tablets.

RESPONSE TO DISRUPTION. The market is dynamic, and in the above example, book publishers looked for another model. Many book publishers worked with Apple on an agency approach, in which the publishers would set the price for Apple and receive 70 percent of the revenue, while Apple received 30 percent. The approach is similar to the Apple App Store pricing model for iOS applications in which developers set a price for applications and Apple retains a percentage of the revenue.

Use of the agency model was intended to give publishers the leverage to raise e-book prices for retailers. Under the agency model, publishers could increase their e-book profits and price e-book more closely to prices of print books. Publishers inked their deals with Apple, but how could they get Amazon to play ball? For leverage, publishers withheld new releases from Amazon. This forced Amazon to raise prices on newly released e-books in line with the agency model to around $14.95.

LEGAL CONFLICTS. The rapid development of business models, especially in response to disruption, can lead producers to breach existing rules of commerce. In the above example, the publishers' response prompted an antitrust investigation. In 2012 the Department of Justice determined that Apple and major publishers had conspired to raise prices of e-books. To settle the legal action, each publisher involved negotiated new deals with retailers, including Amazon. A year later, Apple was found guilty of colluding with several major book publishers to fix prices on e-books and had to change its agency model.[42]

5.3 ◄► Implications for the Strategist

In this chapter, we discussed how to measure and assess competitive advantage using three traditional approaches: accounting profitability, shareholder value creation, and economic value creation. We then introduced two conceptual frameworks to help us understand competitive advantage in a more holistic fashion: the balanced scorecard and the triple bottom line. Exhibit 5.10 summarizes the concepts discussed.

Several managerial implications emerged from our discussion of competitive advantage and firm performance:

- No *best* strategy exists—only *better* ones (better in comparison with others). We must interpret any performance metric relative to those of competitors and the industry average. True performance can be judged only in comparison to other contenders in the field or the industry average, not on an absolute basis.

- The goal of strategic management is to integrate and align each business function and activity to obtain superior performance at the business unit and corporate levels. Therefore, competitive advantage is best measured by criteria that reflect *overall business unit performance* rather than the performance of specific departments. For example, although the functional managers in the marketing department may (and should) care greatly about the success or failure of their recent ad campaign, the *general* manager cares most about the performance implications of the ad campaign at the business unit level for which she has profit-and-loss responsibility. Metrics that aggregate upward and reflect overall firm and corporate performance are most useful to assess the effectiveness of a firm's competitive strategy.

- Both *quantitative and qualitative* performance dimensions matter in judging the effectiveness of a firm's strategy. Those who focus on only one metric will risk being blindsided by poor performance on another. Rather, managers need to rely on a more holistic perspective when assessing firm performance, measuring different dimensions over different time periods.

- A firm's business model is critical to achieving a competitive advantage. How a firm does business is as important as what it does.

This concludes our discussion of competitive advantage, firm performance, and business models, and completes Part 1—strategy analysis—of the AFI framework. In Part 2, we turn our attention to the next steps in the AFI framework—strategy formulation. In Chapters 6 and 7, we focus on business strategy: *How should the firm compete (cost leadership, differentiation, or value innovation)?* In Chapters 8 and 9, we study corporate strategy: *Where should the firm compete (industry, markets, and geography)?* Chapter 10 looks at global strategy: *How and where (local, regional, national, and international) should the firm compete around the world?*

EXHIBIT 5.10 / How Do We Measure and Assess Competitive Advantage?

Competitive advantage is reflected in superior firm performance.

- We always assess competitive advantage *relative* to a benchmark, either using competitors or the industry average.
- Competitive advantage is a multifaceted concept.
- We can assess competitive advantage by measuring accounting profit, shareholder value, or economic value.
- The balanced-scorecard approach harnesses multiple internal and external performance dimensions to balance a firm's financial and strategic goals.
- More recently, competitive advantage has been linked to a firm's triple bottom line, the ability to maintain performance in the economic, social, and ecological contexts (profits, people, planet) to achieve a sustainable strategy.

CHAPTER**CASE 5** / Consider This...*

GIVEN MICROSOFT'S LACKLUSTER performance since 2000, the once dominant company is now in turnaround mode. Over time, its competitive advantage turned into a competitive disadvantage, lagging behind Apple by a wide margin. Satya Nadella's strategic focus is to move Microsoft away from its Windows-only business model to compete more effectively in a "mobile-first, cloud-first world," the mantra he used in his appointment e-mail as CEO. Under his leadership, Microsoft made the Office Suite available on Apple iOS and Android mobile devices. Office 365, its cloud-based software offering, is now available as a subscription service starting at $6.99 per month for personal use and $69.99 for business use. Software applications can be accessed on any device, any time, with online storage, combined with Skype's global calling feature. Yet, Nadella needs to work hard to ensure Microsoft's future viability since Windows and Office were cash cows for so long. They are still generating almost half of revenues and some 60 percent of profits, but both continue to decline. The problem he faces is that the gross margin of "classic" PC-based Office is an astronomical 90 percent (due to Microsoft's "monopoly" position), while the gross margin for Office 365 is only around 50 percent. The cloud

computing space with Google, Amazon, Apple, IBM, and others is fiercely competitive.[43]

Questions

1. Why is it so hard to gain a competitive advantage? Why is it even harder to sustain a competitive advantage?

2. Looking at the different ways to assess competitive advantage discussed in this chapter, does Apple have a competitive advantage over Microsoft using any of the approaches? Why or why not? In which approach is Microsoft looking "the best"? Explain.

3. Microsoft's new CEO, Satya Nadella, has made drastic changes to Microsoft's strategy. What was Microsoft's strategy before Nadella was appointed CEO? What is it now under his leadership? Do you agree that Nadella has formulated a promising strategy? Why or why not?

4. How much longer do you think Apple can sustain its competitive advantage (not just over Microsoft, but in general)? Explain.

*A strategic financial analysis exercise related to this **ChapterCase** is available in Connect.

TAKE-AWAY CONCEPTS

This chapter demonstrated three traditional approaches for assessing and measuring firm performance and competitive advantage, as well as two conceptual frameworks designed to provide a more holistic, albeit more qualitative, perspective on firm performance. We also discussed the role of business models in translating a firm's strategy into actions.

LO 5-1 / Conduct a firm profitability analysis using accounting data to assess and evaluate competitive advantage.

- To measure competitive advantage, we must be able to (1) accurately assess firm performance, and (2) compare and benchmark the focal firm's performance to other competitors in the same industry or the industry average.

- To measure accounting profitability, we use standard metrics derived from publicly available accounting data.

- Commonly used profitability metrics in strategic management are *return on assets (ROA), return on equity (ROE), return on invested capital (ROIC)*, and *return on revenue (ROR)*. See the key financial ratios in five tables in the "How to Conduct a Case Analysis" guide.

- All accounting data are historical and thus backward-looking. They focus mainly on tangible assets and do not consider intangibles that are hard or impossible to measure and quantify, such as an innovation competency.

LO 5-2 / Apply shareholder value creation to assess and evaluate competitive advantage.

- Investors are primarily interested in total return to shareholders, which includes stock price appreciation plus dividends received over a specific period.

- Total return to shareholders is an external performance metric; it indicates how the market views all publicly available information about a firm's past, current state, and expected future performance.

- Applying a shareholders' perspective, key metrics to measure and assess competitive advantage are the return on (risk) capital and market capitalization.

- Stock prices can be highly volatile, which makes it difficult to assess firm performance. Overall macroeconomic factors have a direct bearing on stock prices. Also, stock prices frequently reflect the psychological mood of the investors, which can at times be irrational.

- Shareholder value creation is a better measure of competitive advantage over the *long term* due to the "noise" introduced by market volatility, external factors, and investor sentiment.

LO 5-3 / Explain economic value creation and different sources of competitive advantage.

- The relationship between economic value creation and competitive advantage is fundamental in strategic management. It provides the foundation upon which to formulate a firm's competitive strategy of cost leadership or differentiation.

- Three components are critical to evaluating any good or service: value (V), price (P), and cost (C). In this perspective, cost includes opportunity costs.

- Economic value created is the difference between a buyer's willingness to pay for a good or service and the firm's cost to produce it $(V - C)$.

- A firm has a competitive advantage when it is able to create more economic value than its rivals. The source of competitive advantage can stem from higher perceived value creation (assuming equal cost) or lower cost (assuming equal value creation).

LO 5-4 / Apply a balanced scorecard to assess and evaluate competitive advantage.

- The balanced-scorecard approach attempts to provide a more integrative view of competitive advantage.

- Its goal is to harness multiple internal and external performance dimensions to balance financial and strategic goals.

- Managers develop strategic objectives for the balanced scorecard by answering four key questions: (1) How do customers view us? (2) How do we create value? (3) What core competencies do we need? (4) How do shareholders view us?

LO 5-5 / Apply a triple bottom line to assess and evaluate competitive advantage.

- Noneconomic factors can have a significant impact on a firm's financial performance, not to mention its reputation and customer goodwill.

- Managers are frequently asked to maintain and improve not only the firm's economic performance but also its social and ecological performance.

- Three dimensions—economic, social, and ecological, also known as *profits, people,* and *planet*—make up the triple bottom line. Achieving positive results in all three areas can lead to a sustainable strategy—a strategy that can endure over time.

- A sustainable strategy produces not only positive financial results, but also positive results along the social and ecological dimensions.

- Using a triple-bottom-line approach, managers audit their company's fulfillment of its social and ecological obligations to stakeholders such as employees, customers, suppliers, and communities in as serious a way as they track its financial performance.

- The triple-bottom-line framework is related to stakeholder theory, an approach to understanding a firm as embedded in a network of internal and external constituencies that each make contributions and expect consideration in return.

LO 5-6 / Outline how business models put strategy into action.

- The translation of a firm's strategy (*where and how to compete for competitive advantage*) into action takes place in the firm's business model (*how to make money*).

- A business model details how the firm conducts its business with its buyers, suppliers, and partners.

- How companies do business is as important to gaining and sustaining competitive advantage as what they do.

- Some important business models include *razor-razorblade, subscription, pay as you go,* and *freemium.*

KEY TERMS

Balanced scorecard *(p. 157)*

Business model *(p. 160)*

Consumer surplus *(p. 153)*

Economic value created *(p. 151)*

Market capitalization *(p. 149)*

Opportunity costs *(p. 155)*

Producer surplus *(p. 153)*

Profit *(p. 153)*

Reservation price *(p. 151)*

Risk capital *(p. 149)*

Shareholders *(p. 149)*

Sustainable strategy *(p. 160)*

Total return to shareholders *(p. 149)*

Triple bottom line *(p. 160)*

Value *(p. 153)*

DISCUSSION QUESTIONS

1. Domino's Pizza has been in business over 50 years and claimed to be "#1 Worldwide in Pizza Delivery" in 2013. Visit the company's business-related website (www.dominosbiz.com) and read the company profile under the "Investors" tab. Does the firm focus on the accounting, shareholder, or economic perspective in describing its competitive advantage in the profile?

2. For many people, the shareholder perspective is perhaps the most familiar measure of competitive advantage for publicly traded firms. What are some of the disadvantages of using shareholder value as the sole point of view for defining competitive advantage?

3. Interface, Inc., is discussed in Strategy Highlight 5.1. It may seem unusual for a business-to-business carpet company to be using a triple-bottom-line approach for its strategy. What other industries do you think could productively use this approach? How would it change customers' perceptions if it did?

4. The chapter highlights several firms that are developing business models around a "sharing economy." The idea being that assets not currently in use by their owners (cars, car seats, homes, rooms, etc.) can be rented to (shared with) others. What other industries can you think of that can be disrupted by this new business model? Where do you see "excess" space or other assets that could perhaps be utilized more efficiently?

ETHICAL/SOCIAL ISSUES

1. You work as a supervisor in a manufacturing firm. The company has implemented a balanced-scorecard performance-appraisal system and a financial bonus for exceeding goals. A major customer order for 1,000 units needs to ship to a destination across the country by the end of the quarter, which is two days away from its close. This shipment, if it goes well, will have a major impact on both your customer-satisfaction goals and your financial goals.

   With 990 units built, a machine breaks. It will take two days to get the parts and repair the machine. You realize there is an opportunity to load the finished units on a truck tomorrow with paperwork for the completed order of 1,000 units. You can have an employee fly out with the 10 remaining parts and meet the truck at the destination city once the machinery has been repaired. The 10 units can be added to the pallet and delivered as a complete shipment of 1,000 pieces, matching the customer's order and your paperwork. What do you do?

2. The chapter mentions that accounting data do not consider off–balance sheet items. A retailer that owns its stores will list the value of that property as an asset, for example, while a firm that leases its stores will not. What are some of the accounting and shareholder advantages of leasing compared to owning retail locations?

3. How do the perspectives on competitive advantage differ when comparing brick-and-mortar stores to online businesses (e.g., Best Buy vs. Amazon, Barnes & Noble vs. Amazon, The Gap vs. Threadless (noted in Strategy Highlight 1.1), Nordstrom vs. Zappos, and so on)? Make recommendations to brick-and-mortar stores as to how they can compete more effectively with online firms. What conclusions do you draw?

SMALL GROUP EXERCISES

//// Small Group Exercise 1

As discussed in the chapter, a balanced scorecard views the performance of an organization through four lenses: customer, innovation and learning, internal business, and financial. According to surveys from Bain & Company (a consulting firm), in recent years about 60 percent of firms in both public and private sectors have used a balanced scorecard for performance measures.[44]

With your group, create a balanced scorecard for the business school at your university. You might start by looking at your school's web page for a mission or vision statement. Then divide up the four perspectives among the team members to develop key elements for each one. It may be helpful to remember the four key balanced-scorecard questions from the chapter:

1. How do customers view us? (Hint: First discuss the following: Who are the customers? The students? The companies that hire students? Others?)
2. How do we create value?
3. What core competencies do we need?
4. How do shareholders view us? (For public universities, the shareholders are the taxpayers who invest their taxes into the university. For private universities, the shareholders are the people or organizations that endow the university.)

//// Small Group Exercise 2

At the next big family gathering, you want to impress your grandparents with the innovative ideas you have learned in business school. They have decades of experience in investing in the stock market and, from their college days, believe that economic profitability is a business's primary responsibility. You would like to convince them that a triple-bottom-line approach is the modern path to stronger economic performance. With your group members, prepare a casual yet informative speech that you can use to persuade them. They probably will not listen for more than two minutes, so you know you have to be clear and concise with interesting examples. You may want to reinforce your argument by consulting "The Bottom Line of Corporate Good," published in *Forbes*.[45] Present your speech in whatever way your instructor requests—to your group, the entire class, or post a video on YouTube.

STRATEGY TERM PROJECT

Mc Graw Hill Education connect®

The HP Running Case, *a related activity for each strategy term project module, is available in Connect.*

//// Module 5: Competitive Advantage Perspectives

1. Based on information in the annual reports or published on the firm's website, summarize what the firm views as the reasons for its successes (either past or expected in the future). Search for both quantitative and qualitative success factors provided in the report.

2. Does the firm seem most focused on accounting profitability, shareholder value creation, or economic value creation? Give quotes or information from these sources to support your view.

3. Many firms are now including annual corporate social responsibility (CSR) reports on their websites. See whether your firm does so. If it does not, are there other indications of a triple-bottom-line approach, including social and ecological elements, in the firm's strategies?

*my*STRATEGY

How Much Is an MBA Worth to You?

The *my*Strategy box at the end of Chapter 2 asked how much you would be willing to pay for the job you want—for a job that reflects your values. Here, we look at a different issue relating to worth: How much is an MBA worth over the course of your career?

Alongside the traditional two-year full-time MBA program, many business schools also offer evening MBAs and executive MBAs. Let's assume you know you want to pursue an advanced degree, and you need to decide which program format is better

for you (or you want to evaluate the choice you already made). You've narrowed your options to either (1) a two-year full-time MBA program, or (2) an executive MBA program at the same institution that is 18 months long with classes every other weekend. Let's also assume the price for tuition, books, and fees is $30,000 for the full-time program and $90,000 for the executive MBA program.

Which MBA program should you choose? Consider in your analysis the value, price, and cost concepts discussed in this chapter. Pay special attention to opportunity costs attached to different MBA program options.

ENDNOTES

1. For an in-depth discussion of Apple, see Rothaermel, F.T. and D. King, Case MHE-FTR-031- 1259420477, "Apple Inc." (2015), http://create.mheducation.com/; Rothaermel, F.T., MiniCase XX: "Competing on Business Models: Google vs. Microsoft"; and "Microsoft at middle age: Opening Windows," *The Economist,* April 4, 2015.

2. This debate takes place in the following discourses, among others: Misangyi, V.F., H. Elms, T. Greckhamer, and J.A. Lepine (2006), "A new perspective on a fundamental debate: A multilevel approach to industry, corporate, and business unit

effects," *Strategic Management Journal* 27: 571–590; McNamara, G., F. Aime, and P. Vaaler (2005), "Is performance driven by industry- or firm-specific factors? A reply to Hawawini, Subramanian, and Verdin," *Strategic Management Journal* 26: 1075–1081; Hawawini, G., V. Subramanian, and P. Verdin (2005), "Is performance driven by industry- or firm-specific factors? A new look at the evidence: A response to McNamara, Aime, and Vaaler," *Strategic Management Journal* 26: 1083–1086; Rumelt, R.P. (2003), "What in the world is competitive advantage?" *Policy Working Paper 2003-105;* McGahan,

A.M., and M.E. Porter (2002), "What do we know about variance in accounting profitability?" *Management Science* 48: 834–851; Hawawini, G., V. Subramanian, and P. Verdin (2003), "Is performance driven by industry- or firm-specific factors? A new look at the evidence," *Strategic Management Journal* 24: 1–16; McGahan, A.M., and M.E. Porter (1997), "How much does industry matter, really?" *Strategic Management Journal* 18: 15–30; Rumelt, R.P. (1991), "How much does industry matter?" *Strategic Management Journal* 12: 167–185; Porter, M.E. (1985), *Competitive Advantage: Creating and*

Sustaining Superior Performance (New York: Free Press); and Schmalensee, R. (1985), "Do markets differ much?" *American Economic Review* 75: 341–351;

3. Rumelt, "What in the world?"

4. For a discussion see: McGahan, A.M., and M. E. Porter (2002), "What do we know about variance in accounting profitability?" *Management Science,* 48: 834–851.

5. *(Net profits / Invested capital)* is short-hand for *(Net operating profit after taxes [NOPAT]/Total stockholders' equity + Total debt − Value of preferred stock)*. See discussion of profitability ratios in Table 1, "When and How to Use Financial Measures to Assess Firm Performance," of the "How to Conduct a Case Analysis" the guide to conducting a case analysis that concludes Part IV of the text.

6. This example is based on the 2014 SEC 10-K reports for Apple and Microsoft.

7. "The second coming of Apple through a magical fusion of man—Steve Jobs—and company, Apple is becoming itself again: The little anticompany that could," *Fortune,* November 9, 1998.

8. Prahalad, C.K., and G. Hamel (1990), "The Core Competence of the Corporation," *Harvard Business Review,* May–June.

9. Baruch, L. (2001), *Intangibles: Management, Measurement, and Reporting* (Washington, DC: Brookings Institution Press).

10. Cameron, W.B. (1967), *Informal Sociology: A Casual Introduction to Sociological Thinking* (New York: Random House).

11. Friedman, M. (2002), *Capitalism and Freedom,* 40th anniversary edition (Chicago, IL: University of Chicago Press).

12. Beechy, M., D. Gruen, and J. Vickrey (2000), "The efficient market hypothesis: A survey," Research Discussion Paper, Federal Reserve Bank of Australia; and Fama, E. (1970), "Efficient capital markets: A review of theory and empirical work," *Journal of Finance* 25: 383–417.

13. The three broad categories of companies by market cap are *large cap* (over $10 billion), *mid cap* ($2 billion to $10 billion), and *small cap* (less than $2 billion).

14. Alexander, J. (2007), *Performance Dashboards and Analysis for Value Creation* (Hoboken, NJ: Wiley-Interscience).

15. Microsoft 2012 Annual Report.

16. This section draws on: Christensen, C.M., and M.E. Raynor (2003), *The Innovator's Solution: Creating and Sustaining Successful Growth* (Boston, MA: Harvard Business School Press).

17. "Satya Nadella: Mobile first, cloud first press briefing," Microsoft press release, March 27, 2014.

18. Speech given by Alan Greenspan on December 5, 1996, at the American Enterprise Institute.

19. "Irrational gloom," *The Economist,* October 11, 2002.

20. Olivarez-Giles, N., "What makes the apple Watch tick," *The Wall Street Journal,* April 30, 2015.

21. "Microsoft at middle age: Opening Windows"; and Amazon.com, various annual reports.

22. Kaplan, R.S., and D.P. Norton (1992), "The balanced scorecard: Measures that drive performance," *Harvard Business Review,* January–February: 71–79.

23. Ibid.

24. Govindarajan, V., and J.B. Lang (2002), *3M Corporation,* case study, Tuck School of Business at Dartmouth.

25. Rothaermel, F.T., and A.M. Hess (2010), "Innovation strategies combined," *MIT Sloan Management Review,* Spring: 12–15.

26. Huston, L., and N. Sakkab (2006), "Connect & Develop: Inside Procter & Gamble's new model for innovation," *Harvard Business Review,* March: 58–66.

27. Kaplan, R.S. (1993), "Implementing the balanced scorecard at FMC Corporation: An interview with Larry D. Brady," *Harvard Business Review,* September–October: 143–147.

28. Norreklit, H. (2000), "The balance on the balanced scorecard—A critical analysis of some of its assumptions," *Management Accounting Research* 11: 65–88; Jensen, M.C. (2002), "Value Maximization, Stakeholder Theory, and the Corporate Objective Function," in *Unfolding Stakeholder Thinking,* ed. Andriof, J., et al. (Sheffield, UK: Greenleaf Publishing).

29. Kaplan, R.S., and D.P. Norton (2007), "Using the balanced scorecard as a strategic management system," *Harvard Business Review,* July–August; and Kaplan and Norton, "The balanced scorecard: Measures that drive performance."

30. Lawrie, G., and I. Cobbold (2002), "Development of the 3rd generation balanced scorecard: Evolution of the balanced scorecard into an effective strategic performance management tool," *2GC Working Paper,* 2GC Limited, Berkshire, UK.

31. Senge, P.M., B. Bryan Smith, N. Kruschwitz, J. Laur, and S. Schley, (2010), *The Necessary Revolution: How Individuals and Organizations Are Working Together to Create a Sustainable World* (New York: Crown).

32. GE 2014 Annual Report, http://www.ge.com/ar2014.

33. Anderson, R.C. (2009), *Confessions of a Radical Industrialist: Profits, People, Purpose—Doing Business by Respecting the Earth* (New York: St. Martin's Press).

34. Norman, W., and C. MacDonald (2004), "Getting to the bottom of 'triple bottom line,'" *Business Ethics Quarterly* 14: 243–262.

35. Collins, J.C., and J.I. Porras (1994), *Built to Last: Successful Habits of Visionary Companies* (New York: HarperBusiness), 93.

36. Anderson, *Confessions of a Radical Industrialist,* 5; TED talk, "Ray Anderson on the business logic of sustainability," www.ted.com; and Perkins, J. (2009), *Hoodwinked: An Economic Hit Man Reveals Why the World Financial Markets Imploded—and What We Need to Do to Remake Them* (New York: Crown Business), 107.

37. This discussion is based on: Adner, R. (2012), *The Wide Lens. A New Strategy for Innovation* (New York: Portfolio/Penguin); and Amit, R., and C. Zott (2012), "Creating value through business model innovation," *MIT Sloan Management Review,* Spring: 41–49; see also Gassmann, O., K. Frankenberger, and M. Csik (2015), *The Business Model Navigator: 55 Models That Will Revolutionise Your Business* (Harlow, UK: FT Press).

38. "Zipcar: Entrepreneurial genius, public-company failure," *The Wall Street Journal,* January 2, 2013.

39. Lunden, I., "Airbnb is raising a monster round at a $20B valuation," *TechCrunch,* February 27, 2015; MacMillan, D., M. Spector, and E.M. Rusli, "Airbnb weighs employee stock sale at $13 billion valuation," *The Wall Street Journal,* October 23, 2014; "The rise of the sharing economy," *The Economist,* March 9, 2013; and "All eyes on the sharing economy," *The Economist,* March 9, 2013.

40. For a fully dedicated and more in-depth treatment of business models, see Gassmann, et al., *The Business Model Navigator: 55 Models That Will Revolutionise Your Business.*

41. Anderson, C. (2009), *Free: The Future of a Radical Price* (New York: Hyperion).

42. Bray, C., J. Palazzolo, and I. Sherr, "U.S. judge rules Apple colluded on e-books," *The Wall Street Journal,* July 13, 2013.

43. "Microsoft at middle age: Opening Windows."

44. See www.thepalladiumgroup.com for examples.

45. www.forbes.com/sites/causeintegration/2012/09/14/the-bottom-line-of-corporate-good/.

Formulation

The AFI Strategy Framework

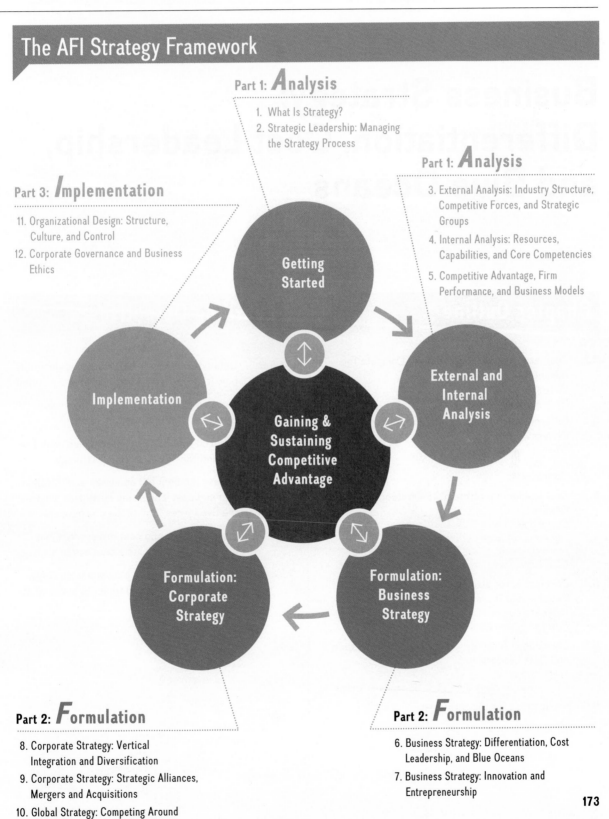

Part 1: Analysis

1. What Is Strategy?
2. Strategic Leadership: Managing the Strategy Process

Part 1: Analysis

3. External Analysis: Industry Structure, Competitive Forces, and Strategic Groups
4. Internal Analysis: Resources, Capabilities, and Core Competencies
5. Competitive Advantage, Firm Performance, and Business Models

Part 3: Implementation

11. Organizational Design: Structure, Culture, and Control
12. Corporate Governance and Business Ethics

Part 2: Formulation

8. Corporate Strategy: Vertical Integration and Diversification
9. Corporate Strategy: Strategic Alliances, Mergers and Acquisitions
10. Global Strategy: Competing Around the World

Part 2: Formulation

6. Business Strategy: Differentiation, Cost Leadership, and Blue Oceans
7. Business Strategy: Innovation and Entrepreneurship

Getting Started

External and Internal Analysis

Formulation: Business Strategy

Formulation: Corporate Strategy

Implementation

Gaining & Sustaining Competitive Advantage

173

Chapter 6

Business Strategy: Differentiation, Cost Leadership, and Blue Oceans

Learning Objectives

LO 6-1 Define business-level strategy and describe how it determines a firm's strategic position.

LO 6-2 Examine the relationship between value drivers and differentiation strategy.

LO 6-3 Examine the relationship between cost drivers and the cost-leadership strategy.

LO 6-4 Assess the benefits and risks of differentiation and cost-leadership strategies vis-à-vis the five forces that shape competition.

LO 6-5 Evaluate value and cost drivers that may allow a firm to pursue a blue ocean strategy.

LO 6-6 Assess the risks of a blue ocean strategy, and explain why it is difficult to succeed at value innovation.

JetBlue: "Stuck in the Middle"?

ENTREPRENEUR DAVID NEELEMAN, at the age of 25, co-founded Morris Air, a charter air service that in 1993 was purchased by Southwest Airlines (SWA). Morris Air was a low-fare airline that pioneered many cost-saving practices that later became standard in the industry, such as e-ticketing. After working as an airline executive for

SWA, Neeleman founded another airline, JetBlue Airways, in 1998. When Neeleman established JetBlue, his strategy was to provide air travel at even lower costs than SWA. At the same time, he wanted to offer better service and more amenities.

JetBlue copied and improved upon many of SWA's cost-reducing activities. For example, it started by using just one type of airplane (the Airbus A320) to lower the costs of aircraft maintenance and pilot training. It also chose to fly point to point, directly connecting highly trafficked city pairs. In contrast, legacy airlines such as Delta, United, and American use a hub-and-spoke system; such systems connect many different locations via layovers at airport hubs. The point-to-point business model focuses on directly connecting fewer but more highly trafficked city pairs. This operating system lowers costs by not offering baggage transfers and schedule coordination with other airlines. In addition, JetBlue flew longer distances and transported more passengers per flight than SWA, further driving down its costs. Initially, JetBlue enjoyed the lowest cost per available seat-mile (an important performance metric in the airline industry) in the United States.

At the same time, JetBlue also attempted to enhance its differential appeal by driving up its perceived value. Its intent was to combine high-touch—to enhance the customer experience—and high-tech—to drive down costs.

Among high-profile incidents affecting JetBlue's overall reputation as a quality airline was the 2014 emergency landing at Long Beach Airport, after instruments identified a potentially overheated engine. Four passengers were injured in the evacuation.
© AP Photo/KABC-TV

Some of JetBlue's value-enhancing features include high-end 100-seat Embraer regional jets with leather seats, free movie and television programming via DirecTV, XM Satellite Radio, along with friendly and attentive on-board service. Other amenities include its recently added Mint class, which offers personal check-in and early boarding, free bag checking and priority bag retrieval after flight, and complimentary gourmet food and alcoholic beverages in flight. It also features small private suites with a lie-flat bed up to 6 feet 8 inches long, a 15-inch high-resolution personal screen, and free in-flight high-speed Wi-Fi ("Fly-Fi"). JetBlue is also adding the newer Airbus 321 to its fleet, which scores significantly higher in customer satisfaction surveys than the older Airbus 320.

Also, because roughly one-third of customers prefer speaking to a live reservation agent, despite a highly functional website for reservations and other travel-related services, JetBlue decided to employ stay-at-home parents in the United States instead of following industry best practice by outsourcing its reservation system to India. The company suggests this "home sourcing" is more productive than outsourcing; it also says that customers' appreciation of the reservation experience more than makes up for the wage differential between the United States and India. To sum it up, JetBlue's "Customer Bill of Rights" declares its dedication to "bringing humanity back to air travel."

Several high-profile incidents, however, damaged JetBlue's outstanding customer service record. In early 2007, JetBlue's reputation took a major hit: Several flights were delayed due to a snowstorm in which the airline kept passengers on board the aircraft; some sat on the tarmac for up to nine hours. Many wondered whether JetBlue was losing its magic touch. A few months later, David

Neeleman left JetBlue.[1] Another reputation-damaging incident for JetBlue occurred in 2010 when a flight attendant, upset because a passenger refused to apologize after striking him with luggage when disembarking the plane, allegedly used the airplane's PA system to hurl obscenities at passengers. Then, he grabbed a couple of cold beers from the galley, deployed and slid down the emergency escape chute, before disappearing in a terminal at New York's JFK airport and proceeding to drive home (where he was later arrested). In 2012, a JetBlue flight to Las Vegas was diverted to Texas because of the pilot's erratic behavior during the flight. Among other bizarre behavior, the mentally unstable pilot told the co-pilot that "we need to take a leap of faith," and that "we're not going to Vegas." The co-pilot locked the pilot out of the cockpit and diverted the flight to Texas, where it landed safely. The issue of pilot mental health and the responsibilities of an airline have taken on new urgency in light of the 2015 deliberate crash into the French Alps of a Germanwings flight with 150 people on board by a co-pilot suffering from documented mental health issues.

For JetBlue, trying to combine a cost-leadership position with a differentiation strategy has meant that despite early years of competitive advantage, it is now struggling. As a consequence of several high-profile mishaps combined with the difficulty in resolving the trade-offs inherent in driving costs down while providing superior customer service and in-flight amenities, JetBlue has experienced a sustained competitive disadvantage since 2007.[2]

You will learn more about JetBlue by reading the chapter; related questions appear on page 200.

THE CHAPTERCASE illustrates how JetBlue ran into trouble by trying to combine two different business strategies at the same time—a *cost-leadership* strategy, focused on low cost, and a *differentiation* strategy, focused on delivering unique features and service. Although the idea of combining different business strategies seems appealing, it is quite difficult to execute a cost-leadership and differentiation position at the same time. This is because cost leadership and differentiation are distinct strategic positions. Pursuing them simultaneously results in trade-offs that work against each other. For instance, higher perceived customer value (e.g., providing leather seats throughout the entire aircraft and free Wi-Fi) comes with higher costs.

JetBlue attempts to be both a cost leader and differentiator. Many firms that attempt to combine cost-leadership and differentiation strategies end up being *stuck in the middle,* that is, the managers have failed to carve out a clear *strategic position.* In their attempt to be everything to everybody, these firms end up being neither a low-cost leader nor a differentiator. This common strategic failure contributed to JetBlue's sustained competitive disadvantage in recent years. Managers need to be aware to not end up being *stuck in the middle* between distinct strategic positions. A clear strategic position—either as differentiator or low-cost leader—can form the basis for competitive advantage.

This chapter, the first in Part 2 on strategy *formulation,* takes a close look at business-level strategy. It deals with *how* to compete for advantage. Based on the analysis of the external and internal environments (presented in Part 1), the second step in the *AFI Strategy Framework* (see page 175) is to formulate a business strategy that enhances the firm's chances of achieving a competitive advantage.

We begin our discussion of strategy formulation by defining *business-level strategy, strategic position,* and *generic business strategies.* We then look at two key generic business strategies: *differentiation* and *cost leadership.* We pay special attention to value and cost drivers that managers can use to carve out a clear strategic profile. Next, we relate the two business-level strategies to the external environment, in particular, to the five forces in order to highlight their respective benefits and risks. We then introduce the notion of *blue ocean strategy*—using *value innovation* to combine a differentiation and cost-leadership strategic position. We also look at changes in competitive positioning over time before concluding with practical "Implications for the Strategist."

6.1 Business-Level Strategy: How to Compete for Advantage

Business-level strategy details the goal-directed actions managers take in their quest for competitive advantage when competing in a single product market.[3] It may involve a single product or a group of similar products that use the same distribution channel. It concerns the broad question, "How should we compete?" To formulate an appropriate business-level strategy, managers must answer the who, what, why, and how questions of competition:

- *Who*—which customer segments will we serve?
- *What* customer needs, wishes, and desires will we satisfy?
- *Why* do we want to satisfy them?
- *How* will we satisfy our customers' needs?[4]

To formulate an effective business strategy, managers need to keep in mind that competitive advantage is determined jointly by *industry* and *firm* effects. As shown in Exhibit 6.1, one route to competitive advantage is shaped by *industry effects,* while a second route is determined by *firm effects.* As discussed in Chapter 3, an industry's profit potential can be assessed using the five forces framework plus the availability of complements. Managers need to be certain that the business strategy is aligned with the five forces that shape competition. They can evaluate performance differences among clusters of firms in the same industry by conducting a strategic-group analysis. The concepts introduced in Chapter 4 are key in understanding firm effects because they allow us to look inside firms and explain why they differ based on their resources, capabilities, and competencies. It is also important to note

LO 6-1

Define business-level strategy and describe how it determines a firm's strategic position.

business-level strategy
The goal-directed actions managers take in their quest for competitive advantage when competing in a single product market.

EXHIBIT 6.1 / Industry and Firm Effects Jointly Determine Competitive Advantage

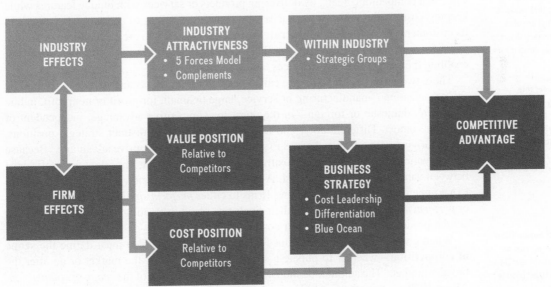

that industry and firm effects are not independent, but rather they are *interdependent,* as shown by the two-pointed arrow connecting industry effects and firm effects in Exhibit 6.1. At the firm level, performance is determined by value and cost positions *relative* to competitors. This is the firm's *strategic position,* to which we turn next.

STRATEGIC POSITION

We noted in Chapter 5 that competitive advantage is based on the difference between the *perceived value* a firm is able to create for consumers (V), captured by how much consumers are willing to pay for a product or service, and the total cost (C) the firm incurs to create that value. The greater the *economic value created* ($V - C$), the greater is a firm's potential for competitive advantage. To answer the business-level strategy question of how to compete, managers have two primary competitive levers at their disposal: value (V) and cost (C).

A firm's business-level strategy determines its *strategic position*—its strategic profile based on value creation and cost—in a specific product market. A firm attempts to stake out a valuable and unique position that meets customer needs while simultaneously creating as large a gap as possible between the value the firm's product creates and the cost required to produce it. Higher value creation tends to require higher cost. To achieve a desired strategic position, managers must make **strategic trade-offs**—choices between a cost *or* value position. Managers must address the tension between value creation and the pressure to keep cost in check so as not to erode the firm's economic value creation and profit margin. As shown in the ChapterCase, JetBlue experienced a competitive disadvantage because it was unable to effectively address the strategic trade-offs inherent in pursuing a cost-leadership *and* differentiation strategy at the same time. A business strategy is more likely to lead to a competitive advantage if a firm has a clear strategic profile, either as differentiator *or* a low-cost leader.

strategic trade-offs
Choices between a cost *or* value position. Such choices are necessary because higher value creation tends to generate higher cost.

GENERIC BUSINESS STRATEGIES

There are two fundamentally different generic business strategies—*differentiation* and *cost leadership*. A **differentiation strategy** seeks to create higher value for customers than the value that competitors create, by delivering products or services with unique features while keeping costs at the same or similar levels, allowing the firm to charge higher prices to its customers. A **cost-leadership strategy**, in contrast, seeks to create the same or similar value for customers by delivering products or services at a lower cost than competitors, enabling the firm to offer lower prices to its customers.

differentiation strategy
Generic business strategy that seeks to create higher value for customers than the value that competitors create.

These two business strategies are called *generic strategies* because they can be used by any organization—manufacturing or service, large or small, for-profit or nonprofit, public or private, domestic or foreign—in the quest for competitive advantage, independent of industry context. Differentiation and cost leadership require distinct strategic positions, and in turn increase a firm's chances to gain and sustain a competitive advantage.[5] Because value creation and cost tend to be positively correlated, however, important trade-offs exist between value creation and low cost. A business strategy, therefore, is more likely to lead to a competitive advantage if it allows firms to either *perform similar activities differently* or *perform different activities* than their rivals that result in creating more value or offering similar products or services at lower cost.[6]

cost-leadership strategy
Generic business strategy that seeks to create the same or similar value for customers at a lower cost.

When considering different business strategies, managers also must define the **scope of competition**—whether to pursue a specific, narrow part of the market or go after the broader market.[7] The automobile industry provides an example of the *scope of competition.* Alfred P. Sloan, longtime president and CEO of GM, defined the carmaker's mission as

scope of competition
The size—narrow or broad—of the market in which a firm chooses to compete.

providing *a car for every purse and purpose.* GM was one of the first to implement a multi-divisional structure in order to separate the brands into strategic business units, allowing each brand to create its unique strategic position (and profit and loss responsibility) within the broad automotive market. For example, GM's product lineup ranges from the low-cost-positioned Chevy brand to the differentiated Cadillac brand. In this case, Chevy is pursuing a broad cost-leadership strategy, while Cadillac is pursuing a broad differentiation strategy. The two different business strategies are integrated at the corporate level at GM (more on *corporate strategy* in Chapters 8 and 9). On the other hand, Tesla Motors, the maker of all-electric cars (featured in ChapterCase 3), offers a highly differentiated product and pursues only a small market segment. At this point, it uses a *focused differentiation strategy.* In particular, Tesla focuses on environmentally conscious consumers who are willing to pay a premium price. Taken together, GM's competitive scope is broad—with a focus on the mass automotive market—while Tesla's competitive scope is narrow—with a focus on high-end (all-electric) luxury cars.

Now we can combine the dimensions describing a firm's strategic position (*differentiation vs. cost*) with the scope of competition (*narrow vs. broad*). As shown in Exhibit 6.2, by doing so we get the two major broad business strategies (*cost leadership* and *differentiation*), shown as the top two boxes in the matrix, and the *focused* version of each (shown as the bottom two boxes in the matrix). The focused versions of the two business strategies—**focused cost-leadership strategy** and **focused differentiation strategy**—are essentially the same as the broad generic strategies *except* that the competitive scope is narrower. For example, the manufacturing company BIC pursues a focused cost-leadership strategy, designing and producing disposable pens and cigarette lighters at a low cost, while Mont Blanc pursues a focused differentiation strategy, offering exquisite pens—what it calls "writing instruments"—priced at several hundred dollars.

As discussed in ChapterCase 6, JetBlue attempted to combine a focused cost-leadership position with a focused differentiation position. Although initially successful, JetBlue has been consistently outperformed for the past few years by airlines that do not attempt to straddle different strategic positions, but rather have a clear strategic profile. For example, Southwest Airlines competes clearly as a broad cost leader (and would be placed squarely in the upper-left quadrant of Exhibit 6.2). The legacy carriers—Delta, American, and United—all compete as broad differentiators (and would be placed in the upper-right quadrant of Exhibit 6.2). Regionally, we find smaller airlines that are ultra low cost, such as Allegiant Air, Frontier Airlines, or Spirit Airlines, with a very clear strategic position (and would be placed in the lower-left quadrant of Exhibit 6.2 because they are pursuing a focused cost-leadership strategy). Based on a clear strategic position, these airlines have outperformed JetBlue over the last few years. The reason is that JetBlue is stuck between different strategic positions, trying to combine a focused cost-leadership position with focused differentiation. As JetBlue grew, the problems inherent in an attempt to straddle different strategic

focused cost-leadership strategy Same as the cost-leadership strategy except with a narrow focus on a niche market.

focused differentiation strategy Same as the differentiation strategy except with a narrow focus on a niche market.

EXHIBIT 6.2 / Strategic Position and Competitive Scope: Generic Business Strategies

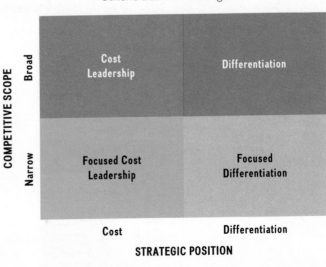

Source: Adapted from M.E. Porter (1980), *Competitive Strategy. Techniques for Analyzing Industries and Competitors* (New York: Free Press).

positions grew more severe because JetBlue now attempts to also straddle the (broad) cost-leadership position with the (broad) differentiation position, thus trying to be everything to everybody. Being *stuck in the middle* of different strategic positions is a recipe for inferior performance and competitive disadvantage—and this is exactly what JetBlue has experienced since the mid-2000s.

6.2 Differentiation Strategy: Understanding Value Drivers

The goal of a differentiation strategy is to add unique features that will increase the perceived value of goods and services in the minds of consumers so they are willing to pay a higher price. Ideally, a firm following a differentiation strategy aims to achieve in the minds of consumers a level of value creation that its competitors cannot easily match. The focus of competition in a differentiation strategy tends to be on unique product features, service, and new product launches, or on marketing and promotion rather than price. For example, the carpet company Interface is a leader in sustainability and offers innovative products such as its Cool Carpet, the world's first carbon-neutral floor covering. Interface's customers reward it with a willingness to pay a higher price for its environmentally friendly products.[8]

A company that uses a differentiation strategy can achieve a competitive advantage as long as its economic value created $(V - C)$ is greater than that of its competitors. Firm A in Exhibit 6.3 produces a generic commodity. Firm B and Firm C represent two efforts at differentiation. Firm B not only offers greater value than Firm A, but also maintains *cost parity,* meaning it has the same costs as Firm A. However, even if a firm fails to achieve cost parity (which is often the case because higher value creation tends to go along with higher costs in terms of higher-quality raw materials, research and development, employee training to provide superior customer service, and so on), it can still gain a competitive advantage if its economic value creation exceeds that of its competitors. Firm C represents just such a competitive advantage. For the approach shown *either* in Firm B or Firm C,

EXHIBIT 6.3

Differentiation Strategy: Achieving Competitive Advantage

Under a differentiation strategy, firms that successfully differentiate their products enjoy a competitive advantage. Firm A's product is seen as a generic commodity with no unique brand value. Firm B has the same cost structure as Firm A but creates more economic value, and thus has a competitive advantage over both Firm A and Firm C because $(V - C)_B > (V - C)_C > (V - C)_A$. Although, Firm C has higher costs than Firm A and B, it still generates a significantly higher economic value than Firm A.

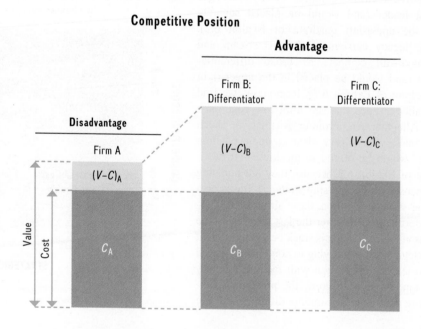

economic value creation, $(V - C)_B$ or $(V - C)_C$, is greater than that of Firm A $(V - C)_A$. Either Firm B or C, therefore, achieves a competitive advantage because it has a higher value gap over Firm A $[(V - C)_B > (V - C)_A$, or $(V - C)_C > (V - C)_A]$, which allows it to charge a premium price, reflecting its higher value creation. To complete the relative comparison, although both companies pursue a differentiation strategy, Firm B also has a competitive advantage over Firm C because although both offer identical value, Firm B has lower cost, thus $(V - C)_B > (V - C)_C$.

Although increased value creation is a defining feature of a differentiation strategy, managers must also control costs. Rising costs reduce economic value created and erode profit margins. Indeed, if cost rises too much as the firm attempts to create more perceived value for customers, its value gap shrinks, negating any differentiation advantage. One reason JetBlue could not maintain an initial competitive advantage was because it was unable to keep its costs down sufficiently. JetBlue's new management team immediately put measures in place to lower the airline's cost structure such as charging fees for checked bags and reducing leg space to increase passenger capacity on each of its planes. These cost-saving initiatives should increase its economic value creation.

Although a differentiation strategy is generally associated with premium pricing, managers have an important second pricing option. When a firm is able to offer a differentiated product or service and can control its costs at the same time, it is able to gain market share from other firms in the industry by charging a similar price but offering more perceived value. By leveraging its differentiated appeal of superior customer service and quality, for example, Marriott offers a line of different hotels: its flagship Marriott full-service business hotel equipped to host large conferences; Residence Inn for extended stay; Marriott Courtyard for business travelers; and Marriott Fairfield Inn for inexpensive leisure and family travel.[9] Although these hotels are roughly comparable to competitors in price, they generally offer a higher perceived value. With this line of different hotels, Marriott can benefit from economies of scale and scope, and thus keep its cost structure in check. *Economies of scale* denote decreases in cost per unit as output increases (more in the next section when we discuss cost-leadership strategy). **Economies of scope** describe the savings that come from producing two (or more) outputs at less cost than producing each output individually, even though using the same resources and technology. This larger difference between cost and value allows Marriott to achieve greater economic value than its competitors, and thus to gain market share and post superior performance.

> **economies of scope**
> Savings that come from producing two (or more) outputs at less cost than producing each output individually, despite using the same resources and technology.

Managers can adjust a number of different levers to improve a firm's strategic position. These levers either increase perceived value or decrease costs. Here, we will study the most salient *value drivers* that managers have at their disposal (we look at cost drivers in the next section).[10] They are:

■ Product features

■ Customer service

■ Complements

These value drivers are related to a firm's expertise in, and organization of, different internal value chain activities. Although these are the most important value drivers, no such list can be complete. Applying the concepts introduced in this chapter should allow managers to identify other important value and cost drivers unique to their business.

When attempting to increase the perceived value of the firm's product or service offerings, managers must remember that the different value drivers contribute to competitive advantage *only if* their increase in value creation (ΔV) exceeds the increase in costs (ΔC). The condition of $\Delta V > \Delta C$ must be fulfilled if a differentiation strategy is to strengthen a firm's strategic position and thus enhance its competitive advantage.

Trader Joe's is a chain of more than 400 stores, half of which are in California and the rest in another 38 states plus Washington, D.C. The chain is known for good products, value for money, clerks in Hawaiian shirts— and great customer service. As just one example, stores happily stock local products as requested by their communities.[14]
© Karsten Moran/Aurora Photos/Alamy

PRODUCT FEATURES

One of the obvious but most important levers that managers can adjust is product features, thereby increasing the perceived value of the product or service offering. Adding unique product attributes allows firms to turn commodity products into differentiated products commanding a premium price. Strong R&D capabilities are often needed to create superior product features. In the kitchen-utensil industry, OXO follows a differentiation strategy, highlighting product features. By adhering to its "philosophy of making products that are easy to use for the widest spectrum of possible users,"[11] OXO differentiates its kitchen utensils through its patent-protected ergonomically designed soft black rubber grips.

CUSTOMER SERVICE

Managers can increase the perceived value of their firms' product or service offerings by focusing on customer service. For example, the online retailer Zappos earned a reputation for superior customer service by offering free shipping both ways: to the customer and for returns.[12] Zappos' managers didn't view this as an additional expense but rather as part of their marketing budget. Moreover, Zappos does not outsource its customer service, and its associates do not use predetermined scripts. They are instead encouraged to build a relationship of trust with each individual customer. There seemed to be a good return on investment as word spread through the online shopping community. Competitors took notice, too; Amazon bought Zappos for over $1 billion.[13]

COMPLEMENTS

When studying industry analysis in Chapter 3, we identified the availability of complements as an important force determining the profit potential of an industry. Complements add value to a product or service when they are consumed in tandem. Finding complements, therefore, is an important task for managers in their quest to enhance the value of their offerings.

The introduction of AT&T U-verse is an example of leveraging complements to increase the perceived value of a service offering.[15] AT&T's U-verse service bundles high-speed Internet access, phone, and TV services. Service bundles can be further enhanced by DVR capabilities that allow users to pause live TV, to record live TV shows, and to access video on demand. A DVR by itself is not very valuable, but included as a "free" add-on to subscribers, it turns into a complement that significantly enhances the perceived value of the service bundle. Leveraging complementary products allowed AT&T to break into the highly competitive television services market, significantly enhancing the value of its service offerings.

As you have just seen, the differentiation strategy covers a great deal of ground, so let's summarize what we have learned. By choosing the differentiation strategy as the strategic position for a product, managers focus their attention on adding value to the product through its unique features that respond to customer preferences, customer service during and after the sale, or effective marketing that communicates the value of the product's features. Although this positioning involves increased costs (for example, higher-quality inputs or innovative research and development activities), customers will be willing to pay a premium price for the product or service that satisfies their needs and preferences. In the next section, we will discuss how managers formulate a cost-leadership strategy.

6.3 Cost-Leadership Strategy: Understanding Cost Drivers

LO 6-3

Examine the relationship between cost drivers and the cost-leadership strategy.

The goal of a cost-leadership strategy is to reduce the firm's cost below that of its competitors while offering adequate value. The *cost leader,* as the name implies, focuses its attention and resources on reducing the cost to manufacture a product or deliver a service in order to offer lower prices to its customers. The cost leader attempts to optimize all of its value chain activities to achieve a low-cost position. Although staking out the lowest-cost position in the industry is the overriding strategic objective, a cost leader still needs to offer products and services of acceptable value. As an example, GM and Korean car manufacturer Kia offer some models that compete directly with one another, yet Kia's cars tend to be produced at lower cost, while providing a similar value proposition.

A cost leader can achieve a competitive advantage as long as its economic value created $(V - C)$ is greater than that of its competitors. Firm A in Exhibit 6.4 produces a product with a cost structure vulnerable to competition. Firms B and C show two different approaches to cost leadership. Firm B achieves a competitive advantage over Firm A because Firm B not only has lower cost than Firm A, but also achieves *differentiation parity* (meaning it creates the same value as Firm A). As a result, Firm B's economic value creation, $(V - C)_B$, is greater than that of Firm A, $(V - C)_A$. For example, as the low-cost leader, Walmart took market share from Kmart, which subsequently filed for bankruptcy.

What if a firm fails to create differentiation parity? Such parity is often hard to achieve because value creation tends to go along with higher costs, and Firm B's strategy is aimed at lower costs. A firm can still gain a competitive advantage as long as its economic value creation exceeds that of its competitors. Firm C represents this approach to cost leadership. Even with lower value (no differentiation parity) but lower cost, Firm C's economic value creation, $(V - C)_C$, still is greater than that of Firm A, $(V - C)_A$.

EXHIBIT 6.4 /

Cost-Leadership Strategy: Achieving Competitive Advantage

Under a cost-leadership strategy, firms that can keep their cost at the lowest point in the industry while offering acceptable value are able to gain a competitive advantage. Firm A has not managed to take advantage of possible cost savings, and thus experiences a competitive disadvantage. The offering from Firm B has the same perceived value as Firm A but through more effective cost containment creates more economic value (over both Firm A and Firm C because $(V - C)_B > (V - C)_C > (V - C)_A$. The offering from Firm C has a lower perceived value than that of Firm A or B and has the same reduced product cost as with Firm B; as a result, Firm C still generates higher economic value than Firm A.

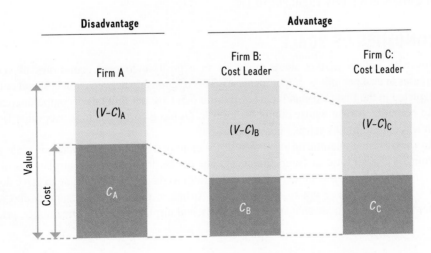

Competitive Position

In both approaches to cost leadership in Exhibit 6.4, Firm B's economic value creation is greater than that of Firm A and Firm C. Yet, both firms B and C achieve a competitive advantage over Firm A. Either one can charge prices similar to its competitors and benefit from a greater profit margin per unit, or it can charge lower prices than its competition and gain higher profits from higher volume. Both variations of a cost-leadership strategy can result in competitive advantage. Although Firm B has a competitive advantage over both Firms A and C, Firm C has a competitive advantage in comparison to Firm A.

Although companies successful at cost leadership must excel at controlling costs, this doesn't mean that they can neglect value creation. Kia signals the quality of its cars with a five-year, 60,000-mile warranty, one of the more generous warranties in the industry. Walmart offers products of acceptable quality, including many brand-name products.

The most important *cost drivers* that managers can manipulate to keep their costs low are:

- Cost of input factors.
- Economies of scale.
- Learning-curve effects.
- Experience-curve effects.

However, this list is only a starting point; managers may consider other cost drivers, depending on the situation.

COST OF INPUT FACTORS

One of the most basic advantages a firm can have over its rivals is access to lower-cost input factors such as raw materials, capital, labor, and IT services. In the market for international long-distance travel, the greatest competitive threat facing U.S. legacy carriers—American, Delta, and United—comes from three fast-growing airlines located in the Persian Gulf states—Emirates, Etihad, and Qatar. These airlines achieve a competitive advantage over their U.S. counterparts thanks to lower-cost inputs—raw materials (access to cheaper fuel), capital (interest-free government loans), labor—and fewer regulations (for example, regarding nighttime takeoffs and landings, or in adding new runways and building luxury airports with swimming pools, among other amenities).[16] To benefit from lower-cost IT services, the gulf carriers also outsource some value chain activities such as booking and online customer service to India. Together, these distinct cost advantages across several key input factors add up to create a greater economic value creation for the gulf carriers vis-à-vis U.S. competitors, leading to a competitive advantage (more on the gulf carriers in Strategy Highlight 10.1).

ECONOMIES OF SCALE

economies of scale
Decreases in cost per
unit as output increases.

Firms with greater market share might be in a position to reap **economies of scale**, decreases in cost per unit as output increases. This relationship between unit cost and output is depicted in the first (left-hand) part of Exhibit 6.5: Cost per unit falls as output increases up to point Q_1. A firm whose output is closer to Q_1 has a cost advantage over other firms with less output. In this sense, bigger is better.

In the airframe-manufacturing industry, for example, reaping economies of scale and learning is critical for cost-competitiveness. The market for commercial airplanes is often not large enough to allow more than one competitor to reach sufficient scale to drive down unit cost. Boeing chose not to compete with Airbus in the market for superjumbo jets; rather, it decided to focus on a smaller, fuel-efficient airplane (the 787 Dreamliner, priced

EXHIBIT 6.5 /

Economies of
Scale, Minimum
Efficient Scale, and
Diseconomies of
Scale

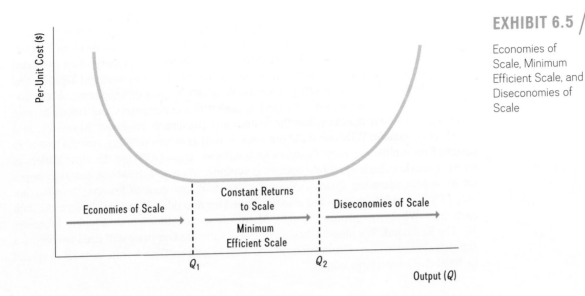

at roughly $250 million) that allows for long-distance, point-to-point connections. By 2015, it had built over 250 Dreamliners with more than 1,000 orders for the new airplane.[17] Boeing can expect to reap significant economies of scale and learning, which will lower per-unit cost. At the same time, Airbus had delivered over 150 A380 superjumbos (sticker price: $430 million) with more than 310 orders on its books.[18] If both companies would have chosen to compete head-on in each market segment, the resulting per-unit cost for each airplane would have been much higher because neither could have achieved significant economies of scale (overall their market share split is roughly 50–50).

What causes per-unit cost to drop as output increases (up to point Q_1)? Economies of scale allow firms to:

■ Spread their fixed costs over a larger output.

■ Employ specialized systems and equipment.

■ Take advantage of certain physical properties.

SPREADING FIXED COSTS OVER LARGER OUTPUT. Larger output allows firms to spread their fixed costs over more units. That is why gains in market share are often critical to drive down per-unit cost. This relationship is even more pronounced in many high-tech industries because most of the cost occurs before a single product or service is sold. Take operating systems software as an example. Between 2007 and 2009, Microsoft spent approximately $25 billion on R&D, a significant portion of it on its new Windows 7 operating system.[19] This R&D expense was a fixed cost Microsoft had to incur before a single copy of Windows 7 was sold. However, once the initial version of the new software was completed, the marginal cost of each additional copy was basically zero, especially for copies sold in digital form online. Given that Microsoft dominates the operating system market for personal computers (PCs) with more than 90 percent market share, it sold several hundred million copies of Windows 7, thereby spreading its huge fixed cost of development over a large output. Moreover, Microsoft's large installed base of Windows operating systems throughout the world allowed it to capture a large profit margin for each copy of Windows sold, after recouping its initial investment.

Microsoft's advantage based on its large installed base on personal computers, however, is no longer as valuable.[20] Due to the shift to mobile computing, demand for PCs has been in free-fall in recent years. Before 2010, growth in the PC industry often exceeded more than 20 percent a year. Since then, the market for PCs has declined rapidly. The launch of Microsoft's next operating system—Windows 8—was disappointing. A key feature of Windows 8 was the ability to straddle both personal computers and mobile devices by providing a dual interface, but the feature left consumers confused. Moreover, in a mobile environment, Windows 8 did not work as well as other operating systems that were designed for mobile use only; Google (Android) and Apple (iOS) are the clear leaders in terms of market share in mobile operating systems. Microsoft, however, has high hopes for its newest operating system—Windows 10—with the goal of bringing together not only PCs and mobile devices but also the Xbox One and other Windows devices. As with each prior Windows operating system, Microsoft spent billions in developing Windows 10. The Redmond, Washington-based computer software company will need to capture a significant market share (from Android and iOS) to gain sufficient scale in order to spread its fixed cost over a large output.

EMPLOYING SPECIALIZED SYSTEMS AND EQUIPMENT.

Larger output also allows firms to invest in more specialized systems and equipment, such as enterprise resource planning (ERP) software or manufacturing robots. As discussed in ChapterCase 3, Tesla's strong demand for its Model S sedan allowed it to employ cutting-edge robotics in its Fremont, California, manufacturing plant to produce cars of the highest quality at large scale.

TAKING ADVANTAGE OF CERTAIN PHYSICAL PROPERTIES.

Economies of scale also occur because of certain physical properties. One such property is known as the *cube-square rule:* The volume of a body such as a pipe or a tank increases disproportionately more than its surface. This same principle makes big-box retail stores such as Walmart, Best Buy, The Home Depot, and Toys "R" Us cheaper to build and run. They can also stock much more merchandise and handle inventory more efficiently. Their huge size makes it difficult for department stores or small retailers to compete on cost and selection.

minimum efficient scale (MES) Output range needed to bring down the cost per unit as much as possible, allowing a firm to stake out the lowest-cost position that is achievable through economies of scale.

Look again at Exhibit 6.5. The output range between Q_1 and Q_2 in the figure is considered the **minimum efficient scale (MES)** in order to be cost-competitive. Between Q_1 and Q_2, the returns to scale are constant. It is the output range needed to bring the cost per unit down as much as possible, allowing a firm to stake out the lowest-cost position achievable through economies of scale. If the firm's output range is less than Q_1 or more than Q_2, the firm is at a cost disadvantage.

With more than 6 million Prius cars sold since its introduction in 1997, Toyota has been able to reach the minimum efficient scale part of the per-unit cost curve. This allows the company to offer the car at a relatively low price and still make a profit.

The concept of minimum efficient scale applies not only to manufacturing processes but also to managerial tasks such as how to organize work. Due to investments in specialized technology and equipment (e.g., electric arc furnaces), Nucor is able to reach MES with much smaller batches of steel than larger, fully vertically integrated steel companies using older technology. Nucor's optimal plant size is about 500 people, which is much smaller than at larger integrated steelmakers such as U.S. Steel (which often employs thousands of workers per plant).[21] Of course, minimum efficient scale depends on the specific industry: The average per-unit cost curve, depicted conceptually in Exhibit 6.5, is a reflection of the underlying production function, which is determined by technology and other input factors.

Benefits to scale cannot go on indefinitely, though. Bigger is not always better; in fact, sometimes bigger is worse. Beyond Q_2 in Exhibit 6.5, firms experience **diseconomies of scale**—increases in cost as output increases. As firms get too big, the complexity of managing and coordinating raises the cost, negating any benefits to scale. Large firms tend to become overly bureaucratic, with too many layers of hierarchy. They grow inflexible and slow in decision making. To avoid problems associated with diseconomies of scale, Gore Associates, maker of GORE-TEX fabric, Glide dental floss, and many other innovative products, breaks up its company into smaller units. Gore Associates found that employing about 150 people per plant allows it to avoid diseconomies of scale. It uses a simple decision rule:[22] "We put 150 parking spaces in the lot, and when people start parking on the grass, we know it's time to build a new plant."[23]

Finally, there are also physical limits to scale. Airbus is pushing the envelope with its A380 aircraft, which can hold more than 850 passengers and fly up to 8,200 miles (enough to travel nonstop from Boston to Hong Kong at about 600 mph). The goal, of course, is to drive down the cost of the average seat-mile flown (CASM, a standard cost metric in the airline industry). It remains to be seen whether the A380 superjumbo will enable airlines to reach minimum efficient scale or will simply be too large to be efficient. For example, boarding and embarking procedures must be streamlined to accommodate more than 850 people in a timely and safe manner. Many airports around the world will need to be retrofitted with longer and wider runways to allow the superjumbo to take off and land.

Taken together, *scale economies* are critical to driving down a firm's cost and strengthening a cost-leadership position. Although managers need to increase output to operate at a minimum efficient scale (between Q_1 and Q_2 in Exhibit 6.5), they also need to be watchful not to drive scale beyond Q_2, where they would encounter diseconomies. Monitoring the firm's cost structure closely over different output ranges allows managers to fine-tune operations and benefit from economies of scale.

> **diseconomies of scale**
> Increases in cost per unit when output increases.

LEARNING CURVE

Do learning curves go up or down? Looking at the challenge of learning, many people tend to see it as an uphill battle, and assume the learning curve goes up. But if we consider our productivity, learning curves go down, as it takes less and less time to produce the same output as we learn how to be more efficient—learning by doing drives down cost. As individuals and teams engage repeatedly in an activity, whether writing computer code, developing new medicines, or building submarines, they learn from their cumulative experience.[24] *Learning curves* were first documented in aircraft manufacturing as the United States ramped up production in the 1930s, prior to its entry into World War II.[25] Every time production was doubled, the per-unit cost dropped by a predictable and constant rate (approximately 20 percent).[26] This important relationship is captured in Exhibit 6.6, where we see two different learning curves. The steeper the learning curve, the more learning has taken place. As cumulative output increases, firms move down the learning curve, reaching lower per-unit costs.

In particular, Exhibit 6.6 depicts a 90 percent and an 80 percent learning curve. In a 90 percent learning curve, per-unit cost drops 10 percent every time output is doubled. The steeper 80 percent learning curve indicates a 20 percent drop every time output is doubled (this was the case in the aircraft manufacturing example above). It is important to note that the learning-curve effect is driven by increasing cumulative output within the existing technology over time. That implies that the only difference between two points on the same learning curve is the size of the cumulative output. The underlying technology remains the same. The speed of learning determines the slope of the learning curve, or how steep the learning curve is (e.g., 80 percent is steeper than a 90 percent learning curve, because costs decrease by 20 percent versus a mere 10 percent each time output doubles). In this

EXHIBIT 6.6 / Gaining Competitive Advantage through Leveraging Learning- and Experience-Curve Effects

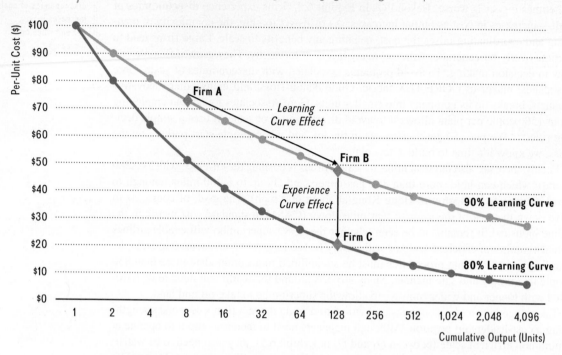

perspective, economies of learning allow movement down a *given* learning curve based on current production technology.

By moving further down a given learning curve than competitors, a firm can gain a competitive advantage. For example, Exhibit 6.6 shows that Firm B is further down the 90 percent learning curve than Firm A. Firm B leverages economies of learning due to larger cumulative output to gain an advantage over Firm A. The only variable that has changed is cumulative output; the technology underlying the 90 percent learning curve remained the same. Let's continue with the example of manufacturing airframes. To be more precise, as shown in Exhibit 6.6, Firm A produces eight aircraft and reaches a per-unit cost of $73 million per aircraft.[27] Firm B produces 128 aircraft using the same technology as Firm A (because both firms are on the same [90 percent] learning curve), but given a much larger cumulative output, its per unit-cost falls to only $48 million. Thus, Firm B has a clear competitive advantage over Firm A (assuming similar or identical quality in output). (We will discuss Firm C when we formally introduce the impact of changes in technology and process innovation.)

It is not surprising that a learning curve was first observed in aircraft manufacturing. Highly complex, a modern commercial aircraft can contain more than 5 million parts, compared with a few thousand for a car. The more complex the underlying process to manufacture a product or deliver a service, the more learning effects we can expect. As cumulative output increases, managers learn how to optimize the process, and workers improve their performance through repetition.

Learning curves are a robust phenomenon that have been observed in many industries, not only in manufacturing processes but also in alliance management, franchising, and health care.[28] For example, physicians who perform only a small number of cardiac surgeries per year can have a patient mortality rate five times higher than physicians who perform the same surgery more frequently.[29] Strategy Highlight 6.1 features Dr. Devi Shetty of India who reaped huge benefits by applying learning-curve principles to open-heart surgery, driving down cost while improving quality at the same time!

Strategy Highlight 6.1

Dr. Shetty: "The Henry Ford of Heart Surgery"

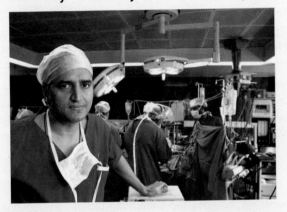

Dr. Devi Shetty
© Namas Bhojani

Open-heart surgeries are complex medical procedures, and loaded with risk. While well-trained surgeons using high-tech equipment are able to reduce mortality rates, costs for cardiac surgeries in the United States have climbed. Difficult heart surgeries can cost $100,000 or more. A heart surgeon in India has driven the costs down to an average of $2,000 per heart surgery, while delivering equal or better outcomes in terms of quality.

Dr. Devi Shetty's goal is to be "the Henry Ford of heart surgery." Just like the great American industrialist who applied the learning curve to drive down the cost of an automobile to make it affordable, so Dr. Shetty is reducing the costs of health care and making some of the most complex medical procedures affordable to the world's poorest. A native of Mangalore, India, Dr. Shetty was trained as a heart surgeon at Guy's Hospital in London, one of Europe's best medical facilities. He first came to fame in the 1990s when he successfully conducted an open-heart bypass surgery on Mother Teresa, after she suffered a heart attack.

Dr. Shetty believes that the key to driving down costs in health care is not product innovation, but process innovation. He is able to drive down the cost of complex medical procedures from $100,000 to $2,000 not by doing one big thing, but rather by focusing on doing 1,000 small things. Dr. Shetty is applying the concept of the learning curve to make a complex procedure routine and comparatively inexpensive. Part of the Narayana Health group, Dr. Shetty's hospital in Bangalore, India, performs so many cardiac procedures per year that doctors are able to get a great deal of experience quickly, which allows them to specialize in one or two complex procedures. The Narayana surgeons perform two or three procedures a day for six days a week, compared to U.S. surgeons who perform one or two procedures

a day for five days a week. The difference adds up. Some of Dr. Shetty's surgeons perform more specialized procedures by the time they are in their 30s than their U.S. counterparts will perform throughout their entire careers. This volume of experience allows the cardiac surgeons to move down the learning curve quickly, because the more heart surgeries they perform, the more their skills improve. With this skill level, surgical teams develop robust standard operating procedures and processes, where team members become experts at their specific tasks.

This expertise improves outcomes while the learning-curve effects of performing the same procedures over time also save money (see Exhibit 6.6). Other factors provide more cost savings. At the same time, Dr. Shetty pays his cardiac surgeons the going rate in India, between $110,000 and $250,000 a year, depending on experience. Their U.S. counterparts earn two to three times the average Indian salary.

Dr. Shetty's health group also reduces costs through economies of scale. By performing thousands of heart surgeries a year, high fixed costs such as the purchase of expensive medical equipment can be spread over a much larger volume. The Narayana hospital in Bangalore has 1,000 beds and some 20 operating rooms that stay busy pretty much around the clock, many times larger than the average U.S. hospital with 160 beds. This scale allows the Narayana heart clinic to cost-effectively employ specialized high-tech equipment. Given the large size of Dr. Shetty's hospital, he also has significant buying power, driving down the costs of the latest high-tech equipment from top-notch vendors such as GE. Wherever possible, Dr. Shetty sources lower-cost inputs such as sutures locally, rather than from the more expensive companies such as Johnson & Johnson. Further, the Narayana heart clinic shares common services, such as laboratories and blood bank and more mundane services such as catering, with the 1,400-bed cancer clinic next door. Taken together, all of these small changes result in significant cost savings, and so create a reinforcing system of low-cost value chain activities.

While many worry that high volume compromises quality, the data suggest the opposite: Narayana Health's medical outcomes in terms of mortality rate are equal to or even lower than the best hospitals in the United States. The American College of Cardiology frequently sends surgeons and administrators to visit the Narayana heart clinic. The college concluded that the clinic provides high-tech and high-quality care at low cost. Dr. Shetty now brings top-notch care at low cost to the masses in India. Narayana Health runs a chain of over 30 hospitals in 20 locations throughout India and performs some 100,000 heart surgeries a year.[30]

Learning effects differ from economies of scale (discussed earlier) as shown:

- **Differences in timing.** Learning effects occur *over time* as output accumulates, while economies of scale are captured at *one point in time* when output increases. Although learning can decline or flatten (see Exhibit 6.6), there are no *diseconomies to learning* (unlike *diseconomies to scale* in Exhibit 6.5).

- **Differences in complexity.** In some production processes (e.g., the manufacture of steel rods), effects from economies of scale can be quite significant, while learning effects are minimal. In contrast, in some professions (brain surgery or the practice of estate law), learning effects can be substantial, while economies of scale are minimal.

Managers need to understand such differences to calibrate their business-level strategy. If a firm's cost advantage is due to economies of scale, a manager should worry less about employee turnover (and a potential loss in learning) and more about drops in production runs. In contrast, if the firm's low-cost position is based on complex learning, a manager should be much more concerned if a key employee (e.g., a star researcher) was to leave.

EXPERIENCE CURVE

In the *learning curve* just discussed, we assumed the underlying technology remained constant, while only cumulative output increased. In the *experience curve,* in contrast, we now change the underlying technology while holding cumulative output constant.[31]

In general, technology and production processes do not stay constant. *Process innovation*—a new method or technology to produce an existing product—may initiate a new and steeper curve. Assume that Firm C, on the same learning curve as Firm B, implements a new production process (such as lean manufacturing). In doing so, Firm C initiates an entirely new and steeper learning curve. Exhibit 6.6 shows this *experience-curve effect* based on a process innovation. Firm C jumps down to the 80 percent learning curve, reflecting the new and lower-cost production process. Although Firm B and Firm C produce the same cumulative output (each making 128 aircraft), the per-unit cost differs. Firm B's per-unit cost for each airplane, being positioned on the less-steep 90 percent learning curve is $48 million.[32] In contrast, Firm C's per-unit cost, being positioned on the steeper 80 percent learning curve because of process innovation, is only $21 million per aircraft, and thus less than half of that of Firm B. Clearly, Firm C has a competitive advantage over Firm B based on lower cost per unit (assuming similar quality).

Learning by doing allows a firm to lower its per-unit costs by moving down a given learning curve, while experience-curve effects based on process innovation allow a firm to leapfrog to a steeper learning curve, thereby driving down its per-unit costs.

In Strategy Highlight 6.1, we saw how Dr. Shetty leveraged learning-curve effects to save lives while driving down costs. One could argue that his Narayana Health group not only moved down a given learning curve using best industry practice, but it also jumped down to a new and steeper learning curve through process innovation. Dr. Shetty sums up his business strategy based on cost leadership: "Japanese companies reinvented the process of making cars (by introducing lean manufacturing). That's what we're doing in health care. What health care needs is process innovation, not product innovation."[33]

In a cost-leadership strategy, managers must focus on lowering the costs of production while maintaining a level of quality acceptable to the customer. If firms can share the benefits of lower costs with consumers, cost leaders appeal to the bargain-conscious buyer, whose main criterion is price. By looking to reduce costs in each value chain activity, managers aim for the lowest-cost position in the industry. Thus they strive to offer lower prices than competitors and to attract increased sales. Cost leaders such as Walmart ("Every Day Low Prices"), can profit from this strategic position over time.

6.4 Business-Level Strategy and the Five Forces: Benefits and Risks

The business-level strategies introduced in this chapter allow firms to carve out strong strategic positions that enhance the likelihood of gaining and sustaining competitive advantage. The five forces model introduced in Chapter 3 helps managers assess the forces—threat of entry, power of suppliers, power of buyers, threat of substitutes, and rivalry among existing competitors—that make some industries more attractive than others. With this understanding of industry dynamics, managers use one of the generic business-level strategies to protect themselves against the forces that drive down profitability.[34] Exhibit 6.7 details the relationship between competitive positioning and the five forces. In particular, it highlights the benefits and risks of differentiation and cost-leadership business strategies, which we discuss next.

EXHIBIT 6.7 / Competitive Positioning and the Five Forces: Benefits and Risks of Differentiation and Cost-Leadership Business Strategies

Competitive Force	Differentiation		Cost Leadership	
	Benefits	**Risks**	**Benefits**	**Risks**
Threat of entry	• Protection against entry due to intangible resources such as a reputation for innovation, quality, or customer service	• Erosion of margins • Replacement	• Protection against entry due to economies of scale	• Erosion of margins • Replacement
Power of suppliers	• Protection against increase in input prices, which can be passed on to customers	• Erosion of margins	• Protection against increase in input prices, which can be absorbed	• Erosion of margins
Power of buyers	• Protection against decrease in sales prices, because well-differentiated products or services are not perfect imitations	• Erosion of margins	• Protection against decrease in sales prices, which can be absorbed	• Erosion of margins
Threat of substitutes	• Protection against substitute products due to differential appeal	• Replacement, especially when faced with innovation	• Protection against substitute products through further lowering of prices	• Replacement, especially when faced with innovation
Rivalry among existing competitors	• Protection against competitors if product or service has enough differential appeal to command premium price	• Focus of competition shifts to price • Increasing differentiation of product features that do not create value but raise costs • Increasing differentiation to raise costs above acceptable threshold	• Protection against price wars because lowest-cost firm will win	• Focus of competition shifts to non-price attributes • Lowering costs to drive value creation below acceptable threshold

Source: Based on M.E. Porter (2008), "The five competitive forces that shape strategy," *Harvard Business Review*, January; and M.E. Porter (1980), *Competitive Strategy: Techniques for Analyzing Industries and Competitors* (New York: Free Press).

DIFFERENTIATION STRATEGY: BENEFITS AND RISKS

A differentiation strategy is defined by establishing a strategic position that creates higher perceived value while controlling costs. The successful differentiator stakes out a unique strategic position, where it can benefit from imperfect competition (as discussed in Chapter 3) and command a premium price. A well-executed differentiation strategy reduces rivalry among competitors.

A successful differentiation strategy is likely to be based on unique or specialized features of the product, on an effective marketing campaign, or on intangible resources such as a reputation for innovation, quality, and customer service. A rival would need to improve the product features as well as build a similar or more effective reputation in order to gain market share. The threat of entry is reduced: Competitors will find such intangible advantages time-consuming and costly, and maybe impossible, to imitate. If the source of the differential appeal is intangible rather than tangible (e.g., reputation rather than observable product and service features), a differentiator is even more likely to sustain its advantage.

Moreover, if the differentiator is able to create a significant difference between perceived value and current market prices, the differentiator will not be so threatened by increases in input prices due to powerful suppliers. Although an increase in input factors could erode margins, a differentiator is likely able to pass on price increases to its customersas long as its value creation exceeds the price charged. Since a successful differentiator creates perceived value in the minds of consumers and builds customer loyalty, powerful buyers demanding price decreases are unlikely to emerge. A strong differentiated position also reduces the threat of substitutes, because the unique features of the product have been created to appeal to customer preferences, keeping them loyal to the product. By providing superior quality beverages and other food items combined with a great customer experienceand a global presence, Starbucks has built a strong differentiated appeal. It has cultivated a loyal following of customers who reward it with repeat business.

The viability of a differentiation strategy is severely undermined when the focus of competition shifts to price rather than value-creating features. This can happen when differentiated products become commoditized and an acceptable standard of quality has emerged across rival firms. Although the iPhone was a highly differentiated product when first introduced in 2007, touch-based screens and other once-innovative features are now standard in smartphones. Indeed, Android-based smartphones held more than 80 percent market share in 2015, while Apple's iOS held 15 percent.[35] Several companies including Samsung and low-cost leader Xiaomi of China are attempting to challenge Apple's ability to extract significant profits from the smartphone industry based on its iPhone franchise. A differentiator also needs to be careful not to overshoot its differentiated appeal by adding product features that raise costs but not perceived value in the minds of consumers. For example, any additional increase in screen resolution beyond Apple's retina display cannot be detected by the human eye at a normal viewing distance. Finally, a differentiator needs to be vigilant that its costs of providing uniqueness do not rise above the customer's willingness to pay.

COST-LEADERSHIP STRATEGY: BENEFITS AND RISKS

A cost-leadership strategy is defined by obtaining the lowest-cost position in the industry while offering acceptable value. The cost leader, therefore, is protected from other competitors because of having the lowest cost. If a price war ensues, the low-cost leader will be the last firm standing; all other firms will be driven out as margins evaporate. Since reaping economies of scale is critical to reaching a low-cost position, the cost leader is likely to have a large market share, which in turn reduces the threat of entry.

A cost leader is also fairly well isolated from threats of powerful suppliers to increase input prices, because it is more able to absorb price increases through accepting lower profit margins. Likewise, a cost leader can absorb price reductions more easily when demanded by powerful buyers. Should substitutes emerge, the low-cost leader can try to fend them off by further lowering its prices to reinstall relative value with the substitute. For example, Walmart tends to be fairly isolated from these threats. Walmart's cost structure combined with its large volume allows it to work with suppliers in keeping prices low, to the extent that suppliers are often the party who experiences a profit margin squeeze.

Although a cost-leadership strategy provides some protection against the five forces, it also carries some risks. If a new entrant with new and relevant expertise enters the market, the low-cost leader's margins may erode due to loss in market share while it attempts to learn new capabilities. For example, Walmart faces challenges to its cost leadership. The Dollar Store has drawn customers who prefer a smaller format than the big box of Walmart. The risk of replacement is particularly pertinent if a potent substitute emerges due to an innovation. Leveraging e-commerce, Amazon has become a potent substitute and thus a powerful threat to many brick-and-mortar retail outlets including Barnes & Noble, Best Buy, The Home Depot, and even Walmart. Powerful suppliers and buyers may be able to reduce margins so much that the low-cost leader could have difficulty covering the cost of capital and lose the potential for a competitive advantage.

The low-cost leader also needs to stay vigilant to keep its cost the lowest in the industry. Over time, competitors can beat the cost leader by implementing the same business strategy, but more effectively. Although keeping its cost the lowest in the industry is imperative, the cost leader must not forget that it needs to create an acceptable level of value. If continuously lowering costs leads to a value proposition that falls below an acceptable threshold, the low-cost leader's market share will evaporate. Finally, the low-cost leader faces significant difficulties when the focus of competition shifts from price to non-price attributes.

We have seen how useful the five forces model can be in industry analysis. None of the business-level strategies depicted in Exhibit 6.2 (cost leadership, differentiation, and focused variations thereof) is inherently superior. The success of each depends on context and relies on two factors:

- How well the strategy leverages the firm's internal strengths while mitigating its weaknesses.
- How well it helps the firm exploit external opportunities while avoiding external threats.

There is no single correct business strategy for a specific industry. The deciding factor is that the chosen business strategy provides a strong position that attempts to maximize economic value creation and is effectively implemented.

6.5 Blue Ocean Strategy: Combining Differentiation and Cost Leadership

So far we've seen that firms can create more economic value and their likelihood of gaining and sustaining competitive advantage in one of two ways—either increasing perceived consumer value (while containing costs) or lowering costs (while offering acceptable value). Should managers try to do both at the same time? To accomplish this, they would need to integrate two different strategic positions: differentiation *and* low cost.[36] In general the answer is *no*. Managers should not pursue this complex strategy because of the inherent trade-offs in different strategic positions, unless they are able to reconcile the conflicting requirements of each generic strategy.

To meet this challenge, the strategy scholars Kim and Mauborgne advance the notion of a **blue ocean strategy**, which is a business-level strategy that successfully combines differentiation and cost-leadership activities using value innovation to reconcile the inherent trade-offs in those two distinct strategic positions.[37] They use the metaphor of an ocean to denote market spaces. *Blue oceans* represent untapped market space, the creation of additional demand, and the resulting opportunities for highly profitable growth. In contrast, *red oceans* are the known market space of existing industries. In *red oceans* the rivalry among existing firms is cut-throat because the market space is crowded and competition is a zero-sum game. Products become commodities, and competition is focused mainly on price. Any market share gain comes at the expense of other competitors in the same industry, turning the oceans bloody red.

A blue ocean strategy allows a firm to offer a differentiated product or service at low cost. As one example of a blue ocean strategy, consider Trader Joe's, the regional grocer introduced earlier in the chapter. Trader Joe's has much lower costs than Whole Foods for the same market of patrons desiring high value and health-conscious foods, and the chain scores exceptionally well in customer service and other areas. When a blue ocean strategy is successfully formulated and implemented, investments in differentiation and low cost are not substitutes but are complements, providing important positive spill-over effects. A successfully implemented blue ocean strategy allows firms two pricing options: First, the firm can charge a higher price than the cost leader, reflecting its higher value creation and thus generating greater profit margins. Second, the firm can lower its price below that of the differentiator because of its lower-cost structure. If the firm offers lower prices than the differentiator, it can gain market share and make up the loss in margin through increased sales.

blue ocean strategy
Business-level strategy that successfully combines differentiation and cost-leadership activities using value innovation to reconcile the inherent trade-offs.

value innovation
The simultaneous pursuit of differentiation and low cost in a way that creates a leap in value for both the firm and the consumers; considered a cornerstone of blue ocean strategy.

Canny managers may use *value innovation* to move to blue oceans, that is, to new and uncontested market spaces. (Shown here is the famous "blue hole" just off Belize.)

© Mlenny/Getty Images RF

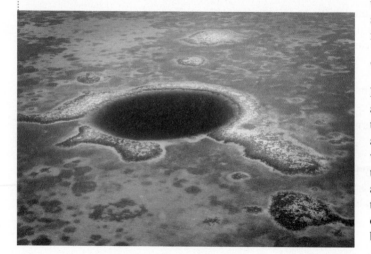

VALUE INNOVATION

For a blue ocean strategy to succeed, managers must resolve trade-offs between the two generic strategic positions—low cost and differentiation.[38] This is done through **value innovation**, aligning innovation with total perceived consumer benefits, price and cost (also see the discussion in Chapter 5 on *economic value creation*). Instead of attempting to out-compete your rivals by offering better features or lower costs, successful value innovation makes competition irrelevant by providing a leap in value creation, thereby opening new and uncontested market spaces.

Successful value innovation requires that a firm's strategic moves lower its costs and at the same increase the perceived value for buyers (see Exhibit 6.8). Lowering a firm's costs is primarily achieved by eliminating and reducing the taken-for-granted factors that the firm's rivals in their industry compete on. Perceived buyer value is increased by raising existing key success factors and by creating new elements that the industry has not offered previously. To initiate a strategic move that allows a firm to open a new and uncontested market space through value innovation, managers must answer the four key questions below when formulating a blue ocean business strategy.[39] In terms of achieving successful value innovation, note that the first two questions focus on lowering costs, while the other two questions focus on increasing perceived consumer benefits.

LO 6-5

Evaluate value and cost drivers that may allow a firm to pursue a blue ocean strategy.

Value Innovation—Lower Costs

1. *Eliminate.* Which of the factors that the industry takes for granted should be eliminated?
2. *Reduce.* Which of the factors should be reduced well below the industry's standard?

Value Innovation—Increase Perceived Consumer Benefits

3. *Raise.* Which of the factors should be raised well above the industry's standard?
4. *Create.* Which factors should be created that the industry has never offered?

The international furniture retailer IKEA, for example, has used value innovation based on the *eliminate-reduce-raise-create* framework to initiate its own blue ocean and to achieve a sustainable competitive advantage.[40]

ELIMINATE. IKEA eliminated several taken-for-granted competitive elements: salespeople, expensive but small retail outlets in prime urban locations and shopping malls, long wait after ordering furniture, after-sales service, and other factors. In contrast, IKEA displays its products in a warehouse-like setting, thus reducing inventory cost. Customers serve themselves and then transport the furniture to their homes in IKEA's signature flat-packs for assembly. IKEA also uses the big-box concept of locating super-sized stores near major metropolitan areas.

REDUCE. Because of its do-it-yourself business model from furniture selection, transporting it home, and assembly, IKEA drastically reduced the need for staff in its mega-stores. Strolling through an IKEA store, you encounter few employees. IKEA also reduced several other taken-for-granted competitive elements: 25-year warranties on high-end custom

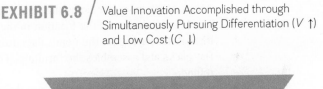

EXHIBIT 6.8 / Value Innovation Accomplished through Simultaneously Pursuing Differentiation ($V \uparrow$) and Low Cost ($C \downarrow$)

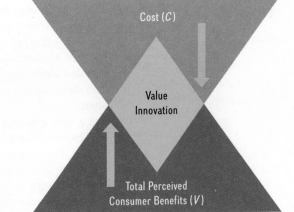

Source: Adapted from C.W. Kim and R. Mauborgne (2005), *Blue Ocean Strategy: How to Create Uncontested Market Space and Make Competition Irrelevant* (Boston, MA: Harvard Business School Publishing).

Inside IKEA's self-service warehouse
© Alex Segre/Alamy

furniture, high degree of customization in selection of options such as different fabrics and patterns, and use of expensive materials such as leather or hardwoods, among other elements.

RAISE. IKEA raised several competitive elements: It offers tens of thousands of home furnishing items in each of its big-box stores (some 300,000 square feet, roughly five football fields), versus a few hundred at best in traditional furniture stores; it also offers more than furniture, including a range of accessories such as place mats, laptop stands, and much more; each store has hundreds of rooms fully decorated with all sorts of IKEA items, each with a detailed tag explaining the item in detail. Moreover, rather than sourcing its furniture from wholesalers or other furniture makers, IKEA manufactures all of its furniture at fully dedicated suppliers, thus tightly controlling the design, quality, functionality, and cost of each product.

IKEA also raised the customer experience by laying out its stores in such a way that customers see and can touch basically all of IKEA's products, from wineglasses (six for $2.99) to bookshelves (for less than $100).

CREATE. IKEA created a new way for people to shop for furniture. The customer strolls through a predetermined path winding through the fully furnished showrooms. She can compare, test, and touch all the things in the showroom. The price tag on each item contains other important information: type of material, weight, and so on. Once an item is selected, the customer notes the item number (the store provides a pencil and notepad). The tag also indicates the location in the warehouse where the customer can pick up the item. After paying for the items, the customer transports the products in IKEA's signature flat-packs and assembles the furniture. The customer has 90 days to return items for a full refund.

In traditional furniture shopping, the customer visits a small retail outlet where salespeople swarm around him. After a purchase, the customer has to wait generally a few weeks before the furniture is shipped to his house. This is because many furniture makers do not produce items such as expensive leather sofas unless they are paid for in advance. Finely crafted couches and chairs cost thousands of dollars (while IKEA's fabric couches retail for $399). When shopping at a traditional furniture store, the customer also pays for delivery of the furniture.

IKEA also created a new approach to pricing its products. Rather than using a "cost plus margin approach" like traditional furniture stores when pricing its items, IKEA begins with the retail price first. For example, it sets the price for an office chair at $150, and IKEA's designers figure out how to meet this goal. They need to consider the chair from start to finish, including not only design but also raw materials and the way the product will be displayed and transported to meet that goal, including a profit margin. Only then will products go into production.

IKEA also created several other new competitive elements that allow it to offer more value to its customers: It provides on-site child care; it features a restaurant offering delicious food options including Swedish delicatessen such as smoked salmon at low prices;

stores have convenient and ample parking, often in garages under the store, where escalators bring customers directly into the showrooms.

Taken together, with all these steps to eliminate, reduce, raise, and create, IKEA orchestrates different internal value chain activities to reconcile the tension between differentiation and cost leadership in order to create a unique market space. IKEA uses innovation in multiple dimensions—in furniture design, engineering, and store design—to solve the trade-offs between value creation and production cost. An IKEA executive highlights the difficulty as follows: "Designing beautiful-but-expensive products is easy. Designing beautiful products that are inexpensive and functional is a huge challenge."[41] IKEA leverages its deep design and engineering expertise to offer furniture that is stylish and functional and that can be easily assembled by the consumer. In this way, IKEA can pursue a blue ocean strategy based on value innovation to increase the perceived value of its products, while simultaneously lowering its cost and offering competitive prices. It opened up a new market serving a younger demographic than traditional furniture stores. When young people the world over move into their own apartment or house, they frequently furnish it from IKEA.

BLUE OCEAN STRATEGY GONE BAD: "STUCK IN THE MIDDLE"

LO 6-6

Assess the risks of a blue ocean strategy, and explain why it is difficult to succeed at value innovation.

Although appealing in a theoretical sense, a blue ocean strategy can be quite difficult to translate into reality. The reason is that differentiation and cost leadership are distinct strategic positions that require important trade-offs.[42] A blue ocean strategy is difficult to implement because it requires the reconciliation of fundamentally different strategic positions—differentiation and low cost—which in turn require distinct internal value chain activities (see Chapter 4) so the firm can increase value *and* lower cost at the same time.

Exhibit 6.9 suggests how a successfully formulated blue ocean strategy based on *value innovation* combines both a differentiation and low-cost position. It also shows the consequence of a blue ocean strategy gone bad—the firm ends up being *stuck in the middle,* meaning the firm has neither a clear differentiation nor a clear cost-leadership profile. Being *stuck in the middle* leads to inferior performance and a resulting competitive disadvantage. Strategy Highlight 6.2 illustrates how JCPenney failed at a blue ocean strategy and ended up in the red ocean of cut-throat competition.

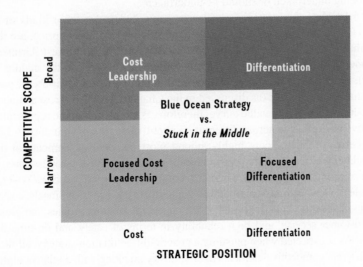

EXHIBIT 6.9

Value Innovation vs. *Stuck in the Middle*

Strategy Highlight 6.2

How JCPenney Sailed Deeper into the Red Ocean

JCPenney under its (former) CEO, Ron Johnson, learned the hard way how difficult it is to change a strategic position. When hired as JCPenney's CEO in 2011, Johnson was hailed as a star executive. He was poached from Apple, where he had created and led Apple's retail stores since 2000. Apple's stores are the most successful retail outlets globally in terms of sales per square foot. No other retail outlet, not even luxury jewelers, achieves more.

Once on board with JCPenney, Johnson immediately began to change the company's strategic position from a cost-leadership to a *blue ocean strategy*, attempting to combine the cost-leadership position with a differentiation position. In particular, he tried to reposition the department store more toward the high end by providing an improved customer experience and more exclusive merchandise through in-store boutiques. CEO Johnson ordered all clearance racks with steeply discounted merchandise, common in JCPenney stores, to be removed. He also did away with JCPenney's long-standing practice of mailing discount coupons to its customers. Rather than following industry best practice by testing the more drastic strategic moves in a small number of selected stores, Johnson implemented them wholesale in all 1,800 stores at once. When one executive raised the issue of pretesting, Johnson bristled and responded: "We didn't test at Apple." Under his leadership, JCPenney also got embroiled in a legal battle with Macy's because of Johnson's attempt to lure away homemaking maven Martha Stewart and her exclusive merchandise collection.

The envisioned blue ocean strategy failed badly, and JCPenney ended up being stuck in the middle. Within 12 months with Johnson at the helm, JCPenney's sales dropped by 25 percent. In a hypercompetitive industry such as retailing where every single percent of market share counts, this was a landslide. In 2013, JCPenney's stock performed so poorly it was dropped from the S&P 500 index. Less than 18 months into his new job, Johnson was fired. Myron Ullman, his predecessor, was brought out of retirement as a replacement.

JCPenney failed at its attempted blue ocean strategy and instead sailed deeper into the *red ocean* of bloody competition. This highlights the perils of attempting a blue ocean strategy because of the inherent trade-offs in the underlying generic business strategies of cost leadership and differentiation. As a result, JCPenney continues to experience a sustained competitive disadvantage as of this writing.[43]

---

value curve
Horizontal connection of the points of each value on the strategy canvas that helps strategists diagnose and determine courses of action.

strategy canvas
Graphical depiction of a company's relative performance vis-à-vis its competitors across the industry's key success factors.

The **value curve** is the basic component of the **strategy canvas**. It graphically depicts a company's relative performance across its industry's factors of competition. A strong value curve has focus and divergence, and it can even provide a kind of tagline as to what strategy is being undertaken or should be undertaken.

Exhibit 6.10 plots the strategic profiles or value curves for three kinds of competitors in the U.S. airline industry. On the left-hand side, descending in price, are the legacy carriers (think Delta), JetBlue, and low-cost airlines such as Southwest Airlines (SWA). We also show the different strategic positions (differentiator, stuck in the middle, and low-cost leader). Trace the value curves as they rank high or low on a variety of parameters. JetBlue is stuck in the middle (as discussed in the ChapterCase). Low-cost airlines follow a cost-leadership strategy. The value curve, therefore, is simply a graphic representation of a firm's relative performance across different competitive factors in an industry.

Legacy carriers tend to score highly among most competitive elements in the airline industry, including different seating class choices (such as first class, business class, economy comfort, basic economy, and so on), a high level of in-flight amenities such as Wi-Fi, personal video console to view movies or play games, complimentary drinks and meals, coast-to-coast coverage via connecting hubs, plush airport lounges, international routes and global coverage, high customer service, and high reliability in terms of safety and on-time departures and arrivals. As is expected when pursuing a generic differentiation strategy, all these scores along the different competitive elements in an industry go along with a relative high price.

EXHIBIT 6.10 / Strategy Canvas of JetBlue vs. Low-cost Airlines and Legacy Carriers.

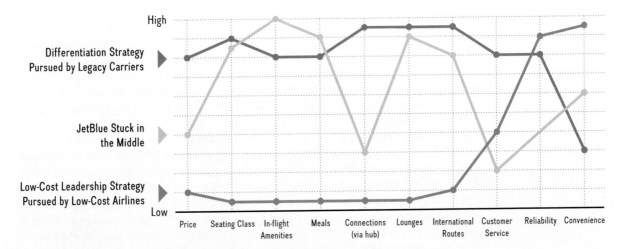

In contrast, the low-cost airlines tend to hover near the bottom of the strategy canvas, indicating low scores along a number of competitive factors in the industry, with no assigned seating, no in-flight amenities, no drinks or meals, no airport lounges, few if any international routes, low to intermediate level of customer service. A relatively low price goes along with a generic low-cost leadership strategy.

This strategy canvas also reveals key strategic insights. Look at the few competitive elements where the value curves of the differentiator and low-cost leader diverge. Interestingly, some cost leaders (e.g., SWA) score much higher than some differentiators (e.g., Delta) in terms of reliability and convenience, offering frequent point-to-point connections to conveniently located airports, often in or near city centers. This key divergence between the two strategies explains why generic cost leaders have frequently outperformed generic differentiators in the U.S. airline industry. Overall, both value curves show a consistent pattern representative of a more or less clear strategic profile as either differentiation or low-cost leader.

Now look at JetBlue's value curve. Rather than being consistent such as the differentiation or low-cost value curves, the JetBlue value curve follows a zigzag pattern and is thus "all over the place." JetBlue attempts to achieve parity or even out-compete differentiators in the U.S. airline industry along the competitive factors such as different seating classes (e.g., the high-end Mint offering discussed in the ChapterCase), higher level of in-flight amenities, higher-quality beverages and meals, plush airport lounges, and a large number of international routes (mainly with global partner airlines). JetBlue, however, looks more like a low-cost leader in terms of the ability to provide only a few connections via hubs domestically, and it recently has had a poor record of customer service, mainly because of some high-profile missteps as documented in the ChapterCase. JetBlue's reliability is somewhat mediocre, but it does provide a larger number of convenient point-to-point flights than a differentiator such as Delta, but fewer than a low-cost leader such as SWA.

A value curve that zigzags across the strategy canvas indicates a lack of effectiveness in its strategic profile. The curve visually represents how JetBlue is *stuck in the middle* and as a consequence experienced inferior performance and thus a sustained competitive disadvantage vis-à-vis airlines with a stronger strategy profile such as SWA and Delta, among others.

6.7 ◄► Implications for the Strategist

Strategy is never easy, even when, as in achieving competitive advantage, only a handful of strategic options are available (i.e., low cost or differentiation, broad or narrow, or blue ocean). The best managers work hard to make sure they understand their firm and industry effects, and the opportunities they reveal. They work even harder to fine-tune strategy formulation and execution. When well-formulated and implemented, a firm's business strategy enhances a firm's chances of obtaining superior performance. Strategic positioning requires making important trade-offs (think Walmart versus J. Crew in clothing).

In rare instances, a few exceptional firms might be able to change the competitive landscape by opening previously unknown areas of competition. To do so requires the firm reconcile the significant trade-offs between increasing value and lowering costs by pursuing both business strategies (differentiation and low cost) simultaneously. Such a blue ocean strategy tends to be successful only if a firm is able to rely on a value innovation that allows it to reconcile the trade-offs mentioned. Toyota, for example, initiated a new market space with its introduction of lean manufacturing, delivering cars of higher quality and value at lower cost. This value innovation allowed Toyota a competitive advantage for a decade or more, until this new process technology diffused widely. JCPenney, on the other hand, stumbled and found itself failing on most fronts, resulting in a competitive disadvantage.

CHAPTER**CASE 6** ⁄ Consider This...

Early in its history JetBlue achieved a competitive advantage based on *value innovation*. In particular, JetBlue was able to drive up perceived costumer value while lowering costs. This allowed it to carve out a strong strategic position and move to a non-contested market space. This implies that no other competitors in the U.S. domestic airline industry were able to provide such value innovation at that point in time. Rather than directly competing with other airlines, JetBlue created a blue ocean.

Although JetBlue was able to create an initial competitive advantage, it was unable to sustain it over time. Because JetBlue failed in reconciling the strategic trade-offs inherent in combing differentiation and cost leadership, it was unable to continue its blue ocean strategy, despite initial success. Since 2007 JetBlue experienced a sustained competitive disadvantage, at one point in 2014 lagging the S&P 500 index by more than 100 percentage points.

A new leadership team CEO Robin Hayes put in place in early 2015 is attempting to reverse this trend. The new team made quick changes to improve the airline's flagging profitability. It decided to start charging $50 per checked bag instead of offering it as a free service. Moreover, it also removed the additional legroom JetBlue was famous for in the industry, adding 10 percent more seats on its airplanes. It remains to be seen if JetBlue's strategic repositioning will be successful.

Questions

1. Despite its initial success, why was JetBlue unable to sustain a blue ocean strategy?

2. JetBlue's chief marketing officer, Marty St. George, was asked by *The Wall Street Journal*, "What is the biggest marketing challenge JetBlue faces?" His response: "We are flying in a space where our competitors are moving toward commoditization. We have taken a position that air travel is not a commodity but a services business. We want to stand out, but it's hard to break through to customers with that message."

   A. Given St. George's statement, which strategic position is JetBlue trying to accomplish: differentiator, cost leader, or blue ocean strategy? Explain why.

   B. Which strategic moves has the new CEO, Robin Hayes, put in place? Do these moves correspond to St. George's understanding of JetBlue's strategic position? Why or why not? Explain.

3. Consider JetBlue's value curve in Exhibit 6.10. Why is JetBlue experiencing a competitive advantage? What recommendations would you offer to JetBlue to strengthen its strategic profile? Be specific.

TAKE-AWAY CONCEPTS

This chapter discussed two generic business-level strategies: *differentiation* and *cost leadership*. Companies can use various tactics to drive one or the other of those strategies, either narrowly or broadly. *Blue ocean strategy* attempts to find a competitive advantage by creating a new competitive area, which it does (when successful) by value innovation, reconciling the trade-offs between the two generic business strategies discussed. These concepts are summarized by the following learning objectives and related take-away concepts.

LO 6-1 / Define business-level strategy and describe how it determines a firm's strategic position.

- Business-level strategy determines a firm's strategic position in its quest for competitive advantage when competing in a single industry or product market.
- Strategic positioning requires that managers address strategic trade-offs that arise between value and cost, because higher value tends to go along with higher cost.
- Differentiation and cost leadership are distinct strategic positions.
- Besides selecting an appropriate strategic position, managers must also define the scope of competition—whether to pursue a specific market niche or go after the broader market.

LO 6-2 / Examine the relationship between value drivers and differentiation strategy.

- The goal of a differentiation strategy is to increase the perceived value of goods and services so that customers will pay a higher price for additional features.
- In a differentiation strategy, the focus of competition is on value-enhancing attributes and features, while controlling costs.
- Some of the unique value drivers managers can manipulate are product features, customer service, customization, and complements.
- Value drivers contribute to competitive advantage only if their increase in value creation (ΔV) exceeds the increase in costs, that is: $(\Delta V) > (\Delta C)$.

LO 6-3 / Examine the relationship between cost drivers and the cost-leadership strategy.

- The goal of a cost-leadership strategy is to reduce the firm's cost below that of its competitors.
- In a cost-leadership strategy, the focus of competition is achieving the lowest possible cost position, which allows the firm to offer a lower price than competitors while maintaining acceptable value.
- Some of the unique cost drivers that managers can manipulate are the cost of input factors, economies of scale, and learning- and experience-curve effects.
- No matter how low the price, if there is no acceptable value proposition, the product or service will not sell.

LO 6-4 / Assess the benefits and risks of differentiation and cost-leadership strategies vis-à-vis the five forces that shape competition.

- The five forces model helps managers use generic business strategies to protect themselves against the industry forces that drive down profitability.
- Differentiation and cost-leadership strategies allow firms to carve out strong strategic positions, not only to protect themselves against the five forces, but also to benefit from them in their quest for competitive advantage.
- Exhibit 6.7 details the benefits and risks of each business strategy.

LO 6-5 / Evaluate value and cost drivers that may allow a firm to pursue a blue ocean strategy.

- To address the trade-offs between differentiation and cost leadership at the business level, managers must employ value innovation, a process that will lead them to align the proposed business strategy with total perceived consumer benefits, price, and cost.
- Lowering a firm's costs is primarily achieved by eliminating and reducing the taken-for-granted factors on which the firm's industry rivals compete.
- Increasing perceived buyer value is primarily achieved by raising existing key success factors and by creating new elements that the industry has not yet offered.
- Managers track their opportunities and risks for lowering a firm's costs and increasing perceived value vis-à-vis their competitors by use

of a strategy canvas, which plots industry factors among competitors (see Exhibit 6.10).

LO 6-6 / Assess the risks of a blue ocean strategy, and explain why it is difficult to succeed at value innovation.

■ A successful blue ocean strategy requires that trade-offs between differentiation and low cost be reconciled.

■ A blue ocean strategy often is difficult because the two distinct strategic positions require internal value chain activities that are fundamentally different from one another.

■ When firms fail to resolve strategic trade-offs between differentiation and cost, they end up being "stuck in the middle." They then succeed at neither business strategy, leading to a competitive disadvantage.

KEY TERMS

Blue ocean strategy *(p. 194)*

Business-level strategy *(p. 177)*

Cost-leadership strategy *(p. 178)*

Differentiation strategy *(p. 178)*

Diseconomies of scale *(p. 187)*

Economies of scale *(p. 184)*

Economies of scope *(p. 181)*

Focused cost-leadership strategy *(p. 179)*

Focused differentiation strategy *(p. 179)*

Minimum efficient scale (MES) *(p. 186)*

Scope of competition *(p. 178)*

Strategic trade-offs *(p. 178)*

Strategy canvas *(p. 198)*

Value curve *(p. 198)*

Value innovation *(p. 194)*

DISCUSSION QUESTIONS

1. What are some drawbacks and risks to a broad generic business strategy? To a focused strategy?

2. How can a firm attempting to have a blue ocean business-level strategy manage to avoid being "stuck in the middle"?

3. In Chapter 4, we discussed the internal value chain activities a firm can perform in its business model (see Exhibit 4.8). The value chain priorities can be quite different for firms taking different business strategies. Create examples of value chains for three firms: one using cost leadership, another using differentiation, and a third using value innovation business-level strategy.

4. The chapter notes there are key differences between economies of scale and learning effects. Let us put that into practice with a brief example.

A company such as Intel has a complex design and manufacturing process. For instance, one fabrication line for semiconductors typically costs more than $1.5 billion to build. Yet the industry also has high human costs for research and development (R&D) departments. Semiconductor firms spend an average of 17 percent of revenues on R&D. For comparison the automobile industry spends a mere 3 percent of sales on R&D.[44] Thus Intel's management must be concerned with both scale of production and learning curves. When do you think managers should be more concerned with large-scale production runs, and when do you think they should be most concerned with practices that would foster or hinder the hiring, training, and retention of key employees?

ETHICAL/SOCIAL ISSUES

1. Suppose Procter & Gamble (P&G) learns that a relatively new start-up company Method (www .methodhome.com) is gaining market share with a new laundry detergent in West Coast markets.

In response, P&G lowers the price of its Tide detergent from $18 to $9 for a 150-ounce bottle only in markets where Method's product is for sale. The goal of this "loss leader" price drop is to encourage Method to leave the laundry detergent market. Is this an ethical business practice? Why or why not?

2. In the chapter discussion on value innovation, IKEA is noted as a firm that has successfully applied these techniques. What roles, if any, do sustainability and triple-bottom-line factors have in the success of IKEA as a leader in the furniture industry? (See Chapter 5.)

SMALL GROUP EXERCISES

//// Small Group Exercise 1

Ryanair based in Dublin, Ireland, has been renowned in Europe as a firm that can make a profit on a $20 ticket by imposing numerous fees and surcharges. The airline has sought to be the lowest of the low-cost providers in the EU with a "no frills get you from point A-to-B-model." More recently Ryanair is on record as saying it wants to be the "Amazon.com of travel in Europe" by bringing in competitors' price comparison, hotel discounts, and even concert tickets.[45] Check out the company website (www.ryanair.com) and consider the questions that follow.

1. If you were a competitor in the European market, such as British Airways or Lufthansa, how would you compete against Ryanair, knowing your cost structure would not allow price parity? If you were a low-cost leader like EasyJet, how would you compete against Ryanair?

2. What similarities and differences do you find about RyanAir compared to Jet Blue from the ChapterCase?

//// Small Group Exercise 2

1. The table that follows includes a list of prominent firms. Select one of the five categories of generic business-level strategies—broad cost leadership, focused cost leadership, broad differentiation, focused differentiation, and value innovation—that you would apply to each firm. Add that strategy to the table, and explain your choices.

2. What are some common features of the firms you have placed within each category?

Firm	Business-Level Strategy	Firm	Business-Level Strategy
Ann Taylor		LVMH	
BIC		McKinsey & Co.	
Big Lots		Netflix	
Black & Decker		Nike	
C.F. Martin & Co.		Patek Philippe	
Clif Bar		Porsche	
Coca-Cola		Rhapsody	
Dollar stores (e.g., Dollar Tree, Family Dollar Stores, or Dollar General)		Rolls-Royce	
Ferrari		Ryanair	
Google		Samuel Adams	
Goya Foods		Singaporwe Airlines	
Greyhound Lines		Target	
Hyundai		Toyota	
Kia Motors		Vanguard Group	
Lands' End		Victoria's Secret	
Liberty Mutual		Zara	

STRATEGY TERM PROJECT

connect *The* HP Running Case, *a related activity for each strategy term project module, is available in Connect.*

//// Module 6: Business Strategy

In this module, we will look at the business model your selected company uses and analyze its business-level strategy to see if it is appropriate for the strategic position. If your firm is a large multi-business entity, you will need to choose one of the major businesses (strategic business unit, or SBU) of the firm for this analysis. In prior chapters, you collected information about this firm's external environment and some of its internal competitive advantages. Using this information and any other you have gathered, address the following questions.

1. Does your selected business have differentiated products or services? If so, what is the basis for this differentiation from the competition?

2. Does your firm have a cost-leadership position in this business? If so, can you identify which cost drivers it uses effectively to hold this position?

3. What is your firm's approach to the market? If it segments the market, identify the scope of competition it is using.

4. Using the answers to the preceding questions, identify which generic business strategies your firm is employing. Is the firm leveraging the appropriate value and cost drivers for the business strategy you identified? Explain why or why not.

5. As noted in the chapter, each business strategy is context-dependent. What do you see as positives and negatives with the selected business strategy of your firm in its competitive situation?

6. What suggestions do you have to improve the firm's business strategy and strategic position?

7. Create a strategy canvas (see Exhibit 6.10) for your firm. Set on the horizontal axis an appropriate selection of the value curve items and on the vertical axis, set the other industry segments (such as strategic groups) for comparison.

*my*STRATEGY

Low-Cost and Differentiated Workplaces

We have studied the differences in business-level strategies closely in this chapter, but how might these differences relate directly to you? As you've learned, firms using a differentiation strategy will focus on drivers such as product features and customer service, while firms using a cost-leadership strategy will prioritize cost of inputs and economies of scale. These strategic decisions can have an impact on an employee's experience with the firm's work environment and culture.

Nordstrom, Whole Foods Market, and Wegmans Food Markets are companies that routinely end up on *Fortune's* list of "100 Best Places to Work." These companies use a differentiation business strategy. In contrast, Amazon and Walmart use the cost-leadership strategy; and as low-cost leaders, they do not rate nearly as well. According to inputs from the employee review site Glassdoor.com, only 50 percent of the employees working at Walmart would recommend the firm to a friend. Compare this to the 72 percent who would recommend both Nordstrom and Whole Foods, and the 80 percent who would recommend Wegmans Food Markets.

As you seek options for starting or growing your career, carefully consider the strategy the firm takes in the marketplace. By no means should you avoid low-cost leaders in lieu of strong differentiators (nor should you deem all differentiators as great places to work). Fast-paced organizations that focus on driving tangible results for the organization offer much to learn. For example, Amazon has been a very successful company for the past decade, and many employees have had multiple opportunities to learn enormous amounts in a short period of time. While the environment is challenging and intense, some employees love it. For others, though, the demands of the workplace are overpowering and far too combative. Many of them leave after a year or two. Amazon had the shortest employee tenure among the Fortune 500 firms, according to a 2013 salary analysis by PayScale.

Amazon employees are encouraged to criticize each other's ideas openly in meetings; they work long days and on weekends; and they strive to meet "unreasonably high" standards. "When you're shooting for the moon, the nature of the work is really challenging. For some people it doesn't work," says Susan Harker, a top recruiter for Amazon. The high standards and relentless pace are a draw for many employees who are motivated to push themselves to learn, grow, and create—perhaps beyond their perceived limits. Many former employees say the nimble and productive environment is great for learning and the Amazon experience has really helped their careers expand. Now consider the following questions.

1. Employees and consultants say the Amazon workplace is the epitome of a "do more for less cost" environment. We recognize this is a hallmark goal of a cost-leadership business strategy. But ask yourself this key question, *Is it*

the type of high-pressure work environment in which YOU would thrive?

2. By 2020 Amazon is planning to have space for 50,000 employees in its Seattle office buildings (an increase of three times the number of employees in 2013). They will be offering bold new ideas and moving Amazon toward being the first trillion-dollar retailer under an intense pressure to deliver on their goals. The allure from this type of success is compelling and offers tremendous rewards to many employees, shareholders, and customers. What aspects of success are you seeking in your professional career?

3. Before you launch into a new project, job, or firm, or even before you make a change in industry in the effort to move forward in your career, always consider the trade-offs that you would and would NOT be willing to make.[46]

ENDNOTES

1. Ever the entrepreneur, David Neeleman went on to found Azul, a Brazilian airline, in 2008.

2. Nicas, J., "Pilot sues JetBlue for allegedly letting him fly while mentally unfit," *The Wall Street Journal,* March 27, 2015; Vranica, S., "JetBlue's plan to repair its brand," *The Wall Street Journal,* February 22, 2015; Harris, R.L., "On JetBlue, passengers can use ApplePay," *The New York Times,* February 11, 2015; Rosenbloom, S., "Flying deluxe domestic coast-to-coast for around $1,000," *The New York Times,* January 23, 2015; Nicas, J., "JetBlue to add bag fees, reduce legroom," *The Wall Street Journal,* November 19, 2014; Gardiner, S., "Flight attendant grabs two beers, slides down the emergency chute," *The Wall Street Journal,* August 10, 2010; "Can JetBlue weather the storm?" *Time,* February 21, 2007; "Held hostage on the tarmac: Time for a passenger bill of rights?" *The New York Times,* February 16, 2007; Bryce, D.J., and J.H. Dyer (2007), "Strategies to crack well-guarded markets," *Harvard Business Review,* May; Friedman, T. (2005), *The World Is Flat: A Brief History of the Twenty-First Century* (New York: Farrar, Strauss and Giroux); and Neeleman, D. (2003), "Entrepreneurial thought leaders lecture," *Stanford Technology Ventures Program,* April 30.

3. This discussion is based on: Porter, M.E. (2008), "The five competitive forces that shape strategy," *Harvard Business Review,* January; Porter, M.E. (1996), "What is

strategy?" *Harvard Business Review,* November–December; Porter, M.E. (1985), *Competitive Advantage: Creating and Sustaining Superior Performance* (New York: Free Press); and Porter, M.E. (1980), *Competitive Strategy: Techniques for Analyzing Industries and Competitors* (New York: Free Press).

4. These questions are based on: Priem, R. (2007), "A consumer perspective on value creation," *Academy of Management Review* 32: 219–235; Abell, D.F. (1980), *Defining the Business: The Starting Point of Strategic Planning* (Englewood Cliffs, NJ: Prentice-Hall); and Porter, "What is strategy?"

5. The discussion of generic business strategies is based on: Porter, *Competitive Strategy;* Porter, *Competitive Advantage;* Porter, "What is strategy?"; and Porter, "The five competitive forces that shape strategy."

6. Porter, "What is strategy?"

7. To decide if and how to divide the market, you can apply the market segmentation techniques you have acquired in your marketing and microeconomics classes.

8. Anderson, R.C., and R. White (2009), *Confessions of a Radical Industrialist: Profits, People, Purpose—Doing Business by Respecting the Earth* (New York: St. Martin's Press).

9. Christensen, C.M., and M.E. Raynor (2003), *The Innovator's Solution: Creating and Sustaining Successful Growth* (Boston, MA: Harvard Business School Press).

10. The interested reader is referred to the strategy, marketing, and economics literatures. A good start in the strategy literature is the classic work of M.E. Porter: Porter, *Competitive Strategy: Techniques for Analyzing Industries and Competitors;* Porter, *Competitive Advantage: Creating and Sustaining Superior Performance;* and Porter, "The five competitive forces that shape strategy."

11. www.oxo.com/about.jsp.

12. Hsieh, T. (2010), *Delivering Happiness: A Path to Profits, Passion, and Purpose* (New York: Business Plus).

13. "Amazon opens wallet, buys Zappos," *The Wall Street Journal,* July 23, 2009.

14. "Where in the Dickens can you find a Trader Joe's," store listing at www.traderjoes.com/pdf/locations/all-llocations.pdf; "Ten companies with excellent customer service," *Huffington Post,* August 15, 2014, http://www.huffingtonpost.com/2013/08/15/best-customer-service_n_3720052.html.

15. www.att.com/u-verse/.

16. "Flights of hypocrisy," *The Economist,* April 25, 2015.

17. "Boeing 787: Orders and Deliveries (updated monthly)," *The Boeing Company,* March 2015, www.boeing.com.

18. www.airbus.com/en/aircraftfamilies/a380/home/.

19. Kevin Turner, COO Microsoft, keynote speech at Microsoft's Worldwide Partner Conference, New Orleans, July 15, 2009.

20. "Microsoft concedes Windows 8 misses expectations," *The Wall Street Journal,* May 7, 2013; "Windows 8 is only the beginning of Microsoft's problems," *The Economist,* May 11, 2013.

21. "Nucor's new plant project still on hold," Associated Press, July 23, 2009; www.nucor.com.

22. On strategy as simple rules, see Sull, D., and K.M. Eisenhardt (2015), *Simple Rules: How to Thrive in a Complex World* (New York: Houghton Mifflin Harcourt).

23. Gladwell, M. (2002), *The Tipping Point: How Little Things Can Make a Big Difference* (New York: Back Bay Books), 185.

24. Levitt, B., and J.G. March (1988), "Organizational learning,"*Annual Review of Sociology* 14: 319–340.

25. For insightful reviews and syntheses on the learning-curve literature, see: Argote, L., and G. Todorova (2007), "Organizational learning: Review and future directions," *International Review of Industrial and Organizational Psychology* 22: 193–234; and Yelle, L.E. (1979), "The learning curve: Historical review and comprehensive survey," *Decision Sciences* 10: 302–308.

26. Wright, T.P. (1936), "Factors affecting the cost of airplanes," *Journal of Aeronautical Sciences* 3: 122–128.

27. The exact data for learning curves depicted in Exhibit 6.6 are depicted below. A simplifying assumption is that the manufacturing of one aircraft costs $100 million, from there the two different learning curves set in. Noteworthy, that while making only one aircraft costs $100 million, when manufacturing over 4,000 aircraft the expected per-unit cost falls to only $28 million (assuming a 90 percent learning curve) and only $7 million (assuming an 80 percent learning curve).

Data underlying Exhibit 6.6

Units	Learning Curves Per-Unit Cost*	
	90%	**80%**
1	$100	$100
2	90	80
4	81	64
8	73	51
16	66	41
32	59	33
64	53	26
128	48	21
256	43	17
512	39	13
1,024	35	11
2,048	31	9
4,096	28	7

* Rounded to full dollar value in million $.

28. This discussion is based on: Gulati, R., D. Lavie, and H. Singh (2009), "The nature of partnering experience and the gain from alliances," *Strategic Management Journal* 30: 1213–1233; Thompson, P. (2001), "How much did the liberty shipbuilders learn? New evidence from an old case study," *Journal of Political Economy* 109: 103–137; Edmondson, A.C., R.M. Bohmer, and G.P. Pisano (2001), "Disrupted routines: Team learning and new technology implementation in hospitals," *Administrative Science Quarterly* 46: 685–716; Pisano, G.P., R.M. Bohmer, and A.C. Edmondson (2001), "Organizational differences in rates of learning: Evidence from the adoption of minimally invasive cardiac surgery," *Management Science* 47: 752–768; Rothaermel, F.T., and D.L. Deeds (2006), "Alliance type, alliance experience, and alliance management capability in high-technology ventures," *Journal of Business Venturing* 21: 429–460; Hoang, H., and F.T. Rothaermel (2005), "The effect of general and partner-specific alliance experience on joint R&D project performance," *Academy of Management Journal* 48: 332–345; Zollo, M., J.J. Reuer, and H. Singh (2002), "Interorganizational routines and performance in strategic alliances," *Organization Science* 13: 701–713; King, A.W., and A.L. Ranft (2001), "Capturing knowledge and knowing through improvisation: What managers can learn from the thoracic surgery board certification process," *Journal of Management* 27: 255–277; and Darr, E.D., L. Argote, and D. Epple (1995), "The acquisition, transfer and depreciation of knowledge in service organizations: Productivity in franchises," *Management Science* 42: 1750–1762.

29. Ramanarayanan, S. (2008), "Does practice make perfect: An empirical analysis of learning-by-doing in cardiac surgery." Available at SSRN: http://ssrn.com/abstract=1129350.

30. "Coronary artery bypass grafting," (2015), healthcarebluebook.com, doi:10.1016/B978-1-84569-800-3.50011-5; Gokhale, K., "Heart surgery in India for $1,583 Costs $106,385 in U.S., *Bloomberg Businessweek,* July 29, 2013; and Anand, G., "The Henry Ford of heart surgery," *The Wall Street Journal,* November 25, 2009. See also "Cardiac Surgeon Salary (United States)," *Payscale.com,* survey updated July 18, 2015.

31. Boston Consulting Group (1972), *Perspectives on Experience* (Boston, MA: Boston Consulting Group).

32. See data presented in Footnote 27.

33. Anand, "The Henry Ford of heart surgery."

34. This discussion is based on: Porter, M.E. (1979), "How competitive forces shape strategy," *Harvard Business Review,* March–April: 137–145; Porter, *Competitive Strategy. Techniques for Analyzing Industries and Competitors;* and Porter, "The five competitive forces that shape strategy."

35. "Android creator Andy Rubin rekindles Redpoint relationship," *The Wall Street Journal,* April 7, 2015.

36. This discussion is based on: Kim, C.W., and R. Mauborgne (2005), *Blue Ocean Strategy: How to Create Uncontested Market Space and Make Competition Irrelevant* (Boston, MA: Harvard Business School Publishing); Miller, A., and G.G. Dess (1993), "Assessing Porter's model in terms of its generalizability, accuracy, and simplicity," *Journal of Management Studies* 30: 553–585; andHill, C.W.L. (1988), "Differentiation versus low cost or differentiation and low cost: A contingency framework," *Academy of Management Review* 13: 401–412.

37. Kim and Mauborgne, *Blue Ocean Strategy.*

38. Ibid.

39. Ibid.

40. The IKEA example is drawn from: "IKEA: How the Swedish retailer became a global cult brand," *Bloomberg Businessweek,* November 14, 2005; Edmonds, M., "How Ikea works" (accessed May 6, 2015), http://money.howstuffworks.com/; and www.ikea.com.

41. "IKEA: How the Swedish retailer became a global cult brand."

42. This discussion is based on: Porter, *Competitive Strategy;* and Porter, "What is strategy?": 61–78.

43. "For Penney's heralded boss, the shine is off the apple," *The Wall Street Journal,* February 24, 2013; "Macy's CEO: Penney, Martha Stewart deal made me 'sick,'" *The Wall Street Journal,* February 25, 2013; and "Penney CEO out, old boss back in," *The Wall Street Journal,* April 8, 2013.

44. "McKinsey on Semiconductors," McKinsey & Co., Autumn 2011.

45. Whyte, P., "Ryanair plans to become 'Amazon' of European travel," TTGDigital, August 14, 2015.

46. Sources for this myStrategy include: Kantor, J., and D. Streitfeld, "Inside Amazon: Wrestling big ideas in a bruising workplace," *The New York Times,* August 15, 2015; "100 best companies to work for," *Fortune,* 2014, 2015; and www.glassdoor.com.

Chapter 7

Business Strategy:
Innovation and Entrepreneurship

Learning Objectives

LO 7.1 Outline the four-step innovation process from idea to imitation.

LO 7.2 Apply strategic management concepts to entrepreneurship and innovation.

LO 7.3 Describe the competitive implications of different stages in the industry life cycle.

LO 7.4 Derive strategic implications of the crossing-the-chasm framework.

LO 7.5 Categorize different types of innovations in the markets-and-technology framework.

LO 7.6 Compare and contrast closed and open innovation.

Netflix: Disrupting the TV Industry

Just like cable providers disrupted the early broadcast model of television in a wave of innovation, companies streaming video represents the most recent wave of innovation reshaping the television industry.

The disruptive impact of cable played out in the 1980s and 1990s, upsetting a handful of broadcast networks with dozens and then hundreds of channels. The current wave of disruption started in the 2000s and may be reaching its peak. Now, with basically every device from a TV to a PC or laptop and smartphones turning into a TV screen, demand for online streaming is exploding. And Netflix is riding atop the crest of this wave to industry leadership and competitive advantage. During peak hours, Netflix now accounts for more than one-third of all downstream Internet traffic in the United States!

How did Netflix turn from an obscure online rental shop for DVDs sent via postal mail to the dominant content provider of on-demand streaming? After being annoyed at having to pay more than $40 in late fees for a Blockbuster video, Reed Hastings started Netflix in 1997 to offer online rentals of DVDs. At the time, the commercial Internet was in its infancy; Amazon had just made its IPO in the same year. Streaming content was only a distant dream in the era of dial-up Internet. Selling products online seemed rather straightforward, but how could a business rent DVDs through the web? In 1999 Netflix rolled out a monthly subscription model, with unlimited rentals for a single monthly rate (and no late fees!). Rental

House of Cards, a Netflix original series, starring Kevin Spacey and Robin Wright.
© A-Pix Entertainment/Photofest

DVDs were sent in distinctive red envelopes, with pre-printed return envelopes. New rentals would not be sent until the current rental was returned.

Despite an innovative business model, Netflix got off to a slow start. By 2000, it had only about 300,000 subscribers and was losing money. Hastings approached Blockbuster, at the time the largest brick-and-mortar video rental chain with almost 8,000 stores in the United States. He proposed selling Blockbuster 49 percent of Netflix and rebranding it as Blockbuster.com. Basically the idea was that Netflix would become the online presence for the huge national chain. The dot.com bubble had just burst, and Blockbuster didn't see value in having a presence online. Blockbuster turned Netflix down cold. Netflix, however, survived the dot.com bust, and by 2002, the company was profitable and went public. Blockbuster began online rentals in 2004, but by this time, Netflix had built a subscriber base of almost 4 million and a strong brand identity.

Blockbuster lost 75 percent of its market value between 2003 and 2005. From there it went from bad to worse. In 2010, the once mighty Blockbuster filed for bankruptcy.

So Netflix was at the forefront of the current wave of disruption in the TV industry as it began streaming content over the Internet in 2007. And it stayed at the forefront. It adjusted quickly to the new options consumers had to receive content, making streaming available on a large number of devices including mobile phones, tablets, game consoles, and new devices dedicated to Internet content streaming such as Roku, Apple TV, and Google Chromecast. At the same time the market for Internet-connected, large, high-definition flat-screen TVs began to take off. Within just two years, Netflix subscriptions (then priced at $7.99 per month) jumped to 12 million. Despite the impending wave of disruption, old-line media executives continued to dismiss Netflix as a threat. In 2010, Time Warner CEO Jeff Bewkes snubbed Netflix by saying, "It's a little bit like, is the Albanian army going to take over the world? I don't think so."[1]

Even Reed Hastings called what Netflix provided "rerun TV." But behind their bravado, the broadcast networks were awaking to the threat Netflix posed. They stopped distributing content to Netflix and instead made it available through Hulu.com, an online content website that is jointly owned by several of the major networks. In 2011, Hulu began offering original content that was not available on broadcast or cable television. The lower-cost structure afforded by Hulu's streaming model meant that the networks saw Hulu as a place to test new series ideas with minimal financial risk. In response, Netflix announced a move to create and stream original content online.

Since content streaming was Netflix's main business, it devoted significant resources to produce high-quality content. In 2013, Netflix first released the political drama *House of Cards,* followed by the comedy-drama *Orange Is the New Black*. Both of these shows proved tremendous hits, and both have received many awards including Emmys and Golden Globes.

In 2015, Netflix had more than 60 million subscribers worldwide, with 50 million in the United States. Its revenues were $6 billion, and its market cap was $38 billion. Indeed, over the past decade, Netflix's stock appreciated by over 4,100 percentage points, while the tech-heavy NASDAQ 100 index grew by "only" 193 percentage points over the same period. By innovating on many different dimensions, Netflix was able to not only disrupt the TV industry, but also to gain a competitive advantage.[2]

You will learn more about Netflix by reading the chapter; related questions appear on page 242.

INNOVATION—the successful introduction of a new product, process, or business model—is a powerful driver in the competitive process. The ChapterCase provides an example of how innovations in technology and business models can make existing competitors obsolete, and how they allowed Netflix to gain a competitive advantage.

Continued innovation forms the bedrock of Netflix's business strategy. Using big data analytics, in particular, Netflix introduced a number of early innovations in the video rental business. One of the more ingenious moves by Netflix was to have each user build a queue of movies he or she wanted to watch next. This allowed Netflix to predict future demand for specific movies fairly accurately. Another innovation was to create a "personalized recommendation engine" for each user that would predict what each subscriber might want to watch next based not only on a quick rating survey and the subscriber's viewing history, but also what movies users with a similar profile had watched and enjoyed. Based on Netflix's proprietary learning algorithm, the recommendations would improve over time as the user's preferences become more clear. This also allowed Netflix to steer users away from hit movies (where wait times for DVD rentals were long because the company only had a limited number in its library) to lesser-known titles in its catalog. The ability to bring in the "long tail"[3] of demand delighted not only viewers, as they enjoyed lesser-known, but often critically acclaimed films, but also movie studies, which could now make additional money on movies that would otherwise not be in demand. Moreover, in contrast to other players in the media industry, Netflix was fast to catch the wave of content streaming via the Internet.

Innovation allows firms to redefine the marketplace in their favor and achieve a competitive advantage.[4] That's why we focus on innovation and the related topic of entrepreneurship in this chapter—to celebrate innovation as a powerful competitive weapon for business strategy formulation. We begin this chapter by detailing how competition is a process driven by continuous innovation. Next we discuss strategic and social entrepreneurship. We then take a deep dive into the industry life cycle. This helps us to formulate a more dynamic business strategy as the industry changes over time. We also introduce the crossing-the-chasm framework, highlighting the difficulties in transitioning through different stages of the industry life cycle. We then move into a detailed discussion of different types of innovation using the markets-and-technology framework. We also present different ways to organize for innovation. As with every chapter, we conclude with practice-oriented "Implications for the Strategist."

7.1 Competition Driven by Innovation

Competition is a process driven by the "perennial gale of creative destruction," in the words of famed economist Joseph Schumpeter.[5] The continuous waves of market leadership changes in the TV industry, detailed in the ChapterCase, demonstrate the potency of innovation as a competitive weapon: It can simultaneously create and destroy value. Firms must be able to innovate while also fending off competitors' imitation attempts. A successful strategy requires both an effective offense and a hard-to-crack defense.

Many firms have dominated an early wave of innovation only to be challenged and often destroyed by the next wave. Examples include:

- *The explosion of television-viewing options:* As highlighted in the ChapterCase, traditional television networks (ABC, CBS, and NBC) have been struggling to maintain viewers and advertising revenues as cable and satellite providers offered innovative programming. Those same cable and satellite providers are trying hard to hold on to viewers as more and more people gravitate toward customized content online. To exploit such opportunities, Google acquired YouTube, while Comcast, the largest U.S. cable operator, purchased NBCUniversal.[6] Comcast's acquisition helps it integrate delivery services and content, with the goal of establishing itself as a new player in the media industry. In turn, both traditional TV and cable networks are currently under threat from content providers that stream via the Internet, such as Netflix, YouTube, and Amazon.

- *The move from typewriters to PCs to mobile devices:* Wang Laboratories, a computer company that led the market for word-processing machines, destroyed typewriter companies such as Smith Corona and Underwood. It then was undone by computer makers such as IBM and Compaq. Today, IBM has exited the personal computer market, selling its PC division to the Chinese technology company Lenovo, and Compaq has been acquired by HP. The computer industry, however, has not been standing still either. Once-successful PC makers such as HP and Dell are now under threat by companies that are innovating in the mobile device space, such as Apple, Samsung, Google, and the Chinese start-up Xiaomi.

As the adage goes, change is the only constant—and the rate of technological change has accelerated dramatically over the past hundred years. Changing technologies spawn new industries, while others die. This makes innovation a powerful strategic weapon in order to gain and sustain competitive advantage. Exhibit 7.1 shows how many years it took for different technological innovations to reach 50 percent of the U.S. population (either through ownership or usage). As an example, it took 84 years for half of the U.S. population to own a car, but only 28 years for half the population to own a TV. The pace of the adoption rate of recent innovations continues to accelerate. It took 19 years for the PC to reach 50 percent ownership, but only 6 years for MP3 players to accomplish the same diffusion rate.

EXHIBIT 7.1 / Accelerating Speed of Technological Change

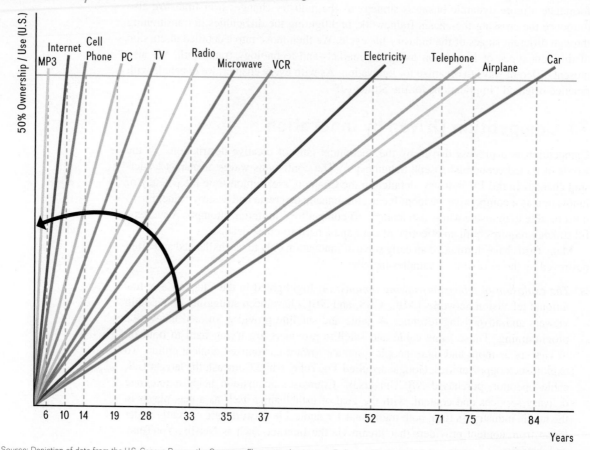

Source: Depiction of data from the U.S. Census Bureau, the Consumer Electronics Association, *Forbes*, and the National Cable and Telecommunications Association.

What factors explain increasingly rapid technological diffusion and adoption? One determinant is that initial innovations such as the car, airplane, telephone, and the use of electricity provided the necessary infrastructure for newer innovations to diffuse more rapidly. Another reason is the emergence of new business models that make innovations more accessible. For example, Dell's direct-to-consumer distribution system improved access to low-cost PCs, and Walmart's low-price, high-volume model used its sophisticated IT logistics system to fuel explosive growth. In addition, satellite and cable distribution systems facilitated the ability of mass media such as radio and TV to deliver advertising and information to a wider audience. The speed of technology diffusion has accelerated further with the emergence of the Internet, social networking sites, and viral messaging. The accelerating speed of technological changes has significant implications for the competitive process and firm strategy. We will now take a close look at the innovation process unleashed by technological changes.

LO 7-1

Outline the four-step innovation process from idea to imitation.

THE INNOVATION PROCESS

Broadly viewed, innovation describes the discovery, development, and transformation of new knowledge in a four-step process captured in the *four I's: Idea, Invention, Innovation,* and *Imitation* (see Exhibit 7.2).[7]

EXHIBIT 7.2 /

The Four I's: Idea, Invention, Innovation, and Imitation

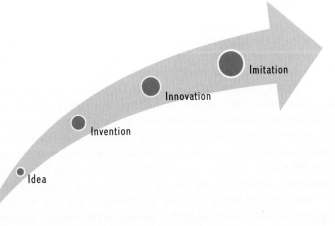

The innovation process begins with an *idea*. The idea is often presented in terms of abstract concepts or as findings derived from basic research. Basic research is conducted to discover new knowledge and is often published in academic journals. This may be done to enhance the fundamental understanding of nature, without any commercial application or benefit in mind. In the long run, however, basic research is often transformed into applied research with commercial applications. For example, wireless communication technology today is built upon the fundamental science breakthroughs Albert Einstein accomplished over 100 years ago in his research on the nature of light.[8]

In a next step, **invention** describes the transformation of an idea into a new product or process, or the modification and recombination of existing ones. The practical application of basic knowledge in a particular area frequently results in new technology. If an invention is *useful, novel,* and *non-obvious* as assessed by the U.S. Patent and Trademark Office, it can be patented.[9] A **patent** is a form of *intellectual property,* and gives the inventor exclusive rights to benefit from commercializing a technology for a specified time period in exchange for public disclosure of the underlying idea (see also the discussion on *isolating mechanisms* in Chapter 4). In the United States, the time period for the right to exclude others from the use of the technology is 20 years from the filing date of a patent application. Exclusive rights often translate into a *temporary monopoly position* until the patent expires. For instance, many pharmaceutical drugs are patent protected.

Strategically, however, patents are a *double-edged sword.* On the one hand, patents provide a temporary monopoly as they bestow exclusive rights on the patent owner to use a novel technology for a specific time period. Thus, patents may form the basis for a competitive advantage. Because patents require full disclosure of the underlying technology and know-how so that others can use it freely once the patent protection has expired, however, many firms find it strategically beneficial *not* to patent their technology. Instead they use **trade secrets**, defined as valuable proprietary information that is not in the public domain and where the firm makes every effort to maintain its secrecy. The most famous example of a trade secret is the Coca-Cola recipe, which has been protected for over a century.[10] The same goes for Ferrero's Nutella, whose secret recipe is said to be known by even fewer than the handful of people who have access to the Coca-Cola recipe.[11]

Avoiding public disclosure and thus making its underlying technology widely known is precisely the reason Netflix does not patent its recommendation algorithm or Google its PageRank algorithm. Netflix has an advantage over competitors because its recommendation algorithm works best; the same goes for Google—its search algorithm is the best available. Disclosing the information how exactly these algorithms work would nullify their advantage.

invention
The transformation of an idea into a new product or process, or the modification and recombination of existing ones.

patent
A form of *intellectual property* that gives the inventor exclusive rights to benefit from commercializing a technology for a specified time period in exchange for public disclosure of the underlying idea.

trade secret
Valuable proprietary information that is not in the public domain and where the firm makes every effort to maintain its secrecy.

innovation
The commercialization of any new product or process, or the modification and recombination of existing ones.

Innovation concerns the *commercialization* of an invention.[12] The successful commercialization of a new product or service allows a firm to extract temporary monopoly profits. As detailed in the ChapterCase, Netflix began its life with a business model innovation, offering unlimited DVD rentals via the Internet, without any late fees. What really aided Netflix, however, to gain an early lead was the application of big data analytics to its user preferences to not only predict future demand but also to provide highly personalized viewing recommendations. The success of the latter is evident by the fact that movies that were recommended to viewers scored higher than on what they were scored previously. To sustain a competitive advantage, however, a firm must continuously innovate—that is, it must produce a string of successful new products or services over time. In this spirit, Netflix further developed its business model innovation, moving from online DVD rentals to directly streaming content via the Internet. Moreover, it innovated further in creating proprietary content such as *House of Cards* and *Orange Is the New Black*.

first-mover advantages
Competitive benefits that accrue to the successful innovator.

Successful innovators can benefit from a number of **first-mover advantages,**[13] including economies of scale as well as experience and learning-curve effects (as discussed in Chapter 6). First movers may also benefit from *network effects* (see discussion of Apple in discussion of the Introduction Stage later in this chapter). Moreover, first movers may hold important intellectual property such as critical patents. They may also be able to lock in key suppliers as well as customers through increasing switching costs. For example, users of Microsoft Word might find the switching costs entailed in moving to a different word-processing software prohibitive. Not only would they need to spend many hours learning the new software, but collaborators would also need to have compatible software installed and be familiar with the program to open and revise shared documents.

Google (by offering Google Docs, a free web-based suite of application software such as word-processing, spreadsheet, and presentation programs) is attempting to minimize switching costs by leveraging *cloud computing*—a real-time network of shared computing resources via the Internet (Google Drive). Rather than requiring each user to have the appropriate software installed on his or her personal computer, the software is maintained and updated in the cloud. Files are also saved in the cloud, which allows collaboration in real time globally wherever one can access an Internet connection.

EXHIBIT 7.3 / Innovation: A Novel and Useful Idea That Is Successfully Implemented

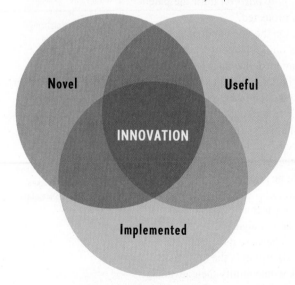

Innovation need not be high-tech in order to be a potent competitive weapon, as P&G's history of innovative new product launches such as the Swiffer line of cleaning products shows. P&G uses the *razor-razorblade business model* (introduced in Chapter 5), where the consumer purchases the handle at a low price, but must pay a premium for replacement refills and pads over time. As shown in Exhibit 7.3, an innovation needs to be novel, useful, and successfully implemented in order to help firms gain and sustain a competitive advantage.

The innovation process ends with *imitation.* If an innovation is successful in the marketplace, competitors will attempt to imitate it. Although Netflix has some 50 million U.S. subscribers, imitators are set to compete its advantage away. Amazon offers its Instant Video service to its estimated 50 million Prime subscribers ($99 a year or $8.25 a month), with selected titles free. In addition, Prime members receive free two-day shipping on Amazon purchases. Hulu Plus ($7.99 a month), a video-on-demand service jointly owned by NBC, Fox, and Disney, has some 6 million subscribers. One advantage Hulu Plus has over Netflix and Amazon is that it typically makes the latest episodes of popular TV shows available the day following broadcast, on Hulu, while often delayed by several months before offered by Netflix or Amazon. A joint venture of NBCUniversal Television Group (Comcast), Fox Broadcasting (21st Century Fox) and Disney—ABC Television Group (The Walt Disney Company), Hulu Plus uses advertisements along with its subscription fees as revenue sources. Finally, Google's YouTube with its over 1 billion users is evolving into a TV ecosystem, benefiting not only from free content uploaded by its users but also creating original programming. As of 2015, the most subscribed channels were by PewDiePie (36 million) and YouTube Spotlight, its official channel (23 million) used to highlight videos and events such as YouTube Music Awards and YouTube Comedy Week. Google's business is, of course, ad supported. Only time will tell whether Netflix will be able to sustain its competitive advantage given the imitation attempts by a number of competitors.

7.2 Strategic and Social Entrepreneurship

Entrepreneurship describes the process by which change agents (entrepreneurs) undertake economic risk to innovate—to create new products, processes, and sometimes new organizations.[14] Entrepreneurs innovate by commercializing ideas and inventions.[15] They seek out or create new business opportunities and then assemble the resources necessary to exploit them.[16] If successful, entrepreneurship not only drives the competitive process, but it also creates value for the individual entrepreneurs and society at large.

Although many new ventures fail, some achieve spectacular success. Examples of successful entrepreneurs are:

- **Reed Hastings,** founder of Netflix featured in the ChapterCase. Hastings grew up in Cambridge, Massachusetts. He obtained an undergraduate degree in math from Bowdoin College, a small liberal arts college. Hastings then volunteered for the Peace Corps for two years, teaching high school math in Swaziland (Africa). Next, he enrolled at Stanford University to pursue a master's degree in computer science, which brought him to Silicon Valley. Reed Hastings declared his love affair with writing computer code, but emphasized, "The big thing that Stanford did for me was to turn me on to the entrepreneurial model."[17] His net worth today is an estimated $1 billion.

- **Jeff Bezos,** the founder of Amazon.com (featured in ChapterCase 8), the world's largest online retailer. The stepson of a Cuban immigrant, Bezos graduated from Princeton and then worked as a financial analyst on Wall Street. In 1994, after reading that the Internet was growing by 2,000 percent a month, he set out to leverage the Internet as a new distribution channel. Listing products that could be sold online, he finally settled on books because that retail market was fairly fragmented, with huge inefficiencies in its distribution system. Perhaps even more important, books represent a perfect commodity, because they are identical regardless of where a consumer buys them. This reduced uncertainty when introducing online shopping to consumers. In a comprehensive research study that evaluated the long-term performance of CEOs globally, Jeff Bezos was ranked number two, just behind the late Steve Jobs (Apple), but ahead of Yun Jong-Yong (Samsung).[18]

- **Oprah Winfrey,** best-known for her self-titled TV talk show, and founder and CEO of Harpo Productions, a multimedia company. Some of Harpo's well-known products include *The Oprah Winfrey Show, Dr. Phil, The Rachael Ray Show, The Dr. Oz Show,*

LO 7-2

Apply strategic management concepts to entrepreneurship and innovation.

entrepreneurship
The process by which people undertake economic risk to innovate—to create new products, processes, and sometimes new organizations.

Oprah Winfrey, a highly successful entrepreneur and business person in many areas including as talk show host, actress, producer, media proprietor, and philanthropist.
© Randall Michelson/ WireImage/Getty Images

Oprah.com, O, The Oprah Magazine, and *O at Home.* In 2011, she launched a new cable TV channel jointly with Discovery Communications: OWN, The Oprah Winfrey Network.[19] A graduate of Tennessee State University, Winfrey used her entrepreneurial talents to rise from poverty and an abusive childhood to become one of the most successful entrepreneurs in the multimedia business, with a net worth of over $2 billion.[20] Also in 2011, Winfrey ended her record-setting talk show to devote her entrepreneurial talents to OWN. To make OWN more successful, she took over the position as CEO in addition to chief creative officer. OWN is now available to some 82 million pay television households in the United States (70 percent of households).

■ **Elon Musk,** an engineer and serial entrepreneur with a deep passion to "solve environmental, social, and economic challenges."[21] We featured him in his role as leader of Tesla Motors in ChapterCase 3. Musk left his native South Africa at age 17. He went to Canada and then to the United States, where he completed a bachelor's degree in economics and physics at the University of Pennsylvania. After only two days in a PhD program in applied physics and material sciences at Stanford University, Musk left graduate school to found Zip2, an online provider of content publishing software for news organizations. Four years later, in 1999, computer maker Compaq acquired Zip2 for $341 million (and was in turn acquired by HP in 2002). Elon Musk moved on to co-found PayPal, an online payment processor. When eBay acquired PayPal for $1.5 billion in 2002, Musk had the financial resources to pursue his passion to use science and engineering to solve social and economic challenges. He is leading three new ventures simultaneously: electric cars with Tesla Motors, renewable energy with SolarCity, and space exploration with SpaceX.[22]

entrepreneurs
The agents that introduce change into the competitive system.

Entrepreneurs are the agents who introduce change into the competitive system. They do this not only by figuring out how to use inventions, but also by introducing new products or services, new production processes, and new forms of organization. Entrepreneurs can introduce change by starting new ventures, such as Reed Hastings with Netflix or Mark Zuckerberg with Facebook. Or they can be found within existing firms, such as A.G. Lafley at Procter & Gamble (P&G), who implemented an *open-innovation model* (which we'll discuss later). When innovating within existing companies, change agents are often called *intrapreneurs:* those pursuing *corporate entrepreneurship.*[23]

Entrepreneurs who drive innovation need just as much skill, commitment, and daring as the inventors who are responsible for the process of invention.[24] As an example, the engineer Nikola Tesla invented the alternating-current (AC) electric motor and was granted a patent in 1888 by the U.S. Patent and Trademark Office.[25] Because this breakthrough technology was neglected for much of the 20th century and Tesla did not receive the recognition he deserved in his lifetime, the entrepreneur Elon Musk is not just commercializing Tesla's invention but also honoring Tesla with the name of his company, Tesla Motors, a new venture formed to design and manufacture all-electric automobiles. Tesla Motors launched several all-electric vehicles based on Tesla's original invention.

strategic entrepreneurship
The pursuit of innovation using tools and concepts from strategic management.

Strategic entrepreneurship describes the pursuit of innovation using tools and concepts from strategic management.[26] We can leverage innovation for competitive advantage by applying a strategic management lens to entrepreneurship. The fundamental question of strategic entrepreneurship, therefore, is how to combine entrepreneurial actions, creating new opportunities or exploiting existing ones with strategic actions taken in the pursuit of competitive advantage.[27] This can take place within new ventures such as Tesla Motors or within established firms such as Apple. Apple's continued innovation in mobile devices is an example of strategic entrepreneurship: Apple's managers use strategic analysis, formulation, and implementation when deciding which new type of mobile device to research and develop, when to launch it, and how to implement the necessary organizational changes to support the new product launch. Each new release is an innovation; each is therefore an act of entrepreneurship—planned and executed using strategic management concepts. In 2015, for example, Apple entered the market for computer wearables by introducing the Apple Watch.

Social entrepreneurship describes the pursuit of social goals while creating profitable businesses. Social entrepreneurs evaluate the performance of their ventures not only by financial metrics but also by ecological and social contribution (*profits, planet,* and *people*). They use a *triple-bottom-line* approach to assess performance (discussed in Chapter 5). Examples of social entrepreneurship ventures include Teach For America (see MiniCase 2), TOMS Shoes (which gives a pair of shoes to an economically disadvantaged child for every pair of shoes it sells), Better World Books (an online bookstore that "harnesses the power of capitalism to bring literacy and opportunity to people around the world"),[28] and Wikipedia (see following and MiniCase 17).

> **social entrepreneurship**
> The pursuit of social goals while creating a profitable business.

The founder of Wikipedia, Jimmy Wales, typifies social entrepreneurship.[29] Raised in Alabama, Wales was educated by his mother and grandmother who ran a nontraditional school. In 1994, he dropped out of a doctoral program in economics at Indiana University to take a job at a stock brokerage firm in Chicago. In the evenings he wrote computer code for fun and built a web browser. During the late 1990s' Internet boom, Wales was one of the first to grasp the power of an open-source method to provide knowledge on a very large scale. What differentiates Wales from other web entrepreneurs is his idealism: Wikipedia is free for the end user and supports itself solely by donations and not, for example, by online advertising. Wikipedia has 35 million articles in 288 languages, including some 5 million items in English. About 500 million people use Wikipedia each month. Wales' idealism is a form of social entrepreneurship: His vision is to make the entire repository of human knowledge available to anyone anywhere for free.

Since entrepreneurs and the innovations they unleash frequently create entire new industries, we now turn to a discussion of the industry life cycle to derive implications for competitive strategy.

7.3 Innovation and the Industry Life Cycle

LO 7-3

Describe the competitive implications of different stages in the industry life cycle.

Innovations frequently lead to the birth of new industries. Innovative advances in IT and logistics facilitated the creation of the overnight express delivery industry by FedEx and that of big-box retailing by Walmart. The Internet set online retailing in motion, with new companies such as Amazon and eBay taking the lead, and it revolutionized the advertising industry first through Yahoo, and later Google and Facebook. Advances in nanotechnology are revolutionizing many different industries, ranging from medical diagnostics and surgery to lighter and stronger airplane components.[30]

Industries tend to follow a predictable **industry life cycle**: As an industry evolves over time, we can identify five distinct stages: *introduction, growth, shakeout, maturity,* and *decline*.[31] We will illustrate how the type of innovation and resulting strategic implications change at each stage of the life cycle as well as how innovation can initiate and drive a new life cycle.

> **industry life cycle**
> The five different stages—introduction, growth, shakeout, maturity, and decline—that occur in the evolution of an industry over time.

The number and size of competitors change as the industry life cycle unfolds, and different types of consumers enter the market at each stage. That is, both the supply and demand sides of the market change as the industry ages. Each stage of the industry life cycle requires different competencies for the firm to perform well and to satisfy that stage's unique customer group. We first introduce the life cycle model before discussing different customer groups in more depth when introducing the crossing-the-chasm concept later in this chapter.[32]

Exhibit 7.4 depicts a typical industry life cycle, focusing on the smartphone industry in emerging and developed economies. In a stylized industry life cycle model, the horizontal axis shows time (in years) and the vertical axis market size. In Exhibit 7.4, however, we are taking a snapshot of the global smartphone industry in the year 2016. This implies that we are joining two different life cycles (one for emerging economies and one for developed economies) in the same exhibit at one point in time.

The development of most industries follows an S-curve. Initial demand for a new product or service is often slow to take off, then accelerates, before decelerating, and eventually turning to zero, and even becoming negative as a market contracts.

As shown in Exhibit 7.4, in emerging economies such as Argentina, Brazil, China, India, Indonesia, Mexico, and Russia, the smartphone industry is in the growth stage (in 2016). The market for smartphones in these countries is expected to grow rapidly over the next few years. More and more of the consumers in these countries with very large populations are expected to upgrade from a simple mobile phone to a smartphone such as the Apple iPhone, Samsung Galaxy, or Xiaomi's popular Mi2S phone.

In contrast, the market for smartphones is in the maturity stage in 2016 in developed economies such as Australia, Canada, Germany, Japan, South Korea, the United Kingdom, and the United States. This implies that developed economies moved through the prior three stages of the industry life cycle (introductory, growth, and shakeout) some years earlier. Because the smartphone industry is mature in these markets, little or no growth in market size is expected over the next few years because most consumers own smartphones. This implies that any market share gain by one firm comes at the expense of others, as users replace older smartphones with newer models. Competitive intensity is expected to be high.

Each stage of the industry life cycle—introduction, growth, shakeout, maturity, and decline—has different strategic implications for competing firms. We now discuss each stage in detail.

EXHIBIT 7.4 /

Industry Life Cycle: The Smartphone Industry in Emerging and Developed Economies

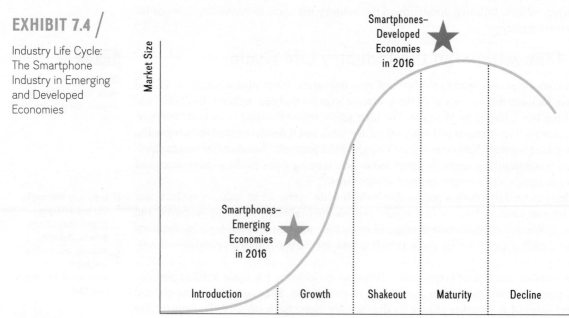

INTRODUCTION STAGE

When an individual inventor or company launches a successful innovation, a new industry may emerge. In this introductory stage, the innovator's core competency is R&D, which is necessary to creating a new product category that will attract customers. This is a capital-intensive process, in which the innovator is investing in designing a unique product, trying new ideas to attract customers, and producing small quantities—all of which contribute to a high price when the product is launched. The initial market size is small, and growth is slow.

In this introductory stage, when barriers to entry tend to be high, generally only a few firms are active in the market. In their competitive struggle for market share, they emphasize unique product features and performance rather than price.

Although there are some benefits to being early in the market (as previously discussed), innovators also may encounter *first-mover disadvantages.* They must educate potential customers about the product's intended benefits, find distribution channels and complementary assets, and continue to perfect the fledgling product. Although a core competency in R&D is necessary to create or enter an industry in the introductory stage, some competency in marketing also is helpful in achieving a successful product launch and market acceptance. Competition can be intense, and early winners are well-positioned to stake out a strong position for the future. As one of the main innovators in software for mobile devices, Google's Android operating system for smartphones is enjoying a strong market position and substantial lead over competitors.

The strategic objective during the introductory stage is to achieve market acceptance and seed future growth. One way to accomplish these objectives is to initiate and leverage **network effects**,[33] the positive effect that one user of a product or service has on the value of that product for other users. Network effects occur when the value of a product or service increases, often exponentially, with the number of users. If successful, network effects propel the industry to the next stage of the life cycle, the growth stage (which we discuss next).

network effects
The positive effect (externality) that one user of a product or service has on the value of that product for other users.

Apple effectively leveraged the network effects generated by numerous complementary software applications (apps) available via iTunes to create a tightly integrated ecosystem of hardware, software, and services, which competitors find hard to crack. The consequence has been a competitive advantage for over a decade, beginning with the introduction of the iPod in 2001 and iTunes in 2003. Apple launched its enormously successful iPhone in the summer of 2007. A year later, it followed up with the Apple App Store, which boasts, for almost anything you might need, "there's an app for that." *Apps* are small software programs developed to provide mobile users with inexpensive business and personal services wherever they may be. Popular apps allow iPhone users to access their business contacts via LinkedIn, hail a ride via Uber, call colleagues overseas via Skype, check delivery of their Zappos packages shipped via UPS, get the latest news on Twitter, and engage in customer relationship management using Salesforce.com. You can stream music via Pandora, post photos using Instagram, watch Netflix, access Facebook to check on your friends, or video message using Snapchat.

Even more important is the effect that apps have on the value of an iPhone. Arguably, the explosive growth of the iPhone is due to the fact that the Apple App Store offers the largest selection of apps to its users. The 1.5 million apps available were downloaded 75 billion times as of spring 2015. Moreover, Apple argues that users have a better experience because the apps take advantage of the tight integration of hardware and software provided by the iPhone. The availability of apps, in turn, leads to network effects that increase the value of the iPhone for its users. Exhibit 7.5 shows how. Increased value creation, as we know from Chapter 6, is positively related to demand, which in turn

EXHIBIT 7.5 / Leveraging Network Effects to Drive Demand: Apple's iPhone

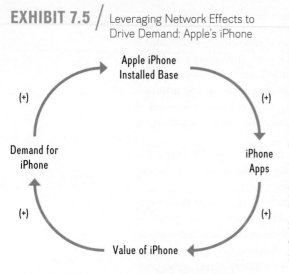

increases the installed base, meaning the number of people using an iPhone. As of the spring of 2015, Apple had sold more than 75 million iPhone 6 models, introduced just six months prior. As the installed based of iPhone users further increases, this incentivizes software developers to write even more apps. Making apps widely available strengthened Apple's position in the smartphone industry. Based on positive feedback loops, a virtuous cycle emerges where one factor positively reinforces another. Apple's ecosystem based on integrated hardware, software, and services providing a superior user experience is hard to crack for competitors. Apple now hopes that its vast App Store in combination with a seamless user experience will now also ignite a virtuous cycle of continuous demand based on network effects for its Apple Watch, introduced in early 2015.[34]

GROWTH STAGE

Market growth accelerates in the growth stage of the industry life cycle (see Exhibit 7.4). After the initial innovation has gained some market acceptance, demand increases rapidly as first-time buyers rush to enter the market, convinced by the proof of concept demonstrated in the introductory stage.

standard
An agreed-upon solution about a common set of engineering features and design choices.

As the size of the market expands, a **standard** signals the market's agreement on a common set of engineering features and design choices.[35] Standards can emerge bottom-up through competition in the marketplace or be imposed top-down by government or other standard-setting agencies such as the Institute of Electrical and Electronics Engineers (IEEE) that develops and sets industrial standards in a broad range of industries, including energy, electric power, biomedical and health care technology, IT, telecommunications, consumer electronics, aerospace, and nanotechnology.

An agreed-upon standard, such as the IBM PC, ensures that all components of the system work well together, regardless of who developed them. It also helps legitimize the new technology by reducing uncertainty and confusion. A standard tends to capture a larger market share and can persist for a long time.

In the 1980s, the Wintel standard (a portmanteau of Windows and Intel) marked the beginning of exponential growth in the personal computer industry; it still holds some 90 percent of market share in personal computers. In the 2000s we saw a standards war between the HD-DVD format and the higher-definition rival, the Blu-ray Disc (BD). Blu-ray, backed by an association of electronics companies including Sony, Panasonic, and others, bested the HD-DVD format backed by Toshiba. Some argue that Sony's PlayStation 3 acted as a catalyst for adopting the Blu-ray format. A tipping point in favor of the Blu-ray format may have been the decision in 2008 by Warner Bros. to release discs only in Blu-ray format. Leading retailers such as Walmart and Best Buy began carrying DVDs in Blu-ray format and did not stock as large a selection in the HD-DVD format; Netflix and Blockbuster also fell in line. As a consequence, many companies stopped making HD-DVD players. Barriers to entry fell as technological uncertainties were overcome, and many new and established firms rushed to participate in the growth opportunity. As a side note, Sony and others never reaped the full rewards of this victory. Today the HD-DVD format still prevails, and wars on media formats have been overshadowed by delivery through video on demand (VOD) and streaming.

Government bodies or industry associations can also set standards by making top-down decisions. The European Union determined in the 1980s that GSM (Global System for Mobile Communications) should be the standard for cell phones in Europe. The United States relied instead on a market-based approach, and CDMA (Code Division Multiple Access), a proprietary standard developed by Qualcomm, emerged as an early leader. While North American manufacturers and service providers such as AT&T, Verizon, Motorola, and others were fighting a format war, Scandinavian companies such as Nokia and Ericsson faced no such uncertainty, and they leveraged their early lead into a temporary competitive advantage. Today, about 80 percent of the global mobile market uses the GSM standard.

Since demand is strong during the growth phase, both efficient and inefficient firms thrive; the rising tide lifts all boats. Moreover, prices begin to fall, often rapidly, as standard business processes are put in place and firms begin to reap economies of scale and learning. Distribution channels are expanded, and complementary assets in the form of products and services become widely available.[36]

After a standard is established in an industry, the basis of competition tends to move away from product innovations toward process innovations.[37] **Product innovations**, as the name suggests, are new or recombined knowledge embodied in new products—the jet airplane, electric vehicle, smartphones, and wearable computers. **Process innovations** are new ways to produce existing products or to deliver existing services. Process innovations are made possible through advances such as the Internet, lean manufacturing, Six Sigma, biotechnology, nanotechnology, and so on.

Process innovation must not be high-tech to be impactful, however. The invention of the standardized shipping container, for instance, has transformed global trade.[38] By loading goods into uniform containers that could easily be moved between trucks, rail, and ships, significant savings in cost and time were accomplished. Before containerization was invented some 60 years ago, it cost almost $6 to load a ton of (loose) cargo, and theft was rampant. After containerization, the cost for loading a ton of cargo had plummeted to $0.16 and theft all but disappeared (because containers are sealed at the departing factory). Efficiency gains in terms of labor and time were even more impressive. Before containerization, dock labor could move 1.7 tons per hour onto a cargo ship. After containerization, this had jumped to 30 tons per hour. Ports are now able to accommodate much larger ships, and travel time across the oceans has fallen in half. As a consequence, costs for shipping goods across the globe have fallen rapidly. Moreover, containerization enabled optimization of global supply chains and set the stage for subsequent process innovations such as *just-in-time (JIT) operations management*. Taken together, a set of research studies estimated that containerization alone more than tripled international trade within five years of adopting this critical process innovation.[39]

Exhibit 7.6 shows the level of product and process innovation throughout the entire life cycle.[40] In the introductory stage, the level of *product* innovation is at a maximum because new features increasing perceived consumer value are critical to gaining traction in the market. In contrast, process innovation is at a minimum in the introductory stage because companies produce only a small number of products, often just prototypes or beta versions. The main concern is to commercialize the invention—that is, to demonstrate that the product works and that a market exists.

The relative importance, however, reverses over time. Frequently, a standard emerges during the growth stage of the industry life cycle (see the second column, "Growth," in Exhibit 7.6). At that point, most of the technological and commercial uncertainties about the new product are gone. After the market accepts a new product, and a standard for the new technology has emerged, *process* innovation rapidly becomes more important than

product innovation
New or recombined knowledge embodied in new products.

process innovation
New ways to produce existing products or deliver existing services.

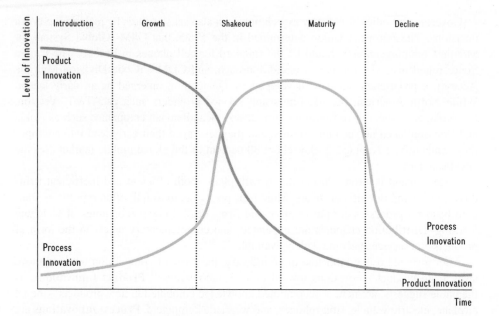

product innovation. As market demand increases, economies of scale kick in: Firms establish and optimize standard business processes through applications of lean manufacturing, Six Sigma, and so on. As a consequence, product improvements become incremental, while the level of process innovation rises rapidly.

During the growth stage, process innovation ramps up (at increasing marginal returns) as firms attempt to keep up with rapidly rising demand while attempting to bring down costs at the same time. The core competencies for competitive advantage in the growth stage tend to shift toward manufacturing and marketing capabilities. At the same time, the R&D emphasis tends to shift to process innovation for improved efficiency. Competitive rivalry is somewhat muted because the market is growing fast.

Since market demand is robust in this stage and more competitors have entered the market, there tends to be more strategic variety: Some competitors will continue to follow a *differentiation* strategy, emphasizing unique features, product functionality, and reliability. Other firms employ a *cost-leadership strategy* in order to offer an acceptable level of value but lower prices to consumers. They realize that lower cost is likely a key success factor in the future, because this will allow the firm to lower prices and attract more consumers into the market. When introduced in the spring of 2010, for example, Apple's first-generation iPad was priced at $829 for 64GB with a 3G Wi-Fi connection.[41] Just three years later, in spring 2013, the same model was priced at only one-third of the original price, or $275.[42] Access to efficient and large-scale manufacturing operations (such as those offered by Foxconn in China, the company that assembles most of Apple's products) and effective supply chain capabilities are key success factors when market demand increases rapidly. By 2015, Gazelle, an ecommerce company that allows people to sell their electronic devices and to buy pre-certified used ones, offered $30 for a "flawless" first-generation iPad.

The key objective for firms during the growth phase is to stake out a strong strategic position not easily imitated by rivals. In the fast-growing shapewear industry, start-up company Spanx has staked out a strong position. In 1998, Florida State University graduate Sara Blakely decided to cut the feet off her pantyhose to enhance her looks when wearing pants.[43] Soon after she obtained a patent for her bodyshaping undergarments, and

Spanx began production and retailing of its shapewear in 2000. Sales grew exponentially after Blakely appeared on *The Oprah Winfrey Show.* By 2015, Spanx had grown to 150 employees and sold millions of Spanx "power panties," with revenues exceeding $250 million. To stake out a strong position and to preempt competitors, Spanx now offers over 200 products ranging from slimming apparel and swimsuits to bras and activewear. Moreover, it now designs and manufactures bodyshaping undergarments for men ("Spanx for Men—Manx"). Spanx products are now available in over 50 countries globally via the Internet. Moreover, to strengthen its strategic position and brand image in the United States, Spanx is opening retail stores across the country.

Sara Blakely, founder and long-time CEO of Spanx. World's youngest female billionaire.
© Zuma Press, Inc/Alamy

The shapewear industry's explosive growth has attracted several other players: Flexees by Maidenform, BodyWrap, and Miraclesuit, to name a few. They are all attempting to carve out positions in the new industry. Given Spanx's ability to stake out a strong position during the growth stage of the industry life cycle and the fact that it continues to be a moving target, it might be difficult for competitors to dislodge the company.

Taking the risk paid off for Spanx's founder: After investing an initial $5,000 into her startup, Blakely became the world's youngest self-made female billionaire. Blakely was also listed in the Time 100, the annual list of the most influential people in the world.

SHAKEOUT STAGE

Rapid industry growth and expansion cannot go on indefinitely. As the industry moves into the next stage of the industry life cycle, the rate of growth declines (see Exhibit 7.4). Firms begin to compete directly against one another for market share, rather than trying to capture a share of an increasing pie. As competitive intensity increases, the weaker firms are forced out of the industry. This is the reason this phase of the industry life cycle is called the shakeout stage: Only the strongest competitors survive increasing rivalry as firms begin to cut prices and offer more services, all in an attempt to gain more of a market that grows slowly, it at all. This type of cut-throat competition erodes profitability of all but the most efficient firms in the industry. As a consequence, the industry often consolidates, as the weakest competitors either are acquired by stronger firms or exit through bankruptcy.

The winners in this increasingly competitive environment are often firms that stake out a strong position as cost leaders. Key success factors at this stage are the manufacturing and process engineering capabilities that can be used to drive costs down. The importance of process innovation further increases (albeit at diminishing marginal returns), while the importance of product innovation further declines.

Assuming an acceptable value proposition, price becomes a more important competitive weapon in the shakeout stage, because product features and performance requirements tend to be well-established. A few firms may be able to implement a blue ocean strategy, combining differentiation and low cost, but given the intensity of competition, many weaker firms are forced to exit. Any firm that does not have a clear strategic profile is likely to not survive the shakeout phase.

MATURITY STAGE

After the shakeout is completed and a few firms remain, the industry enters the maturity stage. During the fourth stage of the industry life cycle, the industry structure morphs into an oligopoly with only a few large firms. Most of the demand was largely satisfied in the prior shakeout stage. Any additional market demand in the maturity stage is limited. Demand now consists of replacement or repeat purchases. The market has reached its maximum size, and industry growth is likely to be zero or even negative going forward. This decrease in market demand increases competitive intensity within the industry. In the maturity stage, the level of process innovation reaches its maximum as firms attempt to lower cost as much as possible, while the level of incremental product innovation sinks to its minimum (see Exhibit 7.6).

Generally, the firms that survive the shakeout stage tend to be larger and enjoy economies of scale, as the industry consolidated and most excess capacity was removed. As shown in Exhibit 7.4, the smartphone industry in the United States and other developed economies is in the maturity stage. Competitive intensity is likely to increase even further going forward.

The domestic airline industry has been in the maturity stage for a long time. The large number of bankruptcies as well as the wave of mega-mergers, such as those of Delta and Northwest, United and Continental, and American Airlines and US Airways, are a consequence of low or zero growth in a mature market characterized by significant excess capacity.

DECLINE STAGE

Changes in the external environment (such as those discussed in Chapter 3 when presenting the PESTEL framework) often take industries from maturity to decline. In this final stage of the industry life cycle, the size of the market contracts further as demand falls, often rapidly. At this final phase of the industry life cycle, innovation efforts along both product and process dimensions cease (see Exhibit 7.6). If a technological or business model breakthrough emerges that opens up a *new* industry, however, then this dynamic interplay between product and process innovation starts anew.

If there is any remaining excess industry capacity in the decline stage, this puts strong pressure on prices and can further increase competitive intensity, especially if the industry has high exit barriers. At this final stage of the industry life cycle, managers generally have four strategic options: *exit, harvest, maintain,* or *consolidate:*[44]

- **Exit.** Some firms are forced to *exit* the industry by bankruptcy or liquidation. The U.S. textile industry has experienced a large number of exits over the last few decades, mainly due to low-cost foreign competition.
- **Harvest.** In pursuing a *harvest strategy,* the firm reduces investments in product support and allocates only a minimum of human and other resources. While several companies such as IBM, Brother, Olivetti, and Nakajima still offer typewriters, they don't invest much in future innovation. Instead, they are maximizing cash flow from their existing typewriter product line.
- **Maintain.** Philip Morris, on the other hand, is following a *maintain strategy* with its Marlboro brand, continuing to support marketing efforts at a given level despite the fact that U.S. cigarette consumption has been declining.
- **Consolidate.** Although market size shrinks in a declining industry, some firms may choose to *consolidate* the industry by buying rivals. This allows the consolidating firm to stake out a strong position—possibly approaching monopolistic market power, albeit in a declining industry.

Although chewing tobacco is a declining industry, Swedish Match has pursued a number of acquisitions to consolidate its strategic position in the industry. It acquired, among other firms, the Pinkerton Tobacco Company of Owensboro, Kentucky, maker of the Red Man brand. Red Man is the leading chewing tobacco brand in the United States. Red Man has carved out a strong strategic position built on a superior reputation for a quality product and by past endorsements of Major League Baseball players since 1904. Despite gory product warnings detailing the health risk of chewing tobacco and a federally mandated prohibition on marketing, the Red Man brand has remained not only popular, but also profitable.

CROSSING THE CHASM

The industry life cycle model assumes a more or less smooth transition from one stage to another. This holds true for most continuous innovations that require little or no change in consumer behavior. But not all innovations enjoy such continuity.

In the influential bestseller *Crossing the Chasm*[45] Geoffrey Moore documented that many innovators were unable to successfully transition from one stage of the industry life cycle to the next. Based on empirical observations, Moore's core argument is that *each stage of the industry life cycle is dominated by a different customer group.* Different customer groups with distinctly different preferences enter the industry at each stage of the industry life cycle. Each customer group responds differently to a technological innovation. This is due to differences in the psychological, demographic, and social attributes observed in each unique customer segment. Moore's main contribution is that the significant differences between the *early* customer groups—who enter during the introductory stage of the industry life cycle—and *later* customers—who enter during the growth stage—can make for a difficult transition between the different parts of the industry life cycle. Such differences between customer groups lead to a big gulf or *chasm* into which companies and their innovations frequently fall. Only companies that recognize these differences and are able to apply the appropriate competencies at each stage of the industry life cycle will have a chance to transition successfully from stage to stage.

Exhibit 7.7 shows the **crossing-the-chasm framework** and the different customer segments. The industry life cycle model (shown in Exhibit 7.4) follows an S-curve leading up to 100 percent total market potential that can be reached during the maturity

LO 7-4

Derive strategic implications of the crossing-the-chasm framework.

crossing-the-chasm framework Conceptual model that shows how each stage of the industry life cycle is dominated by a different customer group.

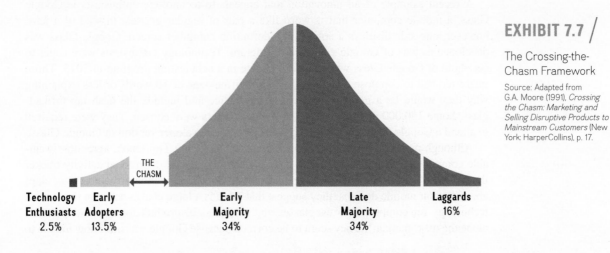

EXHIBIT 7.7

The Crossing-the-Chasm Framework

Source: Adapted from G.A. Moore (1991), *Crossing the Chasm: Marketing and Selling Disruptive Products to Mainstream Customers* (New York: HarperCollins), p. 17.

Technology Enthusiasts 2.5% | Early Adopters 13.5% | Early Majority 34% | Late Majority 34% | Laggards 16%

THE CHASM

stage. In contrast, the *chasm framework* breaks down the 100 percent market potential into different customer segments, highlighting the *incremental* contribution each specific segment can bring into the market. This results in the familiar bell curve. Note the big gulf, or *chasm,* separating the early adopters from the early and late majority that make up the mass market. Social network sites have followed a pattern similar to that illustrated in Exhibit 7.7. Friendster was unable to cross the big chasm. MySpace was successful with the early majority, but only Facebook went on to succeed with the late majority and laggards. Each stage customer segment, moreover, is also separated by smaller chasms. Both the large competitive chasm and the smaller ones have strategic implications.

Both new technology ventures and innovations introduced by established firms have a high failure rate. This can be explained as a failure to successfully cross the chasm from the early users to the mass market because the firm does not recognize that the business strategy needs to be fine-tuned for each customer segment. Formulating a business strategy for each segment guided by the *who, what, why, and how* questions of competition (Who to serve? What needs to satisfy? Why and how to satisfy them?), introduced in Chapter 6, the firm will find that the core competencies to satisfy each of the different customer segments are quite different. If not recognized and addressed, this will lead to the demise of the innovation as it crashes into the chasm between life cycle stages.

We first introduce each customer group and map it to the respective stage of the industry life cycle. To illustrate, we then apply the chasm framework to an analysis of the mobile phone industry.

TECHNOLOGY ENTHUSIASTS. The customer segment in the introductory stage of the industry life cycle is called *technology enthusiasts.*[46] The smallest market segment, it makes up some 2.5 percent of total market potential. Technology enthusiasts often have an engineering mind-set and pursue new technology proactively. They frequently seek out new products before the products are officially introduced into the market. Technology enthusiasts enjoy using beta versions of products, tinkering with the product's imperfections and providing (free) feedback and suggestions to companies. For example, many software companies such as Google and Microsoft launch beta versions to accumulate customer feedback to work out bugs before the official launch. Moreover, technology enthusiasts will often pay a premium price to have the latest gadget. The endorsement by technology enthusiasts validates the fact that the new product does in fact work.

A recent example of an innovation that appeals to technology enthusiasts is Google Glass, a mobile computer that is worn like a pair of regular glasses. Instead of a lens, however, one side displays a small, high-definition computer screen. Google Glass was developed as part of Google's wild-card program. Technology enthusiasts were eager to get ahold of Google Glass when made available in a beta testing program in 2013. Those interested had to compose a Google+ or Twitter message of 50 words or less explaining why they would be a good choice to test the device and include the hash tag #ifihad-glass. Some 150,000 people applied and 8,000 winners were chosen. They were required to attend a Google Glass event and pay $1,500 for the developer version of Google Glass.

Although many industry leaders, including Apple's CEO Tim Cook, agree that wearable computers like the Apple Watch or the Nike + FuelBand (a physical activity tracker that is worn on the wrist; data are integrated into an online community and phone app) are important mobile devices, they suggest that there is a large chasm between the current technology for computerized eyeglasses and a successful product for early adopters let alone the mass market.[47] They seem to be correct, because Google was until now unable to cross the chasm between technology enthusiasts and early adopters, even after spending $10 billion on R&D per year.[48]

EARLY ADOPTERS. The customers entering the market in the growth stage are *early adopters.* They make up roughly 13.5 percent of the total market potential. Early adopters, as the name suggests, are eager to buy early into a new technology or product concept. Unlike technology enthusiasts, however, their demand is driven by their imagination and creativity rather than by the technology per se. They recognize and appreciate the possibilities the new technology can afford them in their professional and personal lives. Early adopters' demand is fueled more by intuition and vision rather than technology concerns. These are the people that lined up at Apple Stores in the spring of 2015 when it introduced Apple Watch. Since early adopters are not influenced by standard technological performance metrics but by intuition and imagination (What can this new product do for me or my business?), the firm needs to communicate the product's potential applications in a more direct way than when it attracted the initial technology enthusiasts. Attracting the early adopters to the new offering is critical to opening any new high-tech market segment.

Google Glass allows the wearer to use the Internet and smartphone-like applications via voice commands (e.g., conduct online search, stream video, and so on). © AP Photo/Google/ Rex Features

EARLY MAJORITY. The customers coming into the market in the shakeout stage are called *early majority.* Their main consideration in deciding whether or not to adopt a new technological innovation is a strong sense of practicality. They are pragmatists and are most concerned with the question of what the new technology can do for them. Before adopting a new product or service, they weigh the benefits and costs carefully. Customers in the early majority are aware that many hyped new product introductions will fade away, so they prefer to wait and see how things shake out. They like to observe how early adopters are using the product. Early majority customers rely on endorsements by others. They seek out reputable references such as reviews in prominent trade journals or in magazines such as *Consumer Reports.*

Because the early majority makes up roughly one-third of the entire market potential, winning them over is critical to the commercial success of the innovation. They are on the cusp of the mass market. Bringing the early majority on board is the key to catching the growth wave of the industry life cycle. Once they decide to enter the market, a *herding effect* is frequently observed: The early majority enters in large numbers.[49]

The significant differences in the attitudes toward technology of the early majority when compared to the early adopters signify the wide competitive gulf—*the chasm*—between these two consumer segments (see Exhibit 7.7). Without adequate demand from the early majority, most innovative products wither away.

Fisker Automotive, a California-based designer and manufacturer of premium plug-in hybrid vehicles, fell into the chasm because it was unable to transition to early adopters, let alone the mass market. Between its founding in 2007 and 2012, Fisker sold some 1,800 of its Karma model, a $100K sports car, to technology enthusiasts. It was unable, however, to follow up with a lower-cost model to attract the early adopters into the market. In addition, technology and reliability issues for the Karma could not be overcome. By 2013, Fisker had crashed into a chasm, filing for bankruptcy. The assets of Fisker Automotive were purchased by Wanxiang, a Chinese auto parts maker.[50]

Tesla Motors CEO Elon Musk, left, in front of a Tesla Roadster; Fisker Automotive CEO Henrik Fisker, right, in front of a Fisker Karma.
© Misha Gravenor

In contrast, Tesla Motors, the maker of all-electric vehicles introduced in ChapterCase 3, and a fierce rival of Fisker at one time, was able to overcome some of the early chasms. The Tesla Roadster was a proof-of-concept car that demonstrated that electric vehicles could achieve an equal or better performance than the very best gasoline-engine sports cars. The 2,400 Roadsters that Tesla built between 2008 and 2012 were purchased by technology enthusiasts. Next, Tesla successfully launched the Model S, a family sedan, sold to early adopters. The Tesla Model S received a strong endorsement as the 2013 *Motor-Trend* Car of the Year and the highest test scores ever awarded by *Consumer Reports*. This may help in crossing the chasm to the early majority, because consumers would now feel more comfortable in considering and purchasing a Tesla vehicle. Tesla is hoping to cross the large competitive chasm between early adopters and early majority with its Model X (a minivan, SUV crossover) and its new, lower-priced Model 3, coming out in 2017.

LATE MAJORITY. The next wave of growth comes from buyers in the *late majority* entering the market in the maturity stage. Like the early majority, they are a large customer segment, making up approximately 34 percent of the total market potential. Combined, the early adopters and early majority make up the lion's share of the market potential. Demand coming from just two groups—early and late majority—drives most industry growth and firm profitability.

Members of the early and late majority are also quite similar in their attitudes toward new technology. The late majority shares all the concerns of the early majority. But there are important differences. Although members of the early majority are confident in their ability to master the new technology, the late majority is not. They prefer to wait until standards have emerged and are firmly entrenched, so that uncertainty is much reduced. The late majority also prefers to buy from well-established firms with a strong brand image rather than from unknown new ventures.

LAGGARDS. Finally, *laggards* are the last consumer segment to come into the market, entering in the declining stage of the industry life cycle. These are customers who adopt a new product only if it is absolutely necessary, such as first-time cell phone adopters in the United States today. These customers generally don't want new technology, either for personal or economic reasons. Given their reluctance to adopt new technology, they are generally not considered worth pursuing. Laggards make up no more than 16 percent of the total market potential. Their demand is far too small to compensate for reduced demand from the early and late majority (jointly almost 70 percent of total market demand), who are moving on to different products and services.

CROSSING THE CHASM: APPLICATION TO THE MOBILE PHONE INDUSTRY. Let's apply the crossing-the-chasm framework to one specific industry. In this model, the transition from stage to stage in the industry life cycle is characterized by different competitive chasms that open up because of important differences between customer groups. Although the large chasm between early adopters and the early majority is the main cause of demise for technological innovations, other smaller mini-chasms open between each stage.

Exhibit 7.8 shows the application of the chasm model to the mobile phone industry. The first victim was Motorola's Iridium, an ill-fated satellite-based telephone system.[51] Development began in 1992 after the spouse of a Motorola engineer complained about being unable to get any data or voice access to check on clients while vacationing on a remote island. Motorola's solution was to launch 66 satellites into low orbit to provide global voice and data coverage. In late 1998, Motorola began offering its satellite phone service, charging $5,000 per handset (which was almost too heavy to carry around) and up to $14 per minute for calls.[52] Problems in consumer adoption beyond the few technology enthusiasts became rapidly apparent. The Iridium phone could not be used inside buildings or in cars. Rather, to receive a satellite signal, the phone needed an unobstructed line of sight to a satellite. Iridium crashed into the first chasm, never moving beyond technology enthusiasts (see Exhibit 7.8). For Motorola, it was a billion-dollar blunder. Iridium was soon displaced by cell phones that relied on Earth-based networks of radio towers. The global satellite telephone industry never moved beyond the introductory stage of the industry life cycle.

The first Treo, a fully functioning smartphone combining voice and data capabilities, was released in 2002 by Handspring. The Treo fell into the main chasm that arises between early adopters and the early majority (see Exhibit 7.8). Technical problems, combined with a lack of apps and an overly rigid contract with Sprint as its sole service provider, prevented the Treo from gaining traction in the market beyond early adopters. For these reasons, the Treo was not an attractive product for the early majority, who rejected it. This caused the Treo to plunge into the chasm. Just a year later, Handspring was folded into Palm, which in turn was acquired by HP for $1 billion in 2010.[53] HP shut down Palm in 2011 and wrote off the acquisition.[54]

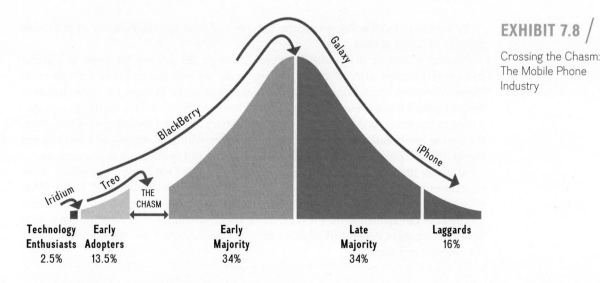

EXHIBIT 7.8

Crossing the Chasm: The Mobile Phone Industry

Research in Motion (RIM)[55] introduced its first fully functioning BlackBerry smartphone in 2000. It was a huge success—especially with two key consumer segments. First, corporate IT managers were early adopters. They became product champions for the BlackBerry because of its encrypted security software and its reliability in always staying connected to a company's network. This allowed users to receive e-mail and other data in real time, anywhere in the world where wireless service was provided. Second, corporate executives were the early majority pulling the BlackBerry over the chasm because it allowed 24/7 access to data and voice. RIM was able to create a beachhead to cross the chasm between the technology enthusiasts and early adopters on one side and the early majority on the other.[56] RIM's managers identified the needs of not only early adopters (e.g., IT managers) but also the early majority (e.g., executives), who pulled the BlackBerry over the chasm. By 2005, the BlackBerry had become a corporate executive status symbol. As a consequence of capturing the first three stages of the industry life cycle, between 2002 and 2007, RIM enjoyed no less than 30 percent year-over-year revenue growth as well as double-digit growth in other financial performance metrics such as return on equity. RIM enjoyed a temporary competitive advantage.

In 2007, RIM's dominance over the smartphone market began to erode quickly. The main reason was Apple's introduction of the iPhone. Although technology enthusiasts and early adopters argue that the iPhone is an inferior product to the BlackBerry based on technological criteria, the iPhone enticed not only the early majority, but also the late majority to enter the market. For the late majority, encrypted software security was much less important than having fun with a device that allowed users to surf the web, take pictures, play games, and send and receive e-mail. Moreover, the Apple iTunes Store soon provided thousands of apps for basically any kind of service. While the BlackBerry couldn't cross the gulf between the early and the late majority, Apple's iPhone captured the mass market rapidly. Moreover, consumers began to bring their personal iPhone to work, which forced corporate IT departments to expand their services beyond the BlackBerry. Apple rode the wave of this success to capture each market segment. Likewise, Samsung with its Galaxy line of phones, having successfully imitated the look-and-feel of an iPhone (as discussed in Chapter 4), is enjoying similar success across the different market segments.

This brief application of the chasm framework to the mobile phone industry shows its usefulness. It provides insightful explanations of why some companies failed, while others succeeded—and thus goes at the core of strategy management.

In summary, Exhibit 7.9 details the features and strategic implications of the entire industry life cycle at each stage.

A word of caution is in order, however: Although the industry life cycle is a useful framework to guide strategic choice, industries do not *necessarily evolve* through these stages. Moreover, innovations can emerge at any stage of the industry life cycle, which in turn can initiate a new cycle. Industries can also be rejuvenated, often in the declining stage. Although the motorcycle industry in the United States had been declining for a long time, Harley-Davidson was able to rejuvenate the industry with new designs and an extended lineup of bikes, greater reliability, and a more efficient and professional dealer network.

Although the industry life cycle is a useful tool, it does not explain everything about changes in industries. Some industries may never go through the entire life cycle, while others are continually renewed through innovation. Be aware, too, that other external factors that can be captured in the PESTEL framework (introduced in Chapter 3) such as fads in fashion, changes in demographics, or deregulation can affect the dynamics of industry life cycles at any stage.

EXHIBIT 7.9 / Features and Strategic Implications of the Industry Life Cycle

	Life Cycle Stages				
	Introduction	**Growth**	**Shakeout**	**Maturity**	**Decline**
Core Competency	R&D, some marketing	R&D, some manufacturing, marketing	Manufacturing, process engineering	Manufacturing, process engineering, marketing	Manufacturing, process engineering, marketing, service
Type and Level of Innovation	Product innovation at a maximum; process innovation at a minimum	Product innovation decreasing; process innovation increasing	After emergence of standard: product innovation decreasing rapidly; process innovation increasing rapidly	Product innovation at a minimum; process innovation at a maximum	Product and process innovation ceased
Market Growth	Slow	High	Moderate and slowing down	None to moderate	Negative
Market Size	Small	Moderate	Large	Largest	Small to moderate
Price	High	Falling	Moderate	Low	Low to high
Number of Competitors	Few, if any	Many	Fewer	Moderate, but large	Few, if any
Mode of Competition	Non-price competition	Non-price competition	Shifting from non-price to price competition	Price	Price or non-price competition
Customer	Technology enthusiasts	Early adopters	Early majority	Late majority	Laggards
Business-Level Strategy	Differentiation	Differentiation	Differentiation or blue ocean	Cost-leadership or blue ocean	Cost-leadership, differentiation, or blue ocean
Strategic Objective	Achieving market acceptance	Staking out a strong strategic position; generating "deep pockets"	Surviving by drawing on "deep pockets"	Maintaining strong strategic position	Exit, harvest, maintain, or consolidate

7.4 Types of Innovation

LO 7-5

Categorize different types of innovations in the markets-and-technology framework.

Because of the importance of innovation in shaping competitive dynamics and as a critical component in formulating business strategy, we now turn to a discussion of different types of innovation and the strategic implications of each. We need to know, in particular, along which dimensions we should assess innovations. This will allow us to formulate a business strategy that can leverage innovation for competitive advantage.

One insightful way to categorize innovations is to measure their degree of newness in terms of *technology* and *markets*.[57] Here, *technology* refers to the methods and materials used to achieve a commercial objective.[58] For example, Amazon integrates different types of technologies (hardware, software, microprocessors, the Internet, logistics, and so on) to provide not only the largest selection of retail goods online, but also an array of services and mobile devices (e.g., cloud computing, Kindle tablets, Prime, and so on).

EXHIBIT 7.10 / Types of Innovation: Combining Markets and Technologies

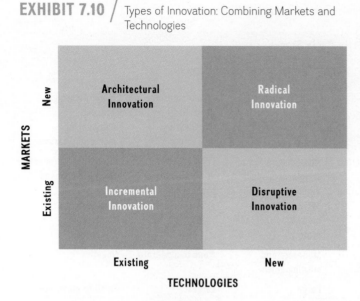

We also want to understand the *market* for an innovation—e.g., whether an innovation is introduced into a new or an existing market—because an invention turns into an innovation only when it is successfully commercialized.[59] Measuring an innovation along these dimensions gives us the **markets-and-technology framework** depicted in Exhibit 7.10. Along the horizontal axis, we ask whether the innovation builds on existing technologies or creates a new one. On the vertical axis, we ask whether the innovation is targeted toward existing or new markets. Four types of innovations emerge: incremental, radical, architectural, and disruptive innovations. As indicated by the color coding in Exhibit 7.10, each diagonal forms a pair: incremental versus radical innovation and architectural versus disruptive innovation.

INCREMENTAL VS. RADICAL INNOVATION

Although radical breakthroughs such as smartphones and magnetic resonance imaging (MRI) radiology capture most of our attention, the vast majority of innovations are actually incremental ones. An **incremental innovation** squarely builds on an established knowledge base and steadily improves an existing product or service offering.[60] It targets existing markets using existing technology.

On the other hand, **radical innovation** draws on novel methods or materials, is derived either from an entirely different knowledge base or from a recombination of existing knowledge bases with a new stream of knowledge. It targets new markets by using new technologies.[61] Well-known examples of radical innovations include the introduction of the mass-produced automobile (the Ford Model T), the X-ray, the airplane, and more recently biotechnology breakthroughs such as genetic engineering and the decoding of the human genome.

Many firms get their start by successfully commercializing radical innovations, some of which, such as the jet-powered airplane, even give birth to new industries. Although the British firm de Havilland first commercialized the jet-powered passenger airplane, Boeing was the company that rode this radical innovation to industry dominance. More recently, Boeing's leadership has been contested by Airbus; each company has approximately half the market. This stalemate is now being challenged by aircraft manufacturers such as Bombardier of Canada and Embraer of Brazil, which are moving up-market by building larger luxury jets that are competing with some of the smaller airplane models offered by Boeing and Airbus.

---

markets-and-technology framework
A conceptual model to categorize innovations along the market (existing/new) and technology (existing/new) dimensions.

incremental innovation
An innovation that squarely builds on an established knowledge base and steadily improves an existing product or service.

radical innovation
An innovation that draws on novel methods or materials, is derived either from an entirely different knowledge base or from a recombination of the existing knowledge bases with a new stream of knowledge.

A predictable pattern of innovation is that firms (often new ventures) use radical innovation to create a temporary competitive advantage. They then follow up with a string of incremental innovations to sustain that initial lead. Gillette is a prime example for this pattern of strategic innovation. In 1903, entrepreneur King C. Gillette invented and began selling the safety razor with a disposable blade. This *radical innovation* launched the Gillette Company (now a brand of Procter & Gamble). To sustain its competitive advantage, Gillette not only made sure that its razors were inexpensive and widely available by introducing the "razor and razorblade" business model, but also continually improved its blades. In a classic example of a string of *incremental innovations,* Gillette kept adding an additional blade with each new version of its razor until the number had gone from one to six! Though this innovation strategy seems predictable, it worked. Gillette holds some 80 percent of the $15 billion market for razors and blades globally. Gillette's newest razor, the Fusion ProGlide with Flexball technology, a razor handle that features a swiveling ball hinge, costs $11.49 (and $12.59 for a battery-operated one) *per* razor![62]

The example shows how radical innovation created a competitive advantage that the company sustained through follow-up incremental innovation. Such an outcome is not a foregone conclusion, though. In some instances, the innovator is outcompeted by second movers that quickly introduce a similar incremental innovation to continuously improve their own offering. For example, although CNN was the pioneer in 24-hour cable news, today Fox News is the most watched cable news network in the United States (although the entire industry is in decline as viewers now stream much more content directly via mobile devices, as discussed in the Netflix ChapterCase). Once firms have achieved market acceptance of a breakthrough innovation, they tend to follow up with incremental rather than radical innovations. Over time, these companies morph into industry incumbents. Future radical innovations are generally introduced by new entrepreneurial ventures. Why is this so? The reasons concern *economic incentives, organizational inertia,* and the firm's embeddedness in an *innovation ecosystem.*[63]

ECONOMIC INCENTIVES. Economists highlight the role of *incentives* in strategic choice. Once an innovator has become an established incumbent firm (such as Google has today), it has strong incentives to defend its strategic position and market power. An emphasis on incremental innovations strengthens the incumbent firm's position and thus maintains high entry barriers. A focus on incremental innovation is particularly attractive once an industry standard has emerged and technological uncertainty is reduced. Moreover, many markets where network effects are important (such as online search), turn into **winner-take-all markets**, where the market leader captures almost all of the market share. As a near monopolist, the winner in these types of markets is able to extract a significant amount of the value created. In the United States, Google handles some 65 percent of all online queries, while it handles more than 90 percent in Europe. As a result, the incumbent firm uses incremental innovation to extend the time it can extract profits based on a favorable industry structure (see the discussion in Chapter 3). Any potential radical innovation threatens the incumbent firm's dominant position.

The incentives for entrepreneurial ventures, however, are just the opposite. Successfully commercializing a radical innovation is frequently the only option to enter an industry protected by high entry barriers. One of the first biotech firms, Amgen, used newly discovered drugs based on genetic engineering to overcome entry barriers to the pharmaceutical industry, in which incumbents had enjoyed notoriously high profits for several decades. Because of differential economic incentives, incumbents often push forward with incremental innovations, while new entrants focus on radical innovations.

winner-take-all markets
Markets where the market leader captures almost all of the market share and is able to extract a significant amount of the value created.

ORGANIZATIONAL INERTIA. From an organizational perspective, as firms become established and grow, they rely more heavily on formalized business processes and structures. In some cases, the firm may experience *organizational inertia*—resistance to changes in the status quo. Incumbent firms, therefore, tend to favor incremental innovations that reinforce the existing organizational structure and power distribution while avoiding radical innovation that could disturb the existing power distribution. Take, for instance, power distribution between different functional areas, such as R&D and marketing. New entrants, however, do not have formal organizational structures and processes, giving them more freedom to launch an initial breakthrough. We discuss the link between organizational structure and firm strategy in depth in Chapter 11.

innovation ecosystem
A firm's embeddedness in a complex network of suppliers, buyers, and complementors, which requires interdependent strategic decision making.

INNOVATION ECOSYSTEM. A final reason incumbent firms tend to be a source of incremental rather than radical innovations is that they become embedded in an **innovation ecosystem**: a network of suppliers, buyers, complementors, and so on.[64] They no longer make independent decisions but must consider the ramifications on other parties in their innovation ecosystem. Continuous incremental innovations reinforce this network and keep all its members happy, while radical innovations disrupt it. Again, new entrants don't have to worry about preexisting innovation ecosystems, since they will be building theirs around the radical innovation they are bringing to a new market.

ARCHITECTURAL VS. DISRUPTIVE INNOVATION

architectural innovation
A new product in which known components, based on existing technologies, are reconfigured in a novel way to attack new markets.

Firms can also innovate by leveraging *existing technologies* into *new markets*. Doing so generally requires them to reconfigure the components of a technology, meaning they alter the overall *architecture* of the product.[65] An **architectural innovation**, therefore, is a new product in which known components, based on existing technologies, are reconfigured in a novel way to create new markets.

As a radical innovator commercializing the xerography invention, Xerox was long the most dominant copier company worldwide.[66] It produced high-volume, high-quality, and high-priced copying machines that it leased to its customers through a service agreement. Although these machines were ideal for the high end of the market such as Fortune 100 companies, Xerox ignored small and medium-sized businesses. By applying an architectural innovation, the Japanese entry Canon was able to redesign the copier so that it didn't need professional service—reliability was built directly into the machine, and the user could replace parts such as the cartridge. This allowed Canon to apply the *razor–razorblade business model* (introduced in Chapter 5), charging relatively low prices for its copiers but adding a steep markup to its cartridges. Xerox had not envisioned the possibility that the components of the copying machine could be put together in an altogether different way that was more user-friendly. More importantly, Canon addressed a need in a specific consumer segment—small and medium-sized businesses and individual departments or offices in large companies—that Xerox neglected.

disruptive innovation
An innovation that leverages new technologies to attack existing markets from the bottom up.

Finally, a **disruptive innovation** leverages *new technologies* to attack *existing markets*. It invades an existing market from the bottom up, as shown in Exhibit 7.11.[67] The dashed blue lines represent different market segments, from Segment 1 at the low end to Segment 4 at the high end. Low-end market segments are generally associated with low profit margins, while high-end market segments often have high profit margins. As first demonstrated by Clayton Christensen, the dynamic process of disruptive innovation begins when a firm, frequently a startup, introduces a new product or process based on a new technology to meet existing customer needs. To be a disruptive force, however, this new technology has to have additional characteristics:

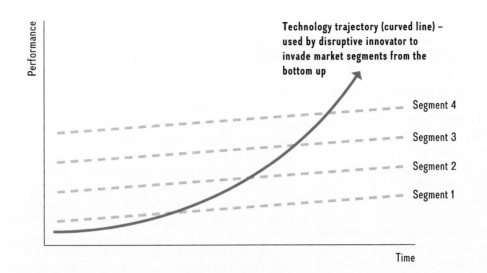

EXHIBIT 7.11

Disruptive Innovation: Riding the Technology Trajectory to Invade Different Market Segments from the Bottom Up

1. It begins as a low-cost solution to an existing problem.
2. Initially, its performance is inferior to the existing technology, but its rate of technological improvement over time is faster than the rate of performance increases required by different market segments. In Exhibit 7.11, the solid curved upward line captures the new technology's trajectory, or rate of improvement over time.

The following examples illustrate disruptive innovations:

■ Japanese carmakers successfully followed a strategy of disruptive innovation by first introducing small fuel-efficient cars and then leveraging their low-cost and high-quality advantages into high-end luxury segments, captured by brands such as Lexus, Infiniti, and Acura. More recently, the South Korean carmakers Kia and Hyundai have followed a similar strategy.

■ Digital photography improved enough over time to provide higher-definition pictures. As a result, it has been able to replace film photography, even in most professional applications.

■ Laptop computers disrupted desktop computers; now tablets and larger-screen smartphones are disrupting laptops.

■ Educational organizations such as Coursera and Udacity are disrupting traditional universities by offering *massive open online courses* (MOOCs), using the web to provide large-scale, interactive online courses with open access.

One factor favoring the success of disruptive innovation is that it relies on a stealth attack: It invades the market from the bottom up, by first capturing the low end. Many times, incumbent firms fail to defend (and sometimes are even happy to cede) the low end of the market, because it is frequently a low-margin business. Google, for example, is using its mobile operating system, Android, as a beachhead to challenge Microsoft's dominance in the personal computer industry, where 90 percent of machines run Windows.[68] Google's Android, in contrast, is optimized to run on mobile devices, the fastest-growing segment in computing. To appeal to users who spend most of their time on the web accessing e-mail and other online applications, for instance, it is designed to start up in a few seconds. Moreover, Google provides Android free of charge.[69] In contrast to Microsoft's proprietary Windows operating system, Android is open-source software, accessible to

Strategy Highlight 7.1

How Dollar Shave Club Is Disrupting Gillette

The Gillette example discussed earlier demonstrated how radical innovation created a competitive advantage that the company sustained through follow-up incremental innovation. In some instances, the innovator might be outmaneuvered by low-cost disruption. One key is that the high-end, highly priced offering of the market leader is not only overshooting what the market demands, but also often priced too high. One wonders if a person really does need six blades on one razor, or wants to pay over $10 for one cartridge!

Seeing this opening provided by Gillette's focus on the high-end, high-margin business of the market, Dollar Shave Club is attempting to establish a low-cost alternative to invade Gillette's market from the bottom up (see Exhibit 7.11). With an $8,000 budget and the help of a hilarious promotional video that went viral with over 20 million views,[70] the entrepreneur Michael Dubin launched Dollar Shave Club, an ecommerce startup that delivers razors by mail. It uses a subscription-based business model.[71] As the company's name suggests, its entry-level membership plan delivers a razor and five cartridges a month for just $1 (plus $2 shipping). The member selects an appropriate plan, pays a monthly fee, and will receive razors every month in the mail. Dollar Shave Club is using a *business model innovation* to disrupt an existing market. Remember earlier, we defined *technology* as the methods and materials used to achieve a commercial objective. The technology or method here is the *business model innovation*, a potent competitive weapon. The entrepreneur identified the need in the market for serving those who don't like to go shopping for razors and certainly don't like to pay the high prices commanded by market leaders such as Gillette.

Dollar Shave Club seems to be off to a great start. After the promotional video was uploaded on YouTube in March 2012, some 12,000 people signed up for Dollar Shave membership within the first 48 hours. It also raised over $20 million in venture capital funding from prominent firms such as Kleiner Perkins Caufield & Byers and Andreessen Horowitz, among others. Dollar Shave Club has also begun advertising on regular television in addition to its online campaigns and has expanded its product lines by the introduction of additional personal grooming products. It remains to be seen, however, if Dollar Shave Club can disrupt the $15 billion wet-shaving industry where Procter & Gamble's subsidiary Gillette holds 80 percent of the world market.

anyone for further development and refinement. In this sense, Google is leveraging *crowdsourcing* in its new product development, just as Threadless uses crowdsourcing to design and market T-shirts, and Wikipedia uses the wisdom of the crowds to collectively edit encyclopedia entries. Google's Android holds an 85 percent market share in mobile operating systems, while Apple's iOS has 12 percent, and the remaining 3 percent is held by Microsoft's Windows.[72]

Strategy Highlight 7.1 shows how the upstart Dollar Shave Club is attempting to disrupt the market leader Gillette in the wet-shaving industry.

Another factor favoring the success of disruptive innovation is that incumbent firms often are slow to change. Incumbent firms tend to listen closely to their current customers and respond by continuing to invest in the existing technology and in incremental changes to the existing products. When a newer technology matures and proves to be a better solution, those same customers will switch. At that time, however, the incumbent firm does not yet have a competitive product ready that is based on the disruptive technology. Although customer-oriented visions are more likely to guard against firm obsolescence than product-oriented ones (see Chapter 2), they are no guarantee that a firm can hold out in the face of disruptive innovation. One of the counterintuitive findings that Clayton Christensen unearthed in his studies is that it can hurt incumbents to listen too closely to their existing customers. Apple is famous for not soliciting customer feedback because it believes it knows what customers need before they even realize it.

Strategy Highlight 7.2

GE's Innovation Mantra: Disrupt Yourself!

GE Healthcare is a leader in diagnostic devices. Realizing that the likelihood of disruptive innovation increases over time, GE decided to disrupt itself. A high-end ultrasound machine found in cutting-edge research hospitals in the United States or Europe costs $250,000. There is not a large market for these high-end, high-price products in developing countries. Given their large populations, however, there is a strong medical need for ultrasound devices.

In 2002, a GE team in China, through a bottom-up strategic initiative, developed an inexpensive, portable ultrasound device, combining laptop technology with a probe and sophisticated imaging software. This light-weight device (11 pounds) was first used in rural China. In spring 2009, GE unveiled the new medical device under the name Venue 40 in the United States, at a price of less than $30,000. There was also high demand from many American general practitioners, who could not otherwise afford the quarter of a million dollars needed to procure a high-end machine (that weighed about 400 pounds). In the fall of 2009, GE Chairman and CEO Jeff Immelt unveiled

the Vscan, an even smaller device that looks like a cross between an early iPod and a flip phone. This wireless ultrasound device is priced around $5,000. GE views the Vscan as the "stethoscope of the 21st century," which a primary care doctor can hang around her neck when visiting with patients.[73]

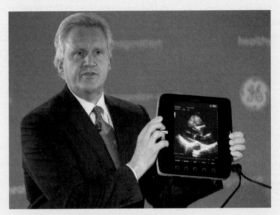

Jeffrey Immelt, GE CEO and chairman, unveils the Vscan.
© Saul Loeb/AFP/Getty Images

HOW TO RESPOND TO DISRUPTIVE INNOVATION? Although these examples show that disruptive innovations are a serious threat for incumbent firms, some have devised strategic initiatives to counter them:

1. *Continue to innovate in order to stay ahead of the competition.* A moving target is much harder to hit than one that is standing still and resting on existing (innovation) laurels. Apple has done this well, beginning with the iPod in 2001, followed by the iPhone and iPad and more recently the Apple Watch in 2015. Amazon is another example of a company that has continuously morphed through innovation,[74] from a simple online book retailer to the largest ecommerce company. It also offers consumer electronics (Kindle tablets), cloud computing, and content streaming, among other offerings.

2. *Guard against disruptive innovation by protecting the low end of the market* (Segment 1 in Exhibit 7.11) by introducing low-cost innovations to preempt stealth competitors. Intel introduced the Celeron chip, a stripped-down, budget version of its Pentium chip, to prevent low-cost entry into its market space. More recently, Intel followed up with the Atom chip, a new processor that is inexpensive and consumes little battery power, to power low-cost mobile devices.[75] Nonetheless, Intel also listened too closely to its existing personal computer customers such as Dell, HP, Lenovo, and so on, and allowed ARM Holdings, a British semiconductor design company (that supplies its technology to Apple, Samsung, HTC, and others) to take the lead in providing high-performing, low-power-consuming processors for smartphones and other mobile devices.

reverse innovation
An innovation that was developed for emerging economies before being introduced in developed economies. Sometimes also called *frugal innovation.*

3. *Disrupt yourself, rather than wait for others to disrupt you.* A firm may develop products specifically for emerging markets such as China and India, and then introduce these innovations into developed markets such as the United States, Japan, or the European Union. This process is called **reverse innovation**,[76] and allows a firm to disrupt itself. Strategy Highlight 7.2 describes how GE Healthcare invented and commercialized a disruptive innovation in China that is now entering the U.S. market, riding the steep technology trajectory of disruptive innovation shown in Exhibit 7.11.

LO 7-6

Compare and contrast closed and open innovation.

OPEN INNOVATION

After discussing the importance of innovation to gaining and sustaining competitive advantage, the question arises: How should firms organize for innovation? During the 20th century, the *closed innovation* approach was the dominant research and development (R&D) approach for most firms: They tended to discover, develop, and commercialize new products internally.[77] Although this approach was costly and time-consuming, it allowed firms to fully capture the returns to their own innovations.

Several factors led to a shift in the knowledge landscape from closed innovation to open innovation. They include:

- The increasing supply and mobility of skilled workers.
- The exponential growth of venture capital.
- The increasing availability of external options (such as spinning out new ventures) to commercialize ideas that were previously shelved or insource promising ideas and inventions.
- The increasing capability of external suppliers globally.

open innovation
A framework for R&D that proposes permeable firm boundaries to allow a firm to benefit not only from internal ideas and inventions, but also from external ones. The sharing goes both ways: some external ideas and inventions are insourced while others are spun out.

Taken together, these factors have led more and more companies to adopt an open innovation approach to research and development. **Open innovation** is a framework for R&D that proposes permeable firm boundaries to allow a firm to benefit not only from internal ideas and inventions, but also from ideas and innovation from external sources. External sources of knowledge can be customers, suppliers, universities, start-up companies, and even competitors.[78] The sharing goes both ways: Some external R&D is insourced (and further developed in-house) while the firm may spin out internal R&D that does not fit its strategy to allow others to commercialize it. Even the largest companies, such as AT&T, IBM, and GE, are shifting their innovation strategy toward a model that blends internal with external knowledge sourcing via licensing agreements, strategic alliances, joint ventures, and acquisitions.[79]

Exhibit 7.12 depicts the closed and open innovation models. In the closed innovation model (Panel A), the firm is conducting all research and development in-house, using a traditional funnel approach. The boundaries of the firm are impenetrable. Outside ideas and projects cannot enter, nor does the firm allow its own research ideas and development projects to leave the firm. Firms in the closed innovation model are extremely protective of their intellectual property. This not only allows the firm to capture all the benefits from its own R&D, but also prevents competitors from benefiting from it. The mind-set of firms in the closed innovation model is that to profit from R&D, the firm must come up with its own discoveries, develop them on its own, and control the distribution channels. Strength in R&D is equated with a high likelihood of benefiting from first-mover advantages. Firms following the closed innovation model,

EXHIBIT 7.12 / Closed Innovation vs. Open Innovation

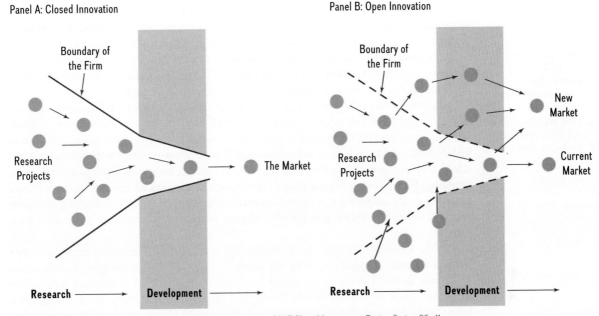

Panel A: Closed Innovation

Panel B: Open Innovation

Source: Adapted from H. Chesbrough (2003), "The area of open innovation," *MIT Sloan Management Review,* Spring: 35–41.

however, are much more likely to fall prone to the *not-invented-here syndrome:*[80] "If the R&D leading to a discovery and a new development project was not conducted in-house, it cannot be good."

As documented, the pharmaceutical company Merck suffers from the *not-invented-here syndrome.*[81] That is, if a product was not created and developed at Merck, it could not be good enough. Merck's culture and organizational systems perpetuate this logic, which assumes that since the company hired the best people, the smartest people in the industry must work for Merck, and so the best discoveries must be made at Merck. The company leads the industry in terms of R&D spending, because Merck believes that if it is the first to discover and develop a new drug, it would be the first to market. Merck is one of the most successful companies by total number of active R&D projects. Perhaps even more important, Merck's researchers had been awarded several Nobel Prizes for their breakthrough research, a considerable point of pride for Merck's personnel.

In the open innovation model, in contrast, a company attempts to commercialize both its own ideas and research from other firms. It also finds external alternatives such as spin-out ventures or strategic alliances to commercialize its internally developed R&D. The boundary of the firm has become porous (as represented by the dashed lines in the Panel B in Exhibit 7.12), allowing the firm to spin out some R&D projects while insourcing other promising projects. Companies using an open innovation approach realize that great ideas can come from both inside and outside the company. Significant value can be had by commercializing external R&D and letting others commercialize internal R&D that does not fit with the firm's strategy. The focus is on building a more effective *business model* to commercialize both internal *and* external R&D, rather than focusing on being first to market.

One key assumption underlying the open innovation model is that combining the best of internal *and* external R&D will more likely lead to a competitive advantage. This requires that the company must continuously upgrade its internal R&D capabilities to enhance its **absorptive capacity**—its ability to understand external technology developments, evaluate them, and integrate them into current products or create new ones.[82] Exhibit 7.13 compares and contrasts open innovation and closed innovation principles.

An example of open innovation is Procter & Gamble's Connect+Develop, or C+D (a play on research and development, or R&D).[83] Because of the maturing of its products and markets, P&G decided it was time to look outside for new ideas. P&G is an $85 billion company whose investors expect it to grow at least 4–6 percent a year, which implies generating between $3 billion and $5 billion in incremental revenue annually. P&G was no longer able to generate this amount of growth through closed innovation. By 2000, P&G's closed innovation machine had stalled, and the company lost half its market value. It needed to change its innovation strategy to drive organic growth.

P&G's Connect+Develop is a web-based interface that connects the company's internal-innovation capability with the distributed knowledge in the global community. From that external community, researchers, entrepreneurs, and consumers can submit ideas that might solve some of P&G's toughest innovation challenges. The C+D model is based on the realization that innovation was increasingly coming from small entrepreneurial ventures and even from individuals. Universities also became much more proactive in commercializing their inventions. The Internet now enables access to widely distributed knowledge from around the globe.

External collaborations fostered through the worldwide Connect+Develop network now play a role in roughly 50 percent of P&G's new products, up from about 15 percent

> **absorptive capacity**
> A firm's ability to understand external technology developments, evaluate them, and integrate them into current products or create new ones.

EXHIBIT 7.13 / Contrasting Principles of Closed and Open Innovation

Closed Innovation Principles	Open Innovation Principles
The smart people in our field work for us.	Not all the smart people work for us. We need to work with smart people inside *and* outside our company.
To profit from R&D, we must discover it, develop it, and ship it ourselves.	External R&D can create significant value; internal R&D is needed to claim (absorb) some portion of that value.
If we discover it ourselves, we will get it to market first.	We don't have to originate the research to profit from it; we can still be first if we successfully commercialize new research.
The company that gets an innovation to market first will win.	Building a better business model is often more important than getting to market first.
If we create the most and best ideas in the industry, we will win.	If we make the best use of internal *and* external ideas, we will win.
We should control our intellectual property (IP), so that our competitors don't profit from it.	We should profit from others' use of our IP, and we should buy others' IP whenever it advances our own business model.

Source: Adapted from H.W. Chesbrough (2003), *Open Innovation: The New Imperative for Creating and Profiting from Technology* (Boston: Harvard Business School Press).

in 2000. Successful product innovations that resulted from P&G's open innovation model include Pringles meets Print (sold for $1.5 billion in 2011), Mr. Clean Magic Eraser, Swiffer Dusters, Crest SpinBrush, and Olay Regenerist.

7.5 ◄► Implications for the Strategist

Innovation drives the competitive process. An effective innovation strategy is critical in formulating a business strategy that provides the firm with a competitive advantage. Successful innovation affords firms a temporary monopoly, with corresponding monopoly pricing power. *Fast Company* named Warby Parker, Apple, Alibaba, Google, and Instagram as the top five on its *2015 Most Innovative Companies.*[84] Continuous innovation fuels the success of these companies.

Entrepreneurs are the agents that introduce change into the competitive system. They do this not only by figuring out how to use inventions, but also by introducing new products or services, new production processes, and new forms of organization. Entrepreneurs frequently start new ventures, but they may also be found in existing firms.

The industry life cycle model and the crossing-the-chasm framework have critical implications for how you manage innovation. To overcome the chasm, you need to formulate a business strategy guided by the who, what, why, and, how questions of competition (Chapter 6) to ensure you meet the distinctly different customer needs inherent along the industry life cycle. You also must be mindful that to do so, you need to bring different competencies and capabilities to bear at different stages of the industry life cycle.

Many of the more successful companies have either adopted or are moving toward an open innovation model. As a strategist, you must actively manage a firm's internal and external innovation activities. Internally, you can *induce innovation* through a top-down process or motivate innovation through *autonomous behavior,* a bottom-up process.[85] In induced innovation, you need to put a structure and system in place to foster innovation. Consider 3M: "A core belief of 3M is that creativity needs freedom. That's why . . . we've encouraged our employees to spend 15 percent of their working time on their own projects. To take our resources, to build up a unique team, and to follow their own insights in pursuit of problem-solving."[86] We discussed *autonomous behavior* in detail in Chapter 2. To not only motivate innovations through autonomous behavior, but also ensure their possible success, *internal champions* need to be willing to support promising projects. In Strategy Highlight 2.2, we detailed how Howard Behar, at that time a senior executive at Starbucks, was willing to support the bottom-up idea of Frappuccino, which turned out to be a multi-billion-dollar business.

Externally, you must manage innovation through cooperative strategies such as licensing, strategic alliances, joint ventures, and acquisitions. These are the vehicles of *corporate strategy* discussed in the next two chapters.

In conclusion, in this and the previous chapter, we discussed how firms can use *business-level strategy*—differentiation, cost leadership, blue ocean, and innovation—to gain and sustain competitive advantage. We now turn our attention to *corporate-level strategy* to help us understand how executives make decisions about *where to compete* (in terms of industries, value chains, and geography) and how to execute it through strategic alliances as well as mergers and acquisitions. A thorough understanding of business and corporate strategy is necessary to formulate and sustain a winning strategy.

CHAPTER**CASE 7** / Consider This...

The impact of Netflix's mega success *House of Cards* in reshaping the TV industry cannot be underestimated. The American political TV drama starring Kevin Spacey and Robin Wright was an innovation that fundamentally changed the existing business model of TV viewing on three fronts.

1. Delivery. *House of Cards* was the first time that a major TV drama was streamed online and thus bypassed the established ecosystem of networks and cable operators.

2. Access. *House of Cards* created the phenomenon of binge watching because it allowed Netflix subscribers to view many or all episodes in one sitting, without any advertising interruptions. As of 2015, spending an estimated $200 million, Netflix produced three seasons for a total of 39 episodes each roughly 45 to 60 minutes long.

3. Management. *House of Cards* was the first time original programming had been developed based on Netflix's proprietary data algorithms and not by more traditional methods. When executive producer David Fincher and actor Kevin Spacey brought the proposed show to Netflix, the company approved the project without a pilot or any test-marketing. "Netflix was the only network that said, 'We believe in you, recalls Spacey. We've run our data and it tells us that our audience would watch this series. We don't need you to do a pilot. How many [episodes] do you wanna do?'"[87]

The success of *House of Cards* created a huge buzz, attracted millions of new subscribers to Netflix, and helped its stock climb to new highs.

The power of directly streaming content to users, so that they can watch whenever they want, how much they want to watch at a time, and on whatever Internet-connected device, was also demonstrated in Netflix's reruns of *Breaking Bad.* Netflix streamed the 62-episode crime drama in ultra HD, and it scored much higher than on its previous run on the cable channel AMC. Indeed, the season finale of *Breaking Bad* on Netflix attracted almost 6 million viewers. This is even more impressive given the fact that *Breaking Bad* was a TV rerun.

Despite riding high, there are some serious challenges for Reed Hastings and Netflix on the horizon. First is the issue of how to ensure that Netflix users' have a seamless, uninterrupted viewing experience, without buffering (and seeing the "spinning wheels"). Recall that Netflix is responsible for more than one-third of all downstream Internet traffic in the United States during peak hours. For a long time, Netflix has been a strong support of *net neutrality,* with the goal of preventing broadband operators such as Comcast from slowing content or blocking access to certain websites. Conceivably, Comcast may have an incentive to slow down Netflix's content and favor its own NBC content. This is the reason Netflix—after refusing to do so for a long time—has begun to pay Comcast directly to ensure a smoother streaming experience for its users. Rather than going through the public Internet, in exchange for payment, Netflix will be able to hook up its servers directly to Comcast's broadband network. This so-called *peering* (creating dedicated and direct connections) between a content provider and a broadband provider is the first in the industry. Given its precedent, Netflix is likely to strike similar deals with other broadband providers, such as AT&T, Verizon, and Time Warner, that control access to Netflix customers.

The second issue for Hastings is how to create sustained future growth. The domestic market seems to be maturing, so growth has to come from international expansion. Problems with a lack of available titles and few places with broadband Internet connections hamper its growth. In 2010, Canadian expansion was off to a slow start because of a small number of titles in the Netflix library because of differences in distribution deals. Of the 10 million international users of Netflix (in 2015), 6 million are in Canada. Although the Latin American market has with some 600 million people, roughly twice the population of the United States, because of the *digital divide* (inequality in access to and speed of the Internet) in many Latin American countries, most Internet connections are slow dial-up, which prohibits effective streaming of content. In 2015, Netflix began negotiations to offer its services in China. One of the issues Netflix will face is potential censoring of its content; *House of Cards* has not only explicit content in terms of nudity and violence, but also features a corrupt Chinese businessman meddling in U.S. politics.

Questions

1. Netflix started to pay one broadband provider (Comcast) to ensure fast and seamless access to its end users. As hinted, other broadband providers (AT&T, Verizon, and Time Warner) will want to extract a similar kind of "toll" from Netflix.

   a. Does this violate net neutrality (the rule Internet service providers should treat all data equally, and not charge differentially by user, content, site, etc.)? Why or why not?

   b. Do you favor net neutrality? Explain why.

   c. As Internet service providers will extract more fees from Netflix, the company continues to invest heavily in its proprietary "Open Connect" network, which allows Netflix to connect its servers directly to those of Internet service providers (via peering). Since most users upgrade their Internet connections to faster broadband in order to watch video, are the incentives of broadband providers aligned with Netflix, or will the broadband providers continue to extract significant value from this industry? Apply a five forces analysis.

2. Netflix growth in the United States seems to be maturing. What other services can Netflix offer that might further demand in the United States?

3. International expansion appears to be a major growth opportunity for Netflix. Elaborate on the challenges Netflix faces going beyond the U.S. market. What can Netflix do to address some of the challenges encountered when going internationally?

TAKE-AWAY CONCEPTS

This chapter discussed various aspects of innovation and entrepreneurship as a business-level strategy, as summarized by the following learning objectives and related take-away concepts.

LO 7-1 / Outline the four-step innovation process from idea to imitation.

- Innovation describes the discovery and development of new knowledge in a four-step process captured in the Four I's: *idea, invention, innovation,* and *imitation.*
- The innovation process begins with an idea.
- An invention describes the transformation of an idea into a new product or process, or the modification and recombination of existing ones.
- Innovation concerns the commercialization of an invention by entrepreneurs (within existing companies or new ventures).
- If an innovation is successful in the marketplace, competitors will attempt to imitate it.

LO 7-2 / Apply strategic management concepts to entrepreneurship and innovation.

- Entrepreneurship describes the process by which change agents undertake economic risk to innovate—to create new products, processes, and sometimes new organizations.
- Strategic entrepreneurship describes the pursuit of innovation using tools and concepts from strategic management.
- Social entrepreneurship describes the pursuit of social goals by using entrepreneurship. Social entrepreneurs use a triple-bottom-line approach to assess performance.

LO 7-3 / Describe the competitive implications of different stages in the industry life cycle.

- Innovations frequently lead to the birth of new industries.
- Industries generally follow a predictable industry life cycle, with five distinct stages: introduction, growth, shakeout, maturity, and decline.

■ Exhibit 7.9 details features and strategic implications of the industry life cycle

LO 7-4 / Derive strategic implications of the crossing-the-chasm framework.

■ The core argument of the crossing-the-chasm framework is that each stage of the industry life cycle is dominated by a different customer group, which responds differently to a new technological innovation.

■ There exists a significant difference between the customer groups that enter early during the introductory stage of the industry life cycle and customers that enter later during the growth stage.

■ This distinct difference between customer groups leads to a big gulf or chasm, which companies and their innovations frequently fall into.

■ To overcome the chasm, managers need to formulate a business strategy guided by the who, what, why, and how questions of competition.

LO 7-5 / Categorize different types of innovations in the markets-and-technology framework.

■ Four types of innovation emerge when applying the existing versus new dimensions of technology and markets: incremental, radical, architectural, and disruptive innovations (see Exhibit 7.10).

■ An incremental innovation squarely builds on an established knowledge base and steadily improves an existing product or service offering (existing market/existing technology).

■ A radical innovation draws on novel methods or materials and is derived either from an entirely different knowledge base or from the recombination of the existing knowledge base with a new stream of knowledge (new market/new technology).

■ An architectural innovation is an embodied new product in which known components, based on existing technologies, are reconfigured in a novel way to attack new markets (new market/existing technology).

■ A disruptive innovation is an innovation that leverages new technologies to attack existing markets from the bottom up (existing market/new technology).

LO 7-6 / Compare and contrast closed and open innovation.

■ Closed innovation is a framework for R&D that proposes impenetrable firm boundaries. Key to success in the closed innovation model is that the firm discovers, develops, and commercializes new products internally.

■ Open innovation is a framework for R&D that proposes permeable firm boundaries to allow a firm to benefit not only from internal ideas and inventions, but also from external ones. The sharing goes both ways: some external ideas and inventions are insourced while others are spun-out.

■ Exhibit 7.13 compares and contrasts principles of closed and open innovation.

KEY TERMS

Absorptive capacity *(p. 240)*

Architectural innovation *(p. 234)*

Crossing-the-chasm framework *(p. 225)*

Disruptive innovation *(p. 234)*

Entrepreneurs *(p. 216)*

Entrepreneurship *(p. 215)*

First-mover advantages *(p. 214)*

Incremental innovation *(p. 232)*

Industry life cycle *(p. 217)*

Innovation *(p. 214)*

Innovation ecosystem *(p. 234)*

Invention *(p. 213)*

Markets-and-technology framework *(p. 232)*

Network effects *(p. 219)*

Open innovation *(p. 238)*

Patent *(p. 213)*

Process innovation *(p. 221)*

Product innovation *(p. 221)*

Radical innovation *(p. 232)*

Reverse innovation *(p. 238)*

Social entrepreneurship *(p. 217)*

Standard *(p. 220)*

Strategic entrepreneurship *(p. 216)*

Trade secret *(p. 213)*

Winner-take-all markets *(p. 233)*

DISCUSSION QUESTIONS

1. Select an industry and consider how the industry life cycle has affected business strategy for the firms in that industry over time. Detail your answer based on each stage: introduction, growth, shakeout, maturity, and decline.

2. Describe a firm you think has been highly innovative. Which of the four types of innovation—radical, incremental, disruptive, or architectural—did it use? Did the firm use different types over time?

3. The chapter discussed the Internet as a disruptive innovation that has facilitated online retailing. It also, however, has presented challenges to brick-and-mortar retailers. How might retailers such as Nordstrom, Neiman Marcus, or Macy's need to change their in-store experience in order to continue to attract a flow of customers into their stores to expand sales using direct selling and store displays of the actual merchandise? If the Internet continues to grow and sales of brick-and-mortar retailers decline, how might the retailers attract, train, and retain high-quality employees if the industry is perceived as in decline?

4. Much has been said about competitive advantage gained from innovations such as the Internet, high-technology gadgets, and apps. The chapter points out, however, that low-technology innovations such as the razor–razorblade business model can also create value with incremental innovation. The chapter also noted that Dollar Shave Club (Strategy Highlight 7.1) is merely using a different business model to try to disrupt Gillette. Think of other low-technology innovations that are/were novel, useful, and successfully implemented so that the innovating firm gained a competitive advantage. Find information about the entrepreneurial story behind the innovation.

ETHICAL/SOCIAL ISSUES

1. You are a co-founder of a start-up firm making electronic sensors. After a year of sales, your business is not growing rapidly, but you have some steady customers keeping the business afloat. A major supplier has informed you it can no longer supply your firm because it is moving to serve large customers only, and your volume does not qualify. Though you have no current orders to support an increased commitment to this supplier, you do have a new version of your sensor coming out that you hope will increase the purchase volume by over 75 percent and qualify you for continued supply. This supplier is important to your plans. What do you do?

2. GE's development of the Vscan provides many benefits as a lower-cost and portable ultrasound device (see Strategy Highlight 7.2). Cardiologists, obstetricians, and veterinarians will be able to use the device in rural areas and developing countries. One of the criticisms of the device, however, is that it also facilitates the use of the technology for gender-selective abortion. In India, for example, there is a cultural preference for males, and the Vscan has been used to identify gender in order to abort an unwanted female fetus. Some argue that gender selection is also used for economic reasons—specifically, to alleviate the financial strain of the common dowry practice. A daughter would require the family to pay a dowry of cash and gifts to the bridegroom's family in order to arrange a suitable marriage, while a son would bring in a dowry of cash, jewelry, gifts, and household items to help the couple start their home. In addition, even though there has been some progress for women in India, others attribute the use of gender selection to women's lack of social, political, and economic empowerment.[88]

To what extent is GE ethically responsible for how—and why—the Vscan is used? (To what extent is any company ethically responsible for how—and why—its product is used?) Note that GE's website states that it is an "Agent of Good." Consider ways that GE might become involved in communities in India to show the company's concern for the underlying problems by improving conditions for women. What other ways might GE influence how its equipment is used?

SMALL GROUP EXERCISES

//// Small Group Exercise 1

Your group works for Warner Music Group (www .wmg.com), a large music record label whose sales are declining largely due to digital piracy. Your supervisor assigns you the task of developing a strategy for improving this situation.

1. What are the key issues you must grapple with to improve the position of Warner Music Group (WMG)?

2. In what phase of the life cycle is the record-label industry?

3. How does this life cycle phase affect the types of innovation that should be considered to help WMG be successful?

//// Small Group Exercise 2

The chapter compares and contrasts closed versus open innovation. It also describes Procter & Gamble's Connect+Develop open innovation system. With your group members, brainstorm to prepare a brief memo with a set of talking points regarding the following questions:

1. What are some of the risks of an open innovation approach that a company should consider before embarking on it?

2. Do you believe P&G's Connect+Develop (C+D) open innovation system has the potential to create a competitive advantage for the firm? How might P&G's capabilities be strengthened as a result? If C+D does have the potential to create a competitive advantage, do you believe it is sustainable? Why or why not?

3. Larry Huston and Nabil Sakkab, (former) executives at P&G, proclaimed, "Connect+Develop will become the dominant innovation model in the 21st century."[89] Do you agree with their statement? Why or why not? If C+D did become the dominant innovation model, how would this affect its potential to create a competitive edge for a firm?

4. Introducing the C+D innovation model requires tremendous organizational change. As Huston and Sakkab described the change effort: "We needed to move the company's attitude from resistance to innovations *'not invented here'* to enthusiasm for those *'proudly found elsewhere.'* And we needed to change how we defined, and perceived, our R&D organization—from 7,500 people inside to 7,500 plus 1.5 million outside, with a permeable boundary between them."[90] Identify some of the major obstacles a manager would encounter attempting this kind of organizational change. For example, how might P&G's research employees react? Although you have not been formally introduced to organizational structure, consider some recommendations for how to accomplish such large-scale organizational change successfully.

STRATEGY TERM PROJECT

McGraw Hill Education connect

The HP Running Case, a related activity for each strategy term project module, is available in Connect.

//// Module 7: Innovation Strategy

In this section, you will study the environment of the firm you have selected for the strategy term project and the firm's susceptibility to technological disruptions from new entrants.

1. Where is your firm's industry on the life cycle exemplified in Exhibit 7.4? What are the strategic implications?

2. What is the firm's innovation strategy? Does it rely on incremental or radical innovations? Disruptive or architectural? What are the competitive implications of the firm's innovation strategies?

3. Are intellectual property rights important for your firm? Can you find what strategies the firm is implementing to protect its proprietary position?

4. Identify a recent innovation by your firm. What is your firm's strategy to cross the chasm(s) to achieve mass market adoption of its innovation?

5. What attributes describe the current major customer segment for your firm? Are these changing? If so, is your firm prepared to meet these new customer demands?

6. How does your firm organize for innovation? Does it use a closed or an open innovation approach? Is its current approach working out well, or does it need changing? If yes, how?

---

*my*STRATEGY

Do You Want to Be an Entrepreneur?

Recent years have seen a sometimes public debate around the question of whether entrepreneurs are better off skipping college. For reasons noted below, we think this is a false debate, and we'll explain why. But before we're done, we will identify an unexpected way in which a higher education can legitimately be seen as limiting one's ability to innovate and start a new business.[91]

Let's start by acknowledging there are complex links between education and entrepreneurship and by explicitly stating our point of view: The right person can become an entrepreneur without the benefit of a college degree. But having a college degree is no impediment to becoming an entrepreneur and can further provide the benefit of formally studying the dynamics of real business—just as we are doing in this class.

One volley in the debate was a provocative article in *Forbes*, titled "The Secret to Entrepreneurial Success: Forget College." Another article listed 100 impressive entrepreneurs, none with a college degree and some with only an elementary school education. And while some famous entrepreneurs neglected higher education (Mark Zuckerberg dropped out of Harvard; Steve Jobs dropped out of Reed College), entrepreneurs are more likely to be better educated than most business owners. Just over half of business owners have a college degree.

And while the very different entrepreneurs in this chapter were chosen for their business success and innovations, and not their education, they all— Jeff Bezos, Sara Blakely, Michael Dublin, Reed Hastings, Elon Musk, Jimmy Wales, and Oprah Winfrey—have college degrees.

On the student side, business majors are drawn to the entrepreneurial role. Over the past 20 years, there has been an explosion of entrepreneurial programs at business schools, all in response to demand. Some 50–75 percent of MBA students from the leading programs are becoming entrepreneurs within 15 years of graduation.

But there is a more likely way in which higher education could be the enemy of entrepreneurship: the crippling impact of large student loans. According to a new report, the higher the student loan debt in an area, the lower the net creation of very small businesses. The correlation of those two factors comes with some caveats:

- These effects tend to affect only the smallest businesses, which are more likely to take on debt that's secured by the founder's own personal credit.

- The authors of the report stop short of claiming that heavy debt burdens hamper an individual's attempt.

- An alternate view of the data would be that students with high debt load go directly to higher paying corporate jobs.

1. Thinking about today's business climate, would you say that now is a good time to start a business? Why or why not?

2. Do you see higher education as a benefit or detriment to becoming a successful entrepreneur? Why or why not?

3. Identify both the up and down sides of taking on personal debt to finance a higher education.

4. Does it matter *where* (in terms of geography) you start your business? Why or why not?

5. Explain how you would apply the strategic management framework to enhance your startup's chances to gain and sustain a competitive advantage.

ENDNOTES

1. Auletta, K., "Outside the box: Netflix and the future of television," *The New Yorker,* February 3, 2014.

2. Ramachandran, S., and T. Stynes, "Netflix steps up foreign expansion," *The Wall Street Journal,* January 20, 2015; Ramachandran, S., and S. Sharma, "NBCU plans subscription comedy video service," *The Wall Street Journal,* March 3, 2015;Vranica, S., "Streaming services hammer cable-TV ratings," *The Wall Street Journal,* March 10, 2015; Lin, L., "Netflix in talks to take content to China," *The Wall Street Journal,* May 15, 2015; Jenkins, H.W., "Netflix is the culprit," *The Wall Street Journal,* March 17, 2015; Jakab, S., "Don't overlook Netflix 's bigger picture," *The Wall Street Journal,* April 14, 2015; Armental, M., and S. Ramachandran, "Netflix gains more users than projected," *The Wall Street Journal,* April 15, 2015; Auletta, "Outside the box: Netflix and the future of television" *The New Yorker,* February 3, 2014; "A brief history of the company that revolutionized watching of movies and TV shows," http://netflix.com; "A brief history of Netflix" (2014), *CNN.com,* www.cnn.com/2014/07/21/showbiz/gallery/netflix-history/; Ramachandran, S., "Netflix to pay Comcast for smoother streaming," *The Wall Street Journal,* February 23, 2014; and Darlin, D., "Falling costs of big-screen TVs to keep falling," *The New York Times,* August 20, 2005.

3. The "long tail" is a business model in which companies can obtain a large part of their revenues by selling a small number of units from among almost unlimited choices. See Anderson, C. (2006), *The Long Tail. Why the Future of Business Is Selling Less of More* (New York: Hachette).

4. Rothaermel, F.T., and A. Hess (2010), "Innovation strategies combined," *MIT Sloan Management Review,* Spring: 12–15.

5. Schumpeter, J.A. (1942), *Capitalism, Socialism, and Democracy* (New York: Harper & Row); Foster, R., and S. Kaplan (2001), *Creative Destruction: Why Companies That Are Built to Last Underperform the Market—and How to Successfully Transform Them* (New York: Currency).

6. "Comcast, GE strike deal; Vivendi to sell NBC stake," *The Wall Street Journal,* December 4, 2009.

7. Rothaermel, F.T., and D.L. Deeds (2004), "Exploration and exploitation alliances in biotechnology: A system of new product development," *Strategic Management Journal* 25: 201–221; Madhavan, R., and R. Grover (1998), "From embedded knowledge to embodied knowledge: New product development as knowledge management," *Journal of Marketing* 62: 1–12; and Stokes, D.E. (1997), *Pasteur's Quadrant: Basic Science and Technological Innovation* (Washington, DC: Brookings Institute Press).

8. Isaacson, W. (2007), *Einstein: His Life and Universe* (New York: Simon & Schuster).

9. A detailed description of patents can be found at the U.S. Patent and Trademark Office's website at www.uspto.gov/.

10. Hallenborg, L., M. Ceccagnoli, and M. Clendenin (2008), "Intellectual property protection in the global economy," *Advances in the Study of Entrepreneurship, Innovation, and Economic Growth* 18: 11–34; and Graham, S.J.H. (2008), "Beyond patents: The role of copyrights, trademarks, and trade secrets in technology commercialization," *Advances in the Study of Entrepreneurship, Innovation, and Economic Growth* 18: 149–171.

11. "Sweet secrets—obituary: Michele Ferrero," *The Economist,* February 21, 2015.

12. Schumpeter, *Capitalism, Socialism, and Democracy.* For an updated and insightful discussion, see Foster and Kaplan, *Creative Destruction.* For a very accessible discussion, see McCraw, T. (2007), *Prophet of Innovation: Joseph Schumpeter and Creative Destruction* (Boston: Harvard University Press).

13. Lieberman, M.B., and D.B. Montgomery (1988), "First-mover advantages," *Strategic Management Journal* 9: 41–58.

14. Schramm, C.J. (2006), *The Entrepreneurial Imperative* (New York: HarperCollins). Dr. Carl Schramm is president of the Kauffman Foundation, the world's leading foundation for entrepreneurship.

15. Schumpeter, *Capitalism, Socialism, and Democracy;* Foster and Kaplan, *Creative Destruction.*

16. Shane, S., and S. Venkataraman (2000), "The promise of entrepreneurship as a field of research," *Academy of Management Review* 25: 217–226; Alvarez, S., and J.B. Barney (2007), "Discovery and creation: Alternative theories of entrepreneurial action," *Strategic Entrepreneurship Journal* 1: 11–26.

17. Auletta, "Outside the box."

18. Hansen, M.T., H. Ibarra, and U. Peyer (2013), "The best-performing CEOs in the world," *Harvard Business Review,* January.

19. "Oprah Winfrey to end her program in 2011," *The Wall Street Journal,* November 19, 2009.

20. *Forbes Special Edition: Billionaires,* March 29, 2010.

21. http://elonmusk.com/.

22. Vance, A. (2015), *Elon Musk: Tesla, SpaceX, and the Quest for a Fantastic Future* (New York: Ecco).

23. Burgelman, R.A. (1983), "Corporate entrepreneurship and strategic management: Insights from a process study," *Management Science* 29: 1349–1364; Zahra, S.A., and J.G. Covin, "Contextual influences on the corporate entrepreneurship-performance relationship: A longitudinal analysis," *Journal of Business Venturing* 10: 43–58.

24. Schumpeter, *Capitalism, Socialism, and Democracy.*

25. U.S. Patent 381968, see www.google.com/patents/US381968.

26. Hitt, M.A., R.D. Ireland, S.M. Camp, and D.L. Sexton (2002), "Strategic entrepreneurship: Integrating entrepreneurial and strategic management perspectives," in ed. M.A. Hitt, R.D. Ireland, S.M. Camp, and D.L. Sexton, *Strategic Entrepreneurship: Creating a New Mindset* (Oxford, UK: Blackwell Publishing); Rothaermel, F.T. (2008), "Strategic management and strategic entrepreneurship," Presentation at the Strategic Management Society Annual International Conference, Cologne, Germany, October 12.

27. Ibid; Bingham, C.B., K.M. Eisenhardt, and N.R. Furr (2007), "What makes a process a capability? Heuristics, strategy, and effective capture of opportunities," *Strategic Entrepreneurship Journal* 1: 27–47.

28. www.betterworldbooks.com/info.aspx?f=corevalues.

29. This discussion is based on: "How Jimmy Wales' Wikipedia harnessed the web as a force for good," *Wired,* March 19, 2013.

30. Rothaermel, F.T., and M. Thursby (2007), "The nanotech vs. the biotech revolution: Sources of incumbent productivity in research," *Research Policy* 36: 832–849; and Woolley, J. (2010), "Technology emergence through entrepreneurship across multiple industries," *Strategic Entrepreneurship Journal* 4: 1–21.

31. This discussion is built on the seminal work by Rogers, E. (1962), *Diffusion of Innovations* (New York: Free Press). For a more recent treatise, see Baum, J.A.C., and A.M. McGahan (2004), *Business Strategy over the Industry Lifecycle, Advances in Strategic Management,* Vol. 21 (Bingley, United Kingdom: Emerald).

32. Moore, G.A. (1991), *Crossing the Chasm. Marketing and Selling Disruptive Products to Mainstream Customers* (New York: HarperCollins).

33. This discussion is based on: Schilling, M.A. (2002), "Technology success and failure in winner-take-all markets: Testing a model of technological lockout," *Academy of Management Journal* 45: 387–398; Shapiro, C., and H.R. Varian (1998), *Information Rules. A Strategic Guide to the Network Economy* (Boston, MA: Harvard Business School Press); Hill, C.W.L. (1997), "Establishing a standard: Competitive strategy and winner-take-all industries," *Academy of Management Executive* 11: 7–25; and Arthur, W.B. (1989), "Competing technologies, increasing returns, and lock-in by historical events," *Economics Journal* 99: 116–131.

34. Wakabayashi, D., 'Staggering' iPhone demand helps lift Apple's quarterly profit by 38%," *The Wall Street Journal,* January 28, 2015; Wakabayashi, D., "Challenge for Apple Watch: Style but no 'killer app,'" *The Wall Street Journal,* March 9, 2015; "The 10 most popular iPhone Apps of all time," *PCMag.com,* May 3, 2013; "Inside the app economy," *Bloomberg Businessweek,* October 22, 2009; Adner, R. (2012), *The Wide Lens. A New Strategy for Innovation* (New York: Portfolio); and www.apple.com/iphone/from-the-app-store/.

35. This discussion is based on: Schilling, M.A. (1998), "Technological lockout: An integrative model of the economic and strategic factors driving technology success and failure," *Academy of Management Review* 23: 267–284; Utterback, J.M. (1994), *Mastering the Dynamics of Innovation* (Boston, MA: Harvard Business School Press); and Anderson, P., and M. Tushman (1990), "Technological discontinuities and dominant designs: A cyclical model of technological change," *Administrative Science Quarterly* 35: 604–634.

36. This discussion is based on: Ceccagnoli, M., and F.T. Rothaermel (2008), "Appropriating the returns to innovation," *Advances in Study of Entrepreneurship, Innovation, and Economic Growth* 18: 11–34; and Teece, D.J. (1986), "Profiting from technological innovation: Implications for integration, collaboration, licensing and public policy," *Research Policy* 15: 285–305.

37. Benner, M., and M.A. Tushman (2003), "Exploitation, exploration, and process management: The productivity dilemma revisited," *Academy of Management Review* 28: 238–256; and Abernathy, W.J., and J.M. Utterback (1978), "Patterns of innovation in technology," *Technology Review* 80: 40–47.

38. "Containers have been more important for globalization than freer trade," *The Economist,* May 18, 2013.

39. "Containers have been more important for globalization than freer trade," *The Economist,*

May 18, 2013, presents findings from the following research studies: Hummels, D. (2007), "Transportation costs and international trade in the second era of globalization," *Journal of Economic Perspectives* 21: 131–154; Baldwin, R. (2011), "Trade and industrialization after globalization's 2nd unbundling: How building and joining a supply chain are different and why it matters," *NBER Working Paper 17716;* and Bernhofen, D., Z. El-Sahli, and R. Keller (2013), "Estimating the Effects of the Container Revolution on World Trade," Working Paper, Lund University.

40. This discussion is based on: Benner, M., and M.A. Tushman (2003), "Exploitation, exploration, and process management: The productivity dilemma revisited," *Academy of Management Review* 28: 238–256; and Abernathy, W.J., and J.M. Utterback (1978), "Patterns of innovation in technology," *Technology Review* 80: 40–47.

41. www.apple.com/ipad/pricing/.

42. www.geeks.com.

43. O'Connor, Clare, "How Sara Blakely of Spanx turned $5,000 into $1 billion," *Forbes,* March 14, 2012. The history of Spanx is documented at www.spanx.com.

44. Harrigan, K.R. (1980), *Strategies for Declining Businesses* (Lexington, MA: Heath).

45. Moore, *Crossing the Chasm.*

46. We follow the customer type category originally introduced by Rogers, E.M. (1962), *Diffusion of Innovations* (New York: Free Press) and also used by Moore, *Crossing the Chasm:* technology enthusiasts (~2.5%), early adopters (~13.5%), early majority (~34%), late majority (~34%), and laggards (~16%). Rogers' book originally used the term *innovators* rather than *technology enthusiasts* for the first segment. Given the specific definition of innovation as commercialized invention in this chapter, we follow Moore (p. 30) and use the term *technology enthusiasts.*

47. "For wearable computers, future looks blurry," *The Wall Street Journal,* May 30, 2013.

48. Barr, A., "Google Lab puts a time limit on innovations," *The Wall Street Journal,* March 31, 2015.

49. Shiller, R. (1995), "Conversation, information, and herd behavior," *American Economic Review* 85: 181–185.

50. Brickley, P., "Creditors agree on Chapter 11 plan with former Fisker Automotive," *The Wall Street Journal,* June 3, 2014; "How the wheels came off for Fisker," *The Wall Street Journal,* April 24, 2013; and "A year of few dull moments," *The New York Times,* December 21, 2012.

51. The Iridium example is drawn from: Finkelstein, S. (2003), *Why Smart Executives*

Fail: And What You Can Learn from Their Mistakes (New York: Portfolio).

52. In inflation-adjusted 2012 U.S. dollars. The original price in 1998 was $3,000 and the cost per minute up to $8.

53. "HP gambles on ailing Palm," *The Wall Street Journal,* April 29, 2010.

54. "What's gone wrong with HP?" *The Wall Street Journal,* November 6, 2012.

55. In 2013, RIM adopted BlackBerry as company name.

56. Moore, *Crossing the Chasm.*

57. Shuen, A. (2008), *Web 2.0: A Strategy Guide* (Sebastopol, CA: O'Reilly Media); Thursby, J., and M. Thursby (2006), *Here or There? A Survey in Factors of Multinational R&D Location* (Washington, DC: National Academies Press).

58. Byers, T.H., R.C. Dorf, and A.J. Nelson (2011), *Technology Entrepreneurship: From Idea to Enterprise* (New York: McGraw-Hill).

59. This discussion is based on: Schumpeter, *Capitalism, Socialism, and Democracy;* Freeman, C., and L. Soete (1997), *The Economics of Industrial Innovation* (Cambridge, MA: MIT Press); and Foster and Kaplan, *Creative Destruction.*

60. The discussion of incremental and radical innovations is based on: Hill, C.W.L., and F.T. Rothaermel (2003), "The performance of incumbent firms in the face of radical technological innovation," *Academy of Management Review* 28: 257–274.

61. Ibid.

62. Luna, T., "The new Gillette Fusion ProGlide Flexball razor, to be available in stores June 9," *The Boston Globe,* April 29, 2014; and "A David and Gillette story," *The Wall Street Journal,* April 12, 2012.

63. This discussion is based on: Hill and Rothaermel, "The performance of incumbent firms in the face of radical technological innovation."

64. Adner, R. (2012), *The Wide Lens. A New Strategy for Innovation* (New York: Portfolio); Brandenburger, A.M., and B.J. Nalebuff (1996), *Co-opetition* (New York: Currency Doubleday); and Christensen, C.M., and J.L. Bower (1996), "Customer power, strategic investment, and the failure of leading firms," *Strategic Management Journal* 17: 197–218.

65. Henderson, R., and K.B. Clark (1990), "Architectural innovation: The reconfiguration of existing technologies and the failure of established firms," *Administrative Science Quarterly* 35: 9–30.

66. This example is drawn from: Chesbrough, H. (2003), *Open Innovation. The New Imperative for Creating and Profiting from*

Technology (Boston, MA: Harvard Business School Press).

67. The discussion of disruptive innovation is based on: Christensen, C.M. (1997), *The Innovator's Dilemma: When New Technologies Cause Great Firms to Fail* (Boston, MA: Harvard Business School Press); and Christensen, C.M., and M.E. Raynor (2003), *The Innovator's Solution: Creating and Sustaining Successful Growth* (Boston, MA: Harvard Business School Press).

68. Android here is used to include Chrome OS. "Introducing the Google Chrome OS," *The Official Google Blog*, July 7, 2009, http://googleblog.blogspot.com/2009/07/introducing-google-chrome-os.html.

69. See the discussion on business models in Chapter 1. See also: Anderson, C. (2009), *Free. The Future of a Radical Price* (New York: Hyperion).

70. Dollar Shave video, www.youtube.com/dollarshaveclub.

71. "A David and Gillette story"; and "Riding the momentum created by a cheeky video," *The New York Times*, April 10, 2013.

72. Winkler, R., "Android market share hits new record," *The Wall Street Journal*, July 31, 2014.

73. This Strategy Highlight is based on: Immelt, J.R., V. Govindarajan, and C. Trimble (2009), "How GE is disrupting itself," *Harvard Business Review*, October; author's interviews with Michael Poteran of GE Healthcare (October 30 and November 4, 2009); and "Vscan handheld ultrasound: GE unveils 'stethoscope of the 21st century,'" *The Huffington Post*, October 20, 2009.

74. Rindova, V., and S. Kotha (2001), "Continuous 'morphing': Competing through dynamic capabilities, form, and function," *Academy of Management Journal* 44: 1263–1280.

75. The new processor not only is inexpensive but also consumes little battery power. Moreover, it marks a departure from the Wintel (Windows and Intel) alliance, because Microsoft did not have a suitable operating system ready for the low-end netbook market. Many of these computers are using free software such as Google's Android operating system and Google Docs for applications.

76. Govindarajan, V., and C. Trimble (2012), *Reverse Innovation: Create Far from Home, Win Everywhere* (Boston, MA: Harvard Business Review Press).

77. The discussion in this section draws mainly on Chesbrough's seminal work, but also on the other insightful sources referenced here. Chesbrough, H.W. (2003), *Open Innovation: The New Imperative for Creating and*

Profiting from Technology (Boston, MA: Harvard Business School Press); Chesbrough, H. (2003), "The area of open innovation," *MIT Sloan Management Review*, Spring: 35–41; Chesbrough, H. (2007), "Why companies should have open business models," *MIT Sloan Management Review*, Winter: 22–28; Chesbrough, H.W., and M.M. Appleyard (2007), "Open innovation and strategy," *California Management Review*, Fall 50: 57–76; Laursen, K., and A. Salter (2006), "Open for innovation: The role of openness in explaining innovation performance among U.K. manufacturing firms," *Strategic Management Journal* 27: 131–150; and West, J., and S. Gallagher (2006), "Challenges of open innovation: The paradox of firm investment in open-source software," *R&D Management* 36: 319–331.

78. See the recent research, for example, by Chatterji, A.K., and K.R. Fabrizio (2013), "Using users: When does external knowledge enhance corporate product innovation?," *Strategic Management Journal* 35: 1427–1445. Using a sample of medical device makers and their collaboration with physicians, this research focuses on the conditions under which user knowledge can contribute most effectively to corporate innovation. The underlying literature in this field identifies both the importance of users to corporate innovation (20 to 80 percent of important innovations across a number of fields were user-sourced) and the unique quality of user-driven innovation (users are highly motivated to fulfill unmet needs that they have experienced). Given that cross-boundary interactions increase administrative costs and communication barriers, the study finds that user-driven open innovation has higher benefits in the early stages of technology life cycle and in the development of radical innovations.

79. Rothaermel, F.T., and M.T. Alexandre (2009), "Ambidexterity in technology sourcing: The moderating role of absorptive capacity," *Organization Science* 20: 759–780; Rothaermel, F.T., and A.M. Hess (2010), "Innovation strategies combined," *MIT Sloan Management Review* 51: 13–15.

80. Katz, R., and T.J. Allen (1982), "Investigating the not invented here (NIH) syndrome: A look at the performance, tenure, and communication patterns of 50 R&D project groups," *R&D Management* 12: 7–20.

81. Horbaczewski, A., and F.T. Rothaermel (2013), "Merck: Open for innovation?" Case Study MH-FTR-009-0077645065, available at: http://create.mcgraw-hill.com.

82. Cohen, W.M., and D.A. Levinthal (1990), "Absorptive capacity: New perspective on learning and innovation," *Administrative Science Quarterly* 35: 128–152; Zahra, S.A.,

and G. George (2002), "Absorptive capacity: A review, reconceptualization, and extension," *Academy of Management Review* 27: 185–203; and Rothaermel and Alexandre, "Ambidexterity in technology sourcing."

83. Lafley, A.G., and R.L. Martin (2013), *Playing to Win: How Strategy Really Works* (Boston, MA: Harvard Business Review Press); Rothaermel and Alexandre, "Ambidexterity in technology sourcing"; Rothaermel and Hess, "Innovation strategies combined"; "Diamond buys P&G's Pringles," *The Wall Street Journal*, April 6, 2011; and Huston, L., and N. Sakkab (2006), "Connect & Develop: Inside Procter & Gamble's new model for innovation," *Harvard Business Review*, March: 58–66.

84. www.fastcompany.com/section/most-innovative-companies-2015.

85. Burgelman, R.A. (1983), "Corporate entrepreneurship and strategic management: Insights from a process study," *Management Science* 29: 1349–1364; Burgelman, R.A. (1991), "Intraorganizational ecology of strategy making and organizational adaptation: Theory and field research," *Organization Science* 2: 239–262; and Burgelman, R.A., and A. Grove (2007), "Let chaos reign, then rein in chaos—repeatedly: Managing strategic dynamics for corporate longevity," *Strategic Management Journal* 28: 965–979.

86. http://solutions.3m.com/innovation/en_US/stories/time-to-think.

87. Auletta, "Outside the box."

88. "Gendercide in India," *The Economist*, April 7, 2011; "Sex-selective abortion," *The Economist*, June 28, 2011; "India women: One dishonourable step backwards," *The Economist*, May 11, 2012; and "India's skewed sex ratios," *The Economist*, December 18, 2012.

89. Huston, L., and N. Sakkab (2006), "Connect & Develop: Inside Procter & Gamble's new model for innovation," *Harvard Business Review*, March: 58–66; Lafley and Martin, *Playing to Win: How Strategy Really Works*.

90. Ibid.

91. Sources for this myStrategy include: "Why more MBAs are becoming entrepreneurs straight out of business school," *Business Insider*, July 24, 2014; "Top 25 colleges for entrepreneurs," *Entrepreneur*, September 15, 2014; "Does college matter for entrepreneurs?" *Entrepreneur*, September 21, 2011; "The secret to entrepreneurial success: Forget college," *Forbes*, July 15, 2013; "Want to be an entrepreneur: Avoid student debt," *The Wall Street Journal*, May 26, 2015; "Full-time MBA programs: Stanford University," *Bloomberg Businessweek*, November 13, 2008.

Chapter 8

Corporate Strategy: Vertical Integration and Diversification

Learning Objectives

LO 8-1 Define corporate strategy and describe the three dimensions along which it is assessed.

LO 8-2 Explain why firms need to grow, and evaluate different growth motives.

LO 8-3 Describe and evaluate different options firms have to organize economic activity.

LO 8-4 Describe the two types of vertical integration along the industry value chain: backward and forward vertical integration.

LO 8-5 Identify and evaluate benefits and risks of vertical integration.

LO 8-6 Describe and examine alternatives to vertical integration.

LO 8-7 Describe and evaluate different types of corporate diversification.

LO 8-8 Apply the core competence–market matrix to derive different diversification strategies.

LO 8-9 Explain when a diversification strategy creates a competitive advantage and when it does not.

How Amazon.com Became the Everything Store

TWENTY YEARS AGO JEFF BEZOS STARTED Amazon.com to sell books online from a garage in a Seattle suburb. He furnished his makeshift office with discarded wood doors for desks. Today, Amazon has become the largest online retailer worldwide, with some 230 million items available, 30 times the number sold by Walmart, the world's largest traditional retailer. Yet, wood doors turning into desks remain a staple at Amazon, where strict cost control is paramount to this day.

Amazon.com is also now a widely diversified technology company; see Exhibit 8.1 for Amazon's key strategic initiatives and stock market valuation over the years. Besides offering every imaginable product online, it sells its own line of Kindle e-book readers, Fire tablets, Fire TV, and Fire phone. The Kindle e-reader has transformed the publishing industry. Amazon holds a two-thirds market share in e-books and now sells more e-books than print books.

Via its Prime Instant Video and Music services, Amazon streams content such as movies, TV shows, and music. Prime members pay an annual $99 fee for unlimited free two-day shipping when buying items on Amazon's site, and they receive the streamed content for free. The estimated 40 million Prime members are Amazon's most loyal customers: They spend roughly $1,300 per year, three times more than non-Prime members. With Amazon Web Services (AWS), the company is now the largest cloud computing service provider globally. It also diversified geographically by establishing country-specific sites not only in the United States, but also in Canada, Brazil, Mexico, Germany, France, Italy, Spain, The Netherlands, the UK, China, India, Japan, and Australia.

Amazon started as an online book retailer but has grown into a massive discount Internet vendor, streaming multimedia from its website, offering cloud computing

© AP Photo/Ted S. Warren

services, and selling its own technology devices. As technology has evolved, traditional boundaries between hardware and software, products and services, and online and brick-and-mortar stores has become increasingly blurred. As a result, Amazon finds itself engaged in a fierce competitive battle for control of the emerging digital ecosystem, pitted against technology giants such as Apple, Google, and Facebook. Moreover, in general retailing Amazon.com competes with Walmart and the Chinese ecommerce company Alibaba. In data services and cloud computing, it competes with Microsoft, IBM, and others.

Amazon's annual sales total almost $100 billion, making it one of the five largest technology companies in the world (with Apple, Microsoft, Google, and Facebook). Yet, profitability still eludes Amazon.com; in 2014 alone, it lost $250 million. With its ability to diversify into business activities that are not necessarily related to its traditional core competencies, the company faces some of the most formidable competitors. Indeed, Amazon's continued diversification into other areas of the technology industry has been part of a broader convergence of industries previously the sole domain of companies such as Apple, Google, and Facebook.

Despite having yet to deliver any profits, Amazon CEO Jeff Bezos seems undaunted. He has continually emphasized that Amazon's focus is on the long run, and that this requires continued diversification and large scale, requiring billion-dollar outlays. Investors seem to believe that Amazon's future is a bright one. In the last 10 years, Amazon's stock appreciated by more than 1,100 percentage points, while the tech-heavy NASDAQ composite index of 100 companies (including Apple, Amazon, Facebook, Google, Microsoft, Netflix, Tesla Motors, and Yahoo) appreciated by a mere 187 percentage points. In summer 2015, Amazon's market capitalization had surpassed $200 billion, making it one of the most valued tech companies globally.[1]

You will learn more about Amazon.com by reading this chapter; related questions appear on page 283.

EXHIBIT 8.1 /

Amazon's Strategic Initiatives and Stock Market Valuation, 1994–2015

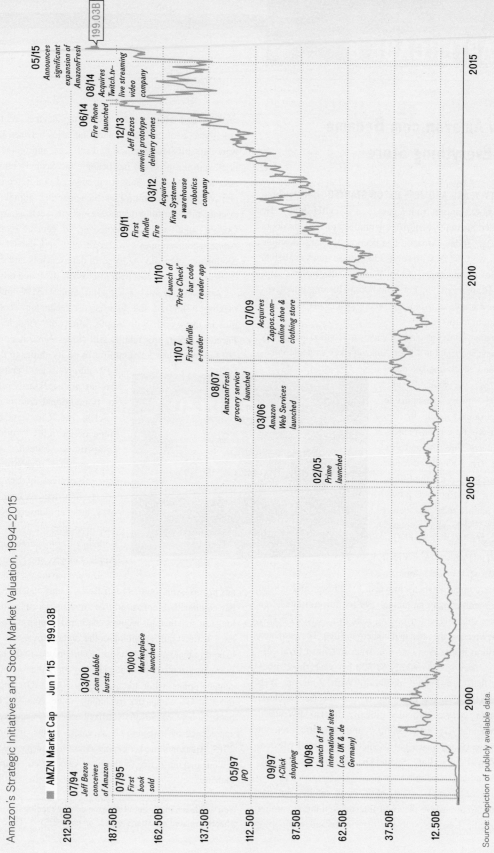

■ AMZN Market Cap   Jun 1 '15   199.03B

07/94 Jeff Bezos conceives of Amazon

07/95 First book sold

05/97 IPO

09/97 1-Click shopping

10/98 Launch of 1st international sites (.co, UK & de Germany)

03/00 .com bubble bursts

10/00 Marketplace launched

02/05 Prime launched

03/06 Amazon Web Services launched

08/07 AmazonFresh grocery service launched

11/07 First Kindle e-reader

07/09 Acquires Zappos.com— online shoe & clothing store

11/10 Launch of "Price Check" bar code reader app

09/11 First Kindle Fire

03/12 Acquires Kiva Systems— a warehouse robotics company

12/13 Jeff Bezos unveils prototype delivery drones

06/14 Fire Phone launched

08/14 Acquires Twitch.tv— live streaming video company

05/15 Announces significant expansion of AmazonFresh

199.03B

212.50B
187.50B
162.50B
137.50B
112.50B
87.50B
62.50B
37.50B
12.50B

2000   2005   2010   2015

Source: Depiction of publicly available data.

OVER TIME AMAZON.COM has morphed from a mere online book retailer into the "everything store."[2] In the process, it transformed into the world's largest online retailer. From books it diversified into consumer electronics, media content, cloud computing services, and other business endeavors. Jeff Bezos decided to compete in a number of different industries, some related to Amazon's core business of online retailing, some unrelated.

How does a business decide exactly *where to compete*? Answers to this important question—in terms of products and services offered, or of geographic markets—are captured in a firm's *corporate strategy*, which we cover in the next three chapters. In this chapter, we define corporate strategy and then look at two fundamental corporate strategy topics: vertical integration and diversification. We conclude the chapter with "Implications for the Strategist," providing a practical application of dynamic corporate strategy at Nike and adidas.

8.1 What Is Corporate Strategy?

LO 8-1

Define corporate strategy and describe the three dimensions along which it is assessed.

Strategy formulation centers around the key questions of *where* and *how* to compete. *Business strategy* concerns the question of *how to compete* in a *single product market*. As discussed in Chapter 6, the two generic business strategies that firms can pursue their quest for competitive advantage are to increase differentiation (while containing cost) *or* lower costs (while maintaining differentiation). If trade-offs can be reconciled, some firms might be able to pursue a blue ocean strategy by increasing differentiation *and* lowering costs. As firms grow, they are frequently expanding their business activities through seeking new markets both by offering new products and services and by competing in different geographies. When this happens, managers must formulate a corporate strategy. To gain and sustain competitive advantage, therefore, any corporate strategy must align with and strengthen a firm's business strategy, whether it is a differentiation, cost-leadership, or blue ocean strategy.

Corporate strategy comprises the decisions that senior management makes and the goal-directed actions it takes in the quest for competitive advantage in several industries and markets simultaneously.[3] It provides answers to the key question of *where to compete*. Corporate strategy determines the boundaries of the firm along three dimensions: vertical integration (along the industry value chain), diversification (of products and services), and geographic scope (regional, national, or global markets).

Executives must determine their corporate strategy by answering three questions:

1. *In what stages of the industry value chain should the company participate (vertical integration)?* The industry value chain describes the transformation of raw materials into finished goods and services along distinct vertical stages.

2. *What range of products and services should the company offer (diversification)?*

3. *Where should the company compete geographically* in terms of regional, national, or international markets (geographic scope)?

In most cases, underlying these three questions is an implicit desire for growth. The need for growth is sometimes taken so much for granted that not every manager understands all the reasons behind it. A clear understanding will help executives pursue growth for the right reasons and make better decisions for the firm and its stakeholders.

corporate strategy
The decisions that senior management makes and the goal-directed actions it takes to gain and sustain competitive advantage in several industries and markets simultaneously.

WHY FIRMS NEED TO GROW

LO 8-2

Explain why firms need to grow, and evaluate different growth motives.

Several reasons explain *why firms need to grow*. These can be summarized as follows:

1. Increase profits.
2. Lower costs.

3. Increase market power.
4. Reduce risk.
5. Motivate management.

Let's look at each reason in turn.

INCREASE PROFITS. Profitable growth allows businesses to provide a higher return for their shareholders, or owners, if privately held. For publicly traded companies, the stock market valuation of a firm is determined to some extent by expected future revenue and profit streams. If firms fail to achieve their growth target, their stock price often falls. With a decline in a firm's stock price comes a lower overall market capitalization, exposing the firm to the risk of a hostile takeover. Moreover, with a lower stock price, it is more costly for firms to raise the required capital to fuel future growth by issuing stock.

LOWER COSTS. Firms are also motivated to grow in order to lower their cost. As discussed in detail in Chapter 6, a larger firm may benefit from *economies of scale,* thus driving down average costs as their output increases. Firms need to grow to achieve minimum efficient scale, and thus stake out the lowest-cost position achievable through economies of scale.

INCREASE MARKET POWER. Firms might be motivated to achieve growth to increase their market share and with it their market power. When discussing an industry's structure in Chapter 3, we noted that firms often consolidate industries through horizontal mergers and acquisitions (buying competitors) to change the industry structure in their favor (we'll discuss mergers and acquisitions in detail in Chapter 9). Fewer competitors generally equates to higher industry profitability. Moreover, larger firms have more bargaining power with suppliers and buyers (see the discussion of the five forces in Chapter 3).

REDUCE RISK. Firms might be motivated to grow in order to diversify their product and service portfolio through competing in a number of different industries. The rationale behind these diversification moves is that falling sales and lower performance in one sector (e.g., GE's oil and gas unit) might be compensated by higher performance in another (e.g., GE's health care unit). Such conglomerates attempt to achieve *economies of scope* (as first discussed in Chapter 6).

MANAGERIAL MOTIVES. Research in behavioral economics suggests that firms may grow to achieve goals that benefit its managers more than their stockholders.[4] As we will discuss in detail when presenting the *principal-agent problem* later in the chapter, managers may be more interested in pursuing their own interests such as empire building and job security—plus managerial perks such as corporate jets or executive retreats at expensive resorts—rather than increasing shareholder value. Although there is a weak link between CEO compensation and firm performance, the CEO pay package often correlates more strongly with firm size.[5]

Finally, we should acknowledge that promising businesses can fail because they grow unwisely—usually too fast too soon, and based on shaky assumptions about the future. There is a small movement counter to the need for growth, seen both in small businesses and social activism. Sometimes small-business owners operate a business for convenience, stability, and lifestyle; growth could threaten those goals. In social entrepreneurship, business micro-solutions are often operated outside of capital motives, where the need to solve a social problem outweighs the need of the firm to insure longevity beyond the solution of the problem.

THREE DIMENSIONS OF CORPORATE STRATEGY

All companies must navigate the three dimensions of vertical integration, diversification, and geographic scope. Although many managers provide input, the responsibility for corporate strategy ultimately rests with the CEO. Jeff Bezos, Amazon's CEO, determined in *what stages of the industry value chain Amazon would participate* (question 1). With its prevalent delivery lockers in large metropolitan areas and its first brick-and-mortar retail store opened in New York City, Amazon moved forward in the industry value chain to be closer to its end customer. With its offering of Amazon-branded electronics and more recently groceries, it also moved backward in the industry value chain toward manufacturing and production.

Bezos also chooses *what range of products and services to offer*, and which not (question 2). ChapterCase 8 discusses Amazon's diversification over time. Finally, Bezos also decided to customize certain country-specific websites despite the instant global reach of ecommerce firms. With this strategic decision, he decided where to compete globally in terms of different geographies beyond the United States. In short, Bezos determined *where Amazon competes geographically* (question 3).

Where to compete in terms of industry value chain, products and services, and geography are the fundamental corporate strategic decisions. The underlying strategic management concepts that will guide our discussion of vertical integration, diversification, and geographic competition are *core competencies, economies of scale, economies of scope,* and *transaction costs.*

- *Core competencies* are unique strengths embedded deep within a firm (as discussed in Chapter 4). Core competencies allow a firm to differentiate its products and services from those of its rivals, creating higher value for the customer or offering products and services of comparable value at lower cost. According to the *resource-based view of the firm,* a firm's boundaries are delineated by its knowledge bases and core competencies.[6] Activities that draw on what the firm knows how to do well (e.g., Google's core competency in developing proprietary search algorithms) should be done in-house, while non-core activities such as payroll and facility maintenance can be outsourced. In this perspective, the internally held knowledge underlying a core competency determines a firm's boundaries.

- *Economies of scale* occur when a firm's average cost per unit decreases as its output increases (as discussed in Chapter 6). Anheuser-Busch InBev, the largest global brewer (producer of brands such as Budweiser, Bud Light, Stella Artois, and Beck's), reaps significant economies of scale. Given its size, it is able to spread its fixed costs over the millions of gallons of beer it brews each year, in addition to the significant buyer power its large market share affords. Larger market share, therefore, often leads to lower costs.

- *Economies of scope* are the savings that come from producing two (or more) outputs or providing different services at less cost than producing each individually, though using the same resources and technology (as discussed in Chapter 6). Leveraging its online retailing expertise, for example, Amazon benefits from economies of scope: It can offer a large range of different product and service categories at a lower cost than it would take to offer each product line individually.

- *Transaction costs* are all costs associated with an economic exchange. The concept is developed in transaction cost economics, a strategic management framework, and enables managers to answer the question of whether it is cost-effective for their firm to expand its boundaries through vertical integration or diversification. This implies taking on greater ownership of the production of needed inputs or of the channels by which it distributes its outputs, or adding business units that offer new products and services.

We continue our study of corporate strategy by drawing on transaction cost economics to explain vertical integration, meaning the choices a firm makes concerning its boundaries. Later, we will explore managerial decisions relating to diversification, which directly affect the firm's range of products and services in multi-industry competition. The third question of geographic scope will receive attention later, especially in Chapter 10.

LO 8-3

Describe and evaluate different options firms have to organize economic activity.

8.2 The Boundaries of the Firm

Determining the boundaries of the firm so that it is more likely to gain and sustain a competitive advantage is the critical challenge in corporate strategy.[7] A theoretical framework in strategic management called **transaction cost economics** explains and predicts the boundaries of the firm. Insights gained from transaction cost economics help managers decide what activities to do in-house versus what services and products to obtain from the external market. This stream of research was first initiated by Nobel Laureate Ronald Coase, who asked a fundamental question: Given the efficiencies of free markets, why do firms even exist? The key insight of transaction cost economics is that different *institutional arrangements*—markets versus firms—have different costs attached.

Transaction costs are all internal and external costs associated with an economic exchange, whether it takes place within the boundaries of a firm or in markets.[8] Exhibit 8.2 visualizes the notion of transaction costs. It shows the respective internal transactions costs within Firm A and Firm B, as well as the external transactions that occur when Firm A and Firm B do business with one another.

The total costs of transacting consist of external and internal transaction costs, as follows:

- When companies transact in the open market, they incur **external transaction costs**: the costs of searching for a firm or an individual with whom to contract, and then negotiating, monitoring, and enforcing the contract.

- Transaction costs can occur within the firm as well. Considered **internal transaction costs**, these include costs pertaining to organizing an economic exchange within a firm—for

EXHIBIT 8.2 /

Internal and External Transaction Costs

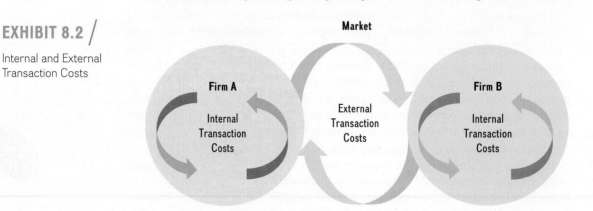

transaction cost economics
A theoretical framework in strategic management to explain and predict the boundaries of the firm, which is central to formulating a corporate strategy that is more likely to lead to competitive advantage.

transaction costs
All internal and external costs associated with an economic exchange, whether within a firm or in markets.

external transaction costs
Costs of searching for a firm or an individual with whom to contract, and then negotiating, monitoring, and enforcing the contract.

internal transaction costs
Costs pertaining to organizing an economic exchange within a hierarchy; also called *administrative costs*.

example, the costs of recruiting and retaining employees; paying salaries and benefits; setting up a shop floor; providing office space and computers; and organizing, monitoring, and supervising work. Internal transaction costs also include administrative costs associated with coordinating economic activity between different business units of the same corporation such as transfer pricing for input factors, and between business units and corporate headquarters including important decisions pertaining to resource allocation, among others. Internal transaction costs tend to increase with organizational size and complexity.

FIRMS VS. MARKETS: MAKE OR BUY?

Transaction cost economics allows us to explain which activities a firm should pursue in-house ("make") versus which goods and services to obtain externally ("buy"). These decisions help determine the boundaries of the firm. In some cases, costs of using the market such as search costs, negotiating and drafting contracts, monitoring work, and enforcing contracts when necessary may be higher than integrating the activity within a single firm and coordinating it through an organizational hierarchy. When the costs of pursuing an activity in-house are less than the costs of transacting for that activity in the market ($C_{in\text{-}house} < C_{market}$), then the firm should *vertically integrate* by owning production of the needed inputs or the channels for the distribution of outputs. In other words, when *firms* are more efficient in organizing economic activity than are *markets,* which rely on contracts among many independent actors, firms should vertically integrate.[9]

For example, rather than contracting in the open market for individual pieces of software code, Google hires programmers to write code in-house. Owning these software development capabilities is valuable to the firm because its costs, such as salaries and employee benefits to in-house computer programmers, are less than what they would be in the open market. More importantly, Google gains economies of scope in software development resources and capabilities and reduces the monitoring costs. Skills acquired in writing software code for its different Internet-based service offerings are transferable to new offerings. Programmers working on the original proprietary software code for the Google search engine leveraged these skills in creating a highly profitable online advertising business (AdWords and AdSense).[10] Although some of Google's software products are open source, such as the Android operating system, many of the company's Internet services are based on closely guarded and proprietary software code. Google, like many leading high-tech companies such as Amazon, Apple, Facebook, and Microsoft, relies on proprietary software code and algorithms, because using the open market to transact for individual pieces of software would be prohibitively expensive. Also, the firms would need to disclose the underlying software code to outside developers, thus negating the value-creation potential.

Firms and markets, as different institutional arrangements for organizing economic activity, have their own distinct advantages and disadvantages, summarized in Exhibit 8.3.

EXHIBIT 8.3 / Organizing Economic Activity: Firms vs. Markets

	Firm	**Markets**
Advantages	• Command and control - Fiat - Hierarchical lines of authority • Coordination • Transaction-specific investments • Community of knowledge	• High-powered incentives • Flexibility
Disadvantages	• Administrative costs • Low-powered incentives • Principal–agent problem	• Search costs • Opportunism - Hold-up • Incomplete contracting - Specifying & measuring performance - Information asymmetries • Enforcement of contracts

The advantages of firms include:

- The ability to make *command-and-control decisions* by fiat along clear hierarchical lines of authority.
- *Coordination* of highly complex tasks to allow for specialized division of labor.
- *Transaction-specific investments,* such as specialized robotics equipment that is highly valuable within the firm, but of little or no use in the external market.
- Creation of a *community of knowledge,* meaning employees within firms have ongoing relationships, exchanging ideas and working closely together to solve problems. This facilitates the development of a deep knowledge repertoire and ecosystem within firms. For example, scientists within a biotech company who worked together developing a new cancer drug over an extended time period may have developed group-specific knowledge and routines. These might lay the foundation for innovation, but would be difficult, if not impossible, to purchase on the open market.[11]

The disadvantages of organizing economic activity within firms include:

- *Administrative costs* because of necessary bureaucracy.
- *Low-powered incentives,* such as hourly wages and salaries. These often are less attractive motivators than the entrepreneurial opportunities and rewards that can be obtained in the open market.
- The *principal–agent problem.*

principal–agent problem
Situation in which an agent performing activities on behalf of a principal pursues his or her own interests.

The **principal–agent problem** is a major disadvantage of organizing economic activity within firms, as opposed to within markets. It can arise when an agent such as a manager, performing activities on behalf of the principal (the owner of the firm), pursues his or her own interests.[12] Indeed, the *separation of ownership and control* is one of the hallmarks of a publicly traded company, and so some degree of the principal–agent problem is almost inevitable.[13] For example, a manager may pursue his or her own interests such as job security and managerial perks (e.g., corporate jets and golf outings) that conflict with the principal's goals—in particular, creating shareholder value. One potential way to overcome the principal–agent problem is to give stock options to managers, thus making them owners. We will revisit the principal–agent problem, with related ideas, in Chapters 11 and 12.

The advantages of markets include:

- *High-powered incentives.* Rather than work as a salaried engineer for an existing firm, for example, an individual can start a new venture offering specialized software. High-powered incentives of the open market include the entrepreneur's ability to capture the venture's profit, to take a new venture through an initial public offering (IPO), or to be acquired by an existing firm. In these so-called *liquidity events,* a successful entrepreneur can make potentially enough money to provide financial security for life.[14]
- *Increased flexibility.* Transacting in markets enables those who wish to purchase goods to compare prices and services among many different providers.

The disadvantages of markets include:

- *Search costs.* On a very fundamental level, perhaps the biggest disadvantage of transacting in markets, rather than owning the various production and distribution activities within the firm itself, entails non-trivial *search costs.* In particular, a firm faces search costs when it must scour the market to find reliable suppliers from among the many firms competing to offer similar products and services. Even more difficult can be the search to find suppliers when the specific products and services needed are not offered by firms currently in the market. In this case, production of supplies would require transaction-specific investments, an advantage of firms.

■ *Opportunism by other parties. Opportunism* is behavior characterized by self-interest seeking with guile (we'll discuss this in more detail later).

■ *Incomplete contracting.* Although market transactions are based on implicit and explicit contracts, all contracts are incomplete to some extent, because not all future contingencies can be anticipated at the time of contracting. It is also difficult to specify expectations (e.g., What stipulates "acceptable quality" in a graphic design project?) or to measure performance and outcomes (e.g., What does "excess wear and tear" mean when returning a leased car?). Another serious hazard inherent in contracting is *information asymmetry* (which we discuss next).

■ *Enforcement of contracts.* It often is difficult, costly, and time-consuming to enforce legal contracts. Not only does litigation absorb a significant amount of managerial resources and attention, but also it can easily amount to several million dollars in legal fees. Legal exposure is one of the major hazards in using markets rather than integrating an activity within a firm's hierarchy.

Frequently, sellers have better information about products and services than buyers, which creates **information asymmetries**, situations in which one party is more informed than another, because of the possession of private information. When firms transact in the market, such unequal information can lead to a *lemons problem.* Nobel Laureate George Akerlof first described this situation using the market for used cars as an example.[15] Assume only two types of cars are sold: good cars and bad cars (lemons). Good cars are worth $8,000 and bad ones are worth $4,000. Moreover, only the seller knows whether a car is good or is a lemon. Assuming the market supply is split equally between good and bad cars, the probability of buying a lemon is 50 percent. Buyers are aware of the general possibility of buying a lemon and thus would like to hedge against it. Therefore, they split the difference and offer $6,000 for a used car. This discounting strategy has the perverse effect of crowding out all the good cars because the sellers perceive their value to be above $6,000. Assuming that to be the case, all used cars offered for sale will be lemons.

The important take-away here is *caveat emptor*—buyer beware. Information asymmetries can result in the crowding out of desirable goods and services by inferior ones. This has been shown to be true in many markets, not just for used cars, but also in e-commerce (e.g., eBay), mortgage-backed securities, and even collaborative R&D projects.[16]

> **information asymmetry**
> Situation in which one party is more informed than another because of the possession of private information.

ALTERNATIVES ON THE MAKE-OR-BUY CONTINUUM

The "make" and "buy" choices *anchor each end of a continuum* from markets to firms, as depicted in Exhibit 8.4. Several alternative hybrid arrangements are available between these two extremes.[17] Moving from transacting in the market ("buy") to full integration ("make"), alternatives include short-term contracts as well as various forms of strategic alliances (long-term contracts, equity alliances, and joint ventures) and parent–subsidiary relationships.

SHORT-TERM CONTRACTS. When engaging in *short-term contracting,* a firm sends out *requests for proposals (RFPs)* to several companies, which initiates competitive bidding for contracts to be awarded with a short duration, generally less than one year.[18] The benefit to this approach lies in the fact that it allows a somewhat longer planning period than individual market transactions. Moreover, the buying firm can often demand lower prices due to the competitive bidding process. The drawback, however, is that firms responding to the RFP have no incentive to make any transaction-specific investments (e.g., buy new machinery

EXHIBIT 8.4 / Alternatives on the Make-or-Buy Continuum

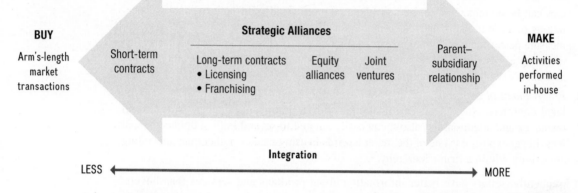

to improve product quality) due to the short duration of the contract. This is exactly what happened in the U.S. automotive industry when GM used short-term contracts for standard car components to reduce costs. When faced with significant cost pressures, suppliers reduced component quality in order to protect their eroding margins. This resulted in lower-quality GM cars, contributing to a competitive advantage vis-à-vis competitors, most notably Toyota but also Ford, which used a more cooperative, longer-term partnering approach with their suppliers.[19]

STRATEGIC ALLIANCES. As we move toward greater integration on the make-or-buy continuum, the next organizational forms are strategic alliances. **Strategic alliances** are voluntary arrangements between firms that involve the sharing of knowledge, resources, and capabilities with the intent of developing processes, products, or services.[20] Alliances have become a ubiquitous phenomenon, especially in high-tech industries. Moreover, strategic alliances can facilitate investments in transaction-specific assets without encountering the internal transaction costs involved in owning firms in various stages of the industry value chain.

 Strategic alliances is an umbrella term that denotes different hybrid organizational forms—among them, long-term contracts, equity alliances, and joint ventures. Given their prevalence in today's competitive landscape as a key vehicle to execute a firm's corporate strategy, we take a quick look at strategic alliances here and then study them in more depth in Chapter 9.

Long-Term Contracts. We noted that firms in short-term contracts have no incentive to make transaction-specific investments. *Long-term contracts,* which work much like short-term contracts but with a duration generally greater than one year, help overcome this drawback. Long-term contracts help facilitate transaction-specific investments. **Licensing,** for example, is a form of long-term contracting in the manufacturing sector that enables firms to commercialize intellectual property such as a patent. The first biotechnology drug to reach the market, Humulin (human insulin), was developed by Genentech and commercialized by Eli Lilly based on a licensing agreement.

 In service industries, **franchising** is an example of long-term contracting. In these arrangements, a franchisor such as McDonald's, Burger King, 7-Eleven, H&R Block, or Subway grants a franchisee (usually an entrepreneur owning no more than a few outlets) the right to use the franchisor's trademark and business processes to offer goods and services that carry the franchisor's brand name. Besides providing the capital to finance the expansion of the chain, the franchisee generally pays an up-front (buy-in) lump sum to the franchisor plus a percentage of revenues.

---

strategic alliances
Voluntary arrangements between firms that involve the sharing of knowledge, resources, and capabilities with the intent of developing processes, products, or services.

licensing
A form of long-term contracting in the manufacturing sector that enables firms to commercialize intellectual property.

franchising
A long-term contract in which a franchisor grants a franchisee the right to use the franchisor's trademark and business processes to offer goods and services that carry the franchisor's brand name.

Equity Alliances. Yet another form of strategic alliance is an *equity alliance*—a partnership in which at least one partner takes partial ownership in the other partner. A partner purchases an ownership share by buying stock or assets (in private companies), and thus making an equity investment. The taking of equity tends to signal greater commitment to the partnership. Strategy Highlight 8.1 describes how soft drink giant Coca-Cola formed an equity alliance with energy-drink maker Monster.

Why is the Coca-Cola Co. forming an equity alliance with Monster Beverage Corporation and not just entering a short- or long-term contract, such as a distribution and profit-sharing agreement? One reason is that an equity investment in Monster might give Coca-Cola an inside look into the company. Gaining more information could be helpful if Coca-Cola decides to acquire Monster in the future. Gaining such private information might not be possible with a mere contractual agreement. Buying time is also helpful so Coca-Cola Co. can see how the wrongful death lawsuits play out, and thus limit the potential downside to Coke's wholesome brand image (as mentioned in Strategy Highlight 8.1).

Moreover, in strategic alliances based on a mere contractual agreement, one transaction partner could attempt to *hold up* the other by demanding lower prices or threatening to

Strategy Highlight 8.1

Is Coke Becoming a Monster?

© David Paul Morris/Bloomberg/Getty Images

While Americans are drinking ever more nonalcoholic beverages, the demand for longtime staples such as the full-calorie Coke or Pepsi are in free fall. More health-conscious consumers are moving away from sugary drinks at the expense of Coke and Pepsi, the two archrivals among regular colas. Unlike in the 1990s, however, Americans are not replacing them with diet sodas, but rather with bottled water and energy drinks. Indeed, Coca-Cola was slow to catch the trend toward bottled water and other more healthy choices such as vitamin water. Protecting its wholesome image, the conservative Coca-Cola Co. shunned energy drinks. The makers of energy drinks, such as 5-hour Energy, Red Bull,

Monster, Rockstar, and Amp Energy, have faced wrongful death lawsuits. PepsiCo, on the other hand, was much more aggressive in moving into the energy-drink business with Amp Energy (owned by PepsiCo) and Rockstar (distributed by PepsiCo).

Albeit late to the party, Coca-Cola decided to not miss out completely on energy drinks, one of the fastest-growing segments in nonalcoholic beverages. After years of deliberation, in 2014 the Coca-Cola Co. formed an equity alliance with Monster Beverage Corporation, spending $2 billion for a 16.7 percent stake in the edgy energy-drink company. This values the privately held Monster Beverage at roughly $12 billion. What might have finally persuaded Coca-Cola to make this decision? Not only was Monster now number one with 40 percent market share of the over $6 billion energy-drink industry, but the company also had settled a number of wrongful death lawsuits out of court. Meanwhile, however, the U.S. Food and Drug Administration is still investigating some 300 "adverse event" reports allegedly linked to the consumption of energy drinks, including 31 deaths. While the Coca-Cola Co. insists that it completed its due diligence before concluding that energy drinks are safe, it hedges its bets with a minority investment in Monster rather than an outright acquisition. This allows the market leader in nonalcoholic beverages to benefit from the explosive growth in energy drinks, while limiting potential exposure of Coca-Cola's wholesome image and brand.[21]

walk away from the agreement (with whatever financial penalties might be included in the contract). This might be a real concern for Monster because Coca-Cola, with about $50 billion in annual sales, is about 20 times larger than Monster with $2.5 billion in revenues. To assuage Monster's concerns, with its equity investment, Coca-Cola made Monster a **credible commitment**—a long-term strategic decision that is both difficult and costly to reverse.

credible commitment
A long-term strategic decision that is both difficult and costly to reverse.

Joint Ventures. In a **joint venture**, which is another special form of strategic alliance, two or more partners create and jointly own a new organization. Since the partners contribute equity to a joint venture, they make a long-term commitment, which in turn facilitates transaction-specific investments. Dow Corning, owned jointly by Dow Chemical and Corning, is an example of a joint venture. Dow Corning focuses on silicone-based technology and employs roughly 10,000 people with $5 billion in annual revenues. That success shows that some joint ventures can be quite large.[22] Hulu, which offers web-based streaming video of TV shows and movies, is also a joint venture, owned by NBC, Fox, and Disney-ABC. Logging 5 million users in 2015, Hulu is a smaller competitor to Netflix with some 50 million users in the United States.

joint venture
A stand-alone organization created and jointly owned by two or more parent companies.

PARENT–SUBSIDIARY RELATIONSHIP. The *parent–subsidiary relationship* describes the most-integrated alternative to performing an activity within one's own corporate family. The corporate parent owns the subsidiary and can direct it via command and control. Transaction costs that arise are frequently due to political turf battles, which may include the capital budgeting process and transfer prices, among other areas. For example, although GM owns its European carmakers (Opel in Germany and Vauxhall in the United Kingdom), it had problems bringing some of their know-how and design of small fuel-efficient cars back into the United States. This failure put GM at a competitive disadvantage vis-à-vis the Japanese competitors when they were first entering the U.S. market with more fuel-efficient cars. In addition, the Japanese carmakers were able to improve the quality and design of their vehicles faster, which enabled them to gain a competitive advantage, especially in an environment of rising gas prices.

The GM versus Opel and Vauxhall parent–subsidiary relationship was burdened by political problems because managers in Detroit did not respect the engineering behind the small, fuel-efficient cars that Opel and Vauxhall made. They were not interested in using European know-how for the U.S. market and didn't want to pay much or anything for it. Moreover, Detroit was tired of subsidizing the losses of Opel and Vauxhall, and felt that its European subsidiaries were manipulating the capital budgeting process.[23] In turn, the Opel and Vauxhall subsidiaries felt resentment toward their parent company: GM had threatened to shut them down as part of its bankruptcy restructuring, whereas they instead hoped to be divested as independent companies.[24]

Having laid a strong theoretical foundation by fully considering transaction cost economics and the boundaries of the firm, we now turn our attention to the firm's position along the vertical industry value chain.

8.3 Vertical Integration along the Industry Value Chain

vertical integration
The firm's ownership of its production of needed inputs or of the channels by which it distributes its outputs.

The first key question when formulating corporate strategy is: In what stages of the industry value chain should the firm participate? Deciding whether to make or buy the various activities in the industry value chain involves the concept of vertical integration. **Vertical integration** is the firm's ownership of its production of needed inputs or of the channels by which it distributes its outputs. Vertical integration can be measured by a firm's value added: What percentage of a firm's sales is generated within the firm's boundaries?[25] The degree of vertical integration tends to correspond to the number of industry value chain stages in which a firm directly participates.

Exhibit 8.5 depicts a generic **industry value chain**. Industry value chains are also called *vertical value chains,* because they depict the transformation of raw materials into finished goods and services along distinct vertical stages. Each stage of the vertical value chain typically represents a distinct *industry* in which a number of different firms are competing. This is also why the expansion of a firm up or down the *vertical* industry value chain is called *vertical* integration.

To explain the concept of vertical integration along the different stages of the industry value chain more fully, let's use your cell phone as an example. This ubiquitous device is the result of a globally coordinated industry value chain of different products and services:

EXHIBIT 8.5 / Backward and Forward Vertical Integration along an Industry Value Chain

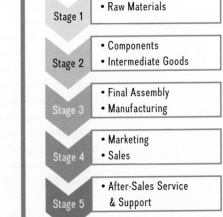

industry value chain
Depiction of the transformation of raw materials into finished goods and services along distinct vertical stages, each of which typically represents a distinct *industry* in which a number of different firms are competing.

- The raw materials to make your cell phone, such as chemicals, ceramics, metals, oil for plastic, and so on, are commodities. In each of these commodity businesses are different companies, such as DuPont (U.S.), BASF (Germany), Kyocera (Japan), and ExxonMobil (U.S.).

- *Intermediate goods and components* such as integrated circuits, displays, touchscreens, cameras, and batteries are provided by firms such as ARM Holdings (UK), Jabil Circuit (U.S.), Intel (U.S.), LG Display (Korea), Altek (Taiwan), and BYD (China).

- *Original equipment manufacturing firms (OEMs)* such as Flextronics (Singapore) or Foxconn (China) typically assemble cell phones under contract for consumer electronics and telecommunications companies such as BlackBerry (Canada), Ericsson (Sweden), Microsoft (U.S., with its acquired Nokia business unit), Samsung (South Korea), and others. If you look closely at an iPhone, for example, you'll notice it says, "Designed by Apple in California. Assembled in China."

- Finally, to get wireless data and voice service, you pick a *service provider* such as AT&T, Sprint, T-Mobile, or Verizon in the United States; América Móvil in Mexico; Oi in Brazil; Orange in France; T-Mobile or Vodafone in Germany; NTT Docomo in Japan; Airtel in India; or China Mobile in China, among others.

In 2015, Google launched a low-cost wireless service in the United States. Called ProjectFi, the wireless service plans offered by Google cost $20 a month for talk and text, including Wi-Fi and international coverage. Each gigabyte of data costs $10 per month. Google's goal is that by providing lower-priced wireless services more people will connect to the Internet, which means more demand for its core online search business and ad-supported YouTube video service. On the downside, initially it is available only with Google phones such as the Nexus 6.[26]

All of these companies—from the raw-materials suppliers to the service providers—make up the global industry value chain that, as a whole, delivers you a working cell phone. Determined by their corporate strategy, each firm decides where in the industry value chain to participate. This in turn defines the vertical boundaries of the firm.

LO 8-4

Describe the two types of vertical integration along the industry value chain: backward and forward vertical integration.

TYPES OF VERTICAL INTEGRATION

Along the industry value chain, there are varying degrees of vertical integration. Some firms participate in only one or a few stages of the industry value chain, while others comprise many if not all stages.

Weyerhaeuser, one of the world's largest paper and pulp companies, is *fully vertically integrated:* All activities are conducted within the boundaries of the firm. Weyerhaeuser owns forests, grows and cuts its timber, mills it, manufactures a variety of different paper and construction products, and distributes them to retail outlets and other large customers. Weyerhaeuser's value added is 100 percent. Weyerhaeuser, therefore, competes in a number of different industries along the entire vertical value chain. As a consequence, it faces different competitors in each stage of the industry value chain.

On the other end of the spectrum are firms that are more or less *vertically disintegrated with a low degree of vertical integration.* These firms focus on only one or a few stages of the industry value chain. Apple, for example, focuses only on design, marketing, and retailing; all other value chain activities are outsourced.

Be aware that *not all industry value chain stages are equally profitable.* Apple captures significant value by designing mobile devices through integration of hardware and software in novel ways, but it outsources the manufacturing to generic OEMs. The logic behind these decisions can be explained by applying Porter's five forces model and the VRIO model. The many small cell phone OEMs are almost completely interchangeable and are exposed to the perils of perfect competition. However, Apple's competencies in innovation, system integration, and marketing are valuable, rare, and unique (non-imitable) resources, and Apple is organized to capture most of the value it creates. Apple's continued innovation through new products and services provides it with a string of temporary competitive advantages.

Exhibit 8.6 displays part of the value chain for smartphones. In this figure, note HTC's transformation from a no-name OEM manufacturer in stage 2 of the value chain to a player in the design, manufacture, and sale of smartphones (stages 1 and 3). It now offers a lineup of innovative and high-performance smartphones under the HTC label.[27]

Firms regularly start out as OEMs and then vertically integrate along the value chain in either a backward and/or forward direction. With these moves, former contractual partners to brand-name phone makers such as Apple and Samsung then become their competitors. OEMs are able to vertically integrate because they acquire the skills needed to compete in adjacent industry value chain activities from their alliance partners, which need to share the technology behind their proprietary phone to enable large-scale manufacturing.

Over time, HTC was able to upgrade its capabilities from merely manufacturing smartphones to also designing products.[28] In doing so, HTC engaged

EXHIBIT 8.6 / HTC's Backward and Forward Integration along the Industry Value Chain in the Smartphone Industry

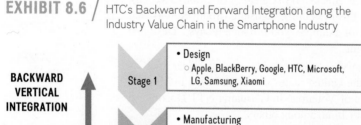

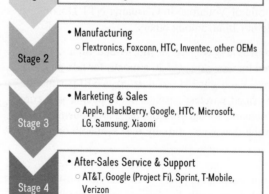

BACKWARD VERTICAL INTEGRATION

HTC

FORWARD VERTICAL INTEGRATION

- **Stage 1**
  - Design
    - Apple, BlackBerry, Google, HTC, Microsoft, LG, Samsung, Xiaomi
- **Stage 2**
  - Manufacturing
    - Flextronics, Foxconn, HTC, Inventec, other OEMs
- **Stage 3**
  - Marketing & Sales
    - Apple, BlackBerry, Google, HTC, Microsoft, LG, Samsung, Xiaomi
- **Stage 4**
  - After-Sales Service & Support
    - AT&T, Google (Project Fi), Sprint, T-Mobile, Verizon

in **backward vertical integration**—moving ownership of activities upstream to the originating inputs of the value chain. Moreover, by moving downstream into sales and increasing its branding activities, HTC has also engaged in **forward vertical integration**—moving ownership of activities closer to the end customer. Although HTC has long benefited from *economies of scale* as an OEM, it is now also benefiting from *economies of scope* through participating in different stages of the industry value chain. For instance, it now can share competencies in product design, manufacturing, and sales, while at the same time attempting to reduce transaction costs.

BENEFITS AND RISKS OF VERTICAL INTEGRATION

To decide the degree and type of vertical integration to pursue, managers need to understand the possible benefits and risks of vertical integration. At a minimum, executives need to proceed with caution, and carefully consider the countervailing risks at the same time they consider the benefits.

BENEFITS OF VERTICAL INTEGRATION. Vertical integration, either backward or forward, can have a number of benefits, including[29]

- Lowering costs.
- Improving quality.
- Facilitating scheduling and planning.
- Facilitating investments in specialized assets.
- Securing critical supplies and distribution channels.

As noted earlier, HTC started as an OEM for brand-name mobile device companies such as Motorola and Nokia and telecom service providers AT&T and T-Mobile. It backwardly integrated into smartphone design by acquiring One & Co., a San Francisco–based design firm.[30] The acquisition allowed HTC to secure scarce design talent and capabilities that it leveraged into the design of smartphones with superior quality and features, enhancing the differentiated appeal of its products. Moreover, HTC can now design phones that leverage its low-cost manufacturing capabilities.

Likewise, forward integration into distribution and sales allows companies to more effectively plan for and respond to changes in demand. HTC's forward integration into sales enables it to offer its products directly to wireless providers such as AT&T, Sprint, and Verizon. HTC even offers unlocked phones directly to the end consumer via its own website. With ownership and control of more stages of the industry value chain, HTC is now in a much better position to respond if, for example, demand for its latest phone should suddenly pick up.

PepsiCo's corporate strategy highlights several benefits to vertical integration. In 2009, PepsiCo forwardly integrated by buying its bottlers in order to obtain more control over its quality, pricing, distribution, and in-store display. This $8 billion purchase reversed a 1999 decision in which PepsiCo sold its bottlers in order to focus on marketing. CEO Indra Nooyi revised PepsiCo's strategic intent to broaden its menu of offerings to include noncarbonated beverages such as flavored water enhanced with vitamins and fruit juices. With an integrated value chain, Nooyi hoped to improve decision making and enhance flexibility to bring these innovative products to market faster, while reducing costs by more than $400 million.[31]

Because of the strategic interdependence of companies in an oligopoly (as studied in Chapter 3), it came as no surprise that only a few months later, in 2010, Pepsi's archrival Coca-Cola responded with its own forward integration move and purchased its bottlers

backward vertical integration
Changes in an industry value chain that involve moving ownership of activities upstream to the originating (inputs) point of the value chain.

forward vertical integration
Changes in an industry value chain that involve moving ownership of activities closer to the end (customer) point of the value chain.

Identify and evaluate benefits and risks of vertical integration.

for $12 billion. Coca-Cola also indicated that more control of manufacturing and distribution was the key driver behind this deal. Moreover, Coca-Cola pegged the expected cost savings at $350 million. Like PepsiCo, Coca-Cola's forward integration represented a major departure from its decade-old business model of large independent bottlers and distributors.[32]

Vertical integration allows firms to increase operational efficiencies through improved coordination and the fine-tuning of adjacent value chain activities. Keeping the downstream value chain activities independent worked well for PepsiCo and Coca-Cola during the 1980s and 1990s, when consumption of soda beverages was on the rise. However, independent bottlers are cost-effective only when doing large-volume business of a few, limited product offerings. With Pepsi's and Coca-Cola's more diversified portfolio of noncarbonated and healthier drinks, the costs of outsourcing bottling and distribution to independent bottlers increased significantly. Some of the independent bottlers even lacked the specialized equipment needed to produce the niche drinks now in demand. In addition, the independent bottlers' direct store-delivery system adds significant costs. To overcome this problem, the soft drink giants had begun to deliver some of their niche products such as Pepsi's Gatorade and SoBe Lifewater and Coca-Cola's Powerade and Glacéau directly to warehouse retailers such as Sam's Club and Costco. By owning the bottlers, both companies can deliver all products through one channel, thus lowering the overall cost of distribution.

Given the increase in costs of using independent bottlers (or the market), the forward integration of PepsiCo and Coca-Cola is in line with predictions derived from transaction cost economics. Controlling the delivery part of the value chain also enhances the soft drink giants' bargaining power when negotiating product price, placement, and promotion. Looking at Porter's five forces model, PepsiCo and Coca-Cola are reducing the bargaining power of buyers and thus shifting the industry structure in their favor. End consumers are likely to benefit from the forward integration in the form of a wider variety of niche drinks. With all these benefits taken together, vertical integration can increase differentiation and reduce costs, thus strengthening a firm's strategic position as the gap between value creation and costs widens.

specialized assets
Unique assets with high opportunity cost: They have significantly more value in their intended use than in their next-best use. They come in three types: site specificity, physical-asset specificity, and human-asset specificity.

Vertical integration along the industry value chain can also facilitate *investments in specialized assets.* What does this mean? **Specialized assets** have a high opportunity cost: They have significantly more value in their intended use than in their next-best use.[33] They can come in several forms:[34]

■ *Site specificity*—assets required to be co-located, such as the equipment necessary for mining bauxite and aluminum smelting.

■ *Physical-asset specificity*—assets whose physical and engineering properties are designed to satisfy a particular customer, such as bottling machinery for Coca-Cola and PepsiCo. Since the bottles have different and often trademarked shapes, they require unique molds. Cans, in contrast, do not require physical-asset specificity because they are generic.

■ *Human-asset specificity*—investments made in human capital to acquire unique knowledge and skills, such as mastering the routines and procedures of a specific organization, which are not transferable to a different employer.

Investments in specialized assets tend to incur high opportunity costs because making the specialized investment opens up the threat of opportunism by one of the partners. *Opportunism* is defined as self-interest seeking with guile.[35] Backward vertical integration is often undertaken to overcome the threat of opportunism and to secure key raw materials.

In an effort to secure supplies and reduce the costs of jet fuel, Delta was the first airline to acquire an oil refinery. In 2012, it purchased a Pennsylvania-based facility from ConocoPhillips. Delta estimates that this backward vertical integration move not only will allow it to provide 80 percent of its fuel internally, but will also save it some $300 million in costs annually. Fuel costs are quite significant for airlines; for Delta, they are almost 40 percent of its total operating cost.[36]

RISKS OF VERTICAL INTEGRATION. It is important to note that the risks of vertical integration can outweigh the benefits. Depending on the situation, vertical integration has several risks, some of which directly counter the potential benefits, including[37]

- Increasing costs.
- Reducing quality.
- Reducing flexibility.
- Increasing the potential for legal repercussions.

A higher degree of vertical integration can lead to increasing costs for a number of reasons. In-house suppliers tend to have higher cost structures because they are not exposed to market competition. Knowing there will always be a buyer for their products reduces their incentives to lower costs. Also, suppliers in the open market, because they serve a much larger market, can achieve economies of scale that elude in-house suppliers. Organizational complexity increases with higher levels of vertical integration, thereby increasing administrative costs such as determining the appropriate transfer prices between an in-house supplier and buyer. Administrative costs are part of internal transaction costs and arise from the coordination of multiple divisions, political maneuvering for resources, the consumption of company perks, or simply from employees slacking off.

The knowledge that there will always be a buyer for their products not only reduces the incentives of in-house suppliers to lower costs, but also can reduce the incentive to increase quality or come up with innovative new products. Moreover, given their larger scale and greater exposure to more customers, external suppliers often can reap higher learning and experience effects and so develop unique capabilities or quality improvements.

A higher degree of vertical integration can also reduce a firm's strategic flexibility, especially when faced with changes in the external environment such as fluctuations in demand and technological change.[38] For instance, when technological process innovations enabled significant improvements in steelmaking, mills such as U.S. Steel and Bethlehem Steel were tied to their fully integrated business models and were thus unable to switch technologies, leading to the bankruptcy of many integrated steel mills. Non-vertically integrated mini-mills such as Nucor and Chaparral, on the other hand, invested in the new steelmaking process and grew their business by taking market share away from the less flexible integrated producers.[39]

U.S. regulators such as the Federal Trade Commission (FTC) and the Justice Department (DOJ) tend to allow vertical integration, arguing that it generally makes firms more efficient and lowers costs, which in turn can benefit customers. However, due to monopoly concerns, vertical integration has not gone entirely unchallenged.[40] The FTC, for example, carefully reviewed PepsiCo's plan to reintegrate its two largest bottlers, which gives the firm full control of about 80 percent of its North American distribution. Before engaging in vertical integration, therefore, managers need to be aware that this corporate strategy can increase the potential for legal repercussions.

WHEN DOES VERTICAL INTEGRATION MAKE SENSE?

U.S. business saw a number of periods of higher than usual vertical integration, and looking back may reveal useful lessons on how a company can make better decisions around its corporate strategy.[41]

In the early days of automobile manufacturing, Ford Motor Company was frustrated by shortages of raw materials and the limited delivery of parts suppliers. In response, Henry Ford decided to own the whole supply chain, so his company soon ran mining operations, rubber plantations, freighters, blast furnaces, glassworks, and its own part manufacturer. In Ford's River Rogue plant, raw materials entered on one end, new cars rolled out the other end. But over time, the costs of vertical integration caught up, both financial costs that undid earlier cost savings and operational costs that hampered the manufacturer's flexibility to respond to changing conditions. Indeed, Ford experienced diseconomies of scale (see Exhibit 6.5) due to its level of vertical integration and the size of its mega-plants.

In the 1970s, the chipmakers and the manufacturers of electronic products tried to move into each others' business. Texas Instruments went downstream into watches and calculators. Bowmar, which at first led the calculator market, tried to go upstream into chip manufacturing and failed. The latter 2000s saw a resurgence of vertical integration. In 2009, General Motors was trying to reacquire Delphi, a parts supplier that it had sold in 1997. In 2010, the major soft drink companies purchased bottling plants (as discussed above).

Rita McGrath suggested that the siren call of vertical integration looms large for companies seeking to completely change the customer's experience: "An innovator who can figure out how to eliminate annoyances and poor interfaces in the chain can build an incredible advantage, based on the customers' desire for that unique solution."[42] So what should company executives do as they contemplate a firm's corporate strategy? As far back as the 1990s, the consulting firm McKinsey was counseling clients that firms had to consider carefully *why* they were looking at integrating along their industry value chain. McKinsey identified the main reason to vertically integrate: failure of vertical markets. **Vertical market failure** occurs when transactions within the industry value chain are too risky, and alternatives to integration are too costly or difficult to administer. This recommendation corresponds with the one derived from transaction cost economics earlier in this chapter. When discussing research on vertical integration, *The Economist* concluded, "Although reliance on [external] supply chains has risks, owning parts of the supply chain can be riskier—for example, few clothing-makers want to own textile factories, with their pollution risks and slim profits." The findings suggest that when a company vertically integrates two or more steps away from its core competency, it fails two-thirds of the time.[43]

The risks of vertical integration and the difficulty of getting it right bring us to look at alternatives that allow companies to gain some of the benefits without the risks of full ownership of the supply chain.

vertical market failure
When the markets along the industry value chain are too risky, and alternatives too costly in time or money.

ALTERNATIVES TO VERTICAL INTEGRATION

LO 8-6

Describe and examine alternatives to vertical integration.

Ideally, one would like to find alternatives to vertical integration that provide similar benefits without the accompanying risks. Taper integration and strategic outsourcing are two such alternatives.

taper integration
A way of orchestrating value activities in which a firm is backwardly integrated but also relies on outside-market firms for some of its supplies and/or is forwardly integrated but also relies on outside-market firms for some of its distribution.

TAPER INTEGRATION. One alternative to vertical integration is **taper integration**. It is a way of orchestrating value activities in which a firm is backwardly integrated, but it also relies on outside-market firms for some of its supplies, and/or is forwardly integrated but also relies on outside-market firms for some if its distribution.[44] Exhibit 8.7 illustrates the concept of taper integration along the vertical industry value chain. Here, the firm sources intermediate goods and components from in-house suppliers as well as outside suppliers. In a similar fashion, a firm sells its products through company-owned retail outlets and through independent retailers. Both Apple and Nike, for example, use taper integration: They own retail outlets but also use other retailers, both the brick-and-mortar type and online.

Taper integration has several benefits:[45]

■ It exposes in-house suppliers and distributors to market competition so that performance comparisons are possible. Rather than hollowing out its competencies by relying too much on outsourcing, taper integration allows a firm to retain and fine-tune its competencies in upstream and downstream value chain activities.[46]

■ Taper integration also enhances a firm's flexibility. For example, when adjusting to fluctuations in demand, a firm could cut back on the finished goods it delivers to external retailers while continuing to stock its own stores.

■ Using taper integration, firms can combine internal and external knowledge, possibly paving the path for innovation.

Based on a study of 3,500 product introductions in the computer industry, researchers have provided empirical evidence that taper integration can be beneficial.[47] Firms that pursued taper integration achieved superior performance in both innovation and financial performance when compared with firms that relied more on vertical integration or strategic outsourcing.

STRATEGIC OUTSOURCING. Another alternative to vertical integration is **strategic outsourcing**, which involves moving one or more internal value chain activities outside the firm's boundaries to other firms in the industry value chain. A firm that engages in strategic outsourcing reduces its level of vertical integration. Rather than developing their own human resource management systems, for instance, firms outsource these non-core activities to companies such as PeopleSoft (owned by Oracle), EDS (owned by HP), or Perot Systems (owned by Dell), which can leverage their deep competencies and produce scale effects.

In the popular media and in everyday conversation, you may hear the term *outsourcing* used to mean sending jobs out of the country. Actually, when outsourced activities take place outside the home country, the correct term is *offshoring* (or *offshore outsourcing*). By whatever name, it is a *huge* phenomenon. For example, Infosys, one of the world's largest technology companies and providers of IT services to many Fortune 100 companies, is located in Bangalore, India. The global offshoring market is estimated to be $1.5 trillion and is expected to grow at a compound annual growth rate of 15 percent. Banking and financial services, IT, and health care are the most active sectors in such offshore outsourcing.[48] More recently, U.S. law firms began to offshore low-end legal work, such as drafting standard contracts and background research, to India.[49] We discuss *global strategy* in detail in Chapter 10.

EXHIBIT 8.7 / Taper Integration along the Industry Value Chain

strategic outsourcing
Moving one or more internal value chain activities outside the firm's boundaries to other firms in the industry value chain.

8.4 Corporate Diversification: Expanding Beyond a Single Market

Early in the chapter, we listed three questions related to corporate strategy and, in particular, the boundaries of the firm. We discussed the first question of defining corporate strategy in detail:

1. *In what stages of the industry value chain should the firm participate?*

Our exploration was primarily in terms of firm boundaries based on the desired extent of vertical integration. We now turn to the second and third questions that determine corporate strategy and the boundaries of the firm:

2. What range of products and services should the firm offer?

3. Where should the firm compete in terms of regional, national, or international markets?

The second question relates to the firm's *degree of diversification:* What range of products and services should the firm offer? In particular, why do some companies compete in a single product market, while others compete in several different product markets? Coca-Cola, for example, focuses on soft drinks and thus on a *single* product market. Its archrival PepsiCo competes directly with Coca-Cola by selling a wide variety of soft drinks and other beverages, and also offering different types of chips such as Lay's, Doritos, and Cheetos, as well as Quaker Oats products such as oatmeal and granola bars. Although PepsiCo is more diversified than Coca-Cola, it has reduced its level of diversification in recent years.

The third and final of the key questions concerns the question of *where to compete* in terms of regional, national, or international markets. This decision determines the firm's geographic focus. For example, why do some firms compete beyond state boundaries, while others are content to focus on the local market? Why do some firms compete beyond their national borders, while others prefer to focus on the domestic market?

Kentucky Fried Chicken (KFC), the world's largest quick-service chicken restaurant chain, operates more than 18,000 outlets in 115 countries.[50] Interestingly, KFC has more restaurants in China with close to 5,000 outlets than in the United States, its birthplace, with some 4,440 outlets. Of course, China has 1.4 billion people and the United States has a mere 320 million. PepsiCo CEO Nooyi was instrumental in spinning out KFC, as well as Pizza Hut and Taco Bell, to reduce PepsiCo's level of diversification. In 1997, the three fast-food chains were established as an independent company under the name Yum Brands. In 2014, Yum Brands had annual revenues of $13 billion. Compare the world's second-largest quick-service chicken restaurant, the privately held Chick-fil-A.[51] KFC and Chick-fil-A are direct competitors in the United States, both specializing in chicken in the fast food market. But Chick-fil-A operates only in the United States; by 2014 it had some 2000 locations across 42 states and earned $5 billion in sales.

Why are KFC and Chick-fil-A pursuing different corporate strategies? Although both companies were founded roughly in the same time period (KFC in 1930 and Chick-fil-A in 1946), one big difference between KFC and Chick-fil-A is the ownership structure. KFC is a publicly traded stock company, as part of Yum Brands; Chick-fil-A is privately owned. Public companies are often expected by shareholders to achieve profitable growth as fast as possible to result in an appreciation of the stock price and thus an increase in shareholder value (see the discussion in Chapter 5). In contrast, private companies generally grow slower than public companies because their growth is mostly financed through retained earnings and debt rather than equity. Before an initial public offering, private companies do not have the option to sell shares (equity) to the public to fuel growth. This is one explanation why KFC focuses on international markets, especially China, where future expected growth continues to be high, while Chick-fil-A focuses on the domestic U.S. market.

Answers to questions about the number of markets to compete in and where to compete geographically relate to the broad topic of **diversification**. A firm that engages in diversification increases the variety of products and services it offers or markets and the geographic regions in which it competes. A *non-diversified company* focuses on a single market, whereas a *diversified company* competes in several different markets simultaneously.[52]

There are various general diversification strategies:

- A firm that is active in several different product markets is pursuing a **product diversification strategy**.

- A firm that is active in several different countries is pursuing a **geographic diversification strategy**.

- A company that pursues *both* a product *and* a geographic diversification strategy simultaneously follows a **product–market diversification strategy**.

Because shareholders expect continuous growth from public companies, managers frequently turn to product and geographic diversification to achieve it. It is therefore not

---

diversification
An increase in the variety of products and services a firm offers or markets and the geographic regions in which it competes.

product diversification strategy
Corporate strategy in which a firm is active in several different product markets.

geographic diversification strategy
Corporate strategy in which a firm is active in several different countries.

product–market diversification strategy
Corporate strategy in which a firm is active in several different product markets *and* several different countries.

surprising that the vast majority of the Fortune 500 companies are diversified to some degree. Achieving performance gains through diversification, however, is not guaranteed. Some forms of diversification are more likely to lead to performance improvements than others. We now discuss which diversification types are more likely to lead to a competitive advantage, and why.

TYPES OF CORPORATE DIVERSIFICATION

LO 8-7

Describe and evaluate different types of corporate diversification.

To understand the different types and degrees of corporate diversification, Richard Rumelt developed a helpful classification scheme that identifies four main types of diversification by looking at two variables:

- The *percentage of revenue* from the dominant or primary business.
- The *relationship of the core competencies* across the business units.

Just knowing the percentage of revenue of the dominant business immediately, (the first variable), lets us identify the first two types. Asking questions about the relationship of core competencies across business units allows us to identify the last two types. The four main types of business diversification are

1. Single business.
2. Dominant business.
3. Related diversification.
4. Unrelated diversification: the conglomerate.

Please note that related diversification (type 3) is divided into two subcategories. We discuss each type of diversification below.

SINGLE BUSINESS. A *single-business firm* derives more than 95 percent of its revenues from one business. The remainder of less than 5 percent of revenue is not (yet) significant to the success of the firm. For example, although Google is active in many different businesses, it obtains more than 95 percent of its revenues ($70 billion in 2014) from online advertising.[53]

>95%

DOMINANT BUSINESS. A *dominant-business firm* derives between 70 and 95 percent of its revenues from a single business, but it pursues at least one other business activity that accounts for the remainder of revenue. The dominant business shares competencies in products, services, technology, or distribution. In the schematic figure shown here, and those to follow the remaining revenue (*R*), is generally obtained in other strategic business units (SBU) within the firm.*

70%-95%

R

RELATED DIVERSIFICATION. A firm follows a **related diversification strategy** when it derives less than 70 percent of its revenues from a single business activity and obtains revenues from other lines of business linked to the primary business activity. The rationale behind related diversification is to benefit from economies of scale and scope: These multi-business firms can pool and share resources as well as leverage competencies across different business lines. The two variations of this type, which we explain next, relate to how much the other lines of business benefit from the core competencies of the primary business activity.

related diversification strategy
Corporate strategy in which a firm derives less than 70 percent of its revenues from a single business activity and obtains revenues from other lines of business that are linked to the primary business activity.

---

* This remaining revenue is by definition less than that of the primary business. Note also that the areas of the boxes in this and following graphics are not scaled to specific percentages.

related-constrained diversification strategy
A kind of related diversification strategy in which executives pursue only businesses where they can apply the resources and core competencies already available in the primary business.

Related-Constrained Diversification. A firm follows a **related-constrained diversification strategy** when it derives less than 70 percent of its revenues from a single business activity and obtains revenues from other lines of business related to the primary business activity. Executives engage in such a new business opportunity only when they can leverage their existing competencies and resources. Specifically, the choices of alternative business activities are limited—constrained—by the fact that they need to be related through common resources, capabilities, and competencies.

ExxonMobil's strategic move into natural gas is an example of related diversification. In 2009, ExxonMobil bought XTO Energy, a natural gas company, for $31 billion.[54] XTO Energy is known for its core competency to extract natural gas from unconventional places such as shale rock—the type of deposits currently being exploited in the United States. ExxonMobil hopes to leverage its core competency in the exploration and commercialization of oil into natural gas extraction. The company is producing nearly equal amounts of crude oil and natural gas, making it the world's largest producer of natural gas. The company believes that roughly 50 percent of the world's energy for the next 50 years will continue to come from fossil fuels, and that its diversification into natural gas, the cleanest of the fossil fuels in terms of greenhouse gas emissions, will pay off. ExxonMobil's strategic scenario may be right on the mark. Because of major technological advances in hydraulic fracking to extract oil and natural gas from shale rock by companies such as XTO Energy, the United States has emerged as the world's richest country in natural gas resources and the third-largest producer of crude oil, just behind Saudi Arabia and Russia.[55]

related-linked diversification strategy
A kind of related diversification strategy in which executives pursue various businesses opportunities that share only a limited number of linkages.

Related-Linked Diversification. If executives consider new business activities that share only a limited number of linkages, the firm is using a **related-linked diversification strategy**. Amazon.com, featured in the ChapterCase, began business by selling only one product: books. Over time, it expanded into CDs and later gradually leveraged its online retailing capabilities into a wide array of product offerings. As the world's largest online retailer, and given the need to build huge data centers to service its peak holiday demand, Amazon decided to leverage spare capacity into cloud computing, again benefiting from economies of scope and scale. Amazon now also offers its Kindle line of tablet computers and proprietary content, as well as instant video streaming via its Prime service. Amazon follows a related-linked diversification strategy.

unrelated diversification strategy
Corporate strategy in which a firm derives less than 70 percent of its revenues from a single business and there are few, if any, linkages among its businesses.

conglomerate
A company that combines two or more strategic business units under one overarching corporation; follows an unrelated diversification strategy.

UNRELATED DIVERSIFICATION: THE CONGLOMERATE. A firm follows an **unrelated diversification strategy** when less than 70 percent of its revenues comes from a single business and there are few, if any, linkages among its businesses. A company that combines two or more strategic business units under one overarching corporation and follows an unrelated diversification strategy is called a **conglomerate**. Some research evidence suggests that an unrelated diversification strategy can be advantageous in emerging economies.[56]

This arrangement helps firms gain and sustain competitive advantage because it allows the conglomerate to overcome institutional weaknesses in emerging economies, such as a lack of capital markets and well-defined legal systems and property rights. Companies such as LG (representing a uniquely South Korean form of organization, the *chaebol*), Berkshire Hathaway, and the Japanese Yamaha group are all considered conglomerates due to their unrelated diversification strategy. Strategy Highlight 8.2 features the Tata group of India, a conglomerate that follows an unrelated diversification strategy.

Exhibit 8.8 summarizes the four main types of diversification—single business, dominant business, related diversification (including its subcategories related-constrained and related-linked diversification), and unrelated diversification.

EXHIBIT 8.8 / Four Main Types of Diversification

Revenues from Primary Business	Type of Diversification	Competencies (in products, services, technology or distribution)	Examples	Graphic
>95%	Single Business	Single business leverages its competencies.	Coca-Cola Google Facebook	>95%
70%–95%	Dominant Business	Dominant and minor businesses share competencies.	Harley-Davidson Nestlé UPS	70%-95% R
<70%	Related Diversification			
	Related-Constrained	Businesses generally share competencies.	ExxonMobil Johnson & Johnson Nike	<70% R — R
	Related-Linked	Some businesses share competencies.	Amazon Disney GE	<70% R — R
	Unrelated Diversification (Conglomerate)	Businesses share few, if any, competencies.	Berkshire Hathaway Yamaha Tata	<70% R R

Note: *R* = Remainder revenue, generally in other strategic business units (SBU) within the firm.

Source: Adapted from R.P. Rumelt (1974), *Strategy, Structure, and Economic Performance* (Boston, MA: Harvard Business School Press).

LEVERAGING CORE COMPETENCIES FOR CORPORATE DIVERSIFICATION

LO 8-8

Apply the core competence–market matrix to derive different diversification strategies.

In Chapter 4, when looking inside the firm, we introduced the idea that competitive advantage can be based on core competencies. Core competencies are unique strengths embedded deep within a firm. They allow companies to increase the perceived value of their product and service offerings and/or lower the cost to produce them.[58] Examples of core competencies are:

- Walmart's ability to effectively orchestrate a globally distributed supply chain at low cost.
- Infosys' ability to provide high-quality information technology services at a low cost by leveraging its global delivery model. This implies taking work to the location where it makes the best economic sense, based on the available talent and the least amount of acceptable risk and lowest cost.

To survive and prosper, companies need to grow. This mantra holds especially true for publicly owned companies, because they create shareholder value through profitable growth. Managers respond to this relentless growth imperative by leveraging their existing core competencies to find future growth opportunities. Gary Hamel and C.K. Prahalad advanced the **core competence–market matrix**, depicted in Exhibit 8.9, as a way to guide

core competence–market matrix
A framework to guide corporate diversification strategy by analyzing possible combinations of existing/new core competencies and existing/new markets.

Strategy Highlight 8.2

The Tata Group:
Integration at the Corporate Level

Tata Nano GenX, starting at $3,100
© Sam Panthaky/AFP/Getty Images

Range Rover, starting at $85,000
© Graeme Lamb/Alamy RF

Founded in 1868 as a trading company by then 29-year-old entrepreneur Jamsetji Nusserwanji Tata, the Tata group today has roughly 500,000 employees and $100 billion in annual revenues. A widely diversified multinational conglomerate, headquartered in Mumbai, India, it is active in industries as wide ranging as tea, hospitality, steel, IT, communications, power, and automobiles. Some of its strategic business units are giants in their own right. The Tata group includes Asia's largest software company (TCS) and India's largest steelmaker. It also owns the renowned Taj Hotels Resorts & Palaces.

In 2008, Tata Motors attracted attention in the automotive world when it bought Jaguar and Land Rover from Ford for $2.3 billion. In 2009, Tata Motors attracted even more attention when it unveiled its Tata Nano, the world's lowest-priced car. It accommodates passengers just over 6 feet tall, goes from zero to 60 mph in 30 seconds, and gets 67 mpg, beating the Toyota Prius for fuel consumption. The Tata Nano, clearly a no-frills car, exemplifies a focused low-cost strategy. It lacks a radio, glove compartment, and operable rear hatch, and its top speed is a little over 60 mph. Nonetheless, being about 50 percent cheaper than the next-lowest-cost car, Tata Motors hopes to find tens of millions of customers in the Indian and Chinese markets. Initial sales were disappointing, however. Apparently low cost alone was not sufficient to lure new buyers into the market. The first Nano models might have provided too little along the value dimension. Tata responded in 2015 with the Nano GenX, which has more options and customizability in an attempt to appeal to younger consumers, including an automatic transmission, Bluetooth compatibility and USB ports for the car's audio system, and a special feature designed to allow the car

to creep forward with the engine at idle when the brake is released—a valuable feature in countries such as China and India where massive traffic jams are the norm.

The Tata group is attempting to carve out different strategic positions in its different segments of the automotive industry. Moreover, the Tata group hopes to integrate distinctly different business strategies at the corporate level. In particular, the luxury division of Tata Motors, with the Jaguar and Land Rover brands, is pursuing a focused differentiation strategy; the Nano car division is pursuing a focused cost-leadership strategy. Although their respective strategic profiles are basically the opposite of one another (differentiation versus low-cost), both business-level strategies are aimed at a specific segment of the market. Jaguar and Land Rover are luxury brands in their respective categories and appeal to affluent buyers; the Nano is clearly a lowest-cost offering, focused on a very specific market niche. Indeed, the Nano focuses on *non-consumption:* Buyers of the Nano will not be replacing other vehicles. They will be first-time car buyers moving up from bicycles and mopeds. Ratan Tata, then chairman of the Tata group, conceived of the Nano while seeing a family of four cramped on a moped in heavy rains.

By offering the Nano, Tata Motors is still hoping to bring millions of new car buyers from emerging countries into the market and thus increase the size of the automobile market. The Nano GenX is an attempt to offer more features and compete in the space occupied by competitors Maruti Suzuki and Hyundai. Taken together, Tata's corporate strategy is attempting to integrate different strategic positions, pursued by different strategic business units, each with its own profit and loss responsibility.[57]

managerial decisions in regard to diversification strategies. The first task for managers is to identify their existing core competencies and understand the firm's current market situation. When applying an existing or new dimension to core competencies and markets, four quadrants emerge, each with distinct strategic implications.

The lower-left quadrant combines existing core competencies with existing markets. Here, managers must come up with ideas of how to leverage existing core competencies to improve the firm's current market position. Bank of America is one of the largest banks in the United States and has at least one customer in 50 percent of U.S. households.[59] Developed from the Bank of Italy and started in San Francisco, California, in 1904, it became the Bank of America and Italy in 1922. Over the next 60 years it grew in California and then nationally into a major banking powerhouse. And then in 1997, in what was the largest bank acquisition of its time, NationsBank bought Bank of America.

You could say that acquisitions were a NationsBank specialty. While still the North Carolina National Bank (NCNB), one of its unique core competencies was identifying, appraising, and integrating acquisition targets. In particular, it bought smaller banks to supplement its organic growth throughout the 1970s and '80s, and from 1989 to 1992, NCNB purchased over 200 regional community and thrift banks to further improve its market position. It then turned its core competency to national banks, with the goal of becoming the first nationwide bank. Known as NationsBank in the 1990s, it purchased Barnett Bank, BankSouth, FleetBank, LaSalle, CountryWide Mortgages, and its eventual namesake, Bank of America. This example illustrates how NationsBank, rebranded as Bank of America since 1998, honed and deployed its core competency of selecting, acquiring, and integrating other commercial banks to grow dramatically in size and geographic scope and emerge as one of the leading banks in the United States. As a key vehicle of corporate strategy, we study acquisitions in more detail in Chapter 9.

The lower-right quadrant of Exhibit 8.9 combines existing core competencies with new market opportunities. Here, managers must strategize about how to redeploy and recombine existing core competencies to compete in future markets. At the height of the financial crisis in the fall of 2008, Bank of America bought the investment bank Merrill Lynch for $50 billion.[60] Although many problems ensued for Bank of America

EXHIBIT 8.9

The Core Competence–
Market Matrix

Source: Adapted from
G. Hamel and C.K. Prahalad
(1994), *Competing for the
Future* (Boston, MA: Harvard
Business School Press).

following the Merrill Lynch acquisition, it is now the bank's investment and wealth management division. Bank of America's corporate managers applied an existing competency (acquiring and integrating) into a new market (investment and wealth management). The combined entity is now leveraging economies of scope through cross-selling when, for example, consumer banking makes customer referrals for investment bankers to follow up.[61]

The upper-left quadrant combines new core competencies with existing market opportunities. Here, managers must come up with strategic initiatives to build new core competencies to protect and extend the company's current market position. For example, in the early 1990s, Gatorade dominated the market for sports drinks, a segment in which it had been the original innovator. Some 25 years earlier, medical researchers at the University of Florida had created the drink to enhance the performance of the Gators, the university's football team, thus the name Gatorade. Stokely-Van Camp commercialized and marketed the drink, and eventually sold it to Quaker Oats. PepsiCo brought Gatorade into its lineup of soft drinks when it acquired Quaker Oats in 2001.

By comparison, Coca-Cola had existing core competencies in marketing, bottling, and distributing soft drinks, but had never attempted to compete in the sports-drink market. Over a 10-year R&D effort, Coca-Cola developed competencies in the development and marketing of its own sports drink, Powerade, which launched in 1990. In 2014, Powerade held about 25 percent of the sports-drink market, making it a viable competitor to Gatorade, which still holds about 70 percent of the market.[62]

Finally, the upper-right quadrant combines new core competencies with new market opportunities. Hamel and Prahalad call this combination "mega-opportunities"—those that hold significant future-growth opportunities. At the same time, it is likely the most challenging diversification strategy because it requires building new core competencies to create and compete in future markets.

Salesforce.com, for example, is a company that employs this diversification strategy well.[63] In recent years, Salesforce experienced tremendous growth, the bulk of it coming from the firm's existing core competency in delivering customer relationship management (CRM) software to its clients. Salesforce's product distinguished itself from the competition by providing software as a service via cloud computing: Clients did not need to install software or manage any servers, but could easily access the CRM through a web browser (a business model called *software as a service,* or *SaaS*). In 2007, Salesforce recognized an emerging market for *platform as a service* (*PaaS*) offerings, which would enable clients to build their own software solutions that are accessed the same way as the Salesforce CRM. Seizing the opportunity, Salesforce developed a new competency in delivering software development and deployment tools that allowed its customers to either extend their existing CRM offering or build completely new types of software. Today, Salesforce's Force.com offering is one of the leading providers of PaaS tools and services.

Taken together, the core competence–market matrix provides guidance to executives on how to diversify in order to achieve continued growth. Once managers have a clear understanding of their firm's core competencies (see Chapter 4), they have four options to formulate corporate strategy:

Four Options to Formulate Corporate Strategy via Core Competencies

1. Leverage existing core competencies to improve current market position.
2. Build new core competencies to protect and extend current market position.
3. Redeploy and recombine existing core competencies to compete in markets of the future.
4. Build new core competencies to create and compete in markets of the future.

CORPORATE DIVERSIFICATION AND FIRM PERFORMANCE

Explain when a diversification strategy creates a competitive advantage and when it does not.

Corporate managers pursue diversification to gain and sustain competitive advantage. But does corporate diversification indeed lead to superior performance? To answer this question, we need to evaluate the performance of diversified companies. The critical question to ask when doing so is whether the individual businesses are worth more under the company's management than if each were managed individually.

The diversification-performance relationship is a function of the underlying type of diversification. A cumulative body of research indicates an inverted U-shaped relationship between the type of diversification and overall firm performance, as depicted in Exhibit 8.10.[64] High and low levels of diversification are generally associated with lower overall performance, while moderate levels of diversification are associated with higher firm performance. This implies that companies that focus on a single business, as well as companies that pursue unrelated diversification, often fail to achieve additional value creation. Firms that compete in single markets could potentially benefit from economies of scope by leveraging their core competencies into adjacent markets.

Firms that pursue unrelated diversification are often unable to create additional value. They experience a **diversification discount** in the stock market: The stock price of such highly diversified firms is valued at less than the sum of their individual business units.[65] For the last decade or so, GE experienced a diversification discount, as its capital unit contributed 50 percent of profits on one-third of the conglomerate's revenues. The presence of the diversification discount in GE's depressed stock price was a major reason GE's CEO, Jeffrey Immelt, decided in 2015 to spin out GE Capital. On the day of the announcement, GE's stock price jumped 11 percent, adding some $28 billion to GE's market capitalization. This provides some idea of the diversification discount that firms pursuing unrelated diversification may experience.[66] Through this restructuring of the corporate portfolio, GE is now better positioned to focus more fully on its core competencies in industrial engineering and management processes.

diversification discount Situation in which the stock price of highly diversified firms is valued at less than the sum of their individual business units.

diversification premium Situation in which the stock price of related-diversification firms is valued at greater than the sum of their individual business units.

The presence of the diversification discount, however, depends on the institutional context. Although it holds in developed economies with developed capital markets, some research evidence suggests that an unrelated diversification strategy can be advantageous in emerging economies as mentioned when discussing the Tata group in Strategy Highlight 8.2.[67] Here, unrelated diversification may help firms gain and sustain competitive advantage because it allows the conglomerate to overcome institutional weaknesses in emerging economies such as a lack of a functioning capital market.

In contrast, companies that pursue related diversification are more likely to improve their performance. They create a **diversification premium**: The stock price of related-diversification firms is valued at greater than the sum of their individual business units.[68]

EXHIBIT 8.10 / The Diversification-Performance Relationship

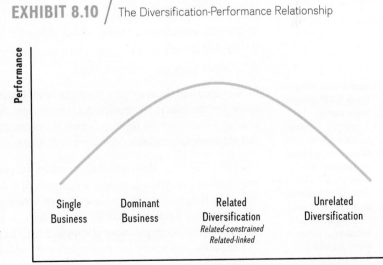

Source: Adapted from L.E. Palich, L.B. Cardinal, and C.C. Miller (2000), "Curvilinearity in the diversification-performance linkage: An examination of over three decades of research," *Strategic Management Journal* 21: 155–174.

Corporate Strategy	Sources of Value Creation (*V*)	Sources of Costs (*C*)
Vertical Integration	• Can lower costs (but can go other way too) • Can improve quality (but can go other way too) • Can facilitate scheduling and planning (but can go other way too) • Facilitating investments in specialized assets • Securing critical supplies and distribution channels	• Can increase costs (but can go other way too) • Can reduce quality (but can go other way too) • Can reduce flexibility (but can go other way too) • Increasing potential for legal repercussions

Related Diversification	• Economies of scope
	
	• Economies of scale
	
	• Financial economies
	   ■ Restructuring
	   ■ Internal capital markets
		• Coordination costs
		• Influence costs

Unrelated Diversification	• Financial economies
	   ■ Restructuring
	   ■ Internal capital markets
		• Influence costs

Why is this so? At the most basic level, a corporate diversification strategy enhances firm performance when its value creation is greater than the costs it incurs. Exhibit 8.11 lists the sources of value creation and costs for different corporate strategies, for vertical integration as well as related and unrelated diversification. For diversification to enhance firm performance, it must do at least one of the following:

■ Provide *economies of scale,* which reduces costs.

■ Exploit *economies of scope,* which increases value.

■ Reduce costs *and* increase value.

We discussed these drivers of competitive advantage—economies of scale, economies of scope, and increase in value and reduction of costs—in depth in Chapter 6 in relation to business strategy. Other potential benefits to firm performance when following a diversification strategy include *financial economies,* resulting from *restructuring* and using *internal capital markets.*

RESTRUCTURING. *Restructuring* describes the process of reorganizing and divesting business units and activities to refocus a company in order to leverage its core competencies more fully. The Belgium-based Anheuser-Busch InBev sold Busch Entertainment, its theme park unit that owns SeaWorld and Busch Gardens, to a group of private investors for roughly $3 billion. This strategic move allows InBev to focus more fully on its core business.[69]

Corporate executives can restructure the portfolio of their firm's businesses, much like an investor can change a portfolio of stocks. One helpful tool to guide corporate portfolio planning is the **Boston Consulting Group (BCG) growth-share matrix,** shown in Exhibit 8.12.[70] This matrix locates the firm's individual SBUs in two dimensions: relative market share (horizontal axis) and speed of market growth (vertical axis). The firm plots its SBUs into one of four categories in the matrix: dog, cash cow, star, and question mark.

Boston Consulting Group (BCG) growth-share matrix
A corporate planning tool in which the corporation is viewed as a portfolio of business units, which are represented graphically along relative market share (horizontal axis) and speed of market growth (vertical axis). SBUs are plotted into four categories (dog, cash cow, star, and question mark), each of which warrants a different investment strategy.

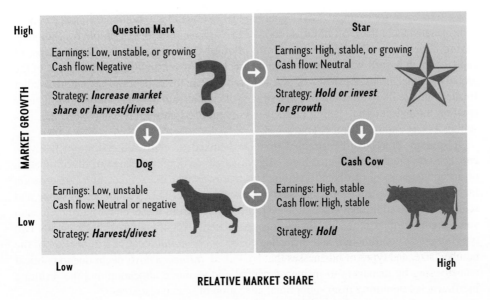

EXHIBIT 8.12 /

Restructuring the Corporate Portfolio: The Boston Consulting Group Growth-Share Matrix

Each category warrants a different investment strategy. All four categories shape the firm's corporate strategy.

SBUs identified as *dogs* are relatively easy to identify: They are the underperforming businesses. Dogs hold a small market share in a low-growth market; they have low and unstable earnings, combined with neutral or negative cash flows. The strategic recommendations are either to *divest* the business or to *harvest* it. This implies stopping investment in the business and squeezing out as much cash flow as possible before shutting it or selling it.

Cash cows, in contrast, are SBUs that compete in a low-growth market but hold considerable market share. Their earnings and cash flows are high and stable. The strategic recommendation is to invest enough into cash cows to hold their current position and to avoid having them turn into dogs (as indicated by the arrow).

A corporation's *star* SBUs hold a high market share in a fast-growing market. Their earnings are high and either stable or growing. The recommendation for the corporate strategist is to invest sufficient resources to hold the star's position or even increase investments for future growth. As indicated by the arrow, stars may turn into cash cows as the market in which the SBU is situated slows after reaching the maturity stage of the industry life cycle.

Finally, some SBUs are *question marks:* It is not clear whether they will turn into dogs or stars (as indicated by the arrows in Exhibit 8.12). Their earnings are low and unstable, but they might be growing. The cash flow, however, is negative. Ideally, corporate executives want to invest in question marks to increase their relative market share so they turn into stars. If market conditions change, however, or the overall market growth slows, then a question-mark SBU is likely to turn into a dog. In this case, executives would want to harvest the cash flow or divest the SBU.

INTERNAL CAPITAL MARKETS. *Internal capital markets* can be a source of value creation in a diversification strategy if the conglomerate's headquarters does a more efficient job of allocating capital through its budgeting process than what could be achieved in external capital markets. Based on private information, corporate managers are in a position to discover which of their strategic business units will provide the highest return on invested capital. In addition, internal capital markets may allow the company to access capital at a lower cost.

Until recently, for example, GE Capital brought in close to $70 billion in annual revenues and generated more than half of GE's profits.[71] In combination with GE's triple-A debt rating, having access to such a large finance arm allowed GE to benefit from a lower cost of capital, which in turn was a source of value creation in itself. In 2009, at the height of the global financial crises, GE lost its AAA debt rating. The lower debt rating and the smaller finance unit are likely to result in a higher cost of capital, and thus a potential loss in value creation through internal capital markets. (As mentioned above, GE announced that it is selling its GE Capital business unit.)

A strategy of related-constrained or related-linked diversification is more likely to enhance corporate performance than either a single or dominant level of diversification or an unrelated level of diversification. The reason is that the sources of value creation include not only restructuring, but also the potential benefits of economies of scope and scale. To create additional value, however, the benefits from these sources of incremental value creation must outweigh their costs. A related-diversification strategy entails two types of costs: coordination and influence costs. *Coordination costs* are a function of the number, size, and types of businesses that are linked. *Influence costs* occur due to political maneuvering by managers to influence capital and resource allocation and the resulting inefficiencies stemming from suboptimal allocation of scarce resources.[72]

8.5 ◄► Implications for the Strategist

An effective corporate strategy increases a firm's chances to gain and sustain a competitive advantage. By formulating corporate strategy, executives make important choices along three dimensions that determine the boundaries of the firm:

- **The degree of vertical integration**—in what stages of the industry value chain to participate.
- **The type of diversification**—what range of products and services to offer.
- **The geographic scope**—where to compete.

EXHIBIT 8.13 / Dynamic Corporate Strategy: Nike vs. adidas

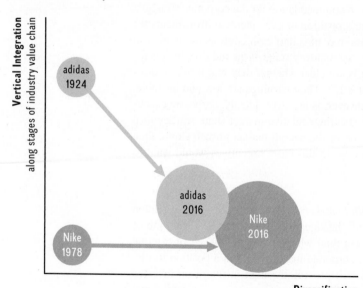

Since a firm's external environment never remains constant over time, *corporate strategy needs to be dynamic over time.* As firms grow, they tend to diversify and globalize to capture additional growth opportunities. Exhibit 8.13 shows the dynamic nature of corporate strategy through decisions made by two top competitors in the sports footwear and apparel industry: Nike and adidas.

Adidas was founded in 1924 in Germany. It began its life in the laundry room of a small apartment. Two brothers focused on one product: athletic shoes. Initially, adidas was a fairly integrated manufacturer of athletic shoes. The big breakthrough for the company came in 1954 when the underdog West Germany won the soccer World Cup in adidas cleats. As the world markets globalized and became more competitive in the decades after World War II, adidas not only vertically disintegrated to focus mainly on the design of athletic shoes but also diversified into sports apparel. Adidas' annual revenues are $20 billion. It is a diversified company active across the globe in sports shoes (40 percent of revenues), sports apparel (50 percent of revenues), and sports equipment (10 percent of revenues). The change in adidas' corporate strategy from a small, highly integrated single business to a disintegrated and diversified global company is shown in Exhibit 8.13.

Nike is the world's leader in sports shoes and apparel with annual sales of $30 billion. Founded in 1978, and thus much younger than adidas, Nike was vertically disintegrated from the very beginning. After moving beyond importing Japanese shoes to the United States, Nike focused almost exclusively on R&D, design, and marketing of running shoes. Although Nike diversified into different lines of business, it stayed true to its vertical disintegration by focusing on only a few activities (see Exhibit 8.13). Nike is a global company and its revenues come from sports shoes (50 percent) and apparel (25 percent), as well as sports equipment and other businesses, such as affiliate brands Cole Haan, Converse, Hurley, and Umbro. The changes in the strategic positions shown in Exhibit 8.13 highlight the dynamic nature of corporate strategy. Also, keep in mind that the relationship between diversification strategy and competitive advantage depends on the *type of diversification*. There exists an inverted U-shaped relationship between the level of diversification and performance improvements. On average, related diversification (either related-constrained or related-linked such as in the Nike and adidas example) is most likely to lead to superior performance because it taps into multiple sources of value creation (economies of scale and scope; financial economies). To achieve a net positive effect on firm performance, however, related diversification must overcome additional sources of costs such as coordination and influence costs.

In the next chapter, we discuss strategic alliances in more depth as well as mergers and acquisitions, both are critical tools in executing corporate strategy. In Chapter 10, we take a closer look at geographic diversification by studying how firms compete for competitive advantage around the world.

CHAPTER**CASE 8** / Consider This...

AMAZON.COM CONTINUES TO diversify at a relentless pace. Besides offering same-day delivery of groceries in some metropolitan areas and testing drones for even faster distribution, Amazon now plans to capture a large piece of the over $10 billion college bookstore market. In a pilot project, Amazon initiated a student-centered program at three large universities: Purdue University, the University of California, Davis, and the University of Massachusetts Amherst. The goal of Amazon Campus is co-branded university-specific websites that offer textbooks, paraphernalia such as the ubiquitous logo sweaters and baseball hats, as well as ramen noodles!

As part of this new campus initiative, Amazon offers its Prime membership to students at a 50 percent discount ($49 a year) and guarantees unlimited next-day delivery of any goods ordered online, besides all the other Prime membership benefits (free streaming of media content, loaning one e-book a month for free, discounts on hardware, etc.). To accomplish next-day delivery, Amazon is building fashionable delivery centers on campus, university co-branded such as "amazon@purdue." Once a package arrives, students receive a text message and can then retrieve it via code-activated lockers or from Amazon employees directly. The on-campus delivery facilities also serve as student return centers.

Amazon's new campus initiative allows it to bind a younger generation of shoppers ever closer into its web of products, services, and content. Next-day delivery makes students less likely to shop at traditional campus bookstores. Amazon also has a history of selling textbooks at a discount in comparison to old-line campus bookstores. All course materials automatically qualify for next-day delivery and do not require a Prime membership. The Amazon Campus initiative is predicted to save students $200 to $400 a year on textbooks and other supplies.

Questions

1. Amazon.com continues to spend billions on seemingly unrelated diversification efforts. Do you believe these efforts contribute to Amazon gaining and sustaining a competitive advantage? Why or why not?

2. Amazon.com is now over 20 years old and makes some $100 billion in annual revenues. As an investor, would it concern you that Amazon.com has yet to deliver any profits? Why or why not? How much longer do you think investors will be patient with Jeff Bezos as he continues to pursue billion-dollar diversification initiatives?

3. One of the most profitable business endeavors that Amazon pursues is its cloud service offering, AWS. In 2014, AWS revenues were an estimated $6 billion, but bringing in $1 billion in profits. What is Amazon's core business? Is AWS related to Amazon's core business? Why or why not? Some investors are pressuring Jeff Bezos to spin out AWS as a standalone company. Do you agree with this corporate strategy recommendation? Why or why not? Hint: Do you believe AWS would be more valuable within Amazon or as a standalone company?

TAKE-AWAY CONCEPTS

This chapter defined corporate strategy and then looked at two fundamental corporate strategy topics—vertical integration and diversification—as summarized by the following learning objectives and related take-away concepts.

LO 8-1 / Define corporate strategy and describe the three dimensions along which it is assessed.

- Corporate strategy addresses "where to compete." Business strategy addresses "how to compete."

- Corporate strategy concerns the boundaries of the firm along three dimensions: (1) industry value chain, (2) products and services, and (3) geography (regional, national, or global markets).

- To gain and sustain competitive advantage, any corporate strategy must support and strengthen a firm's strategic position, regardless of whether it is a differentiation, cost-leadership, or blue ocean strategy.

LO 8-2 / Explain why firms need to grow, and evaluate different growth motives.

- Firm growth is motivated by the following: increasing profits, lowering costs, increasing market power, reducing risk, and managerial motives.

- Not all growth motives are equally valuable.

  - Increasing profits and lowering expenses are clearly related to enhancing a firm's competitive advantage.

  - Increasing market power can also contribute to a greater competitive advantage, but can also result in legal repercussions such as antitrust lawsuits.

  - Growing to reduce risk has fallen out of favor with investors, who argue that they are in a better position to diversify their stock portfolio in comparison to a corporation with a number of unrelated strategic business units.

  - Managerial motives such as increasing company perks and job security are not legitimate reasons a firm needs to grow.

LO 8-3 / Describe and evaluate different options firms have to organize economic activity.

- Transaction cost economics help managers decide what activities to do in-house ("make") versus what services and products to obtain from the external market ("buy").

- When the costs to pursue an activity in-house are less than the costs of transacting in the market

$(C_{in\text{-}house} < C_{market})$, then the firm should vertically integrate.

- Principal–agent problems and information asymmetries can lead to market failures, and thus situations where internalizing the activity is preferred.

- A principal–agent problem arises when an agent, performing activities on behalf of a principal, pursues his or her own interests.

- Information asymmetries arise when one party is more informed than another because of the possession of private information.

- Moving from less integrated to more fully integrated forms of transacting, alternatives include short-term contracts, strategic alliances (including long-term contracts, equity alliances, and joint ventures), and parent–subsidiary relationships.

LO 8-4 / Describe the two types of vertical integration along the industry value chain: backward and forward vertical integration.

- Vertical integration denotes a firm's addition of value—what percentage of a firm's sales is generated by the firm within its boundaries.

- Industry value chains (vertical value chains) depict the transformation of raw materials into finished goods and services. Each stage typically represents a distinct industry in which a number of different firms compete.

- Backward vertical integration involves moving ownership of activities upstream nearer to the originating (inputs) point of the industry value chain.

- Forward vertical integration involves moving ownership of activities closer to the end (customer) point of the value chain.

LO 8-5 / Identify and evaluate benefits and risks of vertical integration.

- Benefits of vertical integration include securing critical supplies and distribution channels, lowering costs, improving quality, facilitating scheduling and planning, and facilitating investments in specialized assets.

- Risks of vertical integration include increasing costs, reducing quality, reducing flexibility, and increasing the potential for legal repercussions.

LO 8-6 / Describe and examine alternatives to vertical integration.

- Taper integration is a strategy in which a firm is backwardly integrated but also relies on outside-market firms for some of its supplies, and/or is forwardly integrated but also relies on outside-market firms for some if its distribution.

- Strategic outsourcing involves moving one or more value chain activities outside the firm's boundaries to other firms in the industry value chain. Offshoring is the outsourcing of activities outside the home country.

LO 8-7 / Describe and evaluate different types of corporate diversification.

- A single-business firm derives 95 percent or more of its revenues from one business.

- A dominant-business firm derives between 70 and 95 percent of its revenues from a single business, but pursues at least one other business activity.

- A firm follows a related diversification strategy when it derives less than 70 percent of its revenues from a single business activity, but obtains revenues from other lines of business that are linked to the primary business activity. Choices within a related diversification strategy can be related-constrained or related-linked.

- A firm follows an unrelated diversification strategy when less than 70 percent of its revenues come from a single business, and there are few, if any, linkages among its businesses.

LO 8-8 / Apply the core competence–market matrix to derive different diversification strategies.

- When applying an existing/new dimension to core competencies and markets, four quadrants emerge, as depicted in Exhibit 8.9.

- The lower-left quadrant combines existing core competencies with existing markets. Here, managers need to come up with ideas of how to leverage existing core competencies to improve their current market position.

- The lower-right quadrant combines existing core competencies with new market opportunities.

Here, managers need to think about how to redeploy and recombine existing core competencies to compete in future markets.

■ The upper-left quadrant combines new core competencies with existing market opportunities. Here, managers must come up with strategic initiatives of how to build new core competencies to protect and extend the firm's current market position.

■ The upper-right quadrant combines new core competencies with new market opportunities. This is likely the most challenging diversification strategy because it requires building new core competencies to create and compete in future markets.

LO 8-9 / **Explain when a diversification strategy creates a competitive advantage and when it does not.**

■ The diversification-performance relationship is a function of the underlying type of diversification.

■ The relationship between the type of diversification and overall firm performance takes on the shape of an inverted U (see Exhibit 8.10).

■ Unrelated diversification often results in a diversification discount: The stock price of such highly diversified firms is valued at less than the sum of their individual business units.

■ Related diversification often results in a diversification premium: The stock price of related-diversification firms is valued at greater than the sum of their individual business units.

■ In the BCG matrix, the corporation is viewed as a portfolio of businesses, much like a portfolio of stocks in finance (see Exhibit 8.12). The individual SBUs are evaluated according to relative market share and the speed of market growth, and are plotted using one of four categories: dog, cash cow, star, and question mark. Each category warrants a different investment strategy.

■ Both low levels and high levels of diversification are generally associated with lower overall performance, while moderate levels of diversification are associated with higher firm performance.

KEY TERMS

Backward vertical integration (p. 267)
Boston Consulting Group (BCG) growth-share matrix (p. 280)
Conglomerate (p. 274)
Core competence–market matrix (p. 277)
Corporate strategy (p. 255)
Credible commitment (p. 264)
Diversification (p. 272)
Diversification discount (p. 279)
Diversification premium (p. 279)
External transaction costs (p. 258)
Forward vertical integration (p. 267)
Franchising (p. 262)

Geographic diversification strategy (p. 272)
Industry value chain (p. 265)
Information asymmetry (p. 261)
Internal transaction costs (p. 258)
Joint venture (p. 264)
Licensing (p. 262)
Principal–agent problem (p. 260)
Product diversification strategy (p. 272)
Product–market diversification strategy (p. 272)
Related-constrained diversification strategy (p. 274)

Related diversification strategy (p. 273)
Related-linked diversification strategy (p. 274)
Specialized assets (p. 268)
Strategic alliances (p. 262)
Strategic outsourcing (p. 271)
Taper integration (p. 270)
Transaction cost economics (p. 258)
Transaction costs (p. 258)
Unrelated diversification strategy (p. 274)
Vertical integration (p. 264)
Vertical market failure (p. 270)

DISCUSSION QUESTIONS

1. When Walmart decided to incorporate grocery stores into some locations and created "supercenters," was this a business-level strategy of differentiation or a corporate strategy of diversification? Why? Explain your answer.

2. How can related diversification create a competitive advantage for the firm? Keeping the advantages of related diversification in mind, think back to the example of Delta's vertical integration decision to acquire an oil refinery—clearly an unrelated

diversification move. What challenges might Delta confront in operating this refinery? Think of the strategic concepts you have learned and how they can help you evaluate Delta's decision.

3. Franchising is widely used in the casual dining and fast food industry, yet Starbucks is quite

successful with a large number of company-owned stores. In 2014 Starbucks had over 7,000 company-owned stores in the United States. How do you explain this difference? Is Starbucks bucking the trend of other food-service stores, or is something else going on?

ETHICAL/SOCIAL ISSUES

1. The chapter notes that some firms choose to outsource their human resource management systems. If a firm has a core value of respecting its employees and rewarding top performance with training, raises, and promotions, does outsourcing HR management show a lack of commitment by the firm? HR management systems are software applications that typically manage payroll, benefits, hiring and training, and performance appraisal. What are the advantages and disadvantages of this decision? Think of ways that a firm can continue to show its commitment to treat employees with respect.

2. Nike is a large and successful firm in the design of athletic shoes. It could easily decide to forward-integrate to manufacture the shoes it designs. Therefore, the firm has a credible threat over its current manufacturers. If Nike has no intention of actually entering the manufacturing arena, is its supply chain management team being ethical with the current manufacturers if the team mentions this credible threat numerous times in annual pricing negotiations? Why or why not? What aspects of Nike's agreement with its manufacturing partners do you believe is emphasized in negotiations?

SMALL GROUP EXERCISES

//// Small Group Exercise 1

Agriculture is one of the largest and oldest industries in the world. In the United States and many other countries, farmers often struggle to turn a profit given the variances of weather and commodity prices. Some working farms are turning to tourism as an additional and complementary revenue source. A study from the U.S. Census of Agriculture in 2007 found nearly 25,000 farms providing some level of agritourism and recreation services. While this number was actually down from the 2002 census, revenues overall had more than doubled, from roughly $202,200 in 2002 to roughly $567,000 in 2007. In 2014, in response to rapid growth, the National Agritourism Professionals Association was formed to help farmers learn how to add this aspect of business to their traditional farms and ranches.

Perhaps one of the most successful large companies leading this marriage of industries is a dairy farm in Indiana: Fair Oaks Farms (www.fofarms.com). Fair Oaks Farms is home to 30,000 cows and produces

enough milk to feed 8 million people. Fair Oaks is also participating in the education market as a popular destination for school field trips. Other attractions include the "Birthing Barn," where calf births can be viewed live; the Cheese Factory; and Mooville, a themed outdoor play area. Each year, Fair Oaks Farms hosts more than 500,000 tourists, who come to see the hands-on adventure center and the working milking operations. A video of the operation by the CEO is available at www.youtube.com/watch?v=Dz_gE4887. Such ingenious business diversification can offer many benefits to the agriculture industry.[73]

1. What other industrial or commercial industries could benefit from such potential tourist or recreational revenues? Discuss what new and complementary capabilities would need to be developed in order to succeed.

2. In your group, list other industry combinations you have seen be successful. Consider why you think the combination has been a success.

//// Small Group Exercise 2

In the ChapterCase 8 *Consider This* section, we learned about the trial rollout of Amazon Campus, an initiative developed to compete directly with university bookstores. This is a good corporate strategy for Amazon for many reasons—among them, it provides the company deeper access into the shopping behavior of college students, as well as of their media viewing purchases and habits. It also represents another large competitive threat to Barnes & Noble, which runs more than 700 campus bookstores (and made $1.7 billion in sales in 2014). To make it beneficial for universities to partner with Amazon, Amazon pays the schools between 0.5 and 2.5 percent of all Amazon purchases made through the university website. Purdue University, one of the first universities to sign on to this initiative, expects to earn $1.7 million from Amazon over the course of its four-year contract.

In June 2015 Barnes & Noble filed papers to spin off its college bookstore unit into a separate company called Barnes & Noble Education (BNED on the NYSE). The firm stated the split would allow each business to focus on its core. Barnes & Noble will focus on the retail business, which has suffered from online shopping and digital books. The new firm will focus on the higher educational market, putting it perhaps in a better position to seek acquisitions on its own.[74]

1. In your small group, discuss any potential ethical issues with Amazon paying the university administration for direct access into the campus's course textbook system.

2. While Amazon as a firm continues to diversify its products, services, and markets under one corporate umbrella, why do firms such as Barnes & Noble choose to split into separate firms for greater focus on each piece of the business? Do these different strategies align with the core competencies of each? It may be helpful to review Exhibit 8.9.

3. If your team was asked to consult for Barnes & Noble Education, which corporate strategies would you recommend to the company's senior leadership?

STRATEGY TERM PROJECT

The HP Running Case, a related activity for each strategy term project module, is available in Connect.

//// Module 8: Vertical Integration

In this module, you will study the boundaries of the firm you have selected for your strategy project in reference to the vertical value chain activities of its industry.

1. Draw the vertical value chain for your firm's industry. List the major firms in each important activity along the chain (see Exhibits 8.5 and 8.6 as examples). Note that a firm's name may appear multiple times in the value chain. This indicates some level of vertical integration by the firm. If your firm is in many different industries (e.g., GE), then choose the dominant industry or the one that intrigues you the most and use only that one for this analysis.

2. Is your firm highly vertically integrated? If yes, does it also employ taper integration?

3. Are any of the vertical value chain operations offshored? If so, list some of the pros and cons of having this part of the value chain outside the home country.

4. Use the preceding vertical value chain to identify the corporate strategy of the firm. In other words, where within the industry has the firm chosen to compete? Based on where it competes, describe what you now see as its corporate strategy.

5. In Module 2, you were asked to identify the mission and major goals for your selected company. Go back to that information now and compare the mission and goals to what you have found as the corporate strategy. Are the mission, goals, and corporate strategy in alignment? Do you see any holes or conflicts among these three elements? Can you relate the performance of the firm to this finding in any way? (If all three are consistent, is this a well-performing unit?) If there is a conflict between the corporate strategy and the mission, does this lack of alignment contribute to performance problems? Why or why not?

*my*STRATEGY

How Diversified Are You?

Corporations diversify by investing time and resources into new areas of business. As individuals, each of us makes choices about how to spend our time and energies. Typically, we could divide our time between school, work, family, sleep, and play. During high-stress work projects, we likely devote more of our time to work; when studying for final exams or a professional board exam (such as the CPA exam), we probably spend more time and effort in the "student learning" mode. This manner of dividing our time can be thought of as "personal diversification." Just as companies can invest in related or unrelated activities, we make similar choices. While we attend college, we may choose to engage in social and leisure activities with campus colleagues, or we may focus on classwork at school and spend our "play time" with an entirely separate set of people.

Using Exhibit 8.8 as a guide, list each of your major activity areas. Think of each of these as a business. (If you are literally "all work and no play," you are a single-business type of personal diversification.) Instead of revenues, estimate the percentage of *time* you spend per week in each activity. (Most people will be diversified, though some may be dominant perhaps in school or work.) To assess your degree of *relatedness* and *unrelatedness*, consider the subject matter and community involved with each activity. For example, if you are studying ballet and working as an accountant, those would be largely unrelated activities (unless you are an accountant for a ballet company!).

1. What conclusions do you derive based on your personal diversification strategy?

2. Do you need to make adjustments to your portfolio of activities? Explain the reasons for your answer.

3. Let's consider dynamics—has your level of diversification changed over time (say, over the last five years)? If so, how and why? If not, why? Looking toward the future, do you expect your level of diversification to change? Why or why not?

ENDNOTES

1. For an in-depth discussion of Amazon.com, see: Rothaermel, F.T., and Michael McKay (2015), Case MHE- MHE-FTR-033-1259420477, "Amazon.com, Inc.," http://create.mheducation.com/. Also see: Bensinger, G., "Amazon plans to add its own line of food," *The Wall Street Journal,* May 28, 2015; Bensinger, G., "Amazon makes a push on college campuses," *The Wall Street Journal,* February 1, 2015; Nicas, J., and G. Bensinger, "Technical hurdles delay drone deliveries," *The Wall Street Journal,* March 20, 2015; Stone, B. (2014), *The Everything Store: Jeff Bezos and the Age of Amazon* (New York: Back Bay Books); "How far can Amazon go?," *The Economist,* June 21, 2014; "Relentless.com," *The Economist,* June 21, 2014; Bensinger, G., "Amazon to open first brick-and-mortar site," *The Wall Street Journal,* October 9, 2014; and O'Connor, C., "The consumer economy: retail, and the people inventing it," *Forbes,* April 23, 2013.

2. Rindova, V.P., and S. Kotha (2001), "Continuous 'morphing': Competing through dynamic capabilities, form, and function," *Academy of Management Journal* 44: 1263–1280.

3. Collis, D.J. (1995), "The scope of the corporation," *Harvard Business School Note,* 9-795-139.

4. For a discussion of behavioral economics in general and executive incentives in particular, see: Kahneman, D. (2011), *Thinking, Fast and Slow* (New York: Farrar, Straus and Giroux); Ariely, D. (2009), *Predictably Irrational: The Hidden Forces That Shape Our Decisions* (New York: Harper Perennial); Kahneman, D. (2003), "Maps of bounded rationality: Psychology for behavioral economics," *The American Economic Review* 93: 1449–1475; and Thaler, R.H., and C.R. Sunstein (2003), *Nudge: Improving Decisions About Health, Wealth, and Happiness* (New York: Farrar, Straus and Giroux).

5. For recent discussion and detailed data on firm performance and CEO pay for some 300 companies, see Lublin, J.S. (2015), "How much the best-performing and worst-performing ceos got paid. WSJ ranking shows top performers aren't the highest paid," *The Wall Street Journal,* June 25, 2015.

6. Kogut, B., and U. Zander (1992), "Knowledge of the firm, combinative capabilities, and the replication of technology," *Organization Science* 3: 383–397; O'Connor, G.C., and M. Rice (2001), "Opportunity recognition and breakthrough innovation in large firms," *California Management Review* 43: 95–116; O'Connor, G.C., and R.W. Veryzer (2001), "The nature of market visioning for technology-based radical innovation," *Journal of Product Innovation Management* 18: 231–224.

7. The literature on transaction cost economics is rich and expanding. For important theoretical and empirical contributions, see: Folta, T.B. (1998), "Governance and uncertainty: The trade-off between administrative control and commitment," *Strategic Management Journal* 19: 1007–1028; Klein, B., R. Crawford, and A. Alchian (1978), "Vertical integration, appropriable rents, and the competitive contracting process," *Journal of Law and Economics* 21: 297–326; Leiblein, M.J., and D.J. Miller (2003), "An empirical examination of transformation- and firm-level influences on the vertical boundaries of the firm," *Strategic Management Journal* 24: 839–859;

Leiblein, M.J., J. J. Reuer, and F. Dalsace (2002), "Do make or buy decisions matter? The influence of organizational governance on technological performance," *Strategic Management Journal* 23: 817–833; Mahoney, J. (1992), "The choice of organizational form: Vertical financial ownership versus other methods of vertical integration," *Strategic Management Journal* 13: 559–584; Mahoney, J.T. (2005), *Economic Foundations of Strategy* (Thousand Oaks, CA: Sage); Williamson, O.E. (1975), *Markets and Hierarchies* (New York: Free Press); Williamson, O.E. (1981), "The economics of organization: The transaction cost approach," *American Journal of Sociology* 87: 548–577; and Williamson, O.E. (1985), *The Economic Institutions of Capitalism* (New York: Free Press).

8. This draws on: Mahoney, *Economic Foundations of Strategy;* Williamson, *Markets and Hierarchies;* Williamson, "The economics of organization: The transaction cost approach"; Williamson, *The Economic Institutions of Capitalism;* and Hart, O., and O. Moore (1990), "Property rights and the nature of the firm," *Journal of Political Economy* 98: 1119–1158.

9. Highlighting the relevance of research on transaction costs, both Ronald Coase (1991) and Oliver Williamson (2009), who further developed and refined Coase's initial insight, were each awarded a Nobel Prize in economics.

10. Levy, S. (2011), *In the Plex: How Google Thinks, Works, and Shapes Our Lives* (New York: Simon & Schuster).

11. Grigoriou, K., and F.T. Rothaermel (2014), "Structural microfoundations of innovation: The role of relational stars," *Journal of Management* 40: 586–615.

12. This is based on: Fama, E. (1980), "Agency problems and the theory of the firm," *Journal of Political Economy* 88: 375–390; Jensen, M., and W. Meckling (1976), "Theory of the firm: Managerial behavior, agency costs and ownership structure," *Journal of Financial Economics* 3: 305–360; and Berle, A., and G. Means (1932), *The Modern Corporation and Private Property* (New York: Macmillan).

13. Berle and Means, *The Modern Corporation and Private Property.*

14. This discussion draws on: Zenger, T.R., and W.S. Hesterly (1997), "The disaggregation of corporations: Selective intervention, high-powered incentives, and molecular units," *Organization Science* 8: 209–222; and Zenger, T.R., and S.G. Lazzarini (2004), "Compensating for innovation: Do small firms offer high-powered incentives that lure talent and motivate effort," *Managerial and Decision Economics* 25: 329–345.

15. This discussion draws on: Akerlof, G.A. (1970), "The market for lemons: Quality uncertainty and the market mechanism," *Quarterly Journal of Economics* 94: 488–500.

16. Pisano, G.P. (1997), "R&D performance, collaborative arrangements, and the market-for-know-how: A test of the 'lemons' hypothesis in biotechnology," *Working Paper No. 97-105,* Harvard Business School; Lerner, J., and R.P. Merges (1998), "The control of technology alliances: An empirical analysis of the biotechnology industry," *Journal of Industrial Economics* 46: 125–156; Huston, J.H., and R.W. Spencer (2002), "Quality, uncertainty and the Internet: The market for cyber lemons," *The American Economist* 46: 50–60; Rothaermel, F.T., and D.L. Deeds (2004), "Exploration and exploitation alliances in biotechnology: A system of new product development," *Strategic Management Journal* 25: 201–221; Downing, C., D. Jaffee, and N. Walla (2009), "Is the market for mortgage-backed securities a market for lemons?" *Review of Financial Studies* 22: 2457–2494.

17. This discussion draws on: Williamson, O. E. (1991), "Comparative economic organization: The analysis of discrete structural alternatives," *Administrative Science Quarterly* 36: 269–296.

18. Since short-term contracts are unlikely to be of strategic significance, they are not subsumed under the term strategic alliances, but rather are considered to be mere contractual arrangements.

19. Dyer, J.H. (1997), "Effective interfirm collaboration: How firms minimize transaction costs and maximize transaction value," *Strategic Management Journal* 18: 535–556.

20. This is based on: Gulati, R. (1998), "Alliances and networks," *Strategic Management Journal* 19: 293–317; Ireland, R.D., M.A. Hitt, and D. Vaidyanath (2002), "Alliance management as a source of competitive advantage," *Journal of Management* 28: 413–446; Hoang, H., and F.T. Rothaermel (2005), "The effect of general and partner-specific alliance experience on joint R&D project performance," *Academy of Management Journal* 48: 332–345; and Lavie, D. (2006), "The competitive advantage of interconnected firms: An extension of the resource-based view," *Academy of Management Review* 31: 638–658.

21. Esterl, M., "Coke says it's ready to let Monster in," *The Wall Street Journal,* May 26, 2015; Esterl, M., "Soft drinks hit 10th year of decline," *The Wall Street Journal,* March 26, 2015; Esterl, M., and J.S. Lublin, "Why didn't Coke buy all of Monster?," *The Wall Street Journal,* August 15, 2014; Esterl, M., "Coca-Cola buys stake in Monster Beverage," *The Wall Street Journal,* August 14,

2014; and McGrath, M., "Coca-Cola buys stake in Monster Beverage for $2 Billion," *Forbes,* August 14, 2014.

22. www.dowcorning.com.

23. "Rising from the ashes in Detroit," *The Economist,* August 19, 2010.

24. "Small cars, big question," *The Economist,* January 21, 2010.

25. Tucker, I., and R.P. Wilder (1977), "Trends in vertical integration in the U.S. manufacturing sector," *Journal of Industrial Economics* 26: 81–97; Harrigan, K.R. (1984), "Formulating vertical integration strategies," *Academy of Management Review* 9: 638–652; Harrigan, K.R. (1986), "Matching vertical integration strategies to competitive conditions," *Strategic Management Journal* 7: 535–555; Rothaermel, F.T., M.A. Hitt, and L.A. Jobe (2006), "Balancing vertical integration and strategic outsourcing: Effects on product portfolios, new product success, and firm performance," *Strategic Management Journal* 27: 1033–1056.

26. Barr, A., and R. Knutson, "Google Project Fi wireless service undercuts phone plans," *The Wall Street Journal,* April 22, 2015.

27. "HTC clones Nexus One, launches 3 new phones," *Wired.com,* February 16, 2010.

28. www.htc.com.

29. Harrigan, K.R. (1984), "Formulating vertical integration strategies," *Academy of Management Review* 9: 638–652; Harrigan, K.R. (1986), "Matching vertical integration strategies to competitive conditions," *Strategic Management Journal* 7: 535–555.

30. "HTC clones Nexus One, launches 3 new phones."

31. "Companies more prone to go vertical," *The Wall Street Journal,* December 1, 2009.

32. This is based on: "Pepsi bids $6 billion for largest bottlers, posts flat profit," *The Wall Street Journal,* April 20, 2009; "PepsiCo buys bottlers for $7.8 billion," *The Wall Street Journal,* August 5, 2009; "Companies more prone to go vertical," *The Wall Street Journal,* December 1, 2009; and "Coca-Cola strikes deal with bottler," *The Wall Street Journal,* February 25, 2010.

33. Williamson, *Markets and Hierarchies;* Williamson, "The economics of organization: The transaction cost approach"; Williamson, *The Economic Institutions of Capitalism;* Poppo, L., and T. Zenger (1998), "Testing alternative theories of the firm: Transaction cost, knowledge based, and measurement explanations for make or buy decisions in information services," *Strategic Management Journal* 19: 853–878.

34. Williamson, *Markets and Hierarchies;* Williamson, "The economics of organization:

The transaction cost approach"; Williamson, *The Economic Institutions of Capitalism.*

35. Williamson, *Markets and Hierarchies.*

36. "Delta to buy refinery in effort to lower jet-fuel costs," *The Wall Street Journal,* April 30, 2012.

37. Harrigan, "Formulating vertical integration strategies"; Harrigan, "Matching vertical integration strategies to competitive conditions"; Afuah, A. (2001), "Dynamic boundaries of the firm: Are firms better off being vertically integrated in the face of a technological change?" *Academy of Management Journal* 44: 1211–1228; Rothaermel, F.T., M.A. Hitt, and L.A. Jobe (2006), "Balancing vertical integration and strategic outsourcing: Effects on product portfolios, new product success, and firm performance," *Strategic Management Journal* 27: 1033–1056.

38. Afuah, "Dynamic boundaries of the firm: Are firms better off being vertically integrated in the face of a technological change?"

39. Ghemawat, P. (1993), "Commitment to a process innovation: Nucor, USX, and thin slab casting," *Journal of Economics and Management Strategy* 2: 133–161; Christensen, C.M., and M.E. Raynor (2003), *The Innovator's Solution: Creating and Sustaining Successful Growth* (Boston, MA: Harvard Business School Press).

40. "Companies more prone to go vertical," *The Wall Street Journal,* December 1, 2009.

41. This section is based on: McGrath, R. (2009), "Why vertical integration is making a comeback," *Harvard Business Review,* December 2; "Vertical integration: Moving on up," *The Economist,* March 7, 2009; Stuckey, J., and D. White, "When and when not to vertically integrate," *McKinsey Quarterly,* August 1993; and Buzzell, R.D. (1983), "Is vertical integration profitable?" *Harvard Business Review,* January.

42. McGrath, "Why vertical integration is making a comeback."

43. "Vertical integration: Moving on up."

44. Harrigan, "Formulating vertical integration strategies."

45. This is based on: Harrigan, "Formulating vertical integration strategies"; and Harrigan, "Matching vertical integration strategies to competitive conditions."

46. This is based on the following: Prahalad and Hamel argued that a firm that outsources too many activities risks hollowing out ("unlearning") its core competencies because the firm no longer participates in key adjacent value chain activities. A similar argument has been made by Prahalad, C.K., and G. Hamel (1990), "The core competence of the corporation," *Harvard Business Review,* May–June; and Teece, D.J. (1986), "Profiting from technological innovation: Implications for integration, collaboration, licensing and public policy," *Research Policy* 15: 285–305.

47. Rothaermel, F.T., et al., "Balancing vertical integration and strategic outsourcing."

48. "Global outsourcing market to be worth $1,430bn by 2009," *Computer Business Review,* August 2007.

49. "Passage to India," *The Economist,* June 26, 2010.

50. KFC and Yum Brands data drawn from 2014 Yum Brands Annual Report (http://yum.com/annualreport/); www.kfc.com/about/; and www.yum.com/investors/restcounts.asp (see downloadable spreadsheet with detailed data).

51. Chick-fil-A data drawn from www.chick-fil-a.com/Company/Highlights-Fact-Sheets.

52. This section is based on: Rumelt, R.P. (1974), *Strategy, Structure, and Economic Performance* (Boston, MA: Harvard Business School Press); Montgomery, C.A. (1985), "Product-market diversification and market power," *Academy of Management Review* 28: 789–798.

53. Google annual reports.

54. This is based on: ExxonMobil Annual Reports; "Oil's decline slows Exxon, Chevron profit growth," *The Wall Street Journal,* January 30, 2009; "The greening of ExxonMobil," *Forbes,* August 24, 2009; Friedman, T.L. (2008), *Hot, Flat, and Crowded. Why We Need a Green Revolution—And How It Can Renew America* (New York: Farrar, Straus and Giroux); "Exxon to acquire XTO Energy in $31 billion stock deal," *The Wall Street Journal,* December 14, 2009; and "ExxonMobil buys XTO Energy," *The Economist,* December 17, 2009.

55. "The shale revolution: What could go wrong?" *The Wall Street Journal,* September 6, 2012; and "U.S. oil notches record growth," *The Wall Street Journal,* June 12, 2013.

56. This is based on: Peng, M.W. (2005), "What determines the scope of the firm over time? A focus on institutional relatedness," *Academy of Management Review* 30: 622–633; Peng, M.W. (2000), *Business Strategies in Transition Economies* (Thousand Oaks, CA: Sage); and Peng, M.W., and P.S. Heath (1996), "The growth of the firm in planned economies in transitions: Institutions, organizations, and strategic choice," *Academy of Management Review* 21: 492–528.

57. The history of the Tata group is documented at: www.tata.com/htm/heritage/HeritageOption1.html; "The Tata group," *The Economist,* March 3, 2011; "Ratan Tata's legacy," *The Economist,* December 1, 2012; and "A new boss at Tata," *The Economist,* December 1, 2012. See also, Dyer, J., H. Gregersen, and C.M. Christensen (2011). *The* *Innovator's DNA: Mastering the Five Skills of Disruptive Innovators* (Boston, MA: Harvard Business Review Press); McLain, S. (2013), "Why the world's cheapest car flopped," *The Wall Street Journal,* October 14, 2013; Abrahams, D. (2015), "Tata's Nano goes upmarket with GenX - IOL Motoring," retrieved May 22, 2015, from www.iol.co.za/motoring/cars/tata/tata-s-nano-goes-upmarket-with-genx-1.1861112#.VV-FdU9Viko; Thakkar, K. (2015), "Launch of GenX Nano a 'make or break' moment for the brand; car to be priced at Rs 2.2-2.9 lakh," retrieved May 22, 2015, from http://articles.economictimes.indiatimes.com/2015-05-19/auto/62369237_1_smart-city-car-tata-nano-girish-wagh

58. Prahalad and Hamel, "The core competence of the corporation."

59. This discussion is based on: Burt, C., and F.T. Rothaermel (2013), "Bank of America and the new financial landscape," in Rothaermel, F.T., *Strategic Management* (New York: McGraw-Hill), http://mcgrawhillcreate.com/rothaermel.

60. Bank of America had long coveted Merrill Lynch, a premier investment bank. Severely weakened by the global financial crisis, Merrill Lynch became a takeover target, and Bank of America made a bid. In the process, Bank of America learned that Merrill Lynch's exposure to subprime mortgages and other exotic financial instruments was much larger than previously disclosed. Other problems included Merrill Lynch's payments of multimillion-dollar bonuses to many employees, despite the investment bank's having lost billions of dollars (in 2008). After learning this new information, Bank of America (under its then-CEO Ken Lewis) attempted to withdraw from the Merrill Lynch takeover. The Federal Reserve Bank, under the leadership of its chairman, Ben Bernanke, insisted that Bank of America fulfill the agreement, noting that the takeover was part of a grand strategy to save the financial system from collapse. Once Bank of America shareholders learned that Lewis had not disclosed the problems at Merrill Lynch, they first stripped him of his chairmanship of the board of directors and later fired him as CEO. For a detailed and insightful discussion on the Merrill Lynch takeover by Bank of America, see Lowenstein, R. (2010), *The End of Wall Street* (New York: Penguin Press).

61. "Bank of America and Merrill Lynch," *The Economist,* April 14, 2010.

62. "In Gatorade war, Pepsi seems to have deliberately given up market share to Coke," *Business Insider,* February 1, 2012; and Sozzi, B., "Gatorade turns 50: What the sports drink must do to keep its edge," *TheStreet.com,* May 12, 2015.

63. "Oracle vs. salesforce.com," Harvard Business School Case Study, 9-705-440; "How to innovate in a downturn," *The Wall Street Journal,* March 18, 2009; and Dyer, Gregersen, and Christensen, *The Innovator's DNA.*

64. Palich, L.E., L.B. Cardinal, and C.C. Miller (2000), "Curvilinearity in the diversification-performance linkage: An examination of over three decades of research," *Strategic Management Journal* 21: 155–174.

65. This is based on: Lang, L.H.P., and R.M. Stulz (1994), "Tobin's *q*, corporate diversification, and firm performance," *Journal of Political Economy* 102: 1248–1280; Martin, J.D., and A. Sayrak (2003), "Corporate diversification and shareholder value: A survey of recent literature," *Journal of Corporate Finance* 9: 37–57; and Rajan, R., H. Servaes, and L. Zingales (2000), "The cost of diversity: The diversification discount and inefficient investment," *Journal of Finance* 55: 35–80.

66. Mann, T., and V. McGrane, "GE to cash out of banking business," *The Wall Street Journal,* April 10, 2015.

67. This is based on: Peng and Heath, "The growth of the firm in planned economies in transitions"; Peng, *Business Strategies in Transition Economies;* and Peng, "What determines the scope of the firm over time? A focus on institutional relatedness."

68. Villalonga, B. (2004), "Diversification discount or premium? New evidence from the business information tracking series," *Journal of Finance* 59: 479–506.

69. This section is based on: "U.S. clears InBev to buy Anheuser," *The Wall Street Journal,* November 15, 2008; and "Blackstone nears deal," *The Wall Street Journal,* October 5, 2009.

70. Boston Consulting Group (1970), *The Product Portfolio* (Boston, MA: Boston Consulting Group); and Shay, J.P., and F.T. Rothaermel (1999), "Dynamic competitive strategy: Towards a multi-perspective conceptual framework," *Long Range Planning* 32: 559–572; and Kiechel, W. (2010), *The Lords of Strategy: The Secret Intellectual History of the New Corporate World* (Boston, MA: Harvard Business School Press).

71. GE annual reports.

72. Milgrom, P., and J. Roberts (1990), "Bargaining costs, influence costs, and the organization of economic activity," in ed. J. Alt and K. Shepsle, *Perspectives on Positive Political Economy* (Cambridge, UK: Cambridge University Press).

73. This Small-Group Exercise is based on: The Rural Community Building website produced by the American Farm Bureau Federation; *America's Heartland* "Episode 311"; and Fair Oaks Farms Dairy (www.fofarms.com).

74. This Small-Group Exercise is based on: Gregory, S. (2009), "Walmart vs. Target: No contest in the recession," *Time,* March 14, 2009; and Food Marketing Institute Annual Financial Report, December 2008.

Chapter 9

Corporate Strategy: Strategic Alliances and Mergers and Acquisitions

Learning Objectives

LO 9-1 Apply the build-borrow-or-buy framework to guide corporate strategy.

LO 9-2 Define strategic alliances, and explain why they are important to implement corporate strategy and why firms enter into them.

LO 9-3 Describe three alliance governance mechanisms and evaluate their pros and cons.

LO 9-4 Describe the three phases of alliance management and explain how an alliance management capability can lead to a competitive advantage.

LO 9-5 Differentiate between mergers and acquisitions, and explain why firms would use either to execute corporate strategy.

LO 9-6 Define horizontal integration and evaluate the advantages and disadvantages of this option to execute corporate-level strategy.

LO 9-7 Explain why firms engage in acquisitions.

LO 9-8 Evaluate whether mergers and acquisitions lead to competitive advantage.

Disney: Building Billion-Dollar Franchises

WITH OVER $50 BILLION in annual revenues, Disney is the world's largest media company. In recent years, Disney has grown through a number of high-profile acquisitions, including Pixar (2006), Marvel (2009), and Lucasfilm (2012), the creator of *Star Wars.* All this was done with the goal to build billion-dollar franchises based on movie sequels, park rides, and merchandise. Let's take a closer look at how an alliance with Pixar turned into an acquisition.

Pixar started as a computer hardware company producing high-end graphic display systems. One of its customers was Disney. To demonstrate the graphic display systems' capabilities, Pixar produced short, computer-animated movies. Despite being sophisticated, Pixar's computer hardware was not selling well, and the new venture was hemorrhaging money. To the rescue rode not Buzz Lightyear, but Steve Jobs. Shortly after being ousted from Apple in 1986, Jobs bought the struggling hardware company for $5 million and founded Pixar Animation Studios, invest-ing another $5 million into the company. The

Elsa from the animated Disney blockbuster hit *Frozen.*
© Moviestore collection Ltd / Alamy

Pixar team led by Edwin Catmull and John Lasseter then transformed the company into a computer animation film studio.

To finance and distribute its newly created computer-animated movies, Pixar entered a strategic alliance with Disney. Disney's distribution network and its stellar repu-tation in animated movies were critical complementary assets that Pixar needed to commercialize its new type of films. In turn, Disney was able to rejuvenate its floun-dering product lineup, retaining the rights to the newly created Pixar characters and to any sequels.

Pixar became successful beyond imagination as it rolled out one blockbuster after another: *Toy Story (1, 2,* and *3), A*

Bug's Life, Monsters, Inc., Finding Nemo, The Incredibles, and *Cars,* grossing several billion dollars. Given Pixar's huge success and Disney's abysmal performance with its own releases during this time, the bargaining power in the alliance shifted dramatically. Renegotiations of the Pixar–Disney alliance broke down in 2004, reportedly because of personality conflicts between Steve Jobs and then-Disney Chairman and CEO Michael Eisner.

After Robert Iger was appointed CEO, Disney acquired Pixar for $7.4 billion in 2006. The success of the alliance demonstrated that the two entities' complementary assets matched, and gave Disney an inside perspective on the value of Pixar's core competencies in the creation of com-puter-animated features. In 2009, Disney turned to acqui-sitions again. The acquisition of Marvel Entertainment for $4 billion added Spiderman, Iron Man, The Incredible Hulk, and Captain America to its lineup of characters. Marvel's superheroes grossed a cumulative $15 billion at the box office, with *The Avengers* bringing in some $2 billion. In 2012, Mickey's extended fam-ily was joined by Darth Vader, Obi-Wan Kenobi, Princess Leia, and Luke Skywalker when Disney acquired Lucasfilm for more than $4 billion.

After taking the reins, Iger transformed a lacklus-ter Disney after a decade or so of inferior perfor-mance by refocusing it around what he calls "franchises," which generally begin with a big movie hit and are fol-lowed up with derivative TV shows, theme park rides, video games, toys, clothing such as T-shirts and PJs, among many other spin-offs. Rather than churning out some 30 movies per year as it did prior to Iger, Disney now pro-duces about 10 movies per year, focusing on box office hits. Disney's annual movie lineup is now dominated by such franchises as *Stars Wars* and Marvel superhero movies and also live-action versions of animated classics such as *Cinderella* and *Beauty and the Beast.* The big-gest Disney franchises that started with a movie hit are *Pirates of Caribbean* (grossing almost $4 billion, with its fifth installment due in 2017), *Toy Story* (some $2 billion with a fourth movie also due in 2017), *Monsters, Inc.* (some $1.5 billion), *Cars* (over $1 billion, with a third sequel rumored to be in the making), and, of course, *Frozen.*

To further build its *Frozen* franchise, Disney is already working on a sequel of its animated movie hit as well as offering *Frozen Ever After,* a new dreamlike ride through the fictional world of Arendelle at Disney World's Epcot Center, which had grown stale. The animated movie *Frozen* (made by Walt Disney Animation Studios run by Pixar execs Catmull and Lasseter) has grossed some $1.5 billion since its release in 2013, making it the most successful animated movie ever![1]

You will learn more about Disney from reading this chapter; related questions appear on page 316.

DISNEY ENTERED STRATEGIC alliances and acquired other media businesses to create theme-based franchises. CEO Iger's corporate strategy around building billion-dollar franchises is certainly paying off: Disney's revenues are up almost 10 percent and it earned some $8 billion in profits in 2015. Its stock has risen by over 230 percent between 2010 and 2015, outperforming its rivals such as Time Warner, Sony's Columbia Pictures, or 21st Century Fox.

As a diversified media company, Disney is active in a wide array of business activities, from movies to amusement parks as well as cable and broadcast television networks (ABC, ESPN, and others), cruises, and retailing. It became the world's leading media company to a large extent by pursuing a corporate strategy of *related-linked diversification* (see Chapter 8). This is because some, but not all, of Disney's business activities share common resources, capabilities, and competencies. As detailed in the ChapterCase, Disney's executives implemented its corporate strategy through the use of strategic alliances and acquisitions.

In Chapter 8, we discussed *why* firms grow. In this chapter we discuss *how* firms grow. In addition to internal organic growth (achieved through reinvesting profits, see discussion of Exhibit 4.3 in Chapter 4), firms have two critical strategic options to execute corporate strategy: alliances and acquisitions. We devote this chapter to the study of these fundamental pathways through which firms implement corporate strategy.

We begin this chapter by introducing the *build-borrow-buy framework* to guide corporate strategy in deciding whether and when to grow *internally (build),* use *alliances (borrow),* or *make acquisitions (buy).* We then take a closer look at strategic alliances before studying mergers and acquisitions. We discuss alliances before acquisitions because alliances are smaller strategic commitments and thus are much more frequent. Moreover, in some cases, alliances may lead to acquisitions later; offering a "try before you buy" approach as in the Disney–Pixar example. We conclude with "Implications for the Strategist," in which we discuss practical applications.

9.1 How Firms Achieve Growth

After discussing in Chapter 8 why firms need to grow, the next question that arises is: *How do firms achieve growth?* Corporate executives have three options at their disposal to drive firm growth: organic growth through internal development, external growth through alliances, or external growth through acquisitions. Laurence Capron and Will Mitchell developed an insightful step-by-step decision model to guide managers in selecting the most appropriate corporate strategy vehicle.[2] Selecting the most appropriate vehicle for corporate strategy in response to a specific strategic challenge also makes successful implementation more likely.

THE BUILD-BORROW-BUY FRAMEWORK

LO 9-1

Apply the build-borrow-or-buy framework to guide corporate strategy.

The **build-borrow-or-buy framework** provides a conceptual model that aids firms in deciding whether to pursue internal development (*build*), enter a contractual arrangement or strategic alliance (*borrow*), or acquire new resources, capabilities, and competencies (*buy*). Firms that are able to learn how to select the right pathways to obtain new resources are more likely to gain and sustain a competitive advantage. Note that in the build-borrow-or-buy model, the term *resources* is defined broadly to include capabilities and competencies (as in the *VRIO model* discussed in Chapter 4). Exhibit 9.1 shows the *build-borrow-or-buy* decision framework.

The starting point is the firm's identification of a strategic resource gap that will impede future growth. The resource gap is *strategic* because closing this gap is likely to lead to a competitive advantage. As discussed in Chapter 4, resources with the potential to lead to competitive advantage cannot be simply bought on the open market. Indeed, if any firm could readily buy this type of resource, its availability would negate its potential for competitive advantage. It would no longer be *rare*, a key condition for a resource to form the basis of competitive advantage. Moreover, resources that are *valuable, rare,* and *difficult to imitate* are often embedded deep within a firm, frequently making up a resource bundle that is hard to unplug whole or in part. The options to close the strategic resource gap are, therefore, to build, borrow, or buy. *Build* in the build-borrow-buy framework refers to internal development; *borrow* refers to the use of strategic alliances; and *buy* refers to acquiring a firm. When acquiring a firm, you buy an entire "resource bundle," not just a specific resource. This resource bundle, if obeying VRIO principles and successfully integrated, can then form the basis of competitive advantage.

Exhibit 9.1 provides a schematic of the build-borrow-or-buy framework. In this approach executives must determine the degree to which certain conditions apply, either

> **build-borrow-or-buy framework** Conceptual model that aids firms in deciding whether to pursue internal development *(build)*, enter a contractual arrangement or strategic alliance *(borrow)*, or acquire new resources, capabilities, and competencies *(buy)*.

EXHIBIT 9.1 / Guiding Corporate Strategy: The Build-Borrow-or-Buy Framework

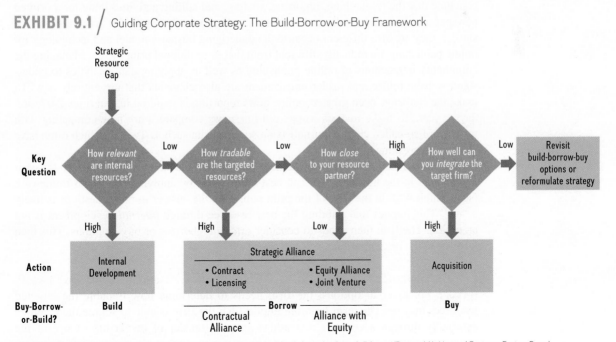

Source: Adapted from L. Capron and W. Mitchell (2012), *Build, Borrow, or Buy: Solving the Growth Dilemma* (Boston, MA: Harvard Business Review Press).

high or low, by responding to up to four questions sequentially before finding the best course. The questions cover issues of *relevancy, tradability, closeness,* and *integration:*

1. **Relevancy.** How *relevant* are the firm's existing internal resources to solving the resource gap?
2. **Tradability.** How *tradable* are the targeted resources that may be available externally?
3. **Closeness.** How *close* do you need to be to your external resource partner?
4. **Integration.** How well can you *integrate* the targeted firm, should you determine you need to acquire the resource partner?

As shown in Exhibit 9.1, the answers to these questions lead to a recommended action or the next question. We'll review each in more depth.

1. HOW *RELEVANT* ARE THE FIRM'S EXISTING INTERNAL RESOURCES TO SOLVING THE RESOURCE GAP?

The firm starts by asking whether the firm's internal resources are high or low in relevance. If the firm's internal resources are highly relevant to closing the identified gap, the firm should itself build the new resources needed through internal development.

But how does a manager know whether the firm's resources are relevant in addressing a new challenge or opportunity? Firms evaluate the relevance of internal resources in two ways: they test whether resources are (1) *similar* to those the firm needs to develop and (2) *superior* to those of competitors in the targeted area.[3] If *both* conditions are met, then the firm's internal resources are relevant and the firm should pursue internal development.

Let's look at both conditions. Managers are often misled by the first test because things that might appear similar at the surface are actually quite different deep down.[4] Moreover, managers tend to focus on the (known) similarities rather than on (unknown) differences. They often don't know how the resources needed for the existing and new business opportunity differ. An executive at a newspaper publisher such as *The New York Times* may conclude that the researching, reporting, writing, and editing activities done for a printed newspaper are similar to those done for an online one. Although the activities may be similar, they are also different because the underlying business model and technology for online publishing are radically different from that of traditional print media. Managing the community interactions of online publishing as well as applying data analytics to understand website traffic and reader engagement are also elements that are entirely new. To make the challenge even greater, online news reporting is required in real time, 24/7, 365 days a year. To make matters worse, old-line news companies are now competing with millions of so-called citizen journalists on social media such as Twitter, which often have an edge on breaking news.[5]

The second test, determining whether your internal resources are *superior* to those of competitors in the targeted area, can best be assessed by applying the VRIO framework (see Exhibit 4.5). In the case of the print publisher, the answer to both questions is likely a "no." This implies that building the new resource through *internal* development is not an option. The firm then needs to consider *external*—borrow or buy—options. This then leads us to the next question.

2. HOW *TRADABLE* ARE THE TARGETED RESOURCES THAT MAY BE AVAILABLE EXTERNALLY?

For external options, the firm needs to determine how tradable the targeted resources may be. The term *tradable* implies that the firm is able to source the resource externally through a contract that allows for the transfer of ownership or use of the resource. Short-term as well as long-term contracts, such as licensing or franchising, are a way to *borrow* resources from another company (see discussion in Chapter 8).

In the biotech-pharma industry, some producers use licensing agreements to transfer knowledge and technology from the licensor's R&D to the licensee's manufacturing. Eli Lilly, for example, has commercialized several breakthrough biotech drugs using licensing agreements with new ventures. The implication is that if a resource is highly tradable, then the resource should be *borrowed* via a licensing agreement or other contractual agreement. If the resource in question is not easily tradable, then the firm needs to consider either a deeper strategic alliance through an equity alliance or a joint venture, or an outright acquisition.

3. HOW *CLOSE* DO YOU NEED TO BE TO YOUR EXTERNAL RESOURCE PARTNER? Many times, firms are able to obtain the required resources to fill the strategic gap through more integrated strategic alliances such as equity alliances or joint ventures (see Exhibit 8.4) rather than through outright acquisition. Mergers and acquisitions are the most costly, complex, and difficult to reverse strategic option. This implies that only if extreme closeness to the resource partner is necessary in order to understand and obtain its underlying knowledge should M&A be considered the *buy* option. Regardless, the firm should always first consider *borrowing* the necessary resources through integrated strategic alliances before looking at M&A.

4. HOW WELL CAN YOU *INTEGRATE* THE TARGETED FIRM, SHOULD YOU DETERMINE YOU NEED TO ACQUIRE THE RESOURCE PARTNER? The final decision question using the build-borrow-buy lens is: *Can you integrate the target firm?* The list of post-integration failure, often due to cultural differences, is long. Multibillion-dollar failures include the Daimler-Chrysler integration, AOL and Time Warner, HP and Autonomy, and Bank of America and Merrill Lynch. More than cultural differences were involved in Microsoft's 2015 decision to write down $7.6 billion in losses on its $9.4 billion acquisition of Nokia (or more than 80 percent) some 15 months earlier. It's now up to Microsoft CEO Satya Nadella to decide how to compete in the mobile device arena after former CEO Steve Ballmer made a desperate gamble on acquiring the Finnish cell phone maker.[6]

Only if the three prior conditions (*low relevancy, low tradability,* and *high need for closeness*) shown in the decision tree in Exhibit 9.1 are met, should the firm consider M&A: If the firm's internal resources are insufficient to *build, and* the resource needed to fill the strategic gap cannot be *borrowed* through a strategic alliance, *and* closeness to the resource partner is needed, then the final question to consider is whether the integration of the two firms using a merger or acquisition will be successful. In all other cases, the firms should consider finding a less costly *borrow* arrangement when *building* is not an option. Since strategic alliances are the less costly and more common tool to execute corporate strategy, we discuss alliances first before mergers and acquisitions. Per the build-borrow-buy decision framework, strategic alliances (*borrow*) also need to be considered before mergers and acquisitions (*buy*).

9.2 Strategic Alliances

Strategic alliances are voluntary arrangements between firms that involve the sharing of knowledge, resources, and capabilities with the intent of developing processes, products, or services.[7] The use of strategic alliances to implement corporate strategy has exploded in the past few decades, with thousands forming each year. As the speed of technological change and innovation has increased (see discussion in Chapter 7), firms have responded by entering more alliances. Globalization has also contributed to an increase in cross-border strategic alliances (see discussion in Chapter 10).

LO 9-2

Define strategic alliances, and explain why they are important to implement corporate strategy and why firms enter into them.

strategic alliance
A voluntary arrangement between firms that involves the sharing of knowledge, resources, and capabilities with the intent of developing processes, products, or services.

Strategic alliances may join complementary parts of a firm's value chain, such as R&D and marketing, or they may focus on joining the same value chain activities. Strategic alliances are attractive because they enable firms to achieve goals faster and at lower costs than going it alone. In contrast to M&A, strategic alliances also allow firms to circumvent potential legal repercussions including potential lawsuits filed by U.S. federal agencies or the European Union.

Firms enter many types of alliances, from small contracts that have no bearing on a firm's competitiveness to multibillion-dollar joint ventures that can make or break the company. An alliance, therefore, qualifies as *strategic* only if it has the potential to affect a firm's competitive advantage. A strategic alliance has the potential to help a firm gain and sustain a competitive advantage when it joins together resources and knowledge in a combination that obeys the VRIO principles (introduced in Chapter 4).[8] The locus of competitive advantage is often not found within the individual firm but within a strategic partnership.

> **relational view of competitive advantage** Strategic management framework that proposes that critical resources and capabilities frequently are embedded in strategic alliances that span firm boundaries.

According to this **relational view of competitive advantage**, critical resources and capabilities frequently are embedded in strategic alliances that span firm boundaries. Applying the VRIO framework, we know that the basis for competitive advantage is formed when a strategic alliance creates resource combinations that are valuable, rare, and difficult to imitate, and the alliance is organized appropriately to allow for value capture. In support of this perspective, over 80 percent of Fortune 1000 CEOs indicated in a recent survey that more than one-quarter of their firm's revenues were derived from strategic alliances.[9]

WHY DO FIRMS ENTER STRATEGIC ALLIANCES?

To affect a firm's competitive advantage, an alliance must promise a positive effect on the firm's economic value creation through increasing value and/or lowering costs (see discussion in Chapter 5). This logic is reflected in the common reasons firms enter alliances.[10] They do so to

- Strengthen competitive position.
- Enter new markets.
- Hedge against uncertainty.
- Access critical complementary assets.
- Learn new capabilities.

STRENGTHEN COMPETITIVE POSITION. Firms can use strategic alliances to change the industry structure in their favor.[11] Firms frequently use strategic alliances when competing in so-called battles for industry standards (see discussion in Chapter 7). Strategy Highlight 9.1 shows how IBM and Apple entered a strategic alliance to strengthen their respective competitive position in mobile computing and business productivity apps. This in turn increases the competitive pressure on rivals of both companies, in particular, Microsoft.

ENTER NEW MARKETS. Firms may use strategic alliances to enter new markets, either in terms of products and services or geography.[12]

Using a strategic alliance, HP and DreamWorks Animation SKG created the Halo Collaboration Studio, which makes virtual communication possible around the globe.[13] Halo's conferencing technology gives participants the vivid sense that they are in the same room. The conference rooms of clients match, down to the last detail, giving participants the impression that they are sitting together at the same table. DreamWorks produced the

Strategy Highlight 9.1

IBM and Apple:
From Big Brother to Alliance Partner

An excerpt from a speech by Apple co-founder Steve Jobs introducing the iconic "1984" Macintosh ad that aired during the Super Bowl XVIII telecast provides a historic perspective about the relationship between Apple and IBM:[14]

> In 1977, Apple, a young fledgling company on the West Coast, invents the Apple II, the first personal computer as we know it today. IBM dismisses the personal computer as too small to do serious computing and unimportant. The early 1980s. Apple II has become the world's most popular computer, and Apple has grown to a $300 million company, becoming the fastest-growing corporation in American business history. IBM enters the personal computer market in 1981. Apple and IBM emerge as the industry's strongest competitors, each selling approximately $1 billion worth of personal computers in 1983. The shakeout is in full swing. The first major firm goes bankrupt, with others teetering on the brink. It is now 1984. IBM wants it all and is aiming its guns on its last obstacle to industry control: Apple. Will Big Blue dominate the entire computer industry—the entire information age? Was George Orwell right about 1984?

Steve Jobs compares IBM to George Orwell's Big Brother, the all-present dictator of a totalitarian state that has absolute power over its inhabitants, including thought control. In the ad, Apple—portrayed by an athletic heroine with a stylized line drawing of Apple's Macintosh on her tank top—is the only hope to save humanity from total oppression and ensure its freedom.

Fast-forward 30 years to 2014. Apple has become the world's most valuable company and IBM is struggling. Although Jobs had a visceral disdain for IBM, Apple CEO Tim Cook took his first job out of college with IBM, where he worked for 12 years. Nonetheless, given their adversarial past and decades as rivals, it came somewhat as a surprise when Apple and IBM announced a strategic alliance to create simple-to-use business productivity apps and to sell

Source: "1984 Apple's Macintosh Commerical," YouTube, posted by Mac History, February 1, 2012

iPhones and iPads to IBM's corporate clients. Why would the former archenemies form a partnership?

Both parties stand to benefit from this arrangement. Although hugely successful, Apple has mainly been a consumer company (B2C). Historically, Apple did not sell directly to business clients. As more and more people bring their mobile devices to work, Apple sees the enterprise business as a huge opportunity for future growth. Cook, for example, claims that he does 80 percent of the work of running the world's most valuable company on his iPad.

In contrast, IBM has long-standing and deep ties as a business-to-business (B2B) company and major seller of tech services, especially in government, banking, finance, and insurance. Yet, IBM has been slow to catch the wave of mobile computing. With this seminal partnership, IBM is hoping to capitalize on the popularity of Apple's devices as it moves more and more of its software productivity tools onto mobile platforms. IBM will be selling and servicing Apple mobile devices to its corporate clients. Together, they plan to create simple to use business apps that bring together Apple's core competency of hardware and software integration to produce a seamless user experience with IBM's core competency in business services and big data analytics. One of the first new business apps resulting from this alliance will help airline pilots determine the right amount of fuel to carry on a particular flight. This task requires significant data analytics displayed in an easily understandable way so that pilots can digest it quickly when glancing at their iPad in a cockpit before departure.[15]

computer-animated movie *Shrek 2* using this new technology for its meetings. People with different creative skills—script writers, computer animators, directors—though dispersed geographically, were able to participate as if in the same room, even seeing the work on each other's laptops. Use of the technology enabled faster decision making, enhanced productivity, reduced (or even eliminated) travel time and expense, and increased job satisfaction. Neither HP nor DreamWorks would have been able to produce this technology breakthrough alone, but moving into the videoconferencing arena together via a strategic alliance allowed both partners to pursue related diversification. Moreover, HP's alliance with DreamWorks Animation SKG enabled HP to compete head on with Cisco's high-end videoconferencing solution, TelePresence. The HP and DreamWorks Animation SKG was motivated by the desire to enter a new market, in terms or products and services offered, that neither could enter alone.[16]

When entering new geographic markets, in some instances, governments such as Saudi Arabia or China may require that foreign firms have a local joint venture partner before doing business in their countries. These cross-border strategic alliances have both benefits and risks. While the foreign firm can benefit from local expertise and contacts, it is exposed to the risk that some of its proprietary know-how may be appropriated by the foreign partner. We will address such issues in Chapter 10 when studying global strategy.

HEDGE AGAINST UNCERTAINTY. In dynamic markets, strategic alliances allow firms to limit their exposure to uncertainty in the market.[17] For instance, in the wake of the biotechnology revolution, incumbent pharmaceutical firms such as Pfizer, Novartis, and Roche entered into hundreds of strategic alliances with biotech startups.[18] These alliances allowed the big pharma firms to make small-scale investments in many of the new biotechnology ventures that were poised to disrupt existing market economics. In some sense, the pharma companies were taking *real options* in these biotechnology experiments, providing them with the right but not the obligation to make further investments when new drugs were introduced from the biotech companies.

A **real-options perspective** to strategic decision making breaks down a larger investment decision (such as whether to enter biotechnology or not) into a set of smaller decisions that are staged sequentially over time. This approach allows the firm to obtain additional information at predetermined stages. At each stage, after new information is revealed, the firm evaluates whether or not to make further investments. In a sense, a real option, which is the right, but not the obligation, to continue making investments allows the firm to buy time until sufficient information for a go versus no-go decision is revealed. Once the new biotech drugs were a known quantity, the uncertainty was removed, and the incumbent firms could react accordingly.

For example, in 1990 the Swiss pharma company Roche initially invested $2.1 billion in an equity alliance to purchase a controlling interest (greater than 50 percent) in the biotech startup Genentech. In 2009, after witnessing the success of Genentech's drug discovery and development projects in subsequent years, Roche spent $47 billion to purchase the remaining minority interest in Genentech, making it a wholly owned subsidiary.[19] Taking a wait-and-see approach by entering strategic alliances allows incumbent firms to buy time and wait for the uncertainty surrounding the market and technology to fade. Many firms in fast-moving markets subscribe to this rationale. Waiting can also be expensive, however. To acquire the remaining less than 50 percent of Genentech some 20 years after its initial investment required a price that was

real-options perspective Approach to strategic decision making that breaks down a larger investment decision into a set of smaller decisions that are staged sequentially over time.

some 24 times higher than the initial investment, as uncertainty settled and the biotech startup turned out to be hugely successful. Besides biotechnology, the use of a *real-options perspective* in making strategic investments has also been documented in nanotechnology, semiconductors, and other dynamic markets.[20]

ACCESS CRITICAL COMPLEMENTARY ASSETS. The successful commercialization of a new product or service often requires complementary assets such as marketing, manufacturing, and after-sale service.[21] In particular, new firms are in need of complementary assets to complete the value chain from upstream innovation to downstream commercialization. This implies that a new venture that has a core competency in R&D, for example, will need to access distribution channels and marketing expertise to complete the value chain. Building downstream complementary assets such as marketing and regulatory expertise or a sales force is often prohibitively expensive and time-consuming, and thus frequently not an option for new ventures. Strategic alliances allow firms to match complementary skills and resources to complete the value chain. Moreover, licensing agreements of this sort allow the partners to benefit from a division of labor, allowing each to efficiently focus on its core competency.

LEARN NEW CAPABILITIES. Firms also enter strategic alliances because they are motivated by the desire to learn new capabilities from their partners.[22] When the collaborating firms are also competitors, *co-opetition* ensues.[23] **Co-opetition** is a portmanteau describing cooperation by competitors. They may cooperate to create a larger pie but then might compete about how the pie should be divided. Such co-opetition can lead to **learning races** in strategic alliances,[24] a situation in which both partners are motivated to form an alliance for learning, but the rate at which the firms learn may vary. The firm that learns faster and accomplishes its goal more quickly has an incentive to exit the alliance or, at a minimum, to reduce its knowledge sharing. Since the cooperating firms are also competitors, learning races can have a positive effect on the winning firm's competitive position vis-à-vis its alliance partner.

NUMMI (New United Motor Manufacturing, Inc.) was the first joint venture in the U.S. automobile industry, formed between GM and Toyota in 1984. Recall from Chapter 8 that joint ventures are a special type of a strategic alliance in which two partner firms create a third, jointly owned entity. In the NUMMI joint venture, each partner was motivated to learn new capabilities: GM entered the equity-based strategic alliance to learn the lean manufacturing system pioneered by Toyota in order to produce high-quality, fuel-efficient cars at a profit. Toyota entered the alliance to learn how to implement its lean manufacturing program with an American work force. NUMMI was a test-run for Toyota before building fully owned *greenfield plants* (new manufacturing facilities) in Alabama, Indiana, Kentucky, Mississippi, Texas, and West Virginia. In this 25-year history, GM and Toyota built some 7 million high-quality cars at the NUMMI plant. In fact, NUMMI was transformed from worst performer (under GM ownership before the joint venture) to GM's highest-quality plant in the United States. In the end, as part of GM's bankruptcy reorganization during 2009–2010, it pulled out of the NUMMI joint venture.

The joint venture between GM and Toyota can be seen as a learning race. Who won? Strategy scholars argue that Toyota was faster in accomplishing its alliance goal—learning how to manage U.S. labor—because of its limited scope.[25] Toyota had already perfected lean manufacturing; all it needed to do was learn how to train U.S. workers in the

co-opetition
Cooperation by competitors to achieve a strategic objective.

learning races
Situations in which both partners in a strategic alliance are motivated to form an alliance for learning, but the rate at which the firms learn may vary.

method and transfer this knowledge to its subsidiary plants in the United States. On the other hand, GM had to learn a completely new production system. GM was successful in transferring lean manufacturing to its newly created Saturn brand (which was discontinued in 2010 as part of GM's reorganization), but it had a hard time implementing lean manufacturing in its *existing* plants. These factors suggest that Toyota won the learning race with GM, which in turn helped Toyota gain and sustain a competitive advantage over GM in the U.S. market.

Also, note that different motivations for forming alliances are not necessarily independent and can be intertwined. For example, firms that collaborate to access critical complementary assets may also want to learn from one another to subsequently pursue vertical integration. In sum, alliance formation is frequently motivated by leveraging economies of scale, scope, specialization, and learning.

LO 9-3

Describe three alliance governance mechanisms and evaluate their pros and cons.

GOVERNING STRATEGIC ALLIANCES

In Chapter 8, we showed that strategic alliances lie in the middle of the make-or-buy continuum (see Exhibit 8.4). Alliances can be governed by the following mechanisms:

- Non-equity alliances
- Equity alliances
- Joint ventures[26]

Exhibit 9.2 provides an overview of the key characteristics of the three alliance types, including their advantages and disadvantages.

non-equity alliance
Partnership based on contracts between firms.

explicit knowledge
Knowledge that can be codified; concerns *knowing about* a process or product.

NON-EQUITY ALLIANCES. The most common type of alliance is a **non-equity alliance**, which is based on contracts between firms. The most frequent forms of non-equity alliances are *supply agreements, distribution agreements,* and *licensing agreements.* As suggested by their names, these contractual agreements are vertical strategic alliances, connecting different parts of the industry value chain. In a non-equity alliance, firms tend to share **explicit knowledge**—knowledge that can be codified. Patents, user manuals, fact sheets, and scientific publications are all ways to capture explicit knowledge, which concerns the notion of *knowing about* a certain process or product.

Licensing agreements are contractual alliances in which the participants regularly exchange codified knowledge. The biotech firm Genentech licensed its newly developed drug Humulin (human insulin) to the pharmaceutical firm Eli Lilly for manufacturing, facilitating approval by the Food and Drug Administration (FDA), and distribution. This partnership was an example of a vertical strategic alliance: One partner (Genentech) was positioned upstream in the industry value chain focusing on R&D, while the other partner (Eli Lilly) was positioned downstream focusing on manufacturing and distribution. This type of vertical arrangement is often described as a "hand-off" from the upstream partner to the downstream partner and is possible because the underlying knowledge is largely explicit and can be easily codified. When Humulin reached the market, it was the first approved genetically engineered human therapeutic drug worldwide.[27] Subsequently, Humulin became a billion-dollar blockbuster drug.

Because of their contractual nature, non-equity alliances are flexible and easy to initiate and terminate. However, because they can be temporary in nature, they also sometimes produce weak ties between the alliance partners, which can result in a lack of trust and commitment.

EXHIBIT 9.2 / Key Characteristics of Different Alliance Types

Alliance Type	Governance Mechanism	Frequency	Type of Knowledge Exchanged	Pros	Cons	Examples
Non-equity (supply, licensing, and distribution agreements)	Contract	Most common	Explicit	• Flexible • Fast • Easy to initiate and terminate	• Weak tie • Lack of trust and commitment	• Genentech–Lilly (exclusive) licensing agreement for Humulin • Microsoft–IBM (nonexclusive) licensing agreement for MS-DOS
Equity (purchase of an equity stake or corporate venture capital, CVC investment)	Equity investment	Less common than non-equity alliances, but more common than joint ventures	Explicit; exchange of tacit knowledge possible	• Stronger tie • Trust and commitment can emerge • Window into new technology (option value)	• Less flexible • Slower • Can entail significant investments	• Renault–Nissan alliance based on cross equity holdings, with Renault owning 44.4% in Nissan; and Nissan owning 15% in Renault • Roche's equity investment in Genentech (prior to full integration)
Joint venture (JV)	Creation of new entity by two or more parent firms	Least common	Both tacit and explicit knowledge exchanged	• Strongest tie • Trust and commitment likely to emerge • May be required by institutional setting	• Can entail long negotiations and significant investments • Long-term solution • JV managers have double reporting lines (2 bosses)	• Hulu, owned by NBC, Fox, and Disney-ABC • Dow Corning, owned by Dow Chemical and Corning

EQUITY ALLIANCES. In an **equity alliance**, at least one partner takes partial ownership in the other partner. Equity alliances are less common than contractual, non-equity alliances because they often require larger investments. Because they are based on partial ownership rather than contracts, equity alliances are used to signal stronger commitments. Moreover, equity alliances allow for the sharing of **tacit knowledge**—knowledge that cannot be codified.[28] Tacit knowledge concerns *knowing how* to do a certain task. It can be acquired only through actively participating in the process. In an equity alliance, therefore, the partners frequently exchange personnel to make the acquisition of tacit knowledge possible.

Toyota used an equity alliance with Tesla Motors, a designer and maker of electric cars (and featured in ChapterCase 3), to learn new knowledge and gain a window into

equity alliance
Partnership in which at least one partner takes partial ownership in the other.

tacit knowledge
Knowledge that cannot be codified; concerns *knowing how* to do a certain task and can be acquired only through active participation in that task.

new technology. In 2010, Toyota made a $50 million equity investment in the California startup. In the same year, Tesla Motors purchased the NUMMI plant in Fremont, California, where it now manufactures its Models S and X. Tesla CEO Elon Musk stated, "The Tesla factory effectively leverages an ideal combination of hardcore Silicon Valley engineering talent, traditional automotive engineering talent, and the proven Toyota production system."[29] Toyota in turn hopes to infuse its company with Tesla's entrepreneurial spirit. Toyota President Akio Toyoda commented, "By partnering with Tesla, my hope is that all Toyota employees will recall that 'venture business spirit' and take on the challenges of the future."[30] Toyoda hoped that a transfer of tacit knowledge would occur, in which Tesla's entrepreneurial spirit would reinvigorate Toyota.[31] This equity-based learning race ended in 2014 when Toyota sold its stake in Tesla.[32] The Japanese automaker is shifting away from electric cars, renewing its focus on hybrid vehicles and exploring fuel-cell technology.

Another governance mechanism that falls under the broad rubric of equity alliances is **corporate venture capital (CVC)** investments, which are equity investments by established firms in entrepreneurial ventures.[33] The value of CVC investments is estimated to be in the double-digit billion-dollar range each year. Larger firms frequently have dedicated CVC units, such as Dow Venture Capital, Siemens Venture Capital, Kaiser Permanente Ventures, and Johnson & Johnson Development Corporation. Rather than hoping primarily for financial gains, as venture capitalists traditionally do, CVC investments create real options in terms of gaining access to new, and potentially disruptive, technologies.[34] Strategy scholars find that CVC investments have a positive impact on value creation for the investing firm, especially in high-tech industries such as semiconductors, computing, and the medical-device sector.[35]

> **corporate venture capital (CVC)**
> Equity investments by established firms in entrepreneurial ventures; CVC falls under the broader rubric of equity alliances.

Taken together, equity alliances tend to produce stronger ties and greater trust between partners than non-equity alliances do. They also offer a window into new technology that, like a real option, can be exercised if successful or abandoned if not promising. Equity alliances are frequently stepping-stones toward full integration of the partner firms either through a merger or an acquisition. Essentially, they are often used as a "try before you buy" strategic option.[36] The downside of equity alliances is the amount of investment that can be involved, as well as a possible lack of flexibility and speed in putting together and reaping benefits from the partnership.

JOINT VENTURES. A *joint venture* (JV) is a standalone organization created and jointly owned by two or more parent companies (as discussed in Chapter 8). For example, Hulu (a video-on-demand service) is jointly owned by NBC, Disney-ABC, and Fox. Since partners contribute equity to a joint venture, they are making a long-term commitment. Exchange of both explicit and tacit knowledge through interaction of personnel is typical. Joint ventures are also frequently used to enter foreign markets where the host country requires such a partnership to gain access to the market in exchange for advanced technology and know-how. In terms of frequency, joint ventures are the least common of the three types of strategic alliances.

The advantages of joint ventures are the strong ties, trust, and commitment that can result between the partners. However, they can entail long negotiations and significant investments. If the alliance doesn't work out as expected, undoing the JV can take some time and involve considerable cost. A further risk is that knowledge shared with the new partner could be misappropriated by opportunistic behavior. Finally, any rewards from the collaboration must be shared between the partners.

ALLIANCE MANAGEMENT CAPABILITY

Strategic alliances create a paradox for managers. Although alliances appear to be necessary to compete in many industries, between 30 and 70 percent of all strategic alliances do not deliver the expected benefits, and are considered failures by at least one alliance partner.[37] Given the high failure rate, effective alliance management is critical to gaining and sustaining a competitive advantage, especially in high-technology industries.[38]

Alliance management capability is a firm's ability to effectively manage three alliance-related tasks concurrently, often across a portfolio of many different alliances (see Exhibit 9.3):[39]

- Partner selection and alliance formation.
- Alliance design and governance.
- Post-formation alliance management.

PARTNER SELECTION AND ALLIANCE FORMATION. When making the business case for an alliance, the expected benefits of the alliance must exceed its costs. When one or more of the five reasons for alliance formation are present—to strengthen competitive position, enter new markets, hedge against uncertainty, access critical complementary resources, or learn new capabilities—the firm must select the best possible alliance partner. Partner compatibility and partner commitment are necessary conditions for successful alliance formation.[40] *Partner compatibility* captures aspects of cultural fit between different firms. *Partner commitment* concerns the willingness to make available necessary resources and to accept short-term sacrifices to ensure long-term rewards.

ALLIANCE DESIGN AND GOVERNANCE. Once two or more firms agree to pursue an alliance, managers must then design the alliance and choose an appropriate governance mechanism from among the three options: non-equity contractual agreement, equity alliances, or joint venture. For example, in a study of over 640 alliances, researchers found that the joining of specialized complementary assets increases the likelihood that the alliance is governed hierarchically. This effect is stronger in the presence of uncertainties concerning the alliance partner as well as the envisioned tasks.[41]

In addition to the formal governance mechanisms, *interorganizational trust* is a critical dimension of alliance success.[42] Because all contracts are necessarily incomplete, trust between the alliance partners plays an important role for effective post-formation alliance management. Effective governance, therefore, can be accomplished only by skillfully combining formal and informal mechanisms.

LO 9-4

Describe the three phases of alliance management and explain how an alliance management capability can lead to a competitive advantage.

alliance management capability
A firm's ability to effectively manage three alliance-related tasks concurrently: (1) partner selection and alliance formation, (2) alliance design and governance, and (3) post-formation alliance management.

Alliance Management Capability

EXHIBIT 9.3

Alliance Management Capability

POST-FORMATION ALLIANCE MANAGEMENT. The third phase in a firm's alliance management capability concerns the ongoing management of the alliance. To be a source of competitive advantage, the partnership needs to create resource combinations that obey the VRIO criteria. As shown in Exhibit 9.4, this can be most likely accomplished if the alliance partners *make relation-specific investments, establish knowledge-sharing routines,* and *build interfirm trust.*[43]

Trust is a critical aspect of any alliance. Interfirm trust entails the expectation that each alliance partner will behave in good faith and develop norms of reciprocity and fairness.[44] Such trust helps ensure that the relationship survives and thereby increases the possibility of meeting the intended goals of the alliance. Interfirm trust is also important for fast decision making.[45] Several firms such as Eli Lilly, HP, Procter & Gamble, and IBM compete to obtain trustworthy reputations in order to become the alliance "partner of choice" for small technology ventures, universities, and individual inventors.

Indeed, the systematic differences in firms' alliance management capability can be a source of competitive advantage.[46] But how do firms build alliance management capability? The answer is to build capability through repeated experiences over time. In support of this idea, several empirical studies have shown that firms move down the learning curve and become better at managing alliances through repeated alliance exposure.[47]

The "learning-by-doing" approach has value for small ventures in which a few key people coordinate most of the firms' activities.[48] However, there are clearly limitations for larger companies. Conglomerates such as ABB, GE, Philips, or Siemens are engaged in hundreds of alliances simultaneously. In fact, if alliances are not managed from a portfolio perspective at the corporate level, serious negative repercussions can emerge.[49] Groupe Danone, a large French food conglomerate, lost its leading position in the highly lucrative and fast-growing Chinese market because its local alliance partner, Hangzhou Wahaha Group, terminated their long-standing alliance.[50] Wahaha accused different Danone business units of subsequently setting up partnerships with other Chinese firms that were a direct competitive threat to Wahaha. This example makes it clear that although alliances are important pathways by which to pursue business-level strategy, they are best managed at the corporate level.

EXHIBIT 9.4 / How to Make Alliances Work

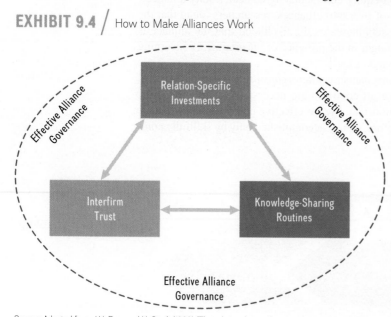

Source: Adapted from J.H. Dyer and H. Singh (1998), "The relational view: Cooperative strategy and the sources of intraorganizational advantage," *Academy of Management Review* 23: 660–679.

To accomplish effective alliance management, strategy scholars suggest that firms create a *dedicated alliance function,*[51] led by a vice president or director of alliance management and endowed with its own resources and support staff. The dedicated alliance function should be given the tasks of coordinating all alliance-related activity in the entire organization, taking a corporate-level perspective. It should serve as a repository of prior experience and be responsible for creating processes and structures to teach and leverage that experience and related knowledge throughout the rest of the organization across all levels. Research shows that firms with a dedicated alliance function are able to create value from their alliances above and beyond what could be expected based on experience alone.[52]

Pharmaceutical company Eli Lilly is an acknowledged leader in alliance management.[53] Lilly's Office of Alliance Management, led by a director and endowed with several full-time positions, manages its far-flung alliance activity across all hierarchical levels and around the globe. Lilly's process prescribes that each alliance is managed by a three-person team: an alliance champion, alliance leader, and alliance manager.

■ The *alliance champion* is a senior, corporate-level executive responsible for high-level support and oversight. This senior manager is also responsible for making sure that the alliance fits within the firm's existing alliance portfolio and corporate-level strategy.

■ The *alliance leader* has the technical expertise and knowledge needed for the specific technical area and is responsible for the day-to-day management of the alliance.

■ The *alliance manager,* positioned within the Office of Alliance Management, serves as an alliance process resource and business integrator between the two alliance partners and provides alliance training and development, as well as diagnostic tools.

Some companies are also able to leverage the relational capabilities obtained through managing alliance portfolios into a successful acquisition strategy.[54] As detailed earlier, Eli Lilly has an entire department at the corporate level devoted to managing its alliance portfolio. Following up on an earlier 50/50 joint venture formed with Icos, maker of the $1 billion-plus erectile-dysfunction drug Cialis, Lilly acquired Icos in 2007. Just a year later, Eli Lilly outmaneuvered Bristol-Myers Squibb to acquire biotech venture ImClone for $6.5 billion. ImClone discovered and developed the cancer-fighting drug Erbitux, also a $1 billion blockbuster in terms of annual sales. The acquisition of these two smaller biotech ventures allowed Lilly to address its problem of an empty drug pipeline.[55]

9.3 Mergers and Acquisitions

LO 9-5

Differentiate between mergers and acquisitions, and explain why firms would use either to execute corporate strategy.

A popular vehicle for executing corporate strategy is mergers and acquisitions (M&A). Hundreds of mergers and acquisitions occur each year, with a cumulative value in the trillions of dollars.[56] Although the terms are often used interchangeably, and usually in tandem, mergers and acquisitions are, by definition, distinct from each other. A **merger** describes the joining of two independent companies to form *a combined entity.* Mergers tend to be friendly; in mergers, the two firms agree to join in order to create a combined entity. In the live event-promotion business, for example, Live Nation merged with Ticketmaster.

An **acquisition** describes the purchase or takeover of one company by another. Acquisitions can be friendly or unfriendly. As discussed in the ChapterCase, Disney's acquisition of Pixar, for example, was a friendly one, in which both management teams believed that joining the two companies was a good idea. When a target firm does not want to be acquired, the acquisition is considered a **hostile takeover**. British telecom company Vodafone's acquisition of Germany-based Mannesmann, a diversified conglomerate with holdings in telephony and Internet services, at an estimated value of $150 billion, was a hostile one.

In defining mergers and acquisitions, size can matter as well. The combining of two firms of comparable size is often described as a merger even though it might in fact be an acquisition. For example, the integration of Daimler and Chrysler was pitched as a merger, though in reality Daimler acquired Chrysler, and later sold it. After emerging from bankruptcy restructuring, Chrysler is now majority-owned by Fiat, an Italian auto manufacturer.

In contrast, when large, incumbent firms such as GE, Cisco, or Microsoft buy start-up companies, the transaction is generally described as an acquisition. Although there is a distinction between mergers and acquisitions, many observers simply use the umbrella term *mergers and acquisitions,* or M&A.

merger
The joining of two independent companies to form a combined entity.

acquisition
The purchase or takeover of one company by another; can be friendly or unfriendly.

hostile takeover
Acquisition in which the target company does not wish to be acquired.

LO 9-6

Define horizontal integration and evaluate the advantages and disadvantages of this option to execute corporate-level strategy.

horizontal integration
The process of merging with competitors, leading to industry consolidation.

WHY DO FIRMS MERGE WITH COMPETITORS?

In contrast to vertical integration, which concerns the number of activities a firm participates in up and down the industry value chain (as discussed in Chapter 8), **horizontal integration** is the process of merging with a competitor at the same stage of the industry value chain. Horizontal integration is a type of corporate strategy that can improve a firm's strategic position in a single industry. As a rule of thumb, firms should go ahead with horizontal integration (i.e., acquiring a competitor) *if the target firm is more valuable inside the acquiring firm than as a continued standalone company.* This implies that the net value creation of a horizontal acquisition must be positive to aid in gaining and sustaining a competitive advantage.

An industry-wide trend toward horizontal integration leads to industry consolidation. In particular, competitors in the same industry such as airlines, banking, telecommunications, pharmaceuticals, or health insurance frequently merge to respond to changes in their external environment and to change the underlying industry structure in their favor.

There are three main benefits to a horizontal integration strategy:

- Reduction in competitive intensity.
- Lower costs.
- Increased differentiation.

Exhibit 9.5 previews the sources of value creation and costs in horizontal integration, which we discuss next.

REDUCTION IN COMPETITIVE INTENSITY. Looking through the lens of Porter's five forces model with a focus on rivalry among competitors (introduced in Chapter 3), horizontal integration changes the underlying industry structure in favor of the surviving firms. Excess capacity is taken out of the market, and competition tends to decrease as a consequence of horizontal integration, assuming no new entrants. As a whole, the industry structure becomes more consolidated and potentially more profitable. If the surviving firms find themselves in an oligopolistic industry structure and maintain a focus on non-price competition (i.e., focus on R&D spending, customer service, or advertising), the industry can indeed be quite profitable, and rivalry would likely decrease among existing firms. The wave of recent horizontal integration in the U.S. airline industry, for example, provided several benefits to the surviving carriers. By reducing excess capacity, the mergers between Delta and Northwest Airlines, United Airlines and Continental, Southwest and AirTran, and American and US Airways lowered competitive intensity in the industry overall.

Horizontal integration can favorably affect several of Porter's five forces for the surviving firms: strengthening bargaining power vis-à-vis suppliers and buyers, reducing the threat of entry, and reducing rivalry among existing firms. Because of the potential to reduce competitive intensity in an industry, government authorities such as the Federal Trade Commission (FTC) in the United States and/or the European Commission usually

EXHIBIT 9.5

Sources of Value Creation and Costs in Horizontal Integration

Corporate Strategy	Sources of Value Creation (*V*)	Sources of Costs (*C*)
Horizontal integration through M&A	• Reduction in competitive intensity • Lower costs • Increased differentiation	• Integration failure • Reduced flexibility • Increased potential for legal repercussions

must approve any large horizontal integration activity. Industry dynamics, however, are in constant flux as new competitors emerge and others fall by the wayside.

In 2005, for example, the FTC did not approve the proposed merger between Staples and Office Depot, arguing that the remaining industry would have only two competitors, with Office Max being the other. Staples and Office Depot argued that the market for office supplies needed to be defined more broadly to include large retailers such as Walmart and Target. The U.S. courts sided with the FTC, which argued that the prices for end consumers would be significantly higher if the market had only two category killers.[57] A few years later, however, the competitive landscape had shifted further as Walmart and Amazon had emerged as ferocious competitors offering rock-bottom prices for office supplies. Subsequently, in 2013, the FTC approved the merger between Staples and Office Max. Just two years later, the FTC also approved the merger between the now much larger Staples and Office Depot.[58]

LOWER COSTS. Firms use horizontal integration to lower costs through economies of scale and to enhance their economic value creation, and in turn their performance.[59] In industries that have high fixed costs, achieving economies of scale through large output is critical in lowering costs. The dominant pharmaceutical companies such as Pfizer, Roche, and Novartis, for example, maintain large sales forces ("detail people") who call on doctors and hospitals to promote their products. These specialized sales forces often number 10,000 or more and thus are a significant fixed cost to the firms, even though part of their compensation is based on commissions. Maintaining such a large and sophisticated sales force (many with MBAs) is costly if the firm has only a few drugs it can show the doctor. As a rule of thumb, if a pharma company does not possess a blockbuster drug that brings in more than $1 billion in annual revenues, it cannot maintain its own sales force.[60] When existing firms such as Pfizer and Wyeth merge, they join their drug pipelines and portfolios of existing drugs. They are likely to have one sales force for the combined portfolio, consequently reducing the size of the sales force and lowering the overall cost of distribution.

INCREASED DIFFERENTIATION. Horizontal integration through M&A can help firms strengthen their competitive positions by increasing the differentiation of their product and service offerings. In particular, horizontal integration can do this by filling gaps in a firm's product offering, allowing the combined entity to offer a complete suite of products and services.

As mentioned in the ChapterCase, Disney acquired Marvel for $4 billion. This acquisition certainly allowed Disney to further differentiate its product offering as an entire new lineup of superheroes was joining Mickey's family, besides being able to offer Marvel superhero themed-rides and merchandise such as clothing (T-shirts, PJs, etc.) and toys. The Marvel acquisition passed an important test of value creation because Marvel is seen as more valuable inside Disney than outside Disney.[61] Because of economies of scope and economies of scale, Marvel is becoming more valuable inside Disney than as a standalone enterprise. The same argument could be made for the other recent Disney acquisitions, including Pixar and Lucasfilm, both highlighted in the ChapterCase.

WHY DO FIRMS ACQUIRE OTHER FIRMS?

LO 9-7

Explain why firms engage in acquisitions.

When first defining the terminology at the beginning of the chapter, we noted that an *acquisition* describes the purchase or takeover of one company by another. Why do firms make acquisitions? Three main reasons stand out:

- ■ To gain access to new markets and distribution channels.
- ■ To gain access to a new capability or competency.
- ■ To preempt rivals.

Strategy Highlight 9.2

Food Fight: Kraft's Hostile Takeover of Cadbury

In 2010, Kraft Foods bought UK-based Cadbury PLC for close to $20 billion in a hostile takeover. Unlike the more diversified food-products company Kraft, Cadbury was focused solely on candy and gum. Hailing to 1824, Cadbury established itself in markets across the globe, in concert with the British Empire.

Kraft was attracted to Cadbury due to its strong position in countries such as India, Egypt, and Thailand and in fast-growing markets in Latin America. Cadbury held 70 percent of the market share for chocolate in India, with more than 1 billion people. Children there specifically ask for "Cadbury chocolate" instead of just plain "chocolate." It is difficult for outsiders like Kraft to break into emerging economies because earlier entrants have developed and perfected their distribution systems to meet the needs of millions of small, independent vendors. To secure a strong strategic position in these fast-growing emerging markets, therefore, Kraft felt that horizontal integration with Cadbury was critical. Kraft continues to face formidable competitors in global markets, including Nestlé and Mars, both of which are especially strong in China.

To focus its different strategic business units more effectively and to reduce costs, Kraft Foods restructured in 2012. It separated its North American grocery-food business from its global snack-food and candy business (including Oreos and Cadbury chocolate), which is now Mondelez International. In 2015, Kraft Foods merged with Heinz (owned

© Keith Homan/Shutterstock.com RF

by Warren Buffett's Berkshire Hathaway and 3G Capital, a Brazilian hedge fund) in a $37 billion merger, creating the fifth-largest food company in the world, behind Nestlé, Mondelez, PepsiCo, and Unilever.

In the U.S. market, the Cadbury acquisition allows the new Kraft Heinz greater access to convenience stores, gives it a new distribution channel, and opens a market for it that is growing fast and tends to have high profit margins. Domestically, Kraft Heinz has to compete with The Hershey Company, the largest U.S. chocolate manufacturer. This battle is intense because Hershey's main strategic focus is squarely on its home market. With the U.S. population growing slowly and becoming more health-conscious, however, Hershey decided to enter the Chinese market in 2013, the world's fastest-growing candy market. Since its founding in 1894, Hershey's entry into China is the company's first new product launch outside the United States. Hershey's sales growth in China, however, has been disappointing so far. Combined with little or no growth in the United States, Hershey announced job cuts in 2015.[62]

TO GAIN ACCESS TO NEW MARKETS AND DISTRIBUTION CHANNELS. Firms may resort to acquisitions when they need to overcome entry barriers into markets they are currently not competing in or to access new distribution channels. Strategy Highlight 9.2 discusses Kraft's acquisition of Cadbury to tap into new distribution channels in both the United States and fast-growing international markets.

TO GAIN ACCESS TO A NEW CAPABILITY OR COMPETENCY. Firms often resort to M&A to obtain new capabilities or competencies. To strengthen its capabilities in server systems and equipment and to gain access to the capability of designing mobile chips for the Internet of things (the concept that everyday objects such as cell phones, wearable devices, temperature controls, household appliances, cars, etc., have network connectivity, allowing them to send and receive data), Intel acquired Altera for $17 billion.[63]

TO PREEMPT RIVALS. Sometimes firms may acquire promising startups not only to gain access to a new capability or competency, but also to preempt rivals from doing so. Let's look at the acquisitions made by two of the leading Internet companies: Facebook and Google.[64]

To preempt rivals Facebook acquired Instagram, a photo- and video-sharing social media site, for $1 billion in 2012. Snapchat, however, spurned a $3 billion offer from Facebook in 2013. Facebook then went on to buy the text messaging service start-up WhatsApp for $22 billion in 2014, making it one of the largest tech acquisitions ever. In the same year, Facebook paid $2 billion to acquire Oculus, a new venture making virtual reality headsets.

Google has made a string of acquisitions of new ventures to preempt rivals. In 2006, Google bought YouTube, the video-sharing website, for $1.65 billion. Google engaged in a somewhat larger acquisition when it bought Motorola's cell phone unit for $12.5 billion (in 2011). This was done to gain access to Motorola's valuable patent holdings in mobile technology. Google later sold the cell phone unit to Lenovo, while retaining Motorola's patents. In 2013, Google purchased the Israeli start-up company Waze for $1 billion. Google acquired Waze to gain access to a new capability and to prevent rivals from gaining access. Waze's claim to fame is its interactive mobile map app. Google is already the leader in online maps and wanted to extend this capability to mobile devices. Perhaps even more importantly, Google's intent was to preempt its competitors Apple and Facebook from buying Waze. Apple and Facebook are each comparatively weaker than Google in the increasingly important interactive mobile map and information services segment.

M&A AND COMPETITIVE ADVANTAGE

> **LO 9-8**
>
> Evaluate whether mergers and acquisitions lead to competitive advantage.

Do mergers and acquisitions create competitive advantage? Despite their popularity, the answer, surprisingly, is that in most cases they do not. In fact, the M&A performance track record is rather mixed. Many mergers destroy shareholder value because the anticipated synergies never materialize.[65] If value is created, it generally accrues to the shareholders of the firm that was taken over (the acquiree), because acquirers often pay a premium when buying the target company.[66] Indeed, sometimes companies get involved in a bidding war for an acquisition; the winner may end up with the prize but may have overpaid for the acquisition—thus falling victim to the *winner's curse.*

Given that mergers and acquisitions, *on average,* destroy rather than create shareholder value, why do we see so many mergers? Reasons include:

- Principal–agent problems.
- The desire to overcome competitive disadvantage.
- Superior acquisition and integration capability.

PRINCIPAL–AGENT PROBLEMS. When discussing diversification in the previous chapter, we noted that some firms diversify through acquisitions due to principal–agent problems (see Chapter 8 discussion of managerial motives behind firm growth).[67] Managers, as agents, are supposed to act in the best interest of the principals, the shareholders. However,

Sometimes the combined value of two companies is less than the value of each company separately. Oatmeal: © McGraw-Hill Education/ Mark Dierker, photographer; Snapple: © George W. Bailey/ Shutterstock.com RF

managerial hubris A form of self-delusion in which managers convince themselves of their superior skills in the face of clear evidence to the contrary.

managers may have incentives to grow their firms through acquisitions—not for anticipated shareholder value appreciation, but to build a larger empire, which is positively correlated with prestige, power, and pay. Besides providing higher compensation and more corporate perks, a larger organization may also provide more job security, especially if the company pursues unrelated diversification.

A related problem is **managerial hubris**, a form of self-delusion in which managers convince themselves of their superior skills in the face of clear evidence to the contrary.[68] Managerial hubris comes in two forms:

1. Managers of the acquiring company convince themselves that they are able to manage the business of the target company more effectively and, therefore, create additional shareholder value. This justification is often used for an unrelated diversification strategy.

2. Although most top-level managers are aware that the majority of acquisitions destroy rather than create shareholder value, they see themselves as the exceptions to the rule.

Managerial hubris has led to many ill-fated deals, destroying billions of dollars. For example, Quaker Oats Company acquired Snapple because its managers thought Snapple was another Gatorade, which was a successful previous acquisition.[69] The difference was that Gatorade had been a standalone company and was easily integrated, but Snapple relied on a decentralized network of independent distributors and retailers who did not want Snapple to be taken over and who made it difficult and costly for Quaker Oats Company to integrate Snapple. The acquisition failed—and Quaker Oats itself was taken over by PepsiCo. Snapple was spun out and eventually ended up being part of the Dr Pepper Snapple Group.

THE DESIRE TO OVERCOME COMPETITIVE DISADVANTAGE. In some instances, mergers are not motivated by gaining competitive advantage, but by the attempt to overcome a competitive disadvantage. For example, to compete more successfully with Nike, the worldwide leader in sports shoes and apparel, adidas (number two) acquired Reebok (number three) for $3.8 billion in 2006. This acquisition allows the now-larger adidas group to benefit from economies of scale and scope that were unachievable when adidas and Reebok operated independently. The hope was that this would help in overcoming adidas' competitive disadvantage vis-à-vis Nike. In the meantime, Under Armour has outperformed adidas in the U.S. market and has become the number two after Nike.

SUPERIOR ACQUISITION AND INTEGRATION CAPABILITY. Acquisition and integration capabilities are not equally distributed across firms. Although there is strong evidence that mergers and acquisitions, *on average,* destroy rather than create shareholder value, it does not exclude the possibility that *some* firms are consistently able to identify, acquire, and integrate target companies to strengthen their competitive positions. Since it is valuable, rare, and difficult to imitate, a superior acquisition and integration capability, together with past experience, can lead to competitive advantage.

Disney has shown superior post-merger integration capabilities after acquiring Pixar, Marvel, and Lucasfilm. Disney managed its new subsidiaries more like alliances rather than attempting full integration, which could have destroyed the unique value of the acquisitions. In Pixar's case, Disney kept the entire creative team in place and allowed its members to continue to work in Pixar's headquarters near San Francisco with minimum interference. The hands-off approach paid huge dividends: Although Disney paid a steep $7.4 billion for Pixar, it made some $10 billion on Pixar's *Toy Story 3* franchise revenues alone. As a consequence, Disney has gained a competitive advantage over its rivals such as Sony and has also outperformed the Dow Jones Industrial Average over the past few years by a wide margin.

9.3 ◀▶ Implications for the Strategist

The business environment is constantly changing.[70] New opportunities come and go quickly. Firms often need to develop new resources, capabilities, or competencies to take advantage of opportunities. Examples abound. Traditional book publishers must transform themselves into digital content companies. Old-line banking institutions with expensive networks of branches must now offer seamless online banking services. They must make them work between a set of traditional and nontraditional payment services on a mobile platform. Energy providers are in the process of changing their coal-fired power plants to gas-fired ones in the wake of the shale gas boom. Pharmaceutical companies need to take advantage of advances in biotechnology to drive future growth. Food companies are now expected to offer organic, all natural, and gluten-free products.

The strategist also knows that firms need to grow to survive and prosper, especially if they are publicly traded stock companies. A firm's corporate strategy is critical in pursuing growth. To be able to grow as well as gain and sustain a competitive advantage, a firm must not only possess VRIO resources but also be able to leverage existing resources, often in conjunction with partners, and build new ones. The question of how to build new resources, capabilities, and competencies to grow your enterprise lies at the center of corporate strategy. Strategic alliances, mergers, and acquisitions are the key tools that the strategist uses in executing corporate strategy.

Ideally, the tools to execute corporate strategy—strategic alliances and acquisitions—should be centralized and managed at the corporate level, rather than at the level of the strategic business unit. This allows the company to not only assess their effect on the overall company performance, but also to harness spillovers between the different corporate development activities. That is, corporate-level managers should not only coordinate the firm's portfolio of alliances, but also leverage their relationships to successfully engage in mergers and acquisitions.[71] Rather than focusing on developing an alliance management capability in isolation, firms should develop a *relational capability* that allows for the successful management of both strategic alliances *and* mergers and acquisitions. In sum, to ensure a positive effect on competitive advantage, the management of strategic alliances and M&A needs to be placed at the corporate level.

We now have concluded our discussion of corporate strategy. Acquisitions and alliances are the key vehicles to execute corporate strategy, each with its distinct advantages and disadvantages. It is also clear from this chapter that strategic alliances, as well as mergers and acquisitions, are a global phenomenon. In the next chapter, we discuss strategy in a global world.

CHAPTER**CASE 9** / Consider This...

THE CORPORATE STRATEGY of creating billion-dollar franchises is Disney's main focus. CEO Iger leads a group of about 20 executives whose sole responsibility is to hunt for new billion-dollar franchises. This group of senior leaders decides top-down which projects are a go and which are not. They also allocate resources to particular projects. Disney even organized its employees in the consumer products group around franchises such as *Frozen, Toy Story, Star Wars,* and other cash cows.

While things seem to be sunny right now in Southern California, there are clouds on the horizon. First, relying on a few big franchises is quite risky. What if the pipeline dries up? Many of Disney's greatest franchises such as *Star Wars* joined the family through an acquisition. (The newly released *Star Wars* sequel *The Force Awakens* is predicted to gross over $1 billion on the big screens, making it the third-bestselling movie ever after *Avatar* and *Titanic*.) An acquisition-led growth strategy, however, may not be sustainable because of the limited number of media companies such as Pixar, Marvel, or Lucasfilm that Disney can acquire. Second, some critics assert that focusing too much on billion-dollar franchises reduces originality and leaves consumers bored more quickly. Disney's recipe of success also becomes too predictable.

Third, and perhaps most important, roughly half of Disney profits come from its TV networks ESPN, ABC, and others. The media industry, however, is being disrupted: People spend much less time and money watching movies on the large screen and spend more time consuming content online via YouTube, Netflix, Hulu, and other streaming services. While ESPN is certainly very successful, the cost of rights to show the big sporting events live has escalated dramatically in recent years. In addition, more and more subscribers have cut their cable cord and get their media online. As a response, cable providers are more likely to unbundle their service offerings, which may create challenges for ESPN, an expensive part of the cable bundle (some estimate $8) with a narrow focus that doesn't appeal to everyone.

Questions

1. Do you think focusing on billion-dollar franchises is a good corporate strategy for Disney? What are pros and cons of this strategy?

2. Given the build-borrow-or-buy framework discussed in the chapter, do you think Disney should pursue alternatives to acquisitions? Why or why not?

3. Why do you think Disney was so successful with the Pixar and Marvel acquisitions, while other media interactions such as Sony's acquisition of Columbia Pictures or News Corp.'s acquisition of MySpace were much less successful?

4. Given Disney's focus on creating and milking billion-dollar franchises, some industry observers now view Disney more as a global consumer products company like Nike rather than a media company. Do you agree with this perspective? Why or why not? What strategic implications would it have if Disney is truly a global consumer products company rather than a media company?

TAKE-AWAY CONCEPTS

This chapter discussed two mechanisms of corporate-level strategy—alliances and acquisitions—as summarized by the following learning objectives and related take-away concepts.

LO 9-1 / Apply the build-borrow-or-buy framework to guide corporate strategy.

▪ The build-borrow-or-buy framework provides a conceptual model that aids strategists in deciding whether to pursue internal development *(build)*, enter a contract arrangement or strategic alliance *(borrow)*, or acquire new resources, capabilities, and competencies *(buy)*.

■ Firms that are able to learn how to select the right pathways to obtain new resources are more likely to gain and sustain a competitive advantage.

LO 9-2 / Define strategic alliances, and explain why they are important to implement corporate strategy and why firms enter into them.

■ Strategic alliances have the goal of sharing knowledge, resources, and capabilities to develop processes, products, or services.

■ An alliance qualifies as strategic if it has the potential to affect a firm's competitive advantage by increasing value and/or lowering costs.

■ The most common reasons firms enter alliances are to (1) strengthen competitive position, (2) enter new markets, (3) hedge against uncertainty, (4) access critical complementary resources, and (5) learn new capabilities.

LO 9-3 / Describe three alliance governance mechanisms and evaluate their pros and cons.

■ Alliances can be governed by the following mechanisms: contractual agreements for non-equity alliances, equity alliances, and joint ventures.

■ There are pros and cons of each alliance governance mechanism, shown in detail in Exhibit 9.2 with highlights as follows:

Non-equity alliance's pros: flexible, fast, easy to get in and out; cons: weak ties, lack of trust/commitment.

Equity alliance's pros: stronger ties, potential for trust/commitment, window into new technology (option value); cons: less flexible, slower, can entail significant investment.

Joint venture pros: strongest tie, trust/commitment most likely, may be required by institutional setting; cons: potentially long negotiations and significant investments, long-term solution, managers may have two reporting lines (two bosses).

LO 9-4 / Describe the three phases of alliance management and explain how an alliance management capability can lead to a competitive advantage.

■ An alliance management capability consists of a firm's ability to effectively manage alliance-related tasks through three phases: (1) partner selection and alliance formation, (2) alliance design and governance, and (3) post-formation alliance management.

■ An alliance management capability can be a source of competitive advantage as better management of alliances leads to more likely superior performance.

■ Firms build a superior alliance management capability through "learning by doing" and by establishing a dedicated alliance function.

LO 9-5 / Differentiate between mergers and acquisitions, and explain why firms would use either to execute corporate strategy.

■ A merger describes the joining of two independent companies to form a combined entity.

■ An acquisition describes the purchase or takeover of one company by another. It can be friendly or hostile.

■ Although there is a distinction between mergers and acquisitions, many observers simply use the umbrella term *mergers and acquisitions*, or M&A.

■ Firms can use M&A activity for competitive advantage when they possess a superior relational capability, which is often built on superior alliance management capability.

LO 9-6 / Define horizontal integration and evaluate the advantages and disadvantages of this option to execute corporate-level strategy.

■ Horizontal integration is the process of merging with competitors, leading to industry consolidation.

■ As a corporate strategy, firms use horizontal integration to (1) reduce competitive intensity, (2) lower costs, and (3) increase differentiation.

LO 9-7 / Explain why firms engage in acquisitions.

■ Firms engage in acquisitions to (1) access new markets and distributions channels, (2) gain access to a new capability or competency, and (3) preempt rivals.

LO 9-8 / Evaluate whether mergers and acquisitions lead to competitive advantage.

■ Most mergers and acquisitions destroy shareholder value because anticipated synergies never materialize.

■ If there is any value creation in M&A, it generally accrues to the shareholders of the firm that is taken over (the acquiree), because acquirers

- often pay a premium when buying the target company.

■ Mergers and acquisitions are a popular vehicle for corporate-level strategy implementation for three reasons: (1) because of principal–agent problems, (2) the desire to overcome competitive disadvantage, and (3) the quest for superior acquisition and integration capability.

KEY TERMS

Acquisition *(p. 309)*

Alliance management capability *(p. 307)*

Build-borrow-or-buy framework *(p. 297)*

Co-opetition *(p. 303)*

Corporate venture capital (CVC) *(p. 306)*

Equity alliance *(p. 305)*

Explicit knowledge *(p. 304)*

Horizontal integration *(p. 310)*

Hostile takeover *(p. 309)*

Learning races *(p. 303)*

Managerial hubris *(p. 318)*

Merger *(p. 309)*

Non-equity alliance *(p. 304)*

Real-options perspective *(p. 302)*

Relational view of competitive advantage *(p. 300)*

Strategic alliance *(p. 299)*

Tacit knowledge *(p. 305)*

DISCUSSION QUESTIONS

1. The chapter identifies three governing mechanisms for strategic alliances: non-equity, equity, and joint venture. List the benefits and downsides for each of these mechanisms.

2. An alliance's purpose can affect which governance structure is optimal. Compare a pharmaceutical R&D alliance with a prescription-drug marketing agreement, and recommend a governing mechanism for each. Provide reasons for your selections.

3. Alliances are often used to pursue business-level goals, but they may be managed at the corporate level. Explain why this portfolio approach to alliance management would make sense.

4. An alliance's purpose can affect which governance structure is optimal. Compare a pharmaceutical R&D alliance with a prescription-drug marketing agreement, and recommend a governing mechanism for each. Provide reasons for your selections.

5. Alliances are often used to pursue business-level goals, but they may be managed at the corporate level. Explain why this portfolio approach to alliance management would make sense.

ETHICAL/SOCIAL ISSUES

1. If mergers and acquisitions quite often end up providing a competitive disadvantage, why do so many of them take place? Given the poor track record, is the continuing M&A activity a result of principal–agent problems and managerial hubris? What can be done to overcome principal–agent problems? Are there other reasons for poor performance?

2. Alliances and acquisitions can sometimes lead to less access or higher prices for consumers. Comcast bought NBC Universal (from GE). When one content provider and the Internet access provider are the same, will this lead to some content being favored over others on the Internet? For example, will Comcast want to send Universal movies (which it owns) with faster download capabilities than it sends, say, a *Harry Potter* movie from Warner Brothers (which it doesn't own)? If you were a Comcast executive, would you want to favor the speed of your own content delivery versus other content providers, including Netflix?[72]

SMALL GROUP EXERCISES

//// Small Group Exercise 1

In this chapter, we studied horizontal integration and the build-borrow-or-buy framework. One industry currently consolidating is furniture manufacturing, with thousands of manufacturers and suppliers. Manufacturers range from large recognizable brands, such as Baker, Steelcase, and La-Z-Boy, to small family-owned companies. Demand for both office furniture and residential furniture is experiencing post-recession growth. Analysts have observed that companies are shopping for acquisitions as consumers are shopping for furniture.

Charter Capital Partners in Grand Rapids, Michigan, is a mergers and acquisitions adviser helping companies initiate, negotiate, and close deals on one company's purchase of another. To take advantage of the increase in M&A activity in the furniture manufacturing industry, Charter recently launched a dedicated furniture practice. Western Michigan is home to the top three office furniture manufacturers, which is a key segment of the industry. The sales of the top three make up half of the industry's $10 billion market.

Charter Capital Partners has hired your small consulting team to do the basic research regarding a client that has recently approached the group. The client is a small manufacturer of office furniture in a medium-sized town in Michigan. The managers are seeking advice as they decide whether to upgrade capabilities in order to expand sales, to find a partner with complementary skills, or to sell to a larger company. The owner has stated that the firm is like a family, and he feels a sense of loyalty to the workers and the community. The firm has had steady sales over its history, although it experienced a slight dip in sales during the recession. The company is aware that other office furniture manufacturers are beginning to integrate technology into the furniture. For example, one competitor is building wireless technology into desk surfaces to power several devices at one time and avoid the need to plug them in. The owner sees the integration of technology as a game changer.

Using the build-borrow-or-buy framework and other strategic concepts, develop a set of questions to ask the managers of this small business in order to gather information regarding a decision as to whether to hire new employees with more sophisticated technology expertise in order to build capabilities *in-house*

or whether to *partner* with another firm that already has these capabilities. Alternatively, consider information that could help the owner decide whether this is the time to sell to a larger company. Your consulting team will need adequate information to help put a value on the firm in order to advise Charter if/when it initiates a search for a partner or buyer.

//// Small Group Exercise 2

The global public relations and communications firm Burson-Marsteller conducted its first study of how the Fortune Global 100 used social media in 2010. It found that 79 percent of the 100 largest companies used Twitter, Facebook, YouTube, or corporate blogs to communicate corporate messages to customers and other stakeholders. Burson-Marsteller wanted to learn how the largest global companies had changed their usage of social media after two years of experience and conducted *The Global Social Media Check-Up 2012*.

The 2012 study focused on the Fortune Global 100 companies' social media activity on Twitter, Facebook, YouTube, Google Plus, and Pinterest. The findings show that companies have gained experience and adapted quickly. Twitter is the most popular platform, as tweets have exploded from 50 million tweets per day in 2010 to 340 million per day in 2012 (over 1 billion every three days). Because of this popularity, 82 percent of the companies have Twitter accounts (up from 65 percent in 2010), and 79 percent are actively engaged in retweeting or @mentions. YouTube has seen the most growth in company usage—79 percent of companies create original content to use on YouTube (up from 50 percent) and average 2 million viewers. Companies are also reacting faster to new social media platforms; Google Plus was launched in November 2011, and 48 percent of the largest companies had accounts by March 2012. Another platform, Pinterest, is joined by invitation, and 48 percent of the Global 100 have accounts there.

The study found that companies now have more accounts on each platform. For example, they may have many Twitter accounts or Facebook pages established in order to communicate more effectively to different stakeholder interests and to highlight different products or services. The companies can provide general news or more specific information about career opportunities or customer service.

In your group, select three firms and research their social media web presence. If you select firms from the same industry, you can more directly compare and contrast their social media expertise.

1. Do the firms seem to do a good job of managing their web identity? If you chose firms from the same industry, is it evident how each firm's web content relates to its competitive position?

2. What differences do you find among the three firms? For example, do some tailor their message for different stakeholders? Are some firms more creative in generating YouTube content?

STRATEGY TERM PROJECT

Connect

The HP Running Case, *a related activity for each strategy term project module, is available in Connect.*

//// Module 9: Strategic Alliance and M&A Strategy

1. Use Exhibit 9.1 as a decision tree guide on your focal firm. Identify a strategic resource gap to study about the firm. Use the related questions to guide your thinking on the appropriate corporate strategy (build, borrow, or buy) to employ to close this gap and move the company forward.

2. Research what strategic alliances your firm has entered in the past three years. If there are several of these, choose the three you identify as the most important for further analysis. Based on company press releases and business journal reports for each alliance, what do you find to be the main reason the firm entered these alliances?

3. Do you think each of the three alliances achieves the original intent and therefore is successful? Why or why not?

4. Does your firm have an identifiable alliance management organization? Can you find any evidence that this organization improves the likelihood of success for these alliances? What responsibilities does this alliance management organization have in your firm?

5. Has your firm participated in any mergers or acquisitions in the past three years? What was the nature of these actions? Did they result in a consolidation of competitors?

*my*STRATEGY

What Is Your Network Strategy for Your Career?

Most of us participate in one or more popular social networks online such as Facebook, LinkedIn, Pinterest, Tumblr, or Twitter. While many of us spend countless hours in these social networks, you may not have given a lot of thought to your network strategy.

Social networks describe the relationships or ties between individuals linked to one another. An important element of social networks is the *different strengths of ties* between individuals. Some ties between two people in a network may be very strong (e.g., "soul mates" or "best friends"), while others are weak (mere acquaintances—"I talk to her briefly in the cafeteria at work").

As a member of a social network, you have access to *social capital*, which is derived from the connections within and between social networks. It is a function of whom you know, and what advantages you can create through those connections. Social capital is an important concept in business. Remember the old adage: *What matters is not what you know, but whom you know.*

Some Facebook users claim to have 2,000 or more "friends." With larger networks, one expects to have greater social capital, right? Though this seems obvious, academic research suggests that humans have the brain capacity to maintain a functional network of only about 150 people. This so-called *Dunbar number* was derived by extrapolating from the brain sizes and social networks of primates.

Far-fetched? Not necessarily. You may have a lot more than 150 friends on Facebook or connections on LinkedIn, but researchers call that number the *social core* of any network. Why is this the case? Even though it takes only a split second to accept a new request on Facebook or LinkedIn, relationships still need to be "groomed." To develop a meaningful relationship, you need to spend some time with this new connection, even in cyberspace.

Social networking sites allow users to broadcast their lives and to passively keep track of more people. They enlarge their social networks, even though many of those ties tend to be weak. It may come as a surprise, however, to learn that research shows new opportunities such as job offers tend to come from weak ties, because it is these weak ties that allow you to access non-redundant and novel information. This phenomenon is called *strength of weak ties*. So, in thinking about how to leverage your social capital more fully as part of your career network strategy, rather than always communicating with the same people, it may pay for you to invest a bit more time in grooming your weak ties.[73]

1. Create a list of up to 12 people at your university (or work environment if applicable) with whom you regularly communicate (in person, electronically, or both). Draw your network (place names or initials next to each node), and connect every node where people you communicate with also talk to one another (i.e., indicate friends of friends). Can you identify strong and weak ties in your network?

2. What is the *degree of closure* in your network? The density of your network reflects the degree of closure. Network density can be calculated in three simple steps.

Step 1: Create a simple matrix in which you list the names of the people in your network on both the horizontal and vertical axis. (This can be easily done in an Excel spreadsheet.) Then put an X in each box, indicating who knows whom in your network. Each X corresponds to a social tie in your network. Count the total number of Xs in your matrix. Let's assume $X = 8$.

Step 2: If your network contains 12 people (including yourself), $N = 12$. The maximum network density is calculated by the following formula: $[N \times (N - 1)] / 2$. If your network size is 12, then your maximum network density is $[12 \times (12 - 1)] / 2 = 66$. This is the maximum number of ties in your network when everybody knows everybody.

Step 3: To calculate your actual network density, divide X by N: Network density $= (X/N)$. In the example with eight ties in a network of 12 people, the network density is 0.67. The closer this number is to 1, the denser the network.

3. Network density is bound by 0 and 1. Is a network density that approaches 1 the most beneficial? Why or why not? Think about weak ties, which can also be indirect connections.

4. Compare your network to that of your group members (two to four people in your class). Do you find any commonalities in your networks? Who has the greatest social capital, and why? What can you do to "optimize" your network structure?

5. Now compare your actual career-related network using a site such as LinkedIn. Are any of your connections linked together? With how many alumni from your university are you linked? These alumni can provide a source of "weak ties" that may help you get a foot in the door at a potential new employer if you leverage them effectively.

ENDNOTES

1. This ChapterCase is based on: Fitz, B., "How Disney Milks Its Hits for Profits Ever After," *The Wall Street Journal,* June 8, 2015; Catmull, E., and A. Wallace (2014), *Creativity, Inc.: Overcoming the Unseen Forces That Stand in the Way of True Inspiration* (New York: Random House); "Superman v Spider-Man," *The Economist,* January 15, 2013; "Disney buys out George Lucas, the creator of 'Star Wars,'" *The Economist,* November 3, 2012; Isaacson, W. (2011), *Steve Jobs* (New York: Simon & Schuster); "Marvel superheroes join the Disney family," *The Wall Street Journal,* August 31, 2009; Paik, K. (2007),

To Infinity and Beyond!: The Story of Pixar Animation Studies (New York: Chronicle Books); and various Disney annual reports.

2. Capron, L., and W. Mitchell (2012), *Build, Borrow, or Buy: Solving the Growth Dilemma* (Boston, MA: Harvard Business Review Press).

3. Ibid., 16.

4. Hoang, H., and Rothaermel, F.T. (2010), "Leveraging internal and external experience: Exploration, exploitation, and R&D project performance," *Strategic Management Journal* 31: 734–758; and Gick, M.L., and

K.J. Holyoak (1987), "The cognitive basis of knowledge transfer," in ed. S.M. Cormier and J. D. Hagman, *Transfer of Learning* (New York: Academic Press): 9–46.

5. Gilbert, C.G. (2005), "Unbundling the structure of inertia: Resource versus routine rigidity," *Academy of Management Journal* 48: 741–763. For an insightful and in-depth discussion of the challenges faced by old-line media companies in making the transition to the Internet, see also: Cozzolino, A. (2015), *Three Essays on Technological Changes and Competitive Advantage: Evidence from the Newspaper Industry* (Milan: Bocconi University).

6. Ovide, S., "Microsoft to cut 7,800 jobs on Nokia woes," *The Wall Street Journal,* July 8, 2015.

7. Gulati, R. (1998), "Alliances and networks," *Strategic Management Journal* 19: 293–317.

8. This discussion draws on: Dyer, J.H., and H. Singh (1998), "The relational view: Cooperative strategy and the sources of interorganizational advantage," *Academy of Management Review* 23: 660–679.

9. Kale, P., and H. Singh (2009), "Managing strategic alliances: What do we know now, and where do we go from here?" *Academy of Management Perspectives* 23: 45–62.

10. For a review of the alliance literature, see: Kale and Singh, "Managing strategic alliances"; Lavie, D. (2006), "The competitive advantage of interconnected firms: An extension of the resource-based view," *Academy of Management Review* 31: 638–658; Ireland, R.D., M.A. Hitt, and D. Vaidyanath (2002), "Alliance management as a source of competitive advantage," *Journal of Management* 28: 413–446; Inkpen, A. (2001), "Strategic alliances," in M.A. Hitt, R.E. Freeman, and J.S. Harrison, *Handbook of Strategic Management* (Oxford, UK: Blackwell-Wiley); Gulati, R. (1998), "Alliances and networks," *Strategic Management Journal* 19: 293–317; and Dyer and Singh, "The relational view: Cooperative strategy and the sources of interorganizational advantage."

11. Kogut, B. (1991), "Joint ventures and the option to expand and acquire," *Management Science* 37: 19–34.

12. Markides, C.C., and P.J. Williamsen (1994), "Related diversification, core competences, and performance," *Strategic Management Journal* 15: 149–165; Kale and Singh, "Managing strategic alliances."

13. The author participated in the HP demo; and "HP unveils Halo collaboration studio: Life-like communication leaps across geographic boundaries," HP press release, December 12, 2005.

14. The source of this transcript is the video of the "1983 Apple Keynote-The '1984' Ad Introduction" speech and can be viewed at www.youtube.com/watch?v=lSiQA6KKyJo (6:42 min). The complete transcript can be viewed at http://lybio.net/steve-jobs-at-a-keynote-in-1983/commercials/. The "1984" ad can be viewed here www.youtube.com/watch?v=2zfqw8nhUwA (1:03 min).

15. Other sources for Strategy Highlight 9.1 include: Wakabayashi, D., "IBM, Apple want consumer apps catered to corporate," *The Wall Street Journal,* July 16, 2014; and "Big Blue Apple," *The Economist,* July 19, 2014.

16. "Bank of America taps Cisco for Tele Presence," *InformationWeek,* March 30, 2010.

17. Tripsas, M. (1997), "Unraveling the process of creative destruction: Complementary assets and incumbent survival in the typesetter industry," *Strategic Management Journal* 18: 119–142.

18. Rothaermel, F.T., and C.W.L. Hill (2005), "Technological discontinuities and complementary assets: A longitudinal study of industry and firm performance," *Organization Science* 16: 52–70; Hill, C.W.L., and F.T. Rothaermel (2003), "The performance of incumbent firms in the face of radical technological innovation," *Academy of Management Review* 28: 257–274; Rothaermel, F.T. (2001), "Incumbent's advantage through exploiting complementary assets via interfirm cooperation," *Strategic Management Journal* 22: 687–699; and Rothaermel, F.T. (2001), "Complementary assets, strategic alliances, and the incumbent's advantage: An empirical study of industry and firm effects in the biopharmaceutical industry," *Research Policy* 30: 1235–1251.

19. Arthaud-Day, M.L., F.T. Rothaermel, and W. Zhang (2013), "Genentech: After the acquisition by Roche," case study, in F.T. Rothaermel, *Strategic Management* (New York: McGraw-Hill), http://mcgrawhillcreate.com/rothaermel, ID# MHE-FTR-014-0077645065.

20. Jiang, L., J. Tan, and M. Thursby (2011), "Incumbent firm invention in emerging fields: Evidence from the semiconductor industry," *Strategic Management Journal* 32: 55–75; Rothaermel, F.T., and M. Thursby (2007), "The nanotech vs. the biotech revolution: Sources of incumbent productivity in research," *Research Policy* 36: 832–849.

21. This discussion is based on: Hess, A.M., and F.T. Rothaermel (2011), "When are assets complementary? Star scientists, strategic alliances and innovation in the pharmaceutical industry," *Strategic Management Journal* 32: 895–909; Ceccagnoli, M., and F.T. Rothaermel (2008), "Appropriating the returns to innovation," *Advances in Study of Entrepreneurship, Innovation, and Economic Growth* 18: 11–34; Rothaermel, F.T., and W. Boeker (2008), "Old technology meets new technology: Complementarities, similarities, and alliance formation," *Strategic Management Journal* 29 (1): 47–77; Rothaermel, F.T. (2001), "Incumbent's advantage through exploiting complementary assets via interfirm cooperation," *Strategic Management Journal* 22 (6–7): 687–699; Tripsas, M. (1997), "Unraveling the process of creative destruction: Complementary assets and incumbent survival in the typesetter industry," *Strategic Management Journal* 18: 51, 119–142; and Teece, D.J. (1986), "Profiting from technological innovation: Implications for integration, collaboration, licensing and public policy," *Research Policy* 15: 285–305.

22. Mowery, D.C., J.E. Oxley, and B.S. Silverman (1996), "Strategic alliances and interfirm knowledge transfer," *Strategic Management Journal* 17: 77–91.

23. Gnyawali, D., and B. Park (2011), "Co-opetition between Giants: Collaboration with competitors for technological innovation," *Research Policy* 40: 650–663; Gnyawali, D., J. He, and R. Madhaven (2008), "Co-opetition: Promises and challenges," in ed. C. Wankel, *21st Century Management: A Reference Handbook* (Thousand Oaks, CA: Sage): 386–398; and Brandenburger, A.M., and B.J. Nalebuff (1996), *Co-opetition* (New York: Currency Doubleday).

24. This discussion is based on: Kale, P., and H. Perlmutter (2000), "Learning and protection of proprietary assets in strategic alliances: Building relational capital," *Strategic Management Journal* 21: 217–237; Khanna, T., R. Gulati, and N. Nohria (1998), "The dynamics of learning alliances: Competition, cooperation, and relative scope," *Strategic Management Journal* 19: 193–210; Larsson, R., L. Bengtsson, K. Henriksson, and J. Sparks (1998), "The interorganizational learning dilemma: Collective knowledge development in strategic alliances," *Organization Science* 9: 285–305; Hamel, G. (1991), "Competition for competence and interpartner learning within international alliances," *Strategic Management Journal* 12: 83–103; and Hamel, G., Y. Doz, and C.K. Prahalad (1989), "Collaborate with your competitors—and win," *Harvard Business Review* (January–February): 190–196.

25. Nti, K.O., and R. Kumar (2000), "Differential learning in alliances," in ed. D. Faulkner and M. de Rond, *Cooperative Strategy. Economic, Business, and Organizational Issues* (Oxford, UK: University Press): 119–134. For an opposing viewpoint, see: Inkpen, A.C. (2008), "Knowledge transfer and international joint ventures: The case of NUMMI and General Motors," *Strategic Management Journal* 29: 447–453.

26. This discussion is based on: Lavie, D. (2006), "The competitive advantage of interconnected firms: An extension of the resource-based view," *Academy of Management Review* 31: 638–658; Hoang, H., and F.T. Rothaermel (2005), "The effect of general and partner-specific alliance experience on joint R&D project performance," *Academy of Management Journal* 48: 332–345; Ireland, R.D., M.A. Hitt, and D. Vaidyanath (2002), "Alliance management as a source of competitive advantage," *Journal of Management* 28: 413–446; and Gulati, R. (1998), "Alliances and networks," *Strategic Management Journal* 19: 293–317.

27. This is based on: Hoang, H., and F.T. Rothaermel (2010), "Leveraging internal and external experience: Exploration, exploitation, and R&D project performance," *Strategic Management Journal* 31 (7): 734–758; and Pisano, G.P., and P. Mang (1993), "Collaborative product development and the market for know-how: Strategies and structures in the biotechnology industry," in ed. R. Rosenbloom and R. Burgelman, *Research on Technological Innovation, Management, and Policy* (Greenwich, CT: J.A.I. Press): 109–136.

28. The distinction of explicit and tacit knowledge goes back to the seminal work by Polanyi, M. (1966), *The Tacit Dimension* (Chicago, IL: University of Chicago Press). For more recent treatments, see: Spender, J.-C. (1996), "Managing knowledge as the basis of a dynamic theory of the firm," *Strategic Management Journal* 17: 45–62; Spender, J.-C., and R.M. Grant (1996), "Knowledge and the firm," *Strategic Management Journal* 17: 5–9; and Crossan, M. M., H.W. Lane, R.E. White (1999), "An organizational learning framework: From intuition to institution," *Academy of Management Review* 24: 522–537.

29. "Toyota and Tesla partnering to make electric cars," *The Wall Street Journal,* May 21, 2010.

30. Ibid.

31. Ibid.

32. White, J.B., "Toyota confirms sale of part of Tesla stake," *The Wall Street Journal,* October 24, 2014.

33. For an insightful treatment of CVC investments, see: Dushnitsky, G., and M.J. Lenox (2005), "When do incumbent firms learn from entrepreneurial ventures? Corporate venture capital and investing firm innovation rates," *Research Policy* 34: 615–639; Dushnitsky, G., and M.J. Lenox (2005), "When do firms undertake R&D by investing in new ventures?" *Strategic Management Journal* 26: 947–965; Dushnitsky, G., and M.J. Lenox (2006), "When does corporate venture capital investment create value?" *Journal of Business Venturing* 21: 753–772; and Wadhwa, A., and S. Kotha (2006), "Knowledge creation through external venturing: Evidence from the telecommunications equipment manufacturing industry," *Academy of Management Journal* 49: 1–17.

34. Benson, D., and R.H. Ziedonis (2009), "Corporate venture capital as a window on new technology for the performance of corporate investors when acquiring startups," *Organization Science* 20: 329–351.

35. Dushnitsky, G., and M.J. Lenox (2006), "When does corporate venture capital investment create value?" *Journal of Business Venturing* 21: 753–772.

36. Higgins, M.J., and D. Rodriguez (2006), "The outsourcing of R&D through acquisition in the pharmaceutical industry," *Journal of Financial Economics* 80: 351–383; Benson, D., and R.H. Ziedonis (2009), "Corporate venture capital as a window on new technology for the performance of corporate investors when acquiring startups," *Organization Science* 20: 329–351.

37. Reuer, J.J., M. Zollo, and H. Singh (2002), "Post-formation dynamics in strategic alliances," *Strategic Management Journal* 23: 135–151.

38. This discussion is based on: Dyer, J.H., and H. Singh (1998), "The relational view: Cooperative strategy and the sources of interorganizational advantage," *Academy of Management Review* 23: 660–679; Ireland, R.D., M.A. Hitt, and D. Vaidyanath (2002), "Alliance management as a source of competitive advantage," *Journal of Management* 28: 413–446; and Lavie, D. (2006), "The competitive advantage of interconnected firms: An extension of the resource-based view," *Academy of Management Review* 31: 638–658.

39. For an insightful discussion of alliance management capability and alliance portfolios, see: Schilke, O., and A. Goerzten (2010), "Alliance management capability: An investigation of the construct and its measurement," *Journal of Management* 36: 1192–1219; Schreiner, M., P. Kale, and D. Corsten (2009), "What really is alliance management capability and how does it impact alliance outcomes and success?" *Strategic Management Journal* 30: 1395–1419; Ozcan, P., and K.M. Eisenhardt (2009), "Origin of alliance portfolios: Entrepreneurs, network strategies, and firm performance," *Academy of Management Journal* 52: 246–279; Hoffmann, W. (2007), "Strategies for managing a portfolio of alliances," *Strategic Management Journal* 28: 827–856;and Rothaermel, F.T., and D.L. Deeds (2006), "Alliance type, alliance experience, and alliance management capability in high-technology ventures," *Journal of Business Venturing* 21: 429–460.

40. Kale and Singh, "Managing strategic alliances."

41. Santoro, M.D., and J.P. McGill (2005), "The effect of uncertainty and asset co-specialization on governance in biotechnology alliances," *Strategic Management Journal* 26: 1261–1269.

42. This is based on: Gulati, R. (1995), "Does familiarity breed trust? The implications of repeated ties for contractual choice in alliances," *Academy of Management Journal* 38: 85–112; and Poppo, L., and T. Zenger (2002), "Do formal contracts and relational governance function as substitutes or complements?" *Strategic Management Journal* 23: 707–725.

43. Dyer, J.H., and H. Singh (1998), "The relational view: Cooperative strategy and the sources of interorganizational advantage," *Academy of Management Review* 23: 660–679.

44. Zaheer, A., B. McEvily, and V. Perrone (1998), "Does trust matter? Exploring the effects of interorganizational and interpersonal trust on performance," *Organization Science* 8: 141–159.

45. Covey, S.M.R. (2008), *The Speed of Trust: The One Thing That Changes Everything* (New York: Free Press).

46. Dyer and Singh, "The relational view"; Ireland, Hitt, and Vaidyanath, "Alliance management as a source of competitive advantage"; Lavie, "The competitive advantage of interconnected firms."

47. This is based on: Anand, B., and T. Khanna (2000), "Do firms learn to create value?" *Strategic Management Journal* 21: 295–315; Sampson, R. (2005), "Experience effects and collaborative returns in R&D alliances," *Strategic Management Journal* 26: 1009–1031; Hoang, H., and F.T. Rothaermel (2005), "The effect of general and partner-specific alliance experience on joint R&D project performance," *Academy of Management Journal* 48: 332–345; and Rothaermel, F.T., and D.L. Deeds (2006), "Alliance type, alliance experience, and alliance management capability in high-technology ventures," *Journal of Business Venturing* 21: 429–460.

48. Rothaermel and Deeds, "Alliance type, alliance experience, and alliance management capability in high-technology ventures."

49. Hoffmann, W. (2007), "Strategies for managing a portfolio of alliances," *Strategic Management Journal* 28: 827–856.

50. Wassmer, U., P. Dussage, and M. Planellas (2010), "How to manage alliances better than one at a time," *MIT Sloan Management Review,* Spring: 77–84.

51. Dyer, J. H., P. Kale, and H. Singh (2001), "How to make strategic alliances work," *MIT Sloan Management Review,* Summer: 37–43.

52. Kale, P., J. H. Dyer, and H. Singh (2002), "Alliance capability, stock market response, and long-term alliance success: The role of the alliance function," *Strategic Management Journal* 23: 747–767.

53. Gueth A., N. Sims, and R. Harrison (2001), "Managing alliances at Lilly," *In Vivo: The Business & Medicine Report* (June): 1–9; Rothaermel and Deeds, "Alliance type, alliance experience, and alliance management capability in high-technology ventures."

54. Dyer, J.H., P. Kale, and H. Singh (2004), "When to ally and when to acquire," *Harvard Business Review,* July–August.

55. Rothaermel, F.T., and A. Hess (2010), "Innovation strategies combined," *MIT Sloan Management Review,* Spring: 12–15.

56. Hitt, M.A., R.D. Ireland, and J.S. Harrison (2001), "Mergers and acquisitions: A value creating or value destroying strategy?" in M.A. Hitt, R.E. Freeman, and J.S. Harrison, *Handbook of Strategic Management* (Oxford, UK: Blackwell-Wiley): 384–408. In 2015 alone, M&A deals valued combined at over $4 trillion were announced, a record high since 2007 prior to the global financial crises, see Mattioli, D., and D. Cimilluca, "Fear of losing out drives deal boom," *The Wall Street Journal,* June 26, 2015.

57. Allen, W.B., N.A. Doherty, K. Weigelt, and E. Mansfield (2005), *Managerial Economics,* 6th ed. (New York: Norton); and Breshnahan, T., and P. Reiss (1991), "Entry and competition in concentrated markets," *Journal of Political Economy* 99: 997–1009.

58. FitzGerald, D., and L. Hoffman, "Staples inks deal to buy Office Depot for $6.3 billion," *The Wall Street Journal,* February 4, 2015.

59. Brush, T.H. (1996), "Predicted change in operational synergy and post-acquisition performance of acquired businesses," *Strategic Management Journal* 17: 1–24.

60. Tebbutt, T. (2010), "An insider's perspective of the pharmaceutical industry," presentation in "Competing in the Health Sciences," Georgia Institute of Technology, January 29. Tebbutt is former president of UCB Pharma.

61. Smith, E., and L.A.E. Schucker, "Disney nabs marvel heroes," *The Wall Street Journal,* September 1, 2009.

62. Strategy Highlight 9.2 is based on: Kraft Foods annual reports; The Hershey Company annual reports; Cimilluca, D., D. Mattioli, and C. Dulaney, "Kraft, Heinz to merge, forming food giant," *The Wall Street Journal,* March 25, 2015; "Mondelez can slim way to success," *The Wall Street Journal,* May 28, 2013;

"Analysts bullish on Mondelez ahead of Kraft split," *The Wall Street Journal,* October 1, 2012; "Cadbury accepts fresh Kraft offer," *The Wall Street Journal,* January 19, 2010; "Kraft wins a reluctant Cadbury with help of clock, hedge funds," *The Wall Street Journal,* January 20, 2010; "Cadbury rejects Kraft's $16.73 billion bid," *The Wall Street Journal,* September 7, 2009; "Food fight," *The Economist,* November 5, 2009; and the author's personal communication with Dr. Narayanan Jayaraman, Georgia Institute of Technology.

63. Clark, D., Cimilluca, D., and D. Mattioli, "Intel agrees to buy Altera for $16.7 billion," *The Wall Street Journal,* June 1, 2015.

64. Examples are drawn from: Dulaney, C., "Facebook completes acquisition of whatsApp," *The Wall Street Journal,* October 6, 2014; Albergotti, R., and I. Sherr, "Facebook to buy virtual reality firm Oculus for $2 billion," *The Wall Street Journal,* March 25, 2014; "Google buys Waze," *The Economist,* June 15, 2013; Rusli, E.M., and D. MacMillan, "Messaging service Snapchat spurned $3 billion Facebook bid," *The Wall Street Journal,* November 13, 2013; "Insta-rich: $1 billion for Instagram," *The Wall Street Journal,* April 10, 2012; "Google's $12.5 billion gamble," *The Wall Street Journal,* August 16, 2011; and "Google in talks to buy YouTube for $1.6 billion," *The Wall Street Journal,* October 7, 2006.

65. Capron, L. (1999), "The long-term performance of horizontal acquisitions," *Strategic Management Journal* 20: 987–1018; Capron, L., and J.C. Shen (2007), "Acquisitions of private vs. public firms: Private information, target selection, and acquirer returns," *Strategic Management Journal* 28: 891–911.

66. Jensen, M.C., and R.S. Ruback (1983), "The market for corporate control: The

scientific evidence," *Journal of Financial Economics* 11: 5–50.

67. This discussion is based on: Finkelstein, S. (2003), *Why Smart Executives Fail, and What You Can Learn from Their Mistakes* (New York: Portfolio); Lambert, R.A., D.F. Larcker, and K. Weigelt (1991), "How sensitive is executive compensation to organizational size?" *Strategic Management Journal* 12: 395–402; and Finkelstein, S., and D.C. Hambrick (1989), "Chief executive compensation: A study of the intersection of markets and political processes, *Strategic Management Journal* 10: 121–134.

68. This discussion is based on: Finkelstein, *Why Smart Executives Fail, and What You Can Learn from Their Mistakes;* and Finkelstein, S., J. Whitehead, and A. Campbell (2009), *Think Again: Why Good Leaders Make Bad Decisions and How to Keep It from Happening to You* (Boston, MA: Harvard Business School Press).

69. Ibid.

70. This section is based on: Capron, L., and W. Mitchell (2012), *Build, Borrow, or Buy: Solving the Growth Dilemma* (Boston, MA: Harvard Business Review Press).

71. Dyer, Kale, and Singh, "When to ally and when to acquire."

72. If so, this would violate a "net-neutrality" policy that has generally been honored—that all information on the Internet is treated equally as far as speed and cost per size of content. Data sourced from "The FCC's crusade to keep the Internet free," *Bloomberg Businessweek,* August 16, 2010.

73. This myStrategy section is based on: Granovetter, M. (1973), "The strength of weak ties," *American Journal of Sociology* 78: 1360–1380; and "Primates on Facebook," *The Economist,* February 26, 2009.

Chapter 10

Global Strategy: Competing Around the World

The Wonder from Sweden: Is IKEA's Success Sustainable?

© DBImages/Alamy

THE WORLD'S MOST profitable retailer is not Walmart, but IKEA—a privately owned home-furnishings company with origins in Sweden. By 2015, IKEA had more than 360 stores worldwide in over 40 countries, employed more than 150,000 people, and earned revenues of 37 billion euros. Exhibit 10.1 shows IKEA's growth in the number of stores and revenues worldwide since 1974.

Known today for its iconic blue-and-yellow big-box retail stores, focusing on flat-pack furniture boxes combined with a large do-it-yourself component, IKEA started as a small retail outlet in 1943 by then-17-year-old Ingvar Kamprad. Now a global phenomenon, it was initially slow to internationalize. It took 20 years before the company expanded beyond Sweden to its neighboring country of Norway. After honing and refining its core competencies of designing modern functional home furnishings at low prices and offering a unique retail experience in its home market, IKEA followed an *international*

EXHIBIT 10.1 / IKEA Stores and Revenues, 1974–2014

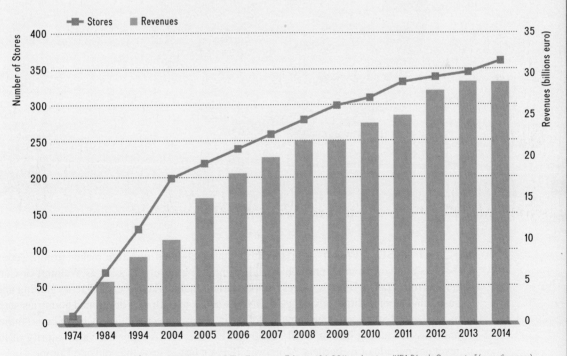

Source: Depiction of data from "The secret of IKEA's success," *The Economist*, February 24, 2011, and various IKEA "Yearly Summaries" (www.ikea.com).

strategy, expanding first to Europe, and then beyond. Using an international strategy allowed IKEA to sell the same types of home furnishings across the globe with little adaptation, although it does make some allowances for country preferences.

Because keeping costs low is critical to IKEA's value innovation (see discussion in Chapter 6), it shifted from an international strategy to a *global-standardization strategy,* in which it attempts to achieve economies of scale through efficiently managing a global supply chain. Although Asia accounts currently for less than 10 percent of its sales, IKEA sources 35 percent of its inputs from this region. To drive costs down further, IKEA has begun to implement production techniques from auto and electronics industries, in which cutting-edge technologies are employed to address complexity while achieving flexibility and low cost.

IKEA's revenues by geographic region are 69 percent from Europe, with the rest from North America (15 percent), Asia and Australia (9 percent), and Russia (7 percent); see Exhibit 10.2. Although IKEA's largest market is in Germany (14 percent of total sales), its fastest-growing markets are the United States, China, and Russia.[1]

You will learn more about **IKEA** by reading this chapter; related questions appear on page 353.

EXHIBIT 10.2 / IKEA's Sales by Geographic Region (2014)

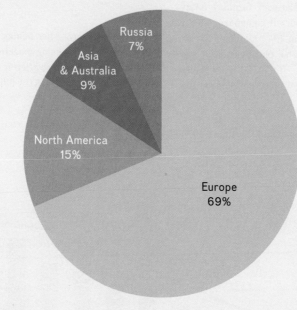

Source: Depiction of data from "IKEA's Yearly Summary FY 2014" (www.ikea.com).

IT IS SOMEWHAT surprising that a privately held furniture maker from Sweden is the world's most profitable retailer and not a behemoth such as Walmart or Carrefour from France. IKEA's success in its international markets is critical to its gaining and sustaining a competitive advantage. IKEA succeeds in both rich developed countries such as the United States and Germany as well as in emerging economies such as China, India, and Russia. Hailing from a small country in Europe, IKEA earns the vast majority of its revenues outside of its borders. Moreover, IKEA's fastest growth is outside Europe.

IKEA's strategic intent is to reach 50 billion euros in sales by 2020, up from 29 billion euros in 2014, and double its 2011 sales of 25 billion euro. IKEA wants to own 500 profitable stores globally by 2020, up from some 360 stores in 2014. To accomplish these lofty goals, IKEA must get its global strategy right, especially in rapidly growing markets such as China and India. Both are countries with more than 1 billion people each and a rapidly growing middle class on which IKEA wants to capitalize.

For more and more U.S. companies, international markets offer the biggest growth opportunities, just as they do for IKEA. Firms from a wide variety of industries—such as Apple, Caterpillar, GE, Intel, and IBM—are global enterprises. They have a global work force and manage global supply chains, and they obtain the majority of their revenues from outside their home market. Once-unassailable U.S. firms now encounter formidable foreign competitors such as Brazil's Embraer (aerospace); China's Alibaba (ecommerce), Haier (home appliances), Lenovo (PCs), and Xiaomi (cell phones); India's ArcelorMittal (steel), Infosys (IT services), and Reliance Group (conglomerate); Germany's Siemens (engineering conglomerate), Daimler, BMW, and VW (vehicles); Japan's Toyota, Honda, and Nissan (vehicles); Mexico's Cemex (cement); Russia's Gazprom (energy); South Korea's LG and Samsung (both in electronics and appliances); and Sweden's IKEA (home furnishings), to name just a few. This chapter is about how firms gain and sustain competitive advantage when competing around the world.

The competitive playing field is becoming increasingly global, as the ChapterCase about the home-furnishings industry indicates. This globalization provides significant opportunities for individuals, companies, and countries. Indeed, you can probably see the increase in globalization on your own campus. The number of students enrolled at universities outside their native countries quadrupled between 1980 and 2014 to over 4 million.[2] The country of choice for foreign students remains the United States, with more than 1 million international students enrolled per year, followed by the UK. The top five countries sending the most students to study abroad are (in rank order): China, India, Korea, Germany, and Saudi Arabia.[3]

In Chapter 8, we looked at the first two dimensions of corporate strategy: managing the degree of vertical integration, and deciding which products and services to offer (the degree of diversification). Now we turn to the third dimension: competing effectively around the world. The world's marketplace—made up of some 200 countries—is a staggering $75 trillion in gross domestic product (GDP), of which the U.S. market is roughly $17 trillion, or about 23 percent.[4]

We begin this chapter by defining globalization and presenting stages of globalization. We then tackle a number of questions that a firm must answer: Why should a company go global? Where and how should it compete? We present the CAGE[5] distance model to answer the question of where the firm should compete globally and the integration-responsiveness framework to link a firm's options of how to compete globally with the different business strategies introduced in Chapter 6 (cost leadership, differentiation, and blue ocean). We then debate the question of why world leadership in specific industries is often concentrated in certain geographic areas. We conclude with the practical "Implications for the Strategist."

10.1 What Is Globalization?

Globalization is a process of closer integration and exchange between different countries and peoples worldwide, made possible by falling trade and investment barriers, advances in telecommunications, and reductions in transportation costs.[6] Combined, these factors reduce the costs of doing business around the world, opening the doors to a much larger market than any one home country. Globalization also allows companies to source supplies at lower costs, to learn new competencies, and to further differentiate products. Consequently, the world's market economies are becoming more integrated and interdependent.

LO 10-1

Define globalization, multinational enterprise (MNE), foreign direct investment (FDI), and global strategy.

globalization
The process of closer integration and exchange between different countries and peoples worldwide, made possible by falling trade and investment barriers, advances in telecommunications, and reductions in transportation costs.

Globalization has led to significant increases in living standards in many economies around the world. Germany and Japan, countries that were basically destroyed after World War II, turned into industrial powerhouses, fueled by export-led growth. The Asian Tigers—Hong Kong, Singapore, South Korea, and Taiwan—turned themselves from underdeveloped countries into advanced economies, enjoying some of the world's highest standards of living. The BRIC countries (Brazil, Russia, India, and China), with more than 40 percent of the world's population and producing roughly half of the world's economic growth over the past decade, continue to offer significant business opportunities.[7] Indeed, China, with over $9 trillion in GDP, has become the second-largest economy worldwide after the United States (with $17 trillion in GDP) and ahead of Japan in third place ($5 trillion GDP), in absolute terms.[8]

multinational enterprise (MNE)
A company that deploys resources and capabilities in the procurement, production, and distribution of goods and services in at least two countries.

foreign direct investment (FDI)
A firm's investments in value chain activities abroad.

global strategy
Part of a firm's corporate strategy to gain and sustain a competitive advantage when competing against other foreign and domestic companies around the world.

The engine behind globalization is the **multinational enterprise (MNE)**—a company that deploys resources and capabilities in the procurement, production, and distribution of goods and services in at least two countries. By making investments in value chain activities abroad, MNEs engage in **foreign direct investment (FDI)**.[9] For example, the European aircraft maker Airbus is investing $600 million in Mobile, Alabama, to build jetliners.[10] It's doing so in order to avoid import restrictions, be closer to customers in North America, and take advantage of business-friendly conditions such as lower taxes, labor cost, and cost of living, plus other incentives provided by host states in the Southern United States. For similar reasons, German carmaker Volkswagen invested $1 billion in its Chattanooga, Tennessee, plant.[11] MNEs need an effective **global strategy** that enables them to gain and sustain a competitive advantage when competing against other foreign and domestic companies around the world.[12]

In the digital age, some companies are *born global*—their founders start them with the intent of running global operations. Internet-based companies such as Alibaba, Amazon, eBay, Google, and LinkedIn by nature have a global presence. Indeed, Facebook, with over 1.5 billion users around the globe, would—were it a country—be the most populous nation worldwide, even ahead of China (1.4 billion) and India (1.3 billion). To better customize their websites to suit local preferences and cultures, these companies tend to establish offices and maintain computer servers in different countries.[13] Amazon.com, for example, customizes its offerings for different markets. You can see country-specific sites at www.amazon.cn (China), www.amazon.de (Germany), and www.amazon.com.br (Brazil).

U.S. MNEs have a disproportionately positive impact on the U.S. economy.[14] Well-known U.S. multinational enterprises include Boeing, Caterpillar, Coca-Cola, GE, John Deere, Exxon Mobil, IBM, P&G, and Walmart. They make up less than 1 percent of the number of total U.S. companies, but they:

- Account for 11 percent of private-sector employment growth since 1990.
- Employ 19 percent of the work force.
- Pay 25 percent of the wages.
- Provide for 31 percent of the U.S. gross domestic product (GDP).
- Make up 74 percent of private-sector R&D spending.

As a business student, you have several reasons to be interested in MNEs. Not only can these companies provide interesting work assignments in different locations throughout the world, but they also frequently offer the highest-paying jobs for college graduates. Even if you don't want to work for an MNE, chances are that the organization you will be working for will do business with one, so it's important to understand how they compete around the globe.

STAGES OF GLOBALIZATION

Since the beginning of the 20th century, globalization has proceeded through three notable stages.[15] Each stage presents a different global strategy pursued by MNEs headquartered in the United States.

GLOBALIZATION 1.0: 1900–1941. Globalization 1.0 took place from about 1900 through the early years of World War II. In that period, basically all the important business functions were located in the home country. Typically, only sales and distribution operations took place overseas—essentially exporting goods to other markets. In some instances, firms procured raw materials from overseas. Strategy formulation and implementation, as well as knowledge flows, followed a one-way path—from domestic headquarters to international outposts. This time period saw the blossoming of the idea of MNEs. It ended with the U.S. entry into World War II.

GLOBALIZATION 2.0: 1945–2000. With the end of World War II came a new focus on growing business—not only to meet the needs that went unfulfilled during the war years but also to reconstruct the damage from the war. From 1945 to the end of the 20th century, in the Globalization 2.0 stage, MNEs began to create smaller, self-contained copies of themselves, with all business functions intact, in a few key countries; notably, Western European countries, Japan, and Australia.

This strategy required significant amounts of foreign direct investment. Although it was costly to duplicate business functions in overseas outposts, doing so allowed for greater local responsiveness to country-specific circumstances. While the U.S. corporate headquarters set overarching strategic goals and allocated resources through the capital budgeting process, local mini-MNE replicas had considerable leeway in day-to-day operations. Knowledge flow back to U.S. headquarters, however, remained limited in most instances.

GLOBALIZATION 3.0: 21ST CENTURY. We are now in the Globalization 3.0 stage. MNEs that had been the vanguard of globalization have since become global-collaboration networks (see Exhibit 10.3). Such companies now freely locate business functions anywhere in the world based on an optimal mix of costs, capabilities, and PESTEL factors. Huge investments in fiber-optic cable networks around the world have effectively reduced communication distances, enabling companies to operate 24/7, 365 days a year. When an engineer in Minneapolis, Minnesota, leaves for the evening, an engineer in Mumbai, India, begins her workday. In the Globalization 3.0 stage, the MNE's strategic objective changes. The MNE reorganizes from a multinational company with self-contained operations in a few selected countries to a more seamless global enterprise with centers of expertise. Each of these centers of expertise is a hub within a global network for delivering products and services. Consulting companies, for example, can now tap into a worldwide network of experts in real time, rather than relying on the limited number of employees in their local offices.

Creating a global network of local expertise is beneficial not only in service industries, but also in the industrial sector. To increase the rate of low-cost innovation that can then be used to disrupt existing markets, GE organizes local growth teams in China, India, Kenya, and many other emerging countries.[16] GE uses the slogan "in country, for country" to describe the local growth teams' autonomy in deciding which products and services to develop, how to make them, and how to shape the business model. Many of these low-cost innovations, first developed to serve local needs, are later introduced in Western markets to become disruptive innovations. Examples include the Vscan, a handheld ultrasound device

EXHIBIT 10.3

Globalization 3.0: 21st Century

Based on an optimal mix of costs, skills, and PESTEL factors, MNEs are organized as global-collaboration networks that perform business functions throughout the world.

Source: Adapted from IBM (2009), "A Decade of Generating Higher Value at IBM," www.ibm.com.

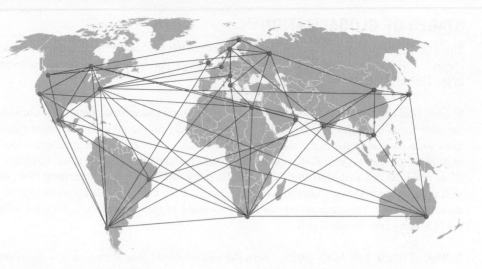

developed in China; the Mac 400, an ECG device developed in India—more details later in the chapter; and the 9100c, an anesthesia system developed in Kenya.[17]

Some new ventures organize as global-collaboration networks from the start. Logitech, the maker of wireless peripherals such as computer mice, presentation "clickers," and video game controllers, started in Switzerland but quickly established offices in Silicon Valley, California.[18] Pursuing a global strategy right from the start allowed Logitech to tap into the innovation expertise contained in Silicon Valley.[19] In 2014, Logitech had sales of over $2 billion, with offices throughout the Americas, Asia, and Europe. Underlying Logitech's innovation competence is a network of best-in-class skills around the globe. Moreover, Logitech can organize work continuously because its teams in different locations around the globe can work 24/7.

Indeed, the trend toward global collaboration networks during the Globalization 3.0 stage raises the interesting question, "What defines a U.S. company?" If it's the address of the headquarters, then IBM, GE, and others are U.S. companies—despite the fact that a majority of their employees work outside the United States. In many instances, the majority of their revenues also come from outside the United States. On the other hand, non-U.S. companies such as carmakers from Japan (Toyota, Honda, and Nissan) and South Korea (Hyundai and Kia) and several engineering companies (Siemens from Germany, and ABB, a Swiss-Swedish MNE) all have made significant investments in the United States and created a large number of well-paying jobs.

STATE OF GLOBALIZATION

Before we delve deeper into the question of why and how firms compete for advantage globally, a cautionary note concerning *globalization* is in order. Although many large firms are more than 50 percent globalized—meaning that more than half of their revenues are from outside the home country—the world itself is far less global.[20] If we look at a number of different indicators, the level of globalization is no more than 10 to 25 percent. For example, only

- 2 percent of all voice-calling minutes are cross-border.[21]
- 3 percent of the world's population are first-generation immigrants.
- 9 percent of all investments in the economy are foreign direct investments.
- 15 percent of patents list at least one foreign inventor.
- 18 percent of Internet traffic crosses national borders.

These data indicate that the world is not quite flat yet,[22] or fully globalized, but at best *semi-globalized.*[23] Pankaj Ghemawat reasons that many more gains in social welfare and living standards can be had through further globalization if future integration is managed effectively through coordinated efforts by governments.[24] The European Union is an example of coordinated economic and political integration by 28 countries, of which 19 use the euro as a common currency. This coordinated integration took place over several decades following World War II, precisely to prevent future wars in Europe. The EU now encompasses more than 500 million people. This makes it one of the largest economic zones in the world; indeed with a GDP of 19 trillion it is a little bit larger than the United States, the largest single country market in the world. Further coordinated integration appears to be one solution to the current eurozone crisis. Although the EU has monetary authority administered through the European Central Bank, it does not have fiscal (i.e., budgetary) authority. This important responsibility remains with national governments, leading to the sovereign debt crisis.

Continued economic development across the globe has two consequences for MNEs. First, rising wages and other costs are likely to negate any benefits of access to low-cost input factors. Second, as the standard of living rises in emerging economies, MNEs are hoping that increased purchasing power will enable workers to purchase the products they used to make for export only.[25] China's labor costs, for example, are steadily rising in tandem with an improved standard of living, especially in the coastal regions, where wages have risen 50 percent since 2005.[26] Some MNEs have boosted wages an extra 30 percent following labor unrest in recent years. Many now offer bonuses to blue-collar workers and are taking other measures to avoid sweatshop allegations that have plagued companies such as Nike, Apple, and Levi Strauss. Rising wages, fewer workers due to the effects of China's one-child-per-family policy, and appreciation of the Chinese currency now combine to lessen the country's advantage in low-cost manufacturing.[27] This shift is in alignment with the Chinese government's economic policy, which wants to see a move from "Made in China" to "Designed in China," to capture more of the value added.[28] The value added of manufacturing an iPhone by Foxconn in China is only about 5 percent.[29] We next discuss in more detail the reasons firms "go global."

10.2 Going Global: Why?

LO 10-2

Explain why companies compete abroad, and evaluate the advantages and disadvantages of a global strategy.

The decision to pursue a global strategy comes from the firm's assessment that doing so enhances its competitive advantage and that the benefits of globalization exceed the costs. Simply put, firms expand beyond their domestic borders if they can increase their economic value creation $(V - C)$ and enhance competitive advantage. As detailed in Chapter 5, firms enlarge their competitive advantage by increasing a consumer's willingness to pay through higher perceived value based on differentiation and/or lower production and service delivery costs. Expanding beyond the home market, therefore, should reinforce a company's basis of competitive advantage—whether differentiation, low-cost, or value innovation. Here we consider both the advantages and disadvantages of expanding beyond the home market.

ADVANTAGES OF GOING GLOBAL

Why do firms expand internationally? The main reasons firms expand abroad are to

- Gain access to a larger market.
- Gain access to low-cost input factors.
- Develop new competencies.

Strategy Highlight 10.1

The Gulf Airlines Are Landing in the United States

Fasten your seat belts Delta, American, and United. Severe turbulence may be ahead.

New entrants into both the domestic and international routes are increasing the competitive pressure on U.S. legacy air carriers. Three airlines—Emirates, Etihad Airways, and Qatar Airways—all from the Persian Gulf, are using a blue ocean strategy to attract new customers. The gulf carriers offer higher quality at lower cost to break into international routes, the last remaining profit sanctuary of U.S. carriers. The legacy carriers have long been squeezed domestically by low-cost competitors such as Southwest, Frontier, Spirit, and others (see Strategy Highlight 3.2). Although most of the future growth is in Asia, the United States remains the world's largest air traffic market, still holding on to one-third of all business.

But look at the latest U.S. competitors. The gulf carriers make flying enjoyable again, getting away from the Greyhound bus feel adopted in the 1980s and persisting today at U.S. carriers. At many U.S. airlines, service has deteriorated as air travel has become a commodity, and price has become the main competitive weapon. The gulf airlines, in contrast, bring back some of the service and glamour that used to be associated with air travel. They offer amenities such as higher-quality complimentary meals and hot towels in economy, in addition, to an open bar in business class, and private suites with showers in first. Their ratio of flight attendants to passengers is also greater, including offering flying nannies to keep kids occupied, happy, and most importantly not crying. In their home base, they build airports reminiscent of luxury hotels with swimming pools above the concourse for laps during layovers, high-speed Wi-Fi, high-end conference rooms with the latest audiovisual equipment, plush lounges, and many other amenities.

Given their location on the Persian peninsula, the gulf airlines offer direct flights to major hubs in Europe, Asia, and the United States, using the newest and most modern aircraft. Their reach via direct flights extends to about 80 percent of the world's population. In particular, the gulf carriers are already connecting Europe and Asia, having taken away major business from European airlines such as Lufthansa of Germany and British Airways. Moreover, traditional international airport hubs such as London, Frankfurt, and Amsterdam all have lost a large share of their business to the new luxury hubs in Dubai, Abu Dhabi, and Doha. The gulf carriers are now attempting to repeat this feat in the United States, offering direct flights to and from Atlanta, Boston, Chicago, Dallas, Houston, Los Angeles, New York, and Orlando.

There are some complaints by U.S. carriers, however, that the Persian Gulf airlines receive unfair subsidies. CEOs of U.S. carriers have turned to politicians in Washington to stem the onslaught of the gulf carriers. They demand that the competition by gulf carriers should be curbed. Customers, however, are voting with their wallets by flocking to the gulf carriers, enjoying competitive prices and a better service experience. Moreover, the gulf carriers counter that U.S. airlines have long enjoyed tightly regulated markets, restricting foreign competition. Moreover, they also remind the public that each of the U.S. legacy carriers has used bankruptcy filings to obtain debt relief, and that some legacy carriers received direct government bailouts. They suggest that the investments made by the government owners of the Persian Gulf carriers are merely equity investments as done by other stockholders.

One thing is clear, the competitive pressure by the gulf carriers on U.S. legacy carriers will only increase. The Persian Gulf states have decided that international air travel is a strategic future industry for the region. To back up their intent, the carriers made strong strategic commitments, not only by building the most modern and luxurious airports in the world, but also by locking up about half of the airframe makers' future production capacity. In particular, they ordered new super-modern, long-range airplanes made by Boeing (such as the new 787 Dreamliner) and Airbus (such as the A-380, the superjumbo). The gulf carriers are already the fastest-growing airlines globally, yet they continue to push into larger markets and more attractive routes. In the meantime, consumers enjoy the benefits of globalization: more choice, more routes, better service and amenities, as well as lower prices.[30]

GAIN ACCESS TO A LARGER MARKET. Becoming an MNE provides significant opportunities for companies, given *economies of scale* and *scope* that can be reaped by participating in a much larger market. Companies that base their competitive advantage on *economies* *of scale* and *economies of scope* have an incentive to gain access to larger markets because this can reinforce the basis of their competitive advantage. This in turn allows MNEs to outcompete local rivals. In Strategy Highlight 6.1, we detailed how Narayana Health, a specialty hospital chain in India, founded and led by Dr. Devi Shetty, obtained a low-cost competitive advantage in complex procedures such as open heart surgery. Narayana Health is now leveraging its low-cost, high-quality position by opening specialty hospitals in the Cayman Islands (to serve U.S. patients) and Kuala Lumpur, Malaysia.

At the same time, some countries with relatively weak domestic demand, such as China, Germany, South Korea, and Japan, focus on export-led economic growth, which drives many of their domestic businesses to become MNEs. For companies based in smaller economies, becoming an MNE may be necessary to achieve growth or to gain and sustain competitive advantage. Examples include Acer (Taiwan), Casella Wines (Australia), IKEA (featured in the ChapterCase), Nestlé (Switzerland), Novo Nordisk (Denmark), Philips (Netherlands), Samsung (South Korea), and Zara (Spain). Unless companies in smaller economies expand internationally, their domestic markets are often too small for them to reach significant economies of scale to compete effectively against other MNEs. Strategy Highlight 10.1 shows how the Persian Gulf airlines (all coming from small countries) are entering the much larger U.S. and international markets, competing directly with legacy carriers such as American, Delta, and United.

GAIN ACCESS TO LOW-COST INPUT FACTORS. MNEs that base their competitive advantage on a low-cost leadership strategy are particularly attracted to go overseas to gain access to low-cost input factors. Access to low-cost raw *materials* such as lumber, iron ore, oil, and coal was a key driver behind Globalization 1.0 and 2.0. During Globalization 3.0, firms have expanded globally to benefit from lower *labor costs* in manufacturing and services. India carved out a competitive advantage in business process outsourcing (BPO), not only because of low-cost labor but because of an abundance of well-educated, English-speaking young people. Infosys, TCS, and Wipro are some of the more well-known Indian IT service companies. Taken together, these companies employ more than 250,000 people and provide services to many of the Global Fortune 500. Many MNEs have close business ties with Indian IT firms. Some, such as IBM, are engaged in foreign direct investment through equity alliances or building their own IT and customer service centers in India. More than a quarter of Accenture's work force, a consultancy specializing in technology and outsourcing, is now in Bangalore, India.[31]

Likewise, China has emerged as a manufacturing powerhouse because of low labor costs and an efficient infrastructure. An American manufacturing worker costs about 20 times more in wages alone than a similarly skilled worker in China.[32] A significant cost differential exists not only for low-skilled labor, but for high-skilled labor as well. A Chinese engineer trained at Purdue University, for example, works for only a quarter of the salary in his native country compared with an engineer working in the United States.[33] Of course, this absolute wage disparity also reflects the relative difference in the two countries' cost of living.

DEVELOP NEW COMPETENCIES. Some MNEs pursue a global strategy in order to develop new competencies.[34] This motivation is particularly attractive for firms that base their competitive advantage on a differentiation strategy. These companies are making foreign direct investments to be part of *communities of learning,* which are often contained in specific geographic regions.[35] AstraZeneca, a Swiss-based pharmaceutical company, relocated its research facility to Cambridge, Massachusetts, to be part of the Boston biotech cluster, in hopes of developing new R&D competencies in biotechnology.[36] Cisco invested more

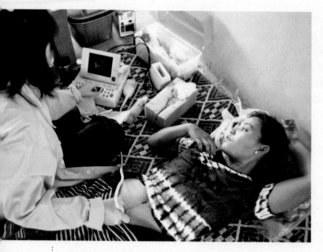

A GE team in China developed the Vscan, an inexpensive, portable ultrasound device, costing some $5,000, rather than $250,000—the cost of a traditional ultrasound machine used in Western hospitals. The Vscan is now widely used in rural areas of developing countries (as shown here in Vietnam), and has made its entry as a disruptive innovation in the United States and other rich countries.
© Thierry Falise/
LightRocket via
Getty Images

than $1.6 billion to create an Asian headquarters in Bangalore and support other locations in India, in order to be in the middle of India's top IT location.[37] Unilever's new-concept center is located in downtown Shanghai, China, attracting hundreds of eager volunteers to test the firm's latest product innovations on-site, while Unilever researchers monitor consumer reactions. In these examples, AstraZeneca, Cisco, and Unilever all reap **location economies**—benefits from locating value chain activities in optimal geographies for a specific activity, wherever that may be.[38]

Many MNEs now are replacing the one-way innovation flow from Western economies to developing markets with a *polycentric innovation strategy*—a strategy in which MNEs now draw on multiple, equally important innovation hubs throughout the world characteristic of Globalization 3.0; see Exhibit 10.3. GE Global Research, for example, orchestrates a "network of excellence" with facilities in Niskayuna, New York (USA); Bangalore (India); Shanghai (China); and Munich (Germany). Indeed, emerging economies are becoming hotbeds for low-cost innovations that find their way back to developed markets.[39] In Bangalore, GE researchers developed the Mac 400, a handheld electrocardiogram (ECG).[40] The device is small, portable, and runs on batteries. Although a conventional ECG machine costs $2,000, this handheld version costs $800 and enables doctors to do an ECG test at a cost of only $1 per patient. The Mac 400 is now entering the United States and other Western markets as a disruptive innovation, with anticipated widespread use in the offices of general practitioners and emergency ambulances.

DISADVANTAGES OF GOING GLOBAL

Companies expanding internationally must carefully weigh the benefits and costs of doing so. If the cost of going global as captured by the following disadvantages exceeds the expected benefits in terms of value added ($C > V$), that is, if the economic value creation is negative, then firms are better off by not expanding internationally. Disadvantages to going global include

location economies
Benefits from locating value chain activities in the world's optimal geographies for a specific activity, wherever that may be.

- Liability of foreignness.
- Loss of reputation.
- Loss of intellectual property.

liability of foreignness
Additional costs of doing business in an unfamiliar cultural and economic environment, and of coordinating across geographic distances.

LIABILITY OF FOREIGNNESS. In international expansion, firms face risks. In particular, MNEs doing business abroad also must overcome the **liability of foreignness**. This liability consists of the additional costs of doing business in an unfamiliar cultural and economic environment, and of coordinating across geographic distances.[41] Strategy Highlight 10.2 illustrates how Walmart underestimated its liability of foreignness when entering and competing in Germany.

LOSS OF REPUTATION. One of the most valuable resources that a firm may possess is its reputation. A firm's reputation can have several dimensions, including a reputation for innovation, customer service, or brand reputation. Apple's brand, for example, stands for innovation and superior customer experience. Apple's brand reputation is also one of its most important resources. Apple's brand is valued at $250 billion, making it the most

Strategy Highlight 10.2

Walmart Retreats from Germany

After losing billions of dollars, Walmart exited Germany in 2006. The massive failure came as a shock to a company that was used to success. What went wrong?

Around 1998, facing a saturated U.S. market, Walmart entered Germany, then the third-largest economy in the world behind the United States and Japan. At that time, the big-box retailer was already active in six foreign countries, with some 500 stores outside U.S. borders. Given the intense pressure for cost reductions in the retail industry and Walmart's superior strategic position as the dominant cost leader in the United States, executives decided to pursue a similar low-cost strategy in Germany.

To enter Germany, Walmart acquired the 21-store Wertkauf chain and 74 hypermarkets from German retailer Spar Handels AG. Next, Walmart attempted to implement its U.S. personnel policies and procedures: the Walmart cheer, a door greeter, every associate within 10 feet of a customer smiling and offering help, bagging groceries at the checkout, video surveillance, a prohibition against dating co-workers, and so on. German employees, however, simply refused to comply. There were no door greeters in the German Walmart stores. The front-line employees behaved as gruffly as they do in other retail outlets in Germany. It also didn't help that the first Walmart boss in Germany was installed from Walmart headquarters in Bentonville, Arkansas. The executive didn't speak any German and simply decreed that English would be the official in-house language.

Significant cultural differences aside, one of the biggest problems Walmart faced in Germany was that, lacking its usual economies of scale and efficient distribution centers, it couldn't get its costs down far enough to successfully implement its trademark cost-leadership strategy. Higher required wages and restrictive labor laws further drove up costs. As a result, the prices at Walmart in Germany were not "always low" as the company slogan suggested, but fell in the medium range. Germany was already home to retail discount powerhouses such as Aldi and Lidl, with thousands of smaller outlets offering higher convenience combined with lower prices. Walmart was unable to be cost-competitive against such tough domestic competition. It also faced Metro, a dominant large-box retailer, that upon entering Germany immediately initiated a price war against Walmart. In the end, a defeated Walmart sold its stores to—guess who?—Metro!

Walmart experienced a similar fate in South Korea, where it also exited in 2006. In addition, Walmart has tried for many years to successfully enter the fast-growing markets in Russia and India, but with little or no success. Walmart's success recipe that worked so well domestically didn't work in Germany, South Korea, Russia, or India—to a large part because of the liability of foreignness.[42]

---

valuable in the world.[43] We detailed in Chapter 4 that a brand can be the basis for a competitive advantage if it is valuable, rare, and difficult to imitate.

Globalizing a supply chain can have unintended side effects. These can lead to a loss of reputation and diminish the MNE's competitiveness. A possible loss in reputation can be a considerable risk and cost for doing business abroad. Because Apple's stellar consumer reputation is critical to its competitive advantage, it should be concerned about any potential negative exposure from its global activities. Problems at Apple's main supplier, Foxconn, brought this concern to the fore.

Low wages, long hours, and poor working and living conditions contributed to a spate of suicides at Foxconn, Apple's main supplier in China.[44] The Taiwanese company, which employs more than a million people, manufactures computers, tablets, smartphones, and other consumer electronics for Apple and other leading consumer electronics companies. The backlash against alleged sweatshop conditions in Foxconn prompted Apple to work with its main supplier to improve working conditions and wages. Tim Cook, Apple's CEO, visited Foxconn in China to personally inspect its manufacturing facility and workers' living conditions. Although conditions at Foxconn have been improving,[45] Apple started to diversify its supplier base by adding Pegatron, another Taiwanese original equipment manufacturer (OEM).[46]

MNEs' search for low-cost labor has had tragic effects where local governments are corrupt and unwilling or unable to enforce a minimum of safety standards. The textile industry is notorious for sweatshop conditions, and many Western companies such as the Gap (U.S.), H&M (Sweden), and Carrefour (France) have taken a big hit to their reputation in factory accidents in Bangladesh and elsewhere in Southeast Asia. Hundreds of factory workers were killed when a textile factory collapsed in Rana Plaza in 2013 on the outskirts of Dhaka, Bangladesh.[47] Although much of the blame lies with the often corrupt host governments not enforcing laws, regulations, and building codes, the MNEs that source their textiles in these factories also receive some of the blame with negative consequences for their reputation. The MNEs are accused of exploiting workers and being indifferent to their working conditions and safety, all in an unending quest to drive down costs.

This challenge directly concerns the MNEs' *corporate social responsibility (CSR)*, discussed in Chapter 2. Since some host governments are either unwilling or unable to enforce regulation and safety codes, MNEs need to rise to the challenge.[48] Walmart responded by posting a public list of "banned suppliers" on its website. These are suppliers that do not meet adequate safety standards and working conditions. Before the Rana Plaza accident, Walmart had already launched a working and fire-safety academy in Bangladesh to train textile workers.

Given the regulatory and legal void that local governments often leave, several Western MNEs have proposed a concerted action to finance safety efforts and worker training as well as structural upgrades to factory buildings. After earlier revelations about the frequent practice of child labor in many developing countries, Western MNEs in the textile industry worked together to ban their suppliers from using child labor. Ensuring ethical sourcing of raw materials and supplies is becoming ever more important. Besides a moral responsibility, MNEs have a market incentive to protect their reputations given the public backlash in the wake of factory accidents, child labor, worker suicides, and other horrific externalities.

LOSS OF INTELLECTUAL PROPERTY. Finally, the issue of protecting intellectual property in foreign markets also looms large. The software, movie, and music industries have long lamented large-scale copyright infringements in many foreign markets. In addition, when required to partner with a foreign host firm, companies may find their intellectual property being siphoned off and reverse-engineered.

Japanese and European engineering companies entered China to participate in building the world's largest network of high-speed trains worth billions of dollars.[49] Companies such as Kawasaki Heavy Industries (Japan), Siemens (Germany), and Alstom (France) were joint venture partners with domestic Chinese companies. These firms now allege that the Chinese partners built on the Japanese and European partners' advanced technology to create their own, next-generation high-speed trains. To make matters worse, they also claim that the Chinese companies now compete against them in other lucrative markets, such as Saudi Arabia, Brazil, and even California, with trains of equal or better capabilities but at much lower prices. This example highlights the *intellectual property exposure* that firms can face when expanding overseas.

LO 10-3

Apply the CAGE distance framework to guide MNE decisions on which countries to enter.

10.3 Going Global: Where and How?

After discussing why companies expand internationally, we now turn to the question of how to guide MNE decisions on which countries to enter and how to then enter those countries.

WHERE IN THE WORLD TO COMPETE?
THE CAGE DISTANCE FRAMEWORK

The question of where to compete geographically is, following vertical integration and diversification, the third dimension of determining a firm's corporate strategy. The primary driver behind firms expanding beyond their domestic market is to strengthen their competitive position by gaining access to larger markets and low-cost input factors and to develop new competencies. So wouldn't companies choose new markets solely based on logical measures, such as per capita consumptions of the product and per capita income?

Yes and no. Consider that several countries and locations can score similarly on such *absolute* metrics of attractiveness. Ireland and Portugal, for example, have similar cost structures, and both provide access to some 500 million customers in the European Union. Both countries use the euro as a common currency, and both have a similarly educated work force and infrastructure. Given these similarities, how does an MNE decide? Rather than looking at absolute measures, MNEs need to consider *relative distance* in the CAGE model.

To aid MNEs in deciding where in the world to compete, Pankaj Ghemawat introduced the **CAGE distance framework**. CAGE is an acronym for different kinds of distance:

- **C**ultural
- **A**dministrative and political
- **G**eographic
- **E**conomic.[50]

Most of the costs and risks involved in expanding beyond the domestic market are created by *distance*. Distance not only denotes geographic distance (in miles or kilometers), but also includes, as the CAGE acronym points out, cultural distance, administrative and political distance, and economic distance. The CAGE distance framework breaks distance into different relative components between any two country pairs that affect the success of FDI.

Although absolute metrics such as country wealth or market size matter to some extent—as we know, for example, that a 1 percent increase in country wealth leads to a 0.8 percent increase in international trade—the relative factors captured by the CAGE distance model matter more. For instance, countries that are 5,000 miles apart trade only 20 percent of the amount traded among countries that are 1,000 miles apart. Cultural distance matters even more. A common language increases trade between two countries by 200 percent over country pairs without one. Thus, in the earlier example regarding which EU country to select for FDI, a U.S. MNE should pick Ireland, while a Brazilian MNE should select Portugal. In the latter case, Brazil and Portugal also share a historic colony–colonizer relationship. This link increases the expected trade intensity between these two countries by yet another 900 percent in comparison to country pairs where absent.

Other CAGE distance factors are significant in predicting the amount of trade between two countries. If the countries belong to the same regional trading bloc, they can expect another 330 percent in trade intensity. Examples include the United States and Mexico in NAFTA, or the 28 member states of the European Union. If the two countries use the same currency it increases trade intensity by 340 percent. An example is use of the euro as the common currency in 19 of 28 EU countries.[51]

Exhibit 10.4 presents the CAGE distance model. In particular, it details factors that increase the overall distance between the two countries and how distance affects different industries or products along the CAGE dimensions.[52] Next, we briefly discuss each of the CAGE distance dimensions.[53]

CAGE distance framework
A decision framework based on the *relative* distance between home and a foreign target country along four dimensions: cultural distance, administrative and political distance, geographic distance, and economic distance.

EXHIBIT 10.4 / The CAGE Distance Framework

Distance	C Cultural	A Administrative and Political	G Geographic	E Economic
between two countries increases with . . .	• Different languages, ethnicities, religions, social norms, and dispositions • Lack of connective ethnic or social networks • Lack of trust and mutual respect	• Absence of trading bloc • Absence of shared currency, monetary or political association • Absence of colonial ties • Political hostilities • Weak legal and financial institutions	• Lack of common border, waterway access, adequate transportation, or communication links • Physical remoteness • Different climates and time zones	• Different consumer incomes • Different costs and quality of natural, financial, and human resources • Different information or knowledge
most affects industries or products . . .	• With high linguistic content (TV) • Related to national and/or religious identity (foods) • Carrying country-specific quality associations (wines)	• That a foreign government views as staples (electricity), as building national reputations (aerospace), or as vital to national security (telecommunications)	• With low value-to-weight ratio (cement) • That are fragile or perishable (glass, meats) • In which communications are vital (financial services)	• For which demand varies by income (cars) • In which labor and other cost differences matter (textiles)

Source: Adapted from P. Ghemawat (2001), "Distance still matters: The hard reality of global expansion," *Harvard Business Review,* September: 137–147.

national culture
The collective mental and emotional "programming of the mind" that differentiates human groups.

CULTURAL DISTANCE. In his seminal research, Geert Hofstede defined and measured **national culture,** the collective mental and emotional "programming of the mind" that differentiates human groups.[54] Culture is made up of a collection of social norms and mores, beliefs, and values. Culture captures the often unwritten and implicitly understood rules of the game.

Although there is no one-size-fits-all culture that accurately describes any nation, Hofstede's work provides a useful tool to proxy cultural distance. Based on data analysis from more than 100,000 individuals from many different countries, four main dimensions of culture emerged: *Power distance, individualism, masculinity–femininity,* and *uncertainty avoidance.*[55] Hofstede's data analysis yielded scores for the different countries, for each dimension, on a range of zero to 100, with 100 as the high end. More recently, Hofstede added two additional cultural dimensions: *long-term orientation* and *indulgence.*[56]

Cultural differences find their expression in language, ethnicity, religion, and social norms. They directly affect customer preferences (see Exhibit 10.4). Because of their religious beliefs, for example, Hindus do not eat beef, while Muslims do not eat pork. In terms of content-intensive service, cultural and language differences are also the reason global Internet companies such as Amazon or Google offer country-specific variations of their sites. Despite these best efforts, they are often outflanked by native providers because of their deeper cultural understanding. For example, in China the leading websites are domestic ones: Alibaba in ecommerce, and Baidu in online search. In Russia, the leading ecommerce site is Ozon, while the leading search engine is Yandex.

Hofstede's national-culture research becomes even more useful for managers by combining the distinct dimensions of culture into an aggregate measure for each country. MNEs then can compare the national-culture measures for any two country pairings to inform their entry decisions.[58] The difference between scores indicates **cultural distance**, the cultural disparity between the internationally expanding firm's home country and its targeted host country. A firm's decision to enter certain international markets is influenced by cultural differences. A greater cultural distance can increase the cost and uncertainty of conducting business abroad. In short, greater cultural distance increases the liability of foreignness.

cultural distance
Cultural disparity between an internationally expanding firm's home country and its targeted host country.

If we calculate the cultural distance from the United States to various countries, for example, we find that some countries are culturally very close to the United States. Australia, for example, has an overall cultural distance score of 0.02. Others are culturally quite distant. Russia has an overall cultural distance score of 4.42. As can be expected, English-speaking countries such as Canada (0.12), Ireland (0.35), New Zealand (0.26), and the UK (0.09) all exhibit a low cultural distance to the United States. Since culture is embedded in language, it comes as no surprise that cultural and linguistic differences are highly correlated.

Culture even matters in the age of Facebook with its global reach of 1.5 billion users. Most Facebook friends are local rather than across borders. This makes sense when one considers that the online social graph that Facebook users develop in their network of friends is actually a virtual network laid above a (pre)existing social network, rather than forming one anew.[59]

ADMINISTRATIVE AND POLITICAL DISTANCE. Administrative and political distances are captured in factors such as the absence or presence of shared monetary or political associations, political hostilities, and weak or strong legal and financial institutions.[60] The 19 European countries in the eurozone, for example, not only share the same currency but also integrate politically to some extent. It should come as no surprise then that most cross-border trade between European countries takes place within the EU. Germany, one of the world's largest exporters, conducts roughly 75 percent of its cross-border business within the EU.[61] Similarly, Canada and Mexico partner with the United States in the North American Free Trade Agreement (NAFTA), increasing trade in goods and services between the three countries. Colony–colonizer relationships also have a strong positive effect on bilateral trade between countries. British companies continue to trade heavily with businesses from its former colonies in the commonwealth; Spanish companies trade heavily with Latin American countries; and French businesses trade with the franc zone of West Africa.

Many foreign (target) countries also erect other political and administrative barriers, such as tariffs, trade quotas, FDI restrictions, and so forth, to protect domestic competitors. In many instances, China, for example, requests the sharing of technology in a joint venture when entering the country. This was the case in the high-speed train developments discussed earlier. Other countries, including the United States and EU members, protect national

In 2000 when Starbucks entered the Chinese market, it moved fast to overcome cultural barriers by handing out key chains to help new customers order! Now it leverages Chinese approaches to social media (WeChat, Weibo, and Jiepang) and fine-tunes its own mobile apps and loyalty programs to lure China's growing middle class. The result? Today China is its second-largest market and growing.[57]
Courtesy of Resonance China

champions such as Boeing or Airbus from foreign competition. Industries that are considered critical to national security—domestic airlines or telecommunications—are often protected. Finally, strong legal and ethical pillars as well as well-functioning economic institutions such as capital markets and an independent central bank reduce distance. Strong institutions, both formal and informal, reduce uncertainty and thus reduce transaction costs.[62]

GEOGRAPHIC DISTANCE. The costs to cross-border trade rise with geographic distance. It is important to note, however, that geographic distance does not simply capture how far two countries are from each other but also includes additional attributes, such as the country's physical size (Canada versus Singapore), the within-country distances to its borders, the country's topography, its time zones, and whether the countries are contiguous to one another or have access to waterways and the ocean. The country's infrastructure, including road, power, and telecommunications networks, also plays a role in determining geographic distance. Geographic distance is particularly relevant when trading products with low value-to-weight ratios, such as steel, cement, or other bulk products, and fragile and perishable products, such as glass or fresh meats and fruits.

ECONOMIC DISTANCE. The wealth and per capita income of consumers is the most important determinant of economic distance. Wealthy countries engage in relatively more cross-border trade than poorer ones. Rich countries tend to trade with other rich countries; in addition, poor countries also trade more frequently with rich countries than with other poor countries. Companies from wealthy countries benefit in cross-border trade with other wealthy countries when their competitive advantage is based on *economies of experience, scale, scope,* and *standardization.* This is because replication of an existing business model is much easier in a country where the incomes are relatively similar and resources, complements, and infrastructure are of roughly equal quality. Although Walmart in Canada is a virtual carbon copy of the Walmart in the United States, Walmart in China is quite different.[63]

Companies from wealthy countries also trade with companies from poor countries to benefit from *economic arbitrage.* The textile industry (discussed earlier) is a prime example. We also highlighted economic arbitrage as one of the main benefits of going global: access to low-cost input factors.

In conclusion, although the CAGE distance framework helps determine the attractiveness of foreign target markets in a more fine-grained manner based on relative differences, it is necessarily only a first step. A deeper analysis requires looking inside the firm (as done in Chapter 4) to see how a firm's strengths and weaknesses work to increase or reduce distance from specific foreign markets. A company with a large cadre of cosmopolitan managers and a diverse work force will be much less affected by cultural differences, for example, than a company with a more insular and less diverse culture with all managers from the home country. Although technology may make the world seem smaller, the costs of distance along all its dimensions are real. The costs of distance in expanding internationally are often very high. Ignoring these costs can be expensive (see Walmart's adventure in Germany, discussed in Strategy Highlight 10.2) and lead to a competitive disadvantage.

HOW DO MNEs ENTER FOREIGN MARKETS?

LO 10-4

Compare and contrast the different options MNEs have to enter foreign markets.

Assuming an MNE has decided why and where to enter a foreign market, the remaining decision is *how* to do so. Exhibit 10.5 displays the different options managers have when entering foreign markets, along with the required investments necessary and the control they can exert. On the left end of the continuum in Exhibit 10.5 are vehicles of foreign

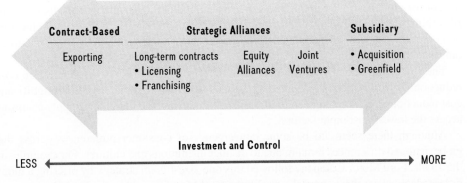

expansion that require low investments but also allow for a low level of control. On the right are foreign-entry modes that require a high level of investments in terms of capital and other resources, but also allow for a high level of control. Foreign-entry modes with a high level of control such as foreign acquisitions or greenfield plants reduce the firm's exposure to two particular downsides of global business: loss of reputation and loss of intellectual property.

Exporting—producing goods in one country to sell in another—is one of the oldest forms of internationalization (part of Globalization 1.0). It is often used to test whether a foreign market is ready for a firm's products. When studying vertical integration and diversification (in Chapter 8), we discussed in detail different forms along the make-or-buy continuum. As discussed in Chapter 9, strategic alliances (including licensing, franchising, and joint ventures) and acquisitions are popular vehicles for entry into foreign markets. Since we discussed these organizational arrangements in detail in previous chapters, we therefore keep this section on foreign-entry modes brief.

The framework illustrated in Exhibit 10.5, moving from left to right, has been suggested as a *stage model* of sequential commitment to a foreign market over time.[64] Though it does not apply to globally born companies, it is relevant for manufacturing companies that are just now expanding into global operations. In some instances, companies are required by the host country to form joint ventures in order to conduct business there, while some MNEs prefer *greenfield operations*—building new, fully owned plants and facilities from scratch, as Motorola did when it entered China in the 1990s.[65]

10.4 Cost Reductions vs. Local Responsiveness: The Integration-Responsiveness Framework

MNEs face two opposing forces when competing around the globe: *cost reductions* versus *local responsiveness* in a way that can affect strategy. Indeed, cost reductions achieved through a global-standardization strategy often reinforce a cost-leadership strategy at the business level. Similarly, local responsiveness increases the differentiation of products and services, reinforcing a differentiation strategy at the business level.

One of the core drivers for globalization is to expand the total market of firms in order to achieve economies of scale and drive down costs. For many business executives, the move toward globalization is based on the **globalization hypothesis**, which states that consumer needs and preferences throughout the world are converging and thus becoming increasingly homogenous.[66] Theodore Levitt stated: "Nothing confirms [the globalization hypothesis] as much as the success of McDonald's from [the] Champs-Élysées to Ginza,

LO 10-5

Apply the integration-responsiveness framework to evaluate the four different strategies MNEs can pursue when competing globally.

globalization hypothesis
Assumption that consumer needs and preferences throughout the world are converging and thus becoming increasingly homogenous.

of Coca-Cola in Bahrain and Pepsi-Cola in Moscow, and of rock music, Greek salad, Hollywood movies, Revlon cosmetics, Sony televisions, and Levi jeans everywhere."[67] In support of the globalization hypothesis, IKEA, as featured in the ChapterCase, sells its home furnishings successfully in over 40 countries. Toyota is selling its hybrid Prius vehicle in 80 countries. Most vehicles today are built on global platforms and modified (sometimes only cosmetically) to meet local tastes and standards.

The strategic foundations of the globalization hypothesis are based primarily on cost reduction. Lower cost is a key competitive weapon, and MNEs attempt to reap significant cost reductions by leveraging economies of scale and by managing global supply chains to access the lowest-cost input factors.

Although there seems to be some convergence of consumer preferences across the globe, national differences remain, due to distinct institutions and cultures. For example, in the 1990s, Ford Motor Company followed this one-size-fits-all strategy by offering a more or less identical car throughout the world: the Ford Mondeo, sold as the Ford Contour and the Mercury Mystique in North America. Ford learned the hard way, by lack of sales, that consumers did not subscribe to the globalization hypothesis at the same level as the Ford executives and were not yet prepared to ignore regional differences.[68] In some instances, MNEs experience pressure for **local responsiveness**—the need to tailor product and service offerings to fit local consumer preferences and host-country requirements; it generally entails higher costs. Walmart sells live animals (snakes, eels, toads, etc.) for food preparation in China. IKEA sells kimchi refrigerators and metal chopsticks in South Korea. McDonald's uses mutton instead of beef in India and offers a teriyaki burger in Japan, even though its basic business model of offering fast food remains the same the world over. Local responsiveness generally entails higher cost, and sometimes even outweighs cost advantages from economies of scale and lower-cost input factors.

Given the two opposing pressures of cost reductions versus local responsiveness, scholars have advanced the **integration-responsiveness framework**, shown in Exhibit 10.6.[69] This framework juxtaposes the opposing pressures for cost reductions and local responsiveness to derive four different strategic positions to gain and sustain competitive advantage when competing globally. The four strategic positions, which we will discuss in the following sections, are

- International
- Multidomestic
- Global-standardization
- Transnational[70]

At the end of that discussion, Exhibit 10.8 summarizes each global strategy.

INTERNATIONAL STRATEGY

An **international strategy** is essentially a strategy in which a company sells the same products or services in both domestic and foreign markets. It enables MNEs to leverage their home-based core competencies in foreign markets. An international strategy is one of the oldest types of global strategies (Globalization 1.0) and is frequently the first step companies take when beginning to conduct business abroad. As shown in the integration-responsiveness framework, it is advantageous when the MNE faces low pressures for both local responsiveness and cost reductions.

An international strategy is often used successfully by MNEs with relatively large domestic markets and with strong reputations and brand names. These MNEs, capitalizing on the fact that foreign customers want to buy the original product, tend to use

---

local responsiveness
The need to tailor product and service offerings to fit local consumer preferences and host-country requirements.

integration-responsiveness framework
Strategy framework that juxtaposes the pressures an MNE faces for cost reductions and local responsiveness to derive four different strategies to gain and sustain competitive advantage when competing globally.

international strategy
Strategy that involves leveraging home-based core competencies by selling the same products or services in both domestic and foreign markets.

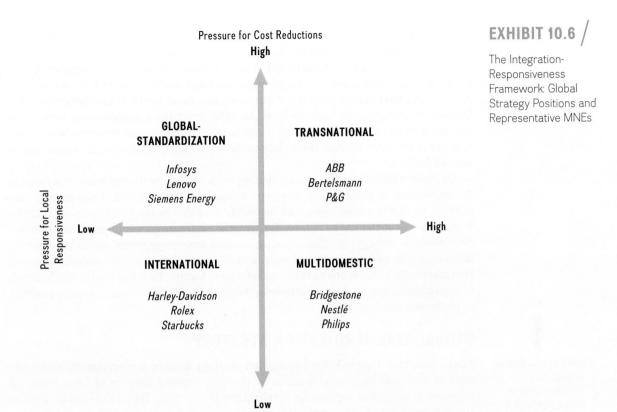

EXHIBIT 10.6 /

The Integration-Responsiveness Framework: Global Strategy Positions and Representative MNEs

differentiation as their preferred business strategy. For example, bikers in Shanghai, China, like their Harley-Davidson motorcycles to roar just like the ones ridden by the Hells Angels in the United States. Similarly, a Brazilian entrepreneur importing machine tools from Germany expects superior engineering and quality. An international strategy tends to rely on exporting or the licensing of products and franchising of services to reap economies of scale by accessing a larger market.

A strength of the international strategy—its limited local responsiveness—is also a weakness in many industries. For example, when an MNE sells its products in foreign markets with little or no change, it leaves itself open to the expropriation of intellectual property (IP). Looking at the MNE's products and services, pirates can reverse-engineer the products to discover the intellectual property embedded in them. In Thailand, for example, a flourishing market for knockoff luxury sports cars (e.g., Ferraris, Lamborghinis, and Porsches) has sprung up.[71] Besides the risk of exposing IP, MNEs following an international strategy are highly affected by exchange-rate fluctuations. Given increasing globalization, however, fewer and fewer markets correspond to this situation—low pressures for local responsiveness *and* cost reductions—that gives rise to the international strategy.

MULTIDOMESTIC STRATEGY

MNEs pursuing a **multidomestic strategy** attempt to maximize local responsiveness, hoping that local consumers will perceive their products or services as local ones. This strategy arises out of the combination of high pressure for local responsiveness and low pressure for cost reductions. MNEs frequently use a multidomestic strategy when entering host countries with large and/or idiosyncratic domestic markets, such as Japan or Saudi Arabia. This is one of the main strategies MNEs pursued in the Globalization 2.0 stage.

multidomestic strategy Strategy pursued by MNEs that attempts to maximize local responsiveness, with the intent that local consumers will perceive them to be domestic companies.

A multidomestic strategy is common in the consumer products and food industries. For example, Swiss-based Nestlé, the largest food company in the world, is known for customizing its product offerings to suit local preferences, tastes, and requirements. Given the strong brand names and core competencies in R&D, and the quality in their consumer products and food industries, it is not surprising that these MNEs generally pursue a differentiation strategy at the business level. An MNE following a multidomestic strategy, in contrast with an international strategy, faces reduced exchange-rate exposure because the majority of the value creation takes place in the host-country business units, which tend to span all functions.

On the downside, a multidomestic strategy is costly and inefficient because it requires the duplication of key business functions across multiple countries. Each country unit tends to be highly autonomous, and the MNE is unable to reap economies of scale or learning across regions. The risk of IP appropriation increases when companies follow a multidomestic strategy. Besides exposing codified knowledge embedded in products, as is the case with an international strategy, a multidomestic strategy also requires exposing tacit knowledge because products are manufactured locally. Tacit knowledge that is at risk of appropriation may include, for example, the process of how to create consumer products of higher perceived quality.

GLOBAL-STANDARDIZATION STRATEGY

global-standardization strategy
Strategy attempting to reap significant economies of scale and location economies by pursuing a global division of labor based on wherever best-of-class capabilities reside at the lowest cost.

MNEs following a **global-standardization strategy** attempt to reap significant economies of scale and location economies by pursuing a global division of labor based on wherever best-of-class capabilities reside at the lowest cost. The global-standardization strategy arises out of the combination of high pressure for cost reductions and low pressure for local responsiveness. MNEs using this strategy are often organized as networks (Globalization 3.0). This lets them strive for the lowest-cost position possible. Their business-level strategy tends to be cost leadership. Because there is little or no differentiation or local responsiveness because products are standardized, price becomes the main competitive weapon. To be price competitive, the MNE must maintain a minimum efficient scale (see Chapter 6).

MNEs that manufacture commodity products such as computer hardware or offer services such as business process outsourcing generally pursue a global-standardization strategy. Lenovo, the Chinese computer manufacturer, is the maker of the ThinkPad line of laptops, which it acquired from IBM in 2005. To keep track of the latest developments in computing, Lenovo's research centers are located in Beijing and Shanghai in China, in Raleigh, North Carolina (in the Research Triangle Park), and in Japan.[72] To benefit from low-cost labor and to be close to its main markets in order to reduce shipping costs, Lenovo's manufacturing facilities are in Mexico, India, and China. The company describes the benefits of its global-standardization strategy insightfully: "Lenovo organizes its worldwide operations with the view that a truly global company must be able to quickly capitalize on new ideas and opportunities from anywhere. By forgoing a traditional headquarters model and focusing on centers of excellence around the world, Lenovo makes the maximum use of its resources to create the best products in the most efficient and effective way possible."[73]

One of the advantages of the global-standardization strategy—obtaining the lowest cost point possible by minimizing local adaptations—is also one of its key weaknesses. The American MTV network cable channel started out with a global-standardization strategy.[74] The main inputs—music videos by vocal artists—were sourced more or less globally based on the prevailing music hits. MTV reasoned that music videos were a commodity product that would attract worldwide audiences. MTV was wrong! As indicated by the CAGE distance model, cultural distance most affects products with high linguistic content such as TV. Even in a music video channel, audiences have a distinct preference for at least some local content.

Keep in mind that strategic positions are not constant; they can change over time. Consider how MTV changed its strategic positions as it attempted to respond to the pressures for both cost reduction and local responsiveness. At first, MTV followed a global standardization strategy. To be more responsive to local audiences, MTV then implemented a multidomestic strategy to meet the need for local responsiveness. This led to a loss of all possible scale effects, especially rolling out expensive content over a large installed base of viewers. In a move a few years later, MTV shifted its strategic position away from a multidomestic strategy and is now pursuing a transnational strategy. Exhibit 10.7 tracks how MTV changed strategic positions in its quest for competitive advantage.

TRANSNATIONAL STRATEGY

MNEs pursuing a **transnational strategy** attempt to combine the benefits of a localization strategy (high local responsiveness) with those of a global-standardization strategy (lowest-cost position attainable). This strategy arises out of the combination of high pressure for local responsiveness and high pressure for cost reductions. A transnational strategy is generally used by MNEs that pursue a blue ocean strategy at the business level by attempting to reconcile product and/or service differentiations at low cost.

transnational strategy
Strategy that attempts to combine the benefits of a localization strategy (high local responsiveness) with those of a global-standardization strategy (lowest-cost position attainable).

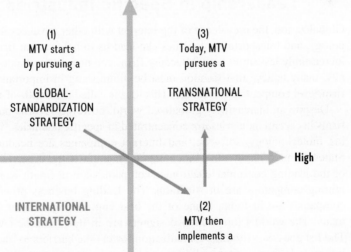

EXHIBIT 10.7 /

Dynamic Strategic Positioning: The MTV Music Chanel

Besides harnessing economies of scale and location, a transnational strategy also aims to benefit from global learning. MNEs typically implement a transnational strategy through a global matrix structure. That structure combines economies of scale along specific product divisions with economies of learning attainable in specific geographic regions. The idea is that best practices, ideas, and innovations will be diffused throughout the world, regardless of their origination. The managers' mantra is to *think globally, but act locally.*

Although a transnational strategy is quite appealing, the required matrix structure is rather difficult to implement because of the organizational complexities involved. High local responsiveness typically requires that key business functions are frequently duplicated in each host country, leading to higher costs. Further compounding the organizational complexities is the challenge of finding managers who can dexterously work across cultures in the ways required by a transnational strategy. We'll discuss organizational structure in more depth in the next chapter.

The German multimedia conglomerate Bertelsmann attempts to follow a transnational strategy. Bertelsmann employs over 100,000 people, with two-thirds of that work force outside its home country. Bertelsmann operates in more than 60 countries throughout the world and owns many regional leaders in their specific product categories, including Random House Publishing in the United States and RTL Group, Europe's second-largest TV, radio, and production company (after the BBC). Bertelsmann operates its over 500 regional media divisions as more or less autonomous profit-and-loss centers but attempts to share best practices across units; global learning and human resource strategies for executives are coordinated at the network level.[75]

As a summary, Exhibit 10.8 provides a detailed description of each of the four global strategies in the integration-responsiveness framework.

10.5 National Competitive Advantage: World Leadership in Specific Industries

Globalization, the prevalence of the Internet with other advances in communications technology, and transportation logistics can lead us to believe that firm location is becoming increasingly less important.[76] Because firms can now, more than ever, source inputs globally, many believe that location must be diminishing in importance as an explanation of firm-level competitive advantage. This idea is called the **death-of-distance hypothesis**.[77]

death-of-distance hypothesis Assumption that geographic location alone should not lead to firm-level competitive advantage because firms are now, more than ever, able to source inputs globally.

Despite an increasingly globalized world, however, it turns out that high-performing firms in certain industries *are* concentrated in specific countries.[78] For example, the leading biotechnology, software, and Internet companies are headquartered in the United States. Some of the world's best computer manufacturers are in China and Taiwan. Many of the leading consumer electronics companies are in South Korea and Japan. The top mining companies are in Australia. The leading business process outsourcing (BPO) companies are in India. Some of the best engineering and car companies are in Germany. The world's top fashion designers are in Italy. The best wineries are in France. The list goes on. Although globalization lowers the barriers to trade and investments and increases human capital mobility, one key question remains: *Why are certain industries more competitive in some countries than in others?* This question goes to the heart of the issue of **national competitive advantage**, a consideration of world leadership in specific industries. That issue, in turn, has a direct effect on firm-level competitive advantage. Companies from home countries that are world leaders in specific industries tend to be the strongest competitors globally.

national competitive advantage World leadership in specific industries.

EXHIBIT 10.8 / International, Multidomestic, Global-Standardization, and Transnational Strategies: Characteristics, Benefits, and Risks

Strategy	Characteristics	Benefits	Risks
International	Often the first step in internationalizing. Used by MNEs with relatively large domestic markets or strong exporters (e.g., MNEs from the United States, Germany, Japan, South Korea). Well-suited for high-end products with high value-to-weight ratios such as machine tools and luxury goods that can be shipped across the globe. Products and services tend to have strong brands. Main business-level strategy tends to be differentiation because exporting, licensing, and franchising add additional costs.	Leveraging core competencies. Economies of scale. Low-cost implementation through: • Exporting or licensing (for products) • Franchising (for services) • Licensing (for trademarks)	No or limited local responsiveness. Highly affected by exchange-rate fluctuations. IP embedded in product or service could be expropriated.
Multidomestic	Used by MNEs to compete in host countries with large and/or lucrative but idiosyncratic domestic markets (e.g., Germany, Japan, Saudi Arabia). Often used in consumer products and food industries. Main business-level strategy is differentiation. MNE wants to be perceived as local company.	Highest-possible local responsiveness. Increased differentiation. Reduced exchange-rate exposure.	Duplication of key business functions in multiple countries leads to high cost of implementation. Little or no economies of scale. Little or no learning across different regions. Higher risk of IP expropriation.
Global-Standardization	Used by MNEs that are offering standardized products and services (e.g., computer hardware or business process outsourcing). Main business-level strategy is cost leadership.	Location economies: global division of labor based on wherever best-of-class capabilities reside at lowest cost. Economies of scale and standardization.	No local responsiveness. Little or no product differentiation. Some exchange-rate exposure. "Race to the bottom" as wages increase. Some risk of IP expropriation.
Transnational	Used by MNEs that pursue a blue ocean strategy at the business level by simultaneously focusing on product differentiation and low cost. Mantra: Think globally, act locally.	Attempts to combine benefits of localization and standardization strategies simultaneously by creating a global matrix structure. Economies of scale, location, experience, and learning.	Global matrix structure is costly and difficult to implement, leading to high failure rate. Some exchange-rate exposure. Higher risk of IP expropriation.

LO 10-6

Apply Porter's diamond framework to explain why certain industries are more competitive in specific nations than in others.

PORTER'S DIAMOND FRAMEWORK

Michael Porter advanced a framework to explain national competitive advantage—why are some nations outperforming others in specific industries. This framework is called Porter's diamond of national competitive advantage. As shown in Exhibit 10.9, it consists of four interrelated factors:

- Factor conditions.
- Demand conditions.
- Competitive intensity in focal industry.
- Related and supporting industries/complementors.

FACTOR CONDITIONS. *Factor conditions* describe a country's endowments in terms of natural, human, and other resources. Other important factors include capital markets, a supportive institutional framework, research universities, and public infrastructure (airports, roads, schools, health care system), among others.

Interestingly, *natural resources* are often not needed to generate world-leading companies, because competitive advantage is often based on other factor endowments such as human capital and know-how. Several of the world's most resource-rich countries (such as Afghanistan,[79] Iran, Iraq, Russia, Saudi Arabia, and Venezuela) are not home to any of the world's leading companies, even though some (though not all) do have in place institutional frameworks allowing them to be a productive member of world commerce. In contrast, countries that lack natural resources (e.g., Denmark, Finland, Israel, Japan, Singapore, South Korea, Switzerland, Taiwan, and the Netherlands) often develop world-class human capital to compensate.[80]

EXHIBIT 10.9

Porter's Diamond of National Competitive Advantage

Source: Adapted from M.E. Porter (1990), "The competitive advantage of nations," *Harvard Business Review*, March–April: 78.

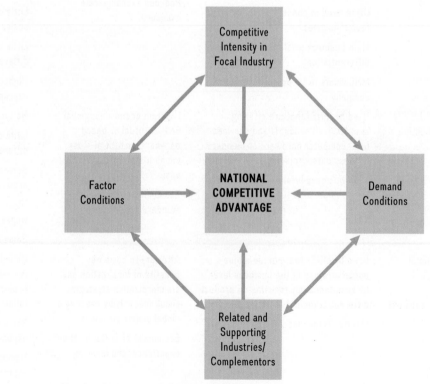

DEMAND CONDITIONS. *Demand conditions* are the specific characteristics of demand in a firm's domestic market. A home market made up of sophisticated customers who hold companies to a high standard of value creation and cost containment contributes to national competitive advantage. Moreover, demanding customers may also clue firms in to the latest developments in specific fields and may push firms to move research from basic findings to commercial applications for the marketplace.

For example, due to dense urban living conditions, hot and humid summers, and high energy costs, it is not surprising that Japanese customers demand small, quiet, and energy-efficient air conditioners. In contrast to the Japanese, Finns have a sparse population living in a more remote countryside. A lack of landlines for telephone service has resulted in the Finnish demand for high-quality wireless services, combined with reliable handsets (and long-life batteries) that can be operated in remote, often hostile, environments. Cell phones have long been a necessity for survival in rural areas of Finland. This situation enabled Nokia to become an early leader in cell phones.[81]

COMPETITIVE INTENSITY IN A FOCAL INDUSTRY. Companies that face a highly competitive environment at home tend to outperform global competitors that lack such intense domestic competition. Fierce domestic competition in Germany, for example, combined with demanding customers and the no-speed-limit autobahn make a tough environment for any car company. Success requires top-notch engineering of chassis and engines, as well as keeping costs and fuel consumption ($9-per-gallon gas) in check. This extremely tough home environment amply prepared German car companies such as Volkswagen (which also owns Audi and Porsche), BMW, and Daimler for global competition.

RELATED AND SUPPORTING INDUSTRIES/COMPLEMENTORS. Leadership in related and supporting industries can also foster world-class competitors in downstream industries. The availability of top-notch *complementors*—firms that provide a good or service that leads customers to value the focal firm's offering more when the two are combined—further strengthens national competitive advantage. Switzerland, for example, leveraged its early lead in industrial chemicals into pharmaceuticals.[82] A sophisticated health care service industry sprang up alongside as an important complementor, to provide further stimulus for growth and continuous improvement and innovation.

The effects of sophisticated customers and highly competitive industries ripple through the industry value chain to create top-notch suppliers and complementors. Toyota's global success in the 1990s and early 2000s was based to a large extent on a network of world-class suppliers in Japan.[83] This tightly knit network allowed for fast two-way knowledge sharing—this in turn improved Toyota's quality and lowered its cost, which it leveraged into a successful blue ocean strategy at the business level.

It is also interesting to note that by 2010, Toyota's supplier advantage had disappeared.[84] It was unable to solve the trade-off between drastically increasing its volume and maintaining superior quality. Toyota's rapid growth in its quest to become the world's leader in volume required quickly bringing on new suppliers outside Japan. Quality standards, however, could not be maintained. Part of the problem lies in path dependence (discussed in Chapter 4), because Chinese and other suppliers could not be found quickly enough, nor could most foreign suppliers build at the required quality levels fast enough. The cultural distance between Japan and China exacerbated these problems. Combined, these factors explain the quality problems Toyota experienced recently and highlight the importance of related and supporting industries to national competitive advantage.

10.6 ◀▶ Implications for the Strategist

In addition to determining the degree of vertical integration and level of diversification, the strategist needs to decide if and how the firm should compete beyond its home market. Decisions along all three dimensions formulate the firm's corporate strategy. Because of increasing global integration in products and services as well as capital markets, the benefits of competing globally outweigh the costs for more and more enterprises. This is true not just for large MNEs, but also for small and medium ones (SMEs). Even small startups are now able to leverage technology such as the Internet to compete beyond their home market.

Strategists have a number of frameworks at their disposal to make global strategy decisions. The CAGE framework allows for a detailed analysis of any country pairing. Rather than looking at simple absolute measures such as market size, the strategist can determine the *relative* distance or closeness of a target market to the home market along cultural, administrative/political, geographic, and economic dimensions. Once the strategist has decided which countries to enter, the *mode* of foreign entry needs to be determined. Considerations of the degree of investment and level of control help in this decision. Higher levels of control, and thus greater protection of IP and a lower likelihood of any loss in reputation, go along with more investment-intensive foreign-entry modes such as acquisitions or greenfield plants (see Exhibit 10.5).

A firm's business-level strategy (discussed in Chapter 6) provides an important clue to possible strategies to be pursued globally. A cost leader, for example, is more likely to have the capabilities to be successful with a global-standardization strategy. In contrast, a differentiator is more likely to be successful in pursuing an international or multidomestic strategy. The same caveats raised concerning a blue ocean strategy at the business level apply at the corporate level: Although attractive on paper, a transnational strategy combining high pressures for cost reductions with high pressures for local responsiveness is difficult to implement because of inherent trade-offs.

Finally, the strategist must be aware of the fact that despite globalization and the emergence of the Internet, firm geographic location has actually maintained its importance. Critical masses of world-class firms are clearly apparent in *regional geographic clusters*. Think of computer technology firms in Silicon Valley, medical device firms in the Chicago area, and biotechnology firms in and around Boston. This is a worldwide phenomenon. Known for their engineering prowess, car companies such as Daimler, BMW, Audi, and Porsche are clustered in southern Germany. Many fashion-related companies (clothing, shoes, and accessories) are located in northern Italy. Singapore is a well-known cluster for semiconductor materials, and India's leading IT firms are in Bangalore. Porter captures this phenomenon succinctly: "Paradoxically, the enduring competitive advantages in a global economy lie increasingly in local things—knowledge, relationships, and motivation that distant rivals cannot match."[85]

This concludes our discussion of global strategy. Moreover, we have now completed our study of the first two pillars of the AFI framework—*strategy analysis* (Chapters 1–5) and *strategy formulation* (Chapters 6–10). Next, we turn to the third and final pillar of the AFI framework—*strategy implementation*. In Chapter 11, we'll study what managers can do to implement their carefully crafted strategies successfully and how to avoid failure. In Chapter 12, we study corporate governance and business ethics.

CHAPTERCASE 10 / Consider This...

DESPITE ITS TREMENDOUS success, IKEA faces significant external and internal challenges going forward. Opening new stores is critical to drive future growth (see Exhibit 10.1). Finding new sources of supply to support more store openings, however, is a significant challenge. Although demand for IKEA's low-cost home furnishings increased during the global financial crisis as more customers became price conscious, IKEA's annual store growth has slowed to less than 10 new stores a year. This is because its global supply chain has become a bottleneck. IKEA has difficulty finding suppliers that are a strategic fit with its highly efficient operations. Related to this issue is the fact that wood remains one of IKEA's main input factors, and the world's consumers are becoming more sensitive to the issue of deforestation and its possible link to global warming. In the near future, IKEA must find low-cost replacement materials for wood. In addition, powerful competitors have taken notice of IKEA's success. Although IKEA is growing in North America, it holds less than 5 percent of the home-furnishings market. To keep IKEA at bay in the United States, Target has recently recruited top designers and launched a wide range of low-priced furnishings. In some European markets, IKEA holds 30 percent market share.

Besides these external challenges, IKEA also faces significant internal ones. Since the company's founding in 1943, no strategic decisions have been made without Kamprad's involvement and explicit approval. In 2013, Kamprad (in his late 80s) stepped down from chairing Inter IKEA, the foundation that owns the company, and passed the position to one of his sons. Many observers compare Kamprad's influence on IKEA's culture and organization to that of the legendary Sam Walton at Walmart. Kamprad's three sons will take on stronger leadership roles at IKEA.

Moreover, IKEA is privately held through a complicated network of foundations and holding companies in the Netherlands, Lichtenstein, and Luxembourg. This arrangement provides benefits in terms of reducing tax exposure, but also creates constraints in accessing large sums of capital needed for rapid global expansion. In addition, many EU countries as well as the United States have become increasingly more sensitive to the issue of tax avoidance schemes by large multinational enterprises. IKEA will need to address these challenges to live up to its strategic intent of doubling its number of yearly openings in an attempt to capture a larger slice of fast-growing markets such as the United States, China, and Russia.

Questions

1. Ingvar Kamprad's influence over IKEA may even be stronger than that of Sam Walton over Walmart because IKEA is privately held, while Walmart is a public company (since 1970). Walmart entered a period of difficulties after Sam Walton stepped down (in 1988 at age 70). Do you anticipate IKEA having similar leadership transition challenges? Why or why not?

2. Did it surprise you to learn that both a rich developed country (the United States) and emerging economies (i.e., China and Russia) are the fastest-growing international markets for IKEA? Does this fact pose any challenges in the way IKEA ought to compete across the globe? Why or why not?

3. What can IKEA do to continue to drive growth globally, especially given its strategic intent to double annual store openings?

4. Assume you are hired to consult IKEA on the topic of *corporate social responsibility* (see the discussion in Chapter 2). Which areas would you recommend the company be most sensitive to, and how should these be addressed?

TAKE-AWAY CONCEPTS

This chapter discussed the roles of MNEs for economic growth; the stages of globalization; why, where, and how companies go global; four strategies MNEs use to navigate between cost reductions and local responsiveness; and national competitive advantage, as summarized by the following learning objectives and related take-away concepts.

LO 10-1 / **Define globalization, multinational enterprise (MNE), foreign direct investment (FDI), and global strategy.**

- Globalization involves closer integration and exchange between different countries and peoples worldwide, made possible by factors such as falling trade and investment barriers, advances in telecommunications, and reductions in transportation costs.

- A multinational enterprise (MNE) deploys resources and capabilities to procure, produce, and distribute goods and services in at least two countries.

- Many MNEs are more than 50 percent globalized; they receive the majority of their revenues from countries other than their home country.

- Product, service, and capital markets are more globalized than labor markets. The level of everyday activities is roughly 10 to 25 percent integrated, and thus *semi-globalized.*

- Foreign direct investment (FDI) denotes a firm's investments in value chain activities abroad.

LO 10-2 / **Explain why companies compete abroad, and evaluate the advantages and disadvantages of going global.**

- Firms expand beyond their domestic borders if they can increase their economic value creation $(V - C)$ and enhance competitive advantage

- Advantages to competing internationally include gaining access to a larger market, gaining access to low-cost input factors, and developing new competencies.

- Disadvantages to competing internationally include the liability of foreignness, the possible loss of reputation, and the possible loss of intellectual capital.

LO 10-3 / **Apply the CAGE distance framework to guide MNE decisions on which countries to enter.**

- Most of the costs and risks involved in expanding beyond the domestic market are created by *distance.*

- The CAGE distance framework determines the *relative* distance between home and foreign target

country along four dimensions: cultural distance, administrative and political distance, geographic distance, and economic distance.

LO 10-4 / **Compare and contrast the different options MNEs have to enter foreign markets.**

- The strategist has the following foreign-entry modes available: exporting, strategic alliances (licensing for products, franchising for services), joint venture, and subsidiary (acquisition or greenfield).

- Higher levels of control, and thus a greater protection of IP and a lower likelihood of any loss in reputation, go along with more investment-intensive foreign-entry modes such as acquisitions or greenfield plants.

LO 10-5 / **Apply the integration-responsiveness framework to evaluate the four different strategies MNEs can pursue when competing globally.**

- To navigate between the competing pressures of cost reductions and local responsiveness, MNEs have four strategy options: international, multidomestic, global-standardization, and transnational.

- An international strategy leverages home-based core competencies into foreign markets, primarily through exports. It is useful when the MNE faces low pressures for both local responsiveness and cost reductions.

- A multidomestic strategy attempts to maximize local responsiveness in the face of low pressure for cost reductions. It is costly and inefficient because it requires the duplication of key business functions in multiple countries.

- A global-standardization strategy seeks to reap economies of scale and location by pursuing a global division of labor based on wherever best-of-class capabilities reside at the lowest cost. It involves little or no local responsiveness.

- A transnational strategy attempts to combine the high local responsiveness of a localization strategy with the lowest-cost position attainable from a global-standardization strategy. It also aims to benefit from global learning. Although appealing, it is difficult to implement due to the organizational complexities involved.

LO 10-6 / Apply Porter's diamond framework to explain why certain industries are more competitive in specific nations than in others.

■ National competitive advantage, or world leadership in specific industries, is created rather than inherited.

■ Four interrelated factors explain national competitive advantage: (1) factor conditions, (2) demand conditions, (3) competitive intensity in a focal industry, and (4) related and supporting industries/complementors.

■ Even in a more globalized world, the basis for competitive advantage is often local.

KEY TERMS

CAGE distance framework *(p. 339)*

Cultural distance *(p. 341)*

Death-of-distance hypothesis *(p. 348)*

Foreign direct investment (FDI) *(p. 330)*

Global-standardization strategy *(p. 346)*

Global strategy *(p. 330)*

Globalization *(p. 329)*

Globalization hypothesis *(p. 343)*

Integration-responsiveness framework *(p. 344)*

International strategy *(p. 344)*

Liability of foreignness *(p. 336)*

Local responsiveness *(p. 344)*

Location economies *(p. 336)*

Multidomestic strategy *(p. 345)*

Multinational enterprise (MNE) *(p. 330)*

National competitive advantage *(p. 348)*

National culture *(p. 340)*

Transnational strategy *(p. 347)*

DISCUSSION QUESTIONS

1. Multinational enterprises (MNEs) have an impact far beyond their firm boundaries. Assume you are working for a small firm that supplies a product or service to an MNE. How might your relationship change as the MNE moves from Globalization 2.0 to Globalization 3.0 operations?

2. Professor Pankaj Ghemawat delivered a TED talk titled "Actually, the World Isn't Flat." Do you agree with his assessment that the world is at most *semi-globalized,* and that we need to be careful not to fall victim to "globalony"? View the talk at: www.ted.com/talks/pankaj_ghemawat_ actually_the_world_isn_t_flat?language=en.

3. The chapter notes that global strategy can change over time for a firm. MTV is highlighted as one example in Exhibit 10.7. Conduct a web search of a firm you know to be operating internationally and determine its current global strategy position. How long has the firm stayed with this approach? Can you find evidence it had a different global strategy earlier?

4. "Licensing patented technology to a foreign competitor is likely to reduce or eliminate the firm's competitive advantage." True or false? Write a paragraph discussing this statement.

ETHICAL/SOCIAL ISSUES

1. A "race-to-the-bottom" process may set in as MNEs search for ever-lower-cost locations. Discuss the trade-offs between the positive effects of raising the standard of living in some of the world's poorest countries with the drawbacks of moving jobs established in one country to another. Does your perspective change in light of the recent accidents in textile factories in Bangladesh, Cambodia, and elsewhere, where the cumulative death was over 1,000 workers? What responsibilities do MNEs have?

2. Will the Globalization 3.0 strategy persist through the 21st century? If not, what will Globalization 4.0 look like? Several American companies such as Apple and GE have realized that they miscalculated the full cost of managing far-flung production operations and are bringing production back to the United States. *Forbes* magazine put the blame on managers who were focused on maximizing shareholder value rather than emphasizing the long-term future of the firm.[86] That is, some managers looked only at labor costs and ignored the hidden costs of time and money trying to communicate quality and design concerns to workers across countries as well as unexpected costs to the supply chain from natural disasters or political threats. These factors combined with the new economics of energy (e.g.,

growing supply of natural gas) and new technologies (robotics, artificial intelligence, 3-D printing, and nanotechnology) are rapidly changing manufacturing and management decisions.

Discuss the factors that managers of Apple or GE may consider as they focus on continuous innovation rather than the cost of manufacturing. How might governments with an interest in generating employment opportunities try to influence the decisions of firms? What other stakeholders may have an interest in bringing jobs back onshore and thus try to influence the decisions of firms? Consider the persuasive arguments and deals that might be struck. With changes to the location of production, what might Globalization 4.0 look like?

SMALL GROUP EXERCISES

//// Small Group Exercise 1

Many U.S. companies have become global players. The technology giant IBM employs over 375,000 people and has revenues of roughly $95 billion. Although IBM's headquarters is in Armonk, New York, the vast majority of its employees (more than 70 percent) actually work outside the United States. IBM, like many other U.S.-based multinationals, now earns the majority of its revenues (roughly two-thirds) outside the United States.[87] Though IBM revenues have been dropping in recent quarters, its global business is still a major focus for the firm.

1. Given that traditional U.S. firms such as IBM have over 70 percent of their employees outside the United States and earn almost two-thirds of their revenues from outside the country, what is an appropriate definition of a "U.S. firm"?

2. Should IKEA be considered a Swedish firm with less than 6 percent of sales garnered from the Swedish market? Discuss why or why not in your groups.

3. Is there any special consideration a firm should have for its "home country"? Is it ethical to keep profits outside the home country in offshore accounts to avoid paying domestic corporate taxes?

//// Small Group Exercise 2

In this exercise, we want to apply the four types of global strategy. Imagine your group works for Clif

Bar (www.clifbar.com). Founded in 1992, the firm makes nutritious, all-natural food and drinks for sport and healthy snacking. Clif Bar is a privately held company with some 400 employees. About 20 percent of the company is owned by the employees through an employee-stock-ownership program (ESOP). The vast majority of Clif Bar's sales are in the United States. The firm has some distribution set up in Canada (since 1996) and the United Kingdom (since 2007). As of 2015, Clif Bar sells limited products only in eight other countries: Austria, Australia, France, Germany, Ireland, Japan, New Zealand, and Switzerland.

Review the company's website for more information about the firm and its products.

1. Apply the CAGE distance framework to the six foreign countries where Clif Bar is operating. What is the *relative* distance of each to the United States? Rank the order of the six countries in terms of *relative* distance.

2. Given the results from the CAGE model, do the six chosen countries make sense? Why or why not?

3. Can you recommend three or four other countries Clif Bar should enter? Support your recommendations.

4. What entrance strategy should the firm employ in expanding the business to new countries? Why?

STRATEGY TERM PROJECT

connect

The HP Running Case, *a related activity for each strategy term project module, is available in Connect.*

//// **Module 10: Global Strategy**

If your firm is already engaged in international activities, answer the following questions:

1. Is your company varying its product or service to adapt to differences in countries? Is the marketing approach different among the nations involved? Should it be?

2. Is your firm working internationally to access larger markets? To gain low-cost input factors? To develop new competencies? Is its approach in all three areas appropriate?

3. Which of the four global strategies is the firm using? Is this the best strategy for it to use? Why or why not? (Exhibit 10.8 provides a summary of the four global strategies.)

If your firm is not *now engaged internationally,* answer the following questions:

1. Would your firm's product or service need to be modified or marketed differently if it expanded beyond the home country?

2. Does your firm have the potential to access larger markets by expanding internationally? Does it have the possibility of lowering input factors with such expansion? Please explain why or why not.

3. If your firm decided to expand internationally, where does the firm reside on the integration-responsiveness framework? (Refer to Exhibit 10.6 if needed.) What does this result say about the "best" global strategy for your firm to use for international expansion?

*my*STRATEGY

How Do You Develop a Global Mind-set?

How can you develop the skills needed to succeed as an international leader? Researchers have developed a personal strategy for building a global mind-set that will facilitate success as an effective manager in a different cultural setting. A global mind-set has three components: *intellectual capital,* the understanding of how business works on a global level; *psychological capital,* openness to new ideas and experiences; and *social capital,* the ability to build connections with people and to influence stakeholders from a different cultural background.[88]

- *Intellectual capital* is considered the easiest to gain if one puts forth the effort. You can gain global business acumen by taking courses, but you can learn a great deal on your own by reading publications with an international scope such as *The Economist,* visiting websites that provide information on different cultures or business operations in foreign countries, or simply watching television programs with an international news or culture focus. Working in global industries with people from diverse cultures is also a complex assignment, requiring the ability to manage complexity and uncertainty.

- *Psychological capital* is gained by being receptive to new ideas and experiences and appreciating diversity. It may be the most difficult to develop, because your ability to change your personality has limits. If you are enthusiastic about adventure and are willing to take risks in new environments, then you have the attitudes needed to be energized by a foreign assignment. It takes self-confidence and a sense of humor to adapt successfully to new environments.

- *Social capital* is based on relationships and is gained through experience. You can gain experience with diversity simply by widening your social circle, volunteering to work with international students, or by traveling on vacation or through a study abroad experience.

Now that you have a description of the three components of a global mind-set and a few ideas about how to develop the attributes necessary for global success, consider some ways you can develop a personal strategy that can be implemented during your college career.

1. So that you have a better idea of where you stand now, list your strengths and weaknesses for each component.

2. Identify your weakest area, and make a list of activities that will help you improve your capital in that area. After generating your own list, check out http://hbr.org/globalize-yourself-list. You will be amazed at the possibilities.

3. Identify courses you could take in international business, economics, politics, history, or art history. While you may be required to be proficient in at least one foreign language, learn a few words in other languages that can help you navigate any new countries you visit.

4. Make a list of at least six activities you could do this week in order to get started. For example, you could choose to work with international students on group projects in class. Or move on to having lunch with them. What questions could you ask that would help you learn about their culture and about doing business in their country? You could go to a museum with an exhibit from another culture, an international movie, or a restaurant with cuisine that is new to you.

If you are interested in more information, go to http://globalmindset.thunderbird.edu/, where you can also take a sample survey to get an idea of the degree to which you have the attributes needed for global success.

ENDNOTES

1. This ChapterCase is based on: Kowitt, B. (2015), "It's Ikea's world. We just live in it," *Fortune,* March 15; "Ingvar Kamprad steps back," *The Economist,* June 5, 2013; "IKEA to accelerate expansion," *The Wall Street Journal,* September 18, 2012; "The secret of IKEA's success," *The Economist,* February 24, 2011; Edmonds, M. (2010), "How Ikea works," http://money.howstuffworks.com/ikea.htm; Peng, M. (2009), *Global Strategy,* 2nd ed. (Mason, OH: South-Western Cengage); "Shocking tell-all book takes aim at Ikea," *Bloomberg Businessweek,* November 12, 2009; "Flat-pack accounting," *The Economist,* May 11, 2006; "IKEA: How the Swedish retailer became a global cult brand," *Bloomberg Businessweek,* November 14, 2005; and various IKEA yearly summaries (www.ikea.com).

2. "Foreign university students," *The Economist,* August 7, 2010; and Haynie, D., "Number of international college students continues to climb," *U.S. News & World Report,* November 17, 2014.

3. McCarthy, N., "These countries have the most students studying abroad," *Forbes,* July 2, 2015.

4. World Bank (2015), *World Development Indicators,* http://data.worldbank.org/data-catalog/world-development-indicators.

5. CAGE is an acronym for *C*ultural, *A*dministrative and political, *G*eographic, and *E*conomic distance. The model was introduced by Ghemawat, P. (2001), "Distance still matters: The hard reality of global expansion," *Harvard Business Review,* September.

6. Stiglitz, J. (2002), *Globalization and Its Discontents* (New York: Norton).

7. "BRICs, emerging markets and the world economy," *The Economist,* June 18, 2009.

8. World Bank (2013), *World Development Indicators,* http://data.worldbank.org/data-catalog/world-development-indicators.

9. Caves, R. (1996), *Multinational Enterprise and Economic Analysis* (New York: Cambridge University Press); and Dunning, J. (1993), *Multinational Enterprises and the Global Economy* (Reading, MA: Addison-Wesley).

10. "Airbus's new push: Made in the U.S.A.," *The Wall Street Journal,* July 2, 2012.

11. "GM's latest nemesis: VW," *The Wall Street Journal,* August 4, 2010.

12. Following Peng (2010: 18), we define global strategy as a "strategy of firms around the globe—essentially various firms' theories about how to compete successfully." This stands in contrast to a narrower alternative use of the term *global strategy,* which implies a global cost-leadership strategy in standardized products. We follow Peng to denote this type of strategy as *global-standardization strategy* (Peng, 2010: 20); Peng, M.W. (2010), *Global Strategy,* 2nd ed. (Mason, OH: Cengage).

13. Kotha, S., V. Rindova, and F.T. Rothaermel (2001), "Assets and actions: Firm-specific factors in the internationalization of U.S. Internet firms," *Journal of International Business Studies* 32: 769–791.

14. McKinsey Global Institute (2010), *Growth and Competitiveness in the United States: The Role of Its Multinational Companies* (London: McKinsey Global Institute).

15. IBM (2009), "A decade of generating higher value at IBM," www.ibm.com; and Friedman, T.L. (2005), *The World Is Flat: A Brief History of the Twenty-First Century* (New York: Farrar, Strauss, and Giroux).

16. Immelt, J.R., V. Govindarajan, and C. Trimble (2009), "How GE is disrupting itself," *Harvard Business Review,* October; author's interviews with Michael Poteran of GE Healthcare (October 30, 2009, and November 4, 2009); and "Vscan handheld ultrasound: GE unveils 'stethoscope of the 21st century,'" *Huffington Post,* October 20, 2009; and Govindarajan, V., and C. Trimble (2012), *Reverse Innovation: Create Far from Home, Win Everywhere* (Boston, MA: Harvard Business Review Press).

17. This process is also referred to as reverse innovation. Govindarajan and Trimble, *Reverse Innovation: Create Far from Home, Win Everywhere.*

18. www.logitech.com. Its two founders, one Swiss and the other Italian, each held master's degrees from Stanford University.

19. Saxenian, A. (1994), *Regional Advantage* (Cambridge, MA: Harvard University Press); and Rothaermel, F.T., and D. Ku (2008), "Intercluster innovation differentials: The role of research universities," *IEEE Transactions on Engineering Management* 55: 9–22.

20. Ghemawat, P. (2011), *World 3.0: Global Prosperity and How to Achieve It* (Boston, MA: Harvard Business Review Press). The data presented are drawn from Ghemawat (2011) and his TED talk "Actually, the world isn't flat," June 2012. You can view this excellent talk at: http://www.ted.com/talks/pankaj_ghemawat_actually_the_world_isn_t_flat.html.

21. The number rises to 6–7 percent if VoIP (such as Skype) is included; Ghemawat, P. (2012), "Actually, the world isn't flat," TED talk.

22. Friedman, *The World Is Flat: A Brief History of the Twenty-First Century.*

23. Ghemawat, *World 3.0: Global Prosperity and How to Achieve It.*

24. Ibid.

25. "The rising power of the Chinese worker," *The Economist,* July 29, 2010.

26. "Supply chain for iPhone highlights costs in China," *The New York Times,* July 5, 2010.

27. Ibid.

28. This is based on: Friedman, *The World Is Flat: A Brief History of the Twenty-First Century;* "Supply chain for iPhone highlights costs in China"; and "The rising power of the Chinese worker."

29. Ghemawat, *World 3.0: Global Prosperity and How to Achieve It.*

30. Strategy Highlight 10.2 is based on: McCartney, S., "Emirates, Etihad and Qatar make their move on the U.S.," *The Wall Street Journal,* November 6, 2014; Carey, S., "Big U.S. Airlines fault Persian Gulf carriers," *The Wall Street Journal,* February 5, 2015; Carey, S., "U.S. airlines battling Gulf carriers cite others' experience," *The Wall Street Journal,* March 16, 2015; Carey, S., "Persian Gulf airlines are winning fans in U.S." *The Wall Street Journal,* March 16, 2015; and "Superconnecting the world." *The Economist,* April 25, 2015.

31. "A special report on innovation in emerging markets," *The Economist,* April 15, 2010.

32. "The rising power of the Chinese worker," *The Economist,* July 29, 2010.

33. Friedman, *The World Is Flat: A Brief History of the Twenty-First Century.*

34. Chang, S.J. (1995), "International expansion strategy of Japanese firms: Capability building through sequential entry," *Academy of Management Journal* 38: 383–407; Vermeulen, F., and H.G. Barkema (1998), "International expansion through start-up or acquisition: A learning perspective," *Academy of Management Journal* 41: 7–26; Vermeulen, F., and H.G. Barkema (2002), "Pace, rhythm, and scope: Process dependence in building a profitable multinational corporation,"

Strategic Management Journal 23: 637–653; and Ghemawat, *World 3.0: Global Prosperity and How to Achieve It.*

35. Brown, J.S., and P. Duguid (1991), "Organizational learning and communities-of-practice: Toward a unified view of working, learning, and innovation," *Organization Science* 2: 40–57.

36. Owen-Smith, J., and W.W. Powell (2004), "Knowledge networks as channels and conduits: The effects of spillovers in the Boston biotech community," *Organization Science* 15: 5–21.

37. Examples drawn from: "A special report on innovation in emerging markets," *The Economist,* April 15, 2010, and "Cisco globalisation centre east: A hotbed of emerging technologies," www.cisco.com

38. Dunning, J.H., and S.M. Lundan (2008), *Multinational Enterprises and the Global Economy,* 2nd ed. (Northampton, MA: Edward Elgar).

39. Govindarajan and Trimble, *Reverse Innovation: Create Far From Home, Win Everywhere.*

40. "A special report on innovation in emerging markets."

41. Zaheer, S. (1995), "Overcoming the liability of foreignness," *Academy of Management Journal* 38: 341–363.

42. Strategy Highlight 10.2 is based on: Knorr, A., and A. Arndt (2003), "Why did Wal-Mart fail in Germany?" in ed. A. Knorr, A. Lemper, A. Sell, and K. Wohlmuth, *Materialien des Wissenschaftsschwerpunktes "Globalisierung der Weltwirtschaft,"* vol. 24 (IWIM—Institute for World Economics and International Management, Universität Bremen, Germany); the author's onsite observations at Walmart stores in Germany; and "Hair-shirt economics: Getting Germans to open their wallets is hard," *The Economist,* July 8, 2010. For a recent discussion of Walmart's global efforts, see: "After early errors, Wal-Mart thinks locally to act globally," *The Wall Street Journal,* August 14, 2009; Sharma, A. and B. Mukherji, "Bad roads, red tape, burly thugs slow Wal-Mart's passage in India," *The Wall Street Journal,* January 12, 2013; Berfield, S., "Where Wal-Mart isn't: Four countries the retailer can't conquer," *Bloomberg Businessweek,* October 10, 2013.

43. Top 100 Most Valuable Global Brands 2015," report by Millward Brown, WPP.

44. "The Foxconn suicides," *The Wall Street Journal,* May 27, 2010.

45. "When workers dream of a life beyond the factory gates," *The Economist,* December 15, 2012.

46. "Apple shifts supply chain away from Foxconn to Pegatron," *The Wall Street Journal,* May 29, 2013.

47. "Disaster at Rana Plaza," *The Economist,* May 4, 2013; "The Bangladesh disaster and corporate social responsibility," *Forbes,* May 2, 2013.

48. Ibid.

49. This example is drawn from: "Train makers rail against China's high-speed designs," *The Wall Street Journal,* November 17, 2010.

50. This section is based on: Ghemawat, P. (2001), "Distance still matters: The hard reality of global expansion," *Harvard Business Review,* September; see also Ghemawat, *World 3.0: Global Prosperity and How to Achieve It.*

51. The euro is the official currency of the European Union and is the official currency in the following member countries: Austria, Belgium, Cyprus, Estonia, Finland, France, Germany, Greece, Ireland, Italy, Latvia, Lithuania, Luxembourg, Malta, the Netherlands, Portugal, Slovakia, Slovenia, and Spain.

52. To obtain scores for any two country pairings and to view interactive CAGE distance maps, go to www.ghemawat.com.

53. The discussion of the CAGE distance frameworks and the attributes thereof is based on: Ghemawat, "Distance still matters: The hard reality of global expansion"; see also Ghemawat, *World 3.0: Global Prosperity and How to Achieve It.*

54. Hofstede, G.H. (1984), *Culture's Consequences: International Differences in Work-Related Values* (Beverly Hills, CA: Sage), p. 21. The description of Hofstede's four cultural dimensions is drawn from: Rothaermel, F.T., S. Kotha, and H.K. Steensma (2006), "International market entry by U.S. Internet firms: An empirical analysis of country risk, national culture, and market size," *Journal of Management* 32: 56–82.

55. The *power-distance dimension* of national culture focuses on how a society deals with inequality among people in terms of physical and intellectual capabilities and how those methods translate into power distributions within organizations. High power-distance cultures, like the Philippines (94/100, with 100 = high), tend to allow inequalities among people to translate into inequalities in opportunity, power, status, and wealth. Low power-distance cultures, like Austria (11/100), on the other hand, tend to intervene to create a more equal distribution among people within organizations and society at large.

The *individualism dimension* of national culture focuses on the relationship between individuals in a society, particularly in regard to the relationship between individual and collective pursuits. In highly individualistic cultures, like the United States (91/100), individual freedom and achievements are highly valued. As a result, individuals are only tied loosely to one another within society. In less-individualistic cultures, like Venezuela (12/100), the collective good is emphasized over the individual, and members of society are strongly tied to one another throughout their lifetimes by virtue of birth into groups like extended families.

The *masculinity–femininity dimension* of national culture focuses on the relationship between genders and its relation to an individual's role at work and in society. In more "masculine" cultures, like Japan (95/100), gender roles tend to be clearly defined and sharply differentiated. In "masculine" cultures, values like competitiveness, assertiveness, and exercise of power are considered cultural ideals, and men are expected to behave accordingly. In more "feminine" cultures, like Sweden (5/100), values like cooperation, humility, and harmony are guiding cultural principles. The masculinity–femininity dimension uncovered in Hofstede's research is undoubtedly evolving over time, and values and behaviors are converging to some extent.

The *uncertainty-avoidance dimension* of national culture focuses on societal differences in tolerance toward ambiguity and uncertainty. In particular, it highlights the extent to which members of a certain culture feel anxious when faced with uncertain or unknown situations. Members of high uncertainty-avoidance cultures, like Russia (95/100), value clear rules and regulations as well as clearly structured career patterns, lifetime employment, and retirement benefits. Members of low uncertainty-avoidance cultures, like Singapore (8/100), have greater tolerance toward ambiguity and thus exhibit less emotional resistance to change and a greater willingness to take risks.

56. See http://geert-hofstede.com/national-culture.html. The available data, however, on the new dimensions are not, at this point, as comprehensive as for the four original dimensions. Alternatively, see the GLOBE cultural dimensions at www.grovewell.com/pub-GLOBE-intro.html.

57. "Strong revenue growth in China & Asia-Pacific drives Starbucks' top-line growth in Q2," *Forbes,* April 28, 2015; "Starbucks," in Resonance Insights, *China Social Branding Report,* November 24, 2014; "Starbucks gets even more social in China, lets fans follow in WeChat app," *Tech in Asia,* September 6, 2012.

58. This is based on: Kogut, B., and H. Singh (1988), "The effect of national culture on the choice of entry mode," *Journal of International Business Studies* 19: 411–432; Rothaermel, F.T., S. Kotha, and H. K. Steensma (2006), "International market entry by U.S. Internet firms: An empirical analysis of country risk, national culture, and market size," *Journal of Management 32:* 56–82. Cultural distance from the United States, for example, is calculated as follows:

$$CD_j = \sum_{i=1}^{4} \{(I_{ij} - I_{iu})^2 / V_i\}/4$$

where I_{ij} stands for the index for the ith cultural dimension and jth country, V_i is the variance of the index of ith dimension, u indicates the United States, and CD_j is the cultural distance difference of the jth country from the United States.

59. Ghemawat, "Actually, the world isn't flat"; and Ghemawat, *World 3.0: Global Prosperity and How to Achieve It.*

60. Ghemawat, "Distance still matters: The hard reality of global expansion."

61. See statistics provided by Eurostat at: http://epp.eurostat.ec.europa.eu.

62. Williamson, O.E. (1975), *Markets and Hierarchies* (New York: Free Press); Williamson, O.E. (1981), "The economics of organization: The transaction cost approach," *American Journal of Sociology* 87: 548–577; and Williamson, O.E. (1985), *The Economic Institutions of Capitalism* (New York: Free Press).

63. Ghemawat, "Distance still matters: The hard reality of global expansion"; Burkitt, L., "Walmart says it will go slow in China," *The Wall Street Journal,* April 29, 2015.

64. Johanson, J., and J. Vahlne (1977), "The internationalization process of the firm," *Journal of International Business Studies* 4: 20–29.

65. Fuller, A.W., and F.T. Rothaermel (2008), "The interplay between capability development and strategy formation: Motorola's entry into China," Georgia Institute of Technology Working Paper.

66. Levitt, T. (1983), "The globalization of markets," *Harvard Business Review,* May–June: 92–102.

67. Ibid.: 93.

68. Mol, M. (2002), "Ford Mondeo: A Model T world car?" in ed. Tan, F.B., *Cases on Global IT Applications and Management: Successes and Pitfalls* (Hershey, PA: Idea Group Publishing), pp. 69–89.

69. Prahalad, C.K., and Y.L. Doz (1987), *The Multinational Mission* (New York: Free Press); and Roth, K., and A.J. Morrison (1990), "An empirical analysis of the integration-responsiveness framework in global industries," *Journal of International Business Studies* 21: 541–564.

70. Bartlett, C.A., S. Ghoshal, and P.W. Beamish (2007), *Transnational Management: Text, Cases and Readings in Cross-Border Management,* 5th ed. (New York: McGraw-Hill).

71. "Ditch the knock-off watch, get the knock-off car," *The Wall Street Journal Video,* August 8, 2010.

72. www.lenovo.com/lenovo/US/en/locations.html.

73. Ibid.

74. Ghemawat, *World 3.0: Global Prosperity and How to Achieve It.*

75. Mueller, H.-E. (2001), "Developing global human resource strategies," paper presented at the European International Business Academy, Paris, December 13–15; Mueller, H.-E. (2001), "Wie Global Player den Kampf um Talente führen," *Harvard Business Manager* 6: 16–25.

76. This section draws on: Rothaermel, F.T., and D. Ku (2008), "Intercluster innovation differentials: The role of research universities," *IEEE Transactions on Engineering Management* 55: 9–22.

77. This is based on: Buckley, P.J., and P.N. Ghauri (2004), "Globalisation, economic geography and the strategy of multinational enterprises," *Journal of International Business Studies* 35: 81–98; Cairncross, F. (1997), *The Death of Distance: How the Communications Revolution Will Change Our Lives* (Boston, MA: Harvard Business School Press); and Friedman, *The World Is Flat: A Brief History of the Twenty-First Century.* For a counterpoint, see: Ghemawat, "Distance still matters: The hard reality of global expansion"; Ghemawat, P. (2007), *Redefining Global Strategy: Crossing Borders in a World Where Differences Still Matter* (Boston, MA: Harvard Business School Press); and Ghemawat, *World 3.0: Global Prosperity and How to Achieve It.*

78. This section is based on: Porter, M.E. (1990), "The competitive advantage of nations," *Harvard Business Review,* March–April: 73–91; and Porter, M.E. (1990), *The Competitive Advantage of Nations* (New York: Free Press).

79. "U.S. identifies vast mineral riches in Afghanistan," *The New York Times,* June 13, 2010.

80. For an insightful recent discussion, see: Breznitz, D. (2007), *Innovation and the State: Political Choice and Strategies for Growth in Israel, Taiwan, and Ireland* (New Haven, CT: Yale University Press).

81. Nokia ceded leadership to RIM (Canada), which subsequently stumbled. Currently, Apple and Samsung (South Korea) are the leaders in the smartphone industry (see discussion in Chapter 7 on the smartphone industry).

82. Murmann, J.P. (2003), *Knowledge and Competitive Advantage* (New York: Cambridge University Press).

83. Dyer, J.H., and K. Nobeoka (2000), "Creating and managing a high-performance knowledge-sharing network: The Toyota case," *Strategic Management Journal* 21: 345–367.

84. This discussion is based on: "Toyota slips up," *The Economist,* December 10, 2009; "Toyota: Losing its shine," *The Economist,* December 10, 2009; "Toyota heir faces crises at the wheel," *The Wall Street Journal,* January 27, 2010; "Toyota's troubles deepen," *The Economist,* February 4, 2010; "The humbling of Toyota," *Bloomberg Businessweek,* March 11, 2010; and "Inside Toyota, executives trade blame over debacle," *The Wall Street Journal,* April 13, 2010.

85. Porter, *The Competitive Advantage of Nations,* p. 77.

86. "Why Apple and GE are bringing back manufacturing," *Forbes,* December 7, 2012.

87. IBM annual reports, various years.

88. This myStrategy item is based on an article by Javidan, M., M. Teagarden, and D. Bowen, (2010), "Making it overseas," *Harvard Business Review,* April: 109–113.

Implementation

The AFI Strategy Framework

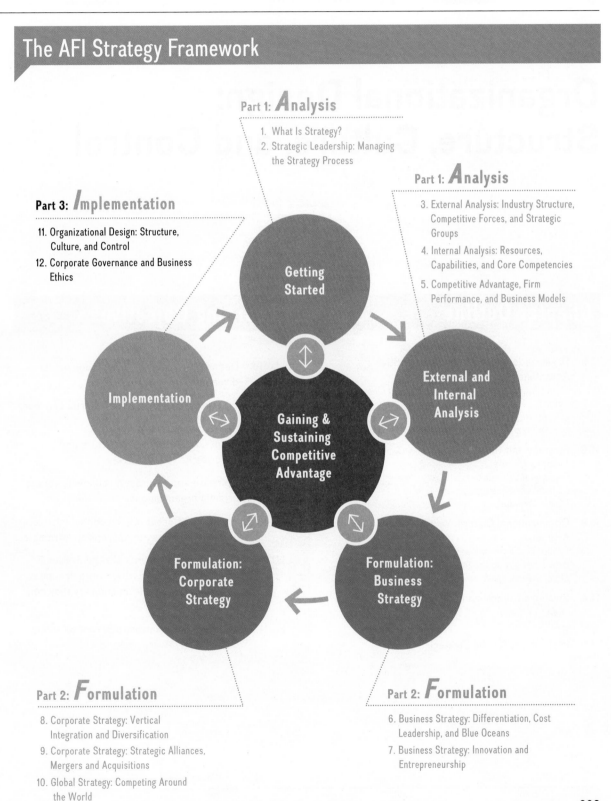

Getting Started

Implementation

Gaining & Sustaining Competitive Advantage

External and Internal Analysis

Formulation: Corporate Strategy

Formulation: Business Strategy

Organizational Design: Structure, Culture, and Control

Zappos: From Happiness to Holacracy

DELIVERING HAPPINESS is the title of *The New York Times* bestseller by Tony Hsieh, CEO of Zappos, the online shoe and clothing store (www.zappos.com). Today, Zappos stocks more than 3 million shoes, handbags, clothing items, eyewear, and accessories from over 1,200 brands. Shoes continue to be the main business for Zappos, bringing in some three-quarters of revenues and making it the world's largest shoe store. Delivering happiness is also Zappos' mission. The company is known for "delivering WOW through service," providing a positive online shopping experience including free shipping to and from its customers, including a generous 365-day return policy.

In addition to making customers happy, Zappos has also made its investors happy. In 2008, just 10 years after its founding, Zappos achieved more than $1 billion in annual sales. In 2009, Amazon.com acquired the company for $1.2 billion. Although now a subsidiary of Amazon, Zappos continues to operate as an independent brand, as Amazon maintains a hands-off policy. Instead of top-down management from Amazon, if anything, new ideas flow from Zappos up to its parent. One example is Zappos' novel approach to weed out cultural misfits by paying employees to leave after the orientation program. Amazon recently implemented a similar program for its warehouse workers.

Zappos has grown so much—receiving over 20 million unique visitors a month to its website—that it sometimes reorganizes to offer the best customer service possible. At one point, to keep the organization flat and responsive to customers, Zappos restructured into 10 separate business units including Zappos.com, Zappos Gift Cards, Zappos IP, and 6pm.com, among others. This step, however, was not sufficient to accommodate the rapid growth, as employee productivity was declining. To continue to make its customers, employees, and other stakeholders happy, Zappos is redesigning its structure radically to create a unique organization that is even more responsive to its customers' needs as well as external and internal changes. Zappos CEO Tony Hsieh decided to implement a radically new structure called *holacracy,* and explains why:

> Research shows that every time the size of a city doubles, innovation or productivity per resident increases by 15 percent. But when companies get bigger, innovation or productivity per employee generally goes down. So we're trying to figure out how to structure Zappos more like a city and less like a bureaucratic corporation. In a city, people and businesses are self-organizing. We're trying to do the same thing by switching from a normal hierarchical structure to a system called Holacracy, which enables employees to act more like entrepreneurs and self-direct their work instead of reporting to a manager who tells them what to do.[1]

A flock of birds in flight, immediately shifting direction with self-regulating unity, frequently serves as a poetic symbol of holacracy in action.
© greatonmywall / Alamy

This focus explains why Zappos is implementing holacracy, but what exactly is it? Often compared to a computer's operating system, holacracy provides a new organizational structure for governing and running a company. Because it greatly changes how workers interact, proponents hail it as a "social technology." It was developed by Brian Robertson in the 2000s, who was working from ideas introduced by Arthur Koestler in the 1967 book, *The Ghost in the Machine,* the work in which Koestler coined the term *holacracy.*[2] Rather than relying on a traditional top-down hierarchical management structure, holacracy attempts to achieve control and coordination by distributing power and authority to self-organizing groups (so-called circles) of employees. Circles of employees are meant to self-organize and own a specific task, such as confirming online orders or authorizing a customer's credit card.

At this point of its reorganization, Zappos grouped its over 1,500 employees in some 400 circles, with each employee in two or more circles. Order is supposed to emerge from the bottom up, rather than rely on top-down command and control as in traditional organizational structures.

How? Rules are explicit in a so-called constitution, which defines the power and authority of each circle. For coordination, the employee circles overlap horizontally, and without vertical hierarchy. Teams in circles of employees self-organize and self-govern. The CEO's last act as the highest-ranking person in the organization is to sign the constitution in a symbolic act, relinquishing all executive powers. Thereafter the former leader becomes the "ratifier of the holacracy constitution." All this is done to serve the overarching goal of achieving rapid organizational evolution and adaptation to constantly changing external and internal environments. Exhibit 11.1 provides an overview comparing a traditional organizational structure with holacracy.

As often happens, a new organizational structure sounds great in theory, but proves hard to implement. In fact, Zappos is the first large corporation to try; previously firms adopting the approach tended to be small startups and nonprofits. Robertson, the inventor of holacracy as organizational form, ran a software company of 12 people where he tested his ideas. Twitter co-founder Evan Williams is a fan; he implemented holacracy—not at Twitter, but at his *new* venture, Medium, a blog-publishing platform. With Zappos the first large corporation attempting to make a wholesale switch to this approach, curiosity remains high as to how it will play out.[3]

You will learn more about Zappos by reading this chapter; related questions appear on page 392.

EXHIBIT 11.1

Traditional Organizational Structure vs. Holacracy

Source: Adapted from Robertson, B. (2015), *Holacracy: The New Management System for a Rapidly Changing World* (New York: Henry Holt).

Traditional Organizational Structure	Holacracy
Static job description	Dynamic roles
Top-down	Self-organizing teams
Hierarchical decision making	Employee senses tension as dissonance between *what is* (current reality) and *what could be* (the purpose). How to resolve tension is worked out in circle meetings.
Formal authority	Distributed authority
Command and control	Employee autonomy
Functional areas	Employee circles
Alignment via politics	Transparent rules defined in constitution
Large scale re-organizations	Rapid, fluid, and constant iterations

ZAPPOS CEO TONY HSIEH believes that about one-half of all retail transactions in the United States will be online soon, and that people will buy from the company with the best customer service and best selection. His strategic intent for Zappos is to be that online store, to differentiate itself from the competition with superior service and selection. Hsieh remains unusually thoughtful about what type of structure, culture, and processes will advance that strategy. He initially designed Zappos as a flat organization to help Zappos provide exceptional service, and he continued to refine its organizational design through trial and error, with transparency, while nurturing a supportive culture by soliciting bottom-up feedback. And he celebrated the emphasis on happiness as noted in his book, with the understanding that happy employees are productive employees.

Yet, a loss of productivity and increased bureaucracy could not be avoided as the company grew and matured. To move Zappos forward, in 2014 Hsieh proposed a new organizational structure called **holacracy**, a form of social technology that Hsieh believes will allow Zappos to pursue its purpose of delivering happiness and WOW through customer service.

This chapter opens the final part of the *AFI framework:* strategy implementation. *Strategy implementation* concerns the organization, coordination, and integration of how work gets done. (See discussion in Chapter 2.)

Effective strategy implementation is critical to gaining and sustaining competitive advantage. Although the discussion of *strategy formulation* (what to do) is distinct from *strategy implementation* (how to do it), formulation and implementation must be part of an interdependent, reciprocal process in order to ensure continued success. That need for interdependence explains why the AFI framework is illustrated as a circle, rather than a linear diagram (see page 365). The design of an organization, the matching of strategy and structure, and its control-and-reward systems determine whether or not an organization that has chosen an effective strategy will be able to gain and sustain a competitive advantage. As discussed in the ChapterCase, Zappos pursues a differentiation strategy at the business level, which it is now implementing internally and structurally through holacracy. Whether Zappos' strategy implementation will be successful or not remains to be seen.

In this chapter, we study the three key levers that managers have at their disposal when designing their organizations for competitive advantage: *structure, culture,* and *control.* Managers employ these three levers to coordinate work and motivate employees across different levels, functions, and geographies. How successful they are in this endeavor determines whether they are able to translate their chosen business, corporate, and global strategy into strategic actions and business models, and ultimately whether the firm is able to gain and sustain a competitive advantage.

We begin our discussion with organizational structure. We discuss different types of organizational structures as well as why and how they need to change over time as successful firms grow in size and complexity. We highlight the critical need to match strategy and structure, and then take a closer look at corporate culture. An organization's culture can either support or hinder its quest for competitive advantage.[4] We next study strategic control systems, which allow managers to receive feedback on how well a firm's strategy is being implemented. We conclude our discussion of how to design an organization for competitive advantage with practical "Implications for the Strategist."

> **holacracy** An organizational structure in which decision-making authority is distributed through loose collections or circles of self-organizing teams.

11.1 Organizational Design and Competitive Advantage

> **LO 11-1**
> Define organizational design and list its three components.

Organizational design is the process of creating, implementing, monitoring, and modifying the structure, processes, and procedures of an organization. The key components of organizational design are structure, culture, and control. The goal is to design an organization that allows managers to effectively translate their chosen strategy into a realized one.

Not surprisingly, the inability to implement strategy effectively is the number-one reason boards of directors fire CEOs.[5] Yahoo's co-founder and CEO Jerry Yang was ousted in 2008 precisely because he failed to implement necessary strategic changes after Yahoo lost its competitive advantage.[6] In the two years leading up to his exit, Yahoo lost more than 75 percent of its market value. Yang was described as someone who preferred consensus among his managers to making tough strategic decisions needed to change Yahoo's structure. That preference, though, led to bickering and infighting. Yang's failure to make the necessary changes to the Internet firm's organizational structure led to a destruction of billions of dollars in shareholder value and thousands of layoffs. Once a leader in online search, Yahoo is struggling to make a comeback. A number of short-term and interim CEOs followed Yang without much success. Then in 2012, as detailed in ChapterCase 2,

> **organizational design** The process of creating, implementing, monitoring, and modifying the structure, processes, and procedures of an organization.

Yahoo tapped former Google executive Marissa Mayer as president and CEO; Mayer's turnaround efforts hinge on improving the user experience to drive mobile advertising revenues. Such changes in strategy required changes in structure as well.

Because strategy implementation transforms strategy into actions and business models, it often requires changes within the organization. However, strategy implementation often fails because managers are unable to make the necessary changes due to the effects on resource allocation and power distribution within an organization.[7] Managers are leery to disturb the status quo.

As demonstrated by business historian Alfred Chandler in his seminal book *Strategy and Structure,* organizational structure must follow strategy in order for firms to achieve superior performance: "Structure can be defined as the design of organization through which the enterprise is administered . . . *structure follows strategy.*"[8] This tenet implies that to implement a strategy successfully, organizational design must be flexible enough to accommodate the formulated strategy and future growth and expansion.

Featured in the ChapterCase, Zappos provides an example of a company with flexible organizational structure. When establishing customer service as a core competency, one of the hardest decisions Hsieh made early was to pull the plug on drop-shipment orders. These are orders for which Zappos would be the intermediary, relaying them to particular shoe vendors who then ship directly to the customer. Such orders were profitable because Zappos would not have to stock all the shoes. They were also appealing because the fledgling startup was still losing money. But the problem was twofold. The vendors were slower than Zappos in filling orders. In addition, they did not accomplish the reliability metric that Zappos wanted for exceptional service: 95 percent accuracy was simply not good enough! Instead, Zappos decided to forgo drop shipments and instead built a larger warehouse in Kentucky to stock a full inventory. This move enabled the firm to achieve close to 100 percent accuracy in its shipments, many of which were overnight. Unlike other online retailers, Zappos stocks everything it sells in its own warehouses—this is the only way to get the merchandise as quickly as possible with 100 percent accuracy to the customer. Strategy, therefore, is as much about deciding what to do as it is about deciding what *not* to do.

ORGANIZATIONAL INERTIA: THE FAILURE OF ESTABLISHED FIRMS

To implement a formulated business strategy successfully, structure must accommodate strategy, not the other way around. In reality, however, a firm's strategy often follows its structure.[9] This reversal implies that some managers consider only strategies that do not change existing organizational structures; they do not want to confront the inertia that often exists in established organizations.[10] **Inertia**, a firm's resistance to change the status quo, can set the stage for the firm's subsequent failure. Successful firms often plant the seed of subsequent failure: They optimize their organizational structure to the current situation. That tightly coupled system can break apart when internal or external pressures occur.

Note that organizational inertia is often the result of success in a particular market during a particular time; it becomes difficult to argue with success. The pattern for successful firms often follows a particular path:

1. Mastery of, and fit with, the current environment.
2. Success, usually measured by financial measurements.
3. Structures, measures, and systems to accommodate and manage size.
4. A resulting organizational inertia that tends to minimize opportunities and challenges created by shifts in the internal and external environment.

What's missing, of course, is the conscious strategic decision to change the firm's internal environment to fit with the new external environment, turning four steps leading to the endpoint of inertia (Option A) into the kind of a virtual circle where the firm essentially reboots and reinvents itself (Option B).

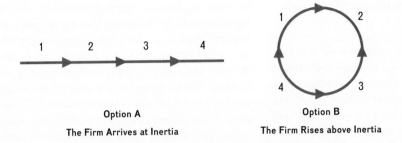

Option A

The Firm Arrives at Inertia

Option B

The Firm Rises above Inertia

Consider that the need for structural reorganization can be especially intense in many industries where the rate of change is high and potential disruption frequent. Consider also that business leaders find it much easier to create and manage within developed structures than to restructure their organizations to be where they will need to be in future.

Exhibit 11.2 shows how success in the current environment can lead to a firm's downfall in the future, when the tightly coupled system of strategy and structure experiences internal or external shifts.[11] First, the managers achieve a mastery of, and fit with, the firm's current environment. Second, the firm often defines and measures success by financial metrics, with a focus on short-term performance (see discussion in Chapter 5). Third, the firm puts in place structures, metrics, and systems to accommodate and

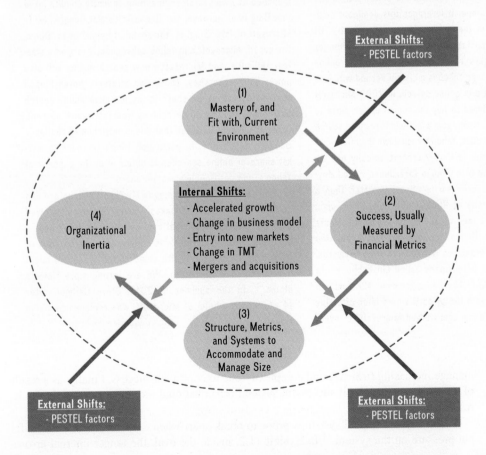

EXHIBIT 11.2 /

Organizational Inertia and the Failure of Established Firms to Respond to Shifts in the External or Internal Environments

Strategy Highlight 11.1

The Premature Death of a Google-like Search Engine at Microsoft

In 1998, 24-year-old Sergey Brin and 25-year-old Larry Page founded Google. At the same time, Microsoft was the most valuable technology company of all time. Brin and Page met as graduate students in computer science at Stanford University, where they began working together on a web crawler, with the goal of improving online searches. What they developed was the PageRank algorithm, which returns the most relevant web pages more or less instantaneously and ranks them by how often they are referenced on other important web pages. A clear improvement over early search engines such as Alta-Vista, Overture, and Yahoo, all of which indexed by keywords, the PageRank algorithm is able to consider 500 million variables and 3 billion terms. What started as a homework assignment launched the two into an entrepreneurial venture when they set up shop in a garage in Menlo Park, California.

Today, Google is the world's leading online search company with 65 percent market share in the United States and over 90 percent in Europe. It leverages this dominant position into leadership in the online advertising industry: Of some $70 billion in annual revenues, more than $60 billion (or 90 percent) of Google's revenues come from paid online search advertising. Though Yahoo is a distant second with less than a 15 percent share in online search, in 2008 Microsoft CEO Steve Ballmer offered to buy the runner-up for close to $50 billion to help his company gain a foothold in the paid-search business where Google rules. Yahoo turned down the offer.

What haunts Ballmer is that Microsoft actually had its own working prototype of a Google forerunner, called Keywords, more than a decade earlier. Scott Banister, then a student at the University of Illinois at Urbana-Champaign, had come up with the idea of adding paid advertisements to Internet searches. He quit college and drove his Geo hatchback to the San Francisco Bay Area to start Keywords, later joining an online ad company called LinkExchange. In 1998, Microsoft bought LinkExchange for some $265 million (about one two-hundredth the price it would later offer for Yahoo). LinkExchange's managers urged Microsoft to invest

in Keywords. Instead, Microsoft executives shut down LinkExchange in 2000 because they did not see a viable business model in it. One LinkExchange manager actually approached Ballmer himself and explained that he thought Microsoft was making a mistake. But Ballmer said he wanted to manage through delegation and would not reverse a decision made by managers three levels below him. This decision put an end to Microsoft's first online advertising venture.

In 2003, Microsoft got a second chance to enter the online advertising business when some mid-level managers proposed buying Overture Services, an innovator in combining Internet searches with advertisements. This time, Ballmer, joined by Microsoft co-founder Bill Gates, decided not to pursue the idea because they thought Overture was overpriced. Shortly thereafter, Yahoo bought Overture for $1.6 billion.

Having missed two huge opportunities to pursue promising strategic initiatives that emerged from lower levels within the firm, Microsoft has been playing catch-up in online search and advertising ever since. In the summer of 2009, it launched its own search engine, Bing. Industry pundits joked that Bing is an acronym for "Because It's Not Google," while Microsoft insists "Bing" is "the sound of found," as in "Bingo, I've got it!" Microsoft and Yahoo subsequently formed a strategic alliance, and Microsoft's new search engine will also power Yahoo searches. These two strategic moves helped Microsoft increase its share in the lucrative online search business to roughly 20 percent, up from just over 8 percent. It seems unlikely, however, that this is sufficient to challenge Google's dominance. In particular, Bing's increase in market share of online searches is obtained at the expense of Yahoo's, and not Google's, market share.

Ballmer admitted problems in Microsoft's structure and culture: "The biggest mistakes I claim I've been involved with are where I was impatient—because we didn't have a business yet in something, we should have stayed patient. If we'd kept consistent with some of the ideas, we might have been in paid search. We are letting more flowers bloom."[12] In the summer of 2014, Steve Ballmer, after 14 years at the helm of Microsoft, was replaced by Satya Nadella as new CEO.[13]

---

manage increasing firm size and complexity due to continued success. Finally, as a result of a tightly coupled albeit successful system, organizational inertia sets in—and with it, resistance to change.

Such a tightly coupled system is prone to break apart when external and internal shifts put pressure on the system.[14] In Exhibit 11.2, inside the oval, the longer internal arrows show the firm's tightly coupled organizational design over time. The shorter internal arrows indicate pressures radiating from internal shifts such as accelerated growth, a change in the business model, entry into new markets, a change in the top management team (TMT), or mergers and acquisitions. Accelerated growth, for example, was the reason for a decline in employee productivity, as discussed in the Zappos ChapterCase. The longest arrows pointing into and piercing the boundary of the firm indicate external pressures, which can stem from any of the PESTEL forces (political, economic, sociocultural, technological, ecological, and legal, as discussed in Chapter 3). Strong external or internal pressure can break apart the current system, which may lead to firm failure. To avoid inertia and possible organizational failure, the firm needs a flexible and adaptive structure to effectively translate the formulated strategy into action. Ideally the firm would maintain a virtuous cycle of reconsidering organization, as implied by Option B earlier in the chapter.

Strategy Highlight 11.1 provides a case in point. It shows how Microsoft's strategy and decision-making process were negatively affected by organizational inertia due to its success and dominance in the Windows-based PC world.

ORGANIZATIONAL STRUCTURE

LO 11-3

Define organizational structure and describe its four elements.

Some of the key decisions managers must make when designing effective organizations pertain to the firm's **organizational structure**. That structure determines how the work efforts of individuals and teams are orchestrated and how resources are distributed. In particular, an organizational structure defines how jobs and tasks are divided and integrated, delineates the reporting relationships up and down the hierarchy, defines formal communication channels, and prescribes how individuals and teams coordinate their work efforts. The key building blocks of an organizational structure are:

organizational structure
A key to determining how the work efforts of individuals and teams are orchestrated and how resources are distributed.

- Specialization
- Formalization
- Centralization
- Hierarchy

SPECIALIZATION. **Specialization** describes the degree to which a task is divided into separate jobs—that is, the *division of labor*. Larger firms, such as Fortune 100 companies, tend to have a high degree of specialization; smaller entrepreneurial ventures tend to have a low degree of specialization. For example, an accountant for a large firm may specialize in only one area (e.g., internal audit), whereas an accountant in a small firm needs to be more of a generalist and take on many different things (e.g., internal auditing, plus payroll, accounts receivable, financial planning, and taxes). Specialization requires a trade-off between breadth and depth of knowledge. While a high degree of the division of labor increases productivity, it can also have unintended side-effects such as reduced employee job satisfaction due to repetition of tasks.

specialization
An organizational element that describes the degree to which a task is divided into separate jobs (i.e., the division of labor).

FORMALIZATION. **Formalization** captures the extent to which employee behavior is steered by explicit and codified rules and procedures. Formalized structures are characterized by detailed written rules and policies of what to do in specific situations. These are often codified in employee handbooks. McDonald's, for example, uses detailed standard operating procedures throughout the world to ensure consistent quality and service.

Formalization, therefore, is not necessarily negative; often it is necessary to achieve consistent and predictable results. Airlines, for instance, must rely on a high degree of formalization to instruct pilots on how to fly their airplanes in order to ensure safety and reliability. Yet a high degree of formalization can slow decision making, reduce creativity and innovation, and hinder customer service.[15] Most customer service reps in call centers, for

formalization
An organizational element that captures the extent to which employee behavior is steered by explicit and codified rules and procedures.

example, follow a detailed script. This is especially true when call centers are outsourced to overseas locations. Zappos deliberately avoided this approach when it made customer service its core competency.

centralization
An organizational element that refers to the degree to which decision making is concentrated at the top of the organization.

CENTRALIZATION. **Centralization** refers to the degree to which decision making is concentrated at the top of the organization. Centralized decision making often correlates with slow response time and reduced customer satisfaction. In decentralized organizations such as Zappos, decisions are made and problems solved by empowered lower-level employees who are closer to the sources of issues.

Different strategic management processes (discussed in Chapter 2) match with different degrees of centralization:

- Top-down strategic planning takes place in highly centralized organizations.
- Planned emergence is found in more decentralized organizations.

Whether centralization or decentralization is more effective depends on the specific situation. During the Gulf of Mexico oil spill in 2010, BP's response was slow and cumbersome because key decisions were initially made in its UK headquarters and not onsite. In this case, centralization reduced response time and led to a prolonged crisis. In contrast, the FBI and the CIA were faulted in the 9/11 Commission Report for *not being centralized enough.*[16] The report concluded that although each agency had different types of evidence that a terrorist strike in the United States was imminent, their decentralization made them unable to put together the pieces to prevent the 9/11 attacks.

hierarchy
An organizational element that determines the formal, position-based reporting lines and thus stipulates who reports to whom.

HIERARCHY. **Hierarchy** determines the formal, position-based reporting lines and thus stipulates *who reports to whom.* Let's assume two firms of roughly equal size: Firm A and Firm B. If many levels of hierarchy exist between the frontline employee and the CEO in Firm A, it has a *tall structure.* In contrast, if there are few levels of hierarchy in Firm B, it has a *flat structure.*

span of control
The number of employees who directly report to a manager.

The number of levels of hierarchy, in turn, determines the managers' **span of control**—how many employees directly report to a manager. In tall organizational structures (Firm A), the span of control is narrow. In flat structures (Firm B), the span of control is wide, meaning one manager supervises many employees. In recent years, firms have de-layered by reducing the headcount (often middle managers), making themselves flatter and more nimble. This, however, puts more pressure on the remaining managers who have to supervise and monitor more direct reports due to an increased span of control.[17] Recent research suggests that managers are most effective at an intermediate point where the span of control is not too narrow or too wide.[18]

LO 11-4

Compare and contrast mechanistic versus organic organizations.

MECHANISTIC VS. ORGANIC ORGANIZATIONS

Several of the building blocks of organizational structure frequently appear together, creating distinct organizational forms—mechanistic or organic organizations.[19]

mechanistic organization
Characterized by a high degree of specialization and formalization and by a tall hierarchy that relies on centralized decision making.

MECHANISTIC ORGANIZATIONS. **Mechanistic organizations** are characterized by a high degree of specialization and formalization and by a tall hierarchy that relies on centralized decision making. The fast food chain McDonald's fits this description quite well. Each step of every job such as deep-frying fries is documented in minute detail (e.g., what kind of vat, the quantity of oil, how many fries, what temperature, how long, and so on). Decision power is centralized at the top of the organization: McDonald's headquarters provides detailed instructions to each of its franchisees so that they provide comparable quality and service across the board although with some local menu variations.

Communication and authority lines are top-down and well defined. To ensure standardized operating procedures and consistent food quality throughout the world, McDonald's operates Hamburger University, a state-of-the-art teaching facility in a Chicago suburb, where 50 full-time instructors teach courses in chemistry, food preparation, and marketing. In 2010, McDonald's opened a second Hamburger University campus in Shanghai, China. Mechanistic structures allow for standardization and economies of scale, and often are used when the firm pursues a cost-leadership strategy at the business level.

ORGANIC ORGANIZATIONS. Organic organizations have a low degree of specialization and formalization, a flat organizational structure, and decentralized decision making. Organic structures tend to be correlated with the following: a fluid and flexible information flow among employees in both horizontal and vertical directions; faster decision making; and higher employee motivation, retention, satisfaction, and creativity. Organic organizations also typically exhibit a higher rate of entrepreneurial behaviors and innovation. Organic structures allow firms to foster R&D and/or marketing, for example, as a core competency. Firms that pursue a differentiation strategy at the business level frequently have an organic structure.

organic organization Characterized by a low degree of specialization and formalization, a flat organizational structure, and decentralized decision making.

Strategy Highlight 11.2 shows how W.L. Gore & Associates uses an organic structure to foster continuous innovation.

Exhibit 11.3 summarizes the key features of mechanistic and organic structures.

Although at first glance organic organizations may appear to be more attractive than mechanistic ones, their relative effectiveness depends on context. McDonald's, with its over 36,000 restaurants across the globe, would not be successful with an organic structure.

EXHIBIT 11.3 / Mechanistic vs. Organic Organizations: Building Blocks of Organizational Structure

	Mechanistic Organizations	**Organic Organizations**
Specialization	• High degree of specialization • Rigid division of labor • Employees focus on narrowly defined tasks	• Low degree of specialization • Flexible division of labor • Employees focus on "bigger picture"
Formalization	• Intimate familiarity with rules, policies, and processes necessary • Deep expertise in narrowly defined domain required • Task-specific knowledge valued	• Clear understanding of organization's core competencies and strategic intent • Domain expertise in different areas • Generalized knowledge of how to accomplish strategic goals valued
Centralization	• Decision power centralized at top • Vertical (top-down) communication	• Distributed decision making • Vertical (top-down and bottom-up) as well as horizontal communication
Hierarchy	• Tall structures • Low span of control • Clear lines of authority • Command and control	• Flat structures • High span of control • Horizontal as well as two-way vertical communication • Mutual adjustment
Business Strategy	• Cost-leadership strategy • Examples: McDonald's; Walmart	• Differentiation strategy • Examples: W.L. Gore, Zappos

Strategy Highlight 11.2

W.L. Gore & Associates: Informality and Innovation

W.L. Gore & Associates is the inventor of path-breaking new products such as breathable GORE-TEX fabrics, Glide dental floss, and Elixir guitar strings. Bill Gore, a former longtime employee of chemical giant DuPont, founded the company with the vision to create an organization "devoted to innovation, a company where imagination and initiative would flourish, where chronically curious engineers would be free to invent, invest, and succeed."[20] When founding the company in 1958, Gore articulated four core values that still guide the company and its associates to this day:

1. Fairness to each other and everyone with whom the firm does business.

2. Freedom to encourage, help, and allow other associates to grow in knowledge, skill, and scope of responsibility.

3. The ability to make one's own commitments and keep them.

4. Consultation with other associates before undertaking actions that could cause serious damage to the reputation of the company ("blowing a hole below the waterline").

W.L. Gore & Associates is organized in an informal and decentralized manner: It has no formal job titles, job descriptions, chains of command, formal communication channels, written rules or standard operating procedures. Face-to-face communication is preferred over e-mail. There is no organizational chart. In what is called a *lattice* or *boundaryless* organizational form, everyone is empowered and encouraged to speak to anyone else in the organization. People who work at Gore are called "associates" rather than employees, indicating professional expertise and status. Gore associates organize themselves in project-based teams that are led by sponsors, not bosses. Associates invite other team members based on their expertise and interests in a more or less ad hoc fashion. Peer control in these multidisciplinary teams further enhances associate productivity. Group members evaluate each other's performance annually, and these evaluations determine each associate's level of compensation. Moreover, all associates at W.L. Gore are also shareholders of the company, and thus are part owners sharing in profits and losses.

Gore's freewheeling and informal culture has been linked to greater employee satisfaction and retention, higher personal initiative and creativity, and innovation at the firm level. Although W.L. Gore's organizational structure may look like something you might find in a small, high-tech startup, the company has 10,000 employees and over $3 billion in revenues, making Gore one of the largest privately held companies in the United States. W.L. Gore is consistently ranked in the top 25 of *Fortune*'s "100 Best Companies to Work For" list (number 17 in 2015), and has been included in every edition of that prestigious ranking.[21]

Similarly, a mechanistic structure would not allow Zappos or W.L. Gore to develop and hone their respective core competencies in customer service and product innovation.

The key point is this: To gain and sustain competitive advantage, structure must follow strategy. Moreover, the chosen organizational form must match the firm's business strategy. We will expand further on the required strategy–structure relationship in the next section.

LO 11-5

Describe different organizational structures and match them with appropriate strategies.

11.2 Strategy and Structure

The important and interdependent relationship between strategy and structure directly impacts a firm's performance. Moreover, the relationship is dynamic—changing over time in a somewhat predictable pattern as firms grow in size and complexity. Successful new ventures generally grow first by increasing sales, then by obtaining larger geographic reach, and finally by diversifying through vertical integration and entering into related and unrelated businesses.[22] Different stages in a firm's growth require different organizational structures. This important evolutionary pattern is depicted in Exhibit 11.4. As we discuss next, organizational structures range from simple to functional to multidivisional to matrix.

SIMPLE STRUCTURE

A **simple structure** generally is used by small firms with low organizational complexity. In such firms, the founders tend to make all the important strategic decisions and run the day-to-day operations. Examples include entrepreneurial ventures such as Facebook in 2004, when the startup operated out of Mark Zuckerberg's dorm room, and professional service firms such as smaller advertising, consulting, accounting, and law firms, as well as family-owned businesses. Simple structures are flat hierarchies operated in a decentralized fashion. They exhibit a low degree of formalization and specialization. Typically, neither professional managers nor sophisticated systems are in place, which often leads to an overload for the founder and/or CEO when the firms experience growth.

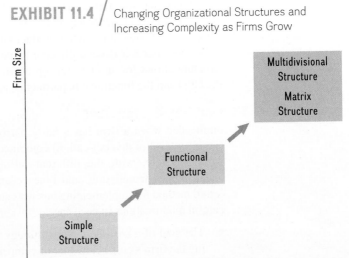

EXHIBIT 11.4 / Changing Organizational Structures and Increasing Complexity as Firms Grow

simple structure
Organizational structure in which the founders tend to make all the important strategic decisions as well as run the day-to-day operations.

functional structure
Organizational structure that groups employees into distinct functional areas based on domain expertise.

FUNCTIONAL STRUCTURE

As sales increase, firms generally adopt a **functional structure,** which groups employees into distinct functional areas based on domain expertise. These functional areas often correspond to distinct stages in the value chain such as R&D, engineering and manufacturing, and marketing and sales, as well as supporting areas such as human resources, finance, and accounting. Exhibit 11.5 shows a functional structure, with the lines indicating reporting and authority relationships. The department head of each functional area reports to the CEO, who coordinates and integrates the work of each function. A business school student generally majors in one of these functional areas such as finance, accounting, IT, marketing, operations, or human resources, and is then recruited into a corresponding functional group.

W.L. Gore began as a company by operating out of Bill Gore's basement and using a simple structure. Two years after its founding, the company received a large manufacturing order for high-tech cable that it could not meet with its ad hoc basement operation. At that point, W.L. Gore reorganized itself into a functional structure. A simple structure could not provide the effective division, coordination, and integration of work required to accommodate future growth.

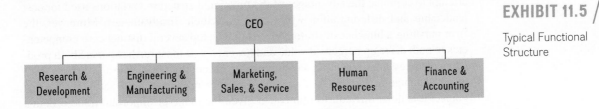

EXHIBIT 11.5 /

Typical Functional Structure

A functional structure allows for a higher degree of specialization and deeper domain expertise than a simple structure. Higher specialization also allows for a greater division of labor, which is linked to higher productivity.[23] While work in a functional structure tends to be specialized, it is centrally coordinated by the CEO (see Exhibit 11.5). A functional structure allows for an efficient top-down and bottom-up communication chain between the CEO and the functional departments, and thus relies on a relatively flat structure.

FUNCTIONAL STRUCTURE AND BUSINESS STRATEGY. A functional structure is recommended when a firm has a fairly narrow focus in terms of product/service offerings (i.e., low level of diversification) combined with a small geographic footprint. It matches well, therefore, with the different *business* strategies discussed in Chapter 6: cost leadership, differentiation, and blue ocean. Although a functional structure is the preferred method for implementing business strategy, different variations and contexts require careful modifications in each case:

- The goal of a *cost-leadership strategy* is to create a competitive advantage by reducing the firm's cost below that of competitors while offering acceptable value. The cost leader sells a no-frills, standardized product or service to the mainstream customer. To effectively implement a cost-leadership strategy, therefore, managers must create a functional structure that contains the organizational elements of a *mechanistic structure*—one that is centralized, with well-defined lines of authority up and down the hierarchy. Using a functional structure allows the cost leader to nurture and constantly upgrade necessary core competencies in manufacturing and logistics. Moreover, the cost leader needs to create incentives to foster process innovation in order to drive down cost. Finally, because the firm services the average customer, and thus targets the largest market segment possible, it should focus on leveraging economies of scale to further drive down costs.

- The goal of a *differentiation strategy* is to create a competitive advantage by offering products or services at a higher perceived value, while controlling costs. The differentiator, therefore, sells a non-standardized product or service to specific market segments in which customers are willing to pay a higher price. To effectively implement a differentiation strategy, managers rely on a functional structure that resembles an *organic organization*. In particular, decision making tends to be decentralized to foster and incentivize continuous innovation and creativity as well as flexibility and mutual adjustment across areas. Using a functional structure with an organic organization allows the differentiator to nurture and constantly upgrade necessary core competencies in R&D, innovation, and marketing. Finally, the functional structure should be set up to allow the firm to reap economies of scope from its core competencies, such as by leveraging its brand name across different products or its technology across different devices.

- A successful *blue ocean strategy* requires reconciliation of the trade-offs between differentiation and low cost. To effectively implement a blue ocean strategy, the firm must be both efficient and flexible. It must balance centralization to control costs with decentralization to foster creativity and innovation. Managers must, therefore, attempt to combine the advantages of the functional-structure variations used for cost leadership and differentiation while mitigating their disadvantages. Moreover, the firm pursuing a blue ocean strategy needs to develop several distinct core competencies to both drive up perceived value and lower cost. It must further pursue both product and process innovations in an attempt to reap economies of scale and scope. All of these challenges make it clear that although a blue ocean strategy is attractive at first glance, it is quite difficult to implement given the range of important trade-offs that must be addressed.

A firm's structure is therefore critical when pursuing a blue ocean strategy. The challenge that managers face is to structure their organizations so that they control cost *and* allow for creativity that can lay the basis for differentiation. Doing both is hard. Achieving a low-cost position requires an organizational structure that relies on strict budget controls, while differentiation requires an organizational structure that allows creativity and customer responsiveness to thrive, which typically necessitates looser organizational structures and controls.

The goal for managers who want to pursue a blue ocean strategy is to build an **ambidextrous organization,** one that enables managers to balance and harness different activities in trade-off situations.[24] Here, the trade-offs to be addressed involve the simultaneous pursuit of low-cost and differentiation strategies. Notable management practices that companies use to resolve this trade-off include flexible and lean manufacturing systems, total quality management, just-in-time inventory management, and Six Sigma.[25] Other management techniques that allow firms to reconcile cost and value pressures are the use of teams in the production process, as well as decentralized decision making at the level of the individual customer.

Ambidexterity describes a firm's ability to address trade-offs not only at one point but also over time. It encourages managers to balance **exploitation**—applying current knowledge to enhance firm performance in the short term—with **exploration**—searching for new knowledge that may enhance a firm's future performance.[26] For example, while Intel focuses on maximizing sales from its *current* cutting-edge microprocessors, it also has several different teams with different time horizons working on *future* generations of microprocessors.[27] In ambidextrous organizations, managers must constantly analyze their existing business processes and routines, looking for ways to change them in order to resolve trade-offs across internal value chain activities and time.[28]

Exhibit 11.6 presents a detailed match between different business strategies and their corresponding functional structures.

DISADVANTAGES. While certainly attractive, the functional structure is not without significant drawbacks. Although the functional structure facilitates rich and extensive communication between members of the *same* department, it frequently lacks effective communication channels *across* departments. Notice in Exhibit 11.5 the lack of links between different functions. The lack of linkage between functions is the reason, for example, why R&D managers often do not communicate directly with marketing managers. In an ambidextrous organization, a top-level manager such as the CEO must take on the necessary coordination and integration work.

To overcome the lack of cross-departmental collaboration in a functional structure, a firm can set up *cross-functional teams.* In these temporary teams, members come from different functional areas to work together on a specific project or product, usually from start to completion. Each team member reports to two supervisors: the team leader and the respective functional department head. As we saw in Strategy Highlight 11.2, W.L. Gore employs cross-functional teams successfully.

A second critical drawback of the functional structure is that it cannot effectively address a higher level of diversification, which often stems from further growth.[29] This is the stage at which firms find it effective to evolve and adopt a multidivisional or matrix structure, both of which we will discuss next.

MULTIDIVISIONAL STRUCTURE

Over time, as a firm diversifies into different product lines and geographies, it generally implements a multidivisional or a matrix structure (as shown in Exhibit 11.4). The **multidivisional structure** (or **M-form**) consists of several distinct strategic business

---

ambidextrous organization
An organization able to balance and harness different activities in trade-off situations.

ambidexterity
A firm's ability to address trade-offs not only at one point but also over time. It encourages managers to balance *exploitation* with *exploration*.

exploitation
Applying current knowledge to enhance firm performance in the short term.

exploration
Searching for new knowledge that may enhance a firm's future performance.

multidivisional structure (M-form)
Organizational structure that consists of several distinct strategic business units (SBUs), each with its own profit-and-loss (P&L) responsibility.

EXHIBIT 11.6

Matching Business Strategy and Structure

Business Strategy	Structure
Cost leadership	**Functional** • Mechanistic organization • Centralized • Command and control • Core competencies in efficient manufacturing and logistics • Process innovation to drive down cost • Focus on economies of scale
Differentiation	**Functional** • Organic organization • Decentralized • Flexibility and mutual adjustment • Core competencies in R&D, innovation, and marketing • Product innovation • Focus on economies of scope
Blue ocean	**Functional** • Ambidextrous organization • Balancing centralization with decentralization • Multiple core competencies along the value chain required: R&D, manufacturing, logistics, marketing, etc. • Process and product innovations • Focus on economies of scale and scope

units (SBUs), each with its own profit-and-loss (P&L) responsibility. Each SBU is operated more or less independently from one another, and each is led by a CEO (or equivalent general manager) who is responsible for the unit's business strategy and its day-to-day operations. The CEOs of each division report to the corporate office, which is led by the company's highest-ranking executive (titles vary and include president or CEO for the entire corporation). Because most large firms are diversified to some extent across different product lines and geographies, the M-form is a widely adopted organizational structure.

Consider that Zappos is an SBU under Amazon, which employs a multidivisional structure. Also, W.L. Gore uses a multidivisional structure to administer its differentiation and related diversification strategies. It has four product divisions (electronic products, industrial products, medical products, and fabrics division) with manufacturing facilities in the United States, China, Germany, Japan, and Scotland, and business activities in 30 countries across the globe.[30]

A typical M-form is shown in Exhibit 11.7. In this example, the company has four SBUs, each led by a CEO. Corporations may use SBUs to organize around different businesses and product lines or around different geographic regions. Each SBU represents a self-contained business with its own hierarchy and organizational structure. Note that in Exhibit 11.7, SBU 2 is organized using a functional structure, while SBU 4 is organized using a matrix structure. The CEO of each SBU must determine which organizational structure is most appropriate to implement the SBU's business strategy.

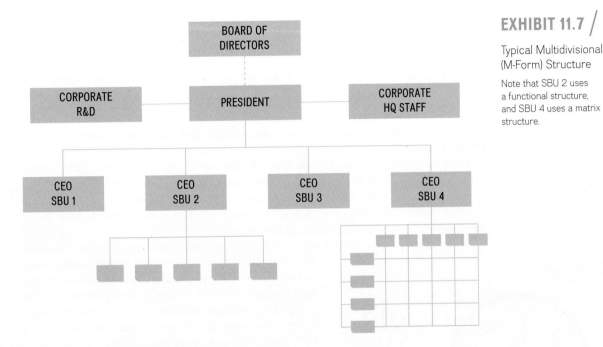

EXHIBIT 11.7 /

Typical Multidivisional
(M-Form) Structure

Note that SBU 2 uses
a functional structure,
and SBU 4 uses a matrix
structure.

A firm's corporate office is supported by company-wide staff functions such as human resources, finance, and corporate R&D. These staff functions support all of the company's SBUs, but are centralized at corporate headquarters to benefit from economies of scale and to avoid duplication within each SBU. Since most of the larger enterprises are publicly held stock companies, the president reports to a board of directors who represents the interests of the shareholders, indicated by the dashed line in Exhibit 11.7.

The president, with support from corporate headquarters staff, monitors the performance of each SBU and determines how to allocate resources across units.[31] Corporate headquarters adds value by functioning as an internal capital market. The goal is to be more efficient at allocating capital through its budgeting process than what could be achieved in external capital markets. This can be especially effective if the corporation overall can access capital at a lower cost than competitors due to a favorable (AAA) debt rating. Corporate headquarters can also add value through restructuring the company's portfolio of SBUs by selling low-performing businesses and adding promising businesses through acquisitions.

M-FORM AND CORPORATE STRATEGY. To achieve an optimal match between strategy and structure, different corporate strategies require different organizational structures. In Chapter 8, we identified four types of corporate diversification (see Exhibit 8.8: *single business, dominant business, related diversification,* and *unrelated diversification.* Each is defined by the percentage of revenues obtained from the firm's primary activity.

- Firms that follow a single-business or *dominant-business strategy* at the corporate level gain at least 70 percent of their revenues from their primary activity; they generally employ a *functional structure.*

- For firms that pursue either *related* or *unrelated diversification,* the *M-form* is the preferred organizational structure.

- Firms using the M-form organizational structure to support a *related-diversification* strategy tend to concentrate decision making at the top of the organization. Doing so allows a high level of integration. It also helps corporate headquarters leverage and transfer across different SBUs the core competencies that form the basis for a related diversification.

■ Firms using the M-form structure to support an *unrelated-diversification* strategy often decentralize decision making. Doing so allows general managers to respond to specific circumstances, and leads to a low level of integration at corporate headquarters.

Exhibit 11.8 matches different corporate strategies and their corresponding organizational structures.

In this understanding we can see how Google was attempting to leverage unrelated diversification and its advantages (decentralized decision making) when it announced its reorganization in 2015.[32] Google split itself and created a diversified multidivisional structure overseen by Alphabet, a new corporate entity. As Google had become much more complex over the years with a number of unrelated lines of businesses (think online search and longevity research), it moved from a functional structure to a multidivisional

© Pawel Kopczynski/
Reuters/Corbis

structure. This is exactly what one would predict based on our discussion around Exhibit 11.4, as firms change their organizational structures as they grow in size and complexity. Alphabet is the new parent company, overseeing seven strategic business units, each with its own CEO and profit-and-loss responsibility.

The seven business units start with Google's core businesses (search, ads, YouTube, Android, Chrome) in a single unit joined by Google X (self-driving cars, delivery drones, Internet balloons), Nest (smart thermostats), Google Fiber (broadband service), Calico (longevity research), Life Sciences (contact lenses), and Google Ventures (start-up investments). This sweeping restructuring allows the company to separate its highly profitable search and advertising business from its "moon shots" such as providing wireless Internet connectivity via high-altitude balloons or developing contact lenses that double as a "computer monitor" and provide real-time information to the wearer.

EXHIBIT 11.8 /

Matching Corporate
Strategy and
Structure

Corporate Strategy	Structure
Single business	Functional structure
Dominant business	Functional structure
Related diversification	Cooperative multidivisional (M-form)
	• Centralized decision making
	• High level of integration at corporate headquarters
	• Co-opetition among SBUs
	– Competition for resources
	– Cooperation in competency sharing
Unrelated diversification	Competitive multidivisional (M-form)
	• Decentralized decision making
	• Low level of integration at corporate headquarters
	• Competition among SBUs for resources

DISADVANTAGES. Moving from the functional structure to the M-form results in adding another layer of corporate hierarchy (corporate headquarters). This goes along with all the known problems of increasing bureaucracy, red tape, and sometimes duplication of efforts. It also slows decision making because in many instances a CEO of an SBU must get approval from corporate headquarters when making major decisions that might affect a second SBU or the corporation as a whole.

Also, since each SBU in the M-form is evaluated as a standalone profit-and-loss center, SBUs frequently end up competing with each other. A high-performing SBU might be rewarded with greater capital budgets and strategic freedoms; low-performing businesses might be spun off. SBUs compete with one another for resources such as capital and managerial talent, but they also need to cooperate to share competencies. *Co-opetition*—competition and cooperation at the same time—among the SBUs is both inevitable and necessary. Sometimes, however, it can be detrimental when a corporate process such as resource allocation or transfer pricing between SBUs becomes riddled with corporate politics and turf wars.

In some instances, spinning out SBUs to make them independent companies is beneficial. As discussed in Chapter 8, the BCG growth-share matrix helps corporate executives when making these types of decisions. In the last few years when owned by eBay, PayPal outperformed its parent company. PayPal's executives (and investors) were tired of subsidizing eBay's stagnant business. EBay had bought PayPal in the aftermath of the dot.com stock market crash in 2002 for $1.5 billion. In 2015, eBay and PayPal were de-merged. PayPal was spun out and became an independent company again. Now, PayPal is able to fully unlock its value. Investors also liked separating eBay and PayPal, giving it a valuation that is estimated to be as high as $100 billion; eBay's standalone valuation is about $35 billion.[33]

MATRIX STRUCTURE

To reap the benefits of both the M-form and the functional structure, many firms employ a mix of these two organizational forms, called a **matrix structure.** Exhibit 11.9 shows an example. In it, the firm is organized according to SBUs along a horizontal axis (like in the

matrix structure
Organizational structure that combines the functional structure with the M-form.

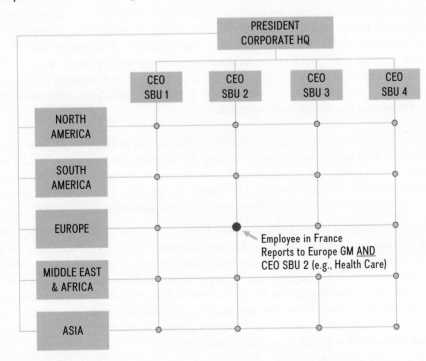

EXHIBIT 11.9

Typical Matrix Structure with Geographic and SBU Divisions

M-form), but also has a second dimension of organizational structure along a vertical axis. In this case, the second dimension consists of different geographic areas, each of which generally would house a full set of functional activities. The idea behind the matrix structure is to combine the benefits of the M-form (domain expertise, economies of scale, and the efficient processing of information) with those of the functional structure (responsiveness and decentralized focus).

The horizontal and vertical reporting lines between SBUs and geographic areas intersect, creating nodes in the matrix. Exhibit 11.9 highlights one employee, represented by a large dot and called out by an arrow. This employee works in a group with other employees in SBU 2, the company's health care unit for the Europe division in France. This employee has two bosses—the CEO of the health care SBU and the general manager (GM) for the Europe division. Both supervisors report to corporate headquarters, which is led by the president of the corporation (indicated in Exhibit 11.9 by the reporting lines from the SBUs and geographic units to the president).

Firms tend to use a *global matrix structure* to pursue a *transnational strategy,* in which the firm combines the benefits of a multidomestic strategy (high local responsiveness) with those of a global-standardization strategy (lowest-cost position attainable). In a global matrix structure, the geographic divisions are charged with local responsiveness and learning. At the same time, each SBU is charged with driving down costs through economies of scale and other efficiencies. A global matrix structure also allows the firm to feed local learning back to different SBUs and thus diffuse it throughout the organization. The specific organizational configuration depicted in Exhibit 11.9 is a global matrix structure.

The matrix structure is quite versatile, because managers can assign different groupings along the vertical and horizontal axes. A common form of the matrix structure uses different projects or products on the vertical axis and different functional areas on the horizontal axis. In that traditional matrix structure, *cross-functional* teams work together on different projects. In contrast to the cross-functional teams discussed earlier in the W.L. Gore example, the teams in a matrix structure tend to be more permanent rather than project-based with a pre-determined time horizon.

Given the advances in computer-mediated collaboration tools, some firms have replaced the more rigid matrix structure with a *network structure.* A network structure allows the firm to connect centers of excellence, whatever their global location (see Exhibit 10.3).[34] The firm benefits from *communities of practice,* which store important organizational learning and expertise. To avoid undue complexity, these network structures need to be supported by corporate-wide procedures and policies to streamline communication, collaboration, and the allocation of resources.[35]

MATRIX STRUCTURE AND GLOBAL STRATEGY. We already noted that a global matrix structure fits well with a transnational strategy. To complete the strategy–structure relationships in the global context, we also need to consider the international, multidomestic, and standardization strategies discussed in Chapter 10. Exhibit 11.10 shows how different global strategies best match with different organizational structures.

- In an *international strategy,* the company leverages its home-based core competency by moving into foreign markets. An international strategy is advantageous when the company faces low pressure for both local responsiveness and cost reductions. Companies pursue an international strategy through a differentiation strategy at the business level. The best match for an international strategy is a *functional* organizational structure, which allows the company to leverage its core competency most effectively. This approach is similar to matching a business-level differentiation strategy with a functional structure (discussed in detail earlier).

Global Strategy	Structure
International	**Functional**
Multidomestic	**Multidivisional**
	• Geographic areas
	• Decentralized decision making
Global standardization	**Multidivisional**
	• Product divisions
	• Centralized decision making
Transnational	**Global matrix**
	• Balance of centralized and decentralized decision making
	• Additional layer of hierarchy to coordinate both:
	— Geographic areas
	— Product divisions

EXHIBIT 11.10

Matching Global
Strategy and
Structure

- When a multinational enterprise (MNE) pursues a *multidomestic strategy*, it attempts to maximize local responsiveness in the face of low pressures for cost reductions. An appropriate match for this type of global strategy is the *multidivisional* organizational structure. That structure would enable the MNE to set up different divisions based on geographic regions (e.g., by continent). The different geographic divisions operate more or less as standalone SBUs to maximize local responsiveness. Decision making is decentralized.

- When following a *global-standardization strategy*, the MNE attempts to reap significant economies of scale as well as location economies by pursuing a global division of labor based on wherever best-of-class capabilities reside at the lowest cost. Since the product offered is more or less an undifferentiated commodity, the MNE pursues a cost-leadership strategy. The optimal organizational structure match is, again, a *multidivisional* structure. Rather than focusing on geographic differences as in the multidomestic strategy, the focus is on driving down costs due to consolidation of activities across different geographic areas.

DISADVANTAGES. Though it is appealing in theory, the matrix structure does have shortcomings. It is usually difficult to implement: Implementing two layers of organizational structure creates significant organizational complexity and increases administrative costs. Also, reporting structures in a matrix are often not clear. In particular, employees can have trouble reconciling goals presented by their two (or more) supervisors. Less-clear reporting structures can undermine accountability by creating multiple principal–agent relationships. This can make performance appraisals more difficult. Adding an additional layer of hierarchy can also slow decision making and increase bureaucratic costs.

As just discussed, the development pattern of how organizational structures tend to change in time as firms grow in size and complexity is fairly predictable: Starting with a simple structure, then moving to functional structure, and finally implementing a multidivisional or matrix structure. As featured in the ChapterCase, Zappos even went a step further. Rapid growth and increasing complexity triggered Zappos' move away from a multidivisional structure with different business units to the radically new organizational structure, holacracy, with its nonhierarchical, over-lapping employee circles. While the organizational structures shown in Exhibit 11.4 have been around for many decades, holacracy as an organizational structure is new and yet untested in a larger firm.

LO 11-6

Describe the elements of organizational culture, and explain where organizational cultures can come from and how they can be changed.

organizational culture
The collectively shared values and norms of an organization's members; a key building block of organizational design.

11.3 Organizational Culture: Values, Norms, and Artifacts

Organizational culture is the second key building block when designing organizations for competitive advantage. Just as people have distinctive personalities, so too do organizations have unique cultures that capture "how things get done around here." **Organizational culture** describes the collectively shared values and norms of an organization's members.[36] *Values* define what is considered important. *Norms* define appropriate employee attitudes and behaviors.[37]

Employees learn about an organization's culture through *socialization,* a process whereby employees internalize an organization's values and norms through immersion in its day-to-day operations.[38] Zappos' new-employee orientation and immersion is now a four-week extensive course. Successful socialization, in turn, allows employees to function productively and to take on specific roles within the organization. *Strong cultures* emerge when the company's core values are widely shared among the firm's employees and when the norms have been internalized.

Corporate culture finds its expression in *artifacts.* Artifacts include elements such as the design and layout of physical space (e.g., cubicles or private offices); symbols (e.g., the type of clothing worn by employees); vocabulary; what stories are told (see the Zappos pizza-ordering example that follows); what events are celebrated and highlighted; and how they are celebrated (e.g., a formal dinner versus a casual BBQ when the firm reaches its sales target).

Exhibit 11.11 depicts the elements of organizational culture—values, norms, and artifacts—in concentric circles. The most important yet least visible element—values—is in the center. As we move outward in the figure, from values to norms to artifacts, culture becomes more observable. Understanding what organizational culture is, and how

EXHIBIT 11.11 / The Elements of Organizational Culture: Values, Norms, and Artifacts

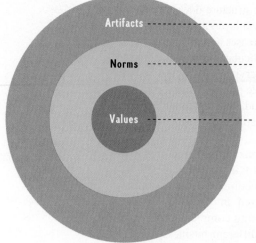

Artifacts - - - - - - - - - - - - - - - At Zappos, even under its previous structure, all employees including CEO Tony Hsieh, worked from a cubicle

Norms - - - - - - - - - - - - - - - Zappos continues to celebrate the norm of happiness; employees are encouraged to promote happiness in the workplace in creative ways.

Values - - - - - - - - - - - - - - - Zappos turned to the employees themselves to articulate company values, conspicuous in orientation, daily operations, and evaluation reviews.

it is created, maintained, and changed, can help you be a more effective manager. A unique culture that is strategically relevant can also be the basis of a firm's competitive advantage.

As Zappos grew, its managers realized that it was critical to explicitly define a set of core values from which to develop the company's culture, brand, and strategy. Zappos CEO Tony Hsieh wanted to make sure that all employees understood the same set of values and expected behaviors. Zappos' list of 10 core values (see Exhibit 11.12) was crafted through a bottom-up initiative, in which all employees were invited to participate.

To live up to its mission of delivering happiness, Zappos decided that exceptional customer service should be its number-one core value. The company put several policies and procedures in place to "deliver WOW through service." For example, shipments to and from customers within the United States are free, allowing customers to order several pairs of shoes and send back (within a liberal 365 days) those that don't fit or are no longer wanted. Repeat customers are automatically upgraded to complimentary express shipping. One of the most important lessons Hsieh learned is "Never outsource your core competency!"[39] Customer service, therefore, is done exclusively in-house.

Perhaps even more importantly, Zappos does not provide a script or measure customer service reps' call times. Rather, the company leaves it up to the individual member of the "Customer Loyalty Team" to deliver exceptional customer service: "We want our reps to let their true personalities shine during each phone call so that they can develop a personal emotional connection with the customer."[40] In fact, one customer service phone call lasted almost six hours! The same trust in the customer service reps applies to e-mail communication. Zappos' official communication policy is to "be real and use your best judgment."[41] Most of Zappos' more than 1,500 employees are in some type of sales function, to maintain constant contact with the customer. The customer call centers are staffed 24/7, seven days a week, 365 days a year.

Zappos third core value, "create fun and a little weirdness," encourages a unique culture based on shared experiences including costume play ("cosplay") at work, parades, fun contests, themed courtyard events, ice cream trucks, Nerf guns, Ping-Pong, live animals, and so on.[42] One of the hardest choices Zapponians need to make each day is choosing which fun event to support, including trivia nights, family picnics, pinewood derby races, talent shows, Foosball, snow sledding, spring break days, pajama days, and karaoke. This is all just part of another day at the Zappos office.

Besides creating a strong culture that binds employees together through shared fun experiences, Zappos believes that encouraging a little weirdness and fun helps people to

EXHIBIT 11.12 / Zappos' 10 Core Values

1. Deliver WOW through service.
2. Embrace and drive change.
3. Create fun and a little weirdness.
4. Be adventurous, creative, and open-minded.
5. Pursue growth and learning.
6. Build open and honest relationships with communication.
7. Build a positive team and family spirit.
8. Do more with less.
9. Be passionate and determined.
10. Be humble.

Source: T. Hsieh (2010), *Delivering Happiness: A Path to Profits, Passion, and Purpose* (New York: Business Plus), pp. 157–160.

© James Leynse/Corbis

think outside the box and thus be more creative and innovative. All this helps to achieve their number-one core value to "deliver WOW through service," but also other core values such as "do more with less." Taken together, employees are more engaged in their work, not only with their hands, but also their minds and hearts, and the company is being more innovative and nimble as a whole.

WHERE DO ORGANIZATIONAL CULTURES COME FROM?

founder imprinting
A process by which the founder defines and shapes an organization's culture, which can persist for decades after his or her departure.

Often, company founders define and shape an organization's culture, which can persist for many decades after their departure. This phenomenon is called **founder imprinting**.[43] Founders set the initial strategy, structure, and culture of an organization by transforming their vision into reality. Famous founders who have left strong imprints on their organizations include Steve Jobs (Apple), Walt Disney (Disney), Michael Dell (Dell), Sergey Brin and Larry Page (Google), Oprah Winfrey (Harpo Productions and *OWN,* the Oprah Winfrey Network), Bill Gates (Microsoft), Larry Ellison (Oracle), Ralph Lauren (Polo Ralph Lauren), Martha Stewart (Martha Stewart Living Omnimedia), and Herb Kelleher (Southwest Airlines).

Walmart founder Sam Walton personified the retailer's cost-leadership strategy. At one time the richest man in America, Sam Walton drove a beat-up Ford pickup truck, got $5 haircuts, went camping for vacations, and lived in a modest ranch home in Bentonville, Arkansas.[44] Everything Walton did was consistent with the low-cost strategy. Walmart stays true to its founder's tradition. Home to one of the largest companies on the planet, the company's Arkansas headquarters in Bentonville was described by Thomas Friedman in his book *The World Is Flat* as "crammed into a reconfigured warehouse . . . a large building made of corrugated metal, I figured it was the maintenance shed."[45]

groupthink
A situation in which opinions coalesce around a leader without individuals critically evaluating and challenging that leader's opinions and assumptions.

The culture that founders initially imprint is reinforced by their strong preference to recruit, retain, and promote employees who subscribe to the same values. In turn, more people with similar values are attracted to that organization.[46] As the values and norms held by the employees become more similar, the firm's corporate culture becomes stronger and more distinct. This in turn can have a serious negative side-effect: **groupthink**, a situation in which opinions coalesce around a leader without individuals critically evaluating and challenging that leader's opinions and assumptions. Cohesive, non-diverse groups are highly susceptible to groupthink, which in turn can lead to flawed decision making with potentially disastrous consequences.

In addition to founder imprinting, a firm's culture also flows from its values, especially when they are linked to the company's reward system. For example, Zappos established its unique organizational culture through explicitly stated values that are connected to its reward system (see Exhibit 11.12). To recruit people that fit with the company's values, Hsieh has all new hires go through a four-week training program. It covers such topics as company history, culture, and vision, as well as customer service.[47] New hires also spend two weeks on the phone as customer service reps. What's novel about Zappos' approach is that at the end of the monthlong employee orientation, the company offers an "exit prize:" one month's pay plus pay for the time already with Zappos. This allows the company to entice people to leave that are qualified for the job but may not fit with Zappos' culture. Individuals who choose to stay despite the enticing offer tend to fit well with and strengthen Zappos' distinct culture.[48]

HOW DOES ORGANIZATIONAL CULTURE CHANGE?

An organization's culture can be one of its strongest assets, but also its greatest liability. An organization's culture can turn from a core competency into a *core rigidity* if a firm relies too long on the competency without honing, refining, and upgrading as the firm and the environment change.[49] (See discussion in Chapter 4.) Over time, the original core competency is no longer a good fit and turns from an asset into a liability. This is the time when a culture needs to change.

GM's bureaucratic culture, combined with its innovative M-form structure, was once hailed as the key to superior efficiency and management.[50] However, that culture became a liability when the external environment changed following the oil-price shocks in the 1970s and the entry of Japanese carmakers into the United States.[51] As a consequence, GM's strong culture led to organizational inertia. This resulted in a failure to adapt to changing customer preferences for more fuel-efficient cars, and it prevented higher quality and more innovative designs. GM lost customers to foreign competitors that offered these features.

Mary Barra, CEO, General Motors
© Jeff Kowalsky/Bloomberg/ Getty Images

More recently, GM's strong culture was again faulted for corporate ineptitude when delaying recalling defective cars.[52] In 2014, over 25 million GM cars were recalled for safety defects, the largest recall ever. In particular, many GM cars were eventually recalled because of a faulty ignition switch, which could turn off the engine while driving and thus disable the airbags. This problem has been linked to more than 120 fatalities in the United States alone.[53] GM is alleged to knowingly have withheld information about the faulty ignition switches and delayed the needed recalls by several years. Indeed, during a U.S. Senate hearing, GM was described as dominated by a "culture of cover-up."[54] In such times of crisis, corporate culture must be changed to avoid such problems in the future and to address a breakdown in the culture-environment fit.

The primary means of cultural change is for the corporate board of directors to bring in new leadership at the top, which is then charged to make changes in strategy and structure. After all, executives shape corporate culture in their decisions on how to structure the organization and its activities, allocate its resources, and develop its system of rewards (see the discussion on strategic leadership in Chapter 2). In 2014, GM's board of directors appointed Mary Barra as CEO with the charge to fix GM's dysfunctional corporate culture and to make the company competitive again.

ORGANIZATIONAL CULTURE AND COMPETITIVE ADVANTAGE

Can organizational culture be the basis of a firm's competitive advantage? For this to occur, the firm's unique culture must help it in some way to increase its *economic value creation* (*V–C*). That is, it must either help in increasing the perceived value of the product/service and/or lower its cost of production/delivery. Moreover, according to the resource-based view of the firm, the resource—in this case, organizational culture—must be *valuable, rare, difficult to imitate,* and the firm must be *organized* to capture the value created. The VRIO principles (see Chapter 4) must apply even as to organizational culture itself.[55]

Let's look at two examples of how culture affects employee behavior and ultimately firm performance:

■ If you have flown with Southwest Airlines (SWA), you may have noticed that things are done a little differently there. Flight attendants might sing a song about the city you're landing in, or they might slide bags of peanuts down the aisle at take-off. Employees celebrate Halloween in a big way by wearing costumes to work. Some argue that SWA's business strategy—being a cost leader in point-to-point air travel—is fairly simple, and that SWA's competitive advantage actually comes from its unique culture.[56] It's not all fun and games, though: Friendly and highly energized employees work across functional and hierarchical levels. Even Southwest's pilots pitch in to help load baggage quickly when needed. As a result, SWA's turn time between flights is only 15 minutes, whereas competitors frequently take two to three times as long.

- Zappos' number-one core value is to "deliver WOW through service." CEO Hsieh shares the following story to illustrate this core value in action: "I was in Santa Monica, California, a few years ago at a Skechers sales conference. . . . [In the early hours of the morning], a small group of us headed up to someone's hotel room to order some food. My friend from Skechers tried to order a pepperoni pizza from the room-service menu but was disappointed to learn that the hotel did not deliver hot food after 11:00 p.m. We had missed the deadline by several hours. . . . A few of us cajoled her into calling Zappos to try to order a pizza. She took us up on our dare, turned on the speakerphone, and explained to the (very) patient Zappos rep that she was staying in a Santa Monica hotel and really craving a pepperoni pizza, that room service was no longer delivering hot food, and that she wanted to know if there was anything Zappos could do to help. The Zappos rep was initially a bit confused by the request, but she quickly recovered and put us on hold. She returned two minutes later, listing the five closest places in the Santa Monica area that were still open and delivering pizzas at that time."[57]

In the SWA example, the company's unique culture helps it keep costs low by turning around its planes faster, thus keeping them flying longer hours (among many other activities that lower SWA's cost structure).[58] In the Zappos example, providing a "wow" customer experience by "going the extra mile" didn't save Zappos money, but in the long run superior experience does increase the company's perceived value and thereby its economic value creation. Indeed, Hsieh makes it a point to conclude the story with the following statement: "As for my friend from Skechers? After that phone call, she's now a customer for life."[59]

Let's consider how an organization's culture can have a strong influence on employee behavior.[60] A positive culture motivates and energizes employees by appealing to their higher ideals. Internalizing the firm's values and norms, employees feel that they are part of a larger, meaningful community attempting to accomplish important things. When employees are intrinsically motivated this way, the firm can rely on fewer levels of hierarchy; thus close monitoring and supervision are not needed as much. Moreover, motivating through inspiring values allows the firms to tap employees' emotions so they use both their heads and their hearts when making business decisions. Strong organizational cultures that are strategically relevant, therefore, align employees' behaviors more fully with the organization's strategic goals. In doing so, they better coordinate work efforts, and they make cooperation more effective. They also strengthen employee commitment, engagement, and effort. Effective alignment in turn allows the organization to develop and refine its core competencies, which can form the basis for competitive advantage.

Applying the VRIO principles to the SWA and Zappos examples, we see that both cultures are *valuable* (lowering costs for SWA and increasing perceived value created for Zappos), *rare* (none of their competitors has an identical culture), *non-imitable* (despite attempts by competitors), and *organized* to capture some part of the incremental economic value created due to their unique cultures. It appears that at both SWA and Zappos, a unique organizational culture can provide the basis for a competitive advantage. These cultures, of course, need to be in sync with and in support of the respective business strategies pursued: cost leadership for SWA and differentiation for Zappos. Moreover, as the firms grow and external economic environments change, these cultures must be flexible enough to adapt.

Once it becomes clear that a firm's culture is a source of competitive advantage, some competitors will attempt to imitate that culture. Therefore, only a culture that cannot be easily copied can provide a competitive advantage. It can be difficult, at best, to imitate the cultures of successful firms, for two reasons: *causal ambiguity* and *social complexity.* While one can observe that a firm has a unique culture, the causal relationships among values, norms, artifacts, and the firm's performance may be hard to establish, even for people who work within the organization. For example, employees may become aware of the effect culture has on performance only after significant organizational changes occur. Moreover, organizational culture is socially complex. It encompasses not only interactions among employees across layers of hierarchy, but also the firm's outside relationships with its customers and suppliers.[61] Such a wide range of factors is difficult for any competing firm to imitate.

It is best to develop a strong and strategically relevant culture in the first few years of a firm's existence. Strategy scholars have documented that the initial structure, culture, and control mechanisms established in a new firm can be a significant predictor of later success.[62] In other empirical research, founder CEOs had a stronger positive imprinting effect than non-founder CEOs.[63] This stronger imprinting effect, in turn, resulted in higher performance of firms led by founder CEOs. In addition, consider that the vehicles of cultural change—changing leadership and M&As—do not have a stellar record of success.[64] Indeed, researchers estimate that only about 20 percent of organizational change attempts are successful.[65] Thus, it is even more important to get the culture right from the beginning and then adapt it as the business evolves.

By combining theory and empirical evidence, we can see that organizational culture can help a firm gain and sustain competitive advantage *if* the culture makes a positive contribution to the firm's economic value creation and obeys the VRIO principles. Organizational culture is an especially effective lever for new ventures due to its malleability. Firm founders, early-stage CEOs, and venture capitalists, therefore, should be proactive in attempting to create a culture that supports a firm's economic value creation.

11.4 Strategic Control-and-Reward Systems

Strategic control-and-reward systems are the third and final key building block when designing organizations for competitive advantage. **Strategic control-and-reward systems** are internal-governance mechanisms put in place to align the incentives of principals (shareholders) and agents (employees). These systems allow managers to specify goals, measure progress, and provide performance feedback.

Zappos restructured its performance-evaluation system to give these values teeth: The firm rewards employees who apply the values (shown in Exhibit 11.11) well in their day-to-day decision making. It created an open market (referred to internally as OM) based on an online scheduling platform that allows Zappos, customer service employees to select their work hours. The novel tweak in the OM system is that it compensates customer service employees based on a surge-pricing payment model (first popularized by the taxi-hailing service, Uber). Hsieh states, "Ideally, we want all 10 core values to be reflected in everything we do, including how we interact with each other, how we interact with our customers, and how we interact with our vendors and business partners. . . . Our core values should always be the framework

LO 11-7

Compare and contrast different strategic control-and-reward systems.

strategic control-and-reward systems Internal-governance mechanisms put in place to align the incentives of principals (shareholders) and agents (employees).

from which we make all of our decisions."[66] Zappos' 10 core values are important to its employees; they define their identity of what it means to be working at Zappos.[67]

Chapter 5 discussed how firms can use the balanced-scorecard framework as a strategic control system. Here, we discuss additional control-and-reward systems: organizational culture, input controls, and output controls.

As just demonstrated, *organizational culture* can be a powerful motivator. It also can be an effective control system. Norms, informal and tacit in nature, act as a social control mechanism. Zappos, for example, achieves organizational control partly through an employee's peer group: Each group member's compensation, including the supervisor's, depends in part on the group's overall productivity. Peer control, therefore, exerts a powerful force on employee conformity and performance.[68] Values and norms also provide control by helping employees address unpredictable and irregular situations and problems (common in service businesses). In contrast, rules and procedures (e.g., codified in an employee handbook) can address only circumstances that can be predicted.

INPUT CONTROLS

input controls
Mechanisms in a strategic control-and-reward system that seek to define and direct employee behavior through a set of explicit, codified rules and standard operating procedures that are considered prior to the value-creating activities.

Input controls seek to define and direct employee behavior through a set of explicit, codified rules and standard operating procedures. Firms use input controls when the goal is to define the ways and means to reach a strategic goal and to ensure a predictable outcome. They are called input controls because management designs these mechanisms so they are considered *before* employees make any business decisions; thus, they are an input into the value-creating activities.

The use of *budgets* is key to input controls. Managers set budgets before employees define and undertake the actual business activities. For example, managers decide how much money to allocate to a certain R&D project before the project begins. In diversified companies using the M-form, corporate headquarters determines the budgets for each division. Public institutions, like some universities, also operate on budgets that must be balanced each year. Their funding often depends to a large extent on state appropriations and thus fluctuates depending on the economic cycle. During recessions, budgets tend to be cut, and they expand during boom periods.

Standard operating procedures, or policies and rules, are also a frequently used mechanism when relying on input controls. The discussion on formalization described how McDonald's relies on detailed operating procedures to ensure consistent quality and service worldwide. The goal is to specify the conversion process from beginning to end in great detail to guarantee standardization and minimize deviation. This is important when a company operates in different geographies and with different human capital throughout the globe but needs to deliver a standardized product or service.

OUTPUT CONTROLS

output controls
Mechanisms in a strategic control-and-reward system that seek to guide employee behavior by defining expected results (outputs), but leave the means to those results open to individual employees, groups, or SBUs.

Output controls seek to guide employee behavior by defining expected results (outputs), but leave the means to those results open to individual employees, groups, or SBUs. Firms frequently tie employee compensation and rewards to predetermined goals, such as a specific sales target or return on invested capital. When factors internal to the firm determine the relationship between effort and expected performance, outcome controls are especially effective. At the corporate level, outcome controls discourage collaboration among different strategic business units. They are best applied when a firm focuses on a single line of business or pursues unrelated diversification.

These days, more and more work requires creativity and innovation, especially in highly developed economies.[69] As a consequence, so-called *results-only-work-environments (ROWEs)* have attracted significant attention. ROWEs are output controls that attempt to tap intrinsic (rather than extrinsic) employee motivation, which is driven by the employee's interest in and the meaning of the work itself. In contrast, extrinsic motivation is driven by external factors such as awards and higher compensation, or punishments like demotions and layoffs (the *carrot-and-stick approach*). According to a recent synthesis of the strategic human resources literature, intrinsic motivation in a task is highest when an employee has:

- Autonomy *(about what to do)*.
- Mastery *(how to do it)*.
- Purpose *(why to do it)*.[70]

Today, 3M is best known for its adhesives and other consumer and industrial products.[71] But its full name reflects its origins: 3M stands for Minnesota Mining and Manufacturing Company. Over time, 3M has relied on the ROWE framework and has morphed into a highly science-driven innovation company. At 3M, employees are encouraged to spend 15 percent of their time on projects of their *own choosing*. If any of these projects look promising, 3M provides financing through an internal venture capital fund and other resources to further develop their commercial potential. In fact, several of 3M's flagship products, including Post-it Notes and Scotch Tape, were the results of serendipity. To foster continued innovation, moreover, 3M requires each of its divisions to derive at least 30 percent of their revenues from products introduced in the past four years.

11.5 ◄► Implications for the Strategist

This chapter has a clear practical implication for the strategist: Formulating an effective strategy is a necessary but not sufficient condition for gaining and sustaining competitive advantage; strategy *execution* is at least as important for success. Successful strategy implementation requires managers to design and shape structure, culture, and control mechanisms. In doing so, they execute a firm's strategy as they put its accompanying business model into action. Strategy formulation and strategy implementation, therefore, are iterative and interdependent activities.

Some argue that strategy implementation is more important than strategy formulation.[72] Often, managers do a good job of analyzing the firm's internal and external environments to formulate a promising business, corporate, and global strategy, but then fail to implement the chosen strategy successfully. That is why some scholars refer to implementation as the "graveyard of strategy."[73]

As a company grows and its operations become more complex, it adopts different organizational structures over time following a generally predictable pattern: beginning with a simple structure, then a functional structure, and followed by a multidivisional or matrix structure.

Organizing for competitive advantage, therefore, is a dynamic and not a static process. As seen in the Zappos example discussed throughout the chapter, in order to maintain competitive advantage, companies need to restructure as they grow and the competitive environment changes.

This concludes our discussion of organizational design. We now move on to our concluding chapter, where we study corporate governance and business ethics.

CHAPTERCASE 11 / Consider This...

ZAPPOS' IMPLEMENTION OF holacracy is not going well. As a consequence, employee morale has plummeted, and Zappos employees are no longer as happy. In 2014, Zappos was ranked seventh in *Fortune's* "100 Best Companies to Work For" list (one of the highest ranking for a relatively young firm). By 2015, after it started implementing holacracy, Zappos had dropped to rank 86! In addition, more than 200 employees, or some 14 percent of Zappos' work force, accepted the offer of a three-month severance package if they didn't like the switch to holacracy and quit. Employees that remain with Zappos complain that the holacracy implementation removes clear career paths for advancement and wonder openly how hiring, firing, and promoting will now be done. They are concerned that relying on employee circles for making decisions will not only induce paralysis, but also make the organization more and not less political. In sum, they find that holacracy forces them to waste time in meetings rather than getting the actual work done.

After the initial implementation struggle, Hsieh remains committed and is doubling down on holacracy implementation. He expressed his frustration about the slow process and lack of productivity gains in a lengthy e-mail to all Zappos employees, which was subsequently leaked to the business press. At the same time, the irony that Hsieh decreed top-down that Zappos would be implementing holacracy (or decided a few years earlier to sell the company to Amazon.com) wasn't lost on the company's workers.

Questions

1. What elements of an organic organization are apparent from the chapter material on Zappos? (Refer to Exhibit 11.3.)

2. What is holacracy, and how does this organizational structure differ from the more traditional ones discussed in this chapter?

3. Why is Zappos experiencing significant implementation problems with holacracy? What else could Zappos do to help implement the new structure more effectively?

4. Do you think that holacracy is a good match with Zappos' business strategy? Why or why not? Explain.

TAKE-AWAY CONCEPTS

This chapter explored the three key levers that managers have at their disposal when designing their firms for competitive advantage—structure, culture, and control—as summarized by the following learning objectives and related take-away concepts.

LO 11-1 / Define organizational design and list its three components.

- Organizational design is the process of creating, implementing, monitoring, and modifying the structure, processes, and procedures of an organization.

- The key components of organizational design are structure, culture, and control.

- The goal is to design an organization that allows managers to effectively translate their chosen strategy into a realized one.

LO 11-2 / Explain how organizational inertia can lead established firms to failure.

- Organizational inertia can lead to the failure of established firms when a tightly coupled system of strategy and structure experiences internal or external shifts.

- Firm failure happens through a dynamic, four-step process (see Exhibit 11.2).

LO 11-3 / Define organizational structure and describe its four elements.

■ An organizational structure determines how firms orchestrate employees' work efforts and distribute resources. It defines how firms divide and integrate tasks, delineates the reporting relationships up and down the hierarchy, defines formal communication channels, and prescribes how employees coordinate work efforts.

■ The four building blocks of an organizational structure are specialization, formalization, centralization, and hierarchy (see Exhibit 11.3).

LO 11-4 / Compare and contrast mechanistic versus organic organizations.

■ Organic organizations are characterized by a low degree of specialization and formalization, a flat organizational structure, and decentralized decision making.

■ Mechanistic organizations are described by a high degree of specialization and formalization, and a tall hierarchy that relies on centralized decision making.

■ The comparative effectiveness of mechanistic versus organic organizational forms depends on the context.

LO 11-5 / Describe different organizational structures and match them with appropriate strategies.

■ To gain and sustain competitive advantage, not only must structure follow strategy, but also the chosen organizational form must match the firm's business strategy.

■ The strategy–structure relationship is dynamic, changing in a predictable pattern—from simple to functional structure, then to multidivisional (M-form) and matrix structure—as firms grow in size and complexity.

■ In a simple structure, the founder tends to make all the important strategic decisions as well as run the day-to-day operations.

■ A functional structure groups employees into distinct functional areas based on domain expertise. Its different variations are matched with different business strategies: cost leadership, differentiation, and blue ocean (see Exhibit 11.6).

■ The multidivisional (M-form) structure consists of several distinct SBUs, each with its own profit-and-loss responsibility. Each SBU operates more or less independently from one another, led by a CEO responsible for the business strategy of the unit and its day-to-day operations (see Exhibit 11.7).

■ The matrix structure is a mixture of two organizational forms: the M-form and the functional structure (see Exhibit 11.9).

■ Exhibits 11.8 and 11.10 show how best to match different corporate and global strategies with respective organizational structures.

LO 11-6 / Describe the elements of organizational culture, and explain where organizational cultures can come from and how they can be changed.

■ Organizational culture describes the collectively shared values and norms of its members.

■ Values define what is considered important, and norms define appropriate employee attitudes and behaviors.

■ Corporate culture finds its expression in artifacts, which are observable expressions of an organization's culture.

LO 11-7 / Compare and contrast different strategic control-and-reward systems.

■ Strategic control-and-reward systems are internal governance mechanisms put in place to align the incentives of principals (shareholders) and agents (employees).

■ Strategic control-and-reward systems allow managers to specify goals, measure progress, and provide performance feedback.

■ In addition to the balanced-scorecard framework, managers can use organizational culture, input controls, and output controls as part of the firm's strategic control-and-reward systems.

■ Input controls define and direct employee behavior through explicit and codified rules and standard operating procedures.

■ Output controls guide employee behavior by defining expected results, but leave the means to those results open to individual employees, groups, or SBUs.

KEY TERMS

Ambidexterity *(p. 377)*

Ambidextrous organization *(p. 377)*

Centralization *(p. 372)*

Exploitation *(p. 377)*

Exploration *(p. 377)*

Formalization *(p. 371)*

Founder imprinting *(p. 386)*

Functional structure *(p. 375)*

Groupthink *(p. 386)*

Hierarchy *(p. 372)*

Holacracy *(p. 367)*

Inertia *(p. 368)*

Input controls *(p. 390)*

Matrix structure *(p. 381)*

Mechanistic organization *(p. 372)*

Multidivisional structure *(M-form)* *(p. 377)*

Organic organization *(p. 373)*

Organizational culture *(p. 384)*

Organizational design *(p. 367)*

Organizational structure *(p. 371)*

Output controls *(p. 390)*

Simple structure *(p. 375)*

Span of control *(p. 372)*

Specialization *(p. 371)*

Strategic control-and-reward systems *(p. 389)*

DISCUSSION QUESTIONS

1. Why is it important for an organization to have alignment between its strategy and structure?

2. The chapter describes the role of culture in the successful implementation of strategy. Consider an employment experience of your own or of someone you have observed closely (e.g., a family member). Describe to the best of your ability the values, norms, and artifacts of the organization. What was the socialization process of embedding the culture? Do you consider this to be an example of an effective culture for contributing to

the organization's competitive advantage? Why or why not?

3. Strategy Highlight 11.2 discusses the informal organizational structure of W.L. Gore & Associates. Go to the firm's website (www.gore.com) and review the company's product scope. What commonalities across the products would likely be enhanced by flexible cross-functional teams? Next look in the "about Gore" section of the website. What would be your expectations of the type of control and rewards systems found at W.L. Gore?

ETHICAL/SOCIAL ISSUES

1. As noted in Chapter 5, many public firms are under intense pressure for short-term (such as quarterly) financial improvements. How might such pressure, in combination with output controls, lead to unethical behaviors?

2. Cultural norms and values play a significant role in all organizations, from businesses in the economic sector to religious, political, and sports organizations. Strong organizational cultures can have many benefits, such as those described in the Zappos example. However, sometimes a strong organizational culture is less positive. Vince Lombardi, renowned coach of the Green Bay Packers, is often quoted as saying, "Winning isn't everything; it's the only thing." Many sports teams from junior sports to professional sports have either explicitly or implicitly touted this attitude as exemplary.

Others, however, argue that this attitude is what's wrong with sports and leads to injury, minor misbehavior, and criminal behavior. It encourages players to do whatever it takes to win—from tripping a player or other unsportsmanlike conduct during middle-school sports to throwing a game as part of gambling. Name other examples of organizational culture leading to business failure, criminal behavior, or civil legal actions.

When a player hears the message as "any action will be tolerated as long as you are winning," there can be serious consequences on and off the field. How could leaders of sports organizations communicate the will to win and develop the necessary skills while maintaining ethical behavior? Think of examples of coaches who coaxed players to play by the rules and maintain high personal ethical standards. What other social-ization experiences could a coach use? What is the role of team leaders in encouraging high ethical standards while building the desire to win?

3. What makes some strong cultures helpful in gain-ing and sustaining a competitive advantage, while other strong cultures are a liability to achieving that goal?

SMALL GROUP EXERCISES

//// Small Group Exercise 1

Your classmates are a group of friends who have decided to open a small retail shop. The team is torn between two storefront ideas. The first idea is to open a high-end antique store selling household items used for decoration in upscale homes. Members of the team have found a location in a heavily pedestrian area near a local coffee shop. The store would have many items authenticated by a team member's uncle, who is a cer-tified appraiser.

In discussing the plan, however, two group members suggest shifting to a drop-off store for online auctions such as eBay. In this "reverse logistics" business model, customers drop off items they want to sell, and the retail store does all the logistics involved—listing and selling the items on eBay or Amazon, and then shipping them to buyers—for a percentage of the sales price. They suggest that a quick way to get started is to become a franchisee for a group such as "I Sold It" (www.877isoldit.com).

1. What is the business strategy for each of these two store concepts?

2. How would the organizational structure be differ-ent for the concepts?

3. What would likely be the cultural differences in the two store concepts?

4. How would the control-and-reward systems be different?

//// Small Group Exercise 2 (Ethical/Social Issues)

The chapter describes Daniel Pink's ROWE theory of motivation, in which he argued that the most powerful motivation occurs when there is an interest in the work and the work itself has meaning. Intrinsic motivation is highest when an employee has *autonomy* (about what to do), *mastery* (how to do it), and *purpose* (why to do it). Assume your group has been asked by your univer-sity to brainstorm ways that the university might apply the ROWE theory. Discuss whether you would be more motivated and better educated if you had more auton-omy in designing your program of study, could deter-mine the best way for you to learn and gain mastery, and could develop your own statement of purpose as to why you were pursuing a particular program of study.

1. How might this change the university's allocation of resources (e.g., would more trained advisers and career counselors be required, and how would they be evaluated)?

2. If large numbers of students decided they would learn some of the core materials best by taking an online course, how might this affect the univer-sity's revenue stream? How might this change the way professors teach courses?

3. Have each group member explain how this approach might change his or her program of study.

4. Consider the potential pitfalls of such an approach and how these might be addressed.

STRATEGY TERM PROJECT

connect · *The* HP Running Case, *a related activity for each strategy term project module, is available in Connect.*

//// Module 11: Organizational Implementation Processes

In this module, you will study the organizational implementation processes of your selected firm. You

will again rely on annual reports, news articles, and press releases for information to analyze and formu-late your answers. You will identify a major strategic change the firm should seriously consider implement-ing, and then follow a six-step process to study the implementation impacts.

Implementation is a critical step in putting a planned action into effect. It often introduces change into the organization and can be met with strong resistance. The six stages outlined in Exhibit 11.13 can help leaders and organizations determine *how* to implement a particular plan.[74] These questions provide a framework for the strategic change. You may be able to find a prior successful strategic change the firm undertook and use this implementation as a guide for your suggested change.

As you progress through the six stages, reflect on what you have learned about your firm in the previous modules. In some cases, you will need to make educated guesses for the answer since you are looking at the implementation from outside the organization. However, over the 10 modules you have completed,

you have already learned much about the firm. Answer the following questions for your selected organization.

1. From your knowledge of the firm, identify a major strategic change the firm should seriously consider. Briefly describe what the goal of the initiative is for the organization.

2. Work your way through the six stages in Exhibit 11.13, answering as many of the questions as you can for the proposed strategic change. As you develop the project plans with specifics for each of the stages, the plan should provide flexibility, allowing for unexpected contingencies to emerge.

EXHIBIT 11.13 / Implementation Framework

Implementation Stage	Key Questions to Ask in This Stage
Stage 1 People, skills, and organizational structure	• When must the strategy/strategic initiative be implemented? (How flexible is that date?) • Who is going to do it? What human skills are needed? • Do affected employees understand their roles? • Will the organization need to hire or lay off people? If so, how should it go about it? • How should the firm be organized? What structure should be implemented? Why and how?
Stage 2 Organizational culture	• What culture in the organization is required for the implementation to be successful? • If the current culture differs from the culture needed for the success of the strategy implementation, how should the firm go about changing its culture?
Stage 3 Reward system	• Is a reward structure in place to accomplish the task? • If not, what type of reward structure needs to be introduced to ensure successful strategy implementation?
Stage 4 Resource requirements	• What resources (financial and otherwise) are needed? • Are they in place? • If not, how can the firm obtain the required resources?
Stage 5 Supporting activities	• How is the implementation to be supported? • What policies, procedures, and IT support are needed? • Does the firm need external help (e.g., consulting services)? If so, what kind of services would the firm need, and why?
Stage 6 Strategic leadership	• What types of strategic leaders are required to make the change happen? • Does the firm have them in-house? • Should the firm hire some strategic leaders from outside? • How should the firm train its managers to create a pipeline of strategic leaders?

*my*STRATEGY

For What Type of Organization Are *You* Best-Suited?

As noted in the chapter, firms can have very distinctive cultures. Recall that Zappos has a standing offer to pay any new hire one month's salary to quit the company during the first month of training. Zappos makes this offer to help ensure that those who stay with the company are comfortable in its "create fun and a little weirdness" environment.

You may have taken a personality test such as Myers-Briggs or The Big Five. These tests may be useful in gauging compatibility of career and personality types. They are often available for both graduate and undergraduate students at university career-placement centers. In considering the following questions, think about your next job and your longer-term career plans.

1. Review Exhibit 11.3 and circle the organizational characteristics you find appealing. Cross out those factors you think you would not like. Do you find a trend toward either the mechanistic or organic organization?

2. Have you been in school or work situations in which your values did not align with those of your peers or colleagues? How did you handle the situation? Are there certain values or norms important enough for you to consider as you look for a new job?

3. As you consider your career after graduation, which control-and-reward system discussed in the concluding section of the chapter would you find most motivating? Is this different from the controls used at some jobs you have had in the past? How do you think you would perform in a holacracy such as Zappos is implementing?

ENDNOTES

1. www.zapposinsights.com/about/holacracy. Also, see video "What is Holacracy?" www.youtube.com/watch?v=MUHfVoQUj54 [1:47 min].

2. Koestler, A. (1968), *The Ghost in the Machine* (New York: Macmillan). Koestler's book was first published in 1967 with the first American edition in 1968. Koestler based his term on the earlier concept of the *holon,* a unit that functions both as a whole and a part of a larger organization.

3. This ChapterCase is based on: Robertson, B. (2015), *Holacracy: The New Management System for a Rapidly Changing World* (New York: Henry Holt); Robertson, B. (2015), "Holacracy: A Radical New Approach to Management," TEDx Grand Rapids talk, www.youtube.com/watch?t=17&v=tJxfJGo-vkI [18:20 min]; Greenfield, R., "How Zappos converts new hires to its bizarre office culture," *Bloomberg Business,* June 30, 2015; Silverman, R.E., "At Zappos, banishing the bosses brings confusion," *The Wall Street Journal,* May 20, 2015; Silverman, R.E., "At Zappos, some employees find offer to leave too good to refuse," *The Wall Street Journal,* May 7, 2015; Greenfield, R.,

"Holawhat? Meet the alt-management system invented by a programmer and used by Zappos," *Fast Company,* March 30, 2015; "The holes in holacracy," *The Economist,* July 5, 2014; Sweeney, C., and J. Gosfield, "No managers required: How Zappos ditched the old corporate structure for something new," *Fast Company,* January 6, 2014; McGregor, J., "Zappos to employees: Get behind our 'no bosses' approach, or leave with severance," *The Washington Post,* March 31; McGregor, J. (2014), "Zappos says goodbye to bosses," *The Washington Post,* January 3, 2014; Denning, S., "Making sense of Zappos and holacracy," *Forbes,* January 15, 2014; Robertson, B. (2012), "Why not ditch bosses and distribute power," TEDx Drexel University talk, www.youtube.com/watch?v=hR-8AOccyj4 [13:00 min]; Hsieh, T. (2010), *Delivering Happiness: A Path to Profits, Passion, and Purpose* (New York: Business Plus); http://about.zappos.com; www.zapposinsights.com/about/holacracy; www.holacracy.org/; and "What is holacracy?" www.youtube.com/watch?v=MUHfVoQUj54 [1:47 min].

4. Barney, J.B. (1986), "Organizational culture: Can it be a source of sustained

competitive advantage?" *Academy of Management Review* 11: 656–665.

5. Bossidy, L., R. Charan, and C. Burck (2002), *Execution: The Discipline of Getting Things Done;* and Herold, D.M., and D.B. Fedor (2008), *Change the Way You Lead Change: Leadership Strategies That Really Work* (Palo Alto, CA: Stanford University Press).

6. "Yang's exit doesn't fix Yahoo," *The Wall Street Journal,* November 19, 2008.

7. Herold and Fedor, *Change the Way You Lead Change.*

8. Chandler, A.D. (1962), *Strategy and Structure: Chapters in the History of American Industrial Enterprise* (Cambridge, MA: MIT Press), p. 14 (italics added).

9. Hall, D.J., and M.A. Saias (1980), "Strategy follows structure!" *Strategic Management Journal* 1: 149–163.

10. Hill, C.W.L., and F.T. Rothaermel (2003), "The performance of incumbent firms in the face of radical technological innovation," *Academy of Management Review* 28: 257–274.

11. I gratefully acknowledge Professor Luis Martins' input on this exhibit.

12. Microsoft CEO Steve Ballmer's quote drawn from "Microsoft bid to beat Google builds on a history of misses," *The Wall Street Journal,* January 16, 2009.

13. This Strategy Highlight is based on: "Opening Windows," *The Economist,* April 4, 2015; "Microsoft CEO Steve Ballmer to retire in 12 months," *The Wall Street Journal,* August 23, 2013; Ovide, S., "Next CEO's biggest job: Fixing Microsoft's culture," *The Wall Street Journal,* August 25, 2013; Levy, S. (2011), *In the Plex: How Google Thinks, Works, and Shapes Our Lives* (New York: Simon & Schuster); "Google, Microsoft spar on antitrust," *The Wall Street Journal,* March 1, 2010; "Microsoft bid to beat Google builds on a history of misses," *The Wall Street Journal,* January 16, 2009; "Yahoo tie-up is latest sign tide turning for Microsoft's Ballmer," *The Wall Street Journal,* July 30, 2009; "Bingoo! A deal between Microsoft and Yahoo!" *The Economist,* July 30, 2009; and "Yahoo to buy Overture for $1.63 billion," *CNET News,* July 14, 2003.

14. In his insightful book, Finkelstein identifies several key transition points that put pressure on an organization and thus increase the likelihood of subsequent failure. See: Finkelstein, S. (2003), *Why Smart Executives Fail: And What You Can Learn from Their Mistakes* (New York: Portfolio).

15. Fredrickson, J.W. (1986), "The strategic decision process and organizational structure," *Academy of Management Review* 11: 280–297; Eisenhardt, K.M. (1989), "Making fast strategic decisions in high-velocity environments," *Academy of Management Journal* 32: 543–576; and Wally, S., and R.J. Baum (1994), "Strategic decision speed and firm performance," *Strategic Management Journal* 24: 1107–1129.

16. *The 9/11 Report. The National Commission on Terrorist Attacks upon the United States* (2004), http://govinfo.library.unt.edu/911/report/index.htm.

17. Child, J., and R.G. McGrath (2001), "Organization unfettered: Organizational forms in the information-intensive economy," *Academy of Management Journal* 44: 1135–1148; and Huy, Q.N. (2002), "Emotional balancing of organizational continuity and radical change: The contribution of middle managers," *Administrative Science Quarterly* 47: 31–69.

18. Theobald, N.A., and S. Nicholson-Crotty (2005), "The many faces of span of control: Organizational structure across multiple goals," *Administration and Society* 36: 648–660.

19. This section draws on: Burns, T., and G.M. Stalker (1961), *The Management of Innovation* (London: Tavistock).

20. Hamel, G. (2007), *The Future of Management* (Boston, MA: Harvard Business School Press), p. 84.

21. This Strategy Highlight is based on: Hamel, *The Future of Management;* Collins, J. (2009), *How the Mighty Fall: And Why Some Companies Never Give In* (New York: Harper-Collins); Collins, J., and M. Hansen (2011), *Great by Choice: Uncertainty, Chaos, and Luck—Why Some Thrive Despite Them All* (New York: HarperCollins); and www .gore.com.

22. Chandler, *Strategy and Structure: Chapters in the History of American Industrial Enterprise.*

23. Ibid. Also, for a more recent treatise across different levels of analysis, see Ridley, M. (2010), *The Rational Optimist: How Prosperity Evolves* (New York: HarperCollins).

24. This discussion is based on: O'Reilly, C.A., III, and M.L. Tushman (2007), "Ambidexterity as dynamic capability: Resolving the innovator's dilemma," *Research in Organizational Behavior* 28: 1–60; Raisch, S., and J. Birkinshaw (2008), "Organizational ambidexterity: Antecedents, outcomes, and moderators," *Journal of Management* 34: 375–409; and Rothaermel, F.T., and M.T. Alexandre (2009), "Ambidexterity in technology sourcing: The moderating role of absorptive capacity," *Organization Science* 20: 759–780.

25. Hamel, G. (2006), "The why, what, and how of management innovation," *Harvard Business Review,* February.

26. March, J.G. (1991), "Exploration and exploitation in organizational learning," *Organization Science* 2: 319–340; and Levinthal, D.A., and J.G. March (1993), "The myopia of learning," *Strategic Management Journal* 14: 95–112.

27. Author's interviews with Intel managers and engineers.

28. Brown, S.L., and K.M. Eisenhardt (1997), "The art of continuous change: Linking complexity theory and time-paced evolution in relentlessly shifting organizations," *Administrative Science Quarterly* 42: 1–34; and O'Reilly, C.A., B. Harreld, and M. Tushman (2009), "Organizational ambidexterity: IBM and emerging business opportunities," *California Management Review* 51: 75–99.

29. Chandler, *Strategy and Structure: Chapters in the History of American Industrial Enterprise.*

30. www.gore.com.

31. Williamson, O.E. (1975), *Markets and Hierarchies* (Free Press: New York); and Williamson, O.E. (1985), *The Economic Institutions of Capitalism* (Free Press: New York).

32. Barr, A., and R. Winkler, "Google creates parent company called Alphabet in

restructuring," *The Wall Street Journal,* August 18, 2015.

33. Bertoni, S., "Elon Musk and David Sacks say PayPal could top $100B away from Ebay," *Forbes,* February 18, 2014; and "EBay's split should make investors happy—and corporate divorces more popular," *The Economist,* July 18, 2015.

34. Bryan, L.L., and C.I. Joyce (2007), "Better strategy through organizational design," *The McKinsley Quarterly* 2: 21–29; Hagel, J., III, J.S. Brown, and L. Davison (2010), *The Power of Pull: How Small Moves, Smartly Made, Can Set Big Things in Motion* (Philadelphia, PA: Basic Books)*;* Majchrzak, A., A. Malhotra, J. Stamps, and J. Lipnack (2004), "Can absence make a team grow stronger?" *Harvard Business Review,* May; Malhotra, A., A. Majchrzak, and B. Rosen (2007), "Leading far-flung teams," *Academy of Management Perspectives,* March.

35. Brown, J.S., and P. Duguid (1991), "Organizational learning and communities-of-practice: Toward a unified view of working, learning, and innovation," *Organization Science* 2: 40–57.

36. This section draws on: Barney, "Organizational culture: Can it be a source of sustained competitive advantage?"; Chatman, J.A., and S. Eunyoung Cha (2003), "Leading by leveraging culture," *California Management Review* 45: 19–34; Kerr, J., and J.W. Slocum (2005), "Managing corporate culture through reward systems," *Academy of Management Executive* 19: 130–138; O'Reilly, C.A., J. Chatman, and D.L. Caldwell (1991), "People and organizational culture: A profile comparison approach to assessing person-organization fit," *Academy of Management Journal* 34: 487–516; and Schein, E.H. (1992), *Organizational Culture and Leadership* (San Francisco: Jossey-Bass).

37. Chatman and Eunyoung Cha (2003), "Leading by leveraging culture," pp. 19–34.

38. Chao, G.T., A.M. O'Leary-Kelly, S. Wolf, H.J. Klein, and P.D. Gardner (1994), "Organizational socialization: Its content and consequences," *Journal of Applied Psychology* 79: 730–743.

39. Hsieh, *Delivering Happiness: A Path to Profits, Passion, and Purpose,* p. 130.

40. Ibid., p. 145.

41. Ibid., p. 177.

42. This section draws on: https://jobs.zappos .com/life-at-zappos.

43. Nelson, T. (2003), "The persistence of founder influence: Management, ownership, and performance effects at initial public offering," *Strategic Management Journal* 24: 707–724.

44. A&E Biography Video (1997), *Sam Walton: Bargain Billionaire.*

45. Friedman, T.L. (2005), *The World Is Flat. A Brief History of the 21st Century* (New York: Farrar, Straus and Giroux), pp. 130–131.

46. Schneider, B., H.W. Goldstein, and D.B. Smith (1995), "The ASA framework: An update," *Personnel Psychology* 48: 747–773.

47. Hsieh, *Delivering Happiness. A Path to Profits, Passion, and Purpose,* p. 145.

48. Less than 1 percent of new hires take Zappos up on the $2,000 offer to quit during the training program.

49. Leonard-Barton, D. (1995), *Wellsprings of Knowledge: Building and Sustaining the Sources of Innovation* (Boston, MA: Harvard Business School Press).

50. Chandler, *Strategy and Structure: Chapters in the History of American Industrial Enterprise.*

51. Birkinshaw, J. (2010), *Reinventing Management. Smarter Choices for Getting Work Done* (Chichester, West Sussex, UK: Jossey-Bass).

52. Boudette, N.E., "GM CEO to testify before House panel," *The Wall Street Journal,* June 17, 2014.

53. Spector, M., and C.M. Matthews, "Investigators narrow GM-switch probe," *The Wall Street Journal,* July 24, 2015.

54. Hughes, S., and J. Bennett, "Senators challenge GM's Barra, push for faster change," *The Wall Street Journal,* April 2, 2014.

55. This section is based on: Barney, "Organizational culture: Can it be a source of sustained competitive advantage?"; Barney, J. (1991), "Firm resources and sustained competitive advantage," *Journal of Management* 17: 99–120; and Chatman and Eunyoung Cha, "Leading by leveraging culture," pp. 19–34.

56. Hoffer Gittel, J. (2003), *The Southwest Airlines Way* (New York: McGraw-Hill); and O'Reilly, C., and J. Pfeffer (1995), "Southwest Airlines: Using human resources for competitive advantage," case study, Graduate School of Business, Stanford University.

57. Hsieh, *Delivering Happiness. A Path to Profits, Passion, and Purpose,* p. 146.

58. See discussion in Chapter 4 on SWA's activities supporting its cost-leadership strategy. SWA has experienced problems with the fuselage of its 737 cracking prematurely. See: "Southwest's solo flight in crisis," *The Wall Street Journal,* April 8, 2011.

59. Hsieh, *Delivering Happiness. A Path to Profits, Passion, and Purpose,* p. 146.

60. Chatman and Eunyoung Cha, "Leading by leveraging culture," pp. 19–34.

61. Hoffer Gittel, J. (2003), *The Southwest Airlines Way* (New York: McGraw-Hill).

62. Baron, J.N., M.T. Hannan, and M.D. Burton (2001), "Labor pains: Change in organizational models and employee turnover in young, high-tech firms," *American Journal of Sociology* 106: 960–1012; and Hannan, M.T., M.D. Burton, and J.N. Baron (1996), "Inertia and change in the early years: Employment relationships in young, high technology firms," *Industrial and Corporate Change* 5: 503–537.

63. Nelson, T. (2003), "The persistence of founder influence: Management, ownership, and performance effects at initial public offering," *Strategic Management Journal* 24: 707–724.

64. See the section on mergers and acquisitions in Chapter 9.

65. Herold and Fedor, *Change the Way You Lead Change: Leadership Strategies That Really Work.*

66. Ibid., pp. 157–160.

67. In this video, Zappos employees speak about what the 10 core values mean to them: http://about.zappos.com/our-unique-culture/zappos-core-values [3.50 min].

68. Hsieh, *Delivering Happiness: A Path to Profits, Passion, and Purpose.*

69. Pink, D.H. (2009), *Drive: The Surprising Truth about What Motivates Us* (New York: Riverhead Books).

70. Ibid.

71 3M Company (2002), *A Century of Innovation: The 3M Story* (Maplewood, MN: The 3M Company).

72. Bossidy, L., R. Charan, and C. Burck (2002), *Execution: The Discipline of Getting Things Done* (New York: Crown Business); and Hrebiniak, L.G. (2005), *Making Strategy Work: Leading Effective Execution and Change* (Philadelphia: Wharton School Publishing).

73. Grundy, T. (1998), "Strategy implementation and project management," *International Journal of Project Management* 16: 43–50.

74. Input for this module is used with the permission of Blaine Lawlor, strategic management professor, University of West Florida.

Chapter 12

Corporate Governance and Business Ethics

Learning Objectives

LO 12-1 Describe the shared value creation framework and its relationship to competitive advantage.

LO 12-2 Explain the role of corporate governance.

LO 12-3 Apply agency theory to explain why and how companies use governance mechanisms to align interests of principals and agents.

LO 12-4 Evaluate the board of directors as the central governance mechanism for public stock companies.

LO 12-5 Evaluate other governance mechanisms.

LO 12-6 Explain the relationship between strategy and business ethics.

Uber: Most Ethically Challenged Tech Company?

IN THE SUMMER of 2015 Uber surpassed a valuation of over $50 billion and became the most valuable private startup ever. Yet in the wake of its business success, Uber leaves a trail of lawsuits and accusations.

RECORD-BREAKING GROWTH

Only one other new venture—Facebook—has ever reached a $50 billion valuation for a private, venture-capital-backed firm. But it took Facebook seven years to reach this mark; Uber only five. For perspective, the valuation of the car rental giant Hertz, with some 150 locations, a fleet of 500,000 cars, and some 30,000 employees, is only about a fifth of Uber's valuation.

Uber reached this astronomical valuation because it successfully expanded both in the United States and globally to more than 300 cities. Uber's popularity grows exponentially, as

Protest against Uber
© Lucy Nicholson/Reuters/Corbis

it already transports millions of riders daily, and continues to expand rapidly here and abroad. Although Uber is still losing money as it continues to subsidize customer fares, its revenues race ahead, from $400 million in 2014 to $2 billion in 2015.

UBER'S BEGINNING

Uber started in 2008 when Travis Kalanick and Garrett Camp were bothered by the inconvenience of getting a cab in San Francisco. The two tech entrepreneurs worked up a prototype of a cab-hailing app and won the first round of funding a year later to further develop the service. They chose the name Uber when inspired by the idea of using a Mercedes limousine and driver instead of a regular cab—the German word *über* means "superior." By 2010, Uber debuted its service in San Francisco.

ETHICALLY CHALLENGED?

Despite its meteoric rise, not all is roses for Uber. Venture capitalist Peter Thiel called Uber the "most ethically challenged company in Silicon Valley."[1] But then, Thiel, the billionaire co-founder of PayPal and Palantir (a big data analytics company), is also an investor in Lyft, Uber's main competitor. Lyft has a valuation of only $2.5 billion. Thiel argues that Uber is pushing the envelope of what is acceptable, ethical, and even legal with all its stakeholders, including its dealings with regulators, government bodies at different levels, freelance drivers, journalists, and competitors. Thiel further argues that Uber is on the cusp of going too far.

ITS OWN RIVAL

Echoing Thiel's assessment, *The Wall Street Journal (WSJ)* argued Uber itself—rather than Lyft or old-line taxi and limo services—is its own biggest threat, thereby functioning as its own biggest rival. The competitive tactics and comments by Uber executives are harming the company's reputation and becoming a liability, the *WSJ* argues. The company's short history provides rich examples for such claims.

- **Open disregard for laws, rules, and regulations.** Within months of its San Francisco launch, the local Metro Transit Authority and the state Public Utilities Commission each ordered Uber to cease and desist. They argued that Uber was operating as a taxi service without proper licensing. Pushback and injunctions followed in major domestic markets, including New York City and Los Angeles, and internationally in Toronto, Paris, London, Berlin, and Delhi. Ignoring such warnings, Uber continues to expand.

- **Dynamic pricing.** While the taxi industry operates under regulation with fixed pricing, Uber opts for the dynamic pricing used by airlines, hotels, and other industries. That is, Uber's fares go up or down based on real-time supply and demand. So during a snowstorm or on New Year's Eve, short Uber rides can cost hundreds of dollars. CEO Kalanick argues that surge pricing efficiently matches supply and demand. But many Uber users see it as price gouging and vent their frustrations on Twitter and Facebook.

■ **Competitive tactics.** Lyft, the competing ride-share app, accused Uber of ordering over 5,000 rides from Lyft, and then canceling, so Lyft drivers lost business from legitimate rides. Reportedly Uber tells its drivers in New York that they cannot work for both Uber and Lyft because of city regulations; the city says Uber's claim is untrue. Accusers say that Uber brand ambassadors actively target successful drivers from Lyft and other competitors to defect.

■ **Poisoning sources of funding.** Kalanick reportedly poisoned Lyft's efforts to raise venture capital, telling investors, "before you decide whether you want to invest in [Lyft], just make sure you know that we are going to be fund-raising immediately after."[2]

■ **Death of a child.** An Uber driver, while between fares, tragically struck and killed 6-year-old Sophia Liu in a crosswalk in San Francisco. Claims arose that the driver was busy using the Uber app at the time and did not see the girl. Uber, rather than dealing with this public relations disaster by expressing condolences to the family for their loss, focused on its legal posture and coldly denied all liability, making sure that people knew that the driver was between Uber jobs.

■ **Sexist ad campaign.** Uber's office in Lyon, France, ran a sexist ad campaign that promised rides with "avions de chasse" as drivers, which is French for fighter jets, but colloquially it means "hot chicks." The ads were accompanied by revealing photos of models. Uber headquarters canceled the ad campaign and apologized for the "clear misjudgment by the local team."

■ **Attacking critics.** In late 2014, Uber senior executive Emil Michael was heard to say that Uber should spend a million dollars to hire private investigators to dig up dirt on journalists who wrote damaging pieces on Uber, with particular focus on Sarah Lacy, of tech blog PandoDaily. When the remarks became public, he apologized. Uber CEO Kalanick said that Michael's comments were "a departure from our values and ideals," but Michaels was not otherwise disciplined.

■ **Stealth tech transfer.** In the spring of 2015, Uber opened its Advanced Tech Center in Pittsburgh to develop autonomous cars and sophisticated mapping services. Uber gained access to scientists when it funded research at Carnegie Mellon University's National Robotics Engineering Center (NREC). A few months later, Uber poached entire NREC research teams with signing bonuses, twice the salaries, and stock options. It is also building a super-modern research center adjacent to the CMU campus. The NREC was left a shell, with its entire future in question. To add insult to injury to Carnegie Mellon, Uber rented a billboard next to its computer science department, reading, "We are looking for the best software engineers in Pittsburgh."

■ **Thumbing its nose.** With the announced agenda of its Advanced Tech Center, Uber moves into direct conflict with one of its biggest partners and investors, Google, the leader in online maps and a pioneer in self-driving cars. After successfully demonstrating an autonomous vehicle on California's highways and cities, Google is hopeful that its self-driving car technology will be viable by 2020 for widespread adoption.[3]

You will learn more about Uber from reading this chapter; related questions appear on page 419.

THE UBER CHAPTERCASE illustrates how intricate and intertwined business ethics issues and competitive advantage can be. With over $50 billion in valuation, Uber is riding high as the world's most valuable private start-up firm. Its huge cash pile fuels its rapid expansion in the United States and abroad. It allows Uber to subsidize fares and to attract more drivers to its platform. All this is done to create network effects based on a large installed base of Uber drivers and users. In what is likely to be a winner-take-all market, Uber is planning to be the winner in the ride-hailing business. Some caution that Uber is risking going too far in its competitive tactics. Uber is certainly pushing the envelope with what is ethical as well as legal in its business practices. This strong-arm approach might harm the company's reputation and negatively impact its competitive advantage.

In this chapter, we wrap up our discussion of strategy implementation and close the circle in the AFI framework by studying two important areas: corporate governance and business ethics. We begin with the *shared value creation framework* to illuminate the link between strategic management, competitive advantage, and society more fully. We then discuss effective *corporate-governance* mechanisms to direct and control the enterprise, which a firm must put in place to ensure pursuit of its intended goals. Next, we study *business ethics,* which enable managers to think through complex decisions in an increasingly dynamic, interdependent, and global marketplace. The vignettes in the ChapterCase documenting controversial decisions, tactics, and statements by Uber highlight the link between business ethics and competitive advantage. We conclude with "Implications for the strategist."

12.1 The Shared Value Creation Framework

The shared value creation framework provides guidance to managers about how to reconcile the economic imperative of gaining and sustaining competitive advantage with corporate social responsibility (introduced in Chapter 1).[4] It helps managers create a larger pie that benefits both shareholders and other stakeholders. To develop the shared value creation framework, though, we first must understand the role of the public stock company.

LO 12-1

Describe the shared value creation framework and its relationship to competitive advantage.

PUBLIC STOCK COMPANIES AND SHAREHOLDER CAPITALISM

The public stock company is an important institutional arrangement in modern, free market economies. It provides goods and services as well as employment, pays taxes, and increases the standard of living. There exists an implicit contract based on trust between society and the public stock company. Society grants the right to incorporation, but in turn expects companies to be good citizens by adding value to society.

To fund future growth, companies frequently need go public. Uber, featured in the ChapterCase, is one of the few companies that achieved a huge valuation prior to an initial public offering. Private start-up companies valued at a billion dollars or more are called *unicorns,* because at one time they seemed as rare as the mythical beast. But their elusiveness has changed. The tech sector now has the lion's share: some 75 unicorns valued at $1 billion or more, for a total of $273 billion.[5] The top five most valuable private start-up companies (as of the summer of 2015) are Uber, Airbnb, Snapchat, Palantir Technologies, and SpaceX (rocket science). These new ventures may eventually go public such as Facebook did in 2012, but as long as they remain private they do not have to follow the stringent financial reporting and auditing requirements that public stock companies do. Consider that there may be a connection between firm structure and the degree that it integrates ethics. Not needing to expose themselves to as much public scrutiny as a publicly traded company also allows unicorns such as Uber to push the envelope in their legal and ethical business practices.

In capital markets, private companies that achieve a valuation of $1 billion or greater are rare enough to be called unicorns.
© Catmando/
Shutterstock.com RF

Exhibit 12.1 depicts the levels of hierarchy within a public stock company. The state or society grants a charter of incorporation to the company's shareholders—its owners, who legally own stock in the company. The shareholders appoint a board of directors to govern

EXHIBIT 12.1 /

The Public Stock
Company: Hierarchy
of Authority

and oversee the firm's management. The managers hire, supervise, and coordinate employees to manufacture products and provide services. The public stock company enjoys four characteristics that make it an attractive corporate form:[6]

1. *Limited liability for investors.* This characteristic means that the shareholders who provide the risk capital are liable only to the capital specifically invested, and not for other investments they may have made or for their personal wealth. Limited liability encourages investments by the wider public and entrepreneurial risk-taking.

2. *Transferability of investor ownership* through the trading of shares of stock on exchanges such as the New York Stock Exchange (NYSE) and NASDAQ,[7] or exchanges in other countries. Each share represents only a minute fraction of ownership in a company, thus easing transferability.

3. *Legal personality*—that is, the law regards a non-living entity such as a for-profit firm as similar to a person, with legal rights and obligations. Legal personality allows a firm's continuation beyond the founder or the founder's family.

4. *Separation of legal ownership and management control.*[8] In publicly traded companies, the stockholders (the principals, represented by the board of directors) are the legal owners of the company, and they delegate decision-making authority to professional managers (the agents).

The public stock company has been a major contributor to value creation since its inception as a new organizational form more than a hundred years ago. Michael Porter and others, however, argue that many public companies have defined value creation too narrowly in terms of financial performance.[9] This in turn has contributed to some of the *black swan events* discussed in Chapter 1, such as large-scale accounting scandals and the global financial crisis. Managers' pursuit of strategies that define value creation too narrowly may have negative consequences for society at large, as evidenced during the global financial crisis. This narrow focus has contributed to the loss of trust in the corporation as a vehicle for value creation, not only for shareholders but also other stakeholders and society.

Nobel laureate Milton Friedman stated his view of the firm's social obligations: "There is one and only one social responsibility of business—to use its resources and engage in activities designed to increase its profits so long as it stays within the rules of the game, which is to say, engages in open and free competition without deception or fraud."[10] This notion is often captured by the term **shareholder capitalism**. According to this perspective, shareholders—the providers of the necessary risk capital and the legal owners of public companies—have the most legitimate claim on profits. When introducing the notion of *corporate social responsibility* (CSR) in Chapter 1, though, we noted that a firm's obligations frequently go beyond the economic responsibility to increase profits, extending to ethical and philanthropic expectations that society has of the business enterprise.[11]

A recent survey measured attitudes toward business responsibility in various countries. The survey asked the top 25 percent of income earners holding a university degree in each country surveyed whether they agree with Milton Friedman's philosophy that "the social responsibility of business is to increase its profits."[12] The results, displayed in Exhibit 12.2, revealed some intriguing national differences. The United Arab Emirates (UAE), a small and business-friendly federation of seven emirates, had the highest level of agreement, at 84 percent. The top five also included a number of Asian countries (Japan, India, South Korea, and Singapore), where roughly two-thirds agreed.

The countries where the fewest people agreed with Friedman's philosophy were China, Brazil, Germany, Italy, and Spain; fewer than 40 percent of respondents in those countries supported an exclusive focus on shareholder capitalism. Although they have achieved a

shareholder capitalism
Shareholders—the providers of the necessary risk capital and the legal owners of public companies—have the most legitimate claim on profits.

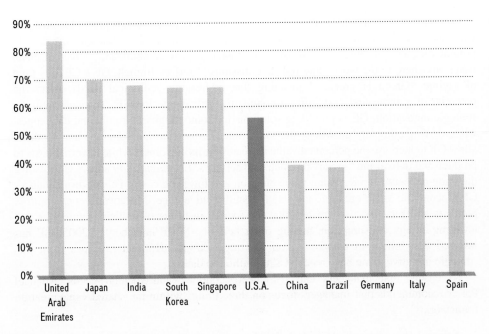

EXHIBIT 12.2 /

Global Survey
of Attitudes
toward Business
Responsibility

The bar chart indicates
the percentage of mem-
bers of the "informed
public" who "strongly
agree/somewhat agree"
with Milton Friedman's
philosophy, "the social
responsibility of business
is to increase its profits."

Source: Author's depiction
of data from Edelman's
(2011) Trust Barometer as
included in "Milton Friedman
goes on tour," The Economist,
January 27, 2011.

high standard of living, European countries such as Germany have tempered the free market system with a strong social element, leading to so-called *social market economies.* The
respondents from these countries seemed to be more supportive of a *stakeholder strategy*
approach to business. Some critics, however, would argue that too strong a focus on the
social dimension contributed to the European debt crisis because sovereign governments
such as Greece, Italy, and Spain took on nonsustainable debt levels to fund social programs
such as early retirement plans, government-funded health care, and so on. The United
States placed roughly in the middle of the continuum. In particular, a bit more than half
(56 percent) of U.S. respondents subscribed to Friedman's philosophy.

CREATING SHARED VALUE

In contrast to Milton Friedman, Porter argues that executives should not concentrate
exclusively on increasing firm profits. Rather, the strategist should focus on creating
shared value, a concept that involves creating economic value for shareholders while
also creating social value by addressing society's needs and challenges. He argues
that managers need to reestablish the important relationship between superior firm
performance and societal progress. This dual point of view, Porter argues, will not only
allow companies to gain and sustain a competitive advantage but also reshape capitalism
and its relationship to society.

The **shared value creation framework** proposes that managers maintain a dual focus
on shareholder value creation and value creation for society. It recognizes that markets
are defined not only by economic needs but also by societal needs. It also advances
the perspective that *externalities* such as pollution, wasted energy, and costly accidents
actually create *internal costs,* at least in lost reputation if not directly on the bottom line.
Rather than pitting economic and societal needs in a trade-off, Porter suggests that the
two can be reconciled to create a larger pie. The shared value creation framework seeks
to enhance a firm's competitiveness by identifying connections between economic and
social needs, and then creating a competitive advantage by addressing these business
opportunities.

**shared value
creation framework**
A model proposing that
managers have a dual
focus on shareholder
value creation and value
creation for society.

GE, for example, has strengthened its competitiveness by creating a profitable business with its "green" *ecomagination* initiative. *Ecomagination* is GE's strategic initiative to provide cleaner and more efficient sources of energy, provide abundant sources of clean water anywhere in the world, and reduce emissions.[13] Jeffrey Immelt, GE's CEO, is fond of saying: "Green is green,"[14] meaning that addressing ecological needs offers the potential of gaining and sustaining a competitive advantage for GE. Through applying strategic innovation, GE is providing solutions for some tough environmental challenges, while driving company growth at the same time. *Ecomagination* solutions and products allow GE to increase the perceived value it creates for its customers while lowering costs to produce and deliver the "green" products and services. *Ecomagination* allows GE to solve the trade-off between increasing value creation and lowering costs. This in turn enhances GE's economic value creation and its competitive advantage. Moreover, *ecomagination* products and services also create value for society in terms of reducing emissions and lowering energy consumption, among other benefits. Since launched in 2005, GE has invested $15 billion in *ecomagination* and reported in 2015 that revenues from this strategic initiative alone have reached $200 billion to date.

To ensure that managers can reconnect economic and societal needs, Michael Porter recommends that managers focus on three things within the shared value creation framework:[15]

1. **Expand the customer base to bring in *nonconsumers*** such as those at the *bottom of the pyramid*—the largest but poorest socioeconomic group of the world's population.

   The bottom of the pyramid in the global economy can yield significant business opportunities, which—if satisfied—could improve the living standard of the world's poorest. Muhammad Yunus, Nobel Peace Prize winner, founded Grameen Bank in Bangladesh to provide small loans (termed *microcredit)* to impoverished villagers, who used the funding for entrepreneurial ventures that would help them climb out of poverty. Other businesses have also found profitable opportunities at the bottom of the pyramid. In India, Arvind Mills offers jeans in a ready-to-make kit that costs only a fraction of the high-end Levi's. The Tata group sells its Nano car for around 150,000 rupees (less than $2,500), enabling more Indian families to move from mopeds to cars and adding up to a substantial business.

2. **Expand traditional internal firm value chains to include more nontraditional partners** such as *nongovernmental organizations* (NGOs).

   NGOs are nonprofit organizations that pursue a particular cause in the public interest and are independent of any governments. Habitat for Humanity and Greenpeace are examples of NGOs.

3. **Focus on creating new *regional clusters*** such as Silicon Valley in the United States, Electronic City in Bangalore, India, and Chilecon Valley in Santiago, Chile.

In line with *stakeholder theory* (discussed in Chapter 1), Porter argues that these strategic actions will lead to a larger pie of revenues and profits that can be distributed among a company's stakeholders. General Electric, for example, recognizes a convergence between shareholders and stakeholders to create shared value. It states in its governance principles: "Both the board of directors and management recognize that the long-term interests of shareowners are advanced by responsibly addressing the concerns of other stakeholders and interested parties, including employees, recruits, customers, suppliers, GE communities, government officials, and the public at large."[16] To ensure that convergence indeed takes place, companies need effective governance mechanisms, which we discuss next.

12.2 Corporate Governance

Corporate governance concerns the mechanisms to direct and control an enterprise in order to ensure that it pursues its strategic goals successfully and legally.[17] Corporate governance is about checks and balances and about asking the tough questions at the right time. The accounting scandals of the early 2000s and the global financial crisis of 2008 and beyond got so out of hand because the enterprises involved did not practice effective corporate governance. As discussed in the ChapterCase, some observers question whether Uber has effective corporate-governance mechanisms in place, or whether its ethically and legally questionable competitive tactics and decisions are part of a larger intended strategy to first dominate the taxi-hailing business and then to address any remaining stakeholder grievances.

Corporate governance attempts to address the *principal–agent problem* (introduced in Chapter 8), which can occur any time an agent performs activities on behalf of a principal.[18] This problem can arise whenever a principal delegates decision making and control over resources to agents, with the expectation that they will act in the principal's best interest.

We mentioned earlier that the separation of ownership and control is one of the major advantages of the public stock companies. This benefit, however, is also the source of the principal–agent problem. In publicly traded companies, the stockholders are the legal owners of the company, but they delegate decision-making authority to professional managers. The conflict arises if the agents pursue their own personal interests, which can be at odds with the principals' goals. For their part, agents may be more interested in maximizing their total compensation, including benefits, job security, status, and power. Principals desire maximization of total returns to shareholders.

The risk of opportunism on behalf of agents is exacerbated by *information asymmetry:* the agents are generally better informed than the principals. Exhibit 12.3 depicts the principal–agent relationship.

Managers, executives, and board members tend to have access to *private information* concerning important company developments that outsiders, especially investors, are not privy to. Often this informational advantage is based on timing—insiders are the first to learn about important developments before the information is released to the public. Although possessing insider information is not illegal and indeed is part of an executive's job, what *is* illegal is acting upon it through trading stocks or passing on the information to others who might do so. Insider-trading cases, therefore, provide an example of egregious exploitation of information asymmetry. The hedge fund Galleon Group (holding assets worth $7 billion under management at its peak) was engulfed in an insider-trading scandal involving private information about important developments at companies such as Goldman Sachs, Google, IBM, Intel, and P&G.[19] Galleon Group's founder, Raj Rajaratnam, the mastermind behind a complex network of informants, was sentenced to 11 years in

LO 12-2

Explain the role of corporate governance.

corporate governance
A system of mechanisms to direct and control an enterprise in order to ensure that it pursues its strategic goals successfully and legally.

EXHIBIT 12.3 / The Principal–Agent Problem

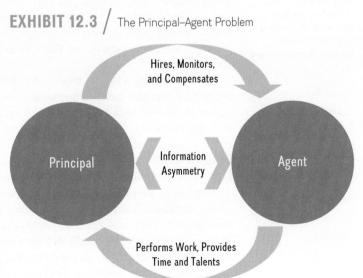

Hires, Monitors, and Compensates

Principal

Information Asymmetry

Agent

Performs Work, Provides Time and Talents

prison and fined more than $150 million. In one instance, an Intel manager had provided Rajaratnam with internal Intel data such as orders for processors and production runs. These data indicated that demand for Intel processors was much higher than analysts had expected. Galleon bought Intel stock well before this information was public to benefit from the anticipated share appreciation.

In another instance, Rajaratnam benefited from insider tips provided by Rajat Gupta, a former McKinsey chief executive who served on Goldman Sachs' board. Often within seconds after a Goldman Sachs board meeting ended, Gupta called Rajaratnam. In one of these phone calls, Gupta revealed the impending multibillion-dollar liquidity injection by Warren Buffett into Goldman Sachs during the midst of the global financial crisis. This information allowed the Galleon Group to buy Goldman Sachs shares before the official announcement about Buffett's investment was made, profiting from the subsequent stock appreciation. In another call, Gupta informed Rajaratnam that the investment bank would miss earnings estimates. Based on this insider information, the Galleon Group was able to sell its holdings in Goldman Sachs' stock prior to the announcement, avoiding a multimillion-dollar loss.[20]

Information asymmetry also can breed *on-the-job consumption,* perquisites, and excessive compensation. Although use of company funds for golf outings, resort retreats, professional sporting events, or elegant dinners and other entertainment is an every-day manifestation of on-the-job consumption, other forms are more extreme. Dennis Kozlowski, former CEO of Tyco, a diversified conglomerate, used company funds for his $30 million New York City apartment (the shower curtain alone was $6,000) and for a $2 million birthday party for his second wife.[21] John Thain, former CEO of Merrill Lynch, spent $1.2 million of company funds on redecorating his office, while he demanded cost cutting and frugality from his employees.[22] Such uses of company funds, in effect, mean that shareholders pay for those items and activities. Thain also allegedly requested a bonus of up to $30 million in 2009 despite Merrill Lynch having lost billions of dollars and being unable to continue as an independent company. Merrill Lynch was later acquired by Bank of America in a fire sale.

AGENCY THEORY

The principal–agent problem is a core part of **agency theory,** which views the firm as a nexus of legal contracts.[23] In this perspective, corporations are viewed merely as a set of legal contracts between different parties. Conflicts that may arise are to be addressed in the legal realm. Agency theory finds its everyday application in employment contracts, for example.

Besides dealing with the relationship between shareholders and managers, principal–agent problems also cascade down the organizational hierarchy (shown in Exhibit 12.3). Senior executives, such as the CEO, face agency problems when they delegate authority of strategic business units to general managers. Uber headquarters staff in the United States claimed that the sexist ad campaign launched by its French office was based on an agency problem, explaining it as a "clear misjudgment of the local team." The local team, however, thought that this type of ad campaign would serve Uber in France well.

Employees who perform the actual operational labor are agents who work on behalf of the managers. Such frontline employees often enjoy an informational advantage over management. They may tell their supervisor that it took longer to complete a project or serve a customer than it actually did, for example. Some employees may be tempted to use such informational advantage for their own self-interest (e.g., spending time on Facebook during work hours, watching YouTube videos, or using the company's computer and Internet connection for personal business).

LO 12-3

Apply agency theory to explain why and how companies use governance mechanisms to align interests of principals and agents.

agency theory
A theory that views the firm as a nexus of legal contracts.

The managerial implication of agency theory relates to the management functions of organization and control: The firm needs to design work tasks, incentives, and employment contracts and other control mechanisms in ways that minimize opportunism by agents. Such governance mechanisms are used to align incentives between principals and agents. These mechanisms need to be designed in such a fashion as to overcome two specific agency problems: *adverse selection* and *moral hazard.*

ADVERSE SELECTION. In general, **adverse selection** occurs when information asymmetry increases the likelihood of selecting inferior alternatives. In principal–agent relationships, for example, adverse selection describes a situation in which an agent misrepresents his or her ability to do the job. Such misrepresentation is common during the recruiting process. Once hired, the principal may not be able to accurately assess whether the agent can do the work for which he or she is being paid. The problem is especially pronounced in team production, when the principal often cannot ascertain the contributions of individual team members. This creates an incentive for opportunistic employees to free-ride on the efforts of others.

> **adverse selection**
> A situation that occurs when information asymmetry increases the likelihood of selecting inferior alternatives.

MORAL HAZARD. In general, **moral hazard** describes a situation in which information asymmetry increases the incentive of one party to take undue risks or shirk other responsibilities because the costs accrue to the other party. For example, bailing out homeowners from their mortgage obligations or bailing out banks from the consequences of undue risk-taking in lending are examples of moral hazard. The costs of default are rolled over to society. Knowing that there is a high probability of being bailed out ("too big to fail") increases moral hazard. In this scenario, any profits remain private, while losses become public.

> **moral hazard**
> A situation in which information asymmetry increases the incentive of one party to take undue risks or shirk other responsibilities because the costs incur to the other party.

In the principal–agent relationship, moral hazard describes the difficulty of the principal to ascertain whether the agent has really put forth a best effort. In this situation, the agent is *able* to do the work but may decide not to do so. For example, a company scientist at a biotechnology company may decide to work on his own research project, hoping to eventually start his own firm, rather than on the project he was assigned.[24] While working on his own research on company time, he might also use the company's laboratory and technicians. Given the complexities of basic research, it is often challenging, especially for nonscientist principals, to ascertain which problem a scientist is working on.[25] To overcome these principal–agent problems, firms put several governance mechanisms in place. We shall discuss several of them next, beginning with the board of directors.

THE BOARD OF DIRECTORS

The shareholders of public stock companies appoint a **board of directors** to represent their interests (see Exhibit 12.1). The board of directors is the centerpiece of corporate governance in such companies. The shareholders' interests, however, are not uniform. The goals of some shareholders, such as institutional investors (e.g., retirement funds, governmental bodies, and so on), are generally the long-term viability of the enterprise combined with profitable growth. Long-term viability and profitable growth should allow consistent dividend payments and result in stock appreciation over time. The goals of other shareholders, such as hedge funds, are often to profit from short-term movements of stock prices. These more proactive investors often demand changes in a firm's strategy, such as spinning out certain divisions or splitting up companies into parts to enhance overall performance. Votes at shareholder meetings, generally in proportion to the amount of ownership, determine whose representatives are appointed to the board of directors.

> **LO 12-4**
>
> Evaluate the board of directors as the central governance mechanism for public stock companies.

> **board of directors**
> The centerpiece of corporate governance, composed of inside and outside directors who are elected by the shareholders.

The day-to-day business operations of a publicly traded stock company are conducted by its managers and employees, under the direction of the chief executive officer (CEO) and the oversight of the board of directors. The board of directors is composed of inside and outside directors who are elected by the shareholders:[26]

inside directors
Board members who are generally part of the company's senior management team; appointed by shareholders to provide the board with necessary information pertaining to the company's internal workings and performance.

- **Inside directors** are generally part of the company's senior management team, such as the chief financial officer (CFO) and the chief operating officer (COO). They are appointed by shareholders to provide the board with necessary information pertaining to the company's internal workings and performance. Without this valuable inside information, the board would not be able to effectively monitor the firm. As senior executives, however, inside board members' interests tend to align with management and the CEO rather than the shareholders.

- **Outside directors**, on the other hand, are not employees of the firm. They frequently are senior executives from other firms or full-time professionals, who are appointed to a board and who serve on several boards simultaneously. Given their independence, they are more likely to watch out for the interests of shareholders.

outside directors
Board members who are not employees of the firm, but who are frequently senior executives from other firms or full-time professionals.

The board is elected by the shareholders to represent their interests. Each director has a *fiduciary responsibility*—a legal duty to act solely in another party's interests—toward the shareholders because of the trust placed in him or her. Prior to the annual shareholders' meeting, the board proposes a slate of nominees, although shareholders can also directly nominate director candidates. In general, large institutional investors support their favored candidates through their accumulated proxy votes. The board members meet several times a year to review and evaluate the company's performance and to assess its future strategic plans as well as opportunities and threats. In addition to general strategic oversight and guidance, the board of directors has other, more specific functions, including:

- Selecting, evaluating, and compensating the CEO. The CEO reports to the board. Should the CEO lose the board's confidence, the board may fire him or her.
- Overseeing the company's CEO succession plan.
- Providing guidance to the CEO in the selection, evaluation, and compensation of other senior executives.
- Reviewing, monitoring, evaluating, and approving any significant strategic initiatives and corporate actions such as large acquisitions.
- Conducting a thorough risk assessment and proposing options to mitigate risk. The boards of directors of the financial firms at the center of the global financial crisis were faulted for not noticing or not appreciating the risks the firms were exposed to.
- Ensuring that the firm's audited financial statements represent a true and accurate picture of the firm.
- Ensuring the firm's compliance with laws and regulations. The boards of directors of firms caught up in the large accounting scandals were faulted for being negligent in their company oversight and not adequately performing several of the functions listed here.

Board independence is critical to effectively fulfilling a board's governance responsibilities. Given that board members are directly responsible to shareholders, they have an incentive to ensure that the shareholders' interests are pursued. If not, they can experience a loss in reputation or can be removed outright. More and more directors are also exposed to legal repercussions should they fail in their fiduciary responsibility. To perform their strategic oversight tasks, board members apply the strategic management theories and concepts presented herein, among other more specialized tools such as those originating in finance and accounting.

To make the workings of a board of directors more concrete, Strategy Highlight 12.1 takes a closer look at corporate governance at General Electric.[27]

Strategy Highlight 12.1

GE's Board of Directors

The GE board is composed of individuals from the business world (chairpersons and CEOs of Fortune 500 companies spanning a range of industries), academia (business school and science professors, deans, and provosts), and government (SEC).[28] Including the board's chairperson, GE's board has 16 members. Experts in corporate governance consider that an appropriate number of directors for a company of GE's size (roughly $260 billion in market capitalization as of the summer of 2015).

At GE (as of 2015), 15 of the 16 board members (94 percent) are independent outside directors. To achieve board independence, experts in corporate governance recommend that two-thirds of its directors be outsiders. GE's board has only one inside director, Jeffrey Immelt, GE's CEO, who also serves as chairman of the board. In roughly half of U.S. public firms, the CEO of the company also serves as chair of the board of directors.

GE's board of directors meets a dozen or more times annually. With increasing board accountability in recent years, boards now tend to meet more often. Moreover, many firms limit the number and type of directorships a board member may hold concurrently. To accomplish their responsibilities, boards of directors are usually organized into different committees. GE's board has five committees, each with its own chair: the audit committee; the management development and compensation committee; the nominating, governance, and affairs committee; the risk committee; and the science and technology committee.

In general, women and minorities remain underrepresented on boards of directors across the United States and throughout most of the world. GE's board is somewhat more diverse in gender when compared with other Fortune 500 companies, which in 2014 averaged 19 percent women on their boards versus 25 percent for GE.

Generally, the larger the company, the greater its gender diversity, as demonstrated in recent years by tracking different levels of the Fortune 1000. For example, in 2014 boards of the Fortune 100 companies averaged 22 percent gender diversity; of Fortune 500 (as noted), 19 percent; and of the bottom half of the Fortune 1000, 16 percent. GE as of this writing ranks number eight in the Fortune 1000 rankings in terms of gender diversity.

Diversity in backgrounds and expertise in the boardroom is considered an asset: More diverse boards are less likely to fall victim to *groupthink*, a situation in which opinions coalesce around a leader without individuals critically challenging and evaluating that leader's opinions and assumptions.

As discussed in Strategy Highlight 12.1, Jeffrey Immelt serves not only as the chief executive officer (CEO) of GE, a roughly $260 billion conglomerate, but also as chairman of the board. This practice of **CEO/chairperson duality**—holding both the role of CEO and chairperson of the board—has been declining somewhat in recent years.[29] Among the largest 500 publicly traded companies in the United States, almost 70 percent of firms had the dual CEO-chair arrangement in 2005 (pre global financial crisis), but this number had declined to 56 percent of companies in 2012 (post global financial crisis).

The functions of the CEO and chairperson of the board roles are distinctly different. A board of directors broadly oversees a company's business activities. The company's CEO reports to the board of directors and acts as a liaison between the company and the board. The CEO has high-level responsibilities of strategy and all other management activities of a company while the functions of the board of directors include approving the annual budget and dealing with stakeholders. Moreover, a CEO is the public face of a company or organization and takes the hit or pat on the back if a company fails or succeeds, while the board of directors is there to steer a company on behalf of shareholders.

Arguments can be made both for and against splitting the roles of CEO and chairperson of the board. On the one hand, the CEO has invaluable inside information that can help in chairing the board effectively. The benefit of a combined CEO and chair of the board is that they can act in unity to streamline and speed the decision-making process

CEO/chairperson duality
Situation where the CEO of a publicly traded company is also the chairperson of the board of directors.

as well as strategy implementation. On the other hand, the chairperson may influence the board unduly through setting the meeting agendas or suggesting board appointees who are friendly toward the CEO. Because one of the key roles of the board is to monitor and evaluate the CEO's performance, there can be a conflict of interest when the CEO actually chairs the board.

OTHER GOVERNANCE MECHANISMS

LO 12-5

Evaluate other governance mechanisms.

While the board of directors is the central governance piece for a public stock company, several other corporate mechanisms are also used to align incentives between principals and agents, including

- Executive compensation.
- The market for corporate control.
- Financial statement auditors, government regulators, and industry analysts.

EXECUTIVE COMPENSATION. The board of directors determines executive compensation packages. To align incentives between shareholders and management, the board frequently grants **stock options** as part of the compensation package. This mechanism is based on agency theory and gives the recipient the right, but not the obligation, to buy a company's stock at a predetermined price sometime in the future. If the company's share price rises above the negotiated strike price, which is often the price on the day when compensation is negotiated, the executive stands to reap significant gains.

stock options
An incentive mechanism to align the interests of shareholders and managers, by giving the recipient the right (but not the obligation) to buy a company's stock at a predetermined price sometime in the future.

The topic of executive compensation—and CEO pay, in particular—has attracted significant attention in recent years. Two issues are at the forefront:

1. The absolute size of the CEO pay package compared with the pay of the average employee.
2. The relationship between CEO pay and firm performance.

Absolute Size of Pay Package. The ratio of CEO to average employee pay in the United States is about 300 to 1, up from roughly 40 to 1 in 1980.[30] Based on a 2014 survey of CEOs among 300 large companies with revenues of at least $9 billion, the average salary for a CEO was $14 million. The five highest paid CEOs were Michael Fries of Liberty Global ($112 million), Satya Nadella of Microsoft ($84 million), Larry Ellison of Oracle ($67 million), Steven Mollenkopf of Qualcomm ($61 million), and Leslie Moonves of CBS ($57 million).[31]

CEO Pay and Firm Performance. Overall, the same survey shows that two-thirds of CEO pay is linked to firm performance.[32] The relationship between pay and performance is positive, but the link is weak at best. Although agency theory would predict a positive link between pay and performance as this aligns incentives, some recent experiments in *behavioral economics* caution that incentives that are too high-powered (e.g., outsized bonuses) may have a negative effect on job performance.[33] That is, when the incentive level is very high, an individual may get distracted from strategic activities because too much attention is devoted to the outsized bonus to be enjoyed in the near future. This can further increase job stress and negatively impact job performance.

THE MARKET FOR CORPORATE CONTROL. Whereas the board of directors and executive compensation are *internal* corporate-governance mechanisms, the *market for corporate control* is an important *external* corporate-governance mechanism. It consists of activist investors who seek to gain control of an underperforming corporation by buying shares of its stock in the open market. To avoid such attempts, corporate managers strive to protect shareholder value by delivering strong share-price performance or putting in place poison pills (discussed later).

Here's how the market for corporate control works: If a company is poorly managed, its performance suffers and its stock price falls as more and more investors sell their shares. Once shares fall to a low enough level, the firm may become the target of a *hostile takeover* (as discussed in Chapter 9) when new bidders believe they can fix the internal problems that are causing the performance decline. Besides competitors, so-called *corporate raiders* (e.g., Carl Icahn and T. Boone Pickens) or *private equity firms* and *hedge funds* (e.g., The Blackstone Group and Pershing Square Capital Management) may buy enough shares to exert control over a company.

In a **leveraged buyout (LBO)**, a single investor or group of investors buys, with the help of borrowed money (leveraged against the company's assets), the outstanding shares of a publicly traded company in order to take it private. In short, an LBO changes the ownership structure of a company from public to private. The expectation is often that the private owners will restructure the company and eventually take it public again through an initial public offering (IPO).

Private companies enjoy certain benefits that public companies do not. Private companies are not required to disclose financial statements. They experience less scrutiny from analysts and can often focus more on long-term viability. In 2013, computer maker Dell Inc. became a takeover target of famed corporate raider Carl Icahn.[34] He jumped into action after Dell's founder and its largest shareholder, Michael Dell, announced in January of that year that he intended a *leveraged buyout* with the help of Silverlake Partners, a private equity firm, to take the company private. In the Dell buyout battle, many observers, including Icahn who is the second-largest shareholder of Dell, saw the attempt by Michael Dell to take the company private as the "ultimate insider trade."

This view implied that Michael Dell, who is also CEO and chairman, had private information about the future value of the company and that his offer was too low. Dell Inc., which had $57 billion in revenues in its fiscal year 2013, has been struggling in the ongoing transition from personal computers such as desktops and laptops to mobile devices and services. Between December 2004 and February 2009, Dell (which until just a few years earlier was the number-one computer maker) lost more than 80 percent of its market capitalization, dropping from some $76 billion to a mere $14 billion. In late 2013, Dell's shareholders approved the founder's $25 billion offer to take the company private, thus avoiding a hostile takeover.

If a hostile takeover attempt is successful, however, the new owner frequently replaces the old management and board of directors in order to manage the company in a way that creates more value for shareholders. In some instances, the new owner will break up the company and sell its pieces. In either case, since a firm's existing executives face the threat of losing their jobs and their reputations if the firm sustains a competitive disadvantage, the market for corporate control is a credible governance mechanism.

To avoid being taken over against their consent, some firms put in place a **poison pill**. These are defensive provisions that kick in should a buyer reach a certain level of share ownership without top management approval. For example, a poison pill could allow existing shareholders to buy additional shares at a steep discount. Those additional shares would make any takeover attempt much more expensive and function as a deterrent. With the rise of actively involved institutional investors, poison pills have become rare because they retard an effective function of equity markets.

Although poison pills are becoming rarer, the market for corporate control is alive and well, as shown in the battle over control of Dell Inc. or the hostile takeover of Cadbury by

leveraged buyout (LBO) A single investor or group of investors buys, with the help of borrowed money (leveraged against the company's assets), the outstanding shares of a publicly traded company in order to take it private.

poison pill Defensive provisions to deter hostile takeovers by making the target firm less attractive.

Kraft (featured in Strategy Highlight 9.2). However, the market for corporate control is a last resort because it comes with significant transaction costs. To succeed in its hostile takeover bid, buyers generally pay a significant premium over the given share price. This often leads to overpaying for the acquisition and subsequent shareholder value destruction—the so-called *winner's curse*. The market for corporate control is useful, however, when internal corporate-governance mechanisms have not functioned effectively and the company is underperforming.

AUDITORS, GOVERNMENT REGULATORS, AND INDUSTRY ANALYSTS. Auditors, government regulators, and industry analysts serve as additional external-governance mechanisms. All public companies listed on the U.S. stock exchanges must file a number of financial statements with the *Securities and Exchange Commission (SEC)*, a federal regulatory agency whose task it is to oversee stock trading and enforce federal securities laws. To avoid the misrepresentation of financial results, all public financial statements must follow *generally accepted accounting principles (GAAP)*[35] and be audited by certified public accountants.

As part of its disclosure policy, the SEC makes all financial reports filed by public companies available electronically via the EDGAR database.[36] This database contains more than 7 million financial statements, going back several years. Industry analysts scrutinize these reports in great detail, trying to identify any financial irregularities and assess firm performance. Given recent high-profile oversights in accounting scandals and fraud cases, the SEC has come under pressure to step up its monitoring and enforcement.

Industry analysts often base their buy, hold, or sell recommendations on financial statements filed with the SEC and business news published in *The Wall Street Journal, Bloomberg Businessweek, Fortune, Forbes,* and other business media such as CNBC. Researchers have questioned the independence of industry analysts and credit-rating agencies that evaluate companies (such as Fitch, Moody's, and Standard & Poor's),[37] because the investment banks and rating agencies frequently have lucrative business relationships with the companies they are supposed to evaluate, creating conflicts of interest. A study of over 8,000 analysts' ratings of corporate equity securities, for example, revealed that investment bankers rated their own clients more favorably.[38]

In addition, an industry has sprung up around assessing the effectiveness of corporate governance in individual firms. Research outfits such as GovernanceMetrics International (now GMI Ratings)[39] provide independent corporate governance ratings. The ratings from these external watchdog organizations inform a wide range of stakeholders, including investors, insurers, auditors, regulators, and others.

Corporate-governance mechanisms play an important part in aligning the interests of principals and agents. They enable closer monitoring and controlling, as well as provide incentives to align interests of principals and agents. Perhaps even more important are the "most internal of control mechanisms": *business ethics*—a topic we discuss next.

12.3 Strategy and Business Ethics

Multiple, high-profile accounting scandals and the global financial crisis have placed business ethics center stage in the public eye. **Business ethics** are an agreed-upon code of conduct in business, based on societal norms. Business ethics lay the foundation and provide training for "behavior that is consistent with the principles, norms, and standards of business practice that have been agreed upon by society."[40] These principles, norms, and standards of business practice differ to some degree in different cultures around the globe. But a large number of research studies have found that some notions—such as fairness, honesty, and reciprocity—are universal norms.[41] As such, many of these values have been codified into law.

Law and ethics, however, are not synonymous. This distinction is important and not always understood by the general public. Staying within the law is a *minimum acceptable standard*. A note of caution is therefore in order: A manager's actions can be completely legal, but ethically questionable. For example, consider the actions of mortgage-loan officers who—being incentivized by commissions—persuaded unsuspecting consumers to sign up for exotic mortgages, such as "option ARMs." These mortgages offer borrowers the choice to pay less than the required interest, which is then added to the principal while the interest rate can adjust upward. Such actions may be legal, but they are unethical, especially if there are indications that the borrower might be unable to repay the mortgage once the interest rate moves up.[42]

To go beyond the minimum acceptable standard codified in law, many organizations have explicit *codes of conduct*. These codes go above and beyond the law in detailing how the organization expects an employee to behave and to represent the company in business dealings. Codes of conduct allow an organization to overcome moral hazards and adverse selections as they attempt to resonate with employees' deeper values of justice, fairness, honesty, integrity, and reciprocity. Since business decisions are not made in a vacuum but are embedded within a societal context that expects ethical behavior, managers can improve their decision making by also considering:

■ When facing an ethical dilemma, a manager can ask whether the intended course of action falls within the *acceptable norms of professional behavior* as outlined in the organization's code of conduct and defined by the profession at large.

■ The manager should imagine whether he or she would feel *comfortable explaining and defending the decision in public.* How would the media report the business decision if it were to become public? How would the company's stakeholders feel about it?

Strategy Highlight 12.2 features Goldman Sachs, which has come under scrutiny and faced tough questions pertaining to its business dealings in the wake of the financial crisis.

In the aftermath of the Abacus debacle (discussed in Strategy Highlight 12.2), Goldman Sachs revised its code of conduct. A former Goldman Sachs employee, Greg Smith, published a book chronicling his career at the investment bank, from a lowly summer intern (in 2000) to head of Goldman Sachs' U.S. equity derivatives business in Europe, the Middle East, and Africa (in 2012).[43] Smith's thesis was that the entire ethical climate within Goldman Sachs changed over that period of time. For its first 130 years, Goldman Sachs was organized as a professional partnership, like most law firms. In this organizational form, a selected group of partners are joint owners and directors of the professional service firms. After years of superior performance, associates in the professional service firms may "make partner"—being promoted to joint owner. During the time when organized as a professional partnership, Goldman Sachs earned a reputation as the best investment bank in the world. It had the best people and put its clients' interests first. Smith describes how Goldman's culture—and with it, employee attitudes—changed after the firm went public (in 1999), from "we are here to serve our clients as honorable business partners, and we have our clients' best interests in mind," to "we [Goldman Sachs and our clients] are all grown-ups and just counter parties to any transaction."[44] In the latter perspective, unsuspecting clients in the Abacus deal were seen just as "counter parties to a transaction," who should have known better.

Some people believe that unethical behavior is limited to a few "bad apples" in organizations.[45] The assumption is that the vast majority of the population—and by extension, organizations—are good, and that we need only safeguard against abuses by a few bad

Strategy Highlight 12.2

Did Goldman Sachs and the "Fabulous Fab" Commit Securities Fraud?

In April 2010, the SEC sued Goldman Sachs and one of its employees, Fabrice Tourre, for securities fraud. The SEC's case focused on one specific, mortgage-related deal during the financial crisis. The deal began in 2006 during the height of the real estate bubble in the United States. The assumption at this time was that house prices could only go up, after years of consistent real estate appreciation. Indeed, real estate prices in the United States had surged, and a speculative bubble had emerged. The real estate bubble was fueled by cheap mortgages, many of them extended to home buyers who really couldn't afford them. John Paulson, founder of the hedge fund Paulson & Co., approached Goldman Sachs with a trading idea to place a billion-dollar bet that the real estate bubble was about to burst. This would occur when borrowers began to default on their mortgages in large numbers. House prices would collapse as distressed borrowers attempted to unload their properties at fire sale prices and banks foreclosed in large numbers. That is exactly what happened.

To benefit from his timely insight, Paulson asked Goldman Sachs to create an investment instrument, later named "Abacus." Goldman Sachs agreed and assigned Tourre to put Abacus together. This investment vehicle was a *collateralized debt obligation (CDO)*. CDOs are made up of thousands of mortgages bundled together into bonds. These bonds provide stable and regular interest payments as long as the borrowers make mortgage payments. CDOs were considered to be much safer investment choices than regular, standalone mortgages because defaults by a few borrowers would not matter much. To make matters worse, rating agencies such as Standard & Poor's, Fitch, and Moody's frequently rated such CDOs as "triple A," which is the highest-quality rating. A triple A rating indicates an "extremely strong capacity" for the borrower to meet its financial obligation. Only a few companies, such as Exxon, Johnson & Johnson, and Microsoft, hold a triple A rating. Given that the Abacus investment vehicle received a triple A rating, many institutional investors such as pension funds bought into it. Everything looked great: Abacus was offered by Goldman Sachs, the number-one investment bank in the world with a stellar reputation, and it had a triple A rating.

But, according to internal e-mails, Paulson and several Goldman Sachs employees, including Tourre, knew otherwise. For example, Tourre, who had earlier been dubbed "fabulous Fab," by a colleague, saw the nickname redound publicly to his discredit when it came out under oath. Specifically, one e-mail was from Tourre to his girlfriend at the time, in which he described himself wistfully in the third person, anticipating the burst of the real estate bubble:

> The entire building is at risk of collapse at any moment. Only potential survivor, the fabulous Fab (. . . even though there is nothing fabulous about me . . .) standing in the middle of all these complex, highly leveraged, exotic trades he created without necessarily understanding all the implications of these monstrosities.[46]

Paulson and Tourre worked together in selecting highly risky CDOs to roll into Abacus. Goldman Sachs then turned around and sold the Abacus CDOs to unsuspecting clients—without, of course, revealing the motivation behind Abacus. Nor did Goldman Sachs reveal that Paulson helped in selecting the riskiest CDOs to be bundled into Abacus. Paulson then took a "short position" in Abacus—meaning he actually bet against its success. Paulson & Co. sold shares that it did not yet own, in anticipation that the value would fall and Paulson would cover its sold shares by buying them at the fallen price. In contrast, institutional investors, often long-term Goldman clients, believed that Abacus was a great investment opportunity. When the real estate bubble burst, Paulson made more than $1 billion from his position in Abacus.

The question that immediately arose was whether Goldman Sachs defrauded investors—as the SEC believed. The SEC argued that the investment bank knowingly misled investors by not revealing its motives in putting Abacus together and not informing them about John Paulson's role in this transaction. Basically, the SEC alleged that Goldman violated its *fiduciary responsibility* and defrauded its clients. Mounting a strong legal defense, Goldman Sachs argued that it is up to the clients to assess the risks involved in any investments. As public pressure mounted, however, Goldman Sachs settled the lawsuit with the SEC by paying a $550 million fine without admitting any wrongdoing. Tourre declined a settlement, and his case went to court. In August 2013, Tourre was convicted of securities fraud.[47]

Tourre ultimately decided not to appeal the decision, stating instead he wished to complete his doctoral studies and hoped to make contributions to scholarship in the field of economics. He is currently pursuing a PhD at the University of Chicago.

actors. According to agency theory, it's the "bad agents" who act opportunistically, and principals need to be on guard against bad actors.

However, research indicates that it is not just the few "bad apples" but entire organizations that can create a climate in which unethical, even illegal behavior is tolerated.[48] While there clearly are some people with unethical or even criminal inclinations, in general one's ethical decision-making capacity depends very much on the organizational context. Research shows that if people work in organizations that expect and value ethical behavior, they are more likely to act ethically.[49] The opposite is also true. Enron's *stated* key values included respect and integrity, and its mission statement proclaimed that all business dealings should be open and fair.[50] Yet, the ethos at Enron was all about creating an inflated share price at any cost, and its employees observed and followed the behavior set by their leaders.

Sometimes, it's the bad barrel that can spoil the apples! This is precisely what Smith argues in regard to Goldman Sachs: The ethical climate had changed for the worse, so that seeing clients as mere "counter parties" to transactions made deals like Abacus possible. One could argue that Tourre simply followed the values held within Goldman Sachs ("profit is king" and "clients are grown-ups"). As a mid-level employee, many view Tourre as the scapegoat in the Abacus case.[51]

Employees take cues from their environment on how to act. Therefore, ethical leadership is critical, and strategic leaders set the tone for the ethical climate within an organization. This is one of the reasons the HP board removed then-CEO Mark Hurd (in 2010) even without proof of illegal behavior or violation of the company's sexual-harassment policy. The forced resignation was prompted by a lawsuit against Hurd by a former adult movie actress who worked for HP as independent contractor alleging sexual harassment. This action goes to show that CEOs of Fortune 500 companies are under constant public scrutiny and ought to adhere to the highest ethical standards. If they do not, they cannot rationally expect their employees to behave ethically. Unethical behavior can quickly destroy the reputation of a CEO, one of the most important assets he or she possesses.

To foster ethical behavior in employees, boards must be clear in their ethical expectations, and top management must create an organizational structure, culture, and control system that values and encourages desired behavior. Furthermore, a company's formal and informal cultures must be aligned, and executive behavior must be in sync with the formally stated vision and values. Employees will quickly see through any duplicity. Actions by executives speak louder than words in vision statements.

Other leading professions have accepted codes of conduct (e.g., the bar association in the practice of law and the Hippocratic oath in medicine); management has not.[52] Some argue that management needs an accepted code of conduct,[53] holding members to a high professional standard and imposing consequences for misconduct. Misconduct by an attorney, for example, can result in being disbarred and losing the right to practice law. Likewise, medical doctors can lose their professional accreditations if they engage in misconduct.

To anchor future managers in professional values and to move management closer to a truly professional status, a group of Harvard Business School students developed an MBA oath (see Exhibit 12.4).[54] Since 2009, over 6,000 MBA students from over 300 institutions around the world have taken this voluntary pledge. The oath explicitly recognizes the role of business in society and its responsibilities beyond shareholders. It also holds managers to a high ethical standard based on more or less universally accepted principles in order to "create value responsibly and ethically."[55] Having the highest personal integrity is of utmost importance to one's career. It takes decades to build a career, but sometimes just a few moments to destroy one. The voluntary MBA oath sets professional standards, but its effect on behavior is unknown, and it does not impose any consequences for misconduct.

EXHIBIT 12.4

The MBA Oath

Source: www.mbaoath.org.

As a business leader I recognize my role in society.

- *My purpose is to lead people and manage resources to create value that no single individual can create alone.*
- *My decisions affect the well-being of individuals inside and outside my enterprise, today and tomorrow.*

Therefore, I promise that:

- *I will manage my enterprise with loyalty and care, and will not advance my personal interests at the expense of my enterprise or society.*
- *I will understand and uphold, in letter and spirit, the laws and contracts governing my conduct and that of my enterprise.*
- *I will refrain from corruption, unfair competition, or business practices harmful to society.*
- *I will protect the human rights and dignity of all people affected by my enterprise, and I will oppose discrimination and exploitation.*
- *I will protect the right of future generations to advance their standard of living and enjoy a healthy planet.*
- *I will report the performance and risks of my enterprise accurately and honestly.*
- *I will invest in developing myself and others, helping the management profession continue to advance and create sustainable and inclusive prosperity.*

In exercising my professional duties according to these principles, I recognize that my behavior must set an example of integrity, eliciting trust and esteem from those I serve. I will remain accountable to my peers and to society for my actions and for upholding these standards.

This oath I make freely, and upon my honor.

12.4 ◂▸ Implications for the Strategist

An important implication for the strategist is the recognition that effective corporate governance and solid business ethics are critical to gaining and sustaining competitive advantage. Governance and ethics are closely intertwined in an intersection of setting the right organizational core values and then ensuring compliance.

A variety of corporate governance mechanisms can be effective in addressing the principal–agent problem. These mechanisms tend to focus on monitoring, controlling, and providing incentives, and they must be complemented by a strong code of conduct and strategic leaders who act with integrity. The strategist must help employees to "walk the talk"; leading by ethical example often has a stronger effect on employee behavior than words alone.

The strategist needs to look beyond shareholders and apply a stakeholder perspective to ensure long-term survival and success of the firm. A firm that does not respond to stakeholders beyond stockholders in a way that keeps them committed to its vision will not be successful. Stakeholders want fair treatment even if not all of their demands can be met. Fairness and transparency is critical to maintaining good relationships within the network of stakeholders the firm is embedded in. Finally, the large number of glaring ethical lapses over the last decade or so makes it clear that organizational core values and a code of conduct are key to the continued professionalization of management. Strategic leaders need to live organizational core values by example.

CHAPTER**CASE 12** / Consider This . . .

SOME CRITICS WOULD argue that Uber's motto seems to be "we don't care for any laws, rules, or regulations; we will deal with the legal fallout later, after we create a large number of happy users and drivers in a city that will support us and will lobby politicians on our behalf." Uber's customers are happy because they can hail rides conveniently and cheaply, often in areas that are underserved by regular taxis, and drivers are happy because they can choose when and how long to work.

Uber is also vehemently defending its policy of dynamic pricing. Without surge pricing, Uber emphasizes, taxis are simply not available during peak times because the limited supply is filled up so quickly. Surge pricing attracts more drivers on the road and helps in matching demand and supply. In further defense of its business model, it stated that the median income of an Uber driver in San Francisco is $75,000 while it is $91,000 in New York City. Meanwhile, Uber is investing heavily in the development of self-driving cars and more sophisticated online mapping systems. The goal appears to be to offer Uber rides by autonomous vehicles, replacing Uber's some 250,000 drivers, at some point in the future. Commenting on this strategic intent, CEO Travis Kalanick stated: "The reason Uber could be expensive is because you're not just paying for the car — you're paying for the other dude in the car. When there's no other dude in the car, the cost of taking an Uber anywhere becomes cheaper than owning a vehicle."[56] After an outcry by Uber drivers on social media such as Facebook and Twitter, Kalanick backpedaled by stating that he doesn't think autonomous cars will be ready for widespread use until 2035. In contrast, Google sees self-driving cars on the road as early as 2020.

Uber is also much more than a simple ride-hailing service. It is the greatest disruptor that the transportation industry has seen since the invention of the automobile. Uber is first disrupting old-line taxi and limo services, often protected by anticompetitive rules and regulations. But Uber also is disrupting transportation more generally. With a fleet of autonomous vehicles offering cheap rides, people don't need to own cars anymore. When car ownership is no longer needed, it will certainly impact the old-line car manufacturers. From there Uber might expand into the "delivery of everything," taking over last-mile deliveries for Amazon. com, Zappos, and other online retailers. Uber might even work in concert with shippers such as UPS and FedEx.

To improve public relations and to lobby politicians, Uber hired David Plouffe, whose claim to fame is being the manager for the 2008 Obama campaign and then a senior adviser to the president. Now senior vice president of policy and strategy at Uber, Plouffe sees Uber as an integral part of the transportation eco system. He argues that as more and more people live and work in cities, Uber will help to address traffic congestion, provide an alternative to personal cars in suburbs, cut down on drunk driving, and provide reliable and safe services to underserved city and suburban areas. Plouffe highlights that one of the reasons people remain trapped in poverty is the lack of reliable transportation, which Uber helps to overcome. Concludes Plouffe, "I don't subscribe to the idea that the company has an image problem. I actually think when you are a disrupter you are going to have a lot of people throwing arrows."[57]

Questions

1. Have you used a ride-hailing service such as Uber or Lyft? How was your experience?

2. Explain Uber's business model and deduce its strategic intent.

3. Do you agree with Peter Thiel's assessment that Uber is the "most ethically challenged company in Silicon Valley"? Why or why not? Explain.

4. Several lawsuits are under way to determine if Uber drivers are independent contractors or employees. The drivers bringing those lawsuits argue that they are employees and should be treated like employees, which would include being reimbursed for expenses such as gas and car maintenance that they currently pay out of pocket.

   - How do you view the so-called sharing economy with companies such as Uber, Airbnb (hospitality), TaskRabbit (house cleaning and odd jobs)?

   - What are the benefits and downsides of being an employee versus an independent contractor? Do you think drivers for Uber (and other ride-hailing services such as Lyft) are independent contractors or are employees?

   - If the ruling of California's labor commissioner should stand that Uber drivers are employees, and this view would prevail in the United States and other countries, what would this do to Uber's business model? Explain.

TAKE-AWAY CONCEPTS

In this final chapter, we looked at stakeholder strategy, corporate governance, business ethics, and strategic leadership, as summarized by the following learning objectives and related take-away concepts.

LO 12-1 / Describe the shared value creation framework and its relationship to competitive advantage.

- By focusing on financial performance, many companies have defined value creation too narrowly.
- Companies should instead focus on creating *shared value,* a concept that includes value creation for both shareholders and society.
- The shared value creation framework seeks to identify connections between economic and social needs, and then leverage them into competitive advantage.

LO 12-2 / Explain the role of corporate governance.

- Corporate governance involves mechanisms used to direct and control an enterprise in order to ensure that it pursues its strategic goals successfully and legally.
- Corporate governance attempts to address the principal–agent problem, which describes any situation in which an agent performs activities on behalf of a principal.

LO 12-3 / Apply agency theory to explain why and how companies use governance mechanisms to align interests of principals and agents.

- Agency theory views the firm as a nexus of legal contracts.
- The principal–agent problem concerns the relationship between owners (shareholders) and managers and also cascades down the organizational hierarchy.
- The risk of opportunism on behalf of agents is exacerbated by information asymmetry: Agents are generally better informed than the principals.
- Governance mechanisms are used to align incentives between principals and agents.
- Governance mechanisms need to be designed in such a fashion as to overcome two specific agency problems: adverse selection and moral hazard.

LO 12-4 / Evaluate the board of directors as the central governance mechanism for public stock companies.

- The shareholders are the legal owners of a publicly traded company and appoint a board of directors to represent their interests.
- The day-to-day business operations of a publicly traded stock company are conducted by its managers and employees, under the direction of the chief executive officer (CEO) and the oversight of the board of directors. The board of directors is composed of inside and outside directors, who are elected by the shareholders.
- Inside directors are generally part of the company's senior management team, such as the chief financial officer (CFO) and the chief operating officer (COO).
- Outside directors are not employees of the firm. They frequently are senior executives from other firms or full-time professionals who are appointed to a board and who serve on several boards simultaneously.

LO 12-5 / Evaluate other governance mechanisms.

- Other important corporate mechanisms are executive compensation, the market for corporate control, and financial statement auditors, government regulators, and industry analysts.
- Executive compensation has attracted significant attention in recent years. Two issues are at the forefront: (1) the absolute size of the CEO pay package compared with the pay of the average employee and (2) the relationship between firm performance and CEO pay.
- The board of directors and executive compensation are internal corporate-governance mechanisms. The market for corporate control is an important external corporate-governance mechanism. It consists of activist investors who seek to gain control of an underperforming corporation by buying shares of its stock in the open market.
- All public companies listed on the U.S. stock exchanges must file a number of financial statements with the Securities and Exchange Commission (SEC), a federal regulatory agency whose task it is to oversee stock trading and enforce

federal securities laws. Auditors and industry analysts study these public financial statements carefully for clues of a firm's future valuations, financial irregularities, and strategy.

LO 12-6 / Explain the relationship between strategy and business ethics.

■ The ethical pursuit of competitive advantage lays the foundation for long-term superior performance.

■ Law and ethics are not synonymous; obeying the law is the minimum that society expects of a corporation and its managers.

■ A manager's actions can be completely legal, but ethically questionable.

■ Some argue that management needs an accepted code of conduct that holds members to a high professional standard and imposes consequences for misconduct.

KEY TERMS

Adverse selection *(p. 409)*

Agency theory *(p. 408)*

Board of directors *(p. 409)*

Business ethics *(p. 414)*

CEO/chairperson duality *(p. 411)*

Corporate governance *(p. 407)*

Inside directors *(p. 410)*

Leveraged buyout (LBO) *(p. 413)*

Moral hazard *(p. 409)*

Outside directors *(p. 410)*

Poison pill *(p. 413)*

Shared value creation framework *(p. 405)*

Shareholder capitalism *(p. 404)*

Stock options *(p. 412)*

DISCUSSION QUESTIONS

1. How can a top management team lower the chances that key managers will pursue their own self-interests at the expense of stockholders? At the expense of the employees? At the expense of other key stakeholders?

2. The Business Roundtable has recommended that the CEO should not also serve as the chairman of the board. Discuss the disadvantages for building a sustainable competitive advantage if the two positions are held by one person. What are the disadvantages for stakeholder management? Are there situations where it would be advantageous to have one person in both positions?

3. The shared value creation framework provides help in making connections between economic needs and social needs in a way that transforms into a business opportunity. Taking the role of consultant to Nike Inc., discuss how Nike might move beyond selling high-quality footwear and apparel and utilize its expertise to serve a social need. Give Nike some advice on actions the company could take in different geographic markets that would connect economic and social needs.

ETHICAL/SOCIAL ISSUES

1. Assume you work in the accounting department of a large software company. Toward the end of December, your supervisor tells you to change the dates on several executive stock option grants from March 15 to July 30. Why would she ask for this change? What should you do?

2. As noted in the chapter, the average compensation for a CEO of a Fortune 500 company was

$14 million, and CEO pay was 300 times the average worker pay. This contrasts with historic values of between 25 and 40 times the average pay. In August 2015 the U.S. Securities and Exchange Commission (SEC) approved a rule mandating that U.S. firms publicly disclose the gap between their CEO annual compensation and the median pay of the firm's other employees.

a. What are the potentially negative effects of this large and increasing disparity in CEO pay?

b. Do you believe that current executive pay packages are justified? Why or why not?

3. The MBA oath (shown in Exhibit 12.4) says in part, "My decisions affect the well-being of individuals inside and outside my enterprise, today and tomorrow."

One example of a large firm reorienting toward this approach is PepsiCo. In the last few years, PepsiCo has been contracting directly with small farmers in impoverished areas (for example, in Mexico). What started as a pilot project in PepsiCo's Sabritas snack food division has now spread to over 1,000 farmers providing potatoes, corn, and sunflower oil to the firm. PepsiCo provides a price guarantee for farmers' crops that is higher and much more consistent than the previous system of using intermediaries. The farmers report that since they have a firm market, they are planting more crops. Output is up about 160 percent, and farm incomes have tripled in the last three years.[58] The program has benefits for PepsiCo as well. A shift to sunflower oil for its Mexican products will replace the 80,000 tons of palm oil it currently imports to Mexico from Asia and Africa, thus slashing transportation and storage costs.

a. What are the benefits of this program for PepsiCo? What are its drawbacks?

b. What other societal benefits could such a program have in Mexico?

c. If you were a PepsiCo shareholder, would you support this program? Why or why not?

SMALL GROUP EXERCISES

//// Small Group Exercise 1

While Uber is a highly valued "unicorn," with a seemingly high disregard for regulations and other external factors that would slow its growth, other competing firms are taking a somewhat different route to the ride-hailing marketplace. For example, Lyft was also started in San Francisco, and since 2012 it has been growing across the country and the globe. Lyft started out as a ride-sharing service (Zimride) targeting college students heading home for the holidays. The firm continues to focus on building a trusting community of drivers and riders—a community that is both social and cost-effective. In fall 2015 Lyft also announced a partnership with China's primary ride-hailing service.[59] Another Uber competitor is Sidecar LLC. Sidecar has a ride-hailing app as well as a carpooling app and an app-enabled delivery service.

In your groups, do some Internet research about Uber competitors (www.lyft.com and www.side.cr will get you started).

1. What similarities and differences do you find in the way these firms have implemented sometimes similar ideas?

2. Discuss why traditional taxi companies, such as Yellow Cabs and those needing medallions (such as in New York City), are choosing to attempt to prohibit these app-enabled, ride-hailing services rather than aggressively implementing their own app-calling systems.

//// Small Group Exercise 2 (Ethical/Social Issues)

It is not unusual for even large corporate boards to have no women or minorities on them. In the United States, women held 19 percent of board seats at Fortune 500 companies in 2012. In her book, *Lean In,* Sheryl Sandberg points out that this number has been flat for 10 years—or, as she puts it, there has been no progress in the past 10 years.[60] In Europe, of the total number of board members in Britain, only 12 percent were women; Spain, France, and Germany all had less than 10 percent.[61] In Norway, by contrast, female members comprised nearly 40 percent of the boards.

So how did Norway do it? In 2003, the government of Norway gave public firms two years to change their boards' composition from 9 percent female to 40 percent female. Is this a good idea? Spain, Italy, France, and the Netherlands must think so: Each country is implementing a similar system. Most recently Germany passed a law requiring that by 2017, 30 percent of non-executive board of director seats of their largest firms be held by women.[62]

1. Discuss in your group to what extent it is a problem that women are proportionally underrepresented on corporate boards. Provide the rationale for your responses.

2. Why has representation by women on U.S. boards not increased over the past 10 years? What actions could be taken by companies to increase participation? What actions could be taken by women who seek to be directors?

3. Would a regulatory quota be a good solution? Why or why not?

4. What other methods could be used to increase female and minority participation on corporate boards? Should it be perceived as a problem when a company seeks minority women as directors so that both statistics rise? What data would you gather in order to verify that such appointments are appropriate?

STRATEGY TERM PROJECT

 *The* HP Running Case, *a related activity for each strategy term project module, is available in Connect.*

//// Module 12: Corporate Governance

In this module, you will study the governance structure of your selected firm. This is also our concluding module, so we will have final questions for you to consider about your firm overall.

1. Find a list of the members of the board of directors for your firm. How large is the board? How many independent (non-employee) members are on the board? Are any women or minorities on the board? Is the CEO also the chair of the board?

2. Who are the largest stockholders of your firm? Is there a high degree of employee ownership of the stock?

3. In reviewing press releases and news articles about your firm over the past year, can you find examples of any actions the firm has taken that, though legal, may be ethically questionable?

4. You have now completed 12 modular assignments about your selected firm. You know a lot about its mission, strategies, competitive advantage, and organization. Is this a company you would like to work for? If you had $1,000 to invest in a firm, would you invest it in the stock of this firm? Why or why not?

*my*STRATEGY

Are You Part of Gen Y, or Will You Manage Gen-Y Workers?

Generation Y (born between 1980 and 2001) is entering the work force and advancing their careers now, as the baby boomers begin to retire in large numbers. Given the smaller size of Gen Y compared to the baby boomers, this generation received much more individual attention from their immediate and extended families. Classes in school were much smaller than in previous generations. The parents of Gen Y placed a premium on achievement, both academically and socially. Gen Y grew up during a time of unprecedented economic growth and prosperity, combined with an explosion in technology (including laptop computers, cell phones, the Internet, e-mail, instant messaging, and online social networks).

Gen Yers are connected 24/7 and are able to work anywhere, frequently multitasking. Due to the unique circumstances of their upbringing, they are said to be tech-savvy, family- and friends-centric, team players, achievement-oriented, but also attention-craving.[63]

Some have called Generation Y the "trophy kids," due in part to the practice of giving all Gen-Y children trophies in competitive activities, not wanting to single out winners and losers. When coaching a group of Gen-Y students for job interviews, a consultant asked them how they believe future employers view them. She gave them a clue to the answer: the letter E. Quickly, the students answered confidently: *excellent, enthusiastic,* and *energetic.* The answer the consultant was looking for was "entitled." Baby boomers believe that Gen Y has an overblown sense of entitlement.

When they bring so many positive characteristics to the workplace, why do baby boomers view Gen-Y employees as entitled? Many managers are concerned that these young workers have outlandish expectations when compared with other employees: They often expect higher pay, flexible work schedules, promotions and significant raises every year, and generous vacation and personal time.[64] Managers also often find that for Gen-Y employees, the traditional annual or semiannual performance evaluations are not considered sufficient. Instead, Gen-Y employees seek more immediate feedback, ideally daily or at least weekly. For many, feedback needs to come in the form of positive reinforcement rather than as a critique.

The generational tension seems a bit ironic, since the dissatisfied baby boomer managers are the same indulgent parents who raised Gen Yers. Some companies, such as Google, Intel, and Sun Microsystems (Sun), have leveraged this tension into an opportunity. Google, for example, allows its engineers to spend one day a week on any project of their own choosing, thus meeting the Gen-Y need for creativity and self-determination. Executives at Intel have learned to motivate Gen-Y employees by sincerely respecting their contributions as colleagues rather than relying on hierarchical or position power. The network-computing company Sun accommodates Gen Yers' need for flexibility through drastically increasing work-from-home and telecommunicating arrangements, so that basically all employees now have a "floating office." Netflix meanwhile has eliminated all tracking of vacation time for employees, essentially allowing unlimited days off—as long as the work still gets done.

1. As this cohort enters the work force, do you expect to see a different set of business ethics take hold?

2. Are efforts such as the MBA oath (discussed in this chapter) reflections of a different approach that Gen Y will take to the business environment, compared with prior generations?

ENDNOTES

1. Peter Thiel, "Uber is most ethically challenged company in Silicon Valley," *CNN Money,* November 18, 2014, http://money.cnn.com/2014/11/18/technology/uber-unethical-peter-thiel/.

2. As quoted in Austin, S., and D. MacMillan, "Is Uber's biggest rival itself? A collection of controversy," *The Wall Street Journal,* November 18, 2014.

3. This ChapterCase is based on: "Potholes ahead," *The Economist,* June 17, 2015; "Driving hard," *The Economist,* June 13, 2015; Ramsey, M., and D. MacMillan, "Carnegie Mellon reels after Uber lures away researchers," *The Wall Street Journal,* May 31, 2015; Austin and MacMillan, "Is Uber's biggest rivals itself? A collection of controversy"; "Uber is most ethically challenged company in Silicon Valley"; "Uber-competitive," *The Economist,* November 22, 2014; "Pricing the surge," *The Economist,* March 29, 2014; and "Tap to hail," *The Economist,* October 19, 2013.

4. Porter, M.E., and M.R. Kramer (2006), "Strategy and society: The link between competitive advantage and corporate social responsibility," *Harvard Business Review,* December: 80–92; Porter, M.E., and M.R. Kramer (2011), "Creating shared value: How to reinvent capitalism—and unleash innovation and growth," *Harvard Business Review,* January–February.

5. "To fly, to fall, to fly again," *The Economist,* July 25, 2015.

6. "The endangered public company," *The Economist,* March 19, 2012; and the classic work by Berle, A., and G. Means (1932), *The Modern Corporation & Private Property* (New York: Macmillan); and Monks, R.A.G., and N. Minow (2008), *Corporate Governance,* 4th ed. (West Sussex, UK: Wiley).

7. NASDAQ was originally an acronym for National Association of Securities Dealers Automated Quotations, but it is now a stand-alone term.

8. Berle and Means, *The Modern Corporation & Private Property;* and Monks and Minow, *Corporate Governance.*

9. This section is based on: Porter and Kramer, "Strategy and society"; Porter and Kramer, "Creating shared value."

10. Friedman, M. (1962), *Capitalism and Freedom* (Chicago, IL: University of Chicago Press), quoted in Friedman, M., "The social responsibility of business is to increase its profits," *The New York Times Magazine,* September 13, 1970.

11. Carroll, A.B., and A.K. Buchholtz (2012), *Business & Society. Ethics, Sustainability, and Stakeholder Management* (Mason, OH: South-Western Cengage).

12. "Milton Friedman goes on tour," *The Economist,* January 27, 2011.

13. For detailed data and descriptions on the GE *ecomagination* initiative, see www.ge.com/about-us/ecomagination.

14. "GE to invest more in 'green' technology," *The New York Times,* May 10, 2005.

15. Porter and Kramer, "Creating shared value."

16. "GE governance principles," p. 1, www.ge.com.

17. Monks and Minow, *Corporate Governance.*

18. Berle and Means, *The Modern Corporation & Private Property;* Jensen, M., and W. Meckling (1976), "Theory of the firm: Managerial behavior, agency costs and ownership structure," *Journal of Financial Economics* 3: 305–360; and Fama, E. (1980), "Agency problems and the theory of the firm," *Journal of Political Economy* 88: 375–390.

19. "Fund titan found guilty," *The Wall Street Journal,* May 12, 2011.

20. Ibid.

21. "Top 10 crooked CEOs," *Time,* June 9, 2009.

22. "Thain ousted in clash at Bank of America," *The Wall Street Journal,* January 23, 2009.

23. Agency theory originated in finance; see Jensen, M., and W. Meckling (1976), "Theory of the firm: Managerial behavior, agency costs and ownership structure," *Journal of Financial Economics* 3: 305–360; and Fama, E. (1980), "Agency problems and the theory of the firm," *Journal of Political Economy* 88: 375–390. For an application to strategic management, see Eisenhardt, K.M. (1989), "Agency theory: An assessment and review," *Academy of Management Review* 14: 57–74; and Mahoney, J.T. (2005), *Economic Foundations of Strategy* (Thousand Oaks, CA: Sage).

24. Fuller, A.W., and F.T. Rothaermel (2012), "When stars shine: The effects of faculty founders on new technology ventures," *Strategic Entrepreneurship Journal*, 6: 220–235.

25. Eisenhardt, K.M. (1989), "Agency theory: An assessment and review," *Academy of Management Review* 14: 57–74.

26. This section draws on: Monks and Minow, *Corporate Governance;* Williamson, O.E. (1984), "Corporate governance," *Yale Law Journal* 93: 1197–1230; and Williamson, O.E. (1985), *The Economic Institutions of Capitalism* (New York: Free Press).

27. This section is based on: "2010 Catalyst census: Fortune 500 women board directors," www.catalyst.org; Baliga, B.R., R.C. Moyer, and R.S. Rao (1996), "CEO duality and firm performance: What's the fuss," *Strategic Management Journal* 17: 41–53; Brickley, J.A., J.L. Coles, and G. Jarrell (1997), "Leadership structure: Separating the CEO and chairman of the board," *Journal of Corporate Finance* 3: 189–220; Daily, C.M., and D.R. Dalton (1997), "CEO and board chair roles held jointly or separately," *Academy of Management Executive* 3: 11–20; "GE governance principles"; Irving, J. (1972), *Victims of Groupthink. A Psychological Study of Foreign-Policy Decisions and Fiascoes* (Boston, MA: Houghton Mifflin); Jensen, M.C. (1993), "The modern industrial revolution, exit, and the failure of internal control systems," *Journal of Corporate Finance* 48: 831–880; "On Apple's board, fewer independent voices," *The Wall Street Journal*, March 24, 2010; "Strings attached to options grant for GE's Immelt," *The Wall Street Journal*, April 20, 2011; Westphal, J.D., and E.J. Zajac (1995), "Who shall govern? CEO board power, demographic similarity and new director selection," *Administrative Science Quarterly* 40: 60–83; and Westphal, J.D., and I. Stern (2007), "Flattery will get you everywhere (especially if you are male Caucasian): How ingratiation, boardroom behavior, and demographic minority status affect additional board appointments at U.S. companies," *Academy of Management Journals* 50: 267–288.

28. For the latest listing of the GE's board of directors, see www.ge.com/about-us/leadership/board-of-directors. For gender diversity among the Fortune 1000, see the advocacy site, 2020 Women on Boards (2020wob.com) and its diversity index.

29. For a research update on the topic of CEO/chairperson duality, see Krause, R., and M. Semadeni (2014), "Last dance or second chance? Firm performance, CEO career horizon, and the separation of board leadership roles," *Strategic Management Journal*, 35: 808–825. This research looks at the three forms of splitting the CEO/chairman roles: apprentice, departure, and demotion. They look at several determinants of the type of split. They find that poor firm performance is more likely to result in a demotion split. The strength of this relationship increases when the board is more independent. The career horizon of the executive is also a determinant. Apprentice shifts involve executives with the shortest career horizons, while demotion shifts are associated with executives with longer career horizons. When performance is poor and boards are independent, the strength of the relationship with career horizon is magnified; see also Flickinger, M., M. Wrage, A. Tuschke, and R. Bresser (2015), "How CEOs protect themselves against dismissal: A social status perspective," *Strategic Management Journal*, March 18.

30. www.faireconomy.org.

31. The data presented here are drawn from Lublin, J. (2015), "How much the best-performing and worst-performing CEOs got paid," *The Wall Street Journal*, June 25, 2015.

32. Lublin, "How much the best-performing and worst-performing CEOs got paid."

33. Ariely, D. (2010), *The Upside of Irrationality: The Unexpected Benefits of Defying Logic at Work and at Home* (New York: HarperCollins).

34. The Dell LBO battle is described in: "Dell buyout pushed to brink," *The Wall Street Journal*, July 18, 2013; and "Monarchs versus managers. The battle over Dell raises the question of whether tech firms' founders make the best long-term leaders of their creations," *The Economist*, July 27, 2013.

35. www.fasb.org: "The term 'generally accepted accounting principles' has a specific meaning for accountants and auditors. The AICPA Code of Professional Conduct prohibits members from expressing an opinion or stating affirmatively that financial statements or other financial data 'present fairly . . . in conformity with generally accepted accounting principles,' if such information contains any departures from accounting principles promulgated by a body designated by the AICPA Council to establish such principles. The AICPA Council designated FASAB as the body that establishes generally accepted accounting principles (GAAP) for federal reporting entities."

36. www.secfilings.com.

37. Lowenstein, R. (2010), *The End of Wall Street* (New York: Penguin Press).

38. Hayward, M.L.A., and W. Boeker (1998), "Power and conflicts of interest in professional firms: Evidence from investment banking," *Administrative Science Quarterly* 43: 1–22.

39. www2.gmiratings.com/.

40. This section draws on and the definition is from: Treviño, L.K., and K.A. Nelson (2011), *Managing Business Ethics: Straight Talk About How to Do It Right,* 5th ed. (Hoboken, NJ: Wiley).

41. Several such studies, such as the "ultimatum game," are described in: Ariely, D. (2008), *Predictably Irrational: The Hidden Forces That Shape Our Decisions* (New York: HarperCollins); and Ariely, *The Upside of Irrationality.*

42. Lowenstein, *The End of Wall Street.*

43. Smith, *Why I Left Goldman Sachs. A Wall Street Story.*

44. Ibid.

45. This section draws on: Treviño and Nelson, *Managing Business Ethics.*

46. Quoted in "'Fab' trader liable in fraud," *The Wall Street Journal*, August 2, 2013.

47. This Strategy Highlight is based on: Smith, G. (2012), *Why I Left Goldman Sachs. A Wall Street Story* (New York: Grand Central Publishing); "The trial of Fabrice Tourre. Not so fabulous," *The Economist*, July 20, 2013; "'Fab' trader liable in fraud"; and "The Abacus trial. No longer fabulous," *The Economist*, August 2, 2013.

48. Treviño, L., and A. Youngblood (1990), "Bad apples in bad barrels: A causal analysis of ethical-decision behavior," *Journal of Applied Psychology* 75: 378–385.

49. Ibid. Also, for a superb review and discussion of this issue, see Treviño and Nelson, *Managing Business Ethics.*

50. McLean, B., and P. Elkind (2004), *The Smartest Guys in the Room: The Amazing Rise and Scandalous Fall of Enron* (New York: Portfolio).

51. "The trial of Fabrice Tourre. Not so fabulous"; "'Fab' trader liable in fraud"; and "The Abacus trial. No longer fabulous."

52. Khurana, R. (2007), *From Higher Aims to Hired Hands: The Social Transformation of American Business Schools and the Unfulfilled Promise of Management as a Profession* (Princeton, NJ: Princeton University Press).

53. Khurana, R., and N. Nohria (2008), "It's time to make management a true profession," *Harvard Business Review*, October: 70–77.

54. For a history of the MBA oath and other information, see www.mbaoath.org. See also

Anderson, M. (2010), *The MBA Oath: Setting a Higher Standard for Business Leaders* (New York: Portfolio).

55. www.mbaoath.org.

56. As quoted in: Austin and MacMillan, "Is Uber's biggest rivals itself?"

57. As quoted in: Swisher, K., "Man and Uber man," *Vanity Fair,* December 2014: 1–11.

58. "For Pepsi, a business decision with social benefit," *The New York Times,* February 21, 2011.

59. Lyft information compiled from: "Is Lyft too cute to fight Uber?" *The New York Times,* December 10, 2014' "Lyft, a year-old startup that helps strangers," *Business Insider,* May 23, 2013; and "Lyft announces deal with Didi Kauidi," *The New York Times,* September 16, 2015.

60. Sandberg, S. (2013), *Lean In: Women, Work, and the Will to Lead* (New York: Knopf).

61. "Skirting the issue," *The Economist,* March 11, 2010.

62. Copley, C., "German parliament approves legal quotas for women on company boards," Reuters March 7, 2015.

63. This *my*Strategy module is based on: "The 'trophy kids' go to work," *The Wall Street Journal,* October 21, 2008; and Alsop, R. (2008), *The Trophy Kids Grow Up: How the Millennial Generation Is Shaking Up the Workplace* (Hoboken, NJ: Jossey-Bass).

64. Survey by CareerBuilder.com.

PART 4

Mini**Cases***

*Interactive case analyses for each of these MiniCases are available on Connect.

Michael Phelps: Strategy Formulation & Implementation

MICHAEL PHELPS, NICKNAMED MP, is the most decorated Olympian of all time. Competing in four Olympic Games,[1] the American swimmer won 22 Olympic medals, including 18 gold! In 2000 at the Sydney Olympics, Phelps at the age of 15 was the youngest U.S. athlete in almost seven decades. In 2008 at the Beijing Olympics, Phelps won an unprecedented eight gold medals, and while doing so set seven world records. Eight short days changed Olympic history and Phelps' life forever, making MP one of the greatest athletes of all time. Immediately after the event, *The Wall Street Journal* reported that Phelps would be likely to turn the eight gold medals into a cash-flow stream of more than $100 million through several product and service endorsements.

Phelps did not rest on his laurels, however. In 2012 at the London Summer Olympics, Michael Phelps added another four gold and two silver medals, elevating him to superstardom. Phelps became an Olympic superhero against long odds. How was he so successful?

Strategy Formulation

In his youth, MP was diagnosed with attention deficit hyperactivity disorder (ADHD). Doctors prescribed swimming to help him release his energy. It worked! Between 2004 and 2008, Michael Phelps attended the University of Michigan, studying marketing and management. He had already competed quite successfully in the 2004 Athens Summer Olympics, where he won eight medals: six gold and two bronze. Right after the Athens Games, the then-19-year-old sat down with his manager, Peter Carlisle, and his longtime swim coach, Bob Bowman, to map out a detailed strategy for the next four years. The explicit goal was to win nothing less than a gold medal in each of the events in which he would compete in Beijing.

Bowman was responsible for getting MP into the necessary physical shape he needed for Beijing and

Michael Phelps, the most decorated Olympian
© DPA Picture Alliance/Alamy

nurturing the mental toughness required to break Mark Spitz's 36-year record of seven gold medals won in the 1972 Munich Olympic Games. Carlisle, meanwhile, conceived of a detailed strategy to launch MP as a world superstar during the Beijing Games. While MP spent six hours a day in the pool, Carlisle focused on exposing him to the Asian market, the largest consumer market in the world, with a special emphasis on the Chinese consumer. MP's wide-ranging presence in the real world was combined with a huge exposure in the virtual world. Phelps posts and maintains his own Facebook page, with 7.6 million "phans." MP is also a favorite of Twitter (1.6 million followers), YouTube, and online blogs, garnering worldwide exposure to an extent never before achieved by an Olympian. The gradual buildup of Phelps over a number of years enabled manager Carlisle to launch MP as a superstar right after he won his eighth gold medal at the Beijing Games. By then, MP had become a worldwide brand.

Frank T. Rothaermel prepared this MiniCase from public sources. This MiniCase is developed for the purpose of class discussion. It is not intended to be used for any kind of endorsement, source of data, or depiction of efficient or inefficient management. All opinions expressed, all errors and omissions are entirely the author's. Revised and updated: August 10, 2015. © Frank T. Rothaermel.

A successful strategy can be based on leveraging unique resources and capabilities. Accordingly, some suggest that MP's success can be explained by his unique physical endowments: his long thin torso, which reduces drag; his arm span of 6 feet 7 inches (204 cm), which is disproportionate to his 6-foot-4-inch (193 cm) height; his relatively short legs for a person of his height; and his size-14 feet, which work like flippers due to hypermobile ankles. While MP's physical attributes are a *necessary* condition for winning, they are *not sufficient*. Many other swimmers, like the Australian Ian Thorpe (who has size-17 feet) or the German "albatross" Michael Gross (with an arm span of 7 feet or 213 cm), also brought extraordinary resource endowments to the swim meet. Yet neither of them won eight gold medals in a single Olympics.

Strategy Implementation

Although Phelps was very disciplined in executing his meticulously formulated strategy to win Olympic gold medals, this is much less true for his strategy implementation to monetize his stardom outside the pool. Following the Beijing Olympics, a photo published by a British tabloid showed Phelps using a bong, a device for smoking marijuana, at a party in South Carolina. Kellogg's immediately withdrew Phelps' endorsement contract. After the London 2012 Olympics, Phelps (then 25) announced his retirement from swimming. After 20 months, he announced that he would come out of retirement. Just a few months later, however, in September 2014, Phelps was arrested for driving under the influence (DUI). In 2004, Phelps had also been arrested for DUI. After the second DUI arrest, Phelps received a one-year suspended jail sentence and 18 months of supervised probation. Phelps also spent 45 days in an in-patient rehab center for alcohol abuse in Arizona. USA Swimming, the national governance body, suspended Phelps for 6 months from all competitions and from representing the United States at the 2015 world championships.

In the spring of 2015, Michael Phelps announced his intention to compete at the 2016 Rio Olympics.

Many experts predict that Phelps has a good chance of winning two more gold medals. What sponsors want to know, however, is whether the promised personal change is real, given that Phelps has made such promises before after his first DUI and then again when photographed smoking a marijuana pipe. Retaining a clean public image will also be critical for Phelps because he just launched his own line of swimwear MP, designed in collaboration with Aqua Sphere, a swimming equipment manufacturer. Phelps grew up idolizing Michael Jordan, and his goal is to change the public image and marketing of swimming to something akin to what Jordan accomplished with his Nike sponsorship in basketball.

DISCUSSION QUESTIONS

1. Olympians generally do not turn into global phenomena. One reason is that they are highlighted only every four years; e.g., not too many people follow competitive swimming or downhill skiing outside the Olympics. How did Michael Phelps (think Lindsey Vonn) turn into a global brand?

2. Which approach to the strategy process did Phelps, his coach, and manager use? Why was this approach successful?

3. Phelps was embroiled in a number of controversies outside the pool. What impact did these shortcomings have on his brand value? What do these incidents tell you about maintaining and increasing brand value over time?

4. What does Phelps need to do if he wants to play a similar transformative role in the marketing and sponsoring of swimming as Michael Jordan achieved in basketball?

Endnote

[1] Sydney in 2000; Athens in 2004; Beijing in 2008; and London in 2012.

Sources: This MiniCase is based on: "Michael Phelps confirms he's aiming to swim at 2016 Olympics," *The Baltimore Sun,* April 15, 2015; "Profile: Michael Phelps—A normal guy from another planet," *Telegraph,* August 15, 2008; "Now, Phelps chases gold on land," *The Wall Street Journal,* August 18, 2008; and "Michael Phelps' agent has been crafting the swimmer's image for years," Associated Press, September 14, 2008.

Teach for America: How to Inspire Future Leaders

TEACH FOR AMERICA describes itself as heading the movement of leaders who work to ensure that youth growing up in poverty get an excellent education. Teach for America (TFA) is a nonprofit organization that recruits college graduates and professionals to teach for two years in economically disadvantaged communities in the United States. The idea behind Teach for America was developed by then-21-year-old Wendy Kopp as her senior thesis at Princeton (in 1989). Kopp was convinced that young people generally search for meaning in their lives by making a positive contribution to society. In the first four months after creating TFA, Kopp received more than 2,500 applicants. Her marketing consisted of flyers in dorm rooms. Corporate America donated $2.5 million in seed grants during TFA's first year. In 2014, TFA's operating budget was $360 million.

The genius of Kopp's idea was to turn on its head the social perception of teaching—to make what appeared to be an unattractive, low-status job into a high-prestige professional opportunity. Kopp established a mission for the organization she had in mind: to eliminate educational inequality by enlisting the nation's most promising future leaders in the effort. Her underlying assumption was that significant numbers of young people have a desire to take on meaningful responsibility in order to have a positive impact on the lives of others. To be chosen for TFA is a badge of honor. Initially, TFA applicants came from Ivy League colleges; in 2014 the top TFA contributors were the University of Michigan, University of California-Berkeley, University of California-Los Angeles, University of Texas at Austin, and the University of North Carolina at Chapel Hill. Today, TFA corps members represent more than 850 colleges and universities throughout the United States. The applicant profile also has changed a bit over time: While initially targeted at college seniors, today, one-third of all TFA corps members applied as graduate students or professionals.

© AP Photo/J.Pat Carter

In 2014, TFA received more than 50,000 applications for only about 5,000 positions across the country. This translates to a mere 10 percent acceptance rate. TFA corps members receive the same pay as other first-year teachers, ranging from $30,000 to $51,500 a year. Since each TFA cohort teaches for two years, in the 2014–15 school year, more than 10,000 corps members taught over 600,000 students. TFA's teaching cohort is also much more diverse than the national average: While less than 20 percent nationwide are teachers of color, about 50 percent of TFA corps members are people of color.

Persuading highly qualified teachers to take up jobs in some inner cities and rural areas has been an elusive goal for many decades. Making TFA highly selective changed the social perception of teaching in underprivileged areas. It is now an honor and great résumé builder to be chosen for TFA. Some notable TFA alumni are now U.S. district judges, state senators, co-founders (of KIPP, Knowledge is Power, college-preparatory schools in disadvantaged communities; and Manhattan GMAT), Olympic medal

Frank T. Rothaermel prepared this MiniCase from public sources. This Mini-Case is developed for the purpose of class discussion. It is not intended to be used for any kind of endorsement, source of data, or depiction of efficient or inefficient management. All opinions expressed, all errors and omissions are entirely the author's. Revised and updated: July 31, 2015. © Frank T. Rothaermel.

winners, chancellors of large public school districts (including the District of Columbia), senior adviser to Hillary Clinton, journalists, actors, and writers. More than 80 percent of TFA's more than 37,000 alumni, however, are still working in the field of education, with the vast majority in public school districts.

Most importantly, TFA makes a significant positive impact on the students. Some 95 percent of all school principals working with TFA members say that these teachers make a positive difference. A detailed and rigorous study commissioned by the U.S. Department for Education finds that students being taught by TFA corps members showed significantly higher achievement, especially in math and science.

DISCUSSION QUESTIONS

1. How did an undergraduate student accomplish what the Department of Education, state and local school boards, and the national Parent-Teacher Association could not achieve despite trying for decades and spending billions of dollars in the process?

2. Applying the Level-5 leadership pyramid, do you believe Wendy Kopp is an effective leader? Why or why not?

3. What are your personal leadership take-aways from Wendy Kopp and the TFA MiniCase? Would you want to apply to be a TFA teaching fellow? Why or why not?

4. How can the frameworks and concepts you studied in strategic management help TFA achieve its mission "to enlist, develop, and mobilize as many as possible of our nation's most promising future leaders to grow and strengthen the movement for educational equality and excellence"?

5. Apply a triple-bottom-line assessment of TFA's performance. How is TFA doing? What are its strong areas, where could its performance be improved? See the TFA site for more information at www.teachforamerica.org.

Sources: This MiniCase is based on: 2014–2015 Teach for America press kit; Simon, S. (2013), "New study finds Teach for America recruits boost student achievement in math," *Politico*, September 10, 2013; Kopp, W. (2011), *A Chance to Make History: What Works and What Doesn't in Providing an Excellent Education for All* (Philadelphia, PA: Public Affairs); Xu, Z., J. Hannaway, and C. Taylor (2008), "Making a difference? The effect of Teach for America on student performance in high school," *Urban Institute*, March 27; www.teachforamerica.org; https://www.teachforamerica.org/tfa-on-the-record; "Wendy Kopp Explains Teach for America," www.youtube.com/watch?v=qLWb_gDIFNk (4.05 min); and Kopp, W. (2001), *One Day, All Children . . .: The Unlikely Triumph of Teach for America and What I Learned Along the Way* (Cambridge, MA: Perseus Book Group).

PepsiCo's Indra Nooyi: Performance with Purpose

"PERFORMANCE WITH PURPOSE is not how we spend the money we make, it's how we make the money," says PepsiCo CEO Indra Nooyi.[1]

As chief executive officer (CEO) of PepsiCo, Nooyi is one of the world's most powerful business leaders. A native of Chennai, India, Nooyi holds multiple degrees: a bachelor's degree in physics, chemistry, and mathematics from Madras Christian College; an MBA from the Indian Institute of Management; and a master's degree in public and private management from Yale University. Prior to joining PepsiCo in 1994, Nooyi worked for Johnson & Johnson, Boston Consulting Group, Motorola, and ABB. She is not your typical Fortune 500 CEO, though: She is well known for walking around the office barefoot and singing—a remnant from her days in an all-girls rock band in high school.

It should come as no surprise, therefore, that Nooyi has been shaking things up at PepsiCo, a company with roughly $67 billion in annual revenues, some 271,000 employees worldwide, and business interests in more than 180 countries. She took the lead role in spinning off Taco Bell, Pizza Hut, and KFC in 1997. Later, she masterminded the acquisitions of Tropicana in 1998 and Quaker Oats, including Gatorade, in 2001. When becoming CEO in 2006, Nooyi declared PepsiCo's vision to be *Performance with Purpose:*

> Performance with Purpose means delivering sustainable growth by investing in a healthier future for people and our planet. . . . We will continue to build a portfolio of enjoyable and healthier foods and beverages, find innovative ways to reduce the use of energy, water and packaging, and provide a great workplace for our associates. . . . Because a healthier future for all people and our planet means a more successful future for PepsiCo. This is our promise.[2]

In particular, *Performance with Purpose* has three dimensions:

1. *Human sustainability.* PepsiCo's strategic intent is to make its product portfolio healthier to combat

Indra Nooyi, chief executive officer of PepsiCo
© Andrey Rudakov/Bloomberg via Getty Images

obesity by reducing sugar, sodium, and saturated fat content in certain key brands. It wants to reduce the salt and fat in its "fun foods" such as Frito-Lay and Doritos brands, and to include healthy choices such as Quaker Oats products and Tropicana fruit juices in its lineup. Nooyi is convinced that if food and beverage companies do not make their products healthier, they will face stricter regulation and lawsuits, as tobacco companies did. Nooyi's goal is to increase PepsiCo's revenues for nutritious foods from $13 billion (approximately 20 percent of the net revenue) today to $30 billion by 2020.

Frank T. Rothaermel prepared this MiniCase from public sources. This MiniCase is developed for the purpose of class discussion. It is not intended to be used for any kind of endorsement, source of data, or depiction of efficient or inefficient management. All opinions expressed, all errors and omissions are entirely the author's. Revised and updated: July 14, 2015. © Frank T. Rothaermel.

2. *Environmental sustainability.* PepsiCo has instituted various initiatives to ensure that its operations don't harm the natural environment. The company has programs in place to reduce water and energy use, increase recycling, and promote sustainable agriculture. The goal is to transform PepsiCo into a company with a net-zero impact on the environment. Nooyi believes that young people today will not patronize or want to work for a company that does not have a strategy that also addresses ecological sustainability.

3. *The whole person at work.* PepsiCo wants to create a corporate culture in which employees do not "just make a living, but also have a life." Nooyi argues that this type of culture allows employees to unleash both their mental and emotional energies.

PepsiCo's vision of Performance with Purpose acknowledges the importance of corporate social responsibility and stakeholder strategy. Nooyi is convinced that companies have a duty to society to "do better by doing better." She subscribes to a triple-bottom-line approach to competitive advantage, which considers not only economic but also social and environmental performance. CEO Nooyi declares that the true profits of an enterprise are not just "revenues *minus* costs" but "revenues *minus* costs *minus* costs to society." Problems such as pollution or the increased cost of health care to combat obesity impose costs on society that companies typically do not bear (externalities). As Nooyi sees it, the time when corporations can just pass on their externalities to society is nearing an end.

The external environment in the soft drink industry, however, has become much more challenging. In the past decade, sales of carbonated soft drinks dropped some 15 percent, reaching the lowest per capita level since 1986. Consumption of bottled water, in contrast, is up some 10 percent since 2013 and predicted to surpass consumptions of carbonated soft drinks in 2017. Energy drinks such as Monster or Red Bull are continuing to grow by double digits in the United States and overseas, making it the hottest category in the soft drink industry.

PepsiCo's archrival Coca-Cola Co. continues to concentrate on its core business in soda and other nonalcoholic beverages. The full-calorie Coke remains America's most popular soda, as more and more people abandon artificial sweetened sodas (number two is PepsiCo's full-calorie cola and number three is Diet Coke). To enhance PepsiCo's strategic focus, critics of

Nooyi propose splitting PepsiCo into two standalone companies. One would focus on beverages (Pepsi, Gatorade, Tropicana); the other would focus on snack foods, several of which such as Lay's or Doritos have become multibillion-dollar brands. This move would unlock additional profit potential, the argument goes, because the well-performing snack food business would no longer need to subsidize underperforming beverages. For the time being, Nooyi has decided that PepsiCo creates more value when both the beverage and snack foods division are together in one corporation, rather than split into two companies.

Although PepsiCo's revenues have remained flat over the past few years, investors see significant future growth potential. Over the last three years, PepsiCo has outperformed Coca-Cola by a relatively wide margin. During this time period, PepsiCo's stock appreciation was more than 32 percentage points higher than that of Coca-Cola (see Exhibit MC3.1). With better than expected financial results, Nooyi certainly stands vindicated after years of criticism. Despite opposition, she stuck by her strategic mantra for PepsiCo—*Performance with Purpose*—and appears to be reaping the rewards.

DISCUSSION QUESTIONS

1. What "grade" would you give PepsiCo CEO Indra Nooyi for her job performance as a strategic leader? What are her strengths and weaknesses? Where would you place Nooyi on the Level-5 pyramid of strategic leadership (see Exhibit 2.4), and why? Support your answers.

2. The first few years after Indra Nooyi took over as PepsiCo's CEO and implemented *Performance with Purpose,* the company underperformed its archrival Coca-Cola Co. by a wide margin. What should a strategic leader do if his or her vision does not seem to lead to an immediate (financial) competitive advantage? What would be your top three recommendations? Support your arguments.

3. Do you agree with Indra Nooyi's philosophy that "performance and purpose are intimately linked and you can't do one without the other"? Support your arguments.

4. PepsiCo's investors require the company to grow about 5 percent or $3.5 billion a year. PepsiCo's top line, however, remained flat for the last few years. Where would future growth for PepsiCo come from?

EXHIBIT MC3.1 / Stock Performance of PepsiCo and Coca-Cola Co., July 2012 to July 2015.

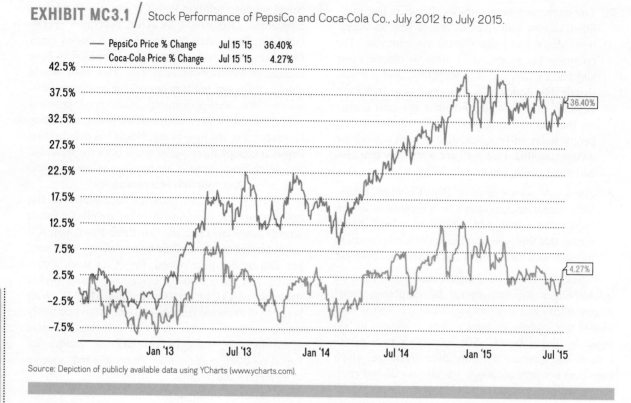

| | PepsiCo Price % Change | Jul 15 '15 | 36.40% |
| | Coca-Cola Price % Change | Jul 15 '15 | 4.27% |

Source: Depiction of publicly available data using YCharts (www.ycharts.com).

Endnotes

[1] As quoted in Safian, K., "It's got to be a passion, it's gotta be your calling: Indra Nooyi," *Fast Company*, October 14, 2014.

[2] www.pepsico.com/Purpose/Overview.html.

Sources: This MiniCase is based on: Esterl, M., "PepsiCo's outlook for year brightens," *The Wall Street Journal*, July 9, 2015; Esterl, M., "Soft drinks hit 10th year of decline," *The Wall Street Journal*, March 26, 2015; Esterl, M., "Monster beverage shares hit high on strong overseas growth," *The Wall Street Journal*, February 27, 2015; Safian, K., "It's got to be a passion, it's gotta be your calling: Indra Nooyi," *Fast Company*, October 14, 2014; "As Pepsi struggles to regain market share, Indra Nooyi's job is on the line," *The Economist*, May 17, 2012; "Should Pepsi break up?" *The Economist*, October 11, 2011; "PepsiCo wakes up and smells the cola," *The Wall Street Journal*, June 28, 2011; "Pepsi gets a makeover," *The Economist*, March 25, 2010; "Keeping cool in hot water," *Bloomberg BusinessWeek*, June 11, 2007; "The Pepsi challenge," *The Economist*, August 17, 2006; PepsiCo shakes it up," *Bloomberg Businessweek*, August 14, 2006; and www.wolframalpha.com and www.ycharts.com.

How the Strategy Process Kills Innovation at Microsoft

SINCE MICROSOFT LAUNCHED Windows 3.0 in 1990, it has dominated the industry for PC operating system (OS) software with a 90 percent market share. Microsoft's huge installed base of Windows operating systems on PCs and its long-term relationships with original equipment manufacturers (OEMs) such as Dell, HP, and Lenovo create tremendous entry barriers for newcomers. Intel's semiconductor chips are the perfect complement to Microsoft's operating system. Every time Microsoft releases a new operating system, demand for Intel's latest microprocessor goes up, because new operating systems require more computing power. Because of the complementary nature of their products, Microsoft's and Intel's alternating advances have created a virtuous cycle, benefiting from network effects. The successful combination of Microsoft's Windows and Intel's processors has produced the *Wintel* (a portmanteau of Windows and Intel) standard in the PC industry. By 1999, Microsoft was the most valuable company on the planet.

Fast-forward to 2015 when Microsoft released Windows 10. For the past quarter century, Microsoft's business model was to establish and maintain the dominance of the Wintel standard in the PC industry. With this standard, Microsoft made money off consumer and business application software such as its ubiquitous Office Suite. Microsoft remains hugely profitable: With some $94 billion in annual revenues (in 2015), it generated over $12 billion in profits! Windows and Office alone generate roughly half of Microsoft's total revenues and 60 percent of profits. The gross margin of "classic" Office is 90 percent, while the new cloud-based Office 365 only has a 50 percent profit margin.

Although Microsoft is highly profitable, its stock price has been flat for most of the 2000s decade, trailing the tech-heavy NASDAQ-100 by a wide margin. Other tech companies such as Google, Apple, or Amazon have created new areas of computing from scratch, and as a consequence, their stock prices have soared. One reason Microsoft's stock price has been

Zune, Microsoft's (failed) digital media player
© David Howells/Corbis

depressed for so many years is that investors don't have high expectations for future growth. This is because since setting the industry standard in personal computing, Microsoft failed to commercialize any category-defining products or services. Why?

Microsoft actually came up with some major breakthroughs, but failed to successfully commercialize them. The root of the problem seems to lie with Microsoft's top-down strategy process. Ever since Windows became the industry standard in 1990, Microsoft's strategy has been defensive: Any new product or extension must strengthen the existing Windows-Office franchise; if not, it will be "killed." Here are some great products and services that Microsoft invented, but never commercialized:

Online Search

Long before Google became the leader in online search, Microsoft had its own working prototype of a

Frank T. Rothaermel prepared this MiniCase from public sources. This Mini-Case is developed for the purpose of class discussion. It is not intended to be used for any kind of endorsement, source of data, or depiction of efficient or inefficient management. All opinions expressed, all errors and omissions are entirely the author's. Revised and updated: August 26, 2015. © Frank T. Rothaermel.

Google forerunner, called Keywords. In 1998, the year Google was founded, Microsoft bought the new venture LinkExchange with its Keywords online search engine. In 2000, Microsoft shut down Keywords because it didn't see a viable business model in online search. After LinkExchange engineers explained to then-CEO Steve Ballmer that Microsoft was making a huge mistake, Ballmer said he wanted to manage through delegation and would not reverse a decision made by managers three levels below him. In 2003, Microsoft had a second chance to innovate in online search. This time it had the opportunity to buy the startup Overture. Microsoft's top management, however, decided that the new venture was overpriced. Yahoo ended up buying Overture and went on to dominate online search for several years, before being eclipsed by Google.

Portable Music Player

In 2001, Apple launched the iPod, a portable music player, with which the floundering company's resurgence began, followed up with the launch of iTunes Music Store with 200,000 songs at 99 cents each in 2003. It laid the foundation of Apple's hugely successful ecosystem combining software, hardware, and services. In 2005, during an employee meeting, one Microsoft engineer asked Steve Ballmer whether Microsoft should compete with Apple's iPod and iTunes. In a sarcastic tone, Ballmer asked the room for a show of hands, "How many people think Microsoft is in the business of selling music?"[1] Not surprisingly, none of the intimidated Microsoft employees raised their hand. More than a year later, Microsoft introduced its own digital music player, the Zune, which flopped.

Tablet Computers

Long before Apple launched the iPad in early 2010, the inventor of Microsoft's highly successful Xbox gaming console had developed a tablet computer called the Courier. The Courier was a fully functioning tablet, which folded like a book, that allowed users to draw on a touchscreen, among other features. Rather than competing against Apple, Ballmer informed the Courier team that he was pulling the plug on the tablet computer because he decided to redirect resources to the next version of Windows. This version's launch was more than two years away. To add insult to injury,

it was Windows 8, Microsoft's failed attempt to straddle desktop and mobile computing.

In the meantime, Apple sold more than 250 million iPads. What's more, the iPad is instrumental in strengthening Apple's ecosystem of tightly integrated software and hardware combined with services. This ecosystem allows Apple to be the world's leader in mobile computing. One other mobile computing invention that Microsoft killed was wearable devices such as smart watches.

Office for iPhone

As soon as Apple released the iPhone in 2007, Microsoft engineers tweaked its PC-based Office Suite to run on the Apple mobile device. Steve Ballmer shut the project down—he had a visceral disdain for Apple, once stomping on an iPhone in an all-employee meeting when he saw a subordinate using the popular Apple device—telling the group that Microsoft needed to focus its resources on Windows 8.

In the meantime, Apple garnered over $500 million in iPhone sales since it was launched in 2007. In 2014, the average price for an iPhone was $625. Although Apple held only 20 percent market share in the smartphone industry, it captured more than 90 percent of the profits. A whopping two-thirds of Apple's annual revenues of some $225 billion is from iPhone sales, surely sufficient to have paid a handsome licensing fee for a Microsoft Office Suite for the iPhone.

Cloud-Based Office Software

Long before cloud-based computing took off, Microsoft developed (in 2000) a fully functioning suite of software applications for the web including an Office-type word-processing software called NetDocs. This project was discontinued in 2001 because Ballmer feared that it would cannibalize sales of the "classic" Office suite. This opened the door for Google to offer cloud-based computing applications such as Google Docs, Google Slides, and Google Sheets, which with Google Drive and Gmail make up the core of Google's cloud-based computing services. This in turn established Google Chrome as the dominant web browser and helped Google's Android to be the leading mobile operating system with some 80 percent market share. In contrast, Microsoft's Windows has some 2 percent market share in mobile computing.

Car Software

In the early 2000s, dozens of Microsoft engineers developed—on their own time—car software that allows drivers to use online maps, have e-mails translated to voice and read to them, as well as play digital music. Ballmer shut the project down, arguing that Microsoft—one of the most cash-rich companies on the planet—could not afford another big bet at the moment. Today, Tesla Motors is as much as a software company as it is a car company, with a market cap of some $30 billion. Moreover, Google is proving that driverless cars (all based on software and sensors) are viable within a few years, and promise to be a multi-billion-dollar industry.

Microsoft's Steve Ballmer admits problems in Microsoft's strategic management process: "The biggest mistakes I claim I've been involved with are where I was impatient—because we didn't have a business yet in something, we should have stayed patient."[2] Steve Ballmer, who served as Microsoft's CEO from 2000 to 2014, was replaced by Satya Nadella. Under its new CEO, Microsoft is attempting to reinvent itself with a new "mobile first, cloud first" strategy. It remains to be seen if Microsoft can once again innovate successfully.

DISCUSSION QUESTIONS

1. Describe the strategic management process at Microsoft under CEO Steve Ballmer (2000–2014).

How are strategic decisions made? What are the strengths and weaknesses of this approach? Explain in detail.

2. Although Microsoft invented some promising computing breakthroughs, and often before competitors, why did Microsoft fail to successfully commercialize them?

3. Why is it so difficult for CEOs of large and successful companies such as Microsoft to balance *exploitation*—applying current knowledge to enhance firm performance in the short term—with *exploration*—searching for new knowledge that may enhance a firm's future performance? What are the trade-offs? How could they be reconciled?

4. What recommendations would you give Microsoft CEO Satya Nadella (since 2014) to redesign Microsoft's strategic management process in order to achieve more successful innovation?

Endnotes

1 Quote drawn from "Next CEO's biggest job: Fixing Microsoft's culture," *The Wall Street Journal,* August 25, 2013.

2 Quote drawn from "Microsoft bid to beat Google builds on a history of misses," *The Wall Street Journal,* January 16, 2009.

Sources: This MiniCase is based on: "Opening Windows," *The Economist,* April 4, 2015; "Next CEO's biggest job: Fixing Microsoft's culture," *The Wall Street Journal,* August 25, 2013; "Microsoft bid to beat Google builds on a history of misses," *The Wall Street Journal,* January 16, 2009; and various annual Microsoft reports.

Strategy and Serendipity: A Billion-Dollar Business

MORE THAN 30 MILLION U.S. men experience some form of erectile dysfunction (ED), and treating the disorder with prescription drugs is a business worth more than $3 billion a year. Was this great pharmaceutical success the result of top-down strategic planning? Far from it. Without serendipity, there would be no success story. Here is how two modern blockbuster drugs were discovered.

In the 1990s, researchers at Pfizer developed the compound UK-95,480 as a potential drug to treat heart disease. In their research, they focused on two things: preventing blood clots and enhancing blood flow. The drug did not achieve the desired effects in human trials, but some men in the test group reported an unexpected side-effect: prolonged erections. Pfizer's managers were quick to turn this unintended result into the blockbuster drug Viagra.

Although the old adage says lightning never strikes the same place twice, it did so in the area of ED drugs. In the mid-1990s, the biotech firm Icos was developing a new treatment for hypertension. Code-named IC-351, the drug moved quickly to clinical trials because of encouraging lab results. Then, unexpected things happened. First was the unusually high compliance rate of patients who took the medication required by the trial, especially males in their 50s, despite the fact that IC-351 turned out to be ineffective in treating hypertension. The second surprise was that many male patients refused to return their surplus pills. The reason: their improved sex life. Icos' IC-351 had failed to treat hypertension but succeeded in treating ED. Marketed as Cialis, it is a major competitor to Viagra, and its success led Lilly to acquire Icos for over $2 billion.

The competition in the ED market is becoming more intense, however, because Pfizer's patent on Viagra is set to expire in 2020. In the meantime, the pharmaceutical company Teva will begin manufacturing and selling a generic version of Viagra in late 2017 under a deal it signed with Pfizer. Lilly's patent

© Miramiska/Shutterstock.com RF

on Cialis is set to expire in late 2017. Lilly is working with the pharmaceutical company Sanofi on a deal that would make Cialis available over-the-counter, and thus the drug could be purchased without a prescription.

DISCUSSION QUESTIONS

1. Do you think "serendipity is random," as some say? Why or why not?

2. What does the discovery of Viagra and Cialis tell us about the strategic management process? About the role of strategic initiatives?

3. Which model of the strategic management process best explains the Viagra/Cialis story? Why? What is the role, if any, of the strategic leader in this process? Explain.

4. If you were to design a strategic management process where "serendipity" is becoming less random, what process would you put in place? Which type of companies could benefits from such a process?

Frank T. Rothaermel prepared this MiniCase from public sources. This Mini-Case is developed for the purpose of class discussion. It is not intended to be used for any kind of endorsement, source of data, or depiction of efficient or inefficient management. All opinions expressed, all errors and omissions are entirely the author's. Revised and updated: July 29, 2015. © Frank T. Rothaermel.

5. Although Viagra is a multibillion-dollar business for Pfizer, what is your prediction concerning Pfizer's profits from Viagra when a generic version is available? What would be a way for Pfizer to respond?

6. Why would Lilly pursue an over-the-counter deal (with Sanofi) rather than a generic drug-licensing deal as Pfizer (with Teva) did?

Sources: This MiniCase is based on: "A plan to sell Cialis, an erectile drug, over the counter," *The New York Times,* May 28, 2014; "Pfizer and Teva settle litigation over Viagra generic," *The Wall Street Journal,* December 17, 2013; "Eli Lilly says Icos acquisition complete," *Reuters,* January 29, 2007; Deeds, D.L., and F.T. Rothaermel (2003), "Honeymoons and liabilities: The relationship between alliance age and performance in R&D alliances," *Journal of Product Innovation Management* 20, no. 6: 468–484; and Mestel, R. (1999), "Sexual chemistry," *Discover,* January: 32.

Apple: What's Next?

IN EARLY 2015, Apple's stock market valuation reached $775 billion, making it the most valuable public company of all time.[1] This made Apple twice as large as Exxon, the number two. Not even 20 years earlier, Apple would likely have gone bankrupt if archrival Microsoft (which enjoyed the same position with a valuation of $615 billion in December 1999) had not invested $150 million in Apple. How did Apple become so successful?

Apple became the world's most successful company based on a powerful competitive strategy. That strategy, conceptualized by co-founder Steve Jobs, combines innovation in products, services, and business models. From near-bankruptcy in 1997, Apple's revitalization really took off in 2001 when it introduced the iPod, a portable digital music player, the same year it opened its first retail stores. Apple's stores now earn the highest sales per square foot of any retail outlets, including luxury stores such as Tiffany & Co. jewelry or LVMH, purveyor of fine handbags and other luxury goods.

In 2003, Apple soared even higher when it opened the online store iTunes. Apple didn't stop there. In 2007, the company revolutionized the smartphone market with the introduction of the iPhone. Just three years later, Apple created the tablet computer industry by introducing the iPad, thus beginning to reshape the publishing and media industries. Further, for each of its iPod, iPhone, and iPad lines of businesses, Apple followed up with incremental product innovations extending each product category. By combining tremendous brainpower, intellectual property, and iconic brand value, Apple has enjoyed dramatic increases in revenues.

A Good Strategy

Why was Apple so successful? Why did Microsoft's once superior market valuation evaporate? Why did Apple's competitors such as Sony, Dell, Hewlett-Packard (HP), Nokia, and BlackBerry struggle or go out of business? The short answer is: Apple had a good strategy. But this begs the question: What is a good strategy?

Apple CEO Tim Cook demos Apple Watch and Apple Pay
© AP Photo/Marcio Jose Sanchez

A good strategy is more than a mere goal or a company slogan. A good strategy defines the competitive challenges facing an organization through a critical

Frank T. Rothaermel prepared this MiniCase from public sources. This Mini-Case is developed for the purpose of class discussion. It is not intended to be used for any kind of endorsement, source of data, or depiction of efficient or inefficient management. All opinions expressed, all errors and omissions are entirely the author's. Revised and updated: July 24, 2015. © Frank T. Rothaermel.

and honest assessment of the status quo. A good strategy also provides an overarching approach (policy) on how to deal with the competitive challenges identified. Last, a good strategy requires effective implementation through a coherent set of actions. A *good strategy*, therefore, consists of three elements:[2]

1. A *diagnosis* of the competitive challenge.
2. A *guiding policy* to address the competitive challenge.
3. A *set of coherent actions* to implement the firm's guiding policy.

THE COMPETITIVE CHALLENGE. First, consider the diagnosis of the competitive challenge. Above, we briefly trace Apple's renewal from the year 2001, when it hit upon the product and business-model innovations of the iPod/iTunes combination. Prior to that, Apple was merely a niche player in the desktop-computing industry and struggling financially. Steve Jobs turned the sinking company around by focusing on only two computer models (one laptop and one desktop) in each of two market segments (the professional market and the consumer market) as opposed to dozens of non-differentiated products within each segment. This streamlining of its product lineup enhanced Apple's strategic focus. Even so, the outlook for Apple was grim. Jobs believed that Apple, with less than 5 percent market share, could not win in the personal computer industry where desktops and laptops had become commoditized gray boxes. In that world, Microsoft, Intel, and Dell were the star performers. Jobs needed to create the "next big thing."[3]

A GUIDING POLICY. Second, let's consider the guiding policy. Apple shifted its competitive focus away from personal computers to mobile devices. In doing so, Apple disrupted several industries through its product and business-model innovations. Combining hardware (i.e., the iPod) with a complementary service product (i.e., the iTunes Store) enabled Apple to devise a new business model. Users could now download individual songs legally (at 99 cents) rather than buying an entire CD or downloading the songs illegally using Napster and other file-sharing services. The availability of the iTunes Store drove sales of iPods. Along with rising sales for the new iPod and iTunes products, demand rose for iMacs. The new products helped disrupt the existing personal computer market, because people wanted to manage their music and photos on a computer that worked seamlessly with their mobile devices. Apple then leveraged the success of the iPod/iTunes business-model innovation, following up with product-category-defining innovations when launching the iPhone (in 2007) and the iPad (in 2010).

COHERENT ACTIONS. Third, Apple implemented its guiding policy with a set of coherent actions. Apple's coherent actions took a two-pronged approach: It drastically streamlined its product lineup through a simple rule—"we will make only one laptop and one desktop model for each of the two markets we serve, professional and consumer." It also disrupted the industry status quo through a potent combination of product and business model innovations, executed at planned intervals. These actions allowed Apple to create a string of temporary competitive advantages (see Exhibit MC6.1). Taken together, this allowed Apple to sustain its superior performance for over a decade.

Past performance, however, is no guarantee of future performance. Microsoft was once the most valuable company in the world but has since struggled to keep up with Apple. At the same time, Microsoft, as well as Google, Samsung, Amazon, and others, is working hard to neutralize Apple's competitive advantage.

The trillion-dollar question is whether Apple can continue to maintain a competitive advantage in the face of increasingly strong competition and rapidly changing industry environments. In both mobile payment systems (Apple Pay launched in 2014) and music streaming (Apple Music launched in 2015), Apple was a later mover. The Apple Watch, introduced in 2015, is the first new product category Apple launched since the iPad in 2010. Although Apple has 55 percent market share and captures over 90 percent of profits in the smartphone industry (as of 2015), over 60 percent of Apple's $225 billion revenues come from the iPhone.

DISCUSSION QUESTIONS

1. Explain Apple's success over the last decade. Think about which industries it has disrupted and how. Also look at Apple's main competitors.

2. Is Apple's success attributable to industry effects or firm effects, or a combination of both? Explain.

EXHIBIT MC6.1 / Apple's Net Income ($ billions) and Key Events, 1978–2015.

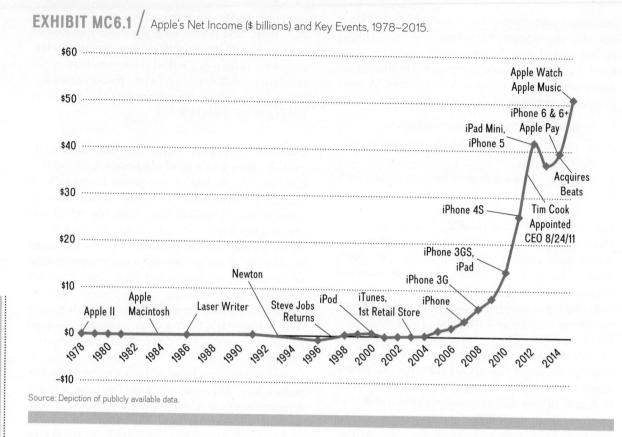

Source: Depiction of publicly available data.

3. What are the greatest challenges Apple is facing? Detail them by internal weaknesses and external threats. How can Apple transform internal weaknesses into strengths, and external threats into opportunities?

4. Apply the three-step process for developing a *good strategy* outlined above (diagnose the competitive challenge, derive a guiding policy, and implement a set of coherent actions) to Apple's situation today. Which recommendations would you have for Apple to outperform its competitors in the future? Be specific.

Endnotes

[1] Apple's valuation is in absolute dollars, not in real (inflation-adjusted) dollars. When adjusted for inflation since 1999, Microsoft's record market valuation would be roughly $850 billion in 2015.

[2] This discussion is based on Rumelt, R. (2011)., *Good Strategy, Bad Strategy* (New York: Crown Business).

[3] Ibid, p. 14.

Sources: This MiniCase is based on: "Apple Earnings Surge 33% on iPhone Sales," *The Wall Street Journal,* April 27, 2015; "Apple, feeling heat from Spotify, to offer streaming music service," *The Wall Street Journal,* June 1, 2015; "Apple's share of smartphone industry's profits soars to 92%," *The Wall Street Journal,* July 12, 2015; "Apple's Market Cap Loses $60 Billion After iPhone Sales Disappoint," *The Wall Street Journal,* July 22, 2015; and Sull, D., K.E. Eisenhardt (2015), *Simple Rules: How to Thrive in a Complex World* (New York: Houghton Mifflin Harcourt); "Apple plans web TV service in fall," *The Wall Street Journal,* March 17, 2015; Kane, I.Y. (2014), *Haunted Empire: Apple After Steve Jobs* (New York: HarperCollins); "An iPopping phenomenon," *The Economist,* March 24, 2012; "From pipsqueak to powerhouse," *The Economist,* August 21, 2012; "iRational?" *The Economist,* March 24, 2012; "Apple market value hits record high," *The Wall Street Journal,* August 20, 2012; "GiantApple," *The Economist,* August 21, 2012; Sull, D., and K.E. Eisenhardt (2012), "Simple rules for a complex world," *Harvard Business Review,* September; Isaacson, W. (2011), *Steve Jobs* (New York: Simon & Schuster); and Rumelt, R. (2011), *Good Strategy, Bad Strategy* (New York: Crown Business).

Starbucks: Schultz Serves Up a Turnaround

INSPIRED BY ITALIAN coffee bars, Starbucks CEO Howard Schultz set out to provide a completely new consumer experience. The trademark of any Starbucks is its ambience—where music and comfortable chairs and sofas encourage customers to sit and enjoy their beverages and, more recently, food and even wine. While hanging out at Starbucks, customers can use the complimentary wireless service or just visit with friends. The barista seems to speak a foreign language as she rattles off the offerings: Caffé Misto, Caramel Macchiato, Cinnamon Dolce Latte, Espresso Con Panna, or Mint Mocha Chip Frappuccino, among some 30 different coffee blends. Dazzled and enchanted, customers pay $4 or more for a venti-sized drink. Starbucks has been so successful in creating its ambience that customers keep coming back for more.

Starbucks' core competency is to create a unique consumer experience the world over. The strategic intent was to create a "third place," between home and work, where people wanted to visit, ideally daily. Customers are paying for the unique experience and ambience, not for the cup of coffee. The consumer experience that Starbucks created is a valuable, rare, and costly to imitate intangible resource. This allowed Starbucks to gain a competitive advantage. Since 2000, Starbucks' revenues have grown 10-fold, from less than $2 billion to some $20 billion in 2015.

While core competencies are often built through learning from experience, they can atrophy through forgetting. This is what happened to Starbucks. Between 2004 and 2008, Starbucks expanded operations rapidly by doubling the number of stores from 8,500 to almost 17,000 stores (see Exhibit MC7.1). It also branched out into ice cream, desserts, sandwiches, books, music, and other retail merchandise, straying from its core business.

Trying to keep up with its explosive growth in both the number of stores and product offerings, Starbucks began to forget what made it unique. It lost the appeal that made it special, and its unique culture got diluted.

China represents a future growth opportunity for Starbucks, assuming it can transfer its core competency successfully.
© Stephen Shaver/Zumapress.com/Alamy Live News

For example, baristas used to grind beans throughout the day whenever a new pot of coffee had to be brewed (which was at least every eight minutes). The grinding sounds and fresh coffee aroma were trademarks of Starbucks stores. Instead, to accommodate its fast growth, many baristas began to grind all of the day's coffee beans early in the morning and store them for the rest of the day. New espresso machines, designed for efficiency, were so tall that they physically blocked interaction between baristas and customers. Although these and other operations changes allowed Starbucks to reduce costs and improve efficiency, they undercut Starbuck's primary reason for success—that going to Starbucks was not simply a stop for caffeine; it was a sensory experience.

Frank T. Rothaermel prepared this MiniCase from public sources. He gratefully acknowledges James Hoadley for research assistance. This MiniCase is developed for the purpose of class discussion. It is not intended to be used for any kind of endorsement, source of data, or depiction of efficient or inefficient management. All opinions expressed, all errors and omissions are entirely the author's. Revised and updated: August 20, 2015. © Frank T. Rothaermel.

EXHIBIT MC7.1 / Total Number of Starbucks Stores and Revenues ($ billions), 1971–2015

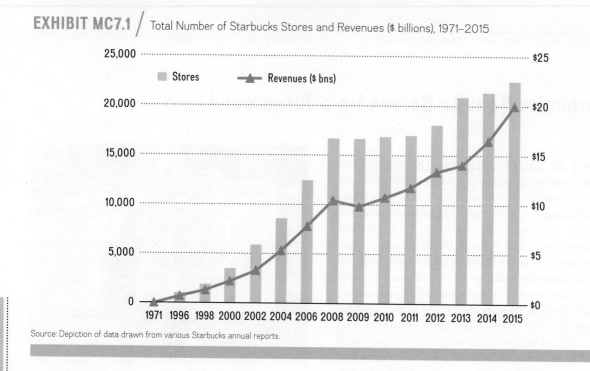

Source: Depiction of data drawn from various Starbucks annual reports.

The negative impact of cost-reduction measures was underscored when Starbucks lost a blind taste-test to fast-food giant McDonald's. Among six coffees tested, Starbucks came in last. Even run-of-the-mill supermarket coffees sold in huge cans were rated higher. Some customers don't like Starbucks coffee and gave the chain the nickname "Charbucks"—because critics say that a lot of the coffee has an overly roasted quality, a dark and bitter taste.

To make matters worse, the global financial crisis (2008–2009) hit Starbucks hard. The first items consumers go without during recession are luxury items such as a $4 coffee at Starbucks (see revenue drop in Exhibit MC7.1).

Coming out of an eight-year retirement, Howard Schultz again took the reins as CEO in January 2008, attempting to re-create what had made Starbucks special. He immediately launched several strategic initiatives to turn the company around. Just a month after coming back, Schultz ordered more than 7,000 Starbucks stores across the United States to close for one day so that baristas could learn the perfect way to prepare coffee. The company lost over $6 million in revenue on that one day. This exacerbated investor jitters, but Schultz felt the importance of relearning

how to create a unique Starbucks experience was key to bringing back its unique corporate culture.

In 2009, Starbucks introduced Via, its new instant coffee, a move that some worried might further dilute the brand. In 2010, Schultz rolled out new customer service guidelines: Baristas would no longer multitask, making multiple drinks at the same time, but would instead focus on no more than two drinks at a time, starting a second one while finishing the first. Schultz also focused on readjusting store managers' goals. Before Schultz's return, managers had been given a mandate to focus on sales growth. Schultz, however, knew that Starbucks' main differentiator was its special customer experience. The CEO instructed managers to focus on what had made the Starbucks brand successful in the first place.

Although its earlier attempt to diversify away from its core business in the mid-2000s failed, under Schultz, Starbucks was able to successfully introduce food items. Attempting to drive more store traffic in other than the morning hours where customers need their daily caffeine shot, the chain has added baked goods, sandwiches, and other food items to its menu. To get more customers into its stores in the late afternoon and early evening—traditionally its slowest time—Starbucks stores now offer items such as vegetables, flatbread pizza, plates of cheese, and desserts. It even introduced alcoholic beverages such as wine and beer, available after 4 p.m. Starbucks' goal is to double its revenues from food over the next few years and to be seen as an evening food-and-wine destination. To symbolize its transition from a traditional coffeehouse, Starbucks dropped the word *coffee* from its logo.

Schultz also pushed the adoption of new technology to engage with customers more intimately and effectively. Starbucks now uses social media platforms Facebook and Twitter to communicate with customers more or less in real time. Its highly successful Starbucks loyalty program has over 10 million regular users. Some 20 percent of all transactions in U.S. stores are now made using mobile devices. The latest tech innovation is a Starbucks app that allows customers to order and pay for drinks and food ahead of time, so that they can bypass standing in line and just need to pick up their order.

Finally, as the U.S. market appears to be saturated with some 12,000 stores, Schultz believes that Starbucks has a great growth opportunity by opening more cafés overseas. Starbucks is planning to have more than 3,000 stores in China by 2019, up from 1,500 in 2015. Starbucks also plans to double its number of cafés elsewhere in Asia to more than 4,000 in the next few years.

As the creator of Starbucks, however, Schultz enjoyed a degree of freedom that an ordinary CEO would not have had. Howard Schultz is to Starbucks much like Steve Jobs was to Apple. Schultz has the reputation and power of personality to implement a change that reduces operational effectiveness in favor of delighting customers. Schultz was able to orchestrate a successful turnaround, and with it Starbucks was able to gain and sustain a competitive advantage.

Since 2009, Starbucks' stock price has appreciated by over 1,000 percent, outperforming the Dow Jones Industrial Average by some 940 percentage points.[1]

DISCUSSION QUESTIONS

1. How did Starbucks create its uniqueness in the first place? Why was it so successful?

2. To be a source of competitive advantage over time, core competencies need to continuously be honed and upgraded. Why and how did Starbucks lose its uniqueness and struggle in the mid-2000s?

3. What strategic initiatives did Howard Schultz put in place to re-create Starbucks' uniqueness after his return in 2008? Detail each strategic initiative, and explain why a specific strategic initiative was successful, if so.

4. What makes Schultz a great strategic leader?

5. How is Starbucks trying to grow in the future? Do you think it will continue to be so successful? Why or why not?

Endnote

1 Between January 1, 2009, and August 20, 2015, Starbucks shares appreciated by 1,030 percent, while the Dow Jones Industrial Average appreciated by 91 percent.

Sources: This MiniCase is based on: "Starbucks raises prices despite declining coffee costs," *The Wall Street Journal,* July 6, 2015; "Starbucks profit jumps, as revenue surges 18%," *The Wall Street Journal,* July 23, 2015; "Starbucks aims to double U.S. food sales," *The Wall Street Journal,* December 4, 2014; "Forty years young: A history of Starbucks," *The Telegraph,* May 11, 2011; "At Starbucks, baristas told no more than two drinks," *The Wall Street Journal,* October 13, 2010; "Latest Starbucks buzzword: 'Lean' Japanese techniques," *The Wall Street Journal,* August 4, 2009; Behar, H. (2007), *It's Not About the Coffee: Leadership Principles from a Life at Starbucks* (New York: Portfolio); Schultz, H., and D.J. Yang (1999), *Pour Your Heart Into It: How Starbucks Built a Company One Cup at a Time* (New York: Hyperion); "Five things Starbucks won't tell you," *The Wall Street Journal* video, http://on.mktw.net/1UVStO6; and http://investor.starbucks.com.

Nike's Core Competency: The Risky Business of Fairy Tales

DURING THE LAST decade, Nike's annual revenues doubled and by 2015 was over $30 billion. Having a globally recognized brand, Nike is the undisputed leader in the athletic shoe and apparel industry. The number-two adidas has some $19 billion in sales, while recent entrant Under Armour reports revenues of $3 billion. Nike is tremendously successful, holding close to a 60 percent market share in running and nearly a 90 percent market share in basketball shoes and apparel.

Nike Co-founders: Bill Bowerman and Phil Knight

The Beaverton, Oregon, company has come a long way from its humble beginnings. It was founded by University of Oregon track and field coach Bill Bowerman and middle-distance runner Phil Knight in 1964 and called Blue Ribbon Sports. In 1971, the company was renamed Nike (Greek mythology's goddess of victory) and the now iconic "swoosh" was designed by a Portland State University student.

Coach Bowerman was a true innovator because he constantly sought ways to give his athletes a competitive edge. He experimented with many factors affecting running performance, from different track surfaces to rehydration drinks. Bowerman's biggest focus, however, was on providing a better running shoe for his athletes. While sitting at the breakfast table one Sunday morning and absentmindedly looking at his waffle iron, Bowerman had an epiphany. He poured hot, liquid urethane into the waffle iron—ruining it in the process but coming up with the now famous waffle-type sole that not only provided better traction but was also lighter than traditional running shoes.

After completing his undergraduate degree at the University of Oregon and serving in the U.S. Army, Phil Knight entered the MBA program at Stanford. One entrepreneurship class required him to come up with a business idea. He wrote a term paper on how

Brazil's National Soccer Team, World Cup 2014 in Brazil
© Jorge Silva/Reuters/Corbis

to disrupt the leading athletic shoemaker, adidas. The research question he came up with was, "Can Japanese sports shoes do to German sports shoes what Japanese cameras have done to German cameras?"[1] At that time, adidas athletic shoes were the gold standard. They were also expensive and hard to find in the United States. After several failed attempts to interest Japanese sneaker makers, Knight struck a distribution agreement with Tiger Shoes. After his first shipment arrived in the United States, Phil Knight sent some of the running shoes to his former coach Bill Bowerman, hoping to make a sale. To his surprise, Bowerman replied that he was interested in becoming a business partner and contributing his innovative ideas on how to improve running shoes, including the waffle design. With an investment of $500 each and a handshake, the venture commenced.

Creating Heroes

Based on a highly successful string of innovations including Nike Air, by 1979 the company had captured

Frank T. Rothaermel prepared this MiniCase from public sources. This MiniCase is developed for the purpose of class discussion. It is not intended to be used for any kind of endorsement, source of data, or depiction of efficient or inefficient management. All opinions expressed, all errors and omissions are entirely the author's. Revised and updated: August 27, 2015. © Frank T. Rothaermel.

more than a 50 percent market share for running shoes in the United States. A year later, Nike went public. In 1984, Nike signed Michael Jordan—whom many consider the greatest basketball player of all time— with an unprecedented multimillion-dollar endorsement deal. Rather than spreading its marketing budget more widely as was common in the sports industry at that time, Nike made the unorthodox move to spend basically its entire budget for a specific sport on a single star athlete. Nike sought to sponsor future superstars that embodied an unlikely success story. Michael Jordan did not make the varsity team as a junior in high school, only to become the greatest basketball player ever. Nike's Air Jordan basketball shoes are all-time classics that remain popular to this day.

In the 1990s and 2000s, Nike continued to sponsor track and field stars such as Marion Jones as well as Kobe Bryant in basketball. With the help of major celebrity endorsements, Nike was also able to move on to different sports and their superstars, including golf with Tiger Woods, cycling with Lance Armstrong, soccer with Wayne Rooney, and football with Michael Vick.

Nike is less about running shoes or sports apparel than about unlocking human potential. This is captured in Nike's mission "to bring inspiration and innovation to every athlete in the world" (and "if you have a body, you are an athlete").[2] Nike uses its heroes to tell a story whose moral is that through sheer will, tenacity, and hard work, anyone can unlock the hero within and achieve amazing things. Nike will help everyone become a hero. *Just Do It!* This type of mythical brand image has allowed Nike to not only enter but often dominate one sport after another, from running to ice hockey. It spends more than $1 billion a year sponsoring athletes. Nike picks athletes that succeeded against the odds—cancer survivor Lance Armstrong, double amputee "blade runner" Oscar Pistorius, and other athletes hailing from disadvantaged backgrounds.

Nike astutely focuses on its core competency in athlete sponsorship and design, while it outsources non-core activities such as manufacturing and much of retailing. To create heroes, Nike has to engage in a number of activities: find athletes that succeed against the odds; identify them before they are well-known superstars; sign the athletes; create products that are closely linked with the athlete; promote the athletes or teams and Nike products through TV ads and social media to create the desired image; and so on. Each

Oscar Pistorius (left), and Lance Armstrong (right), some of Nike's past celebrity endorsements
(left) © Ian Walton/Getty Images; (right) © Epa European Pressphoto Agency b.v./EPA/Alamy

activity contributes to the relative value of the product and service offering in the eyes of potential customers and the firm's relative cost position vis-à-vis its rivals. Over time, Nike developed a deep expertise in creating heroes. More importantly, having consistently better expectations of the future value of resources allows Nike not only to shape the desired image of the athlete, but also to capture some of the value these athletes create.

Although this core competency made Nike highly successful, it has not been without considerable risks. Repeatedly, Nike's "heroes" have become unmasked as cheaters, frauds, and criminals, some of whom have committed serious felonies, such as (culpable) homicide. Long-time CEO and chairman Phil Knight declared that scandals surrounding its superstar endorsement athletes are "part of the game."[3] In some instances, Nike continued to sponsor its athletes involved in various scandals, while in others it terminated its lucrative endorsement contracts. Nike continued to sponsor NBA star Kobe Bryant who was cleared of alleged rape charges. After Tiger Woods was engulfed in an infidelity scandal, Nike continued to sponsor the golf superstar. In 2007, Nike ended its endorsement contract with NFL quarterback Michael Vick after a public outcry and his subsequent felony conviction of running a dog-fighting ring and engaging in animal cruelty. In 2011, after serving a prison sentence and restarting his career at the Philadelphia Eagles, Nike signed a new endorsement deal with Michael Vick. In 2012, Nike terminated its long-term relationship with disgraced cyclist Lance Armstrong. Just before Armstrong's public admission to doping in an interview with Oprah Winfrey, Knight answered,

"Never say never," when asked if Nike would sponsor Armstrong again in the future. In 2013, Nike removed its ads with Oscar Pistorius and the unfortunate tagline "I am the bullet in the chamber," after the homicide charges against the South African track and field athlete.

In 2014, Nike got entangled in the FIFA (the world governing body of soccer) bribery scandal. It began 20 years earlier when Nike decided to gain a stronger presence in soccer after the 1994 World Cup was held in the United States. In 1996, Nike signed a long-term sponsorship agreement with the Brazilian national team worth hundreds of millions of dollars. This was a huge win for Nike because soccer has been the basis of adidas' success, much like running and basketball has been for Nike. Moreover, Brazil won the tournament five times (more than any other nation) and is the only team to have played in every tournament, which is only held every four years.

Nike is now alleged to have paid some $30 million to a middleman, who used that money for bribing soccer officials and politicians in Brazil. This middleman—Jose Hawilla—has admitted a number of crimes including fraud, money laundering, and extortion related to the FIFA soccer investigation by U.S. prosecutors.

Time and time again Nike's heroes have fallen from grace, and the company itself has fallen under suspicion of wrongdoing. Clearly, Nike's approach in building its core competency of creating heroes is not without risks. Too many of these public relations disasters combined with too severe shortcomings of some of Nike's most celebrated heroes could damage the company's reputation and lead to a loss of competitive advantage. As Nike veers from one public relations disaster to the next, disappointment with the brand and its promise may eventually set in, causing customers to go elsewhere.

DISCUSSION QUESTIONS

1. The MiniCase indicates that Nike's core competency is to create heroes. What does this mean? How did Nike build its core competency? Does it obey the *VRIO* attributes (valuable, rare, inimitable, and organized to capture value based on the resource-based view of the firm)?

2. What would it take for Nike's approach to turn from a strength into a weakness? Did this tipping point already occur? Why or why not?

3. What recommendations would you have for Nike? Can you identify a way to reframe the competency of creating heroes? Or a new way to think of heroes, teams, or sports that would continue to build the brand?

4. If you are a competitor of Nike (such as adidas, Under Armour, New Balance, or Li-Ning), how could you exploit Nike's apparent vulnerability? Provide a set of concrete recommendations.

Endnotes

[1] As quoted in: "Knight the king: The founding of Nike," Harvard Business School Case Study, 9-810-077, p. 2.

[2] http://help-en-us.nike.com/app/answers/detail/a_id/113/p/3897.

[3] According to Reuters, cited in: www.sportbusiness.com, December 15, 2009.

Sources: This MiniCase is based on: "Nike's bold push into soccer entangled it in FIFA probe," *The Wall Street Journal,* June 4, 2015; "The big business of fairy tales," *The Wall Street Journal,* February 14, 2013; Sachs, J. (2012), *Winning the Story Wars* (Boston, MA: Harvard Business School Press); Nike, Inc., *History and Heritage,* http://nikeinc.com/pages/history-heritage; and Halberstam, D. (2000), *Playing for Keeps: Michael Jordan and the World* (New York: Broadway Books).

When Will P&G Play to Win Again?

WITH REVENUES OF some $80 billion and business in more than 180 countries, Procter & Gamble (P&G) is the world's largest consumer products company. Some of its category-defining brands include Ivory soap, Tide detergent, Crest toothpaste, and Pampers diapers. Among its many offerings, P&G has more than 20 consumer brands in its lineup that each achieve over $1 billion in annual sales. P&G's iconic brands are a result of a clearly formulated and effectively implemented business strategy. The company pursues a differentiation strategy and attempts to create higher perceived value for its customers than its competitors by delivering products with unique features and attributes. Creating higher perceived value generally goes along with higher product costs due to greater R&D and promotion expenses, among other things. Successful differentiators are able to command a premium price for their products, but they must also control their costs.

Detailing how P&G created many market-winning brands, P&G's long-term CEO A.G. Lafley published (with strategy consultant Roger Martin) the best-selling book *Playing to Win: How Strategy Really Works* (in 2013). In recent years, however, P&G's strategic position has weakened considerably, and P&G seems to be losing rather than winning. P&G lost market share in key "product-country combinations," including beauty in the United States and oral care in China, amid an overall lackluster performance in many emerging economies. As a consequence, profits have declined. P&G posted a sustained competitive advantage in recent years; its stock market valuation has fallen by some $50 billion, while its competitors Unilever, Colgate-Palmolive, and Kimberly-Clark posted strong gains. Many wonder when P&G will play to win again?

Some of P&G's problems today are the result of attempting to achieve growth via an aggressive acquisition strategy in the 2000s. Given the resulting larger P&G revenue base, future incremental revenue growth

Tide detergent, one of P&G's category-defining brands
© John Gress/Reuters/Corbis

for the entire company was harder to achieve. A case in point is P&G's $57 billion acquisition of Gillette in 2005, engineered by then-CEO A.G. Lafley. The value of this acquisition is now being called into question. Although Gillette dominates the retail space of the $3 billion wet shaving industry, P&G was caught off-guard by how quickly razor sales moved online. Turned off by the high prices and the inconvenience of shopping for razors in locked display cases in retail stores, consumers flocked to online options in droves. The online market for razorblades has grown from basically zero just a few years ago to $300 million. Although this is currently only 10 percent of the overall market, the online market continues to grow rapidly. Disruptive startups such as Dollar Shave Club offer low-cost solutions via its monthly subscription plans online.[1]

Perhaps even more troubling is that P&G focused mainly on the U.S. market. Rather than inventing new category-defining products, P&G added more

Frank T. Rothaermel prepared this MiniCase from public sources. This Mini-Case is developed for the purpose of class discussion. It is not intended to be used for any kind of endorsement, source of data, or depiction of efficient or inefficient management. All opinions expressed, all errors and omissions are entirely the author's. Revised and updated: August 19, 2015. © Frank T. Rothaermel.

features to its existing brands, such as Olay's extra-moisturizing creams and ultra-soft and sensitive Charmin toilet paper, while raising prices. Reflecting higher value creation based on its differentiation strategy, P&G generally charges a 20 to 40 percent premium for its products in comparison to retailers' private-label and other brands. The strategic decision to focus on the domestic market combined with incrementally adding minor features to its existing products created two serious problems for P&G.

First, following the deep recession of 2008–2009, U.S. consumers moved away from higher-priced brands, such as those offered by P&G, to lower-cost alternatives. Moreover, P&G's direct rivals in branded goods, including Colgate-Palmolive, Kimberly-Clark, and Unilever, were faster in cutting costs and prices in response to more frugal customers. P&G also fumbled recent launches of reformulated products such as Tide Pods (detergent sealed in single-use pouches) and the Pantene line of shampoos and conditioners. The decline in U.S. demand hit P&G especially hard because the domestic market delivers about one-third of sales, but almost two-thirds of profits. Second, by focusing on the U.S. market, P&G not only missed out on the booming growth years that the emerging economies experienced during the 2000s, but it also left these markets to its rivals. As a consequence, Colgate-Palmolive, Kimberly-Clark, and Unilever all outperformed P&G in recent years.

As a result of its sustained competitive advantage, P&G also had a revolving door in its executive suites. Within a three-year period (from 2013 to 2015), P&G went through three CEOs. After 30 years with P&G, the former Army Ranger Robert McDonald was appointed CEO in 2009, but was replaced in the spring of 2013 in the face of P&G's deteriorating performance. The company's board of directors brought back A.G. Lafley. This was an interesting choice because Lafley had previously served as P&G's CEO from 2000 to 2009, and some of the strategic decisions that led to a weakening of P&G's strategic position were made under his watch. Lafley served a second term as CEO from 2013 to 2015. In late 2015, P&G named David Taylor as new CEO, again promoting from within, while Lafley will continue to serve as executive chairman.

To strengthen its competitive position, P&G launched two strategic initiatives. First, P&G began to refocus its portfolio on the company's 70 to 80 most lucrative product-market combinations, which are responsible for 90 percent of P&G's revenues and almost all of its profits. Some argue that P&G had become too big and spread out to compete effectively in today's dynamic marketplace. To refocus on core products such as Tide, Pampers, and Olay (with these three brands alone accounting for more than 50 percent of the company's revenues), P&G already sold or plans to divest almost 100 brands in its far-flung product portfolio, including well-known brands such Iams pet food, Duracell batteries, Wella shampoos, Clairol hair dye, and CoverGirl makeup, but mainly a slew of lesser known brands.

Part of this strategic initiative is also to expand P&G's presence in large emerging economies. As an example, P&G launched Tide in India and Pantene shampoos in Brazil. Moreover, P&G began to leverage its Crest brand globally, to take on Colgate-Palmolive's global dominance in toothpaste. Yet, the strong dollar in recent years is hurting P&G's international results. Second, P&G implemented strict cost-cutting measures through eliminating all spending not directly related to selling. As part of its cost-cutting initiative, P&G also eliminated thousands of jobs.

The goal of the two strategic initiatives is to increase the perceived value of P&G's brands in the minds of the consumer, while lowering production costs. The combined effort should—if successful—increase P&G's economic value creation ($V - C$). The hope is that P&G's revised business strategy would strengthen its strategic position and help it regain its competitive advantage. It remains to be seen if this will be the case.

DISCUSSION QUESTIONS

1. P&G differentiates itself from competitors by offering branded consumer product goods with distinct features and attributes. This business strategy implies that P&G focuses on increasing the perceived value created for customers, which allows it to charge a premium price. This approach proved quite successful in the past, especially in rich countries such as the United States and many European countries. What went wrong in the recent past? Detail P&G's internal weaknesses and external challenges. Derive recommendations on how to improve P&G's strategic position going forward. Be specific.

2. Given the discussion in the MiniCase about P&G slashing its R&D spending and cutting costs and jobs more generally, does the firm risk being "stuck in the middle"? Why or why not? If yes, why would being "stuck in the middle" be a bad strategic position?

3. Which strategic position should P&G pursue? Which value and/or cost drivers would you focus on to improve P&G's strategic profile? How would you go about implementing your recommended changes? What results would you expect, and why?

4. Given the high turnover of CEOs in recent years as a result of the company's inferior performance and P&G's continued practice to promote company veterans, some argue that P&G's leadership model is broken. Rather than promoting from within, they argue that an outsider might be better positioned to make the necessary changes. Which arguments can be mustered to support sticking with P&G's model to continue promoting from within? Which arguments would support the notion that appointing an outsider as CEO might be advantageous given that P&G has been in a turnaround situation for a number of years now? Where do you come down in this argument?

Endnote

1 Dollar Shave Club's promotional video was a viral hit on YouTube with over 20 million views, see www.youtube.com/watch?v=ZUG9qYTJMsI.

Sources: This MiniCase is based on: "Razor sales move online, away from Gillette," *The Wall Street Journal,* June 23, 2015; "P&G names David Taylor as CEO," *The Wall Street Journal,* July 29, 2015; "P&G to shed more than half its brands," *The Wall Street Journal,* August 1, 2014; "Strong dollar squeezes U.S. firms," *The Wall Street Journal,* January 27, 2014; "Embattled P&G chief replaced by old boss," *The Wall Street Journal,* May 23, 2013; Lafley, A.G., and R.L. Martin (2013), *Playing to Win: How Strategy Really Works* (Boston, MA: Harvard Business Review Press); "A David and Gillette story," *The Wall Street Journal,* April 12, 2012; "P&G's stumbles put CEO on hot seat for turnaround," *The Wall Street Journal,* September 27, 2012; "At Procter & Gamble, the innovation well runs dry," *Bloomberg Businessweek,* September 6, 2012; and "P&G's Billion-Dollar Brands: Trusted, Valued, Recognized," Fact Sheet, www.pg.com.

Trimming Fat at Whole Foods Market

WHEN FOUR YOUNG entrepreneurs opened a small natural-foods store in Austin, Texas, in 1980, they never imagined it would one day turn into an international supermarket chain with stores in the United States, Canada, and the United Kingdom. Some 35 years later, Whole Foods now has more than 420 stores, employs more than 90,000 people, and earned $15 billion in revenue in 2015. Its mission is to offer the finest natural and organic foods available, maintain the highest quality standards in the grocery industry, and remain firmly committed to sustainable agriculture.

Whole Foods differentiates itself from competitors by offering top-quality foods obtained through sustainable agriculture. This business strategy implies that Whole Foods focuses on increasing the perceived value created for customers, which allows it to charge a premium price. In addition to natural and organic foods, it also offers a wide variety of prepared foods and luxury food items, such as $400 bottles of wine. The decision to sell high-ticket items incurs higher costs for the company because such products require more expensive in-store displays and more highly skilled workers, and many fresh items are perishable and require high turnover. Moreover, sourcing natural and organic food is generally done locally, limiting any scale advantages. Taken together, these actions reduce efficiency and drive up costs. The rising cost structure erodes Whole Foods' margin.

Given its unique strategic position as an upscale grocer offering natural, organic, and luxury food items, Whole Foods enjoyed a competitive advantage during the economic boom through early 2008. But as consumers became more budget-conscious in the wake of the deep recession in 2008–2009, the company's performance deteriorated. Competitive intensity also increased markedly because basically every supermarket chain and other retailers now offer organic food. As a result, sales growth of existing Whole Foods stores ("same-store sales," an important performance metric in the grocery business) has been

© Simon Hayter/Toronto Star/Getty Images

declining between 2013 and 2015. To make matters worse, same-store sales growth is now close to zero. Overall, Whole Foods Market has sustained a competitive disadvantage, underperforming not only its competitors, but also the broader market by a wide margin (since 2014).

To revitalize Whole Foods, co-founder and co-CEO John Mackey decided to "trim fat" on two fronts: First, the supermarket chain refocused on its mission to offer wholesome and healthy food options. In Mackey's words, Whole Foods' offerings had included "a bunch of junk," including candy. Mackey is passionate about helping U.S. consumers overcome obesity in order to help reduce heart disease and diabetes. Given that, the new strategic intent at Whole Foods is to become the champion of healthy living not only by offering natural and organic food choices, but also by educating consumers with its new Healthy Eating initiative. Whole Foods Market now has "Take Action Centers" in every store to educate customers on many

Frank T. Rothaermel prepared this MiniCase from public sources. This Mini-Case is developed for the purpose of class discussion. It is not intended to be used for any kind of endorsement, source of data, or depiction of efficient or inefficient management. All opinions expressed, all errors and omissions are entirely the author's. Revised and updated: August 28, 2015. © Frank T. Rothaermel.

food-related topics such as genetic engineering, organic foods, pesticides, and sustainable agriculture.

Yet, a mislabeling "scandal" in New York—city officials found in 2015 that Whole Foods had mislabeled weights of several freshly packaged foods such as chicken tenders and vegetable platters, leading to overcharges of up to $15 an item—reinforced the public's image of Whole Foods as overpriced. Mackey made a video apology and said that this was an unfortunate but isolated incident caused by inadvertent errors of local employees. He also emphasized that the problems were found in only nine out of 425 stores.

Second, Whole Foods is trimming fat by reducing costs. To attract more customers who buy groceries for an entire family or group, Whole Foods now offers volume discounts to compete with Costco, the most successful membership chain in the United States. Whole Foods also expanded its private-label product line, which now includes thousands of products at lower prices. Whole Foods also launched a new store format, "365 by Whole Foods Market," based on its "365 Everyday Value" private label. The 365 stores focus exclusively on Whole Foods' discount private labels, primarily to address the rise of discount competitor Trader Joe's. The risk, however, is that this strategic initiative will cannibalize demand from the higher-end Whole Foods Markets, rather than taking away customers from Trader Joe's.

To offer its private-label line and volume-discount packages, Whole Foods is beginning to rely more on low-cost suppliers and is improving its logistics system to cover larger geographic areas more efficiently.

It still plans to grow threefold in the future and believes that the United States can profitably support some 1,200 Whole Foods stores. Larger scale and more efficient logistics and operations should allow the company to drive down its cost structure. It remains to be seen if Whole Foods can strengthen its economic value creation ($V - C$) to yet again gain and sustain a competitive advantage.

DISCUSSION QUESTIONS

1. Why was Whole Foods successful initially? Why has it lost its competitive advantage and is underperforming its competitors?

2. What value driver is Whole Foods using to remain differentiated in the face of competitors selling organic foods?

3. Given Whole Foods strategic initiatives to reduce its cost structure, does the firm risk being "stuck in the middle"? Why or why not?

4. What other strategic initiatives should/could Whole Foods launch to more successfully drive its business strategy?

Sources: This MiniCase is based on: "Whole Foods 365 takes on Trader Joe's," *Forbes,* June 22, 2015; "Whole Foods sales sour after price scandal," *The Wall Street Journal,* July 29, 2015; "Walter Robb: Whole Foods' other CEO on organic growth," *Fortune,* May 6, 2013; "Whole Foods profits by cutting 'whole paycheck' reputation," *Bloomberg Businessweek,* May 8, 2013; "Walter Robb on Whole Foods' recession lessons," *Bloomberg Businessweek,* August 9, 2012; "Frank talk from Whole Foods' John Mackey," *The Wall Street Journal,* August 4, 2009; "As sales slip, Whole Foods tries to push health," *The Wall Street Journal,* August 5, 2009; "The conscience of a capitalist," *The Wall Street Journal,* October 3, 2009; and www.wholefoodsmarket.com.

Is Porsche Killing the Golden Goose?

One day a farmer going to the nest of his goose found there an egg all yellow and glittering. He took it and found that the egg was pure gold. The farmer could hardly believe his luck! Every morning the same thing occurred, and the farmer grew richer, day by day. Thinking he could get all the gold at once, he killed the goose. After he opened it, he found nothing.

—Aesop's Fable

WHEN PORSCHE REVEALED its 911 sports car design in 1962,[1] it caused a worldwide sensation. Ever since, Porsche has been one of the world's finest performance car manufacturers. The Porsche 911 is a legendary sports car icon. Although focusing on a niche market with a small output every year, Porsche was extremely profitable. Even today, it still enjoys the largest profit margins among all major auto manufacturers, thanks to the hefty premium it can command for its cars.

Brand Proliferation

More than 50 years after its birth, the 911 remains the heart and soul of Porsche. However, it is no longer the company's best-selling model. The number-one spot has been taken by the Cayenne, a five-seat sports utility vehicle (SUV) launched by Porsche in 2002. Porsche views the Cayenne as a way to reduce the company's dependence on the traditional sports models and to provide for future growth in sales and profits. The Cayenne may be the most successful model launch of Porsche since the 911: Porsche sold the 200,000th Cayenne only six years after its debut at the Paris Motor Show. Global sales for the Cayenne reached a record 84,000 units in 2013, accounting for almost two-thirds of the company's overall sales volume (see Exhibit MC11.1). The popularity of the Cayenne is seen across regions, especially in the United States and China, the two largest markets of Porsche overall. In fact, China has become the largest market for Cayenne, and the model will continue to be the strategic sales focus of Porsche in that country. Roughly two-thirds of the 40,000 Porsche vehicles sold annually in China are Cayenne models. This is because wealthy Chinese don't drive themselves, but prefer having a chauffeur.

The Cayenne has made Porsche more appealing to people who are not sports car drivers but are happy to own the sportiest SUV on the market. While the model expansion may upset the purists, Porsche did not stop there. In 2005, Porsche announced its plan to build the Panamera, a premium-category four-seat sports sedan, to further extend its customer base. This new line was launched on time in 2009 and like Cayenne, it outsold the 911 for the first few years after its launch. Porsche kept the model proliferation momentum, and in 2012, it revealed the Macan, a compact SUV. It was launched in 2014 and quickly became the second-best-selling Porsche model behind the Cayenne. In the first year, Porsche sold 45,000 Macans. In total, Porsche sold over 110,000 SUVs in 2014 (Cayenne and Macan) while only 30,000 Porsche 911 models. Its SUV sales now make up close to 70 percent of all Porsche sales. Given the huge success of the Macan in its first year, Porsche is forecasting to sell 72,000 Macans in 2015.

The essence of a Porsche—a high-performance sports car—seems now to take a back seat. Although the company has built "experience centers" in China and the United States to cultivate sports car enthusiasts, Porsche sold only some 30,000 units of the 911

Frank T. Rothaermel prepared this MiniCase from public sources. He gratefully acknowledges the contribution of Carrie Yang on an earlier version and James Hoadley for research assistance. It is developed for the purpose of class discussion. It is not intended to be used for any kind of endorsement, source of data, or depiction of efficient or inefficient management. All opinions expressed, and all errors and omissions, are entirely the author's. Revised and updated: August 25, 2015. © Frank T. Rothaermel.

EXHIBIT MC11.1 / Porsche Annual Sales (units, selected models), 2002–2014

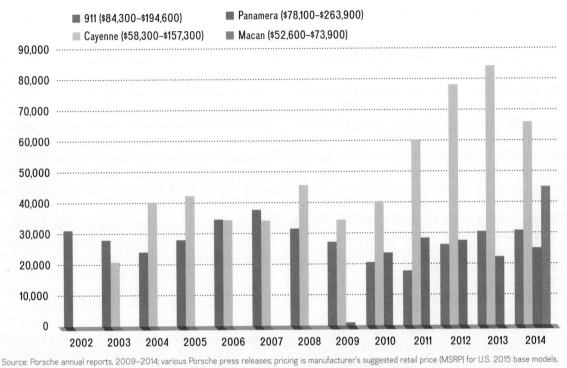

- 911 ($84,300–$194,600)
- Cayenne ($58,300–$157,300)
- Panamera ($78,100–$263,900)
- Macan ($52,600–$73,900)

Source: Porsche annual reports, 2009–2014; various Porsche press releases; pricing is manufacturer's suggested retail price (MSRP) for U.S. 2015 base models, www.porsche.com.

in 2014, or 18 percent of Porsche's total sales volume. Porsche's expansion success has thus far relied largely on its reputation as an iconic sports car maker. However, many of today's Cayenne buyers, such as soccer parents in the United States or Chinese business-people, have no idea about Porsche's true identity as a high-performance sports and race car manufacturer. The same holds true for young urban professionals whether in San Francisco, Stuttgart, or Shanghai—all of who flock to the Macan.

Porsche, now a division of Volkswagen (VW), is clearly gunning for economies of scale as it ramps up unit sales, and VW overall is aiming to be the global leader in sales units. The "new" Porsche developed its own growth blueprint, termed "Strategy 2018," as part of Volkswagen group's grand vision: Porsche plans to increase unit sales to 200,000 per year by 2018, up from 30,000 units in 2002. Given its successful model proliferation, Porsche might achieve this goal early. In 2014, it sold some 166,000 vehicles. Over this time period, it grew by more than 550 percent.

Trouble in the Family

In the years leading up to the global financial crisis in 2008–2009, Porsche was attempting a hostile takeover of the much larger Volkswagen; in terms of market cap, VW (110 billion euro) was more than eight times larger than Porsche (13 billion euro) at that time. Part of the competition was motivated by a bitter family feud resulting from estranged members of the Porsche (and directly related Piëch) families holding leading executive positions in both companies. As the global financial crisis took hold, Porsche collapsed under a heavy debt burden caused by the hostile takeover attempt. VW turned the tables and took over Porsche in 2012.[2]

VW's corporate strategy is not without its critics. They worry that VW has overextended itself in its quest to be number one in the world. They are very much concerned about brand dilution, in particular at Porsche but also of other VW premium brands, including Audi. While serving as chairman of VW's board of directors, Ferdinand Piëch, a grandson of Ferdinand Porsche, the founder of the Porsche car company, publicly criticized VW CEO Martin Winterkorn and asked for his resignation. Winterkorn defended his record, explaining that he increased VW's global reach, and with it its revenues and profits. In addition, VW is set to overtake GM and Toyota as the world's largest car manufacturer in units. Critics, however, lament that although VW's total net income may have increased, the group's profit margins are too low, which necessitated implementation of a company-wide cost-cutting program. In addition, Winterkorn's critics also charge that VW's billion-dollar investments in its Chattanooga, Tennessee, plant have yet to pay off.

In fall 2015, Winterkorn was forced to resign as CEO in light of an emissions cheating scandal and was replaced by Matthias Müller. It was revealed that VW had illegally installed diesel emissions cheat software in more than 11 million vehicles worldwide; in reality, VW's diesel engines were emitting up to 40 times the allowed level of pollutants. Not only must VW now face the repercussions of recalling and retrofitting 11 million vehicles—the world's largest vehicular recall—it must also suffer billions of dollars in lawsuits and fines throughout the world, from which it may take years to recover.

DISCUSSION QUESTIONS

Business Strategy

1. The MiniCase began with Aesop's Fable of "The Goose That Laid the Golden Eggs." What is the take-away of this fable? Is Porsche killing its golden goose?

2. For many decades, Porsche pursued a focused differentiation strategy. Using a clear strategic profile as a focused differentiator, Porsche was very successful and very profitable. More recently, the Porsche brand is repositioning itself from focused differentiation to broad differentiation by changing its competitive scope. What are the risks inherent in such strategic positioning? What are the benefits? Do you think Porsche will be successful in carving out a new strategic position as a broad differentiator? Why or why not?

3. Porsche is expanding rapidly through both related and geographic diversification. Do you consider this business strategy to be successful? Why, or

why not? If you consider Porsche's diversification to be successful, what is the source of Porsche's success?

Corporate Strategy

4. Volkswagen ranks with GM and Toyota as one of the top-three carmakers in the world today in terms of sales volume (in units). It uses its Volkswagen brand, as well as its entire portfolio of other brands, including the luxury marques of Porsche, Audi, Bentley, Bugatti, and Lamborghini, and at the lower end, the Seat, Skoda, and Scania. What type of diversification is Volkswagen pursuing? What are the advantages and disadvantages in VW's corporate strategy?

5. In the recent past, both GM and Toyota ran into problems as they chased the goal of becoming the world's leader in terms of unit sales. GM achieved this goal but lost billions of dollars in the process and ended up in bankruptcy (in 2009). Toyota then pushed output and briefly held the number-one spot in terms of unit sales, but found that the emphasis on increasing output meant that quality issues arose, which then negatively affected its reputation. If you were asked to advise VW, what pitfalls would you point to that may need to be considered when attempting to be the world leader in unit output? How might VW avoid those pitfalls?

Endnotes

[1] Originally, the car's name was the Porsche 901, but Porsche had to change this designation because Peugeot claimed trademark infringement using the numbers "901." Porsche settled on 911—and has used that number ever since. See "1964 Porsche 901 prototype classic drive," *Motor Trend,* December 25, 2012.

[2] Volkswagen (VW) is a stock company owned by the holding company Porsche SE (50.73%), Porsche GmbH (2.37%), Federal State of Lower Saxony (20%), State of Qatar (17%), and the rest is widely distributed (9.90%). Besides its own VW brand, it owns the following brands: Audi, Bentley, Bugatti, Ducati, Giugiaro, Lamborghini, MAN, Porsche, Scania, Seat, and Skoda.

Sources: This MiniCase is based on: Porsche annual reports, 2003–2014; various Porsche press releases; www.porsche.com; "Porsche sales surge on demand for Macan, Cayenne SUVs," *The Wall Street Journal,* January 8, 2015; "Sportwagenbauer stößt in neue Dimensionen vor," *Wirtschaftswoche,* March 15, 2015; "Volkswagen Chairman Ferdinand Piech Resigns," *The Wall Street Journal,* April 25, 2015; "Porsche builds Macan crossover to win over women," *Bloomberg Businessweek,* August 7, 2014; "Is Porsche still a sports car maker?" *The Wall Street Journal,* May 29, 2013; "Porsche puts dollars behind sports cars again after pushing SUV, sedan," *Advertising Age,* April 18, 2011; and "The Porsche story: A fierce family feud," *Der Spiegel,* July 21, 2009.

LEGO's Turnaround: Brick by Brick

IN THE DECADE between 2005 and 2015, LEGO—the famous Danish toy company—grew fivefold from some $1 billion in revenues to $5 billion (see Exhibit MC12.1). Rediscovering, leveraging, and extending its core competence allowed a successful revival for a company that was floundering in the early 2000s. How did LEGO construct a successful turnaround? To answer this question, we first need to understand a bit of the history of this Danish wonder company.

The LEGO company was founded in 1932 by Ole Kirk Kristiansen. The name is a contraction of the Danish words *Leg godt,* which means "play well." Only later did LEGO executives realize that *le go* in Latin also means "I assemble." Throughout its history, LEGO has had numerous formidable competitors, but it has outperformed all of them. Tinkertoys were more complex, Lincoln Logs were limited in what could be constructed, traditional blocks had nothing to hold them together and were too large to show much detail. LEGO bricks were the right balance of simplicity, versatility, and durability.

LEGO competes for the attention of children and their parents who buy the product. Moreover, there is also a sizable group of adult LEGO fans. In the wake of the personal computer revolution in the 1990s, however, the popularity of LEGO began to wane because of attractive alternatives for children such as gaming consoles and computer games. By 1998, LEGO was in trouble. The Danish toymaker hired a highly touted turnaround expert to change its fortune. Unfortunately, he had no background in the toy industry. To make matters worse, the new executive decided that LEGO's hometown of Billund, Denmark, (with 6,000 people) was too provincial. He continued to live in Paris and either commute or run the company remotely.

Things at LEGO went from bad too worse. It started hyperinnovating and diversified into too many areas, too quickly, and too far away from its core. Among a whole slew of other innovation failures, the company created a Saturday morning cartoon called

The *LEGO Movie* was a huge hit: The computer-animated film had a budget of $60 million, but grossed some $500 million at the box office, making it one of the top five movies in 2014.
© Warner Bros./Photofest

"Galidor," which flopped. During this time period, it also decided to become a lifestyle company and to offer LEGO-branded clothing and accessories.

LEGO's Turnaround

By 2003, LEGO was on the verge of bankruptcy. To avoid this fate, the closely held private company, owned by the Kristiansen family since its inception, needed to do something drastic and quickly. Almost out of desperation, it hired Jørgen Vig Knudstorp as CEO. His résumé was quite unusual to say the least: He was only 35 years old (in comparison, the average age for a Fortune 500 CEO is 55 years), held a doctorate in economics, and was a former academic. Knudstorp had transitioned to McKinsey, one of the world's premier strategy consulting firms.

Frank T. Rothaermel prepared this MiniCase from public sources. He gratefully acknowledges James Hoadley for research assistance. This MiniCase is developed for the purpose of class discussion. It is not intended to be used for any kind of endorsement, source of data, or depiction of efficient or inefficient management. All opinions expressed, all errors and omissions are entirely the author's. Revised and updated: August 24, 2015. © Frank T. Rothaermel.

EXHIBIT MC12.1 / Revenues of Mattel, Hasbro, and LEGO ($ billions), 2002–2015

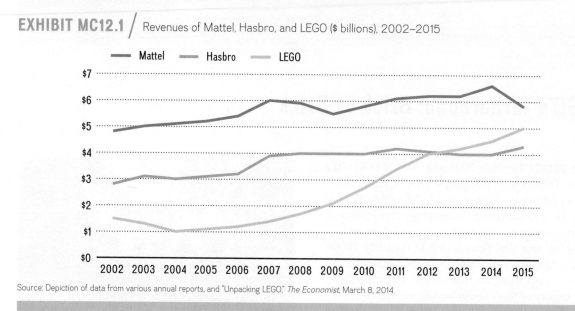

Source: Depiction of data from various annual reports, and "Unpacking LEGO," *The Economist*, March 8, 2014.

Knudstorp decreed that LEGO must "go back to the brick" and focus on core products. As a result of the strategic refocusing, LEGO divested a number of assets including its theme parks. It also drastically culled its product portfolio by almost 50 percent, from some 13,000 pieces to 7,000. At the same time as Knudstorp focused LEGO again on its fundamental strengths, he was also careful to balance exploitation—applying current knowledge to enhance firm performance in the short term—with exploration—searching for new knowledge that may enhance a firm's future performance. This allowed LEGO to improve the performance of traditional product lines, while at the same time to innovate, but this time in a much more disciplined manner.

In particular, LEGO increased sales of its well-known existing products by strengthening the interoperability of various LEGO pieces with other sets to encourage user innovation and creativity. To drive innovation, LEGO has brought its adult fans into the new product development process to leverage crowdsourcing—obtaining ideas from a large fan base using online forums and other Internet-based technologies. To drive future growth, LEGO under Knudstorp has been much more careful with its product extensions. In the past LEGO had licensed its brand freely to other brands, including Star Wars, Indiana Jones, Harry Potter, the Lord of the Rings, Batman, the Simpsons, and Iron Man. The problem was that the benefits from these licensing agreements accrued mainly to the existing brands, because LEGO did not own the more critical intellectual property. Knudstorp focused on owning and leveraging the core intellectual property. As a case in point, *The LEGO Movie* in 2014 was a particular high for the company, grossing $500 million on a $60 million budget in the first year alone. Unlike in previous movie tie-ins, LEGO owned the intellectual property, which meant that LEGO did not need to split profits with existing brands.

Challenges

Although LEGO has grown fivefold since Knudstorp took over, it faces a number of challenges. LEGO needs to strengthen its triple-bottom-line performance (along economic, social, and ecological dimensions) and address globalization challenges.

LEGO must address ecological concerns in the face of growing consumer criticism: Its signature bricks are made from petroleum-based plastic. The company is searching for an environmentally friendly material to replace its bricks that date back to 1963. To overcome its relatively large carbon footprint, the company is spending millions on a 15-year R&D project in hope of finding an eco-friendly alternative. The goal is to invent and then be able to manufacture bricks cost-effectively from a new bio-friendly material that will be virtually indistinguishable from the current blocks. It is a difficult problem to solve because LEGO bricks are precisely engineered to four-thousandths of a millimeter, hold a large range of colors well, and even have a particular sound when two pieces are snapped together.

To continue to grow, LEGO must become stronger in emerging growth markets such as China. LEGO is a comparatively new entry into China because of the fear that knockoff bricks have sufficiently damaged its brand. Knockoffs, which are rampant in China, are of inferior quality and even have injured some consumers. Yet, with growth in Western markets plateauing and a larger number of Chinese entering the middle class, this market opportunity is critical to LEGO's future success. Moreover, Chinese government officials endorse LEGO as a "mind toy," which helps children to develop creativity. The hope is that creative children will grow up to drive innovation in firms, something many critics say Chinese companies lack. In addition, Chinese parents and grandparents are eager to spend money on things that are perceived to help their offspring to excel academically. In general, parents around the globe are more than happy to spend money on games that get their children away from mobile devices, computers, and game consoles.

To take advantage of the growth opportunity in China and other Asian countries such as India and Indonesia, LEGO opened offices in Shanghai and Singapore as well as a factory in Jiaxing, China. To address the globalization challenge more generally, LEGO also needs to internationalize its management. At this point, it is a local, small-town company that happened to be successful globally, especially in the West. LEGO hopes to become a global company that happens to have its headquarters in the 6,000-people town of Billund, Denmark.

DISCUSSION QUESTIONS

1. Why did LEGO face bankruptcy in the early 2000s? In your reasoning, focus on both external and internal factors.

2. What is LEGO's core competence? Explain.

3. Apply the core competence–market matrix to show how LEGO leveraged its core competence into existing and new markets under Jørgen Vig Knudstorp, who was appointed CEO in late 2004.

4. In terms of revenue growth, LEGO experienced a competitive advantage over both Hasbro and Mattel since 2007 because it grew much faster. What explains LEGO's competitive advantage?

5. What must LEGO do to sustain its competitive advantage in the future? One avenue to tackle this question is to think about diversification, both along products but also geography. Another avenue is partnerships such as strategic alliances or even acquisitions. What lessons from LEGO's past should guide its future diversification?

Sources: This MiniCase is based on: "LEGO tries to build a better brick," *The Wall Street Journal,* July 12, 2015; "How LEGO became the Apple of toys," *Fast Company,* January 8, 2015; "LEGO bucks industry trend with profit growth," *The Wall Street Journal,* February 25, 2015; "Unpacking LEGO," *The Economist,* March 8, 2014; "Empire building," *The Economist,* February 13, 2014; "Oh, snap! LEGO's sales surpass Mattel," *The Wall Street Journal,* September 4, 2014; and "How LEGO built up from innovation rubble," *Forbes,* September 23, 2013.

From Good to Great to Gone: The Rise and Fall of Circuit City

IN THE 1990s, Circuit City was the largest and most successful consumer-electronics retailer in the United States. Indeed, Circuit City was so successful that it was included as 1 of only 11 companies featured in Jim Collins's bestseller *Good to Great.* To qualify for this august group of high performers, a company had to attain "extraordinary results, averaging cumulative stock returns 6.9 times the general market in the 15 years following their transition points."[1] Indeed, Circuit City was *the best-performing* company on Collins' good-to-great list, outperforming the stock market 18.5 times during 1982–1997.

How did Circuit City become so successful? The company was able to build and refine a set of core competencies that enabled it to create a higher economic value than its competitors. In particular, Circuit City created world-class competencies in efficient and effective logistics expertise: It deployed sophisticated point-of-sale and inventory-tracking technology, supported by IT investments that enabled the firm to connect the flow of information among geographically dispersed stores. This expertise allowed detailed tracking of customer preferences and thus enabled Circuit City to respond quickly to changing trends. The company also relied on highly motivated, well-trained sales personnel to provide superior service and thus build and maintain customer loyalty. These core competencies enabled Circuit City to implement a "4S business model"—service, selection, savings, and satisfaction—that it applied to big-ticket consumer electronics with an unmatched degree of consistency throughout the United States.

Perhaps even more important during the company's high-performance run, many capable competitors were unable to replicate Circuit City's core competencies. Further underscoring Circuit City's superior performance is the fact, as Collins described it, that "if you had to choose between $1 invested in Circuit City or $1 invested in General Electric on the day that the legendary Jack Welch took over GE in 1981 and held

© Peter Hvizdak/The Image Works

[that investment] to January 1, 2000, you would have been better off with Circuit City—by [a factor of] six times."[2] In the fall of 2008, however, Circuit City filed for bankruptcy. How did Circuit City go from "good to great to gone"?

Circuit City's core competencies lost value because the firm neglected to upgrade and protect them. As a consequence, it was outflanked by Best Buy and online retailers such as Amazon. Moreover, Circuit City's top-management team was also distracted by pursuing noncore activities such as the creation of CarMax, a retail chain for used cars; a foray into providing an alternative to video rentals through its proprietary DivX DVD player; and an attempted merger with Blockbuster, which filed for bankruptcy in 2010.

Perhaps the biggest blunder that Circuit City's top-management team committed was to lay off 3,000 of the firm's highest-paid sales personnel to make the retailer more cost-competitive with Best Buy and, in

Frank T. Rothaermel prepared this MiniCase from public sources. This Mini-Case is developed for the purpose of class discussion. It is not intended to be used for any kind of endorsement, source of data, or depiction of efficient or inefficient management. All opinions expressed, all errors and omissions are entirely the author's. Revised and updated: August 11, 2015. © Frank T. Rothaermel.

particular, the burgeoning online retailers. The problem was that the highest-paid salespeople were also the most experienced and loyal, better able to provide superior customer service. It appears that laying off key human capital—given their valuable, rare, and difficult-to-imitate nature—was a supreme strategic mistake! Not only did Circuit City destroy part of its core competency, but it also allowed its main competitor—Best Buy—to recruit Circuit City's top salespeople. With that shift of personnel to Best Buy went the transfer of important tacit knowledge underlying some of Circuit City's core competencies, which in turn not only mitigated Circuit City's advantage but also allowed Best Buy to upgrade its core competencies. In particular, Best Buy went on to develop its innovative "customer-centricity" model, based on a set of skills that allowed its store employees to identify and more effectively serve specific customer segments. Highlighting the dynamic nature of the competitive process, however, Best Buy now faces its own challenges competing with online retailers such as Amazon.

Employees at Circuit City stores and even at the headquarters in Richmond, Virginia, were shocked and devastated when the firm ceased operations in March 2009. Some 30,000 Circuit City employees lost their jobs. More than a year after the closing, former headquarters workers note that the firm had a good, hardworking, and family-friendly atmosphere. They believed to the end that, in the worst case, another firm would buy Circuit City and perhaps reduce its size but not close the business.

DISCUSSION QUESTIONS

1. Why was Circuit City so successful as featured in *Good to Great*? What was its strategic position during its successful period? How did it contribute to competitive advantage?

2. Why did Circuit City lose its competitive advantage? What was Circuit City's strategic position during the time of competitive disadvantage?

3. What could Circuit City's management have done differently?

4. What is the future of Best Buy as the leader in big-box electronics retailing, especially in light of tough competition by Amazon and other online retailers? What core competencies in big-box retailing are critical to not only survive but also to gain and sustain a competitive advantage?

Endnotes

[1] Collins, J. (2001), *Good to Great: Why Some Companies Make the Leap . . . and Others Don't* (New York: HarperCollins), p. 3.

[2] Ibid, p. 33.

Sources: This MiniCase is based on: Collins, J. (2001), *Good to Great: Why Some Companies Make the Leap . . . and Others Don't* (New York: Harper-Collins); Collins, J. (2009), *How the Mighty Fall: And Why Some Companies Never Give In* (New York: HarperCollins); and *A Tale of Two Cities: The Circuit City Story*, film documentary by Tom Wulf, released November 2010.

Cirque du Soleil: Searching for a New Blue Ocean

Founded in 1984 by two street performers, Guy Laliberté and Gilles Ste-Croix, in an inner-city area of Montreal Canada, Cirque du Soleil (Cirque) today is the largest theatrical producer in the world. With its spectacularly sophisticated shows, Cirque's mission is to "evoke the imagination, invoke the senses, and provoke the emotions of people around the world."[1] Employing some 5,000 people (one-third of them artists) and with annual revenues of about $1 billion, Cirque is hugely successful. Since its founding, some 160 million people worldwide have been dazzled by its high-quality artistic shows, with 15 million viewers alone in 2014. How did Cirque become so successful while most circuses either shut down or barely survive?

Cirque's Blue Ocean Strategy and Value Innovation

Using a *blue ocean strategy* based on *value innovation,* Cirque du Soleil created a new and thus uncontested market space in the entertainment industry. A *blue ocean strategy* attempts to make the competition irrelevant by creating new, uncontested market spaces. For a blue ocean strategy to succeed, managers must resolve trade-offs between the two generic strategic positions—low cost and differentiation. This is done through value innovation, aligning innovation with total perceived consumer benefits, price, and cost. Instead of focusing to compete directly with rivals, attempting to out-compete them by offering better features or lower costs, successful value innovation makes competition more or less irrelevant by providing a leap in value creation, thereby opening new and uncontested market spaces.

Successful value innovation requires that a firm's strategic moves lower its costs and at the same time increase the perceived value for buyers. Lowering a firm's costs is primarily achieved by eliminating and

© AP Photo/Jonathan Short

reducing the taken-for-granted factors that the firm's rivals compete on. Perceived buyer value is increased by raising existing key success factors and by creating new elements that the industry has not offered previously. To initiate a strategic move that allows a firm to open new and uncontested market space through value innovation, managers must answer the four key questions below when formulating a blue ocean business strategy. In terms of achieving successful value innovation, note that the first two questions focus on lowering costs, while the other two questions focus on increasing perceived consumer benefits.

Value Innovation: Lower Costs

1. *Eliminate.* Which of the factors that the industry takes for granted should be eliminated?

2. *Reduce.* Which of the factors should be reduced well below the industry's standard?

Frank T. Rothaermel prepared this MiniCase from public sources. This Mini-Case is developed for the purpose of class discussion. It is not intended to be used for any kind of endorsement, source of data, or depiction of efficient or inefficient management. All opinions expressed, all errors and omissions are entirely the author's. Revised and updated: August 15, 2015. © Frank T. Rothaermel.

Value Innovation: Increase Perceived Consumer Benefits

3. *Raise.* Which of the factors should be raised well above the industry's standard?

4. *Create.* Which factors should be created that the industry has never offered?

Let's take a closer look at how Cirque used the *eliminate-reduce-raise-create* framework to reinvent the circus and to create a blue ocean of uncontested market space where competition is less of a concern.

ELIMINATE. In redefining the circus, Cirque du Soleil eliminated several taken-for-granted elements. First, Cirque did away with all animal shows. In recent years, the public has grown much more concerned about the humane treatment of animals. In addition, animals were the most expensive items for a circus because of their needed care, transportation, medical attention, insurance, and food consumption (a grown male lion can devour some 90 pounds of meat a day). Second, Cirque did away with star performers. They were also expensive; moreover, their name recognition in comparison to movie or sports stars is trivial. Third, it also abolished the standard three-ring venues. They were also expensive since so many performers had to be on stage at the same time, and they frequently created anxiety among circus-goers as they switched their attention rapidly from venue to venue. Finally, it did away with aisle concession sales. They annoyed most circus visitors not only because of the frequent interruptions and interference with the viewing experience, but also because visitors felt taken advantage of because of the vendors' high prices.

REDUCE. Cirque kept the clowns, but reduced their importance in the shows. Moreover, it shifted the clown humor from slapstick and low-brow to a more sophisticated and intellectually stimulating style.

RAISE. Cirque significantly raised the quality of the live performance with its signature acrobatic and aerial stunts to levels never seen before. While many other circuses did away with the luxurious circus tents of old in favor of generic low-cost venues that they rented, Cirque, in contrast, glamorized the circus tent. Using the tent as a unique venue capturing the magic of the circus, Cirque built tents with magnificent exteriors, which attracted the attention of the public, combined with a much higher level of comfort and amenities in the tent's interiors. Given that Cirque attracted consumers who were used to paying much higher ticket prices for live performances at the theater and ballet than what the traveling circus charged, it raised ticket prices (starting at $75 up to $200). This was also possible because Cirque attracted an adult audience rather than several children coming with one adult to the circus.

CREATE. Cirque du Soleil created an entire new entertainment experience. Cirque did this by combining the fun and thrill elements of the traditional circus with the sophistication and high-quality choreographed performances of the theater. Cirque combined a number of unique entertainment features in novel ways. Each show follows a story line characterized by intellectual, sophisticated, highly choreographed dance performances and artistic music. In this sense, Cirque shows are more akin to theater and ballet productions than traditional circuses, which deliver a lineup of unrelated acts. Akin to Broadway shows, Cirque offers multiple productions, playing at all the major venues across the world. In summary, Cirque has created much more sophisticated shows and dramatically increased demand, even at high ticket prices. With multiple productions and changing global venues, visitors now also go to the "circus" more frequently.

A Perfect Storm

Although Cirque du Soleil's venues are still glamorous, the company has fallen on hard times in recent years. A combination of external and internal factors led to a significant decline in performance. Cirque du Soleil was hit hard by the economic downturn during the 2008–2010 global financial crisis. Cirque's management made the situation worse through poor strategic decisions, including offering too many shows that were too little differentiated (at least in the mind of the consumer). As a consequence, Cirque lost its rarity appeal, and its payroll and costs also ballooned. Demand for its European shows dropped as much as 40 percent.

Misfortune also struck: Cirque du Soleil experienced its first fatality as one of its performers fell 95 feet to her death during a live show in Las Vegas. The U.S. Occupational Safety and Health

Administration (OSHA) has issued citations and fines; an in-depth investigation of safety practices at Cirque revealed a very high injury rate. Some Cirque performers claim that the pressure to perform at a high level created a culture where it is difficult to raise concerns about acrobat safety. As a consequence of external threats combined with internal weaknesses, Cirque du Soleil's revenues dropped from $1 billion in 2012 to $850 million in 2013.

Cirque du Soleil is now in search of a new blue ocean. It is attempting to diversify away from its trademark live shows, characterized by creating theatrical spectacles combing high-suspense acrobat stunts. Given its poor safety record, it also revamped its shows to reduce the risk to its performers. Cirque-branded shows now deliver roughly 85 percent of the company's revenues; the company hopes to lower this to no more than 60 percent in 5 to 10 years as it continues to diversify into TV programs, special events, and auxiliary services such as ticketing. To increase its appeal to high-growth markets outside North America, it is infusing Russian and Chinese influences as well as improv comedy.

In 2015, Cirque du Soleil founder Guy Laliberté sold his controlling ownership stake to an investor group led by U.S. private-equity firm TPG. Once valued at close to $3 billion, this deal valued Cirque at $1.5 billion. Once flying high, Cirque du Soleil's valuation had dropped by 50 percent.

DISCUSSION QUESTIONS

1. Cirque du Soleil was able to gain and sustain a competitive advantage for many years. Why was Cirque du Soleil successful in the first place (while most other circuses barely survive)?

2. Which "industry" does Cirque du Soleil compete in? Who are its competitors?

3. Which factors contributed to Cirque du Soleil losing its competitive advantage, and as a consequence led to a 50 percent drop in its valuation? Look at both external and internal factors.

4. A recent report by OSHA concludes that Cirque performers suffered a high number of injuries that required medical attention. One investigation found that Cirque's signature show Kà had 56 injuries per 100 workers, which is four times the injury rate for professional sports teams, according to the Bureau of Labor Statistics. What can Cirque's management do to address the safety concerns of its performers? With more safety measures and less risky shows, do you think Cirque du Soleil will lose its differentiated appeal to audiences? Why or why not?

5. Cirque du Soleil's new owner has retained you (or your study group) as consultants. Which recommendations would you make to address some of the external threats and internal weaknesses to once again gain and sustain a competitive advantage? How would you implement your suggested changes?

Endnote

1 *Cirque du Soleil* at a Glance, www.cirquedusoleil.com/en/home/about-us/at-a-glance.aspx.

Sources: This MiniCase is based on: Kim, W.C., and Mauborgne, R. (2005), *Blue Ocean Strategy: How to Create Uncontested Market Space and Make the Competition Irrelevant* (Boston, MA: Harvard Business Review Press); "Cirque du Soleil's next act: Rebalancing the business," *The Wall Street Journal,* December 1, 2014; "Cirque du Soleil tour revenue tumbles to £40m," *The Telegraph,* February 22, 2015; "Cirque du Soleil being sold to private-equity group," *The Wall Street Journal,* April 20, 2015; "Injuries put safety in spotlight at Cirque du Soleil," *The Wall Street Journal,* April 22, 2015; "The perils of workers' comp for injured Cirque du Soleil performers," *The Wall Street Journal,* April 24, 2015; and *WSJ* video on Cirque du Soleil, www.wsj.com/articles/injuries-put-safety-in-spotlight-at-cirque-du-soleil-1429723558.

Competing on Business Models: Google vs. Microsoft

RIVALS OFTEN USE different business models to compete with one another. Because of competitive dynamics and industry convergence, Google and Microsoft progressively move on to the other's turf. In many areas, Google and Microsoft are now direct competitors. In 2014, Microsoft had $90 billion in revenues and Google $66 billion. Although Google started as an online search and advertising company, it now offers software applications (Google Docs, word processing, spreadsheet, e-mail, interactive calendar, and presentation software) hosted on the cloud (Google Drive), and also operating systems (Chrome OS for the web and Android for mobile applications), among many other online products and services. In contrast, Microsoft began its life by offering an operating system (since 1985, called Windows), then moved into software applications with its Office Suite, and later into online search and advertising with Bing as well as gaming with Xbox One. Both also compete in mobile devices by offering smartphones. The stage is set for a clash of the technology titans.

In competing with each other, Google and Microsoft pursue very different business models, as detailed in Exhibit MC15.1. Google offers its applications software Google Docs and hosting service Google Drive for free to induce and retain as many users as possible for its search engine. Although Google's flagship search engine is free for the end user, Google makes money from sponsored links by advertisers. The advertisers pay for the placement of their ad on the results pages and each time a user clicks through an ad (which Google calls a "sponsored link"). Many billion mini-transactions add up to a substantial business. Exhibit MC15.2 shows how advertising revenues account for some 90 percent of Google's total revenues.

Google uses part of the profits earned from its lucrative online advertising business to subsidize Google Docs (see Exhibit MC15.1). Giving away products and services to induce widespread use allows

Sundar Pichai, Google CEO (top), and Satya Nadella, Microsoft CEO (Bottom)
(top): © Pichi Chuang/Reuters/Corbis; (bottom): © AP Photo/Eric Risberg

Google to benefit from *network effects*—the increase in the value of a product or service as more people use it. Google can charge advertisers for highly targeted and effective ads, allowing it to subsidize other product offerings that compete directly with Microsoft.

Microsoft's business model, however, is almost the reverse of Google's (see the opposing arrows in Exhibit MC15.1). Initially, Microsoft focused on creating a large installed base of users for its PC operating system Windows. It holds some 90 percent market share in operating system software for personal computers worldwide, although the PC has become less important as mobile devices have become more important in

EXHIBIT MC15.1 / Competing Business Models: Google vs. Microsoft

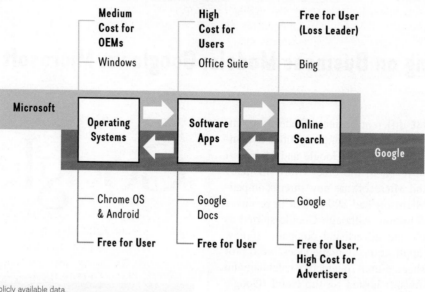

Source: Depiction of publicly available data.

EXHIBIT MC15.2 /

Breakdown of Google's Revenues by Business Segment, ($ millions) 2012–2014

Revenues	2014	2013	2012
Google Websites	$45,085	$37,422	$31,221
Google Network Members' Websites	13,971	13,125	12,465
Total Advertising Revenues	59,056	50,547	43,686
Other Revenues	6,945	4,972	2,354
Total Revenues	66,001	55,519	46,040

Source: Google annual reports.

EXHIBIT MC15.3 /

Breakdown of Microsoft's Revenues by Business Segment, ($ millions) 2013–2015

12 months ending June 30			
Revenues	2015	2014	2013
Devices and Consumer Licensing	$14,969	$19,528	$19,021
Computing and Gaming Hardware	10,183	9,093	6,461
Phone Hardware	7,524	1,982	0
Devices and Consumer Other	8,825	7,014	6,618
Commercial Licensing	41,039	42,085	39,686
Commercial Other	10,836	7,546	5,660
Corporate and Other	204	(415)	403
Total Revenues	93,580	86,833	77,849

Source: Microsoft annual reports.

recent years. Roughly 60 percent of Microsoft's profits are tied to the Windows franchise. Moreover, PC users are locked into a Microsoft operating system that generally comes preloaded with the computer they purchase; they then want to buy applications that run seamlessly with the operating system. The obvious choice for most users is Microsoft's Office Suite containing Word, Excel, PowerPoint, Outlook, and Access. But they need to pay several hundred dollars for the latest standalone version. More recently, Microsoft offers "rental" of its cloud-based Office 365: It costs either $99.99 a year, or $9.99 a month. Exhibit MC15.3 details Microsoft's revenues by business segment.

Currently, Microsoft faces two immediate problems. The first is that people and businesses are buying fewer and fewer PCs (including both desktops and laptops) as personal and business computing move increasingly to mobile devices. The second is the increasing use of cloud-based rather than standalone PC-based computing. The demand for Microsoft's Office is driven by its installed base of Windows. The gross margin for the "classic" Office sitting on your computer is 90 percent, while that for the cloud-hosted Office 365 is only some 50 percent. To maximize the number of users that will upgrade from Windows 7 and the disappointing Windows 8 to Windows 10 launched in summer 2015, users of current versions of the operating system will get a free upgrade. (Microsoft did not offer a Windows 9 version.) On top of the aforementioned problems, Microsoft just wrote off almost $8 billion of its $9.4 billion ill-fated acquisition of smartphone maker Nokia, combined with cutting some 8,000 jobs.

As shown in Exhibit MC15.1, Microsoft uses the profits from its application software business to subsidize its search engine Bing, which is—just like Google's—a free product for the end user. Given Bing's relatively small market share, however, and the tremendous cost in developing the search engine, Microsoft, unlike Google, does not make any money from its online search offering; rather, it is a big money loser. The logic behind Bing is to provide a countervailing power to Google's dominant position in online search. The logic behind Google Docs is to create a threat to Microsoft's dominant position in application software.

The computing industry is undergoing a shift away from personal computers to mobile devices and cloud-based computing. Although Microsoft set the standard and dominates the industry with Windows, Google holds some 75 percent market share in mobile operating systems software with Android, while Microsoft's market share is less than 3 percent. These tactics create *multipoint competition* between the two technology firms. Taken together, Google and Microsoft compete with one another for market share in several different product categories through quite different business models.

As shown in MC15.4, the stock market has valued Google's business model much more highly. Since

EXHIBIT MC15.4 / Stock Performance Comparison of Google, Microsoft, and NASDAQ-100 index, 2004–2015

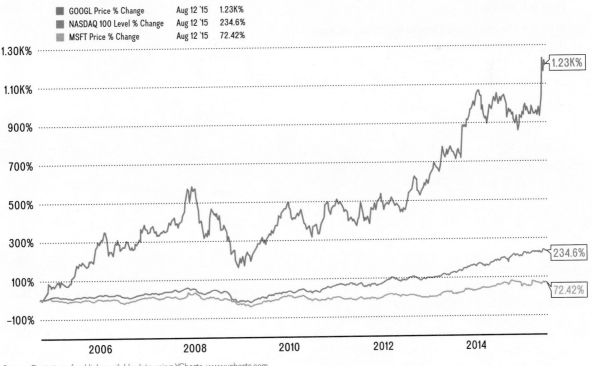

Source: Depiction of publicly available data using YCharts, www.ycharts.com.

its initial public offering in 2004, Google's stock has appreciated by more than 1,200 percent (or 12x), while Microsoft's stock has increased 72 percent over the same period. Also noteworthy is that Google has outperformed the tech-heavy NASDAQ-100 stock market index by a wide margin, while Microsoft has underperformed it. Google was able to gain and sustain a competitive advantage over Microsoft.

Under its new CEO, Satya Nadella, Microsoft is attempting to reinvent itself with a new "mobile first, cloud first" strategy. Microsoft is shifting quickly from being a Windows-only firm to a company offering diversified online services to its customers via the cloud, supported by its strong network of data centers. Nadella realizes that as more computing moves toward the cloud, Microsoft's tried-and-tested model of tightly integrating standalone software with hardware is no longer working. The absence of a sole focus on Windows in Microsoft's new mantra is evidence of where the new CEO sees the future of computing. Nadella is also looking to transform Microsoft's culture into one that is more entrepreneurial. Whether Nadella can engineer a turnaround at Microsoft, which is entering its fifth decade, remains to be seen.

DISCUSSION QUESTIONS

1. How is a strategy different from a business model? How is it similar?

2. Why are Microsoft and Google becoming increasingly direct competitors?

3. Identify other examples of companies that were not competing in the past but are becoming competitors. Why are we seeing such a trend?

4. What recommendations would you give to Satya Nadella, CEO of Microsoft, to compete more effectively against Google? To engineer a turnaround at Microsoft?

5. What recommendations would you give to Sundar Pichai, CEO of Google, to compete more effectively against Microsoft? To continue to sustain its competitive advantage?

Sources: This MiniCase is based on: "Microsoft at middle age: Opening windows," *The Economist,* April 4, 2015; "Microsoft to cut 7,800 jobs on Nokia woes," *The Wall Street Journal,* July 8, 2015; "Google takes stricter approach to costs," *The Wall Street Journal,* July 13, 2015; "Google's share price hits all-time high," *The Wall Street Journal,* July 17, 2015; "The quest for a third mobile platform," *The Wall Street Journal,* May 6, 2013; Adner, R. (2012), *The Wide Lens. A New Strategy for Innovation* (New York: Portfolio); Levy, S. (2011), *In the Plex: How Google Thinks, Works, and Shapes Our Lives* (New York: Simon & Schuster);Anderson, C. (2009), *Free: The Future of a Radical Price* (New York: Hyperion); Gimeno, J. (1999), "Reciprocal threats in multimarket rivalry: Staking out 'spheres of influence' in the U.S. airline industry," *Strategic Management Journal* 20: 101–128; and Gimeno, J., and C.Y. Woo (1999), "Multimarket competition, economies of scale, and firm performance," *Academy of Management Journal* 42: 239–259; Chen, M.J. (1996), "Competitor analysis and interfirm rivalry: Toward a theoretical integration," *Academy of Management Review* 21:100–134; and various Google and Microsoft annual reports.

Assessing Competitive Advantage: Apple vs. BlackBerry*

*A strategic financial analysis (SFA) for this MiniCase is available on Connect.

IN RECENT YEARS, Apple sustained a competitive advantage, while its various competitors struggled to keep up. Before the introduction of the iPhone in 2007, however, the Canadian high-tech company BlackBerry was the global leader in wireless communications. As an innovator, BlackBerry defined the smartphone category and changed the way millions of people around the world live and work. At one point, the iconic Black-Berry smartphone was a corporate status symbol.

Strategy is a set of goal-directed actions a firm takes to gain and sustain competitive advantage. Since competitive advantage is defined as superior performance relative to other competitors in the same industry or the industry average, a firm's managers must be able to accomplish two critical tasks:

1. Accurately assess the performance of their firm.
2. Compare and benchmark their firm's performance to other competitors in the same industry or against the industry average.

One of the most commonly used metrics in assessing firm financial performance is *return on invested capital (ROIC),* where ROIC = (Net profits/Invested capital).[1] ROIC is a popular metric because it is a good proxy for *firm profitability.* In particular, the ratio measures how effectively a company uses its *total invested capital,* which consists of two components: (1) *shareholders' equity* through the selling of shares to the public, and (2) *interest-bearing debt* through borrowing from financial institutions and bond holders. As a rule of thumb, if a firm's ROIC is greater than its *cost of capital,* it generates value; if it is less than the cost of capital, the firm destroys value. To be more precise and to be able to derive strategic implications, however, managers must compare their ROIC to other competitors.

Let's compare the financial performance of Apple and BlackBerry, direct competitors in the smartphone and mobile device industry. Exhibit MC16.1 shows the ROIC for Apple and BlackBerry (for fiscal year 2012, the last year BlackBerry competed without

© Stanca Sanda/Alamy

self-imposed restrictions in the smartphone industry). It further breaks down ROIC into its constituent components. This provides important clues for managers concerning what areas to focus on when attempting to improve firm performance.

Apple's ROIC was 35.0 percent, which was nearly 21 percentage points higher than BlackBerry's (14.1 percent). This means that for every $1.00 invested in Apple, the company returned almost $1.35, while for every $1.00 invested in the company, BlackBerry returned $1.14. Since Apple was 2.5 times more efficient than BlackBerry at generating a return on invested capital, Apple had a clear competitive advantage over BlackBerry.

As shown in Exhibit MC16.1, Apple had a distinct competitive advantage over BlackBerry (in 2012) because Apple's ROIC was much higher than BlackBerry's.

Frank T. Rothaermel prepared this MiniCase from public sources. This Mini-Case is developed for the purpose of class discussion. It is not intended to be used for any kind of endorsement, source of data, or depiction of efficient or inefficient management. All opinions expressed, all errors and omissions are entirely the author's. Revised and updated: August 15, 2015. © Frank T. Rothaermel.

EXHIBIT MC16.1 / Comparing Apple and BlackBerry: Drivers of Firm Profitability (2012)

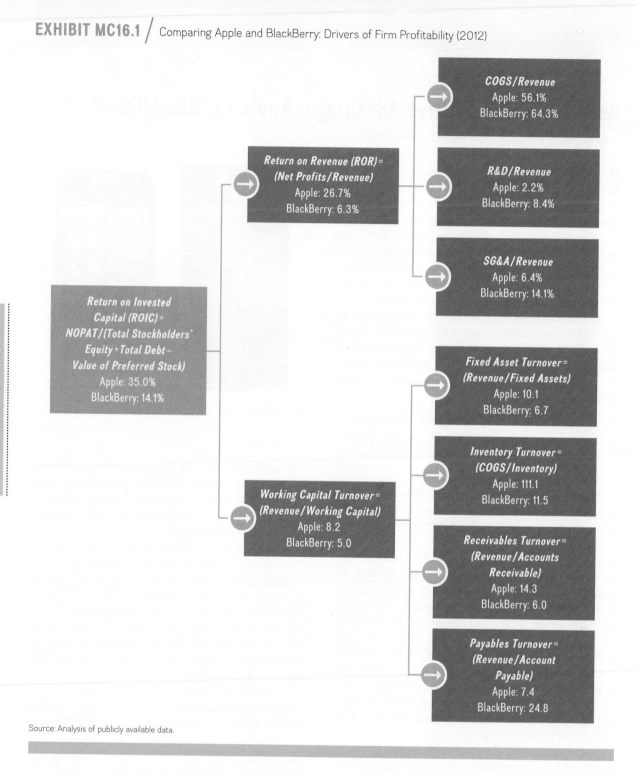

Source: Analysis of publicly available data.

Although this is an important piece of information, managers need to know the underlying factors driving differences in firm profitability. Why is the ROIC for these two companies so different?

Much like detectives, managers look for clues to solve that mystery: They break down ROIC into its constituent parts (as shown in Exhibit MC16.1)—*return on revenue* and *working capital turnover*—to discover the underlying drivers of the marked difference in firm profitability. *Return on revenue (ROR)* indicates how much of the firm's sales are converted into profits. Apple's ROR was more than 20 percentage points higher than that of BlackBerry. For every $100 in revenues, Apple earns $26.70 in profit, while BlackBerry earns only $6.30 in profit. To explore further drivers of this difference, return on revenue is then broken down into three additional financial ratios: *Cost of goods sold (COGS)/Revenue; Research & development (R&D) expense/Revenue;* and *Selling, general, & administrative (SG&A) expense/Revenue.*

The first of these three ratios, *COGS/Revenue,* indicates how efficiently a company can produce a good. Apple is more efficient than BlackBerry (by more than 8 percentage points). This implies that Apple's profit margin is higher than that of Black-Berry because Apple is able to command a greater price premium (higher markup) for its products. In the eyes of the consumer, Apple's products are seen as creating a higher value. Apple is more successful than BlackBerry in differentiating its products through user-friendliness and offering complementary services such as iTunes.

The next ratio, *R&D/Revenue,* indicates how much of each dollar that the firm earns in sales is invested to conduct research and development. A higher percentage is generally an indicator of a stronger focus on innovation to improve current products and services, and to come up with new ones. The third ratio, *SG&A/Revenue,* indicates how much of each dollar that the firm earns in sales is invested in sales, general, and administrative (SG&A) expenses. Generally, this ratio is an indicator of the firm's focus on marketing to promote its products and services. Interestingly, Apple's R&D intensity and marketing intensity are much less than BlackBerry's. Apple spent 2.2 percent on R&D for every dollar of revenue, while BlackBerry spent almost four times as much (8.4 percent R&D intensity). Although BlackBerry's R&D and marketing intensities were multiples of Apple's (in 2012), keep

in mind that Apple was spending much more in absolute dollar terms because it had a much larger revenue. Adjusting financial metrics by size (e.g., revenue), however, allows a direct comparison between different competitors.

Historically, Apple has spent much less on research and development than other firms in the industry, in both absolute and relative terms. Apple's co-founder and CEO, the late Steve Jobs, defined Apple's R&D philosophy as follows: "Innovation has nothing to do with how many R&D dollars you have. When Apple came up with the Mac, IBM was spending at least 100 times more on R&D. It's not about money. It's about the people you have, how you're led, and how much you get it."[2]

In contrast, BlackBerry's R&D and marketing spending had been elevated in 2012 (thus reducing its profitability) in order to complete the development and subsequent launch (in early 2013) of its new mobile operating system (BlackBerry 10) and its newest touchscreen-based smartphone, the BlackBerry Z10. In terms of marketing intensity, BlackBerry spent more than twice as much as Apple (14.1 percent vs. 6.4 percent). The marketing-intensity ratio *(SG&A/Revenue)* indicates how much of each dollar the company takes in as revenue is spent on advertising and sales support.

The second component of ROIC is *working capital turnover* (see Exhibit MC16.1), which is a measure of how effectively capital is being used to generate revenue. For every dollar that BlackBerry puts to work, it realizes $5.00 of sales; for Apple, the conversion rate is more than 1.6 times higher, at $8.20. This relatively large difference provides an important clue for Black-Berry's managers to dig deeper to find the underlying drivers in working capital turnover. This enables managers to uncover which levers to pull in order to improve firm financial performance. In a next step, therefore, managers break down working capital turnover into other ratios, including *fixed asset turnover, inventory turnover, receivables turnover,* and *payables turnover.* Each of these metrics is a measure of how effective a particular item on the balance sheet is contributing to revenue.

Fixed asset turnover (Revenue/Fixed assets) measures how well a company leverages its fixed assets, particularly property, plant, and equipment (PPE). BlackBerry's fixed assets contribute $6.70 of revenue for every dollar spent on PPE, while each dollar of Apple's fixed assets generate $10.10. This ratio indicates how much of a firm's capital is tied up in its fixed assets. Higher fixed assets often go along with lower firm valuations.

The performance difference between Apple and BlackBerry in regard to *inventory turnover (COGS/Inventory)* is even more striking. Cost of goods sold (COGS) captures the firm's production cost of merchandise it *has sold.* Inventory is the cost of the firm's merchandise *to be* sold. This ratio indicates how much of a firm's capital is tied up in its inventory. Apple turned over its inventory 111 times during 2012, which implies that the company had very little capital tied up in its inventory. Apple benefited from strong demand for its products, as well as an effective management of its global supply chain. The vast majority of Apple's manufacturing is done in China by low-cost producer Foxconn, which employs over 1.2 million people. In contrast, BlackBerry has likely higher production costs because it uses higher-cost suppliers than Apple. BlackBerry's suppliers are located in the United States (e.g., Qualcomm and Jabil Circuit) and Luxembourg, countries with a much higher cost structure than that of Foxconn in China.

In stark contrast, BlackBerry turned over its inventory only 11.5 times. In comparison to BlackBerry, Apple turned over its inventory almost 10 times faster! This big difference can be explained by a pronounced decline in demand for BlackBerry products and disappointing new product launches. Consumers continued to migrate away from BlackBerry smartphones to Apple iPhones and Android-based devices. Apple benefited from greater *economies of scale* (a decrease in per-unit cost as output increased) because it sold more than four times as many iPhones as BlackBerry sold smartphones in 2012 (136 million iPhones vs. 33 million BlackBerrys). Moreover, BlackBerry's new product launches such as the Playbook (a tablet computer) flopped. At the same time, demand for the Apple iPad soared.

The final set of financial ratios displayed in Exhibit MC16.1 concerns the effectiveness of a company's receivables and payables. These are part of a company's cash flow management; they indicate the company's efficiency in extending credit, as well as collecting debts. Higher ratios of *receivables turnover (Revenue/Accounts receivable)* imply more efficient management in collecting accounts receivable and shorter durations of interest-free loans to customers (i.e., time until payments are due). In contrast, *payables turnover (Revenue/Accounts payable)* indicates how

fast the firm is paying its creditors and how much it benefits from interest-free loans extended by its suppliers. A lower ratio indicates more efficient management in paying creditors and generating interest-free loans from suppliers. In the two dimensions of cash flow management, Apple displays a clear advantage over BlackBerry. Apple is paid much faster than BlackBerry. This might be explained by the fact that Apple's customers are mainly individual consumers who tend to pay with cash or credit cards at the time of purchase, while BlackBerry's most important customers are corporate IT departments and governments who request to be invoiced, and thus pay later. On the other hand, Apple is taking quite a bit longer to pay its creditors. Due to its stronger negotiating power, Apple might also be able to extend its payment periods, while BlackBerry is required to pay its creditors more quickly.

A deeper understanding of the underlying drivers for differences in firm profitability allows managers to derive strategic implications. Given its higher *COGS/Revenue* ratio, BlackBerry needs to think hard about how to drive down costs, while increasing revenues. With increased marketing spending, BlackBerry is clearly hoping that each dollar spent on marketing and advertising will generate more than one dollar in profits. Since BlackBerry has just completed a major refresh of its mobile phone hardware and operating system, it might reduce R&D intensity going forward. This in turn should improve firm profitability. One of the key pivot points for BlackBerry will be to turn over its inventory much faster. This is, of course, closely tied to consumer demand for its products. Having more attractive products in its lineup and improving its supply chain and logistics should help BlackBerry improve its inventory turnover, and with it, its profitability.

Exhibit MC16.1 presents a firm profitability analysis for Apple and BlackBerry in fiscal year 2012. Although the analysis presented therein allows us to answer the two key questions we set out to accomplish (accurately assess firm performance and compare it to competitors), keep in mind that this is a *static* analysis. It covers only one fiscal year. We basically take a snapshot of a moving target. To obtain a more complete picture, managers need to engage in a *dynamic* analysis, repeating this over a number of years. This will allow you to identify when and where things went wrong (in the case for BlackBerry) and how to get back on track.

EXHIBIT MC16.2 / Key Financial Data for Apple and BlackBerry (fiscal years 2010–2012)

In millions of US$ (except for per share items)	Apple Y/E Sept. 2012	Apple Y/E Sept. 2011	Apple Y/E Sept. 2010	BlackBerry Y/E Mar. 2013	Blackberry Y/E Mar. 2012	Blackberry Y/E Mar. 2011
Total revenue	156,508	108,249	65,225	11,073	18,423	19,907
Cost of revenue, total	87,846	64,431	39,541	7,639	11,848	11,082
Gross profit	68,662	43,818	25,684	3,434	6,575	8,825
Selling/general/admin. expenses, total	10,040	7,599	5,517	2,111	2,600	2,400
Total operating expense	13,421	10,028	7,299	4,669	5,078	4,189
Operating income	55,241	33,790	18,385	−1,235	1,497	4,636
Income before tax	55,763	34,205	18,540	−1,220	1,518	4,644
Income after tax	41,342	25,607	13,896	0	1,429	3,405
Net income	41,733	25,922	14,013	−646	1,164	3,411
Diluted weighted average shares	945	937	925	524	524	538
Dividends per share—common stock	3	0	0	0	0	0
Diluted normalized EPS	44	28	15	−1	2	6
Cash and equivalents	10,746	9,815	11,261	1,549	1,527	1,791
Short-term investments	18,383	16,137	14,359	1,105	247	330
Cash and short-term investments	29,129	25,952	25,620	2,654	1,774	2,121
Accounts receivable—trade, net	10,930	5,369	5,510	2,353	3,062	3,955
Total receivables, net	18,692	11,717	9,924	2,625	3,558	4,279
Total inventory	791	776	1,051	603	1,027	618
Total current assets	57,653	44,988	41,678	7,101	7,071	7,488
Property/plant/equipment, total—net	15,452	7,777	4,768	2,395	2,733	2,504
Accumulated depreciation, total						
Goodwill, net	1,135	896	741	0	304	508
Intangibles, net	4,224	3,536	342	3,448	3,286	1,798
Long-term investments	92,122	55,618	25,391	221	337	577
Other long-term assets, total	5,478	3,556	2,263			
Total assets	176,064	116,371	75,183	13,165	13,731	12,875
Accounts payable	21,175	14,632	12,015	1,064	744	832
Accrued expenses	11,414	9,247	5,723	1,842	2,382	2,511
Other current liabilities, total	5,953	4,091	2,984	542	263	108
Total current liabilities	38,542	27,970	20,722	3,448	3,389	3,630
Total long-term debt	0	0	0	0	0	0
Total debt	0	0	0	0	0	0
Other liabilities, total	22,617	14,191	8,515	542	263	108
Total liabilities	57,854	39,756	27,392	3,705	3,631	3,937
Common stock, total	667	381	283	13	14	66
Additional paid-in capital	0	0	0	0	0	0
Retained earnings (accumulated deficit)	101,289	62,841	37,169	7,267	7,913	6,749
Total equity	118,210	76,615	47,791	9,460	10,100	8,938
Total liabilities and shareholders' equity	176,064	116,371	75,183	13,165	13,731	12,875
Total common shares outstanding	939	929	916	2,431	2,446	2,359

DISCUSSION QUESTIONS

Exhibit MC16.2 shows key financial data for Apple and BlackBerry for the three fiscal years 2010–2012. A strategic financial analysis (SFA) for this MiniCase is available on Connect.

1. Calculate some key profitability, activity, leverage, liquidity, and market ratios for Apple and Black-Berry over time. (If you use the *Strategic Management* text by Frank Rothaermel, refer to the financial ratio tables in the "How to Conduct a Case Analysis" module located at the end of Part 4.)

2. Conduct a *dynamic* firm profitability analysis over time (fiscal years 2008–2012) as shown in Exhibit MC16.2. Can you find signs of performance differentials between these two firms that may have indicated problems at BlackBerry? When did Black-Berry's performance problems become apparent?

3. Make a recommendation to the CEO of Black-Berry about actions that could be taken to improve firm performance.

Endnotes

[1] *(Net profits/Invested capital)* is shorthand for *(Net operating profit after taxes [NOPAT]/Total stockholders' equity + Total debt − Value of preferred stock).* See discussion of profitability ratios in Table 1, "When and How to Use Financial Measures to Assess Firm Performance," of the "How to Conduct a Case Analysis" module.

[2] "The second coming of Apple through a magical fusion of man—Steve Jobs—and company, Apple is becoming itself again: The little anticompany that could," *Fortune,* November 9, 1998.

Sources: This MiniCase is based on: SEC 10-K reports for Apple and Black-Berry (various years); "RIM's new CEO sticks with strategy," *The Wall Street Journal,* January 24, 2012; "Do you know who manufactured your BlackBerry?" *Forbes,* January 13, 2011; "RIM squeezes BlackBerry suppliers as economy stalls," *Bloomberg Businessweek,* April 13, 2009; and http://aaplinvestors.net/stats/iphone/bbvsiphone/.

Wikipedia: Disrupting the Encyclopedia Business

WIKIPEDIA IS OFTEN the first source consulted for information about an unfamiliar topic, but this was not always the case. For almost 250 years, Encyclopaedia Britannica was the gold standard for authoritative reference works, delving into more than 65,000 topics with articles by some 4,000 scholarly contributors, including many by Nobel laureates. The beautiful leather-bound, multivolume set of books made a decorative item in many homes. In the early 1990s, when total sales for encyclopedias were over $1.2 billion annually, Encyclopaedia Britannica was the undisputed market leader, holding more than 50 percent market share and earning some $650 million in revenues. Not surprisingly, its superior differentiated appeal was highly correlated with cost, reflected in its steep sticker price of up to $2,000.

Two innovation waves disrupted the encyclopedia business. Innovation—the successful introduction of a new product, process, or business model—is a powerful driver in the competitive process. The first wave was initiated by the introduction of Encarta. Banking on the widespread diffusion of the personal computer, Microsoft launched its electronic encyclopedia Encarta in 1993 at a price of $99. Although some viewed it as merely a CD-version of the lower-cost and lower-quality Funk & Wagnalls encyclopedia sold in supermarkets, Encarta still took a big bite out of Britannica's market. Within only three years, the market for printed encyclopedias had shrunk by half, along with Britannica's revenues, while Microsoft sold over $100 million worth of Encarta CDs. Sales of the beautiful leather-bound Encyclopaedia Britannica volumes declined from a peak of 120,000 sets in 1990 to a mere 12,000 sets in 2010. As a consequence, Encyclopaedia Britannica announced in 2012 that it no longer would print its namesake books. Its content is now accessible via a paid subscription through its website and apps for mobile devices.

The second wave of innovation is a major disrupter to the encyclopedia business. In January 2001, Internet

© Boris Roessler/EPA/Newscom

entrepreneur Jimmy Wales launched Wikipedia, the free online multilanguage encyclopedia. In Hawaiian, *wiki* means quick, referring to the instant do-it-yourself editing capabilities of the site. Jimmy Wales describes September 11, 2001, as a "Eureka moment" for Wikipedia. Before 9/11, Wikipedia was a small niche site. Immediately following the terrorist attacks, millions of people visited the site and wanted to learn more to complement what they had seen and heard on the news. Massive amounts of queries for search terms such as Al-Qaeda, the World Trade Center, the Pentagon, the different airlines and airports involved, etc., made Wales realize that Wikipedia "could be big." Some 15 years later, Wikipedia is visited some 200 times a second or 500 million times a month! It is one of the top 10 websites by traffic worldwide, just after Google, Facebook, and Amazon, but before Twitter, LinkedIn, Tencent, and Taobao. Wikipedia has 35 million articles in 288 different languages, including

Frank T. Rothaermel prepared this MiniCase from public sources. This Mini-Case is developed for the purpose of class discussion. It is not intended to be used for any kind of endorsement, source of data, or depiction of efficient or inefficient management. All opinions expressed, all errors and omissions are entirely the author's. Revised and updated: August 11, 2015. © Frank T. Rothaermel.

some 5 million entries in English. Roughly 12,000 new pages spring up in a day.

Wikipedia is a nonprofit, free-of-advertising social entrepreneurship venture that is exclusively financed by donations. Wikipedia runs regular calls for donations using slogans such as: "Please help us feed the servers," "We make the Internet not suck. Help us out," and "We are free, our bandwidth isn't!"[1] Calls for donations also come in the form of personal appeals by co-founder Wales. The question arises whether the donation model is sustainable given not only the increasing demand for Wikipedia's services, but also the emergence of competitors. In 2015, people donated more than $50 million in 70 currencies, mostly from a large number of small donations via its website. When asked why Wales wouldn't want to monetize one of the world's most successful websites by placing targeted ads, for example, he responded that running Wikipedia as a charity "just felt right, knowledge should be free for everyone."[2]

Wikipedia's slogan is "the Free Encyclopedia that anyone can edit." Since it is open source, any person, expert or novice, can contribute content and edit pages using the handy "edit this page" button. Although Wikipedia has 26 million registered accounts, and any of these people can edit content, some 100,000 Wikipedians represent the core. They volunteer as editors and authors, representing a global community of widely diverse views.

Although Wikipedia's volume of English entries is more than 500 times greater than that of Britannica, the site is not as error-prone as you might think. The free online encyclopedia relies on the wisdom of the crowds, which assumes "the many" often know more than "the expert." Moreover, user-generated content needs to be verifiable by reliable sources such as links to reputable websites. A peer-reviewed study by *Nature* of selected science topics found that the error rate of Wikipedia and Britannica was roughly the same. Yet, Wikipedia's crowdsourcing approach to display user-generated content is not without criticism. The most serious are that the content may be unreliable and unauthoritative, that it could exhibit systematic bias, and that group dynamics might prevent objective and factual reporting.

DISCUSSION QUESTIONS

1. The MiniCase provides an example of how advancements in technology can render traditional business models obsolete. With introduction of its CD-based Encarta, Microsoft destroyed about half the value created by Britannica. In turn, Wikipedia moved away from Britannica's and Microsoft's proprietary business models to an open-source model powered by user-generated content and available to anyone on the Internet. In doing so, it destroyed Encarta's business, which Microsoft shut down in 2009. At the same time, Wikipedia created substantial benefits for users by shifting to the open-source model for content. Because Wikipedia was able to create value for consumers by driving the price for the end user to zero and making the information instantly accessible on the Internet, there is no future for printed or CD-based encyclopedias.

   a. What are the general take-aways in regard to innovation as driver of competition?

   b. How can existing firms respond to disruptions in their industry?

2. The founder of Wikipedia, Jimmy Wales, is a social entrepreneur. Raised in Alabama, Wales was educated by his mother and grandmother who ran a nontraditional school. In 1994, he dropped out of a doctoral program in economics at Indiana University to take a job at a stock brokerage firm in Chicago. In the evenings he wrote computer code for fun and built a web browser. During the late 1990s Internet boom, Wales was one of the first to grasp the power of an open-source method to provide knowledge on a very large scale. What differentiates Wales from other web entrepreneurs is his idealism: Wikipedia is free for the end user and supports itself solely by donations. Wales' idealism is a form of social entrepreneurship: His vision is to make the entire repository of human knowledge available to anyone, anywhere for free.

   a. If you were the founder of Wikipedia, would you want to monetize the business? Why or why not?

   b. What are the pros and cons of for-profit vs. nonprofit business? Where do you come down?

3. How can Wikipedia maintain and grow its ability to harness the crowdsourcing of its "Wikipedians" to maintain high-quality and quickly updated content?

4. As Wikipedia keeps growing, do you think it can continue to rely exclusively on donations in time and money? Why or why not? What other "business models" could be considered? Would any of those "violate the spirit of Wikipedia"? Why or why not?

5. What, if anything, should Wikipedia do to ensure that its articles present a "neutral point of view"? Shouldn't the crowdsourcing approach ensure objectivity? Does a "neutral point of view" matter to Wikipedia's sustainability? Why or why not?

Endnotes

[1] http://en.wikipedia.org/wiki/Wikipedia:Donation_appeal_ideas.

[2] CBS 60 Minutes video "Wikimania," www.cbsnews.com/news/wikipedia-jimmy-wales-morley-safer-60-minutes/, April 5, 2015.

Sources: This MiniCase is based on: CBS 60 Minutes video "Wikimania," www.cbsnews.com/news/wikipedia-jimmy-wales-morley-safer-60-minutes/, April 5, 2015; "How Jimmy Wales' Wikipedia harnessed the web as a force for good," *Wired,* March 19, 2013; Greenstein, S., and F. Zhu (2012), "Is Wikipedia biased?" *American Economic Review* 102: 343–348; "End of era for Encyclopaedia Britannica," *The Wall Street Journal,* March 14, 2012; Greenstein, S., and F. Zhu (2012), "Is Wikipedia biased?" *American Economic Review* 102: 343–348; www.encyclopediacenter.com; www.alexa.com/topsites; "Wikipedia's old-fashioned revolution," *The Wall Street Journal,* April 6, 2009; Anderson, C. (2009), *Free. The Future of a Radical Price* (New York: Hyperion); "Internet encyclopedias go head-to-head," *Nature,* December 15, 2005; Anderson, C. (2006), *The Long Tail. Why the Future of Business Is Selling Less of More* (New York: Hyperion); Surowiecki, J. (2004), *The Wisdom of Crowds* (New York: Bantam Dell); and, of course, various Wikipedia sources.

Standards Battle: Which Automotive Technology Will Win?

IN THE ENVISIONED FUTURE Transition away from gasoline-powered cars, Nissan CEO Carlos Ghosn firmly believes the next technological paradigm will be electric motors. Ghosn calls hybrids a "halfway technology" and suggests they will be a temporary phenomenon at best. A number of start-up companies, including Tesla Motors in the United States and BYD Auto in China, share Ghosn's belief in this particular future scenario.

One of the biggest impediments to large-scale adoption of electric vehicles, however, remains the lack of appropriate infrastructure: There are few stations where drivers can recharge their car's battery when necessary. With the range of electric vehicles currently limited to some 200 miles, many consider a lack of recharging stations a serious problem (so called "range anxiety"). Tesla Motors and others, however, are working hard to develop a network of charging stations. By the summer of 2015, Tesla had built a network of some 500 supercharger stations throughout the United States.

Nissan's Ghosn believes electric cars will account for 10 percent of global auto sales over the next decade. In contrast, Toyota is convinced gasoline-electric hybrids will become the next dominant technology. These different predictions have significant influence on how much money Nissan and Toyota invest in technology and where. Nissan builds one of its fully electric vehicles, the Leaf (an acronym for *Leading, Environmentally friendly, Affordable, Family car*) at a plant in Smyrna, Tennessee. Toyota is expanding its R&D investments in hybrid technology. Nissan put its money where its mouth is and has spent millions developing its electric-car program since the late 1990s. Since it was introduced in December 2010, the Nissan Leaf has become the best-selling electric vehicle, with more than 180,000 units sold. Toyota, on the other hand, has already sold some 8 million of its popular Prius cars since they were

The Nissan Leaf, the world's best-selling electric vehicle
© Citizen of the Planet/Alamy Stock Photo

introduced in 1997. By 2020, Toyota plans to offer hybrid technology in all its vehicles. Eventually, the investments made by Nissan and Toyota will yield different returns, depending on which predictions prove more accurate.

An alternative outcome is that neither hybrids nor electric cars will become the next paradigm. To add even more uncertainty to the mix, Honda and BMW are betting on cars powered by hydrogen fuel cells. In sum, many alternative technologies are competing to become the winner in setting a new standard for propelling cars. This situation is depicted in Exhibit MC18.1, where the new technologies represent a swarm of new entries vying for dominance. Only time will tell which technology will win this standard battle.

Frank T. Rothaermel prepared this MiniCase from public sources. This MiniCase is developed for the purpose of class discussion. It is not intended to be used for any kind of endorsement, source of data, or depiction of efficient or inefficient management. All opinions expressed, all errors and omissions are entirely the author's. Revised and updated: August 11, 2015. © Frank T. Rothaermel.

EXHIBIT MC18.1 / Several Technologies Competing for Dominance

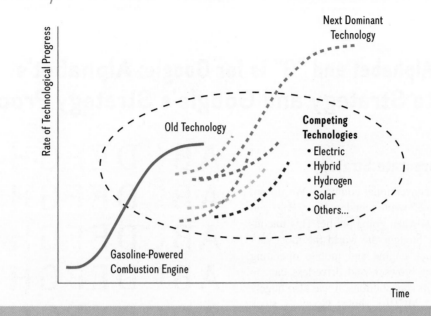

DISCUSSION QUESTIONS

1. Do you believe that the internal combustion engine will lose its dominant position in the future? Why or why not? What time horizon are you looking at?

2. Which factors do you think will be most critical in setting the next industry standard for technology in car propulsion?

3. Which companies do you think are currently best positioned to influence the next industry standard in car-propulsion technology?

4. What would you recommend different competitors (e.g., GM, Toyota, Nissan, and Tesla Motors) do to influence the emerging industry standard?

Sources: This MiniCase is based on: "Propulsion systems: The great powertrain race," *The Economist*, April 20, 2013; "Tesla recharges the battery-car market," *The Economist*, May 10, 2013; www.teslamotors. com/supercharger; "Renault-Nissan alliance sells its 250,000th electric vehicle," www.media.blog.alliance-renault-nissan.com/news/24-juin-10-am/#sthash.lwx1fRYG.dpuf; "Bright sparks," *The Economist*, January 15, 2009; "The electric-fuel-trade acid test," *The Economist*, September 3, 2009; "At Tokyo auto show, hybrids and electrics dominate," *The New York Times*, October 21, 2009; and "Risky business at Nissan," *BusinessWeek*, November 2, 2009.

"A" Is for Alphabet and "G" Is for Google: Alphabet's Corporate Strategy and Google's Strategy Process

Alphabet's Corporate Strategy

"GOOGLE IS NOT a conventional company. We do not intend to become one," wrote founders Larry Page and Sergey Brin in 2004 when going public. This unconventional company brought the world the most successful online search engine and mobile operating system, the Chrome browser, and driverless cars to name just a few of its contributions. It was also hugely successful. Exhibit MC19.1 shows Google's stock performance since its initial public offering (IPO) in 2004 vis-à-vis the tech-heavy NASDAQ 100 stock market index. Google outperformed the NASDAQ 100 by some 1,000 percentage points (or 10 times)!

In the summer of 2015, Google yet again proved that it is not a conventional company, by splitting itself and creating a diversified multidivisional

ABCDEFGHIJK
ABCDEFGHIJK
ABCDEFGHIJK
ABCDEFGHIJK
ABCDEFGHIJK

Frank T. Rothaermel prepared this MiniCase from public sources. This MiniCase is developed for the purpose of class discussion. It is not intended to be used for any kind of endorsement, source of data, or depiction of efficient or inefficient management. All opinions expressed, all errors and omissions are entirely the author's. Revised and updated: August 11, 2015. © Frank T. Rothaermel.

EXHIBIT MC19.1 / Google Stock Performance vis-à-vis NASDAQ 100 Index, 2004–2015

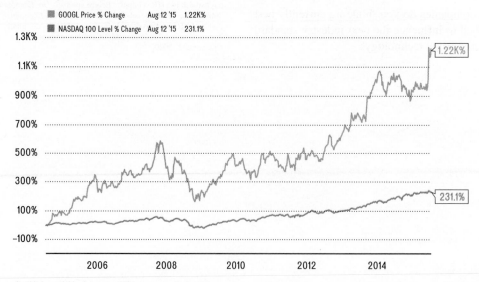

Source: Depiction of publicly available data using YCharts, www.ycharts.com.

structure overseen by Alphabet, a new corporate entity. As Google had become much more complex over the years with a number of unrelated lines of businesses (think online search and longevity research), it moved from a functional structure to a multidivisional structure. Alphabet is the new parent company, overseeing seven strategic business units, each with its own CEO and profit-and-loss responsibility (see Exhibit MC19.2).

The six business units in addition to Google Inc. are: Google X (self-driving cars, delivery drones, Internet balloons), Nest (smart thermostats), Google Fiber (broadband service), Calico (longevity research), Life Sciences (contact lenses), and Google Ventures (start-up investments). This sweeping restructuring allows the company to separate its highly profitable search and advertising business from its "moonshots" such as providing wireless Internet connectivity via high-altitude balloons or contact lenses that double as a "computer monitor" and provide real-time information to the wearer. At the time the restructuring was announced, Google's market capitalization was

some $450 billion. The new structure allows Alphabet to pursue new business far from Google's roots in online search, but that could be worth billions of dollars. Moreover, it also frees Google from huge outlays it occurred funding "moonshots" over the years, of which investors had become much less tolerant.

Larry Page is Alphabet's CEO, while Sergey Brin is president. Former Google CEO Eric Schmidt is executive chairman, and Ruth Porat is CFO, joining Google from Morgan Stanley just a few weeks before the reorganization. Page said he modeled Alphabet's new organizational structure after that of conglomerate Berkshire Hathaway led by Warren Buffett, whom he admires for effectively managing a set of unrelated businesses.

Google, the core business unit, is now being led by Sundar Pichai, who serves as CEO. The Google unit overseas the company's most profitable lines of business including Search, Ads, YouTube, Android, Chrome, and Infrastructure. Of Google's $69 billion in revenues (in 2015), the new Google unit generated $66 billion, or 96 percent. Exhibit MC19.3

EXHIBIT MC19.2 / Alphabet's Corporate Structure

depicts Google's key events and net income since its IPO in 2004 until 2015. Given Google's huge success over the years, let's take a closer look at its strategy process.

Google's Strategy Process

Google is famous for developing many of its most well-known products and services through planned emergence, where the impetus for strategic initiatives emerged from the bottom up through *autonomous actions by lower-level employees*. The Internet company organizes the work of its engineers according to a 70-20-10 rule. The majority of the engineers' work time (70 percent) is focused on its main business, search and ads. Google also allows its engineers to spend one day a week (20 percent) on ideas of their own choosing, and the remainder (10 percent) on total wild cards such as Project Loon (now part of Google X), which is an envisioned network of high-altitude balloons traveling on the edge of space to provide wireless Internet services to the two-thirds of the world's population in rural and remote areas that do not yet have Internet access.

Google reports that half of its new products came from the 20 percent rule, including Gmail, Google Maps, Google News, and Orkut. Even Google's billion-dollar business AdSense, which enables creators of content sites in its network, such as those that publish posts on Google's blogger site, to serve online ads that are targeted to the site's content, came from the 20 percent time. In particular, it started with an experiment by two Google engineers to match the content of e-mail messages in its Gmail system with targeted ads based on the e-mail's content.

Although Google has a stellar track record through its strategy process of planned emergence, it fumbled its social networking opportunity presented by Orkut. In 2002, some two years before Facebook was started (equating to eons in Internet time), Google engineer Orkut Buyukkokten had developed a social network using his 20 percent discretionary time. Marissa Mayer, then Google's vice president in charge of this project, liked what she saw and provided initial support. After adding more engineers to further Orkut's development, Google was astonished at the early success of the social network: within the first month after release, hundreds of thousands of people had signed up.

EXHIBIT MC19.3 / Google's Key Events and Net Income, 1998–2015

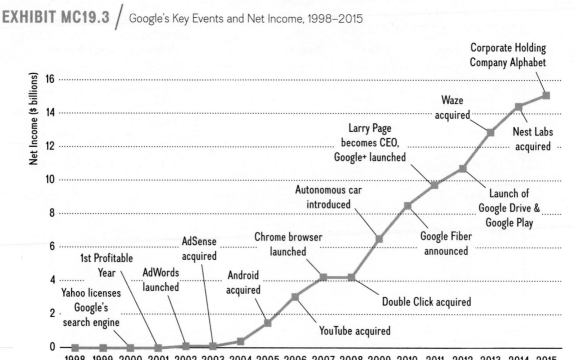

Source: Depiction of publicly available data.

In 2014, Google shut down Orkut. At that time, Orkut had a mere 30 million users, mostly in Brazil and India, which pales in comparison to Facebook's more than 1.5 billion users worldwide.

Why did Google fumble its lead over Facebook? Google had a huge opportunity to become the leader in social networking because MySpace imploded after it was acquired by News Corp. Despite initial support, Google's top executives felt that social networking did not fit its vision *to organize the world's information and make it universally accessible and useful.* Google relied on highly complex and proprietary algorithms to organize the knowledge available on the Internet and serve up targeted search ads. Social networking software, in comparison, is fairly pedestrian. Google's co-founders, Brin and Page, both exceptional computer scientists, looked down on social networking. They felt their Page-Rank algorithm that accounts for hundreds of variables and considers all available websites was far superior in providing *objective* recommendations to users' search queries than *subjective* endorsements by someone's online friends. As a consequence, they snubbed social networking. Moreover, given the many different projects Google was pursuing at that time, Orkut was ranked as a low priority by Google's top executives. Starved of further resources, the social networking site withered, making Facebook the undisputed leader.

In 2011, Google launched Google+, its newest social networking service. By integrating all its services such as Gmail, YouTube, Chrome, and others into one user interface and requiring users of even just one Google product to sign in to its portal, the company tried to catch up with Facebook. Not being able to access Facebook users' activities limits Google's ability to serve targeted ads, and thus cuts into its main line of business. On the other hand, Facebook has a captive audience 1.5 billion strong who spent on average 45 minutes daily on its sites (including Facebook Messenger and photo-sharing app Instagram). AdWords is Google's main online advertising product and garners some 85 percent of Google's total revenues of $66 billion (in 2015). Meanwhile, Facebook's search and mobile advertising business is growing rapidly. While Google still leads and captures roughly 35 percent of the $70 billion mobile advertising industry, Facebook is growing faster.

DISCUSSION QUESTIONS

1. Why did Google restructure itself and create Alphabet? What is it hoping to accomplish? For additional insights, see Larry Page's blog post announcing the restructuring at http://googleblog.blogspot.com/2015/08/google-alphabet.html.

2. Do you think the reorganization is beneficial for Alphabet's "moonshots," now housed in their own business unit with profit-and-loss responsibility?

3. As of the fall of 2015, Alphabet is a "one-trick pony," with Google's online search and advertising business bringing in basically all the profits. Why has Google "failed" to develop other profitable businesses? Is Google's strategy process of planned emergence to blame? Why or why not?

4. Given that Google is now a standalone business run by Sundar Pichai, do you expect that its strategy process will change? Why or why not? If so, how?

Sources: This MiniCase is based on: "Facebook, Google tighten grip on mobile ads," *The Wall Street Journal,* July 29, 2015; "Google creates parent company called Alphabet in restructuring," *The Wall Street Journal,* August 10, 2015; Carlson, N. (2015), *Marissa Mayer and the Fight to Save Yahoo!* (New York: Hachette Book Group); various Google 10-K reports filed with U.S. Securities and Exchange Commission; Edwards, D. (2012), *I'm Feeling Lucky: The Confessions of Google Employee Number 59* (New York: Houghton Mifflin Harcourt); Levy, S. (2011), *In the Plex: How Google Thinks, Works, and Shapes Our Lives* (New York: Simon & Schuster); and www.google.com/loon/.

HP's Boardroom Drama and Divorce

WITH SOME $115 billion annual revenues in 2015, Hewlett-Packard (HP) is one of the largest technology companies in the world. Indeed, HP was once so successful that it was featured as one of a handful of visionary companies in the business bestseller *Built to Last* (published in 1994). These select companies outperformed the stock market by a wide margin over several decades. *Built to Last* opens with a quote by HP's co-founder Bill Hewlett:

> As I look back on my life's work, I'm probably most proud of having helped to create a company that by virtue of its values, practices, and success has had a tremendous impact on the way companies are managed around the world. And I'm particularly proud that I'm leaving behind an ongoing organization that can live on as a role model long after I'm gone.[1]

Hewlett passed away in 2001. Much has changed at HP since then. Within the short 18 months from April 2010 to November 2012, HP's market value dropped by almost 80 percent, wiping out $82 billion in shareholder wealth. Longer term, since early 2010 until summer 2015, HP's stock price declined by 42 percent, while the tech-heavy NASDAQ 100, containing many firms that compete with HP, rose by over 143 percent. This marks a whopping 185 percentage points difference in performance! It turns out that a perfect storm of corporate-governance problems, combined with repeated ethical shortcomings, had been brewing at HP for a decade. The result: a sustained competitive disadvantage.

This development is even more astonishing given that, at one point, HP was much admired for its corporate culture—known as "the HP Way." The core values of the HP Way include business conducted with "uncompromising integrity," as well as "trust and respect for individuals," among others (see Exhibit MC20.1) The HP Way guided the company since its inception in 1938, when it was founded with some $500 of initial investment in Dave Packard's garage in Palo Alto, California. As one of the world's most

Meg Whitman, CEO Hewlett Packard Enterprise
© David Paul Morris/Bloomberg/Getty Images

successful technology companies (think "laser printing"), HP initiated the famous technology cluster known as Silicon Valley. Over the last decade, however, HP's board of directors—a group of individuals that is supposed to represent the interests of the firm's shareholders and oversee the CEO—seemed to forget the HP Way as it violated its core values time and time again. In the process, HP's board of directors acted out a drama series rivaling *House of Cards,* with the season finale not yet in sight.

The first season of the drama "aired" in 2006. The online technology site CNET published an article on HP's strategy. Quoting an anonymous source, the article disclosed sensitive details that could have come only from one of the directors or senior executives at HP. Eager to discover the identity of the leaker, Patricia Dunn, then chair of the board, launched a covert

Frank T. Rothaermel prepared this MiniCase from public sources. He gratefully acknowledges the contribution of Ling Yang on an earlier version. This MiniCase is developed for the purpose of class discussion. It is not intended to be used for any kind of endorsement, source of data, or depiction of efficient or inefficient management. All opinions expressed, all errors and omissions are entirely the author's. Revised and updated: August 3, 2015. © Frank T. Rothaermel.

EXHIBIT MC20.1 / The HP Way

We have trust and respect for individuals.

We approach each situation with the belief that people want to do a good job and will do so, given the proper tools and support. We attract highly capable, diverse, innovative people and recognize their efforts and contributions to the company. HP people contribute enthusiastically and share in the success that they make possible.

We focus on a high level of achievement and contribution.

Our customers expect HP products and services to be of the highest quality and to provide lasting value. To achieve this, all HP people, especially managers, must be leaders who generate enthusiasm and respond with extra effort to meet customer needs. Techniques and management practices which are effective today may be outdated in the future. For us to remain at the forefront in all our activities, people should always be looking for new and better ways to do their work.

We conduct our business with uncompromising integrity.

We expect HP people to be open and honest in their dealings to earn the trust and loyalty of others. People at every level are expected to adhere to the highest standards of business ethics and must understand that anything less is unacceptable. As a practical matter, ethical conduct cannot be assured by written HP policies and codes; it must be an integral part of the organization, a deeply ingrained tradition that is passed from one generation of employees to another.

We achieve our common objectives through teamwork.

We recognize that it is only through effective cooperation within and among organizations that we can achieve our goals. Our commitment is to work as a worldwide team to fulfill the expectations of our customers, shareholders and others who depend upon us. The benefits and obligations of doing business are shared among all HP people.

We encourage flexibility and innovation.

We create an inclusive work environment which supports the diversity of our people and stimulates innovation. We strive for overall objectives which are clearly stated and agreed upon, and allow people flexibility in working toward goals in ways that they help determine are best for the organization. HP people should personally accept responsibility and be encouraged to upgrade their skills and capabilities through ongoing training and development. This is especially important in a technical business where the rate of progress is rapid and where people are expected to adapt to change.

Source: Hewlett-Packard Alumni Association, www.hpalumni.org/hp_way.htm

investigation. She hired an outside security firm to conduct surveillance on HP's board members, select employees, and even some journalists. Although it is common for companies to monitor phone and computer use of their employees, HP's investigation went above and beyond. The private investigators used an illegal spying technique called "pretexting" (impersonating the targets) to obtain phone records by contacting the telecom service providers. The security firm obtained some 300 telephone records covering mobile, home, and office phones of all directors (including Dunn), nine journalists, and several HP employees. Not to leave anything to chance, the security firm also obtained phone records of the spouses and even the children of HP board members and employees. The firm also conducted physical surveillance of the suspected leaker—board member George Keyworth and his spouse—as well as two other directors.

In a May 2006 board meeting, Dunn presented the evidence gathered, implicating Keyworth as the source of the leak. Dunn's disclosure of the investigation infuriated HP director Thomas Perkins, a prominent venture capitalist, so much that he resigned on the spot. Perkins called the HP-initiated surveillance "illegal, unethical, and a misplaced corporate priority."[2] Perkins also forced HP to disclose the spying campaign to the Securities and Exchange Commission (and thus the public) as his reason for resigning. Dunn and Keyworth were dismissed from the board along with six senior HP managers. Despite the boardroom drama, HP came out unscathed financially, largely due to the superior performance of then-CEO Mark Hurd.

Hurd was appointed Hewlett-Packard's CEO in the spring of 2005. He began his business career 25 years earlier as an entry-level salesperson with NCR, a U.S. technology company best known for its bar code scanners in retail outlets and automatic teller machines (ATMs). By the time he worked his way up to the role of CEO at NCR, he had earned a reputation as a low-profile, no-nonsense manager focused on flawless strategy execution. When he was appointed HP's CEO, industry analysts praised its board of directors. Moreover, investors hoped that Hurd would run an efficient and lean operation at HP and return the company to its former greatness and, above all, profitability.

Hurd did not disappoint. By all indications, he was highly successful at the helm of HP. The company became number one in desktop computer sales and increased its lead in inkjet and laser printers to more than 50 percent market share. Through significant cost-cutting and streamlining measures, Hurd turned HP into a lean operation. For example, he oversaw large-scale layoffs and a pay cut for all remaining employees as he reorganized the company. Wall Street rewarded HP shareholders with an almost 90 percent stock price appreciation during Hurd's tenure, outperforming broader stock market indices by a wide margin.

Yet, in the summer of 2010, HP aired the second season of its boardroom soap opera. The HP board found itself caught "between a rock and a hard place," with no easy options in sight. Jodie Fisher, a former adult-movie actress, filed a lawsuit against Hurd, alleging sexual harassment. As an independent contractor, she worked as a hostess at HP-sponsored events. In this function, she screened attending HP customers and personally ensured that Hurd would spend time with the most important ones. With another ethics scandal looming despite Hurd's stellar financial results for the company, HP's board of directors forced him to resign. He left HP in August 2010 with an exit package worth $35 million.

The third season of HP's boardroom drama began in the fall of 2010 when HP announced Leo Apotheker as its new CEO. Apotheker, who came to HP after being let go from the German enterprise software company SAP, proposed a new corporate strategy for HP. He suggested that the company focus on enterprise software solutions and spin out its low-margin consumer hardware business. HP's consumer hardware business resulted from the $25 billion legacy acquisition of Compaq during the tumultuous tenure of CEO Carly Fiorina, prior to Mark Hurd. The hardware business had grown to 40 percent of HP's total revenues. Under Apotheker, HP also exited the mobile device industry, most notably tablet computers. Many viewed this move as capitulating to Apple's dominance.

As part of his new corporate strategy, Apotheker acquired the British software company Autonomy for $11 billion, which analysts saw as grossly overvalued. Shortly thereafter, HP took an almost $9 billion write-down due to alleged "accounting inaccuracies" at Autonomy. HP's stock went into free fall. Under Apotheker's short 11 months at the helm of HP, the share price dropped by almost 50 percent. HP's due diligence process by the board was clearly flawed when acquiring Autonomy. The process itself was truncated. Moreover, the HP board did not heed the red flags thrown up by Deloitte, Autonomy's auditor. Indeed, a few days before the Autonomy acquisition was finalized, Deloitte auditors asked to meet with the board to inform them about a former Autonomy executive who accused the company of accounting irregularities. Deloitte also added that it investigated the claim and did not find any irregularities.

Perhaps most problematic, the board fell victim to groupthink, rallying around Apotheker as CEO and Ray Lane, the board chair, who strongly supported him. Apotheker was eager to make a high-impact acquisition to put his strategic vision of HP as a software and service company into action. In the wake of the Hurd ethics scandal, an outside recruiting firm had proposed Apotheker as CEO and Lane as the new chair of HP's board of directors. The full board never met either of the men before hiring them into key strategic positions! The HP board of directors experienced a major shakeup after the Hurd ethics scandal and then again after the departure of Apotheker. Lane stepped down as chairman of HP's board in the spring of 2013, but remains a director.

After Apotheker was let go, HP did not conduct a search for its next CEO. Instead, in the fall of 2011, the board appointed one of its directors, Meg Whitman, as CEO because the board members were "too exhausted by the fighting."[3] She was formerly the CEO at eBay, had been appointed to HP's board of directors in 2011, and was a director when the Autonomy acquisition was approved. In an effort to regain competitiveness Whitman cut 55,000 jobs at HP.

In 2015, HP split into two firms, one focusing on consumer hardware (PCs and printers) called HP

Inc. ($58 billion in revenues), and the other on business equipment and services called Hewlett Packard Enterprise ($57 billion in revenues). This corporate strategy move is very similar to what Apotheker had suggested three years earlier. This is also a similar move to that IBM undertook a decade earlier, one of HP's main rivals. Whitman will remain as CEO of the new Hewlett Packard Enterprise, which is considered to have higher growth potential than the low-margin computer hardware business.

DISCUSSION QUESTIONS

1. Who is to blame for HP's shareholder-value destruction—the CEO, the board of directors, or both? What recourse, if any, do shareholders have?

2. You are brought in as (a) a corporate governance consultant or (b) a business ethics consultant by HP's CEO. What recommendations would you give the CEO, Meg Whitman? How would you go about implementing them? Be specific.

3. Why is HP splitting itself into two firms, a move that was rejected just three years earlier? Do you think the corporate strategy move of splitting the "old" HP into two companies (HP Inc. and Hewlett Packard Enterprise) will create shareholder value? Why or why not? Which of the two companies would you expect to be the higher performer? Why?

4. Discuss the general lessons in terms of corporate governance and business ethics that can be drawn from this MiniCase.

Endnotes

[1] Bill Hewlett, HP co-founder, as quoted in Collins, J.C., and J.I. Porras (1994), *Built to Last: Successful Habits of Visionary Companies* (New York: HarperCollins), p. 1.

[2] "Suspicions and spies in Silicon Valley," *Newsweek,* September 17, 2006.

[3] "How Hewlett-Packard lost its way," *CNN Money,* May 8, 2012.

Sources: This MiniCase is based on: "As H-P split nears, bosses tick off a surgery checklist," *The Wall Street Journal,* June 30, 2015; "Split today, merge tomorrow," *The Economist,* October 7, 2014; "Inside HP's missed chance to avoid a disastrous deal," *The Wall Street Journal,* January 21, 2013; "The HP Way out," *The Economist,* April 5, 2013; "How Hewlett-Packard lost its way," *CNN Money,* May 8, 2012; "HP shakes up board in scandal's wake," *The Wall Street Journal,* January 21, 2011; "HP CEO Mark Hurd resigns after sexual-harassment probe," *The Huffington Post,* August 6, 2010; "The curse of HP," *The Economist,* August 12, 2010; "Corporate governance: Spying and leaking are wrong," *The Economist,* September 14, 2006; "Corporate governance: Pretext in context," *The Economist,* September 14, 2006; Packard, D. (1995), *HP Way: How Bill Hewlett and I Built Our Company* (New York: Collins); and Collins, J.C., and J.I. Porras (1994), *Built to Last: Successful Habits of Visionary Companies* (New York: HarperCollins).

Hollywood Goes Global

HOLLYWOOD MOVIES HAVE always been a quintessentially American product. Globalization, however, has changed the economics of the movie industry. Foreign ticket sales for Hollywood blockbusters made up 50 percent of worldwide totals in 2000. By 2014, they made up two-thirds, with some movies (e.g., *Transformers: Age of Extinction*) grossing 80 percent of total box-office receipts overseas. Taken together, of the total $26 billion that Hollywood movies grossed in 2014, more than $16 billion came from outside the United States. Today, largely because of the collapse of DVD/Blu-ray sales, Hollywood would be unable to continue producing big-budget movies without foreign revenues. Foreign sales now make or break the success of newly released big-budget movies.

"We Need Movies That Break Out Internationally"

Avatar is the highest-grossing movie to date, earning more than $2.7 billion since its release in 2009. It may surprise you to learn that non-U.S. box-office sales account for almost 75 percent of that number. *Avatar* was hugely popular in Asia, especially in China, where the government gave permission to increase the number of movie theaters showing the film from 5,000 to 35,000. Another of James Cameron's popular films, *Titanic,* grossed almost 70 percent of its $1.8 billion earnings in overseas markets. The trend is clear: Between 2009 and 2013, domestic box-office revenues remained unchanged, but international box-office receipts rose by 33 percent. Exhibit MC21.1 depicts the lifetime revenues of Hollywood's all-time blockbuster movies, broken down into domestic and foreign.

Given the increasing importance of non-U.S. box-office sales, Hollywood studios are changing their business models. Rob Moore, vice chairman of Paramount Pictures, explains: "We need to make movies that have the ability to break out internationally.

For the Chinese audience, Marvel execs added four minutes to *Iron Man 3* with Chinese actors.
© Photofest

That's the only way to make the economic puzzle of film production work today."[1] As a result, studios have changed a number of tactics. Some mega-releases such as Disney's *Monsters University* (the prequel to *Monsters, Inc.*) premiered first in foreign markets before being shown in the United States. *Avengers: Age of Ultron* set the record in 2015 for the biggest overseas opening, surpassing a record set weeks earlier by *Furious 7,* in The Fast and the Furious film series.

Hollywood is also adapting scripts to appeal to global audiences, casting foreign actors in leading roles, and pulling the plug on projects that seem too

Frank T. Rothaermel prepared this MiniCase from public sources. He gratefully acknowledges research assistance by James Hoadley. This MiniCase is developed for the purpose of class discussion. It is not intended to be used for any kind of endorsement, source of data, or depiction of efficient or inefficient management. All opinions expressed, all errors and omissions are entirely the author's. Revised and updated: July 10, 2015. © Frank T. Rothaermel.

EXHIBIT MC21.1 / Lifetime Revenues of Hollywood Blockbuster Movies, > $850 million (release year in parentheses)

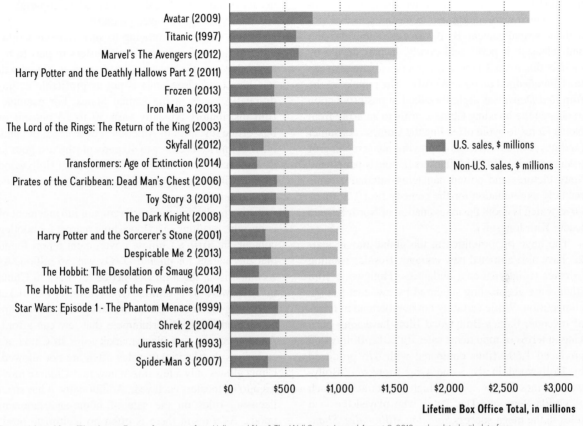

Source: Adapted from "Plot change: Foreign forces transform Hollywood films," *The Wall Street Journal*, August 2, 2010, and updated with data from http://boxofficemojo.com for years 2010–2014.

U.S.-centric. For example, the film *G.I. Joe: The Rise of Cobra* prominently featured South Korean movie star Byung-hun Lee and South African actor Arnold Vosloo. On the other hand, Disney's *Wedding Banned,* a romantic comedy about a divorced couple trying to prevent their daughter from getting married, was axed in the advanced production stage despite several marquee stars (Robin Williams, Anna Faris, and Diane Keaton) because of perceptions that it would not succeed outside the American market.

Although Hollywood has had to release versions of films edited to meet local censorship rules for many years, a recent phenomenon has been the recording of special scenes to cater to audiences in specific markets. Disney's Marvel Studios produced two versions of the 2013 box office hit *Iron Man 3*. One version of the film was produced for general release, and another version specifically targeted the 1.3 billion Chinese

that make up the second-largest film market in the world. This version included bonus footage in Beijing and guest appearances by Chinese movie stars. In addition, the hits *Mission Impossible III* and *Skyfall* were edited for the Chinese markets to take out scenes that Chinese censors thought portrayed China in a negative light, even though several key scenes from these films were set in China. In 2014, only one film grossed more than $300 million domestically (*Guardians of the Galaxy*). Thanks to international releases, however, 2014 was one of the most profitable for Hollywood.

Hollywood's Global Challenges

Although globalization produces a huge upside for Hollywood, this opportunity does not come without its challenges. One serious challenge is content editing by government officials before screening. The Oscar-winning film *Django Unchained* saw its release in China temporarily canceled due to "technical reasons," which were interpreted to mean excessive violent and sexual content. By the time the film was recut and released, it performed poorly, in part driven by the fact that many Chinese filmgoers had already seen the film unedited on pirated DVDs. The remake of the film *Red Dawn* was digitally edited in postproduction to change the invading Chinese army to an army from North Korea to avoid offending the Chinese consumer (and government officials approving the screening of foreign movies). In 2014, hackers famously penetrated Sony Pictures and posted damaging internal e-mails publicly as retaliation for the comedy film *The Interview,* which is about the assassination of North Korean leader Kim Jong-un.

The huge opportunities in the global movie market have also attracted new entrants. Besides wanting to cater to international audiences, Hollywood film studios are also feeling squeezed by low-cost foreign competition. While certainly not number one in terms of revenue, India's Bollywood films have long been king in terms of total ticket sales. In 2012, Bollywood produced 1,602 films compared with 476 produced by Hollywood in the same year. Moreover, Bollywood brings in low-cost but high-impact actors such as Freida Pinto and Dev Patel, who played the lead roles in the mega-success *Slumdog Millionaire. Slumdog*'s budget was merely $14 million, but the movie grossed almost $400 million and won eight Oscars. By comparison, Hollywood's budget for *Home Alone,* a similar success in terms of revenues, was nearly five times as large. Globalization also puts pressure on the pay of Hollywood stars. Given the importance of international audiences and the availability of foreign stars and movies, the days are over when stars such as Tom Hanks, Eddie Murphy, and Julia Roberts could demand 20 percent royalties on total ticket sales.

The fact that Hollywood now garners roughly two-thirds of its revenues internationally is somewhat surprising given several constraints that U.S. films have when selling internationally. Besides potential government interference with content, there are numerous piracy concerns. Even in the European Union (EU), where countries including Britain and France impose fines on producers and buyers of pirated content, other countries, such as Spain, have long been havens for the distribution of illegal movies and music. In 2011, Spain passed a new law to provide better protection

of copyrighted material, but enforcement may be difficult in a country where nearly 50 percent of all Internet users admit to illegally downloading copyrighted content (twice the EU average rate).

Movie studios are moving to simultaneous worldwide releases of expected blockbusters in part to try to cut down on the revenues lost to piracy. Yet growth in China (and elsewhere) is not as profitable as traditional releases in the United States. For example, film distributors typically earn 50 to 55 percent of box-office revenues in America. The average in many other countries is closer to 40 percent (the rest goes to the cinema owner). But in China, a typical Hollywood film distributor gets only 15 percent of the box-office ticket revenue.

China is also infamous for rampant infringement of copyright, resulting in a flourishing market for bootleg content. In 2010, a Chinese government report found that the market for pirated DVDs was $6 billion. As a comparison, the *total* box-office revenues in China in 2010 were $1.5 billion. One reason is that ticket prices for movies in China are steep and movies are considered luxury entertainment that few can afford. Another reason that black-market sales in China are so high is that legitimate sales often are not allowed. China allows only a few dozen new non-Chinese movies into its theaters each year. Additionally, it has strict licensing rules on the sale of home-entertainment goods. As a result there is often no legitimate product competing with the bootleg offerings available via DVD and the Internet in China.

And with the move from physical media like DVDs and Blu-ray discs to digital streaming, China has kept up. While Netflix does not yet do business in China and it blocks Chinese computers from accessing its service, it is estimated that 20 million Chinese access Netflix using proxy servers that mask the actual location of the user's machine. Netflix's original series *House of Cards* has been a huge success not only in the United States but also in China. In 2015, Netflix confirmed that it is in talks with Chinese online streaming companies about bringing its content to China. Netflix content could give Chinese regulators pause, however. The *House of Cards* plotline, for example, involves a corrupt Chinese businessman operating at the highest level of politics.

DISCUSSION QUESTIONS

1. Given the economics of the now global movie industry, what are the strategic implications for

Hollywood studios? What are some opportunities, and what are some threats? How should Hollywood movie studies take advantage of these opportunities, while mitigating the threats?

2. How would you prioritize which nations to expand distribution into if you were working for a major Hollywood movie studio?

3. What alternatives could movie producers develop to help combat the piracy of first-run movies and follow-on DVD and Internet releases?

Endnote

[1] "Plot change: Foreign forces transform Hollywood films," *The Wall Street Journal*, August 2, 2010.

Sources: This MiniCase is based on: Langfitt, F., "How China's censors influence Hollywood," *NPR*, May 18, 2015, www.npr.org/sections/parallels/2015/05/18/407619652/how-chinas-censors-influence-hollywood, retrieved July 5, 2015; Lin, L., "Netflix in talks to take content to China," *The Wall Street Journal*, May 15, 2015; "China's losing battle with Internet censorship," *Chicago Tribune*, January 31, 2015, www.chicagotribune.com/news/opinion/editorials/ct-china-vpn-xi-jinping-internet-beijing-edit-jm-20150130-story.html, retrieved July 5, 2015; Brook, T., "How the global box office is changing Hollywood," October 21, 2014, www.bbc.com/culture/story/20130620-is-china-hollywoods-future, retrieved July 5, 2015; "China's film market is going gangbusters, but it may not help Hollywood much," *Quartz*, March 27, 2014, http://qz.com/192250/chinas-film-market-is-going-gangbusters-but-it-may-not-help-hollywood-much/, retrieved July 5, 2015; McCarthy, N., "Bollywood: India's film industry by the numbers," infographic, *Forbes*, September 3, 2014, www.forbes.com/sites/niallmccarthy/2015/07/10/is-hollywood-sexist-half-of-americans-certainly-think-so-infographic/, retrieved July 5, 2015; Miller, D., "After the controversy, 'Django Unchained' flops in China," *The Los Angeles Times*, June 14, 2014; MacSlarrow, J., "Is Bollywood India's next greatest export?" *Global Intellectual Property Center*, June 7, 2013, www.theglobalipcenter.com/is-bollywood-indias-next-greatest-export/, retrieved July 5, 2015; Takada, K., "China debut of Django Unchained suddenly cancelled for technical reasons," *Reuters*, April 11, 2013, www.reuters.com/article/2013/04/11/us-china-django-cancel-idUSBRE93A06120130411, retrieved July 5, 2015; "'Hobbit' to break $1 billion," *Daily Variety*, January 22, 2013; "China gets its own version of Iron Man 3 after Disney allows the country's film censors onto the set," *MailOnline*, April 14, 2012; Levin, D., and J. Horn, "DVD pirates running rampant in China," *Los Angeles Times*, March 22, 2011; "Ending the open season on artists," *The Economist*, February 17, 2011; "Bigger abroad," *The Economist*, February 17, 2011; "Plot change: Foreign forces transform Hollywood films," *The Wall Street Journal*, August 2, 2010; "Hollywood squeezes stars' pay in slump," *The Wall Street Journal*, April 2, 2009; "News Corporation," *The Economist*, February 26, 2009; and "Slumdog Millionaire wins eight Oscars," *The Wall Street Journal*, February 23, 2009.

Does GM's Future Lie in China?

GIVEN THE SHEER size of the U.S. automotive market, the "old" GM concentrated mainly on its domestic market. GM once held more than 50 percent market share in the United States and was the leader in global car sales (by units) between 1931 and 2007, before filing for bankruptcy in 2009.[1] In its heyday, GM employed 350,000 U.S. workers and was an American icon. The future for the "new" GM may lie overseas, however; most notably in China. Some 70 percent of GM's revenues are now from outside the United States. This is quite a high level of globalization for a company that once was focused on the domestic market only. GM sold more than 3.6 million vehicles in China, 37 percent of total GM cars sold. The Chinese market is becoming more and more important to GM's performance, accounting already for almost 30 percent of total GM revenues of some $155 billion (in 2014).

With a population of 1.4 billion and currently only 11 vehicles per 100 people—compared with a vehicle density of 81 per 100 in the United States—China offers tremendous growth opportunities for the automotive industry. Since China joined the World Trade Organization (WTO) in 2001, its domestic auto market has been growing rapidly and has now overtaken the United States as the largest in the world. Although the growth of the Chinese auto market has slowed in recent years because of the economy's downturn, GM CEO Mary Barra remains convinced that China offers significant long-term growth opportunities.

Unlike some of its main rivals, GM entered the Chinese market early. In 1997, GM formed a joint venture with Shanghai Automotive Industrial Corp. (SAIC), one of the "big four" Chinese carmakers. SAIC is one of the largest companies worldwide and ranked 60th on the Fortune Global 100 list. Over almost 20 years, GM was able to develop *guanxi*—social networks and relationships that facilitate business dealings—with its Chinese business partners and government officials.

Mary Barra, General Motors CEO
© Tomohiro Ohsumi/Bloomberg/Getty Images

GM's China operation has been cost-competitive from day one. The company operates about the same number of assembly plants in China as in the United States, but sells more vehicles while employing about half the number of employees. Chinese workers cost only a fraction of what U.S. workers do, and GM is not weighed down by additional health care and pension obligations.

Although struggling in the United States, GM's Cadillac luxury brand is in high demand in China, where owning a Cadillac is considered a status symbol. GM's best-selling model in China, however, is the Wuling Sunshine, a small, boxy, purely functional "micro van" priced between $5,000 and $10,000 depending on what options the customer chooses. The SAIC-GM joint venture sold almost 2 million Wuling vehicles in China in 2014. The Wuling Sunshine may help GM further penetrate the Chinese market; it also may be an introductory car for other emerging

Frank T. Rothaermel prepared this MiniCase from public sources. This Mini-Case is developed for the purpose of class discussion. It is not intended to be used for any kind of endorsement, source of data, or depiction of efficient or inefficient management. All opinions expressed, all errors and omissions are entirely the author's. Revised and updated: August 18, 2015. © Frank T. Rothaermel.

markets, such as India. GM's low-cost strategy with this vehicle has been so successful that the firm is planning to expand the Wuling product line and offer the vehicle globally. GM already sells the Wuling Sunshine in Brazil under the Buick nameplate.

Taken together, China and other emerging economies in Asia, Latin America, and the Middle East are becoming more and more critical to GM's future performance as it strives to become a lean and low-cost manufacturer of profitable small cars (at least for its non-U.S. markets). To back up its strategic intent, GM has quadrupled its engineering and design personnel in China and is investing a quarter-billion dollars to build a cutting-edge R&D center on its Shanghai campus, home of its international headquarters. Moreover, GM is spending an estimated $14 billion to build five additional manufacturing plants to support anticipated annual sales of 5 million vehicles.

Yet, given the slowdown in the Chinese economy combined with devaluation of the Chinese currency (the yuan), the competitive intensity in the world's largest automobile market is becoming more intense. Moreover, several government-supported domestic car manufacturers in China are initiating a cut-throat price war to gain market share and with it scale. In contrast, low gas prices in the United States have fueled high demand for sport utility vehicles (SUVs) and trucks, where GM and Ford hold strong positions.

DISCUSSION QUESTIONS

1. What explains the resurgence of the "new" GM in the United States? Do you think GM can sustain its competitive advantage in the United States? Why or why not? Buttress your arguments.

2. How important are non-U.S. sales to GM? What implications does this have for GM's global and business strategy? Think about the integration-response framework to inform global strategy and different strategic positions to inform business strategy.

3. In 2014, GM held almost 15 percent market share in China, while Ford held only 3 percent. Why was GM so successful in China, while some of its rivals, including Ford, struggle to gain a stronger position in the world's largest automobile market?

4. What are the challenges GM is currently facing in the Chinese automobile market? How should GM's CEO address them? Be specific.

Endnote

1 Selling a large volume of cars doesn't make a company profitable if the cars are sold at a low margin or even at a loss. In contrast, Ferrari only sells some 7,000 vehicles a year but is highly profitable (not surprising because the sticker price of the entry-level Ferrari is $200,000).

Sources: This MiniCase is based on: "China stocks take GM, Ford on rough ride," *The Wall Street Journal*, July 10, 2015; "Big vehicles power surge in GM's profit," *The Wall Street Journal*, July 23, 2015; "GM, Ford flourish out of the limelight," *The Wall Street Journal*, July 28, 2015; "GM, SAIC plan to jointly design new cars," *The Wall Street Journal*, July 28, 2015; "GM hopes to shift gears after recalls," *The Wall Street Journal*, September 29, 2014; "GM 2012 global sales rise 2.9 percent on strong Chevy demand," *Reuters*, January 14, 2013; "Can China save GM?" *Forbes*, May 10, 2010; Tao, Q. (2009), "Competition in the Chinese automobile industry," in Peng, M.W. (2010), *Global Strategy*, 2e (Independence, KY: Cengage), pp. 419–425; "Cruising into China's booming car market," *The Wall Street Journal*, April 28, 2010; and various GM annual reports.

Flipkart Is Fulfilling Its Wish and Beating Amazon.com

FLIPKART'S MANTRA IS "Ab Har Wish Hogi Poori" or "Every Wish Fulfilled." For the time being, the Indian ecommerce company has fulfilled its own wish. Flipkart (www.flipkart.com/) is valued at more than $15 billion, making it the third most valuable privately held start-up company globally, after U.S. firms Palantir Technologies (data-mining software) and Snapchat (messaging app). The stated goal of the co-founders is to make Flipkart India's first $100 billion ecommerce company.

Flipkart has outperformed Amazon.com in India. How can a new venture beat Amazon.com, the king of ecommerce? Founded in 2007 by Sachin Bansal and Binny Bansal (same last name, but unrelated), Flipkart began its life just like Amazon.com: selling books online at discounted prices. To many observers, this was not surprising because both co-founders worked previously at Amazon.com, where they met. They are also both graduates of India's most prestigious university system: the Indian Institute of Technology (IIT). Flipkart continues to recruit the best and the brightest engineers from India's IITs.

Flipkart had humble beginnings, as Bansal and Bansal set up the company from their two-bedroom apartment in Bangalore with an initial investment of $8,000. What began as selling books is now disrupting retailing in India. In this land of over 1.2 billion people, more than 50 percent of its population is age 25 or younger and more than 65 percent below the age of 35. In 2020, the average Indian will be 29 years old, while the average Chinese will be 37; the average American, 42; and the average Japanese, 48. In addition, English is the country's official language, and most younger Indians are well educated and moving rapidly into the middle class. As their disposable income increases, their time to battle the chaotic Indian traffic and inclination to haggle with obstinate vendors decreases. Instead, they are using the Internet in ever larger numbers and are conducting more and more transactions online (see Exhibit MC23.1 for growth in Internet users).

In 2015, online sales were over $5 billion (see MC23.2). While Flipkart is certainly benefiting from

© Pawan Kumar/Alamy Stock Photo

the explosive growth in Indian ecommerce, it was unique tweaks to its business model that set it apart from other online retailers, including American online giants such as Amazon.com and eBay and also the highly successful Chinese Internet firm Alibaba. In 2014, Alibaba posted the biggest initial public offering ever with $25 billion, as its shares began trading on the New York Stock Exchange.

In a country where fraud is rampant and trust among vendors and customers is low, Flipkart had to first transform the way Indians shopped. It achieved this by tailoring its offerings to the idiosyncrasies of its domestic retail market. Unlike in Western economies such as the United States or Europe, retail transactions in India are mostly in cash. Credit-card penetration is very low (just about 1 percent); however, debit-card usage is growing as more of the population is serviced by the mainstream banking system. Even with the availability of plastic money options, many Indians are wary about the security of online

Frank T. Rothaermel prepared this MiniCase from public sources. He gratefully acknowledges research assistance by Srikanth Prabhu. This MiniCase is developed for the purpose of class discussion. It is not intended to be used for any kind of endorsement, source of data, or depiction of efficient or inefficient management. All opinions expressed, all errors and omissions are entirely the author's. Revised and updated: July 10, 2015. © Frank T. Rothaermel.

EXHIBIT MC23.1 / Internet Users in India ($ millions), 2007–2014

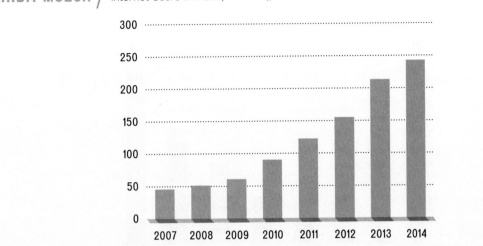

Source: Depiction of data from Internet Live Stats (www.InternetLiveStats.com), Internet & Mobile Association of India (IAMAI), International Telecommunication Union (ITU), World Bank, and United Nations Population Division.

transactions using credit or debit cards. Compounding this problem is that most Indians lack access to credit. To overcome these challenges, Flipkart was one of the first major ecommerce players in India to offer a cash-on-delivery (COD) service to online customers in 2010. This went a long way to build credibility and brand value for Flipkart. Some estimates peg the number of COD transactions in Indian ecommerce as high as 80 percent of all sales.

A second and related problem Flipkart addressed is the custom in India for shoppers to buy goods only after a thorough physical inspection of the product at a brick-and-mortar store, often by multiple family members if a larger purchase is being considered. To overcome this challenge, Flipkart introduced a hassle-free return and exchange policy. This tactic allowed Flipkart to attract many first-time online buyers, who now make up a significant portion of the company's revenues, which were over $1 billion in 2015 (up from only $10 million in 2011, a compound annual growth rate of some 220 percent). Third, Flipkart also introduced an option to purchase expensive items with its EMI (easy monthly installments) program. It accomplished this through associations with all major banks. In 10 urban areas Flipkart offers same-day delivery and guarantees next-day delivery in more than 65 metropolitan areas.

While its business model provided solutions to unique Indian ecommerce challenges, Flipkart diversified quickly into many different product categories. Starting as just an online bookseller, Flipkart now hosts 75 product categories on its platform. Its major product categories include books, electronics and accessories, lifestyle and fashion, home décor, and do-it-yourself products. While books and electronics continue to be its strongholds, lifestyle and fashion are the fastest-growing segments.

Because the Indian government continues to bar foreign direct investment in retail companies, Flipkart (which is financed by non-Indian venture capitalists from the United States, the UK, Russia, and Singapore) had to change its business model. It moved away from Amazon's model of shipping mainly merchandise it owns and that requires storage in its own warehouses to now be more akin to Alibaba, hosting third-party sellers. Flipkart morphed into an online platform that enables other merchants to sell on its website. It makes money by taking a fee on every transaction occurring on its site.

After Amazon lost out to Alibaba in China, it entered India in 2013 to sell books, DVDs, electronic goods, and fashion accessories (www.amazon.in). This made Amazon.com a latecomer to the Indian ecommerce party (see Exhibit MC23.2). Indian ecommerce companies Flipkart and runner-up Snapdeal (www.snapdeal.com) are enjoying early-mover advantages over Amazon. Perhaps, even more important, Flipkart was able to leverage its deep understanding of the Indian retail market and ecommerce into a competitive advantage. The explosive growth in Indian ecommerce is expected to continue, with Morgan Stanley predicting that ecommerce retailing in India will grow to over

EXHIBIT MC23.2 / Ecommerce Sales in India ($ billions), 2005–2016

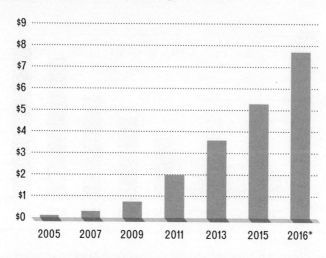

*Prediction

Source: Depiction of data from Euromonitor, McKinsey, and www.eMarketer.com

$100 billion by 2020. And Amazon is catching up fast, having matched many of Flipkart's tactics such as cash on delivery, installment payment plans, and same-day and next-day deliveries. It also offers services that Flipkart cannot yet match, such as the "fulfilled by Amazon" service (where items offered by a third-party seller on Amazon's site are shipped from an Amazon fulfillment center and all Amazon standard shipping rates and policies apply to these items). As an indication how fast Amazon is catching up: It reached sales of $1 billion just one year after it entered India. The same milestone took Snapdeal four years and Flipkart, as first major entrant, seven years to accomplish. It is too early to count out the deep-pocket and relentless Amazon and its CEO, Jeff Bezos, quite yet.

DISCUSSION QUESTIONS

1. Why was Flipkart successful in India? What is the basis of Flipkart's competitive advantage?

2. Will Flipkart be able to sustain its early lead over Amazon, given the deep pockets of the American e-commerce giant and its intentions to invest further in India? What are some of the key advantages that Flipkart has over Amazon? What are some of Flipkart's disadvantages? What would Flipkart need to do to sustain its competitive advantage?

3. Should Flipkart leverage its core competencies outside India to "go global"? If so, which countries do you think would provide the best opportunities for Flipkart, and why?

4. With a valuation of $15 billion, Flipkart is now one of the most valuable privately owned start-ups in the world. Flipkart's investors hail from the United States, United Kingdom, Russia, and Singapore. Venture capitalists (VCs) expect new ventures to file for an initial public offering (IPO) at some point. This event allows the VCs to capture the financial returns to their early-stage and highly risky investments. Do you think Flipkart's business model and strategy would change if it were a publicly traded company? And if so, how? Hint: Look at the Chinese ecommerce firm Alibaba's record IPO in 2014, and see how this has changed the company's strategy.

Sources: This MiniCase is based on: Das, G., "The battle of the big boys—Flipkart vs. Snapdeal vs. Amazon," *Business Standard,* May 24, 2015; Thoppil, D.A., "Flipkart valued at $15 billion after latest funding," *The Wall Street Journal,* May 19, 2015; McLain, S., "Flipkart is worth more than Airbnb," *The Wall Street Journal,* February 19, 2015; Austin, S., C. Canipe, and S. Slobin, "The billion dollar startup club," *The Wall Street Journal,* February 18, 2015; Sood, V., "Amazon India may emerge as fastest e-tailer to touch $2-bn sales mark," *The Economic Times,* January 20, 2015; Bhagavatula, S. (2015), "Creative Disruptions—The story of Indian entrepreneurship," YouTube, NSRCEL, Indian Institute of Management Bangalore (IIMB), www.youtube.com/watch?v=vAFlO9-I5rg (2:53 min); Thoppil, D.A., "India's Flipkart raises $1 billion in fresh funding," *The Wall Street Journal,* July 29, 2014; Fatima, F. (2014), "Flipkart-Myntra; From a merger to an acquisition," *International Journal of Management and International Business Studies* 4: 71–84; Kakroo, U. (2012), "E-commerce in India: Early birds, expensive worms," *McKinsey & Company,* July; and various pages at www.flipkart.com.

LVMH in China: Cracks Its Empire of Desire?

IN JULY 2012, Louis Vuitton, the flagship brand of France's Moët Hennessy Louis Vuitton S.A., better known as LVMH, opened its 16th global Maison at Shanghai's Plaza 66, a huge luxury mall. The Shanghai Maison would house the entire range of Louis Vuitton collections and multiple contemporary artworks created by Chinese and international artists. The grand opening of the Shanghai Maison also coincided with the 20th anniversary of the brand's presence in China; Louis Vuitton opened its first store in the country in 1992, in Beijing's Peninsula Hotel. Indeed, sales in Asia (excluding Japan) accounted for one-third of total revenue by the end of the first quarter of 2015, making Asia LVMH's largest region in terms of revenues (see Exhibit MC24.1).[1] When focusing on countries rather than regions, China is already the world's biggest luxury market (Exhibit MC24.2), having achieved an average annual growth rate of close to 20 percent from 2007 to 2014.

Louis Vuitton loves China; the Chinese love Louis Vuitton too, perhaps even more. In a recent Chinese luxury consumer survey published by the Hurun Research Institute, Louis Vuitton topped the list as the number one and number two preferred luxury brand by Chinese men and women, respectively. Although the brand's heritage and craftsmanship are attractive features to Chinese consumers, they are not solely responsible for opening the wallets of affluent Chinese. Louis Vuitton's steep prices and glamour bestow prestige exclusively on its customers, and this is what Chinese luxury customers value the most—to be recognized as wealthy elites with high social status. To stay apart (or atop) of the crowd is what Chinese customers crave in a densely populated and, technically speaking, an egalitarian and communist society (although much of China's economy is run by capitalist enterprises, some of the biggest are still state-owned). LVMH's image reinforcement is so powerful that even China's middle class aspires to become a Louis Vuitton owner. On average, Chinese Louis

LVMH's Maison in Shanghai, China
© AP Photo/Zhang Haiyan

Vuitton customers are younger than their Western counterparts. Moreover, they spend a significantly higher amount of their disposable income to own LVMH luxury status symbols.

With an eager consumer base and the lack of local competitors, there is probably no better tailwind an international brand could hope for in China: after years of heavy marketing to raise consumer brand recognition, everything Louis Vuitton offers sells well; all stores opened in China are profitable.

LVMH has managed its growth well. Since its formation in 1987, LVMH has become the world's largest luxury conglomerate, owning more than 60 brands and 3,200 stores worldwide.[2] It has a remarkable track record in Asia: 85 percent of Japanese women own a Louis Vuitton product. With an early entry into China, LVMH was also able to take advantage of the country's rise to become the largest luxury market

Frank T. Rothaermel prepared this MiniCase from public sources. He gratefully acknowledges the contribution of Ling Yang on an earlier version and Srikanth Prabhu for research assistance. This MiniCase is developed for the purpose of class discussion. It is not intended to be used for any kind of endorsement, source of data, or depiction of efficient or inefficient management. All opinions expressed, all errors and omissions are entirely the author's. Revised and updated: July 29, 2015. © Frank T. Rothaermel.

497

EXHIBIT MC24.1 / LVMH's Sales by Geographic Region (2002–Q1, 2015)

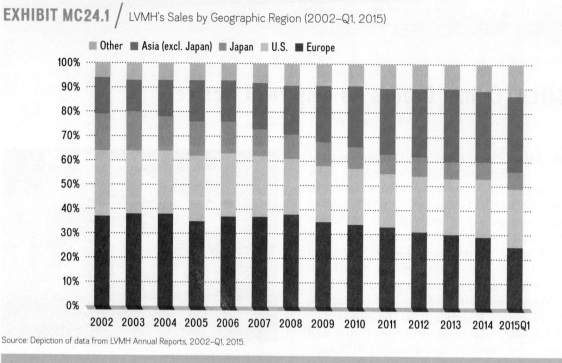

Source: Depiction of data from LVMH Annual Reports, 2002–Q1, 2015.

EXHIBIT MC24.2 / Luxury Market by Consumer Nationality

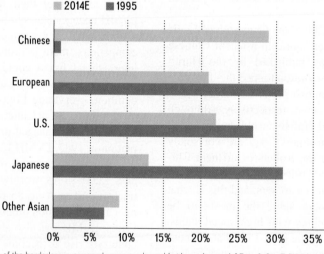

Source: Depiction of data from "The rise of the borderless consumer: Luxury goods worldwide market study," Bain & Co., Fall-Winter 2014.

worldwide. Not only did it capture the luxury lovers in Beijing, Shanghai and the like, LVMH also opened stores in second-tier provincial capitals and wealthier third-tier cities in the west of China, where speedier growth is expected in the coming years. LVMH has 50 stores in China.

After nearly a decade of successful expansion, LVMH recently turned more cautious. LVMH's concern in China is to "avoid becoming too commonplace."[3] Although the new rich in second- and third-tier cities are still craving luxury goods, signs indicate consumers in Beijing and Shanghai are maturing. The more sophisticated consumers now embrace uniqueness and understatement in luxury items; they have become well-traveled global consumers and are shying away from "logo-heavy" mega-brands, such as LVMH handbags. LVMH's reputation is in large part built on the exclusivity and prestige it conveys, but it now faces the threat of brand overexposure.

To respond to changes in consumer taste, LVMH stopped opening stores in China and launched the Shanghai Maison with invitation-only floors. It also offers custom made-to-order bags using exotic skins to project exclusivity for top-end customers. It began to focus on leather products with high value added rather than entry-level canvas logo style. In addition, it has promoted a set of "logo-free" handbags targeted exclusively at high-end Chinese customers.

But LVMH's decision to limit store growth may have another reason: Many Chinese have chosen to buy abroad. The main reasons Chinese consumers cite for shopping overseas, in addition to better selection and greater "show-off" value, are lower prices due to China's high luxury taxes and the weak euro. Taken together, this makes LVMH products in China twice as expensive as they are in Europe. It is quite common to find busloads of Chinese tourists queuing to purchase merchandise outside Louis Vuitton's boutique on Avenue des Champs-Elysées in Paris. Although it has created growth stimulus for LVMH Europe, it also poses significant challenges, such as managing inventory and providing adequate services. Before the holiday season, for example, Louis Vuitton had to put in drastic measures to slow sales. In its flagship Paris stores, LVMH limited the total number of leather products available for purchase for each customer and reduced store hours. In addition, Louis Vuitton's European stores have hired Mandarin-speaking staff trained to better meet Chinese needs and better handle the spikes of tour-bus traffic. Meanwhile, LVMH aims to strengthen its relationship with Chinese customers at home by providing premium services and enhancing their shopping experience. As long as the price difference exists, however, stores abroad will continue to be Chinese customers' preferred shopping destination. Despite all of LVMH's efforts to channel Chinese demand toward domestic outlets, demand at LVMH stores in France and other EU countries has increased significantly as the euro has fallen by 30 percent in five years.

Like all other luxury brands, LVMH has to constantly fight against counterfeiting of its products, especially the Louis Vuitton brand. China's dominance in manufacturing and its lack of intellectual property law enforcement have made the country home to more than 80 percent of the estimated $300 billion counterfeit industry. To keep some control over its intellectual property, LVMH manufactures its leather goods in company-owned factories in France, Switzerland, Germany, Italy, Spain, and the United States. Since the early 2000s, LVMH's Chinese anti-counterfeiting team, together with its global specialists and investigators, has raised public awareness of the illegitimacy of the counterfeits and stemmed the flow of the counterfeits from China to the developed world. It also brought legal actions against pirates who made fake goods and landlords who provided premises to the pirates. LVMH has achieved much success in China, including winning several recent cases in Chinese courts. But as long as the popularity of its Louis Vuitton handbags lasts, the anti-counterfeiting battle goes on, further contributing to a potential loss of exclusivity.

The road ahead in China, however, is becoming more challenging for LVMH. Chinese President Xi Jinping's campaign against corruption has drastically reduced the demand for luxury items that were purchased as "gifts" to curry favor with government officials. In addition, wealthy Chinese have become more cautious in flashing their wealth through conspicuous consumption (spending of money on luxury goods to publicly display wealth and status), given a recent public backlash against wealthy individuals and high-profile trials for corruption. As a consequence, LVMH's sales in China have plateaued over the last three years (Exhibit MC24.3). In addition, the Chinese economy is beginning to slow, and sustaining double-digit growth rates in the future seems unlikely. Volatile stock market swings have also rattled the confidence of Chinese consumers, with the Shanghai composite index losing more than 25 percent of its value during the summer of 2015, despite heavy government intervention to stem the sell-off. Yet, despite the stagnant demand from China, LVMH reported an attractive 16 percent yearly growth in 2015. On the downside, this result was mainly due to the weak euro, and LVMH's net growth was a mere 3 percent after stripping out currency effects.

EXHIBIT MC24.3 / Luxury Market in China, 2007–2014E* (euro's billions)

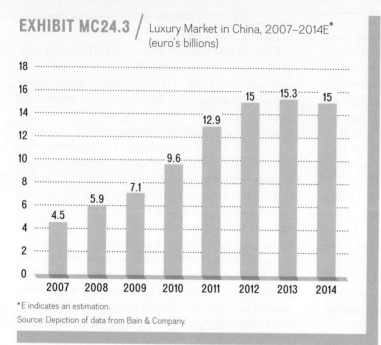

*E indicates an estimation.

Source: Depiction of data from Bain & Company.

DISCUSSION QUESTIONS

1. Why has LVMH been so successful in China? With the Chinese economic slowdown, do you think there are risks to LVMH growing aggressively in China? What do you think should be its strategy in China going forward?

2. Which strategic initiatives does LVMH pursue to strengthen its position in China? In particular, how does LVMH encourage Chinese customers to purchase LVMH products in China rather than abroad? Do you think these strategic initiatives will be successful? Why or why not? What other ideas do you think LVMH should pursue to encourage Chinese customers to purchase LVMH products in China?

3. Louis Vuitton is LVMH's flagship brand. Much of Louis Vuitton's appeal is that it bestows exclusivity on its owners. In the last few years, however, the Louis Vuitton logo has been applied widely with handbags and accessories proliferating at an unprecedented speed. In addition, counterfeiting further leads to a proliferation of the "Louis Vuitton brand." One analyst concluded that LVMH is "way overexposed in China, with too many stores and too much in fixed costs."[4] Is LVMH changing its strategic position of Louis Vuitton from a focused differentiator to a broad differentiator? Is the brand losing its appeal? Does Louis Vuitton risk being "stuck in the middle"? Why or why not?

4. Given the backlash in China against corruption and conspicuous consumption, what recommendations would you give LVMH?

5. LVMH is a diversified conglomerate owning a number of luxury brands including Louis Vuitton (fashion and leather goods), Bulgari and Tag Heuer (watches and jewelry), Moët et Chandon and Dom Pérignon (wines and spirits), and Dior (fashion, perfumes, and cosmetics). Identify core competencies, economies of scale, and economies of scope that would allow LVMH to create value as a diversified conglomerate ("diversification premium"). What factors could lead LVMH to destroy value as a diversified conglomerate ("diversification premium")? Explain.

Endnotes

1 Excluding Japan; LVMH does not break down sales for China.

2 LVMH's famous brands include: Louis Vuitton (fashion and leather goods), Bulgari and Tag Heuer (watches and jewelry), Moët et Chandon and Dom Pérignon (wines and spirits), and Dior (fashion, perfumes, and cosmetics).

3 "Louis Vuitton slows expansion to protect image," *The Globe and Mail,* January 31, 2013.

4 "Weak euro masks lingering woes at LVMH, Kering," *The Wall Street Journal,* July 27, 2015.

Sources: This MiniCase is based on: LVMH's annual reports, 2002-Q1, 2015; "Weak euro masks lingering woes at LVMH, Kering," *The Wall Street Journal,* July 27, 2015; "China stocks tumble as investors doubt Beijing's help," *The Wall Street Journal,* July 15, 2015; "LVMH Moët Hennessy Louis Vuitton quarterly sales rise 5.2%," *The Wall Street Journal,* October 14, 2014; "Louis Vuitton slows expansion to protect image," *The Globe and Mail,* January 31, 2013; "Has luxury peaked in mainland China," *South China Morning Post,* May 22, 2013; "LVMH rushes to keep up with China's changing tastes," *Jing Daily,* May 27, 2013; "For luxury brands targeting China, expansion to lower-tier cities beckons," *Jing Daily,* June 5, 2013; "Luxury goods in China: Beyond bling," *The Economist,* June 8, 2013; "Wealthy Chinese love French luxury goods," *South China Morning Post,* June 21, 2013; "LVMH: the empire of desire," *The Economist,* June 2, 2012; "Event watch: Louis Vuitton Shanghai Maison grand opening," *Jing Daily,* July 10, 2012; "LVMH faces dilemma of success," *Financial Times,* October 19, 2012; "Luxury without borders: China's new class of shoppers take on the world," McKinsey & Co., December 2012; "Made in China on the sly," *The New York Times,* November 23, 2007; and "Louis Vuitton's Steven Lie: Protecting IP in China," *Asialaw,* October 2005.

Sony vs. Apple: Whatever Happened to Sony?

APPLE'S MARKET CAPITALIZATION in 2001 was $7 billion, while Sony's was $55 billion. In other words, Sony was almost eight times larger than Apple. Then most people would have picked Sony as the company to revolutionize the mobile device industry given its stellar innovation track record. Instead that honor goes to Apple, when it introduced the iPod, a portable digital music player, in October 2001, and the iTunes Music Store 18 months later. Through these two strategic moves Apple redefined the music industry, reinventing itself as not only a mobile-device but also a content-delivery company. Signaling its renaissance, Apple changed its name from Apple Computer, Inc., to simply Apple, Inc. Many observers wondered what happened to Sony, the company that created the portable music industry by introducing the Walkman in 1979.

Sony's strategy was to differentiate itself through the vertical integration of content and hardware, driven by its 1988 acquisition of CBS Records (later part of Sony Entertainment) and its 1989 acquisition of Columbia Pictures. This vertical integration strategy contrasted sharply with Sony Music division's desire to protect its lucrative revenue-generating, copyrighted compact discs (CDs). Sony Music's engineers were aggressively combating rampant music piracy by inhibiting the Microsoft Windows media player's ability to rip CDs and by serializing discs (assigning unique ID numbers to discs). The compact disc (CD) became the dominant format for selling music in 1991, replacing analog audiocassettes. The CD had been jointly developed by Sony and European electronics manufacturer Philips.

Media technology, however, soon moved to digital. With the rise of the Internet in the 1990s and use of digital music, illegal file sharing on the Internet was rampant. Napster, for example, allowed peer-to-peer sharing of files, which meant individual users could upload entire albums of music, to be downloaded by anyone, with no payments going to the artists or

Sony's introduction of the Walkman in 1979, the first portable cassette player, revolutionized not only how music was consumed but also launched mobile devices as a new category-defining industry.
© Chris Willson/Alamy Stock Photo

the record companies. Napster, meanwhile, was shut down in 2001 because of copyright infringements.

While Sony focused on preventing media players that could rip CDs, Apple was developing a digital rights management (DRM) system to allow for legal downloads of digital music while protecting

Frank T. Rothaermel prepared this MiniCase from public sources. He gratefully acknowledges research assistance by James Hoadley. A prior version of this MiniCase was prepared in collaboration with Robert Redrow (formerly of Sony Corp.). This MiniCase is developed for the purpose of class discussion. It is not intended to be used for any kind of endorsement, source of data, or depiction of efficient or inefficient management. All opinions expressed, all errors and omissions are entirely the author's. Revised and updated: August 26, 2015. © Frank T. Rothaermel.

copyright at the same time. The iTunes Store enabled users to legally download and own individual songs at an attractive 99 cents. Apple's DRM and iTunes succeeded, protecting the music studios' and artists' interests while creating value that enabled consumers to enjoy portable digital music.

Sony had a long history of creating category-defining electronic devices of superior quality and design. It had all the right competencies to launch a successful counterattack to compete with Apple: electronics, software, music, and computer divisions. Sony even supplied the batteries for Apple's iPod. Cooperation among strategic business units had served Sony well in the past, leading to breakthrough innovations such as the Walkman, PlayStation, CD, and VAIO computer line. In digital music, however, the hardware and content divisions each seemed to have its own idea of what needed to be done. Cooperation among the Sony divisions was also hindered by the fact that their centers of operations were spread across the globe: Music operations were located in New York City and electronics design was in Japan, inhibiting face-to-face communications and making real-time interactions more difficult.

Nobuyuki Idei, then CEO of Sony, learned the hard way that the music division managers were focused on the immediate needs of their recordings competing against the consumer-driven market forces. Idei shared his frustrations with the cultural differences between the hardware and content divisions (in 2002):

> The opposite of soft alliances is hard alliances, which include mergers and acquisitions. Since purchasing the Music and Pictures businesses, more than 10 years have passed, and we have experienced many cultural differences between hardware manufacturing and content businesses. . . . This experience has taught us that in certain areas where hard alliances would have taken 10 years to succeed, soft alliances can be created more easily. Another advantage of soft alliances is the ability to form partnerships with many different companies. We aim to provide an open and easy-to-access environment where anybody can participate and we are willing to cooperate with companies that share our vision. Soft alliances offer many possibilities.[1]

In contrast, Apple organized a small, empowered, cross-functional team to produce the iPod in just a few months. Apple successfully outsourced and integrated many of its components and collaborated across business units. The phenomenal speed and success of the iPod and iTunes development and seamless integration became a structural approach that Apple applied to its successful development and launches of other category-defining products such as the iPhone and iPad.

Having fallen way behind Apple and other competitors in the consumer electronics industry, Sony made drastic changes. From its founding in 1946, Sony's CEOs had all come from inside the company and had all been Japanese. In 2005, Sony appointed its first non-Japanese CEO, Welsh-born Sir Howard Stringer. During Stringer's tenure as head of Sony, however, the company endured a number of high-profile hacking instances that repeatedly brought down the network for the popular PlayStation game console and exposed users' private information.

The most damaging hack of Sony, however, came after Stringer had stepped down as CEO. In 2014, Sony was prepared to release a comedy film titled *The Interview,* starring James Franco and Seth Rogen. The plot of the film was about two men who use the premise of an interview to assassinate North Korean leader Kim Jong-un. According to the FBI, the North Korean government, as retaliation for the film, supported a group of hackers who breached Sony Pictures systems and stole a great deal of information, including personal information of employees and stars who worked on films, and intra-company e-mails. The content of the e-mails proved to be damaging to Sony and resulted in the resignation of several Sony Pictures executives for inappropriate statements made in internal e-mails.

To improve Sony's performance, the company is undergoing a major corporate restructuring. In 2014, Sony's revenues were $71 billion, with Sony's Mobile Products & Communications Division ($11.0 bn), Gaming and Network Services ($11.0 bn), Home Entertainment and Sound ($10.1 bn), Financial Services ($9.0 bn), Devices ($8 bn), Pictures Entertainment ($7.3 bn), Imaging Products ($6.0 bn), Music ($4.5 bn), and "Other" business activities ($4.1 bn) (see Exhibit MC25.1). In terms of profitability, however, Sony's core businesses are underperforming (see Exhibit MC25.2). Sony's most profitable division is its non-core business Financial Services ($1.61 bn), producing 95 percent of all of Sony's profits! In contrast, the Mobile Products & Communications Division, once Sony's claim to fame, lost almost $2 billion.

EXHIBIT MC25.1 / Sony's Revenues by Segment, 2014 ($ billions)

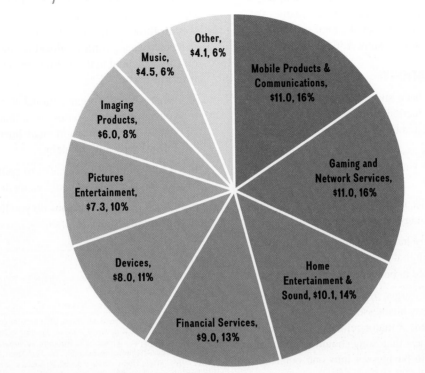

Source: Depiction of data from Sony annual report.

EXHIBIT MC25.2 / Sony's Net Income by Segment, 2014 ($ millions)

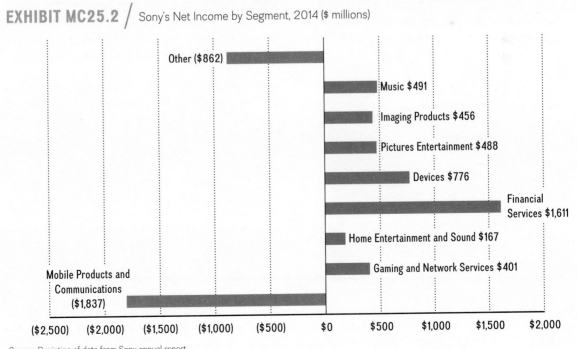

Source: Depiction of data from Sony annual report.

Apple's market capitalization has grown from a paltry $7 billion in 2001 to some $750 billion in 2015. Apple has become the most valuable company ever. In contrast, Sony's market capitalization has dropped from $55 billion in 2001 to some $30 billion in 2015.

DISCUSSION QUESTIONS

1. Why had Sony been successful in the past (e.g., with the introduction of the Walkman, Play Station, the CD, and the VAIO computer line)?

2. What was Idei's assessment of strategic alliances vs. M&As? Do you agree or disagree? Support your assessment.

3. Why do you think Apple succeeded in the digital portable music industry, while Sony failed?

4. What could Sony have done differently to avoid failure in the digital portable music industry? What lessons need to be learned?

5. Activist investors argue that Sony is spread too thin over too many businesses, and that its corporate strategy needs a major refocus. These activist investors request that Sony should combine its music and movie businesses into one entertainment unit, and spin it off as a standalone company. Sony Pictures Entertainment has music artists such as Snoop Dogg, Kelly Clarkson, Justin Timberlake, and Pink under contract. The movie *Skyfall*, Sony's 2012 installment in the James Bond saga, topped the rankings and grossed over $1 billion since its release. This corporate restructuring would allow Sony to focus on its core business in electronics, while unlocking hidden value-creating potential in its entertainment unit, activists investors argue.

a. What is Sony's organizational structure? Do you agree with the assessment that "Sony is spread too thin over too many businesses"? Why or why not? Explain.

b. What would be the benefits of splitting Sony as proposed? What would be its drawbacks?

c. Which recommendations do you have to restructure Sony? Explain.

Endnote

[1] Sony Annual Report 2002, year ended March 31, 2002, Sony Corporation, p. 9.

Sources: This MiniCase is based on: "Sony CEO remains committed to consumer electronics," *The Wall Street Journal*, January 7, 2015; "How Sony makes money off Apple's iPhone," *The Wall Street Journal*, April 28, 2015; "Sony's blunt finance chief takes spotlight," *The Wall Street Journal*, November 16, 2014; "White House deflects doubts on sources of Sony Hack," *The Wall Street Journal*, December 30, 2014; "Behind the scenes at Sony as hacking crisis unfolded," *The Wall Street Journal*, December 30, 2014; "Japan's electronics under siege," *The Wall Street Journal*, May 15, 2013; Hansen, M.T. (2009), *Collaboration: How Leaders Avoid the Traps, Create Unity, and Reap Big Results* (Cambridge, MA: Harvard Business School Press); Sony Corporation Info, www.sony.com; and various Sony annual reports.

Struggling Samsung Electronics

WITH SOME $200 BILLION in revenues in 2015, Samsung is one of the biggest conglomerates globally and the largest *chaebol*[1] in South Korea. (U.S. conglomerate General Electric had some $150 billion in revenues in the same year.) Established in 1938 by Lee Byung-chul as a trading company selling noodles and dried seafood, Samsung has since diversified into various industries, including electronics, chemicals, shipbuilding, financial services, and construction. As a result, Samsung is widely diversified with over 80 standalone subsidiaries. The conglomerate accounts for a fifth of all South Korean exports.

In 1987, Lee Kun-hee, the youngest son of the founder, took over as the chairman of the conglomerate. His strategic intent was to make Samsung a world leader in high-tech industries such as consumer electronics. To execute his strategy, Lee Kun-hee focused first on gaining market share by invading markets from the bottom up with lower-priced products at acceptable value. Over time, quality and consumer perception became more important. Samsung's image, however, was overshadowed by Sony and Motorola, the undisputed world leaders in consumer electronics and mobile phones during this time. During a 1993 trip, Lee Kun-hee saw firsthand how poorly Samsung's electronics were perceived in the United States and Europe, and he vowed to change that. Back in Korea, to show his disappointment and determination alike, he destroyed 150,000 brand-new Samsung cell phones in a large bonfire in front of all 2,000 employees of Samsung's Gami factory. Many employees credit this as the pivotal moment in redefining Samsung Electronics' strategic focus and initiating a successful turnaround.

Samsung Electronics increased spending significantly on R&D as well as on marketing and design. Meanwhile, Lee Kun-hee was undertaking a complete overhaul of the conglomerate's structure to change Samsung's sclerotic culture. To a culture that deeply values seniority, he introduced merit-based pay and

© Jung Yeon-Je/AFP/GettyImages

promotion. Lee Kun-hee, who holds an MBA degree from George Washington University, hired Western managers and designers into leading positions and sent homegrown talent to learn best business practices from other firms wherever they could be found. Lee Kun-hee also set up the Global Strategic Group to assist non-Korean MBAs and PhDs with a smooth transition into their positions in a largely homogenous cadre of Korean executives. Once economies of scale due to a larger market share could be reaped, he moved Samsung to the high end of the market, offering premium consumer electronics such as flat-screen TVs, appliances, semiconductors, and mobile devices such as its famous Galaxy line of smartphones.

In 2007, Apple introduced the iPhone, redefining the entire category of mobile phones and setting the standard of how smartphones looked and felt. Samsung played catch-up again, ratcheting up spending on R&D

Frank T. Rothaermel prepared this MiniCase from public sources. He gratefully acknowledges the contribution of Ling Yang on an earlier version and James Hoadley for research assistance on the current version. This Mini-Case is developed for the purpose of class discussion. It is not intended to be used for any kind of endorsement, source of data, or depiction of efficient or inefficient management. All opinions expressed, all errors and omissions are entirely the author's. Revised and updated: July 29, 2015. © Frank T. Rothaermel.

and marketing. In particular, Samsung Electronics applied its time-tested "follow first, innovate second" rule. Being a key component vendor to other leading technology companies including Apple, Samsung Electronics saw what directions other companies were taking. Within a short time, it had overtaken Motorola, HTC, Blackberry, Nokia, and even Apple to become the number-one vendor of smartphones in the world and the largest technology company by revenues globally (see Exhibit MC26.1). By 2012, with the release of its Galaxy S III phone, Samsung had successfully imitated the look-and-feel of the Apple iPhone. Today, Samsung Electronics is the crown jewel of the Samsung business empire, with its mobile division contributing some 75 percent of the conglomerate's overall profits.

Although Samsung gained a temporary competitive advantage, in recent years it stumbled, with revenues and profits down sharply (see

EXHIBIT MC26.1 / Global Smartphone Market Share (in %), 2010–2015

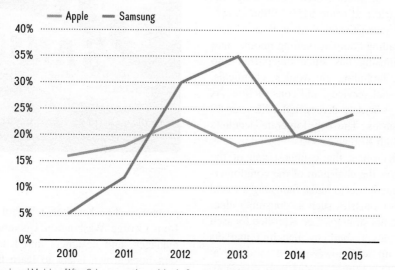

Source: Adapted from Cheng, J., and M.-J. Lee, "After Galaxy smartphone debacle, Samsung questions game plan," *The Wall Street Journal*, May 11, 2015.

EXHIBIT MC26.2 / Samsung Electronics' Revenues (left vertical axis) and Operating Profits (right vertical **axis**), 2000–2014 ($ billions)

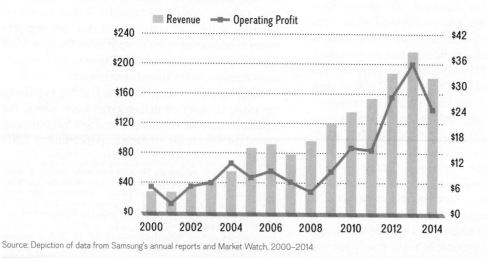

Source: Depiction of data from Samsung's annual reports and Market Watch, 2000–2014.

Exhibit MC26.2). Samsung's competitive advantage was built in large part on its "follow first, innovate second" rule. Although it sells fewer phones than Samsung, Apple's profit margin per phone is much higher. With the introduction of the iPhone 6 in 2014, Apple pulled away from Samsung. With the larger screen on the iPhone 6 Plus, Apple also negated Samsung's lead with its successful Galaxy Note phablets. Since the iPhone 6 and iPhone 6 Plus were introduced, Apple has captured a greater share of the high end of the market. Although Apple's market share in the global smartphone industry is less than 20 percent (see Exhibit MC26.1), it captures a whopping 92 percent of all the profits generated in the industry! In addition, Apple and Samsung have been locked in ongoing court battles over infringement among the various smartphone models. Samsung lost a high-profile case against Apple in a California court, where damages were reduced later to some $500 million.

Samsung Electronics not only lost market share on the high end of the mobile phone market, but also on the low end. Chinese technology companies Lenovo, Huawei, and Xiaomi are becoming more and more popular. In particular, the Chinese start-up Xiaomi, which has only been in existence since 2010, has challenged Samsung and Apple in consumer markets with huge growth potential such as China. By 2014, Xiaomi, often described as China's Apple, had become the number-one seller of smartphones in China by units. Similarly, by launching new smartphones quickly, almost like fashion accessories, India's Micromax had become the number-one seller in its home market.

In summary, Samsung stumbled badly. It is squeezed in the middle. On the high end, it has fallen behind Apple, which continues to pull away with its innovation and design to set new standards for the most profitable segment of the market. On the low end, upstarts from China and India are capturing leading positions in markets with huge growth potential. Samsung's downward spiral coincided with Lee Kun-hee's heart attack in 2014, which left him incapacitated. The 73-year old Lee Kun-hee had ruled Samsung with an iron fist: No strategic or personnel decisions were made without his approval.

Soul-searching about Samsung's future has begun in Seoul. In 2010, Lee Kun-hee set the strategic intent that Samsung should quadruple its revenues from

$100 billion to $400 billion by 2020 (which would be more than the revenues of Apple, Google, Microsoft, and Amazon combined). In 2015, the company sent a survey to all its employees to ask whether the conglomerate's goal of being a $400 billion company by 2020 should be changed.

In addition, the turf battle for Samsung's top job also has begun, with many observers convinced that Lee Kun-hee's son, Lee Jae-yong (who goes by Jay Lee), is the heir apparent. The younger Lee holds the position of vice chairman. At the same time, Samsung Electronics currently has an unusual leadership structure with three co-CEOs (Kwon Oh-Hyun, J.K. Shin, and B.K. Yoon) each acting as the leader for their respective division (components, mobile, and consumer electronics). The involvement of the Lee family in Samsung is persistent throughout the conglomerate, however, with descendants of the company's founder serving in multiple leadership positions. Should Lee Jae-yong get the top job at Samsung Electronics, he will have his work cut out for him to turn around the struggling conglomerate and especially Samsung Electronics, its flagship division.

DISCUSSION QUESTIONS

Corporate Strategy

1. What makes Samsung a conglomerate? What type of diversification does Samsung pursue? Identify possible factors such as core competencies, economies of scale, and economies of scope that were the basis of its past success as a widely diversified conglomerate (*chaebol*). Why is Samsung as a conglomerate struggling today?

2. Despite being a widely diversified conglomerate, Samsung prefers vertical integration: in-house design and development teams, manufacturing in large company-owned factories, and coordinating a sprawling global supply chain. In contrast, Apple concentrates on the design (and retail sales) of high-end mobile devices, while it outsources its production to Foxconn and others. Do you think Samsung's high degree of vertical integration contributed to its recent problems? Why or why not? Explain.

Business Strategy

1. Lee Jae-yong, the 46-year-old grandson of the Samsung founder and heir apparent, was educated

at Seoul National University, Keio University (in Japan), and Harvard Business School. He wrote a master's thesis at Keio University on Japan's struggle to retain its world leadership in manufacturing in the mid-1990s when the country's fast-growing period was ending. He concluded, "Japan's troubles were worsened by its manufacturers' pursuit of scale and market share."[2] Is Samsung Electronics' pursuit of scale and market share to blame for its losing its competitive advantage?

2. Why is Samsung Electronics encountering problems selling its flagship line of smartphones, the Galaxy? How should it compete against premium phone makers such as Apple and low-cost leaders such as Xiaomi and Micromax?

3. What would you recommend Samsung Electronics would need to do to revive and turn around its fledgling mobile division?

Endnotes

[1] A *chaebol* denotes a South Korean multinational business conglomerate.

[2] Cheng, J., and M.-J. Lee, "After Galaxy smartphone debacle, Samsung questions game plan," *The Wall Street Journal,* May 11, 2015.

Sources: This MiniCase is based on: Ovide, S., and D. Wakabayashi, "Apple's share of smartphone industry's profits soars to 92%," *The Wall Street Journal,* July 12, 2015; Bellman, E., and R.J. Krishna, "India's Micromax churns out phones like fast fashion," *The Wall Street Journal,* June 4, 2015; "Samsung: The soft succession," *The Economist,* May 23, 2015; Cheng, J. and M.-J. Lee, "After Galaxy smartphone debacle, Samsung questions game plan," *The Wall Street Journal,* May 11, 2015; Cheng, J., "What to know about Samsung," *The Wall Street Journal,* May 11, 2015; Cheng, J., Samsung unveils Galaxy S6 to answer iPhone 6, *The Wall Street Journal,* March 1, 2015; Cheng, J., "Samsung's primacy is tested in China," *The Wall Street Journal,* October 27, 2014; Lee, M.-J., "Samsung girds for cost cuts after downbeat guidance," *The Wall Street Journal,* October 7, 2014; "Samsung: Waiting in the wings," *The Economist,* September 27, 2014; "How Samsung got big," *TechCrunch,* June 1, 2013; "The rise of Samsung and how it is reshaping the mobile ecosystem," *Business Insider,* March 14, 2013; "Faster, higher, stronger: The rise and rise of Samsung," *The Sydney Morning Herald,* August 13, 2012; "Samsung: the next big bet," *The Economist,* October 1, 2011; "Samsung and its attractions: Asia's new model company," *The Economist,* October 1, 2011; Khanna, T., J. Song, and K. Lee (2011), "The paradox of Samsung's rise," *Harvard Business Review,* July–August; and various Samsung annual reports.

Alibaba and China's ECommerce: Reality Bites

TODAY, ALIBABA GROUP is the largest Chinese ecommerce company. In the original Arabic tale of *Ali Baba and the Forty Thieves,* Ali Baba, the poor woodcutter, opened the cave with hidden treasure by calling the magic words "Open Sesame." Alibaba's founder selected the name to open up opportunities for small Chinese manufacturers to sell their goods around the world, with the hope of finding treasures for Alibaba's users and shareholders. Today, Alibaba is a family of ecommerce businesses, which *The Wall Street Journal* described as "comparable to eBay, Amazon, and PayPal all rolled into one, with a stake in Twitter-like Weibo thrown in to boot."[1] Alibaba's main trading platforms are Taobao and Tmall.

Just like Ali Baba in the folk tale, Alibaba had humble beginnings. In 1999, a former English teacher named Jack Ma started the company with a team of 18 in his apartment in Hangzhou, a city some 100 miles southwest of Shanghai. At this time, China's explosive growth of Internet users was just beginning (see Exhibit MC 27.1). By 2015, China's Internet users had grown to 675 million. Alibaba rode this wave of exponential growth to success. In comparison, the United States has some 260 million Internet users (less than 40 percent of Chinese Internet users).

The number of Internet users in China seems to be reaching a plateau in recent years. Nonetheless, given the low percentage of online transactions in comparison to China's total commerce, huge growth in per capita spending online is expected in the future.

Initially, Alibaba's website was a business-to-business (B2B) platform where China's small and medium-sized businesses could showcase their products to buyers around the world. Alibaba was not the first company to explore opportunities in introducing China's manufacturing to global demand, but it was the first to do so online. In its first year of operation, Alibaba signed up new members at a rate of 1,200 per day. By 2002, the young startup was already profitable. By 2012, Alibaba facilitated transactions in nearly every country around the world.

Alibaba had the most successful initial public offering ever, surpassing a valuation of over $230 billion on its first day of trading, September 19, 2014.
© Tomohiro Ohsumi/Bloomberg/Getty Images

Alibaba vs. eBay

At the same time as Alibaba was started, EachNet, another Chinese Internet venture, was launched in Shanghai. EachNet was founded by two Harvard MBAs who wanted to create a Chinese eBay, an auction site for locals to sell and bid for goods. By 2003, EachNet had 2 million users and 85 percent market share in China's consumer-to-consumer (C2C) transactions. At the time, eBay was actively looking to expand in China and eventually acquired EachNet as its China operation for $180 million in 2003.

Fearing eBay would lure small businesses away, Alibaba launched a competing C2C platform Taobao (meaning "digging treasure" in Chinese) as a defensive strategy. Unlike EachNet, which charged listing and transaction fees from sellers, Taobao was free for sellers. But Taobao's free services did not erode EachNet's loyal customer base. EachNet's dominant market

Frank T. Rothaermel prepared this MiniCase from public sources. He gratefully acknowledges the contribution of Ling Yang on an earlier version. This MiniCase is developed for the purpose of class discussion. It is not intended to be used for any kind of endorsement, source of data, or depiction of efficient or inefficient management. All opinions expressed, all errors and omissions are entirely the author's. Revised and updated: August 26, 2015. © Frank T. Rothaermel.

EXHIBIT MC27.1 / China's Internet Users (millions), 2000–2018E*

The moving trend line (dotted) follows a typical S-curve, suggesting a slowdown in the growth of Chinese Internet users.

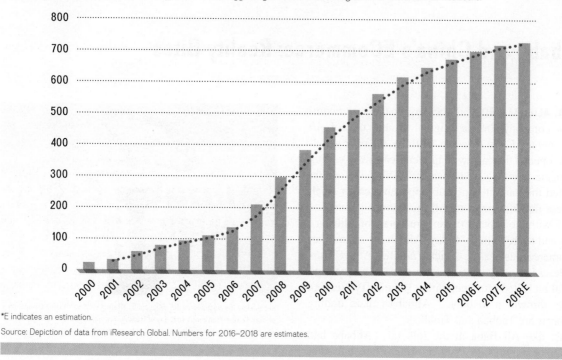

*E indicates an estimation.

Source: Depiction of data from iResearch Global. Numbers for 2016–2018 are estimates.

position meant more products and more opportunities for both buyers and sellers to trade. Although EachNet was competing head-to-head with Taobao on advertising campaigns, eBay made a decision to terminate EachNet's homegrown technology platform and move all EachNet users to eBay's U.S. platform in 2004. At eBay, the internal term for this was "migration." The intent was to create one global trading platform that would allow eBay users to trade with each other, no matter where they located.

The problem was that eBay's U.S. platform did not offer features that EachNet needed to compete in China. The online data that once freely flowed within China suddenly became cross-border traffic and had to pass through the Chinese government's firewall. The speed to load EachNet's web pages slowed significantly. Frustrated users left EachNet in droves and turned to Taobao for a better alternative. While most decisions at EachNet had to go to eBay's U.S. headquarters for approval, Alibaba swiftly launched a number of innovative services to assist transactions on Taobao, including Aliwangwang, an instant messaging service helping buyers and sellers interact in real time, and Alipay, an escrow payment system to reduce online transaction

risks. Just three months after eBay's migration, Taobao captured 60 percent of the C2C market share, leaving EachNet at 30 percent. In 2006, eBay shut down EachNet and closed its China operation. Commenting on Alibaba's competition with eBay, founder Ma noted, "eBay may be a shark in the ocean, but I am a crocodile in the Yangtze River. If we fight in the ocean, we lose, but if we fight in the river, we win."[2]

Alibaba continued to build its ecommerce venture around Taobao. In 2007, it set up Alisoft, where Taobao sellers could buy customized third-party software to help with their day-to-day operations, and Alimama, where Taobao sellers could post ads on a network of specialized websites. Anticipating a growing share of business-to-consumer (B2C) transactions of online retailing, Taobao launched TMall, a dedicated B2C platform to complement Taobao in 2008. Today, Alibaba has a massive footprint in the largest and fastest growing ecommerce market globally.

Most Successful IPO Ever

On September 19, 2014, Alibaba went public on the New York Stock Exchange (NYSE). It had the most successful initial public offering ever, surpassing a stock market valuation of over $230 billion on its first day of trading. In 2015, Alibaba employed more than 25,000 people, had $13 billion in revenues, and remained highly profitable, capturing more than 50 percent of its revenues as profits. At the same time, Alibaba's market presence is still predominantly in China. In a survey of American Internet shoppers, almost 9 out of 10 had never heard of Alibaba.

Lost Magic?

In the summer of 2015, not yet one year after its IPO, Alibaba's market valuation had dropped by $50 billion (22 percent) to some $180 billion. Its stock price had fallen to an all-time low. It appears that the Alibaba fairy tale lost some of its magic. What happened?

Alibaba is facing a number of internal and external challenges. Alibaba delivered slower than anticipated growth. Alibaba also reorganized its operation by folding its consumer sites Taobao and Tmall with group-buying site Juhuasuan into one business unit. Moreover, Alibaba continues to heavily invest in expanding beyond the Chinese market to become a truly global player. It also invests heavily in cloud computing to compete more effectively with Amazon, and just spent almost $5 billion to buy a 20 percent stake in Suning, China's largest electronics retailer. This should allow Alibaba to compete more effectively with its domestic rival JD.com, which is especially strong in electronics. Moreover, it also creates a retail presence throughout China—much like what Amazon is doing in the United States—to facilitate pick-ups and returns of merchandise.

Since Alibaba is still mainly focused on the Chinese market, facilitating ecommerce transactions to consumers, it was hit hard by China's slowing economy. Moreover, the Chinese government decided to devalue its currency (the yuan), which makes international products such as Nike running shoes or Procter & Gamble consumer products such as Tide much more expensive for Chinese consumers and is thus hurting Alibaba's sales. Moreover, some of Alibaba's domestic rivals, including JD.com, Tencent, Baidu, and WeChat, are getting stronger, especially on mobile platforms (Alibaba is not as strong as the competitors mentioned here.) Indeed, most Chinese Internet users (86 percent) are accessing the Internet through a mobile device. (See Exhibit MC27.2). Foreign competitors such as Amazon, which has $90 billion in annual revenues and is thus more than seven times larger than Alibaba, is also beginning to focus more on the Chinese market.

EXHIBIT MC27.2 / China's PC and Mobile Internet Economy Revenues, 2011–2018E* ($ millions)

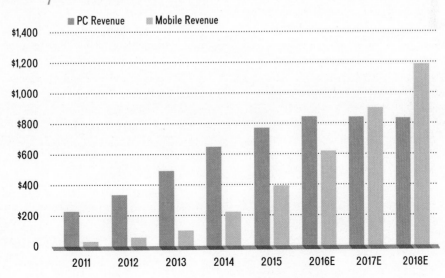

*E indicates an estimation.

Source: Depiction of data from iResearch Global.

DISCUSSION QUESTIONS

1. Why did eBay lose out to Alibaba in China? What lessons can be learned for non-Chinese ecommerce companies such as Amazon?

2. How was Alibaba able to become the most successful ecommerce company in China? Think about standards, network effects, and the crossing-the-chasm framework to inform your reasoning.

3. What factors contributed to Alibaba's loss in performance? Detail internal weaknesses and external threats.

4. How can Alibaba mitigate some of the external threats? Make some recommendations to Alibaba's CEO.

5. Apply the integration-responsiveness framework to determine:

   a. Which global strategy position would you recommend Alibaba should pursue when attempting to create a stronger foothold in the United States, and why?

   b. Which global strategy positions would you recommend U.S. ecommerce companies such as eBay, Amazon, and others should pursue when competing in China, and why?

Endnotes

[1] "China changes won't face Alibaba," *The Wall Street Journal,* July 5, 2013.

[2] As quoted in "Standing Up to a Giant," *Forbes,* April 25, 2005.

Sources: This MiniCase is based on: Company overview, news on Alibaba.com; "Alibaba faces fresh threat from rivals," *The Wall Street Journal,* August 17, 2015; "Reality hits Alibaba's results," *The Wall Street Journal,* August 12, 2015; "Clicks to bricks," *The Economist,* August 15, 2015; "Alibaba debut makes a splash," *The Wall Street Journal,* September 19, 2014; "Alibaba: The world's greatest bazaar," *The Economist,* March 23, 2013; "E-commerce in China: The Alibaba phenomenon," *The Economist,* March 23, 2013; "Microsoft Considered Building E-Commerce Market," *Fox Business,* June 2013; "Yahoo's Marissa Mayer Hits One-Year Mark," *The Wall Street Journal,* July 15, 2013; "Yahoo's ad struggles persist," *The Wall Street Journal,* April 16, 2013; "How Taobao bested eBay in China," *Financial Times,* March 12, 2012; "How eBay failed in China," *Forbes,* September 12, 2010; "How eBay lost the China market," *Global Times,* August 10, 2009; "E-commerce with Chinese characteristics," *The Economist,* November 15, 2007; and "The Jack who would be king," *The Economist,* August 24, 2000.

UBS: A Pattern of Ethics Scandals

UBS WAS FORMED in 1997 when the Swiss Bank Corp. merged with the Union Bank of Switzerland. After acquiring Paine Webber, a 120-year-old U.S. wealth management firm in 2000, combined with aggressive hiring for its investment banking business, UBS soon became one of the top financial services companies in the world and the biggest bank in Switzerland. Between 2008 and 2015, however, UBS's reputation was severely tarnished by a series of ethics scandals. These scandals cost the bank billions of dollars in fines and lost profits, not to mention a severely diminished reputation. Even more important, these ethics scandals don't seem to be isolated instances, but appear to resemble a troubling pattern.

© Sebastian Derungs/AFP/Getty Images

Ethics Scandal No. 1: U.S. Tax Evasion

Swiss banks have long enjoyed a competitive advantage brought by the Swiss banking privacy laws that make it a criminal offense to share clients' information with any third parties. The exceptions are cases of criminal acts such as accounts linked to terrorists or tax fraud. Merely not declaring assets to tax authorities (tax evasion), however, is not considered tax fraud. After the acquisition of Paine Webber, UBS entered into a qualified intermediary (QI) agreement with the Internal Revenue Service (IRS), the federal tax agency of the U.S. government. Like other foreign financial institutions under a QI agreement, UBS agreed to report and withhold taxes on accounts receiving U.S.-source of income. Reporting on non-U.S. accounts with U.S.-source of income is done on an aggregate basis. This protects the identity of the non-U.S. account holders.

In mid-2008, it came to light that since 2000, UBS had actively participated in helping its U.S. clients evade taxes. To avoid QI reporting requirements, UBS's Switzerland-based bankers had assisted the U.S. clients to structure their accounts by divesting U.S. securities and setting up sham entities offshore to acquire non-U.S. account holder status. Aided by Swiss bank privacy laws, UBS successfully helped its U.S. clients conceal billions of dollars from the IRS. In addition, UBS aggressively marketed its "tax-saving" schemes by sending its Swiss bankers to the United States to develop clientele, even though those bankers never acquired proper licenses from the U.S. Securities and Exchange Commission (SEC) to do so.

The U.S. prosecutors pressed charges on UBS for conspiring to defraud the United States by impeding the IRS. In a separate suit, the U.S. government requested the UBS to reveal the names of 52,000 U.S. clients who were believed to be tax evaders. In February 2009, UBS paid $780 million in fines to settle the charges. Although it initially resisted the pressure to turn over clients' information, citing the Swiss bank privacy laws, UBS eventually agreed to disclose some 5,000 account details, including individual names, after intense negotiations involving

Frank T. Rothaermel prepared this MiniCase from public sources. He gratefully acknowledges the contribution of Ling Yang on an earlier version. This MiniCase is developed for the purpose of class discussion. It is not intended to be used for any kind of endorsement, source of data, or depiction of efficient or inefficient management. All opinions expressed, all errors and omissions are entirely the author's. Revised and updated: August 8, 2015. © Frank T. Rothaermel.

officials from both countries. Clients left UBS in droves: Operating profit from the bank's wealth management division declined by 60 percent, or $4.4 billion, in 2008 alone; it declined by another 17 percent, or $504 million, in 2009.

The UBS case has far-reaching implications for the bank's wealth management business and the Swiss banking industry as a whole, especially the prided bank secrecy. To close loopholes in the QI program and crack down on tax evasion in countries with strict bank secrecy traditions, President Obama signed into law the Foreign Account Tax Compliance Act (FATCA) in 2010. The law requires all foreign financial institutions to report offshore accounts and activities of their U.S. clients with assets over $50,000, and to impose a 30 percent withholding tax on U.S. investments or to exit the U.S. business. Switzerland has agreed to implement the FATCA. The annual compliance cost for each Swiss bank is estimated to be $100 million.

Ethics Scandal No. 2: Rogue Trader

On September 15, 2011, UBS announced that a rogue trader named Kweku Adoboli at its London branch had racked up an unauthorized trading loss of $2.3 billion over a period of three years. Nine days later, UBS CEO Oswald Grübel resigned "to assume responsibility for the recent unauthorized trading incident."[1] After more than a year of joint investigation by the U.K. and Swiss regulators, the case was concluded with findings that systems and controls at UBS were "seriously defective."[2] As a result, Adoboli, a relatively junior trader, was able to take highly risky positions with vast amounts of money. More alarmingly, all three of Adoboli's desk colleagues admitted that they knew more or less of his unauthorized trades. Moreover, Adoboli's two bosses had shown a relaxed attitude toward breaching daily trading limits. UBS was fined $47.6 million in late 2012.

Ethics Scandal No. 3: LIBOR Manipulation

LIBOR, or the London Interbank Offered Rate, is the interest rate at which international banks based in London would lend to each other. LIBOR is set daily: A panel of banks submits rates to the British Bankers' Association based on their perceived unsecured borrowing cost; the rate is then calculated using a "trimmed" average, which excludes the highest and lowest 25 percent of the submissions. LIBOR is the most frequently used benchmark reference rate worldwide, setting prices on financial instruments worth about $800 trillion, including mortgage rates, term loans, and many others.

UBS, as one of the panel banks, was fined $1.5 billion in December 2012 by the U.S., U.K., and Swiss regulators for manipulating LIBOR submissions from 2005 to 2010. Besides the fine, UBS pleaded guilty to U.S. prosecutors for committing wire fraud. During the said period, UBS acted on its own or colluded with other panel banks to adjust LIBOR submissions to benefit UBS's own trading positions. In addition, during the second half of 2008, UBS instructed its LIBOR submitters to keep submissions low to make the bank look stronger. At least 40 people, including several senior managers at UBS were involved in the manipulation. One major conviction was handed down to date, while other traders will stand trial in the future.

In particular, 35-year-old Tom Hayes, a former UBS (and Citibank) trader was sentenced to 14 years in prison for fraudulently rigging the LIBOR. The jail sentence is much longer than what was expected. The judge presiding over the case stated that the court wanted to send a powerful message to banks around the world that financial crime will be severely punished and will no longer just be settled with a fine (paid by the bank). The autistic mathematician Hayes argues that he is the scapegoat for senior management failings: "I refute that my actions constituted any wrong doing . . . I wish to reiterate that my actions were consistent with those of others at senior levels . . . senior management was aware of my actions and at no point was I told that my actions could or would constitute any wrongdoing."[3] In contrast, prosecutors maintained that Hayes was the mastermind behind a corrupt ring of traders and brokers globally, motivated by making his performance look stronger. Just a few years earlier, Hayes was considered to be one of the most talented traders in the banking industry, whom Goldman Sachs tried to poach from UBS with the promise of a $3 million signing bonus.

Ethics Scandal No. 4: UBS "Did It Again"

In 2015, the U.S. Department of Justice voided the $1.5 billion settlement from 2012 with UBS in the wake of the LIBOR rigging scandal, adding another $200 million in fines. Perhaps more damaging, UBS is pleading guilty to allegations that UBS traders (including Tom Hayes) had manipulated LIBOR. UBS had avoided prosecution in 2012 by agreeing to cooperate with authorities and promising not to engage in rate rigging and other illegal activities in the future. The Department of Justice alleges that UBS had violated terms of the agreement and "did it again." This time, prosecutors allege that UBS manipulated foreign-exchange rates. In particular, UBS and other banks are accused of having colluded in moving foreign-exchange rates for their own benefit and to the detriment of their clients. The Justice Department views UBS as a "repeat offender," especially in light of a 2011 settlement related to antitrust violations in the municipal-bond investments market.

Since its high in 2007, UBS's stock price has lost almost 70 percent of its value, while the S&P 500, representing the broader stock market, is up 40 percent.

DISCUSSION QUESTIONS

1. This MiniCase details several ethics scandals at UBS in recent years. What does that tell you about UBS?

2. Given UBS's repeated ethics failings, who is to blame? The CEO? The board of directors? The individuals directly involved? Who should be held accountable? Is it sufficient just to fine the bank?

3. Given the information herein, do you think that the 14-year jail sentence for Tom Hayes was harsh? Did he serve as a scapegoat?

4. What lessons in terms of business ethics and competitive advantage can be drawn from this MiniCase?

5. What can UBS do to avoid more ethics failures in the future and repair its damaged reputation?

Endnotes

1 "Memo to UBS staff from interim CEO, chairman," *Reuters*, September 24, 2011.

2 "UBS fined £29.7m over rogue trader," *Financial Times,* November 26, 2012.

3 "LIBOR rate-probe spotlight shines on higher-ups at Citigroup, other banks," *The Wall Street Journal,* August 28, 2013.

Sources: This MiniCase is based on: UBS annual reports, various years; "Former trader Tom Hayes sentenced to 14 years for LIBOR rigging," *The Wall Street Journal,* August 3, 2015; "Justice Department to tear up past UBS settlement," *The Wall Street Journal,* May 14, 2015; "Goldman Sachs offered Tom Hayes $3 million bonus to quit UBS," *Bloomberg Businessweek,* May 28, 2015; "Demise of Swiss banking secrecy heralds new era," *Financial Times,* May 19, 2013; "UBS ex-official gets 18 months in muni bond-rigging case," *The Wall Street Journal,* July 24, 2013; "LIBOR rate-probe spotlight shines on higher-ups at Citigroup, other banks," *The Wall Street Journal,* August 28, 2013; "Swiss and U.S. move forward on tax compliance," Swissinfo.ch, June 21, 2012; "The LIBOR scandal: The rotten heart of finance," *The Economist,* July 7, 2012; "UBS fined £30m over rogue trader," *The Guardian,* November 26, 2012; "UBS fined £29.7m over rogue trader," *Financial Times,* November 26, 2012; "Final notice to UBS AG," *Financial Services Authority,* December 19, 2012; Cantley, B.G. (2011), "The U.B.S. Case: The U.S. Attack on Swiss Banking Sovereignty," *Brigham Young University International Law & Management Review* 7 (Spring) available at SSRN: http://ssrn.com/abstract=1554827; "Rogue trader causes $2 billion loss at UBS," Associated Press, September 15, 2011; "Ending an era of Swiss banking secrecy: The facts behind FATCA," *American Criminal Law Review,* September 18, 2011; "UBS enters into Deferred Prosecution Agreement," The United States Department of Justice Release, February 18, 2009; "UBS to give 4,450 names to U.S.," *The Wall Street Journal,* August 20, 2009; and "Tax haven banks and U.S. tax compliance," United States Senate, July 17, 2008;.

How to Conduct a Case Analysis

THE CASE STUDY is a fundamental learning tool in strategic management. We carefully wrote and chose the cases in this book to expose you to a wide variety of key concepts, industries, protagonists, and strategic problems.

In simple terms, cases tell the story of a company facing a strategic dilemma. The firms may be real or fictional in nature, and the problem may be current or one that the firm faced in the past. Although the details of the cases vary, in general they start with a description of the challenge(s) to be addressed, followed by the history of the firm up until the decision point, and then additional information to help you with your analysis. The strategic dilemma is often faced by a specific manager, who wonders what he or she should do. To address the strategic dilemma, you will use the AFI framework to conduct a case analysis using the tools and concepts provided in this textbook. After careful analysis, you will be able to formulate a strategic response and make recommendations about how to implement it.

Why Do We Use Cases?

Strategy is something that people learn by doing; it cannot be learned simply by reading a book or listening carefully in class. While those activities will help you become more familiar with the concepts and models used in strategic management, the only way to improve your skills in analyzing, formulating, and implementing strategy is to *practice*.

We encourage you to take advantage of the cases in this text as a "laboratory" in which to experiment with the strategic management tools you have been given, so that you can learn more about how, when, and where they might work in the "real world." Cases are valuable because they expose you to a number and variety of situations in which you can refine your strategic management skills without worrying about making mistakes. The companies in these cases will not

lose profits or fire you if you miscalculate a financial ratio, misinterpret someone's intentions, or make an incorrect prediction about environmental trends.

Cases also invite you to "walk in" and explore many more kinds of companies in a wider array of industries than you will ever be able to work at in your lifetime. With this strategy content, you will find MiniCases (i.e., shorter cases) about athletes (Michael Phelps), social networks (Facebook), fashion (LVMH), and entertainment (Cirque du Soleil), among others, as well as longer cases with complete financial data about companies such as Google, Tesla Motors, Apple, to name just a few. Your personal organizational experiences are usually much more limited, defined by the jobs held by your family members or by your own forays into the working world. Learning about companies involved in so many different types of products and services may open up new employment possibilities for you. Diversity also forces us to think about the ways in which industries (as well as people) are both similar and yet distinct, and to critically examine the degree to which lessons learned in one forum transfer to other settings (i.e., to what degree are they "generalizable"). In short, cases are a great training tool, and they are fun to study.

You will find that many of our cases are written from the perspective of the CEO or general manager responsible for strategic decision making in the organization. While you do not need to be a member of a top management team to utilize the strategic management process, these senior leaders are usually responsible for determining strategy in most of the organizations we study. Importantly, cases allow us to put ourselves "in the shoes" of strategic leaders and invite us to view the issues from their perspective. Having responsibility for the performance of an entire organization is quite different from managing a single project team, department, or functional area. Cases can help you see the *big picture* in a way that most of us are not accustomed to in our daily, organizational lives. We recognize that most undergraduate students and even MBAs do not land immediately in the corporate boardroom. Yet having a basic understanding of the types of conversations going on in the boardroom not only increases your current value as an employee, but also improves your chances of getting there someday, should you so desire.

Finally, cases help give us a *long-term* view of the firms they depict. Corporate history is immensely helpful in understanding how a firm got to its present position and why people within that organization think the way they do. Our case authors (both the author of this book and authors of cases from respected third-party sources) have spent many hours poring over historical documents and news reports in order to re-create each company's heritage for you, a luxury that most of us do not have when we are bombarded on a daily basis with homework, tests, and papers or project team meetings, deadlines, and reports. We invite you not just to learn from but also to savor reading each company's story.

STRATEGIC CASE ANALYSIS. The first step in analyzing a case is to *skim it for the basic facts.* As you read, jot down your notes regarding the following basic questions:

- What company or companies is the case about?
- Who are the principal actors?
- What are the key events? When and where do they happen (in other words, what is the timeline)?

Second, go back and reread the case in greater detail, this time with a focus on *defining the problem.* Which facts are relevant and why? Just as a doctor begins by interviewing the patient ("What hurts?"), you likewise gather information and then piece the clues together in order to figure out what is wrong. Your goal at this stage is to identify the "symptoms" in order to figure out which "tests" to run in order to make a definitive "diagnosis" of the main "disease." Only then can you prescribe a "treatment" with confidence that it will actually help the situation. Rushing too quickly through this stage often results in "malpractice" (that is, giving a patient with an upset stomach an antacid when she really has the flu), with effects that range from unhelpful to downright dangerous. The best way to ensure that you "do no harm" is to analyze the facts carefully, fighting the temptation to jump right to proposing a solution.

The third step, continuing the medical analogy, is to determine which analytical tools will help you to most accurately diagnose the problem(s). Doctors may choose to run blood tests or take an X-ray. In doing case analysis, we follow the steps of the *strategic management process.* You have any and all of the following models and frameworks at your disposal:

1. Perform an **external environmental analysis** of the:
   - Macro-level environment (PESTEL analysis).
   - Industry environment (e.g., Porter's five forces).
   - Competitive environment.
2. Perform an **internal analysis** of the firm using the resource-based view:
   - What are the firm's resources, capabilities, and competencies?
   - Does the firm possess valuable, rare, costly to imitate resources, and is it organized to capture value from those resources (VRIO analysis)?
   - What is the firm's value chain?
3. Analyze the firm's current **business-level** and **corporate-level** strategies:
   - Business-level strategy (product market positioning).
   - Corporate-level strategy (diversification).
   - International strategy (geographic scope and mode of entry).
   - How are these strategies being implemented?
4. Analyze the firm's **performance**:
   - Use both financial and market-based measures.
   - How does the firm compare to its competitors as well as the industry average?
   - What trends are evident over the past three to five years?
   - Consider the perspectives of multiple stakeholders (internal and external).
   - Does the firm possess a competitive advantage? If so, can it be sustained?

CALCULATING FINANCIAL RATIOS. Financial ratio analysis is an important tool for assessing the outcomes of a firm's strategy. Although financial performance is not the only relevant outcome measure, long-term profitability is a necessary precondition for firms to remain in business and to be able to serve the needs of all of their stakeholders. Accordingly, at the end of this introductory module, we have provided a table of financial measures that can be used to assess firm performance (see Table 1).

All of the following aspects of performance should be considered, because each provides a different type of information about the financial health of the firm:

- Profitability ratios—how efficiently a company utilizes its resources.
- Activity ratios—how effectively a firm manages its assets.
- Leverage ratios—the degree to which a firm relies on debt versus equity (capital structure).
- Liquidity ratios—a firm's ability to pay off its short-term obligations.
- Market ratios—returns earned by shareholders who hold company stock.

MAKING THE DIAGNOSIS. With all of this information in hand, you are finally ready to *make a "diagnosis."* Describe the problem(s) or opportunity(ies) facing the firm at this time and/or in the near future. How are they interrelated? (For example, a runny nose, fever, stomach upset, and body aches are all indicative of the flu.) Support your conclusions with data generated from your analyses.

The following general themes may be helpful to consider as you try to pull all the pieces together into a cohesive summary:

- Are the firm's value chain (primary and support) activities mutually reinforcing?
- Do the firm's resources and capabilities fit with the demands of the external environment?
- Does the firm have a clearly defined strategy that will create a competitive advantage?
- Is the firm making good use of its strengths and taking full advantage of its opportunities?
- Does the firm have serious weaknesses or face significant threats that need to be mitigated?

Keep in mind that "problems" can be positive (how to manage increased demand) as well as negative (declining stock price) in nature. Even firms that are currently performing well need to figure out how to maintain their success in an ever-changing and highly competitive global business environment.

Formulation: Proposing Feasible Solutions

When you have the problem figured out (your diagnosis), the next step is to *propose a "treatment plan"* or solution. There are two parts to the treatment plan: the *what* and the *why.* Using our medical analogy: The *what* for a patient with the flu might be antiviral medication, rest, and lots of fluids. The *why:* antivirals attack the virus directly, shortening the duration of illness; rest enables the body to recuperate naturally; and fluids are necessary to help the body fight fever and dehydration. *The ultimate goal is to restore the patient to wellness.* Similarly, when you are doing case analysis, your task is to figure out *what* the leaders of the company should do and *why* this is an appropriate course of action. Each part of your proposal should be justifiable based on your analyses.

One word of caution about the formulation stage: By nature, humans are predisposed to engage in "local" and "simplistic" searches for solutions to the problems they face.[1] On the one hand, this can be an efficient approach to problem solving, because relying on past experiences (what worked before) does not waste time reinventing the wheel. The purpose of doing case analysis, however, is to *look past* the easy answers and to help us figure out not just what works (satisficing) but what might be the *best* answer (optimizing). In other words, do not just take the first idea that comes to your mind and run with it. Instead, write down that idea for subsequent consideration but then think about what other solutions might achieve the same (or even better) results. Some of the most successful companies engage in scenario planning, in which they develop several possible outcomes and estimate the likelihood that each will happen. If their first prediction turns out to be incorrect, then they have a Plan B ready and waiting to be executed.

Plan for Implementation

The final step in the AFI framework is to develop a plan for implementation. Under formulation, you came up with a proposal, tested it against alternatives, and used your research to support why it provides the best solution to the problem at hand. To demonstrate its feasibility, however, you must be able to explain *how to put it into action.* Consider the following questions:

1. *What activities need to be performed?* The value chain is a very useful tool when you need to

figure out how different parts of the company are likely to be affected. What are the implications of your plan with respect to both primary activities (e.g., operations and sales/marketing/service) and support activities (e.g., human resources and infrastructure)?

2. *What is the timeline?* What steps must be taken first and why? Which ones are most critical? Which activities can proceed simultaneously, and which ones are sequential in nature? How long is your plan going to take?

3. *How are you going to finance your proposal?* Does the company have adequate cash on hand, or does it need to consider debt and/or equity financing? How long until your proposal breaks even and pays for itself?

4. *What outcomes is your plan likely to achieve?* Provide goals that are "SMART": specific, measurable, achievable, realistic, and timely in nature. Make a case for how your plan will help the firm to achieve a strategic competitive advantage.

In-Class Discussion

Discussing your ideas in class is often the most valuable part of a case study. Your professor will moderate the class discussion, guiding the AFI process and asking probing questions when necessary. Case discussion classes are most effective and interesting when everybody comes prepared and participates in the exchange.

Actively listen to your fellow students; mutual respect is necessary in order to create an open and inviting environment in which people feel comfortable sharing their thoughts with one another. This does not mean you need to agree with what everyone else is saying, however. Everyone has unique perspectives and biases based on differences in life experiences, education and training, values, and goals. As a result, no two people will interpret the same information in exactly the same way. Be prepared to be challenged, as well as to challenge others, to consider the case from another vantage point. Conflict is natural and even beneficial as long as it is managed in constructive ways.

Throughout the discussion, you should be prepared to support your ideas based on the analyses you conducted. Even students who agree with you on the general steps to be taken may disagree on the order of importance. Alternatively, they may like your plan in

principle but argue that it is not feasible for the company to accomplish. You should not be surprised if others come up with an altogether different diagnosis and prescription. For better or worse, a good idea does not stand on its own merit—you must be able to convince your peers of its value by backing it up with sound logic and support.

Things to Keep in Mind while Doing Case Analysis

While some solutions are clearly better than others, it is important to remember that there is no single correct answer to any case. Unlike an optimization equation or accounting spreadsheet, cases cannot be reduced to a mathematical formula. Formulating and implementing strategy involves people, and working with people is inherently messy. Thus, the best way to get the maximum value from case analysis is to maintain an open mind and carefully consider the strengths and weaknesses of all of the options. Strategy is an iterative process, and it is important not to rush to a premature conclusion.

For some cases, your instructor may be able to share with you what the company actually did, but that does not necessarily mean it was the best course of action. Too often students find out what happened in the "real world" and their creative juices stop flowing. Whether due to lack of information, experience, or time, companies quite often make the most expedient decision. With your access to additional data and time to conduct more detailed analyses, you may very well arrive at a different (and better) conclusion. Stand by your findings as long as you can support them with solid research data. Even Fortune 500 companies make mistakes.

Unfortunately, to their own detriment, students sometimes discount the value of cases based on fictional scenarios or set some time in the past. One significant advantage of fictional cases is that everybody has access to the same information. Not only does this level the playing field, but it also prevents you from being unduly biased by actual events, thus cutting short your own learning process. Similarly, just because a case occurred in the past does not mean it is no longer relevant. The players and technology may change over time, but many questions that businesses face are timeless in nature: how to adapt to a changing environment, the best way to compete against other firms, and whether and how to expand.

Case Limitations

As powerful a learning tool as case analysis can be, it does come with some limitations. One of the most important for you to be aware of is that case analysis relies on a process known as *inductive reasoning,* in which you study specific business cases in order to derive general principles of management. Intuitively, we rely on inductive reasoning across almost every aspect of our lives. We know that we need oxygen to survive, so we assume that all living organisms need oxygen. Similarly, if all the swans we have ever seen are white, we extrapolate this to mean that all swans are white. While such relationships are often built upon a high degree of probability, it is important to remember that they are not empirically proven. We have in fact discovered life forms (microorganisms) that rely on sulfur instead of oxygen. Likewise, just because all the swans you have seen have been white, black swans do exist.

What does this caution mean with respect to case analysis? First and foremost, do not assume that just because one company utilized a joint venture to commercialize a new innovation, another company will be successful employing the same strategy. The first company's success may not be due to the particular organizational form it selected; it might instead be a function of its competencies in managing interfirm relationships or the particularities of the external environment. Practically speaking, this is why the analysis step is so fundamental to good strategic management. Careful research helps us to figure out all of the potential contributing factors and to formulate hypotheses about which ones are most likely critical to success. Put another way, what happens at one firm does not necessarily generalize to others. However, solid analytical skills go a long way toward enabling you to make informed, educated guesses about when and where insights gained from one company have broader applications.

In addition, we have a business culture that tends to put on a pedestal high-performance firms and their leaders. Critical analysis is absolutely essential in order to discern the reasons for such firms' success. Upon closer inspection, we have sometimes found that their image is more a mirage than a direct reflection of sound business practices. Many business analysts have been taken in by the likes of Enron, WorldCom, and Bernie Madoff, only to humbly retract their praise when the company's shaky foundation crumbles. We selected many of the firms in these cases because of their unique stories and positive performance, but we would be remiss if we let students interpret their presence in this book as a wholehearted endorsement of all of their business activities.

Finally, our business culture also places a high premium on benchmarking and best practices. Although we present you with a sample of firms that we believe are worthy of in-depth study, we would again caution you against uncritical adoption of their activities in the hope of emulating their achievements. Even when a management practice has broad applications, strategy involves far more than merely copying the industry leader. The company that invents a best practice is already far ahead of its competitors on the learning curve, and even if other firms do catch up, the best they can usually hope for is to match (but not exceed) the original firm's success. By all means, learn as much as you can from whomever you can, but use that information to strengthen your organization's *own* strategic identity.

Frequently Asked Questions about Case Analysis

1. *Is it OK to utilize outside materials?*

   Ask your professor. Some instructors utilize cases as a springboard for analysis and will want you to look up more recent financial and other data. Others may want you to base your analysis on the information from the case only, so that you are not influenced by the actions actually taken by the company.

2. *Can I talk about the case with other students?*

   Again, you should check with your professor, but many will strongly encourage you to meet and talk about the case with other students as part of your preparation process. The goal is not to come to a group consensus, but to test your ideas in a small group setting and revise them based on the feedback you receive.

3. *Is it OK to contact the company for more information?*

   If your professor permits you to gather outside information, you may want to consider contacting the company directly. If you do so, it is imperative that you represent yourself and your school in the most professional and ethical manner possible. Explain to them that you are a student studying the firm and that you are seeking additional information, with your instructor's permission. Our experience is that some companies are quite receptive to student inquiries; others are not. You cannot know how a particular company will respond unless you try.

4. *What should I include in my case analysis report?*

Instructors generally provide their own guidelines regarding content and format, but a general outline for a case analysis report is as follows: (1) analysis of the problem; (2) proposal of one or more alternative solutions; and (3) justification for which solution you believe is best and why. The most important thing to remember is not to waste precious space repeating facts from the case. You can assume that your professor has read the case carefully. What he or she is most interested in is your analysis of the situation and your rationale for choosing a particular solution.

Endnote

1. Cyert, R.M., and J.G. March (2001), *A Behavioral Theory of the Firm,* 2nd ed. (Malden, MA: Blackwell Publishers Inc.).

TABLE 1 / When and How to Use Financial Measures to Assess Firm Performance

Overview: We have grouped the financial performance measures into five main categories:

Table 1a: Profitability: How profitable is the company?

Table 1b: Activity: How efficient are the operations of the company?

Table 1c: Leverage: How effectively is the company financed in terms of debt and equity?

Table 1d: Liquidity: How capable is the business of meeting its short-term obligations as they fall due?

Table 1e: Market: How does the company's performance compare to other companies in the market?

Table 1a: Profitability Ratios	Formula	Characteristics
Gross margin (or EBITDA, EBIT, etc.)	(Sales − COGS) / Sales	Measures the relationship between sales and the costs to support those sales (e.g., manufacturing, procurement, advertising, payroll, etc.)
Return on assets (ROA)	Net income / Total assets	Measures the firm's efficiency in using assets to generate earnings
Return on equity (ROE)	Net income / Total stockholders' equity	Measures earnings to owners as measured by net assets
Return on invested capital (ROIC)	Net operating profit after taxes / (Total stockholders' equity + Total debt − Value of preferred stock)	Measures how effectively a company uses the capital (owned or borrowed) invested in its operations
Return on revenue (ROR)	Net profits / Revenue	Measures the profit earned per dollar of revenue
Dividend payout	Common dividends / Net income	Measures the percent of earnings paid out to common stockholders

Limitations

1. Static snapshot of balance sheet.
2. Many important intangibles not accounted for.
3. Affected by accounting rules on accruals and timing. One-time nonoperating income/expense.
4. Does not take into account cost of capital.
5. Affected by timing and accounting treatment of operating results.

TABLE 1 / When and How to Use Financial Measures to Assess Firm Performance *(continued)*

Table 1b: Activity Ratios

Activity Ratios	Formula	Characteristics
Inventory turnover	COGS inventory	Measures inventory management
Receivables turnover	Revenue / accounts receivable	Measures the effectiveness of credit policies and the needed level of receivables investment for sales
Payables turnover	Revenue / accounts payable	Measures the rate at which a firm pays its suppliers
Working capital turnover	Revenue / working capital	Measures how much working (operating) capital is needed for sales
Fixed asset turnover	Revenue / fixed assets	Measures the efficiency of investments in net fixed assets (property, plant, and equipment after accumulated depreciation)
Total asset turnover	Revenue / total assets	Represents the overall (comprehensive) efficiency of assets to sales
Cash turnover	Revenue / cash (which usually includes marketable securities)	Measures a firm's efficiency in its use of cash to generate sales

Limitations

Good measures of cash flow efficiency, but with the following limitations:

1. Limited by accounting treatment and timing (e.g., monthly/quarterly close)

2. Limitations of accrual vs. cash accounting

TABLE 1 / When and How to Use Financial Measures to Assess Firm Performance *(continued)*

Table 1c: Leverage Ratios	Formula	Characteristics
Debt to equity	Total liabilities / Total stockholders' equity	Direct comparison of debt to equity stakeholders and the most common measure of capital structure
Debt to assets	Total liabilities / Total assets	Debt as a percent of assets
Interest coverage (times interest earned)	(Net income + Interest expense + Tax expense) / Interest expense	Direct measure of the firm's ability to meet interest payments, indicating the protection provided from current operations
Long-term debt to equity	Long-term liabilities / Total stockholders' equity	A long-term perspective of debt and equity positions of stakeholders
Debt to market equity	Total liabilities at book value / Total equity at market value	Market valuation may represent a better measure of equity than book value. Most firms have a market premium relative to book value.
Bonded debt to equity	Bonded debt / Stockholders' equity	Measures a firm's leverage in terms of stockholders' equity
Debt to tangible net worth	Total liabilities / (Common equity − Intangible assets)	Measures a firm's leverage in terms of tangible (hard) assets captured in book value
Financial leverage index	Return on equity / Return on assets	Measures how well a company is using its debt
Limitations	Overall good measures of a firm's financing strategy; needs to be looked at in concert with operating results because	
	1. These measures can be misleading if looked at in isolation.	
	2. They can also be misleading if using book values as opposed to market values of debt and equity.	

TABLE 1 / When and How to Use Financial Measures to Assess Firm Performance *(continued)*

Table 1d: Liquidity Ratios	Formula	Characteristics
Current	Current assets / Current liabilities	Measures short-term liquidity. Current assets are all assets that a firm can readily convert to cash to pay outstanding debts and cover liabilities without having to sell hard assets. Current liabilities are a firm's debt and other obligations that are due within a year.
Quick (acid-test)	(Cash + Marketable securities + Net receivables) / Current liabilities	Eliminates inventory from the numerator, focusing on cash, marketable securities, and receivables.
Cash	(Cash + Marketable securities) / Current liabilities	Considers only cash and marketable securities for payment of current liabilities.
Operating cash flow	Cash flow from operations / Current liabilities	Evaluates cash-related performance (as measured from the statement of cash flows) relative to current liabilities
Cash to current assets	(Cash + Marketable securities) / Current assets	Indicates the part of current assets that are among the most fungible (i.e., cash and marketable securities).
Cash position	(Cash + Marketable securities) / Total assets	Indicates the percent of total assets that are most fungible (i.e., cash).
Current liability position	Current liabilities / Total assets	Indicates what percent of total assets the firm's current liabilities represent.

Limitations

Liquidity measures are important, especially in times of economic instability, but they also need to be looked at holistically along with financing and operating measures of a firm's performance.

1. Accounting processes (e.g., monthly close) limit efficacy of these measures when you want to understand daily cash position.
2. No account taken of risk and exposure on the liability side.

TABLE 1 / When and How to Use Financial Measures to Assess Firm Performance *(continued)*

Table 1e: Market Ratios	Formula	Characteristics
Book value per share	Total stockholders' equity / Number of shares outstanding	Equity or net assets, as measured on the balance sheet
Earnings-based growth models	$P = kE / (r - g)$, where E = earnings, k = dividend payout rate, r = discount rate, and g = earnings growth rate	Valuation models that discount earnings and dividends by a discount rate adjusted for future earnings growth
Market-to-book	(Stock price × Number of shares outstanding) / Total stockholders' equity	Measures accounting-based equity
Price-earnings (PE) ratio	Stock price / EPS	Measures market premium paid for earnings and future expectations
Price-earnings growth (PEG) ratio	PE / Earnings growth rate	PE compared to earnings growth rates, a measure of PE "reasonableness"
Sales-to-market value	Sales / (Stock price × Number of shares outstanding)	A sales activity ratio based on market price
Dividend yield	Dividends per share / Stock price	Direct cash return on stock investment
Total return to shareholders	Stock price appreciation plus dividends	
Limitations	Market measures tend to be more volatile than accounting measures but also provide a good perspective on the overall health of a company when used holistically with the other measures of financial performance. 1. Market volatility/noise is the biggest challenge with these measures. 2. Understanding what is a result of a firm strategy/decision vs. the broader market is challenging.	

COMPANY INDEX

NAME INDEX

Note: Page numbers followed by *n* indicate material in chapter endnotes. Page numbers beginning with C indicate material in case studies.

Note: Page numbers followed by *n* indicate material in chapter endnotes. Page numbers beginning with C indicate material in case studies.

FINANCIAL RATIOS USED IN CASE ANALYSIS

	Formula
Profitability Ratios: "How profitable is the company?"	
Gross Margin (or EBITDA, EBIT, etc.)	(Sales − COGS) / Sales
Return on Assets (ROA)	Net Income / Total Assets
Return on Equity (ROE)	Net Income / Total Stockholders' Equity
Return on Invested Capital (ROIC)	Net Operating Profit After Taxes / (Total Stockholders' Equity + Total Debt − Value of Preferred Stock)
Return on Revenue (ROR)	Net Profits / Revenue
Dividend Payout	Common Dividends / Net Income
Activity Ratios: "How efficient are the operations of the company?"	
Inventory Turnover	COGS / Inventory
Receivables Turnover	Revenue / Accounts Receivable
Payables Turnover	Revenue / Accounts Payable
Working Capital Turnover	Revenue / Working Capital
Fixed Asset Turnover	Revenue / Fixed Assets
Total Asset Turnover	Revenue / Total Assets
Cash Turnover	Revenue / Cash (which usually includes marketable securities)
Leverage Ratios: "How effectively is the company financed in terms of debt and equity?"	
Debt to Equity	Total Liabilities / Total Stockholders' Equity
Financial Leverage Index	Return on Equity / Return on Assets
Debt Ratio	Total Liabilities / Total Assets
Interest Coverage (Times Interest Earned)	(Net Income + Interest Expense + Tax Expense) / Interest Expense
Long-Term Debt to Equity	Long-Term Liabilities / Total Stockholders' Equity
Debt to Market Equity	Total Liabilities at Book Value / Total Equity at Market Value
Bonded Debt to Equity	Bonded Debt / Stockholders' Equity
Debt to tangible net worth	Total Liabilities / (Common Equity − Intangible Assets)
Liquidity Ratios: "How capable is the company of meeting its short-term obligations?"	
Current	Current Assets / Current Liabilities
Quick (Acid-Test)	(Cash + Marketable Securities + Net Receivables) / Current Liabilities
Cash	(Cash + Marketable Securities) / Current Liabilities
Operating Cash Flow	Cash Flow from Operations / Current Liabilities
Cash to Current Assets	(Cash + Marketable Securities) / Current Assets
Cash Position	Cash / Total Assets
Current Liability Position	Current Liabilities / Total Assets
Market Ratios: "How does the company's performance compare to other companies?"	
Book Value per Share	Total Stockholders' Equity / Number of Shares Outstanding
Earnings-Based Growth Models	$P = kE / (r − g)$, where E = Earnings, k = Dividend Payout Rate, r = Discount Rate, and g = Earnings Growth Rate
Market-to-Book	(Stock Price × Number of Shares Outstanding) / Total Stockholders' Equity
Price-Earnings (PE) Ratio	Stock Price / EPS
Price-Earnings Growth (PEG) Ratio	PE / Earnings Growth Rate
Sales-to-Market Value	Sales / (Stock Price × Number of Shares Outstanding)
Dividend Yield	Dividends per Share / Stock Price
Total Return to Shareholders	Stock Price Appreciation + Dividends